Lecture Notes in Computer Science 1150

Edited by G. Goos, J. Hartmanis and J. van Leeuwen

Advisory Board: W. Brauer   D. Gries   J. Stoer

Springer
Berlin
Heidelberg
New York
Barcelona
Budapest
Hong Kong
London
Milan
Paris
Santa Clara
Singapore
Tokyo

Andrzej Hlawiczka   João Gabriel Silva
Luca Simoncini   (Eds.)

Dependable Computing – EDCC-2

Second European
Dependable Computing Conference
Taormina, Italy, October 2-4, 1996
Proceedings

Springer

Series Editors

Gerhard Goos, Karlsruhe University, Germany

Juris Hartmanis, Cornell University, NY, USA

Jan van Leeuwen, Utrecht University, The Netherlands

Volume Editors

Andrzej Hlawiczka
Silesian Technical University, Instytut Elektroniki
ul. Akademicka 16, 44 100 Gliwice, Poland

João Gabriel Silva
Polo II - Universidade, Dep. Eng. Informática
Pinhal de Marrocos, 3030 Coimbra, Portugal
E-mail: jgabriel@dei.uc.pt

Luca Simoncini
Universitá di Pisa, Dip. di Ingegneria dell'Informazione
Via Diotisalvi 2, I-56126 Pisa, Italy
E-mail: simon@iet.unipi.it

Cataloging-in-Publication data applied for

Die Deutsche Bibliothek - CIP-Einheitsaufnahme

Dependable computing : proceedings / EDCC-2, Second
European Dependable Computing Conference, Taormina, Italy,
October 2 - 4, 1996. Andrzej Hlawiczka ... (ed.). - Berlin ;
Heidelberg ; New York ; Barcelona ; Budapest ; Hong Kong ;
London ; Milan ; Paris ; Santa Clara ; Singapore ; Tokyo :
Springer, 1996
  (Lecture notes in computer science ; Vol. 1150)
  ISBN 3-540-61772-8
NE: Hlawiczka, Andrzej [Hrsg.]; EDCC <2, 1996, Taormina>; GT

CR Subject Classification (1991): B.1.3, B.2.3, B.3.4, B.4.5, C.3-4, D.2.4,
D.2.8, D.4.5, E.4, J.7

ISSN 0302-9743
ISBN 3-540-61772-8 Springer-Verlag Berlin Heidelberg New York

© Springer-Verlag Berlin Heidelberg 1996
Printed in Germany

Typesetting: Camera-ready by author
SPIN 10513762   06/3142 – 5 4 3 2 1 0   Printed on acid-free paper

Foreword

The Second European Dependable Computing Conference continues the forum for dependable computing started with the first successful event, held in Berlin in October 1994. EDCC has been generated by merging two former conference series – the International Conference on Fault Tolerant Computing Systems held in the Federal Republic of Germany until 1991 and the International Conference on Fault-Tolerant Systems and Diagnostics held in the countries of Eastern Europe until 1990.

Dependability, and all its attributes of reliability, availability, safety, security and integrity, is challenging for every computing system, in particular for those whose service is either time constrained or critical. Theoretical and experimental research form the scientific background to enable such applications.

The EDCC conference is becoming a meeting point for the exchange of ideas, models, designs and results from all over the world. European research institutions, academia and industries have well established know-how in dealing with both research and applications and are at the frontier in exploiting novel techniques and designs.

The work on dependability is supported by interest groups in several European countries. They agreed to set up EDCC as their common platform. The unification of their previous activities is also important from a political point of view, encouraging exchange of experiences matured in different realities and strengthening co-operation between all European countries, with no other limit than the scientific relevance of the work submitted and discussed. In effect this vision of Europe as a "common house" has been enforced also in the EEC co-operative research programmes which see a growing participation of East European countries.

The East-West unification character of EDCC is underlined by the composition of the program committee, the external referees, the session chairs, the two program co-chairs and by the fact that the program committee meeting was held in Gliwice, Poland, at the Silesian Technical University.

EDCC-2 would not be possible without the substantial contributions of many persons. First, the dedication of the two program co-chairs João Gabriel Silva and Andrzej Hlawiczka who did excellent work in both paper processing and running the program committee. Thanks are also due to all external referees and to the members of the program committee who reliably performed very serious and dedicated work in the difficult part of evaluating the papers. Ettore Ricciardi contributed a lot in publicising and disseminating information about the conference.

The organisation was supported by the AICA Working Group on Dependability in Computing Systems, by the University of Pisa, and IEI and CNUCE of the Italian CNR. Their help is gratefully acknowledged.

The conference has received generous financial support from several organisations: the Office of Naval Research Europe, Ansaldo Transporti, and the Italian National Council of Research. With their support it was possible to offer the participants warm hospitality to make the scientific exchange possible in a relaxed and nice setting.

Final thanks are due to Springer-Verlag for publishing the conference proceedings in the well-known series Lecture Notes in Computer Science.

I hope that EDCC-2 will be a successful continuation of this series and that the participants will find its technical and scientific contribution interesting.

I also hope that all participants will enjoy Taormina and Sicily for their outstanding beauty and the hospitality of the Italian island.

July 1996   Luca Simoncini
                                                              General Chairman

Preface

Europe is certainly an exciting place to live at this end of the millennium. The big wall that divided us has fallen, but it is not all roses on the other side. Other potential walls lurk at each turn of the road that, we hope, leads to a Europe of peace and prosperity for all its inhabitants. The second European Dependable Computing Conference, EDCC-2, is a contribution of the dependable computing community to strengthen what unites us and keep away the devils that have turned us against each other so many times in the past. Without any isolationism — the conference is European just because it is promoted mostly by Europeans on European soil, otherwise it is totally open to contributions from all over the world.

May the smooth collaboration between the two program co-chairs, one from Central Europe and the other from Western Europe, be an indication of what lies ahead for Europe.

As the second conference of a series, the program committee had the added responsibility of keeping up with the high scientific standards set forth by the first. For us, program co-chairs, it was a great honor to be considered capable of maintaining that standard, and we certainly did our best for it. The 66 received papers were subjected to rigorous reviewing by 146 referees from 24 countries. All regular papers were reviewed by at least four different people, except 4 that were reviewed by three people. The industrial track submissions were reviewed by three members of the program committee.

The program committee, that comprised 41 people from 20 countries, was in charge of the final decision on acceptance and rejection. It should come as no surprise that the discussion was very lively when it met in Gliwice, Poland, on May 13 and 14, in the premises of the University Club of the Silesian Technical University. In the end, 26 papers were accepted, 4 of them on the industrial track. On next day, May 15, many of us attended, also in Gliwice, the EDCC-2 Companion Workshop. There we had the opportunity to listen to short presentations on the current research activities of many of the program committee members, and we had the privilege of witnessing the formation of the Polish Association for Dependability. We wish it a long and fruitful life.

The industrial track, where less demanding papers from industry could be submitted, reporting on the problems and successes of using dependability techniques in industrial practice, managed to attract a small number of good quality papers that otherwise would not be considered. It is our view that they enrich the conference, and we recommend that such a track be maintained in the future.

For the conference itself the single track structure was maintained, with ample time for presentation and discussion of each paper, and industrial and regular papers in the same sections. We hope that very interesting discussions will take place.

The selected papers cover most of the areas of dependable computing, from evaluation and modeling to testing, from design and distribution to security, from replication and diagnosis to safety. The breath of the program will, we hope, appeal to most researchers in the field.

We would also like to acknowledge the continued support of the Prof. Luca Simoncini, conference chair, and of Dr. David Powell, Program Chair of EDCC-1. David's database was essential to solve many tasks in the lengthy process that leads to a conference program; more relevant still, his wise advice enabled us to avoid many pitfalls and solve more satisfactorily many of the problems encountered.

Finally, we hope that EDCC-2 has given a significant contribution to help establish EDCC as a high quality conference series.

July 1996

João Gabriel Silva
Andrzej Hlawiczka
Program Co-Chairs

Organization Committee

General Chair

Luca Simoncini
University of Pisa
Italy

Program Co-Chairs

João Gabriel Silva
University of Coimbra
Portugal

Andrzej Hlawiczka
Silesian Technical University
Poland

Finance and Local Arrangements Chair

Ettore Ricciardi
IEI - CNR, Pisa
Italy

International Liaison Chairs

North America:
Ravi Iyer
University of Illinois at Urbana
Champaign
USA

Asia:
Hideo Fujiwara
Nara Institute of Science and
Technology
Japan

Program Committee

Sergio Arevalo, Spain
Algirdas Avizienis, Lithuania
Andrea Bondavalli, Italy
Pierre Jacques Courtois, Belgium
Klaus Echtle, Germany
Elena Gramatova, Slovakia
Boudewijn Haverkort, Netherlands
Jan Hlavicka, Czech Republic
Hubert Kirrmann, Switzerland
Henryk Krawczyk, Poland
Bev Littlewood, U.K.
Erik Maehle, Germany
Miroslaw Malek, Germany
Gilles Muller, France
David Powell, France
Michel Renovell, France
Santosh Shrivastava, U.K.
Janusz Sosnowski, Poland
Pascale Thevenod-Fosse, France
Paulo Verissimo, Portugal

Jean Arlat, France
Dimitri Avreski, Bulgaria
Andrea Clematis, Italy
Yves Deswarte, France
Michael Goessel, Germany
Karl Erwin Grosspietch, Germany
Bjarne Helvik, Norway
Johan Karlsson, Sweden
Andrzej Krasniewski, Poland
Jean Claude Laprie, France
Henrique Madeira, Portugal
Piero Maestrini, Italy
Giorgio Mongardi, Italy
Andras Pataricza , Hungary
Anders P. Ravn, Denmark
Ernst Schmitter, Germany
Egor S. Sogomonian, Russia
Bernd Straube, Germany
Rajmund Ubar, Estonia

External Referees

Altman J.
Amir Y.
Andersen H.R.
Arevalo S.
Arlat J.
Avresky D.R
Banerjee P.
Belli F.
Bernardeschi C.
Bertolino A.
Bertrand Y.
Bidan C.
Bondawalli A.
Bruck J.
Buchs D.
Carrasco J.
Carreira J.
Chojcan J.
Ciardo G.
Ciufoletti A.
Clematis A.
Courtois P.-J.
Cunha J.C.
Dal Cin M.
de Lemos R.
Deconinck G
Decotignie J.-D.
Deswarte Y.
Di Giandomenico F.
Dilger E.
Drabek V.
Draber S.
Echtle K.
Escherman B.
Ezhilchelvan P.
Fernandez E.B.
Frankl P.
Fujiwara E.
Gantenbein R.
Gaudel M.-C.
Geisselhardt W.
Girard P.
Gössel M.

Gramatova E.
Grosspietsch K.-E
Guerraoui. R.
Guthoff J.
Harari S.
Harbour M.G.
Haverkort B.R.
Helvik B.E.
Hiltunen M.
Hlavicka J.
Issarny V.
Joubert P.
Juanole G.
Kaiser J.
Kanawati G.A.
Karlsson J.
Kemnitz G.
Kikuno T.
Kirrman H.
Kopetz H.
Krasniewski A.
Krawczyk H.
Krumm H.
Kunz W.
Landrault C.
Laprie J.-C.
Leveugle R.
Littlewood B.
Lo J.-C.
Lotti G.
Lovric T.
Madeira H.
Maehle E.
Maestrini P.
Majzik I.
Malek M.
Marie R.
Mitrani I.
Mittal R.
Mongardi G.
Morin C.
Moustefaoui A.
Muller G.

Nett E.
Ni L.M.
Nicolaidis M.
Novak O.
Nusbaumer H.J.
Pataricza A.
Pleinevaux P.
Powel D.
Pravossoudovitch S.
Prinetto P.
Puente J.D.L.
Randell B.
Ravn A.P.
Raynal M.
Renovell M.
Rodrigues L.
Rosenberg H.A.
Rufino J.
Rushby J.
Sanders W.
Santucci J.-F.
Sapiecha K.
Schlichting R.
Schmitter E.
Schneeweiss W.G.
Schoitsch E.
Schwartz M.
Selenyi E.
Sens P.
Sericola B.
Shrivastava S.K.
Siegrist T.
Sieh V.
Sifakis J.
Silva L.M.
Slimani Y.
Sogomonian E.S.
Soler J.-L.
Sosnowski J.
Sparmann U.
Stalhane T.
Steininger A.
Stopp A.

Table of Contents

Session 7: Verification   283
Chair: Ernst Schmitter, Siemens AG, Germany

Session 8: Replication and Distribution   333
Chair: Gilles Muller, IRISA, France

Session 9: System Level Diagnosis   383
Chair: Henryk Krawczyk, Technical University of Gdansk,
    Poland

Author Index   439

Session 1

Distributed Fault Tolerance

Chair: Erik Maehle, University of Lübeck, Germany

FRIENDS: A Flexible Architecture for Implementing Fault Tolerant and Secure Distributed Applications

Jean-Charles Fabre[*]   and   Tanguy Pérennou[**]

*LAAS-CNRS & INRIA   **LAAS-CNRS
7, Avenue du Colonel Roche, 31077 Toulouse cedex - France

Abstract. 𝓕𝓡𝓘𝓔𝓝𝓓𝓢 is a software-based architecture for implementing fault-tolerant and, to some extent, secure applications. This architecture is composed of sub-systems and libraries of metaobjects. Transparency and separation of concerns is provided not only to the application programmer but also to the programmers implementing metaobjects for fault tolerance, secure communication and distribution. Common services required for implementing metaobjects are provided by the sub-systems. Metaobjects are implemented using object-oriented techniques and can be reused and customised according to the application needs, the operational environment and its related fault assumptions. Flexibility is increased by a recursive use of metaobjects. Examples and experiments are also described.

1 Introduction

The dependability research community has designed and experimented a number of mechanisms which have now reached full maturity. Nevertheless, in practice, the integration of such mechanisms within applications still raises several problems. A flexible implementation of dependable applications requires the following properties: *transparency* of the mechanisms for the application programmer; *independence* of the mechanisms with respect to each other; *composability* of mechanisms on a case-by-case basis; *reusability* of existing mechanisms to derive new ones.

None of the solutions traditionally used manages to ensure all these properties at the same time. The approach which is developed and illustrated in this paper aims at providing a good balance among the properties identified above. It is based on object-orientation, metaobject protocols and also, to some extent, micro-kernel technology. The notions of reflection and metaobject protocols in object-oriented languages [1, 2] emerged recently and proved to be both efficient and elegant for the integration of application-orthogonal concerns in a highly flexible way. Among many other examples, PCLOS implements persistent objects [3], R^2 allows inclusion of soft real-time constraints in object-oriented applications [4], Object Communities provides distribution transparency [5].

As some other researchers in the dependability community, we believe that the use of metaobject protocols can yield the same benefits for the integration of dependability concerns within distributed applications. This idea has already been introduced and used in previous works [6, 7], but needs more investigation in order to state on the usefulness, practicality and efficiency of this approach to build dependable

This work was partially supported by the *DEVA* Esprit project n°20072.

applications. This paper describes to what extent metaobject protocols can simplify such an integration and presents *FRIENDS*, a prototype software architecture to build dependable distributed systems.

Section 2 describes related work on the integration of fault tolerance mechanisms within applications, describes what is a metaobject protocol and delineates what is expected from its use. Section 3 describes the architecture of a system supporting dependable applications using a metaobject protocol. Section 4 describes our application model and stresses the separation of concerns obtained when programming fault tolerance or some security mechanisms[1] using multiple meta-levels. This allows the application programmer to concentrate only on the functionalities of its program. Section 5 illustrates and discusses this approach with examples of application objects and metaobjects. Section 6 discusses the identified advantages and limits of this approach. Section 7 briefly sketches out our experiments.

2 Problem Statement and Metaobject Protocols

2.1 Related Work

The approach presented in this paper is an evolution, with more flexibility in mind, of previous work on the integration of fault tolerance mechanisms within distributed systems, either at the system level through system services or at the user level through the use of libraries.

System Approach. When fault tolerance mechanisms are embedded in the underlying runtime system they are (almost) transparent to the application programmer. For example the system Delta-4 [8] offers several replication protocols based on a multicast communication system supporting error detection and voting protocols. The communication system is based on fail-silent specialised hardware components, i.e. network attachment controllers. This approach inherently lacks flexibility in particular concerning the replication protocols which are embedded within the system. Another drawback of this approach is composability of various mechanisms dealing with various fault classes. Adding various types of mechanisms to the application on a case-by-case basis, for instance client-server authentication, is not easy.

Library Approach. Pre-defined libraries of basic mechanisms enable more flexibility to be obtained in the sense that users can tailor their own fault tolerance mechanisms to suit their needs by using constructs and primitives from some library. Thus Isis [9] offers the *coordinator-cohort* software construct, group management and atomic broadcast primitives on top of which primary/backup and active replication for example can be built. In this approach it is the programmer's responsibility to use library functions at appropriate places to implement a given fault tolerance mechanism, which may require a good knowledge of fault tolerance techniques.

The object-oriented development of such libraries provides the user with classes rather than functions. Inheritance then makes it easier to adapt fault tolerance mechanisms to specific needs or to add new features. Examples of such a use of inheritance can be found in Avalon/C++ [10] and Arjuna [11].

---

[1] In this paper, the term "security" must mainly be understood as "secure communication".

So on one hand, a system approach provides transparency and on the other hand object-oriented libraries provide reusability, but none of these approaches manages to combine both properties. As a matter of fact, a careful observation of the code written by library users reveals that functions are used almost systematically in dedicated places such as object creation and deletion, beginning and ending of methods. This is the kind of problem a metaobject protocol can solve in an elegant way.

2.2 Metaobject Protocols

The essence of metaobject protocols (MOP) is to give to the user the ability to adjust the language implementation to suit its particular needs. Metaobject protocols are based on reflection [1] and object-orientation. Reflection exposes the language implementation at a high level of abstraction, making it understandable for the user while preserving the efficiency and portability of the default language implementation. Object-orientation provides an interface to the language implementation in the form of classes and methods so that variants of the default language implementation can be produced, using specialisation by inheritance. Instances of such classes are called *metaobjects*. The notion of *protocol* relates here to the interaction between object and metaobject. In class-based reflective languages, this interface generally comprises at least instance creation and deletion, attribute read or write access, method call.

An a priori argument at the expenses of reflection-based languages and metaobject protocols is that they are not efficient. A counter-example is ABCL/R2, an object-oriented concurrent reflective language that in terms of performance compares with C used with lightweight processes [12].

2.3 Using a Metaobject Protocol for Dependability

The ability to adapt some aspects of the language implementation can be delegated to a third party rather than the user, e.g. a fault tolerance or security specialist. In this way, a clean separation of concerns between the application and mechanisms for fault tolerance or secure communication can be achieved. This approach enables the role of different programmers with a different basic knowledge to be clearly identified and made easier: the application programmer, the fault tolerance programmer, the security programmer, the distribution programmer. All of them share the same knowledge of object-oriented programming and some about metaobject protocols.

In the present paper a recursive use of metaobjects is investigated so that addition of some dependability-related mechanism takes place in a simple and convenient conceptual framework: a specific programmer only deals with the mechanisms he is responsible for and their implementation using the underlying object model.

Nevertheless metaobject protocols are not a panacea and it is not claimed here that they can be used on their own to build dependable distributed systems. Several basic services must be implemented at the system level, like error detection (to ensure high asymptotic coverage of the failure mode assumptions [13]) or a security kernel (that must be always invoked and tamper proof). Other system services like group management and atomic multicast protocols, authentication and authorisation servers are also necessary. The respective roles of metaobjects and system services in the presence of multiple mechanisms are discussed in Section 3.

2.4 Motivations and Previous Work

In our previous work [14], the use of metaobjects for implementing fault tolerance mechanisms was experimented with only one meta-level. Several metaobjects classes for various replication strategies were developed and experimented with simple application examples. This was very promising and showed that transparency and separation of concerns could be obtained for the application programmer.

However, a single-level approach suffers from several drawbacks. First of all, the interaction between replicas at the meta-level was rather complex because of the use of system calls to group management services. Likewise, remote interaction between application objects was implemented at the base-level and thus very dependent on the communication mechanisms used. A second problem was the difficulty to add transparently some security aspects (authentication, ciphering and signature checking). All security-related statements would have been mixed in the source code with fault tolerance and group management aspects.

In both cases, problems arise from the fact that remote interaction or security are not handled as separate and independent abstractions, which also limited very much the flexibility and the reusability of metaobjects that were initially developed. The separation of abstractions improves the flexibility of the approach and the recursive use of several meta-levels allows composability to be exploited as much as possible.

3 System Architecture and Assumptions

The architecture of the system is composed of several layers: (i) the kernel layer which can be either a Unix kernel or better a micro-kernel, such as Chorus [15], (ii) the system layer composed of several dedicated sub-systems, one for each abstraction, and finally (iii) the user layer dedicated to the implementation of applications.

3.1 System Layer

The system layer is organised as a set of sub-systems. In micro-kernel technology a sub-system corresponds to a set of services implementing any software system, for instance an operating system on top of the micro-kernel (e.g. Unix on Chorus). In *FRIENDS* each sub-system provides services for fault tolerance, or secure communication, or distribution. Any sub-system may be hardware- and software-implemented. The three necessary sub-systems are the following:

- *FTS* (Fault Tolerance Sub-system) provides basic services mandatory in fault-tolerant computing, in particular error detection and failure suspectors which must be implemented as low level entities. This sub-system also includes configuration and replication domains management facilities and a stable storage support.

- *SCS* (Secure Communication Sub-system) provides basic services that must obviously be implemented as trusted entities within the system (notion of Trusted Computing Base). These services should include in particular an authentication server, but also an authorisation server, a directory server, an audit server.

- *GDS* (Group-based Distribution Sub-system) provides basic services for implementing a distribution support for object-oriented applications where objects can be replicated using groups. These basic services include group management facilities and atomic multicast protocols.

Every sub-system provides basic services required by the mechanisms implemented with metaobjects. These services can be seen as *Software Replaceable Units* (SRU). Using micro-kernel technology, the system layer can easily be composed of the required sub-systems, each of them using the appropriate SRUs.

3.2 User Layer

The user layer is divided into two sub-layers, the application layer and the metaobject layer controlling the behaviour of application objects. Some libraries of metaobject classes for the implementation of fault-tolerant and secure distributed applications are implemented on top of the corresponding sub-system and provide the user with mechanisms that can be adjusted, using object-oriented techniques.

- *libft_mo* provides metaobject classes for various fault tolerance strategies (based on stable storage or replication) with respect to physical faults considering today fail-silent nodes.

- *libsc_mo* provides metaobject classes for various secure communication protocols using ciphering techniques, signature computation and verification based on secret or public key cryptosystems.

- *libgd_mo* provides metaobject classes for handling remote object interaction, which can be implemented with groups. The combination of these metaobjects and GDS provides a runtime support for distributed object-oriented applications.

We also suppose that application objects have a "deterministic behaviour". Any method invocation with identical input parameters will produce the same results on any of the object replicas. Concurrency and other sources of non determinism within objects have not been considered yet.

3.3 Overall Architecture

The static view of the overall architecture of the system is illustrated in figure 1. The implementation environment provided by *FRIENDS* corresponds to the whole set of sub-systems and libraries of metaobject classes.

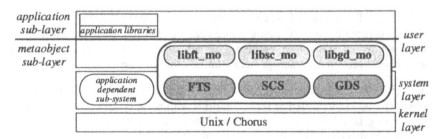

Fig. 1. Overall system architecture

The implementation of any abstraction (fault tolerance, secure communication, distribution) is thus divided into a library of metaobjects classes and the corresponding sub-system, thus spanning at least partially the user and the system layers.

4 Multi-Level Application Model

4.1 Distributed Application Model

An application is regarded as a collection of communicating objects developed using an object-oriented programming language (currently C++). Any application object is mapped by GDS on a runtime object, depending on entities handled by the underlying operating system (Unix processes or Chorus actors). Each runtime object is not only composed of an application object, but also contains one or several metaobjects within the same address space.

```
RT_object = {A, FT, SC, GD}  with:
    A    : application object
    FT   : fault tolerance metaobject
    SC   : secure communication metaobject
    GD   : group-based distribution metaobject
```

The set of metaobjects depends on the properties that must be added to the application and includes at least one metaobject, GD, for distributed interaction. Ideally, adding properties to an application involves adding other metaobjects to the set. The notion of *metaobjects set* is similar to the notion of *metaspace* defined in Apertos [16] and also to the notion of *reflective object tower* [12]. Figure 2 below depicts our application model on a distributed system configuration.

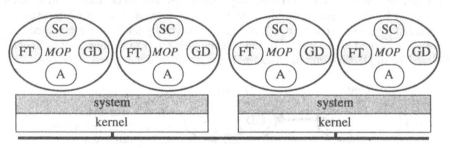

Fig. 2. A distributed application using $\mathcal{FRIENDS}$

Within one runtime object, the interaction between the application object and the metaobjects is done through the MOP. The interaction of runtime objects is based on the client-server model. For a given abstraction, this interaction is performed by two metaobjects, one for the client behaviour and the other for the server behaviour: a protocol takes place between both metaobjects. The application programmers just writes the application objects and selects the set of appropriate metaobjects.

4.2 The Multi-Level Approach

In order to solve the problems mentioned in Section 2.4, a *three meta-level* application model was defined. Any (runtime) object is organised using several levels: the first level or the base-level (the application object), several intermediate meta-levels (metaobjects for fault tolerance and secure communication) and finally the last meta-level responsible for handling objects interaction. This structure of the application implies a sequence of interactions through the MOP as shown in figure 3.

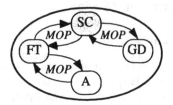

Fig. 3. Base and meta-level interaction

The minimal specifications of the MOP (see Section 5.1 for a more complete description) that we need and that we have used are the following:

- object creation/deletion: some operations can be done when creating/deleting an object;

- invocation trapping: the method invocation semantics can be implemented in a different way, e.g. as group-based remote procedure call;

- base-level access: base-level methods and attributes can be manipulated from the meta-level.

From Single To Multi-Level.

Considering just one meta-level handling distribution, any server method invocation is trapped by the client metaobject on the client side, an invocation message is forwarded to the server side, this message is received by the server metaobject and finally the method is executed at the base-level. This protocol is illustrated in figure 4 below. The implementation of an example using this model is given in Section 5.2.

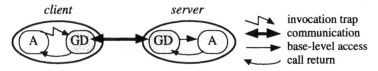

Fig. 4. Using metaobjects for distribution

Considering now several intermediate levels, each server method invocation is trapped by the next meta-level. This is recursively done until the last meta-level (GD) where an invocation message is forwarded to the server. The invocation message is received by the server meta-level (GD) and the invocation is propagated recursively through intermediate levels to the base-level where the method is finally executed. This is illustrated in figure 5 below.

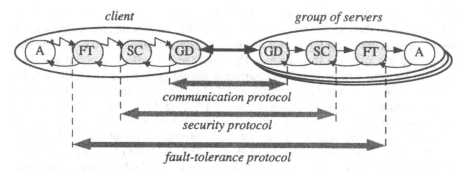

Fig. 5. Multi-level implementation of the client-server protocol

This figure also shows the various underlying protocols between a client object and a replicated server object. With this application structure any intermediate meta-level can be added or removed quite easily, thus adding or removing the corresponding underlying protocol.

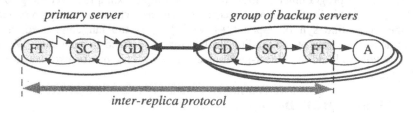

Fig. 6. Multi-level implementation of the primary-backup protocol

This multi-level model is also used in the implementation of inter-replica protocols on the server side. For instance, the interaction between the primary and the group of backup replicas is such that the primary is a client of the group of backup replicas. The primary replica captures the state of the base-level object and invokes transparently an update_state method of the backup replicas (figure 6).

Intermediate Levels and Properties.

The order of levels may vary according to the properties that must be guaranteed. Except for the last meta-level (responsible for communications) and the base-level (application object), a permutation of all intermediate levels seems possible and sound. Although it could be done from a practical viewpoint (similar interface of metaobject classes), this actually depends on the expected properties that the final application should have. For instance, if message integrity must be guaranteed (e.g. by means of signature computation and verification) also on information added during methods invocation by the fault tolerance meta-level, then the security meta-level must be invoked after the fault tolerance meta-level. If message integrity must just be guaranteed on the application information during the method invocation (method and parameters), then one would expect the security meta-level to be put straight after the base-level. Suppose then that the intermediate levels are organised in the following order: the security meta-level is put straight after the application level, then the fault tolerance meta-level, leading thus to the following sequence (A; SC; FT; GD). When the primary takes a checkpoint of the application object, the access to the base-level state should go through the security meta-level. This implies that the security meta-level is able to propagate this access down to its base-level which is not possible with the metaobject protocol that we use. Updating the backup state would also be a problem because writing base-level attributes should go again through the security meta-level. With the current solution (A; FT; SC; GD) and the simple MOP used, reading or writing base-level attributes is easily achieved. Moreover, errors detected by the security meta-level, such as authentication error after multiple retries, can be delivered to security base-level, i.e. the fault tolerance meta-level which handles recovery actions. Actually, according to the expected properties of the application, this is the only suitable sequence of intermediate levels if both fault tolerance and secure communication are required.

5 Metaobjects Implementation Issues

The objective of this section is to show how objects and metaobjects can be programmed and bound using a simple MOP. The transparency of the mechanisms for the application programmer is illustrated by a simple example. According to the models presented in Section 4, metaobjects for each abstraction are briefly presented in an Open C++-like syntax. Open C++ v1.2 [17] is the language used in our experiments. The role of the binding declarations is defined in each case. We also illustrate how to build the object-metaobject stack with no, one or two intermediate meta-levels.

5.1 A Simple MOP Definition

The following simple MOP is used throughout the rest of this section: each object is controlled by a unique metaobject and the binding is done on a class-by-class basis. The binding between an application class A and a metaobject class M is realised by the statement: //MOP reflect A: M. All metaobject classes inherit from the pre-defined class MetaObj and have the following interface:

```
class MetaObj {
public:
  void Meta_StartUp ();
  void Meta_CleanUp ();
  void Meta_MethodCall (int m_id, ArgPac args, ArgPac reply);
  void Meta_Read (int var_id, ArgPac value);
  void Meta_Assign (int var_id, ArgPac value);
private:
  void Meta_HandleMethodCall (int m_id, ArgPac args, ArgPac reply);
  void Meta_HandleRead (int var_id, ArgPac value);
  void Meta_HandleAssign (int var_id, ArgPac value);
};
```

Methods Meta_StartUp and Meta_CleanUp are called respectively after creation and before deletion of the base-level object; between creation and deletion, object and metaobject can refer to each other. Meta_MethodCall is called when a base-level method is invoked: m_id identifies the method, args packs its input arguments and reply is supposed to pack the results when Meta_MethodCall returns. Meta_Read is called when an attribute identified by var_id is read and value is supposed to contain the result of the read access. Meta_Assign is called when an attribute identified by var_id is written and value is the value that should be assigned. Private methods implement the default behaviour of the language: Meta_HandleMethodCall, Meta_HandleRead, Meta_HandleAssign enable the meta-level to invoke a base-level method or access (read, write) a base-level attribute, respectively. Finally, ArgPac is a stack-like class that may contain all types of objects (including ArgPac objects). Figure 7 illustrates how invocation is trapped and can be adjusted with this MOP.

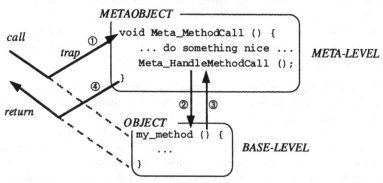

Fig. 7. Invocation trapping

Classes that are not bound to a metaobject class have the default class behaviour. This MOP is a simplified version of the Open C++ MOP [5]. Nevertheless, any reflective object-oriented language providing this MOP could be used instead.

5.2 Handling Distribution

The idea here is to provide a set of metaobjects classes providing access to remote, replicated and/or shared objects. These metaobjects use other classes, based on GDS, providing an object-oriented interface to group management services. A server is seen by the client through a local representative, a proxy. This proxy is bound to a client metaobject whereas the server itself is bound to a server metaobject. The client_GD_MO and server_GD_MO metaobject classes provide (almost) transparent access to remote groups of objects.

Client source code	Server source code
```class Customer {protected: BankAccount account ("Bob");public: Customer () { account.Credit (1000); account.Debit (500); printf (account.Balance()); }};//MOP reflect BankAccount: client_GD_MO;int main () { Customer client;}```	```class BankAccount {protected: int val;public: BankAccount() { val = 0; } void Credit(int x) { val = val + x; } void Debit(int x) { val = val - x; } int Balance() { return val; }};//MOP reflect BankAccount: server_GD_MO;int main() { BankAccount server("Bob");}```

Fig. 8. A client-server application using metaobjects

Figure 8 shows a simplistic client-server application example. The extra argument "Bob" passed to the server constructor is a group identifier automatically transmitted to the meta-level client_GD_MO and server_GD_MO constructors. It is used to identify the underlying group dedicated to this service. Nodes where server replicas are created are declared in a configuration file (notion of replication domain). The server is created on the appropriate nodes and shared if different clients use the same identifier. The user only runs the client; then, the constructor of client_GD_MO creates all remote server replicas when necessary. Likewise, the destructor of client_GD_MO is responsible for the deletion of all server replicas. A simple service called factory was developed in order to deal with the creation of remote objects.

The extra task of the application programmer just corresponds to some declaration statements. To use an additional meta-level, say fault tolerance, the programmer only has to change //MOP reflect BankAccount: client_GD_MO into //MOP reflect BankAccount: client_FT_MO in the client source code, and //MOP reflect Bank-Account: server_GD_MO into //MOP reflect BankAccount: server_FT_MO in the server source code. The declaration of metaobjects handling distribution is then delegated to the next meta-level. These declarations may be inserted automatically as discussed in Section 6.

5.3 Fault Tolerance

Several fault tolerance mechanisms have been implemented in the form of metaobject classes implemented on FTS: a mechanism based on stable storage, primary-backup and leader-follower replication protocols[2]. In most cases, from the fault tolerance programmer viewpoint, the development of metaobject classes is done using the same class pattern. Figure 9 shows a simplified view of the client_LFR_MO and server_LFR_MO classes implementing the leader-follower mechanism [8].

client_LFR_MO	server_LFR_MO
```class client_LFR_MO {` `protected:` ` server_LFR_MO FT_server;` `public:` ` Meta_StartUp () {...}` ` Meta_MethodCall (...) {` `` `    ...` `    FT_server.FT_Call (...);` `    ...` `  }` `};` `` `` `//MOP reflect server_LFR_MO:` ` client_GD_MO;```	```class server_LFR_MO {` `protected:` ` server_IRP_LFR_MO Followers;` `public:` ` Meta_StartUp () {...}` ` FT_Call (...) {` ` ...` ` Meta_HandleMethodCall(...);` ` ...` ` Followers.FT_Notify (...);` ` }` ` FT_Notify (...) {...}` ` FT_Recover (...) {...}` `};` `//MOP reflect server_LFR_MO:` ` server_GD_MO;` `//MOP reflect` ` server_IRP_LFR_MO:` ` client_GD_MO;```

Fig. 9. Fault tolerance metaobject classes

---

[2] Only server failure is tolerated by these mechanisms.

The client class defines mainly how a method invocation is handled: Meta_MethodCall(). The method invocation is propagated to the server metaobject using a simple statement: FT_server.FT_Call(). The server metaobject is transparently invoked from the client metaobject thanks to the use of the upper distribution meta-level. The server is declared as a local attribute FT_server of class server_LFR_MO. This class is bound to client_GD_MO handling the client behaviour at the distribution meta-level.

The server class holds methods for handling the invocation (all replicas execute the method in this case) and the inter-replica protocol (IRp). The FT_Call() method is responsible for handling the server method invocation at the base-level. This is done using Meta_HandleMethodCall(). The FT_Notify method enables the leader to synchronise with the followers by telling them that a given method was executed[3]. This is done after any base-level method execution, by Followers.FT_Notify(). The followers are invoked transparently from the leader, again thanks to the use of the distribution meta-level.

In all replication mechanisms, a replica crash is detected by FTS which in turn activates the FT_Recover method of one of the alive replicas. In the example given here, if the leader crashes then the FT_Recover involves a follower to become a leader and the creation of a new replica within the appropriate replication domain.

Two declarations are mandatory: //MOP reflect server_LFR_MO: server_GD_MO and //MOP reflect server_IRP_LFR_MO: server_GD_MO indicate that the server and the followers are respectively bound to a server metaobject and a client metaobject at the distribution meta-level. The latter declaration enables the leader to transparently invoke the followers during the inter-replica protocol, as already mentioned. This frees fault tolerance metaobjects from handling distribution problems such as remote creation/deletion, group management and atomic multicast message passing. When implementing metaobjects for replication protocols, the programmer only assumes that all server replicas receive the same invocation requests in the same order even when the server is shared by multiple clients.

In this example, no secure communication level is used and thus fault tolerance metaobjects are bound to distribution metaobjects. If such a level is used then binding declarations must be updated accordingly.

5.4 Secure Communication

The interface of metaobject classes at this level is similar to the class interface defined in the previous section, as shown in figure 10. Based on this model, metaobject classes responsible for the authentication of the client user and the computation/verification of signatures have been implemented. Currently, authentication is based on the Needham-Schroeder protocol [18] upon client creation. Computation and verification of DES-based signatures are performed upon every server invocations.

---

[3] In the primary-backup metaobject, the method FT_Update is used instead of FT_Notify to update the base-level state after each base-level method invocation. This method writes the base-level state of backup replicas using Meta_HandleAssign.

client_SC_MO	server_SC_MO
| ```
class client_SC_MO {
protected:
  server_SC_MO SC_server;
  session_key  SK;
public:
  Meta_StartUp () {
    // get SK from the
    // authentication server
    SC_server.SC_GetSessionKey(SK);

    ...
  }
  Meta_MethodCall (...) {
    ...
    SC_server.SC_Call (...);
    ...
  }
};
//MOP reflect server_SC_MO:
                client_GD_MO;
``` | ```
class server_SC_MO {
protected:
  session_key SK;

public:
  Meta_StartUp () {...}
  SC_GetSessionKey (...) {...}
  SC_Call (...) {
    ...
    Meta_HandleMethodCall(...);
    ...
  }
};



//MOP reflect server_SC_MO:
                server_GD_MO;
``` |

Fig. 10. Secure communication metaobject classes

On the client side, Meta_StartUp authenticates the client and receives a session key. This session key is transparently propagated (in a ticket) to the server by the invocation SC_Server.SC_GetSessionKey(). Within Meta_MethodCall, every server method invocation is signed and propagated transparently to the server by SC_Server.SC_Call(). On the server side, SC_Call verifies the signature and, if it is correct, the invocation is propagated to the base-level by Meta_HandleMethodCall(). The base-level can be the fault tolerance or the application level.

6 Discussion

According to our experiments, the approach presented here provides the expected properties. The current support for applications is extensible by simply adding new metaobjects for fault tolerance and secure communication to the provided libraries. As soon as the reflective compiler is available on a new system platform, then most of the metaobjects can be easily ported. Nevertheless, this involves porting the sub-systems on the new platform which is a more conventional work. We have shown that the use of metaobjects was transparent to the application programmer who is just supposed to be involved in some declarations. Actually, those declarations could be done by a *system configuration officer*, independently and transparently from the application programmer through the use of included files containing all the //MOP reflect declarations at compile time. Conversely, application functionalities are transparent to all types of programmers and the system configuration officer. As shown by the examples, the metaobjects classes can be developed independently from each other and from any use in application programs. The interface of these classes are similar and their public interface is defined by the MOP, enabling classes from various abstractions to be composed quite easily. Finally, the defined classes can be reused and specialised using object-oriented technique to derive new variants of existing mechanisms. The design of the provided mechanisms using object-oriented design methods is one of our current activities.

The limits and drawbacks that we have been identified essentially relate to the MOP that was used. To overcome a problem due to the static binding of application classes to metaobject classes, several names must be given to application classes defining the same behaviour. In addition, Open C++ provides limited meta-information and thus application objects have not been implemented using inheritance. Another point concerns the abstractions dealt with. The organisation of the metaobject stack is possible because neither the security level nor the communication level need to access the application level. This is not typical to these abstractions and others, like soft real-time aspects, could be handled easily in this stack. Nevertheless, if two meta-levels need to access the application level, then their respective behaviour must be handled at a single meta-level. Another lesson that we have learnt from this experience is that the order of levels in the stack, whenever possible, leads to different properties. This must be carefully analysed when using several meta-levels because this could lead to unexpected side effects as shown in the last part of Section 4.2.

In this architecture, the frontier between metaobjects and sub-systems depends very much on the abstraction which is considered. The identification of this frontier was easier for fault tolerance than for security. In the former, replication and other strategies can easily be handled as metaobjects based on basic services that must be implemented within the underlying operating system. In the latter, just secure communication are handled by metaobjects: authentication protocol, signature computation and verification, use of any cryptosystem. Those involve authentication services that are difficult to handle at the application level because of their trusted underlying property. This property must be enforced by their implementation within the operating system.

Several other problems are also not easy to solve but they are not, to our viewpoint, due to the use of metaobjects (handling multiple replies, view changes are they to be considered as failures, etc.).

7 Current Status and Performance Issues

7.1 Current Status

Our experiments are done on an Ethernet network of Sun IPX workstations with SunOS 4, using Open C++ v1.2. Several fault tolerance mechanisms (stable storage, primary-backup and leader-follower replication) have been implemented using the multi-level approach presented in this paper. GDS includes an object-oriented extension of the xAMp package [19] (version 3.1) and the metaobject library provides a support for distributed applications. The library comprises several basic classes (handling creation/deletion of objects, group registration and naming, message management, etc.) used for implementing group-based distribution metaobjects. The size of the source code we developed for all metaobjects libraries is about 10000 lines of C++. This does not include neither xAMp nor libraries of cryptographic functions.

Fault tolerance mechanisms have been designed and implemented using inheritance. Metaobjects using a stable storage approach have been implemented first, then a primary-backup strategy and finally a leader-follower strategy was implemented. Metaobjects implementing the leader-follower strategy have been derived from the previous one quite easily. In both replication examples, the inter-replica protocol was implemented with a multi-level approach. This is of course a key aspect of the implementation of all distributed fault tolerance mechanisms. In FTS, the Unix file system is used as a stable storage service and failure detection is performed today by means of station failure signals provided by the xAMp package. Finally, a service manages system configuration and replication domains in a very simple way.

A first version of the metaobjects handling secure communications has been implemented, based on the Needham-Schroeder authentication protocol with secret keys. Thus, SCS contains today a simple implementation of a Needham-Schroeder authentication server used in our examples; this first implementation will be upgraded later on to be in accordance with the Kerberos authentication protocol. SCS will be also completed with other elements: the highly dependable authentication server that was developed several years ago [20] will be soon included in SCS.

Sub-systems are not totally independent from each other and cooperate for several tasks, such as failure detection, configuration management, stable storage. The role of the sub-systems is also to hold some information shared between meta-levels, groups for instance. This could be perceived as a limit of this approach, although this problem arises in any multi-layer architecture. A distributed application for the management of bank accounts has developed recently. All kinds of metaobjects have been tested with this application in different experiments: first, only distribution metaobjects have been used, then secure communication and distribution metaobjects or fault tolerance and distribution metaobjects, and finally fault tolerance, secure communication and distribution metaobjects. These various configurations were obtained by simply changing //MOP reflect associations between objects and metaobjects at compile-time. In these experiments we have also simulated physical faults (crash failure) and authentication faults (authentication error, session key expiration). Testing several configurations according to various situations is still under way.

Porting $\mathcal{FRIENDS}$ to our experimental platform of Chorus-based PCs is one of our on-going work. The xAMp package has been ported on top of Chorus and the Open C++ compiler is currently being ported: as soon as it is completed, the libraries of metaobject classes will be available on the Chorus platform. The authentication server previously developed at LAAS has also been ported on Chorus.

7.2 Performance Issues

At the time of writing no exhaustive performance measurements have been made. The cost of fault tolerance and secure communication services in the context of a distributed application based on atomic multicast protocols largely outweighs the extra cost due to the use of an efficient compiled MOP-based language like Open C++. To substantiate this idea a first simple experiment was made: the time spent in trapping invocations was compared to the time spent in group communications (i.e. forwarding the invocation message to a group of 3 replicas). For an invocation with 1 kb of parameters, the time for trapping the invocation is about 0.1 ms, most of this time (80%) being used for packing the parameters in an ArgPac object. This packing time is obviously mandatory in the client-server model, whatever the way the interaction between the object and the fault tolerance mechanisms is realised. On the other hand, the time being spent in forwarding the message to the group using the atomic multicast protocol was about 4 ms and computation and verification of a signed invocation message was about 2 ms.

According to these timing values, one can see that the cost of the meta-level indirection is negligible with respect to the cost of both group communication and authentication. Actually, this is not surprising at all. Indeed, the trapping of an invocation corresponds to a C++ method invocation, namely Meta_MethodCall within the metaobject. The interaction between the application object and its meta-level (say the fault tolerance level) is thus nearly identical to any other approach (library function calls, middleware system calls automatically inserted by an IDL pre-compiler). Indeed, group communication appears to be the bottleneck of distributed fault tolerance whatever the approach used for implementing such mechanisms. Finally, it is clear that a more compact and conventional implementation can lead to better performance, but this is the price to pay for flexibility.

8 Conclusion

FRIENDS stands for *Flexible and Reusable Implementation Environment for your Next Dependable System*: its components can be reused and customised to develop a next version of a dependable system. This environment is currently composed of Open C++, several class libraries of metaobjects, the corresponding underlying sub-systems and multicast communication protocols. A first prototype version is now available on a standard Unix platform (SunOS) and later on Chorus. The first experiments have shown that the approach used provides flexibility, in the sense of transparency, independence, composition and reusability of the mechanisms implemented as metaobjects. Because of the compile-time metaobject protocol used, binding of metaobjects to objects is static. A different implementation of the same MOP interface would enable dynamic binding to be done, at the expense of some additional overhead. Performance penalty is always due when new properties are required.

Our next activities first encompass the final development and testing of the first version of *FRIENDS* and its use in a sizeable distributed application. Performance evaluation and a more detailed analysis of the properties must be done now. Indeed, this platform will enable more aspects of object-oriented technology to be investigated for the development of dependable systems. Metaobject classes will be reused to derive new variants of existing mechanisms; for instance, various synchronisation policies can be implemented according to the leader-follower model. The identification of classes reused, the impact of modifications on other classes, the knowledge required about existing classes for doing that job, are some of the aspects we are interested in. Currently, the inheritance hierarchy has been produced with the BON (Business Object Notation) design method [21] using static and dynamic diagrams in order to identify common behaviour among the mechanisms. The use of object-oriented design methods in the development of metaobjects will be continued, in order to evaluate how far reuse can be driven, when new assumptions concerning faults classes and the operational environment are considered. Today, we have not yet considered the use of standard object-oriented execution supports; the GDS sub-system and its companion metaobject library constitute a home-made runtime support for distributed (group of) objects. The use of standard object oriented layers will be investigated using COOL-ORB on Chorus, a CORBA-compliant object-oriented layer on microkernel.

Acknowledgements

The authors wish to thank very much our friends, Brian Randell, Robert Stroud and Zhixue Wu in the PDCS and DeVa projects who participated in the elaboration of these ideas, Paulo Veríssimo and Henrique Fonseca for xAMp, Shigeru Chiba for Open C++ and Marc Rozier for his advices on porting the xAMp package on top of Chorus. Vincent Nicomette, Françoise Cabrolié, Frédéric Salles, Cyril Delamare and Frédéric Melle have contributed to the development of $\mathcal{FRIENDS}$ and must be acknowledged. Finally, we would like to thank Jean-Claude Laprie for his comments on an early version of this paper.

References

[1]   Maes P., "Concepts and Experiments in Computational Reflection", in *Proc. of OOPSLA'87*, Orlando, USA, 1987, pp. 147-155.

[2]   Kiczales G., des Rivières J. and Bobrow D.G., *The Art of the Metaobject Protocol*, MIT Press, 1991.

[3]   Paepcke A., "PCLOS: Stress Testing CLOS — Experiencing the Metaobject Protocol", in *Proc. of OOPSLA'90*, 1990, pp. 194-211.

[4]   Honda Y. and Tokoro M., "Soft Real-Time Programming through Reflection", in *Proc. of the Int. Workshop on Reflection and Meta-level Architecture*, November 1992, pp. 12-23.

[5]   Chiba S. and Masuda T., "Designing an Extensible Distributed Language with Meta-level Architecture", in *Proc. of ECOOP '93, LNCS 707*, Springer-Verlag, Kaiserslautern, Germany, 1993, pp. 482-501.

[6]   Agha G., Frølund S., Panwar R. and Sturman D., "A Linguistic Framework for Dynamic Composition of Dependability Protocols", in *Proc. of DCCA-3*, 1993, pp. 197-207.

[7]   Stroud R.J., "Transparency and Reflection in Distributed Systems", *ACM Operating Systems Review*, 22 (2), April 1993, pp. 99-103.

[8]   Powell D., "Distributed Fault Tolerance — Lessons Learnt from Delta-4", in *Hardware and Software Architecture for Fault Tolerance: Experiences and Perspectives (M. Banâtre and P.A. Lee, Eds.), LNCS 774*, Springer Verlag, 1994, pp.199-217.

[9]   Birman K.J., "Replication and Fault tolerance in the Isis System", *ACM Operating Systems Review*, 19 (5), 1985, pp. 79-86.

[10] Detlefs D., Herlihy M.P. and Wing J.M., "Inheritance of Synchronization and Recovery Properties in Avalon/C++", *Computer*, 21 (12), December 1988, pp. 57-69.

[11] Shrivastava S.K., Dixon G.N. and Parrington G.D., "An Overview of the Arjuna Distributed Programming System", *IEEE Software*, 8 (1), 1991, pp. 66-73.

[12] Masuhara H., Matsuoka S., Watanabe T. and Yonezawa A., "Object-Oriented Concurrent Reflective Languages can be Implemented Efficiently", in *Proc. of OOPSLA'92*, 1992, pp. 127-144.

[13] Powell D., "Failure Mode Assumptions and Assumption Coverage", in *Proc. of FTCS-22*, Boston, USA, 1992, pp. 386-395.

[14] Fabre J.C., Nicomette V., Pérennou T., Wu Z. and Stroud R.J., "Implementing Fault-tolerant Applications using Reflective Object-Oriented Programming", in *Proc. of FTCS-25*, Pasadena, USA, June 1995, pp. 489-498.

[15] Rozier M., Abrossimov V., Armand F., Boule I., Gien M., Guillemont M., Hermann F., Kaiser C., Langlois S., Leonard P. and Neuhauser W., "Overview of the Chorus Distributed Operating System", Chorus Systèmes Technical Report CS-TR-90-25, 1990, 45 p.

[16] Yokote Y., "The Apertos Reflective Operating System: The Concept and Its Implementation", in *Proc. of OOPSLA'92*, 1992, pp. 414-434.

[17] Chiba S.,"Open C++ Release 1.2 Programmer's Guide", Technical Report No. 93-3, Dept. of Information Science, University of Tokyo, 1993.

[18] Needham R.M. and Schroeder M.D., "Using Encryption for Authentication in Large Networks of Computers", *Comm. of the ACM*, 21 (12), December 1978, pp. 993-999

[19] Rodrigues L. and Veríssimo P., "xAMp: A Protocol Suite for Group Communication", in *Proc. of SRDS-11*, 1992, pp. 112-121.

[20] Deswarte Y., Blain L. and Fabre J.C., "Intrusion Tolerance in Distributed Computing Systems", *Proc. of the 1991 IEEE Symp. on Research in Security and Privacy*, Oakland, USA, 1991, pp.110-121.

[21] Waldén K. and Nerson J.M., *Seamless Object-Oriented Software Architecture, Analysis and Design of Reliable Systems*, The Object-Oriented Series, Prentice Hall, 1995, 438 p.

Adaptable Fault Tolerance for Distributed Process Control Using Exclusively Standard Components

Jürgen Bohne[*], Reny Grönberg[*]

Abstract. This paper describes an adaptable fault tolerance architecture for distributed process control which uses exclusively standard hardware, standard system software and standard protocols. It offers a quick and low cost solution to provide non-safety critical, technical facilities and plants with continuous service. Thereby a maximum of practicability for the application engineers is achieved. The architecture is composed from well known fault tolerance methods under the constraints of real-time requirements. The latitude of non-safety critical applications is carefully used to minimize the fault tolerance overhead. Because of the transparency of the fault tolerance each functional part of the process control, which is represented by an application task, can be implemented without regard to non-determinism and executing hosts. The configuration of a control system is easy and simply done by naming hosts, tasks and groups in a file, wherein every individual task has to be declared with the selected fault tolerance strategy.

It can be expected by a fault-tolerant system that reconfiguration, following a fault, is done automatically. The present system does more: it reintegrates repaired hosts automatically and re-establishes the redundant operation, while the entire system is working.

Introduction

It is often required or at least beneficial to equip computer-controlled facilities, such as manufacturing plants, waterworks, traffic control, material transport, or energy distribution systems, with fault-tolerant process control that provides continuous service. However, the costs of special fault-tolerant hardware or facility-specific fault-tolerant software using redundant standard hardware are prohibitive, and may be much higher than the costs resulting from down-time of a poorly controlled system. To trace out a low cost fault tolerance architecture, which is worth applying to the above mentioned facilities, the following extra requirements must be considered: the fault tolerance (ft) must

- produce a minimum of run-time and communication overhead,
- run on a standard operating system and use standard communication protocols,
- use standard hardware without special additions,
- work in a heterogeneous world (different hardware and operating systems),
- be easily adaptable to any application and
- offer a way to migrate the existing control software into the ft-environment.

On the other hand, it is adequate for this type of facilities to assume that only one error occurs during the recovery time, i.e., the interval between error detection and redundancy restoration. Moreover, control systems of this type leave some latitude for the fault tolerance. For example, a rare false output to the technical process has often no or sometimes just a small and unimportant effect, *if the control system continues to work.* This is either due to the periodical execution of the software itself, or the periodicity of the technical process.

[*] Daimler-Benz AG, Research and Technology, Alt-Moabit 96a, D-10559 Berlin
e-mail: {bohne,groen,heiner}@DBresearch–berlin.de, fax: (+49 30) 39982 107

The requirements listed above demand software-implemented fault tolerance. This approach is best suited for applications without hard real-time constraints, which can tolerate short outage times. But up to now there is no fault tolerance support available on the market or offered within the scientific community that fulfills these requirements.

When our project was started in 1991, two recent software-implemented fault-tolerant systems intended for distributed (commercial) transaction processing – ISIS [1,2] and Arjuna [3,4] – were strongly discussed in the scientific community. Both systems are based on redundant servers respectively objects which are members of groups. They are provided with a broadcast communication which guarantees delivery of messages, global ordering and atomicity of message transfer to any active member of a group. The members may be connected over any communication infrastructure (including wide area networks). Our real-time applications do not need all of these guarantees and are typically connected to a bus based local area network. Nevertheless, ISIS and Arjuna have been installed and tested in our institute and found to be too slow in normal (fault free) operation, with too much message overhead.

We therefore decided to design and implement our own ft-architecture for our real-time applications. Our aim was to combine fast reliable message handling, a consistent state service and distributed execution supervision into a complete ft-architecture, that covers the most probable failures with a minimum of overhead and a maximum of flexibility for the application engineers. We used as a starting point the comprehensive overview of distributed fault tolerant systems carried out by the Delta-4 project [5]. The results of our development have been described in the first ft-architecture report [6], which outlines a fault-tolerant system that fulfills the listed requirements. In addition, a strategy is provided to (re-)establish the redundant operation, without halting the control system. Later on, redundancy management has been added, that makes optimal use of the existing hardware.

1 Fault-Tolerant System Architecture

A fault-tolerant control system consists of standard control computers, graphic stations and front end computers, which are directly connected by a possibly redundant bus. The ft-software layer is built on top of the standard operating systems at all of these hosts. It forms a virtual ft-platform upon which the application tasks are executed in different ft-strategies. The operations inside the ft-platform and the communication infrastructure are mostly invisible and are not required to be known by the application.

The application tasks have to use a reliable real-time transport service, provided by the ft-platform. Every task or task-group is identified by a symbolic name. Messages are sent to and received from tasks or task-groups without knowledge of executing hosts. For tasks running a "high level" ft-strategy, it is guaranteed that no input is lost and no inconsistent output becomes valid, even in the presence of a failure. Moreover, the ft-layer guarantees the consistency of the internal states after such tasks fail.

Fault Model

The ft-platform masks permanent and transient hardware faults and non-reproducible software faults. The smallest fault containment unit is a task. The model of the ft-platform is based on the fail-stop processor approach [7]. Proceeding from the precise definitions of a fail-stop processor by Schneider [8], results were found which exploit the latitude of the technical facilities and reduce the implementation constraints and the overhead for totally fail-stop processors. Fail-stop processors are defined in [8] to have three properties: *halt on failure*, *failure status* and *stable storage*. In the ft-platform all these properties are realized with some weakness. The following engineering data and assumptions about failure modes make this weakness bearable.

Halt on failure property: Nowadays modern standard computers are largely equipped with error detection hardware, invisible to the programmer. The probability of detection is rarely below 75% [9][10][11]. In case of a revelation the current activity is stopped immediately by the operating system. About 15% of the transient errors remain undetected and become ineffective (not used, dismissed, corrected) within the subsequent software flow. The rest, about 10% [10] are undetected errors that lead to a violation of the halt on failure assumption, i.e., the host produces incorrect output. These rare remaining effective errors are accepted[1] for our type of facilities because of two facts. First, their detection would cost too much and second, as stated before, the false output, which could be given to the technical process, has just a small and unimportant effect, *if the system continues to work.* Because the latter is guaranteed by the ft-platform, the effect is corrected within the next control cycle(s). If one wants to catch more of the effective errors then dedicated error detection techniques, like compiler generated run-time assertions and double execution as used in the MARS architecture [11][12], may be added.

Failure status property: Commercial computers do not provide a failure status. Permanent hardware errors, like a sudden loss of a total host, must be detected by a time-out mechanism. According to the given overhead limits and to the restriction on (non-real-time) standard operating systems the time within the platform can not strongly be synchronized. Therefore the time-out intervals have to be configured generously.

Stable storage property: For limited overhead we keep a single redundant storage area (per task) on an independent host. Remember, we have the assumption of one error within the recovery interval.

Error Recovery

On revelation of an error, the affected task is terminated by the operating system or by the task cycle time-out mechanism, which is offered to each application task by the ft-platform, and then restarted at the same host. That is why redundancy and non-redundant functionality are not unnecessarily released. A permanent fault is assumed when a second error occurs at the same host within a given time interval. An error during the run-time of the operating system or the ft-management is immediately treated like a permanent fault. In the case of a permanent fault, all tasks on the faulty host, which are executed in a "stand-by" strategy, are switched to another host, i.e., are restarted and provided with consistent state or simply take over control, depending on the chosen ft-strategy. When a repaired host comes up again it is reintegrated into the ft-platform and is used at once, if there is a lack of redundancy, or later, after a permanent fault occurs at another host. The redundant state is recovered without halting the control system.

---

[1] Remember, the low cost fault tolerance platform was never thought for safety critical applications.

2 Fault Tolerance Strategies

Why use different execution strategies? Fault tolerance does not come for nothing, it costs additional CPU-time, space and message transfer and it costs time and money to implement a task in a special structure. The strategies vary in cost and the application engineer normally knows very well what is sufficient for a part of the technical facility that is controlled by a task. Thus, any application task can be configured to run the ft-strategy which is satisfactory to fulfill its requirements. There are seven major strategies which are characterized by the following diagram:

communicates by messages	survives transient faults	survives permanent faults	recovers consistently after faults	operates continuously	strategies
✓	✓	✓	✓	✓	hot stand-by
✓	✓	✓	✓		warm stand-by
✓	✓	✓			cold stand-by
✓	✓				restart, degrade
✓					start once, manual
		✓	✓		external cold standby
		✓			external restart/degrade

Figure 1   Fault tolerance strategies

Tasks in the two highest ft-strategy classes, *hot* and *warm stand-by*, have to adhere to a prescribed cyclic software structure with two calls of the ft-layer at fixed positions of their structure. However, they may choose their work in a non-deterministic way, like all other tasks in any class. Both structures will be discussed in the next sections.

Tasks running *cold stand-by*, *restart* or *degrade* are restarted, after they fail, using their initial state. *Cold stand-by* tasks migrate to another host after a permanent fault is recognized, whilst the others survive only transient faults. *Degrade* tasks halt operations in favor of important tasks when a lack of capacity is found following a permanent fault.

Next is a non-ft strategy class, wherein tasks can communicate with other application tasks, but they are started once and/or can be started manually and therefore are not totally controlled by the ft-management.

The last two classes are "external" strategies. A task executed in an external strategy is treated like a *cold stand-by* or *restart* task, but it does not use the ft-communication. Normally, such tasks are pre-fabricated software products which cannot be changed later on. For example, this could be a graphic display processor, which communicates by a common buffer with its clients. This task type can be connected to the control system by a possibly stateless "connection" task, which must be implemented by the application. An external task and its connection task have to be executed in associated ft-strategies. They can be bound together, so that both tasks restart or degrade away after one task fails.

2.1 *Warm Stand-by* Strategy

The *warm stand-by* strategy is a backward error recovery strategy using checkpoints of the task state. According to the requirement for easy adaptability, the prescribed task structure is cyclic and very simple.

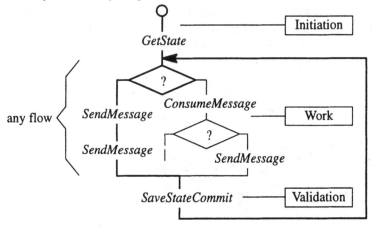

Figure 2   Structure of a *warm stand-by* task

When the program is started it runs in the initiation phase, where it loads its state variables, creates objects etc. In the case of a task restart the initial state will be overwritten with the last remotely saved state at the end of this phase by calling *GetState*. If the saved state changed in length, the ft-layer automatically allocates or reallocates memory before the state is written. The task then enters its task cycle and operates possibly non-deterministically. It may consume messages, read the clock and choose any path, where it may change its task state and send messages. At the end of the task cycle, *SaveStateCommit* is called. At first – as the name suggests – all parts of the state, i.e., memory pages, that have been changed within the task cycle are saved. Secondly, the new state and all produced messages become valid and all consumed messages are deleted. This is done in an atomic action using a special two phase commit protocol (see chapter 3.2). If anything went wrong within the cycle, e.g., a produced message has not arrived at its destination, the application task is restarted. On calling *GetState*, all unconfirmed work of the task is thrown away. Therefore a crash of the task is tolerated at any point.

Normally a problem exists for crashed tasks using a backward error recovery strategy: the domino effect, where partner tasks also have to roll back if communication took place. This effect is evaded by the *warm stand-by* strategy by not validating output and not deleting input within a possibly unfinished task cycle. The reverse of the coin is a weakness with synchronous remote procedure calls.[2] They must be implemented in two task cycles – send and validate the request message in the first cycle and receive the reply message in the second cycle – or they are restricted to informational calls, where a special send flag may be set, so that the request message becomes valid immediately.

---

[2] The existing control software systems and real world applications of our industrial project partners are implemented without synchronous RPCs.

The *warm stand-by* architecture is useful for tasks with time constraints in the range of a second and upwards, depending mainly on the length of the application task state and the duration of the load and initiation phase. *Warm stand-by* tasks are easy to implement and they can be configured to run any ft-strategy, except *hot stand-by*.

2.2 *Hot Stand-by* Strategy

Running a task in "hot stand-by" means that two incarnations of the same program run simultaneously on different hosts. To ensure replica determinism, the twin tasks must be synchronized, which is necessary only once per task cycle using our strategy. For that reason *hot stand-by* tasks need a more complex task structure, wherein the monolithic task cycle is broken into two phases (see Figure 3).

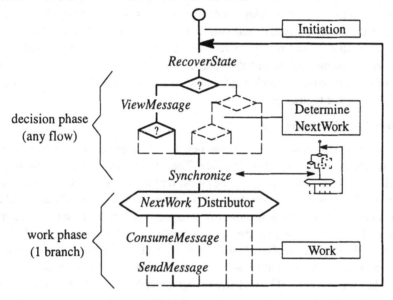

Figure 3   Structure of a *hot stand-by* task

In the first phase, the decision phase, such tasks decide from their actual state, current time and existing messages, what single branch they have to take in the second phase, the work phase, by computing a *NextWork* value. In the decision phase the special receive function *ViewMessage* must be used to get messages without deleting them, because the messages are needed again in the working phase.

The synchronization, which is done by the *Synchronize* call, is given the *NextWork* value and some information that has to be adjusted (like the current time). If, because of non-determinism, leader- and follower-task decide to go different ways, one task, the leader, is defined to be right. The divergent follower must take the same branch as the leader in its work phase and therefore it must ask for the messages, which the leader task "viewed" in its decision phase. *Synchronize* returns the common *NextWork* value and the adjusted information.

Subsequently the *NextWork* value is used to select the work branch. Messages which have been "viewed" before may be consumed on that branch. *ConsumeMessage* returns only messages that are viewed in the leader decision phase. The message content, as well as the adjusted (leader) information, can be used to change the task state and for the computation of new message content. *SendMessage* is handled differently by leader and follower tasks. The leader sends its message requesting an acknowledgment for itself and its twin partner. Both twins wait for the broadcast reply. If no acknowledgment is received within a short time the follower task sends its message instead and both twins continue.

The call to *RecoverState* at the beginning of the task cycle allows redundant operation to be re-established when the task twin comes up (again).

The *hot stand-by* strategy is more complicated to implement, but is necessary if short time constraints must be respected. It is useful for certain types of control functions which would produce too much overhead in *warm stand-by* operation, e.g., in case of a short task cycle. The possible control delay after an error occurs is governed by the real-time capability of the operating system and may be less than half a second for the highest priority task running with a preemptive real-time kernel. The length of the application task state and the duration of the initiation phase has no effect for recovery, such as with *warm stand-by*. *Hot stand-by* implemented tasks can be configured to run also in *warm stand-by* or any other ft-strategy.

2.3 Connection with Process IO

Our idea[3] how to connect process input and output is, to implement a reusable "transformer" task for each type of process interface. These tasks should receive ft-messages, take the contained information and generate output for their specific process (or process-bus) interface. They should also take the input from their interface, compute and send information to the control tasks by means of ft-messages. Such tasks must be configured to execute in the *restart* mode or in the *warm setup* mode on the IO-hosts, i.e., the hosts which contain the process interface. *Warm setup* is a minor execution strategy for *warm stand-by* implemented tasks, that helps to survive transient faults with consistent state. Special IO-hosts, like CPLCs (Computerized Programmable Logical Control), can be integrated into the ft-platform by allocating at least one transformer task to each of it. In this case the task has to transform commands and replies to and from the CPLC software.

After an IO-host permanently fails, the connected part of the technical facility falls out of control, but all other parts continue to function. The ft-platform informs the application software if a destination task of a *SendMessage* call is inactive and cannot be activated, because it is fixed to a specific unavailable host.

Nevertheless, continuous service for front-end parts can be provided by the application engineer, who may install redundant (switchable) process interface in different IO-hosts. In this case, two principle procedures are possible. First, the application control software may switch over, after the primary IO-host and transformer task permanently fail, and send messages to the alternative task on the redundant IO-host. Second (and better), the ft-platform automatically restarts the failed task on the redundant host. This can be done by configuring the transformer task to execute in *warm* or *cold stand-by* mode fixed to the redundant IO-hosts.

---

[3] Some similar ideas to the ft-platform and fault-tolerant process IO are given by Silva et al. [13].

3 Details of the Fault Tolerance Design and Implementation

The most important parts of the ft-layer are the ft-manager task, four types of ft-servers and the application interface, as shown in Figure 4. The monitoring and operating task MonOp shows which hosts are alive and what tasks are being executed at those hosts.

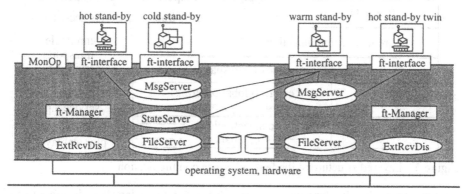

Figure 4   Elements of fault tolerance layer

3.1 System Startup

When a host is powered up, the ft-manager is started and reads in a globally consistent configuration file, naming all hosts, tasks, execution modes and parameters of the control system. The ft-manager creates a routing table used by the ft-communication which is part of the ft-layer. It inserts the first static information relating to all configured ft-managers and starts the external-receive-dispatcher (ExtRcvDis). This ft-server gets all messages from the network and dispatches them to the final destinations inside the host. Thereafter, the ft-manager tries to connect to the partner ft-managers using the ft-communication. All active ft-managers confirm a common view of the ft-platform and take the active manager with the highest configured rank as commanding manager.

Based on this view, a host selection takes place by the commanding manager for all configured application tasks, taking into account their ft-strategies. A task can be given a fixed or a preferable place for execution in the configuration file. Usually, this predetermined host is taken. If no host is given, or if the preferable host is off line, an executor host is chosen by scanning the host service attributes, e.g., types, devices, connections, or special functions. The attributes must match the requirement attributes of the application task (for details see chapter 4). In addition, a potential host must possess enough free capacity at selection time. After the host selection is finished and a global distribution is committed, each manager completes the routing table by adding all information relating to the distribution. Then it starts, supervises, controls and restarts all the ft-servers and application tasks which are chosen to be executed by the local host.

Before an application task is started, it must be sure that all necessary ft-servers are running. Each task is given a local message-server which works as its input queue. *Hot stand-by* and *warm stand-by* tasks are provided with a redundant message-server pair. All *warm stand-by* tasks are also associated with a state-server running on a remote host. Redundant file servers are created and associated dynamically, on demand of an application task.

3.2 Fault Tolerance Communication

Application tasks, ft-servers and ft-managers send and receive their messages using the fault tolerance communication, which is shown in Figure 5.

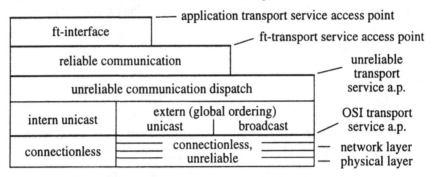

Figure 5   Layered structure of the fault tolerance communication

On top, the *application transport service* is located in the ft-interface. It offers three access points to the application software: "no wait send", "wait receive time-out" and "wait receive time-out and consume". The latter means delete the message after reception. Application tasks may address tasks, task groups and objects inside the tasks. Application messages are extended to ft-messages by the ft-interface. In this way the alphanumeric addressing at the application level is transformed into ft-identifiers (ft-id).

Any addressable part inside the ft-layer is given such an unambiguous ft-id, consisting of an index and a type which is, for instance: task, server or group. All ft-messages are led by a destination ft-id or an ft-id list. A destination ft-id names an ft-group, an ft-server or a task. A group ft-id points to a static ft-group, for example a message-server group derived from a group of application tasks, configured at the application level. An ft-id list is used when a dynamic group must be addressed. An example for a dynamic group is "the assembly of the state-server plus all message-servers which have been addressed in the last cycle of a *warm stand-by* task". All these servers, including the redundant ones, are "pushed" by a single external broadcast message.

The ft-interface itself uses the *ft-transport service*, which provides reliable communication. The ft-transport service is also used by the ft-servers and the ft-manager.

Synchronization problems in distributed systems can be solved by putting the events in a total order. The basic solution, adding logical clocks to events, is described by Lamport in [14]. However, totally ordering events is accompanied by overhead. Our analysis of the existing application control software did not show any decision, which was based on the ordering of messages coming from different tasks. Nevertheless, causality and atomicity – in the sense of the ABCAST definition given by Birman in [1] – is guaranteed by the ft-transport service for all application messages with one exception. We cannot guarantee these attributes if a Byzantine transfer failure (e.g., an incoming link failure) appears, which happens, however, very rarely. In order to provide the attributes, the ft-transport service systematically sends application messages over the network (even if the destinations are internal), exploiting the global physical bus as a serializing single point.

Furthermore the service ensures the fifo-order of all messages by adding a logical input clock and an unequivocal output message stamp, consisting of the producer task ft-id and its logical output clock (both are part of the saved task state), to every message. The additional information is also used to detect duplicate or missing messages. The service requests acknowledgement by setting a flag in the output message if the transfer is not assured otherwise (e.g., by the commit protocol or in case of only host-internal destinations by the host-hardware). Acknowledgement messages are sent by the destination part of the layer and contain the output message stamp. The source part receives the acknowledgement message(s), compares the stamp(s) and marks the ft-id of each correct replier in its replier list. The list was derived from the leading ft-id or ft-id list of the output message (members of static groups are commonly known). The output message is retransmitted once if a replier is left unmarked after acknowledgement time-out. The application is informed of a replier which does not acknowledge both transfers.

The communication flow then passes to the *unreliable transport service*, where messages are dispatched using the routing table, which was generated by the ft-manager. Messages directed to a group ft-id or an ft-id list are broadcasted in any case, all others are sent as unicast messages to their host-internal or external destination. External unicast and broadcast messages, including all such messages from the local host, are caught by the external-receive-dispatcher (ExtRcvDis), an ft-server that is part of the ft-communication. The dispatcher forwards external messages to their final destinations, using the unreliable transport service. If a message is directed to a group ft-id or an id-list, the dispatcher copies the message and forwards it to all group members running inside its host. An external broadcast message is dismissed if no final destination is located at the host. This construction, together with the ability to broadcast a message in an indivisible whole over a bus-based network (for example IEEE 802.3), guarantees the causal order for all external messages and the atomicity for external broadcast messages.

Commit Protocol

The commit protocol, which executes every time the commit point of a *warm stand-by* task is reached, needs a special quick solution with a minimum of external messages. A two phase commit protocol was composed, which uses the unreliable transport service to transfer its messages: external broadcast commit-open, internal unicast commit-acknowledge (sent by the involved state- and message-servers and collected by their ft-managers), external unicast commit-reply (sent by the remote ft-managers which *must* have got commit-acknowledge) and external broadcast commit-close.

The protocol was completed by the following precautions to break up a possible deadlock after a commit-close message is lost: Every commit-open message contains the preceding commit code (CONFIRM or ABORT), so that – because of the period of the control software – pending commit servers, which haven't got the commit-close, have a good chance to close correctly with delay. Each server with pending commit, which neither gets a commit-close nor a commit-open message within the scalable commit time interval, "auto-confirms" and closes the commit by itself. The rare commit-close messages with code ABORT are given by sending two redundant broadcast messages within a few milliseconds delay.

3.3 Recovery and Restoration

Any task or server is restarted at its former host after it has crashed. When a permanent fault is detected or supposed, a new executor host must be found and the level of redundancy must be re-established. A new host selection takes place, as described in chapter 3.1, and the routing tables are partially changed by all active ft-managers. The subsequent restoration of the redundant state is carried out while the system is working.

Hot stand-by Recovery

In an error-free state, a *hot stand-by* process consists of two twin partner tasks: the leader and the follower. Both twins normally synchronize very quick. The leader sends its decision which the follower receives and acknowledges. After the twins have got their message they continue. If the leader has got no reply after the synchronization time interval has passed, it sends its decision once again. A twin changes to simplex state as soon as the synchronization time interval and an additional small reaction time interval ends and no message has arrived. Thereafter it sends a notice to the partner and continues with its own decision. If the partner has not crashed it receives this notice after calling an ft-interface function and terminates. This may happen, for instance, to a simply delayed partner or to a follower partner if the synchronization reply to the leader was lost.

The inactive partner is restarted on the former host or, in the case of a permanent fault, on a new host and enters *RecoverState* after the initiation phase. The state is updated when the active partner begins a new cycle and also enters *RecoverState*. If the time constraints of the task can be met, the state is transferred in one piece. Otherwise a step by step strategy is used to update the state in more than one cycle. In any case, the *hot stand-by* task is delayed for a short time. Thus the application software can suppress a restoration in time-critical situations of control.

Warm stand-by Recovery

Normally, before a *warm stand-by* task is started, a redundant executor host and a host for its remote state-server is selected. Upon a permanent fault, a *warm stand-by* task is restarted on its preselected redundant executor host. On this executor host, CPU-time and memory was reserved for the *warm stand-by* task, or given to a *degrade* task which can be aborted on demand. A new host must be searched for if no redundant host was found before, or if the redundant host went off line in the meantime, or if the capacity was given to another task which was hit by a permanent fault. If there exists no host which owns free capacity, the host running the remote state-server is used for restart. In that case the state-server stops after recovery in order to make memory available. Every time a repaired host comes up again, the redundancy management is informed. It restarts the state-server as soon as possible and tries to reserve redundant execution capacity for the task.

Server Recovery

If a redundant message-server must be restarted, it recovers from its active message-server partner. Non-redundant message-servers lose their messages when they are stopped or crashed and are empty on restart. When a state-server is started or restarted, it requests a complete state save. The redundant state will be produced when its *warm stand-by* client task reaches the *SaveStateCommit* point.

4 Capability and Configuration of the Fault-Tolerant Platform

The configuration of a distributed control system is very easy. The application engineer has to fill in a configuration file and dispatch it to all hosts consistently. A configuration file consists of HOST, TASK, and GROUP lines. All hosts of the ft-platform have to be named together with their provided attributes enclosed in angle brackets. Every individual task has to be declared naming the execution mode and the required attributes. In our example, the configured ft-platform covers 7 hosts and 8 tasks have to be executed:

```
#*********************************************
HOST    Zeus            <sun>;
HOST    Hera            <sun,bigdisk>;
HOST    Athena          <sun,graphic,bigdisk>;
HOST    Cassandra       <sgi,graphic>;
HOST    Hermes          <sgi,graphic>;
HOST    Hades;
HOST    Persephone;

TASK    Alarm           h@*<sun>;
TASK    Control         h@Zeus|Hera;
TASK    Strategy        w@*<sun&bigdisk>;
TASK    MMI             c@Hermes|*<graphic>;
TASK    PlantDetails    d@*<sgi>;
TASK    GraphicSys      D@{PlantDetails};
TASK    FrontEnd1       r@Hades;
TASK    FrontEnd2       r@Persephone;
TASK    MonOp           m@*;

GROUP   PlantInfo       Control,Alarm;
#*********************************************
```

- The first application task, Alarm, has to be executed in _hot stand-by_ as a twin task. The twins may run on each host (wild-card star for host) provided with the attribute <sun>, these are Zeus, Hera and Athena.

- The next task is also a _hot stand-by_ task: Control. But in this case, the task twins are forced to run on Zeus and Hera. If one host dies, no redundancy can be provided for Control, in contrast to the Alarm task above.

- Strategy is a _warm stand-by_ task, which may run on any <sun> host with a <bigdisk>, which are Hera and Athena; it also could be declared as: w@Hera|Athena.

- The MMI is executed in _cold stand-by_. If available, (leftmost) host Hermes is selected preferably to execute MMI, otherwise it executes at one of the other <graphic> hosts.

- PlantDetails are shown, as long as one of the two <sgi> hosts works and is not otherwise being used. If, for example, Hermes and Athena go off line, MMI must be switched to Cassandra, the only host left with a <graphic> attribute, and PlantDetails "degrades" away.

- GraphicSys is a graphic processor, only available in binary code. Therefore it is configured as an external task (uppercase _D_ = _external degrade_) and is bound (as indicated by the braces) to its connection task PlantDetails. Thus, it always executes at the same host, where PlantDetails executes, or "degrades" away.

- The process-IO transformer tasks FrontEnd1 and FrontEnd2 are forced to run at their hosts Hades and Persephone and are restarted on transient faults.
- The ft-monitoring and operating task MonOp can be started manually at any host.

Finally an application message group is configured. If a message is sent to the group PlantInfo, it is transferred to the tasks Alarm and Control. If a task reads a message and uses the selector PlantInfo, it gets a messages from task Alarm or Control.

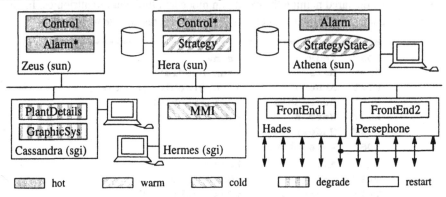

Figure 6   Possible startup distribution of the example configuration file[4]

5 Concluding Remarks

Current Implementation: A prototype of the fault tolerance platform has been implemented using the POSIX.1 environment. The external communication protocol is UDP/IP. The ft-platform consists of about 23000 lines of code and was tested by tasks of any ft-strategy and in any combination with up to six hosts. The ft-platform executes on Sun (SOLARIS), SiliconGraphics (IRIX), DEC-Alpha (Digital-UNIX), HP (HPUX) and PCs (LINUX). For demonstration purposes two control systems have been implemented with tasks of different ft-strategies. The first is a conventional system, that controls a baggage transportation system. It was written in C using 2 SGIs and 2 SUNs. The second is an object oriented system which is implemented in Smalltalk. It controls the disposition of a plant with several injection molding machines and needs 3 SUNs to work.

Performance Measurement: A performance test was implemented by our industrial project partner. An extract of the evaluation with SUN Sparc10/30 hosts is given as follows.

Message round trip time of 2 remote running tasks, message length up to 1024 bytes:

hot stand-by ≈ 12 ms

warm stand-by ≈ 22 ms (+ 1.5 ms / KByte state to save)

restart, cold stand-by ≈ 7 ms

Recovery time:

hot stand-by = 1 s (scalable) synchronization time-out

warm stand-by ≈ 200 ms + 0.8 ms/KByte State (transient error, same host)

+ 3 s (scalable) heart beat time-out (perm. error, host crash)

---

[4] For clarity some parameter types are left out in the example configuration file, but have an influence on the startup and reconfiguration selection. Memory and CPU-speed parameters, for example, are points provided by each host from which the requirement points of each task are subtracted.

Evaluation: An industrial team successfully integrated the fault tolerance platform into a part of a commercial control system, which has been operational for a long time and controls gas, water and energy distribution. They recommend the ft-platform for the next generation of the control system in general.

Conclusion: In this paper a software-implemented platform has been described that provides fault tolerance and continuous service in an inexpensive way. The ft-platform is composed from well known fault tolerance methods under the constraints of real-time requirements. Additionally the following strong requirements have been fulfilled: The ft-platform is exclusively based on standard system software and protocols. Application software, even existing packages, are easily adaptable. Only standard hardware is necessary which may even be heterogeneous.

References

[1]   K. Birman, R. Cooper, K. Marzullo: *ISIS and META Projects Progress Report*, 1990

[2]   K. P. Birman: *Reliable Enterprise Computing Systems*, Lecture Notes in Comp. Science: HW and SW Architectures for Fault Tolerance, Springer 1994, pp. 140–150

[3]   S. K. Shrivastava, G. N. Dixon, G. D. Parrington: *An Overview of the Arjuna Distributed Programming System*, IEEE Software, pp. 66–73, January 1991

[4]   S. K. Shrivastava: *Arjuna and Voltan: Case Studies in Building Fault-Tolerant Distributed Systems Using Standard Components*, Lecture Notes in Comp. Science: HW and SW Architectures for Fault Tolerance, Springer 1994, pp. 218–226

[5]   D. Powell (Editor): *Delta-4: A generic Architecture for Dependable Distributed Computing.* Research Reports ESPRIT, Project 818/2252, Springer 1991

[6]   J. Bohne: *Task-specific Fault Tolerance for Distributed Control Systems*, Daimler-Benz Technical Report, May 1992

[7]   J. C. Laprie (ed.) IFIP WG 10.4 (Dependable Computing and Fault Tolerance): *Dependability: Basic Concepts and Terminology*, Springer 1992

[8]   F. B. Schneider: Byzantine Generals in Action: *Implementing Fail-Stop Processors*, ACM Transaction on Computer Systems, Vol.2, No.2, 5/1984

[9]   H. Madeira, G. Quadros, J. Gabriel: *Experimental Evaluation of a Set of Simple Error Detection Techniques*, Microprocessing and Microprogramming No.30, 1990

[10] J. G. Silva, L. M. Silva, H. Madeira, J. Bernardino: *Experimental Evaluation of the Fail-Silent Behavior in Computers Without Error Masking*, FTCS-24, June 1994

[11] J. Karlson, P. Folkesson, J. Arlat, Y. Crouzet, G. Leber: *Integration and Comparison of Three Physical Fault Injection Techniques*, Esprit Basic Research Series: Predictably Dependable Computing Systems 1994

[12] H. Kopetz, H. Kants, G. Grünsteidl, P. Puschner, J. Reisinger: *Tolerating Transient Faults in MARS*, FTCS-20, June 1990

[13] J. G. Silva, L. M. Silva, H. Madeira, J. Bernadino: *A Fault-Tolerant Mechanism for Simple Controllers*, Dependable Computing – EDCC-1, October 1994

[14] L. Lamport: *Time, clocks, and the ordering of events in a distributed system*, Communications ACM 21, 7/1978

Session 2

Fault Injection

Chair: Johan Karlsson, Chalmers University of Technology, Sweden

On Stratified Sampling for High Coverage Estimations*

David Powell, Michel Cukier, Jean Arlat

LAAS-CNRS
7 Avenue du Colonel Roche
31077 Toulouse - France

Abstract. This paper addresses the problem of estimating the coverage of a fault tolerance mechanism through statistical processing of observations collected in fault-injection experiments. In an earlier paper, several techniques for sampling the fault/activity input space of a fault tolerance mechanism were presented. Various estimators based on simple sampling in the whole space and stratified sampling in a partitioned space were studied; confidence limits were derived based on a normal approximation. In this paper, the validity of this approximation is analyzed, especially for high coverage systems. The theory of confidence regions is then introduced to estimate the coverage without approximation when, for practical reasons, stratification is used. Three statistics are considered for defining confidence regions. It is shown that one of these statistics — a vectorial statistic — is often more conservative than the other two. However, only the vectorial statistic is computationally tractable. The results obtained are compared with those based on approximation by means of three hypothetical example systems.

1 Introduction

Fault-tolerance mechanisms, like any other human-engineered artefact, are never perfect. Residual imperfections in their design are usually the limiting factor to the degree of dependability that can be achieved by a fault-tolerant system [1]. If such a system is to be used in critical applications, it is particularly important to assess the efficiency of the underlying mechanisms. One measure of this efficiency is their fault tolerance coverage, defined as the probability of system recovery given that a fault exists [2]. This paper addresses the problem of estimating fault tolerance coverage by processing the observations collected in a set of fault-injection experiments [3-9].

A single fault-injection experiment consists of injecting a fault condition into a simulation or a prototype of a fault-tolerant system and observing the behavior of the system to determine whether or not the injected fault has been properly handled by the system's fault tolerance mechanisms. In practical systems, it is not feasible to inject all fault conditions that could possibly occur during the system's operational life. Coverage evaluation is therefore usually carried out by statistical estimation, where inferences about the behavior of the system regarding the complete fault population are based on a sample observation. Since the effect of a fault is dependent on system activity at the moment the fault is sensitized, we consider a sampling space consisting of the combination of the fault space and the set of system "activities" at the moment of fault sensitization.

There have been several previous studies on statistical techniques based on fault injection for evaluating the effectiveness of fault-tolerant systems. Agrawal [10] and Daehn [11] have studied *simple sampling* techniques (in the complete "fault/activity" sample

---

*   This work was partially supported by the DεVΛ project (ESPRIT n°20072).

space) for decreasing the number of fault simulation experiments necessary to determine the effectiveness of hardware-fault test patterns. In these studies, the effectiveness of a set of test patterns is quantified by the "fault coverage" defined as the *proportion* of a finite fault set that is successfully detected. This is quite a different viewpoint to the one studied in this paper, where we are concerned with the coverage of on-line error-detection and fault tolerance mechanisms defined as a *conditional probability*.

Partitioning of the sample space into *classes* or *strata* is called *stratified sampling* and was first studied in the context of fault injection in [12]. Wang *et al.* [13] used stratified sampling to introduce *equivalence classes*, defined as a set of faults that can be determined — in advance — to have the same effect on system behavior. The aim of Wang *et al.* was to reduce the number of fault-injection experiments necessary to obtain a statistically significant estimate of coverage while only injecting one fault in each equivalence class. However, it was concluded that no benefit could be obtained from this approach in practical systems for which each equivalence class constitutes a very small proportion of the overall sample space.

Constantinescu [14] performed statistical experiments in a multidimensional finite space of events (each dimension being an attribute of a fault/activity). Multistage and stratified sampling are considered, as well as a combination of both. Constantinescu assumed that the fault/activities have the same occurrence probability, so the author estimated the *coverage factor* for the particular case when it is equal to the *coverage proportion*. The normal distribution approximation has been used to estimate the coverage confidence limits.

In [12], several coverage estimation techniques based on *simple sampling* and on *stratified sampling* were considered. It was concluded that stratified sampling techniques were of particular interest. An *a priori* representative stratification, in which the number of experiments carried out in each class of the input space is pre-determined according to the probability of real fault/activity occurrences in each class, leads to an estimator whose variance is less than or equal to that of the estimator for representative sampling in the complete space. It was assumed that the estimation can be approximated by a normal distribution by applying the central limit theorem. The coverage confidence limit estimations presented in that paper were based on this approximation.

This paper presents some completely new work on the theory of estimation for systems with very high coverage, i.e., ones for which most if not all injected faults are successfully handled. We first discuss the validity of the normal distribution approximation when estimating the coverage confidence limits. It is argued that this approximation is no longer valid for systems with high coverage so new methods without this approximation are introduced. These methods lead to new results that can be in contradiction with previous statistical lore based on the normal distribution approximation. The new methods are tested by means of three hypothetical systems whose characteristics are purposely chosen to stress the considered estimation techniques to determine their range of applicability.

We place particular emphasis on *stratified sampling* techniques since there are several practical reasons for partitioning the sample space. First, stratification can simplify the fault injection process. For example, in physical pin-level fault injection, a fault-injection probe is physically placed on each integrated circuit that is to be faulted. Moving the probe from one circuit to another usually requires manual intervention so it is natural to group together all the fault-injection experiments concerning a single circuit, and consider these faults as a class. Stratification can be used to *re-interpret the results* of a fault-injection campaign should, for example, new knowledge be acquired about the actual distribution of real faults. Without stratification, use of such new knowledge would require a whole new fault-injection campaign since the distribution of injected faults must reflect the actual distribution of real faults. This point is also relevant with respect to data obtained from tests aimed at removing deficiencies in the fault tolerance mechanisms. If some parts of the system are tested more than others, then stratified estimation can be used to make use of all extra data for estimating coverage. Third, under certain conditions, stratified sampling allows for the *composition of results* of fault-injection experiments. Consider the situation in which part of an already-tested system has been replaced by a new version. If we can assume that the fault-handling behavior of the unchanged part of the system is not affected by the introduction of the new sub-system [15], stratification allows re-use of the previously obtained results, with new experiments carried out only for the new sub-system.

As an example of how the methods presented in this paper might be used, consider the following scenario:

A self-checking system S is composed of two self-checking subsystems, S_1 and S_2. Suppose that 10,000 faults have been injected into S_1, and 5,000 faults into S_2, and that none of the faults injected into S_1 went undetected but there were 2 faults injected into S_2 that were not detected. Given that the probabilities of real faults occurring in S_1 and S_2 are 0.9 and 0.1 respectively, what can we say about the overall non-coverage of the composite system S and with what degree of confidence?

We will show in this paper how a lower confidence limit can be estimated for the coverage of the composite system S.

The remainder of the paper is organized as follows. Sections 2 and 3 recapitulate some notions from [12] concerning basic definitions and two categories of sampling techniques: simple sampling and stratified sampling. Two point estimators are introduced for the latter case. Section 4 gives the coverage confidence limit estimators obtained with both sampling strategies when applying the normal distribution approximation. Section 5 then tackles the problem of exact sampling distributions for both sampling methods. We introduce, for stratified sampling, the theory of confidence regions. A vectorial statistic is introduced and compared with the previously defined point estimators. Section 6 compares the results obtained for three hypothetical examples with both simple sampling and stratified sampling, and using both approximate and exact sampling distributions. Finally, Section 7 concludes the paper.

2 Coverage factor

Let H be a variable characterizing the handling of a particular fault, such that $H = 1$ if the mechanism correctly handles the fault and $H = 0$ otherwise.

The effect of a given fault is dependent on system activity at the moment of, and following, the sensitization of the fault, so the complete input space of a fault tolerance mechanism consists not only of the considered *fault space F* but also the *activity space A* due to the system's functional inputs. We can thus formally define the *coverage factor* of a fault tolerance mechanism in terms of the complete input space defined as the Cartesian product $G = F \times A$:

$$c = \Pr\{H = 1 | g \in G\} \tag{1}$$

i.e., the conditional probability of correct fault handling, given the occurrence of a fault/activity pair $g \in G$.

H is a discrete random variable that can take the values 0 or 1 for each element of the fault/activity space G. Let $h(g)$ denote the value of H for a given point $g \in G$ and let $p(g)$ be the *probability of occurrence* of g. Expression (1) can then be rewritten as [12]:

$$c = \sum_{g \in G} h(g)p(g) \tag{2}$$

i.e., the expected value of H. It should be stressed that the distribution $p(g)$ is an inherent part of the very *definition* of coverage as a conditional probability parameter. Without knowledge about $p(g)$, one cannot make meaningful statements about the coverage factor of a system. This point was also clearly stressed in [16], when analyzing the results of fault injection experiments on a system decomposed into subsystems. At best, one may use the *coverage proportion*, $\tilde{c} = \dfrac{1}{|G|} \sum_{g \in G} h(g)$, to describe the effectiveness of a given fault tolerance mechanism, but one can only use such a measure of effectiveness as a branching probability parameter for predicting system dependability (e.g., in stochastic Markov chain models) if it can be assumed that all fault/activity pairs in G are equally probable, i.e., $p(g) = 1/|G|$.

The most accurate way to determine c would be to submit the system to all $g \in G$ and to observe all events $h(g)$. However, such exhaustive testing is only possible under very restrictive hypotheses. For this reason, coverage evaluation is in practice carried out by submitting the system to a subset of fault/activity occurrences $G^* \subset G$ obtained by random sampling in the space G and then using statistics to estimate c.

3 Sampling strategies

Extending on the theory presented in [12], we consider the theory of coverage factor estimation by sampling first in a non-partitioned sampling space and then in a partitioned sampling space.

3.1 Sampling in a non-partitioned space

We consider sampling with replacement of a sub-set G^* of n fault/activity pairs in G. To each element of G is assigned a *selection probability*, $t(g)$, such that $\forall g \in G$, $t(g) > 0$ and $\sum_{g \in G} t(g) = 1$. Note that the sampling experiments are Bernoulli trials with outcome $H = 1$ with probability θ and $H = 0$ with probability $1 - \theta$ where $\theta = \sum_{g \in G} h(g)t(g)$. By setting $t(g)$ equal to:

- $1/|G|$, we obtain a *uniform sample* and $\theta = \tilde{c}$, the coverage *proportion*,
- $p(g)$, we obtain a *representative sample* and $\theta = c$, the coverage *factor*.

Let Γ_i denote the ith fault/activity pair added to the sample. The selection probability of the ith fault/activity pair is independent from the value of i: $\forall i$, $\Pr\{\Gamma_i = g\} = t(g)$.

Let $\tau(\Gamma_i)$ and $\pi(\Gamma_i)$ respectively denote the values of the selection probability $t(g)$ and the occurrence probability $p(g)$ for the ith fault/activity pair, and let $h(\Gamma_i)$ be the outcome of the experiment (the observed value of the fault tolerance predicate H). An unbiased point estimator for c is given by [12]:

$$\hat{c}(\Gamma_1, ..., \Gamma_n) = \frac{1}{n}\sum_{i=1}^{n} h(\Gamma_i) \frac{\pi(\Gamma_i)}{\tau(\Gamma_i)} \tag{3}$$

With representative sampling, we have $\forall i \in \{1..n\}$, $\tau(\Gamma_i) = \pi(\Gamma_i)$ and (3) may be

rewritten as:
$$\hat{c}(\Gamma_1, ..., \Gamma_n) = \frac{1}{n}\sum_{i=1}^{n} h(\Gamma_i)$$

Equivalently, an unbiased estimator of the system non-coverage $\bar{c}$ $(=1-c)$ is given by:

$$\boxed{\hat{\bar{c}}(X) = \frac{X}{n}} \tag{4}$$

where $X = n - \sum_{i=1}^{n} h(\Gamma_i)$ is the number of fault tolerance deficiencies observed for n injected fault/activity pairs. In the sequel, we refer to the random variable X as the *deficiency number* and an observation of X is noted x.

3.2 Sampling in a partitioned space

For the sampling techniques that follow, the sampling space G is considered as partitioned into M *classes* or *strata*:

$$G = \bigcup_{i=1}^{M} G_i \text{ such that } \forall i,j, \ i \neq j, \ G_i \cap G_j = \varnothing$$

We can rewrite the coverage factor definition (2) as follows:

$$c = \sum_{i=1}^{M} \sum_{g \in G_i} h(g)p(g) = \sum_{i=1}^{M} p(g \in G_i) \sum_{g \in G_i} h(g)p(g|g \in G_i) = \sum_{i=1}^{M} p_i c_i$$

where $p(g \in G_i) \equiv p_i$ is the relative probability of fault/activity occurrences in class G_i and c_i is the corresponding coverage factor:

$$c_i = \sum_{g \in G_i} h(g)p(g|g \in G_i)$$

A target system can be characterized by:

- $\mathbf{p} = [p_1,...,p_M]$, the vector of fault/activity occurrence probabilities in each class of the fault/activity space G;

- $\bar{\mathbf{c}} = [\bar{c}_1,...,\bar{c}_M]$, the (unknown) vector of class non-coverages;

such that the overall non-coverage is given by the scalar product:

$$\boxed{\bar{c} = \sum_{i=1}^{M} p_i \bar{c}_i = \mathbf{p}.\bar{\mathbf{c}}^T}$$

In a stratified fault-injection campaign, a fixed number of experiments are carried out in each class (using representative sampling within each class, cf. Section 3.1). The random variables characterizing the deficiency number X_i for each class together constitute a random *deficiency vector* **X**. A stratified fault-injection campaign is therefore defined by:

- $\mathbf{n} = [n_1,\dots,n_M]$, the number of fault/activity pairs injected per class;
- $\mathbf{x} = [x_1,\dots,x_M]$, the observed value of the deficiency vector **X**.

We first consider two estimators defined respectively by the *arithmetic* and *weighted* averages of the elements of the deficiency vector **X**:

$$Y_A(\mathbf{X}) = \frac{1}{n}\sum_{i=1}^{M} X_i \qquad\qquad Y_W(\mathbf{X}) = \sum_{i=1}^{M} \frac{p_i}{n_i} X_i$$

and two stratified allocations of n experiments corresponding respectively to a *representative* and a *homogeneous* allocation:

$$\mathbf{n}_R = [p_1 n, \dots, p_M n] \qquad\qquad \mathbf{n}_H = \left[\frac{n}{M}, \dots, \frac{n}{M}\right]$$

When each statistic is considered with each allocation, three point estimation techniques can be considered:

$$
\begin{array}{|ll|}
\hline
Y_A(\mathbf{X})\text{ or }Y_W(\mathbf{X})\text{ with }\mathbf{n_R} \Rightarrow & \hat{\bar{c}}_R(\mathbf{X}) = \dfrac{1}{n}\sum_{i=1}^{M} X_i = \dfrac{X}{n} \\[2ex]
Y_W(\mathbf{X})\text{ with }\mathbf{n}_H \Rightarrow & \hat{\bar{c}}_{WH}(\mathbf{X}) = \dfrac{M}{n}\sum_{i=1}^{M} p_i X_i \\[2ex]
Y_A(\mathbf{X})\text{ with }\mathbf{n}_H \Rightarrow & \hat{\bar{c}}_{AH}(\mathbf{X}) = \dfrac{1}{n}\sum_{i=1}^{M} X_i = \dfrac{X}{n} \\[1ex]
\hline
\end{array}
\qquad (5)
$$

The latter technique is called naive stratification since the estimate it provides is biased (its expected value is in fact the average class non-coverage). By extension, we call $Y_A(\mathbf{X})$ the naive estimator and $Y_W(\mathbf{X})$ the stratified estimator since only the latter includes the fault/activity occurrence distribution and is therefore always unbiased.

In [12] it is shown that the variance of the stratified estimator with a representative allocation, $\hat{\bar{c}}_R(\mathbf{X})$, is never greater than that of the estimator for simple sampling, $\hat{\bar{c}}(X)$.

4 Confidence limits using approximations

Based on the confidence limit expressions presented in [12], we successively consider simple sampling and stratified sampling.

4.1 Confidence limit with simple sampling

An upper $100\gamma\%$ confidence limit estimator for $\bar{c}$ is defined by:

$$\bar{c}_\gamma^\uparrow(X) \;:\; \Pr\!\left[\bar{c} \le \bar{c}_\gamma^\uparrow(X) \mid \bar{c}\right] = \gamma \qquad (6)$$

i.e., if a large number of individual values x of the deficiency number X are considered, $\bar{c}_\gamma^\uparrow(x)$ will be greater than the unknown value $\bar{c}$ $100\gamma\%$ of the time.

A classic way of defining such a confidence limit is to assume that, due to the central limit theorem, the non-coverage point estimator $\hat{\bar{c}}(X)$ is normally distributed around its expected value which leads to the well-known form for the confidence limit estimator:

$$\bar{c}_\gamma^\uparrow(X) = \hat{\bar{c}}(X) + z_\gamma \sqrt{V\{\hat{\bar{c}}(X)\}} \tag{7}$$

where $V\{\hat{\bar{c}}(X)\}$ is the variance of the non-coverage estimator and z_γ is the 100γth standard normal percentile.

Substituting for $\hat{\bar{c}}(X)$ from (4) and replacing $V\{\hat{\bar{c}}(X)\}$ by its unbiased estimator [12],

(7) becomes:
$$\bar{c}_\gamma^\uparrow(X) = \frac{X}{n} + \frac{z_\gamma}{n}\sqrt{\frac{X(n-X)}{n-1}} \tag{8}$$

4.2   Confidence limit with stratified sampling

As with simple sampling, due the central limit theorem, the non-coverage estimators are assumed to be normally distributed around their expected values. With this approximation, a $100\gamma\%$ upper confidence limit for $\bar{c}$ is given by:

$$\bar{c}_\gamma^\uparrow(\mathbf{X}) = \hat{\bar{c}}_@(\mathbf{X}) + z_\gamma \sqrt{V\{\hat{\bar{c}}_@(\mathbf{X})\}} \tag{9}$$

where @ is R, WH or AH, as defined in (5).

Replacing $V\{\hat{\bar{c}}(\mathbf{X})\}$ by its corresponding estimator [12], (9) becomes:

$$\bar{c}_\gamma^\uparrow(\mathbf{X}) = \hat{\bar{c}}_@(\mathbf{X}) + z_\gamma \sqrt{\sum_{i=1}^{M}\left(\frac{p_i}{n_i}\right)^2\left(\frac{X_i(n_i - X_i)}{n_i - 1}\right)} \tag{10}$$

5   Confidence limits without approximation

It can be easily demonstrated that, even for modest coverage values, the previous confidence limits based on the normal approximation are only valid for large total sample sizes. Moreover, when coverage is very high, it is very likely that one or more classes will not reveal any deficiencies, i.e., for some classes we will have $x_i = 0$. Expression (10) would appear to imply that such classes do not contribute *any* uncertainty to the overall estimate. This is clearly not a very satisfactory implication. These problems can be avoided if we use, for both sampling strategies, the true sampling distribution instead of an approximation. In this section, we will develop the theory of confidence regions for sampling in a partitioned space. We apply the theory first to estimators which are positive functions of $\mathbf{X}$ and then to a special vectorial statistic. The well-known result for simple sampling will also be recapitulated as a special degenerate case of stratified sampling in which there is only one class.

A *confidence region* for the non-coverage parameter vector $\bar{c} = [\bar{c}_1, ..., \bar{c}_M]$ is a function $I_\gamma(\mathbf{X})$ of the deficiency vector $\mathbf{X}$ such that for any given value of the vector $\bar{c}$: $\Pr[I_\gamma(\mathbf{X}) \ni \bar{c}|\bar{c}] = \gamma$, i.e., if a large number of individual values $\mathbf{x}$ of the random vector $\mathbf{X}$ are considered, $I_\gamma(\mathbf{x})$ will contain the unknown value of the parameter vector $\bar{c}$ $100\gamma\%$ of the time. The frontier values of a confidence region are *confidence limits*.

Since the *overall* non-coverage is defined by the scalar product $\bar{c} = \mathbf{p}.\bar{\mathbf{c}}^T$, an upper $100\gamma\%$ confidence limit estimator on $\bar{c}$ is given by:

$$\bar{c}_\gamma^\uparrow(\mathbf{X}) = \max_{\bar{\mathbf{c}} \in I_\gamma(\mathbf{X})}\left(\mathbf{p}.\bar{\mathbf{c}}^T\right) \tag{11}$$

5.1 Estimators $Y_A(X)$ and $Y_W(X)$

Estimators $Y_A(\mathbf{X})$ and $Y_W(\mathbf{X})$ have a common property in that they are positive functions of X_i. We will note $Y(\mathbf{X})$ a general estimator with this property and let $y_\gamma(\bar{\mathbf{c}})$ be the value of $Y(\mathbf{X})$ that satisfies:

$$F_{Y(\mathbf{X})}\left(y_\gamma(\bar{\mathbf{c}})|\bar{\mathbf{c}}\right) = 1 - \gamma \tag{12}$$

Since sampling experiments in each class are Bernoulli trials, the deficiency number of each class X_i is distributed according to the binomial distribution $B(n_i, \bar{c}_i)$. The cumulative distribution of each X_i is thus a decreasing function of $\bar{c}_i$. Since $Y(\mathbf{X})$ is a positive function of the X_i ($i=1, ..., M$), its cumulative distribution $F_{Y(\mathbf{X})}(y|\bar{\mathbf{c}})$ is also a decreasing function of the $\bar{c}_i$ ($i=1, ..., M$).

Furthermore, by definition of a cumulative distribution, $F_{Y(\mathbf{X})}(y|\bar{\mathbf{c}})$ is an increasing function[1] of y. This means that, for $F_{Y(\mathbf{X})}(y|\bar{\mathbf{c}})$ to remain constant, any positive variation of a $\bar{c}_i$ must be compensated by a positive variation of y. Therefore, $y_\gamma(\bar{\mathbf{c}})$ defined by the solution of (12) is an increasing function of $\bar{\mathbf{c}}$.

We will now successively consider the special cases $M=1$ and $M=2$.

Case M=1: This special case corresponds to simple (non-stratified) sampling. We have $\bar{\mathbf{c}} = \bar{c}$ and equation (12) becomes:

$$y_\gamma(\bar{c}) \quad : \quad F_{Y(\mathbf{X})}\left(y_\gamma(\bar{c})|\bar{c}\right) = 1 - \gamma \tag{13}$$

The solution of this equation, $y_\gamma(\bar{c})$, is typically of the form illustrated in Fig. 1.

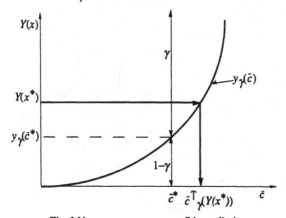

Fig. 1 Non-coverage upper confidence limit

---

[1] Since the X_i, and therefore $Y(\mathbf{X})$, are discrete, the distribution $F_{Y(\mathbf{X})}(y|\bar{c})$ is a staircase function. However, for simplicity of explanation, we will use a continuous representation of this function.

We will now show that an upper $100\gamma\%$ confidence limit on $\bar{c}$ is given by the inverse of function $y_\gamma(\bar{c})$, that is: $\bar{c}_\gamma(Y(x)) = \bar{c}$: $F_{Y(x)}(Y(x)|\bar{c}) = 1 - \gamma$ (14)

For a given value $\bar{c}^*$ of $\bar{c}$, Fig. 1 shows that the estimate $Y(x)$ will be greater than $y_\gamma(\bar{c}^*)$ for $100\gamma\%$ of the time, and less than $y_\gamma(\bar{c}^*)$ for $100(1 - \gamma)\%$ of the time. Consequently, the inverse function $\bar{c}_\gamma(Y(x))$ will lead to a value on the $\bar{c}$ axis that falls to the right of $\bar{c}^*$ $100\gamma\%$ of the time, and to the left $100(1 - \gamma)\%$ of the time.

We observe that the random variable $\bar{c}_\gamma(X)$ that is so defined satisfies the requirement for an upper $100\gamma\%$ confidence limit given by (6). So, for $M=1$, $\bar{c}_\gamma^\uparrow(X) = \bar{c}_\gamma(X)$.

For this special case, expression (6) can be rewritten in its well-known form:

$$\bar{c}_\gamma^\uparrow(X) \quad : \quad \sum_{j=0}^{x} \binom{n}{j}\left(\bar{c}_\gamma^\uparrow(X)\right)^j\left(1 - \bar{c}_\gamma^\uparrow(X)\right)^{n-j} = 1 - \gamma \tag{15}$$

This equation can be solved analytically. By introducing $100\gamma\%$ percentile points, $F_{v_1, v_2, \gamma}$, of an F distribution with v_1, v_2 degrees of freedom [17, p. 59], we obtain:

$$\boxed{\bar{c}_\gamma^\uparrow(X) = \frac{(X+1)F_{2(X+1),2(n-X),\gamma}}{(n-X)+(X+1)F_{2(X+1),2(n-X),\gamma}}} \tag{16}$$

Case M=2: The solution $y_\gamma(\bar{c})$ of equation (12) in the space $(y, \bar{c}_1, \bar{c}_2)$ defines a surface around the $Y(x)$ axis, typically of the form shown in Fig. 2.

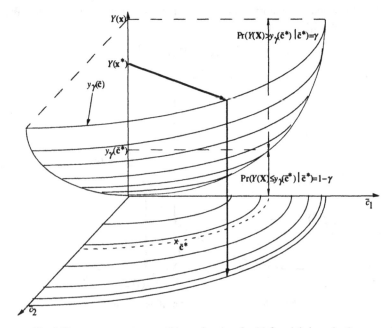

Fig. 2 Non-coverage upper confidence frontiers for $M=2$ and their projections

The contours on this surface are solutions $y_\gamma(\bar{\mathbf{c}})$ corresponding to different values of $Y(\mathbf{X})$. These contours can be projected onto the plane $(\bar{c}_1, \bar{c}_2)$ as shown in Fig. 2. They represent the inverse of function $y_\gamma(\bar{\mathbf{c}})$, noted $\bar{\mathbf{c}}_\gamma(\mathbf{x})$, defined by:

$$\bar{\mathbf{c}}_\gamma(Y(\mathbf{x})) = \bar{\mathbf{c}} \quad : \quad F_{Y(\mathbf{x})}(Y(\mathbf{x}) \,|\, \bar{\mathbf{c}}) = 1 - \gamma \tag{17}$$

For a given value $\bar{\mathbf{c}}^*$ of $\bar{\mathbf{c}}$, the region delimited by $\bar{\mathbf{c}}_\gamma(Y(\mathbf{x}))$ and the $(\bar{c}_1, \bar{c}_2)$ axes, which can be denoted $I_\gamma(\mathbf{x})$, will include $\bar{\mathbf{c}}^*$ $100\gamma\%$ of the time, and exclude it $100(1 - \gamma)\%$ of the time. $I_\gamma(\mathbf{X})$ is thus a $100\gamma\%$ confidence region estimator for the vector $\bar{\mathbf{c}}$. An upper $100\gamma\%$ confidence limit estimator on $\bar{c}$ is obtained by (11). Since $\bar{c}$ is a positive function of $\bar{c}_i$, the value of $\bar{\mathbf{c}}$ which maximizes $\mathbf{p}.\bar{\mathbf{c}}^T$ is on the contour $\bar{\mathbf{c}}_\gamma(Y(\mathbf{x}))$.

General case: For any $M > 0$, the solution $y_\gamma(\bar{\mathbf{c}})$ of the expression (12) defines a hypersurface around the $Y(\mathbf{x})$ axis and the inverse function $\bar{\mathbf{c}}_\gamma(Y(\mathbf{x}))$ defines the limit of a confidence region around the origin:

$$\bar{\mathbf{c}}_\gamma(Y(\mathbf{x})) = \bar{\mathbf{c}} \quad : \quad F_{Y(\mathbf{x})}(Y(\mathbf{x}) \,|\, \bar{\mathbf{c}}) = 1 - \gamma \tag{18}$$

As it was stated before, an upper $100\gamma\%$ confidence limit estimator on $\bar{c}$ is obtained for a vector $\bar{\mathbf{c}}$ on the frontier $\bar{\mathbf{c}}_\gamma(Y(\mathbf{x}))$.

Since the elements X_i of $\mathbf{X}$ are independently and binomially distributed with parameters $\bar{c}_i$ and n_i, (18) can be re-written as:

$$\boxed{\bar{\mathbf{c}} \quad : \quad F_{\mathbf{X}}(Y(\mathbf{x}) | \bar{\mathbf{c}}) = \sum_{\mathbf{x}' : Y(\mathbf{x}') \leq Y(\mathbf{x})} f_{\mathbf{X}}(\mathbf{x}' | \bar{\mathbf{c}}) = 1 - \gamma} \tag{19}$$

with $f_{\mathbf{X}}(\mathbf{x}' | \bar{\mathbf{c}}) = \prod_{i=1}^{M} \binom{n_i}{x_i'} \bar{c}_i^{x_i'} (1 - \bar{c}_i)^{n_i - x_i'}$

The computation of $\bar{c}_\gamma^{\uparrow}(\mathbf{x})$ can thus be expressed as the following maximization problem with constraints:

Maximization of $\bar{c} = \mathbf{p}.\bar{\mathbf{c}}^T$ under the constraints:

- given by the confidence region frontier $\bar{\mathbf{c}}_\gamma(Y(\mathbf{x}))$ for $\bar{\mathbf{c}}$:

$$\bar{\mathbf{c}} \quad : \quad \sum_{\mathbf{x}' : Y(\mathbf{x}') \leq Y(\mathbf{x})} \prod_{i=1}^{M} \binom{n_i}{x_i'} \bar{c}_i^{x_i'} (1 - \bar{c}_i)^{n_i - x_i'} = 1 - \gamma \tag{20}$$

- given by the limits of the parameter space:

$$\forall i \in \{1..M\}, \bar{c}_i \in [0,1]$$

5.2 Vectorial statistic

We now consider an alternative formulation in which each element of the deficiency vector is used individually to define an upper confidence limit on the non-coverage of its corresponding class.

For each class i, we can use (15) to define an upper $100\gamma_i\%$ confidence limit estimator:

$$\bar{c}_{i\gamma_i}^{\uparrow}(X_i) \quad : \quad \sum_{j=0}^{x_i} \binom{n_i}{j}\left(\bar{c}_{i\gamma_i}^{\uparrow}(X_i)\right)^{j}\left(1-\bar{c}_{i\gamma_i}^{\uparrow}(X_i)\right)^{n_i-j} = 1-\gamma_i \quad \forall i=1,\dots,M \qquad (21)$$

If we choose the M values of γ_i such that: $\prod_{i=1}^{M}\gamma_i = \gamma$ \qquad (22)

then the hypercube in the parameter space formed by the axes and the $\bar{c}_{i\gamma_i}^{\uparrow}(x_i)$ is a $100\gamma\%$ confidence region for which the corresponding upper $100\gamma\%$ confidence limit

on $\bar{c}$ is given by: $$\bar{c}_{\gamma}^{\uparrow}(\mathbf{x})\Big|_{(\gamma_1,\gamma_2,\dots,\gamma_M)} = \sum_{i=1}^{M} p_i\bar{c}_{i\gamma_i}^{\uparrow}(x_i) \qquad (23)$$

corresponding to the value of $\bar{c}$ at the apex of the confidence region hypercube.

Among the infinite number of ways of choosing the γ_i such that (22) is satisfied, we are looking for the one leading to the lowest value of $\bar{c}_{\gamma}^{\uparrow}(\mathbf{x})\Big|_{(\gamma_1,\gamma_2,\dots,\gamma_M)}$. Thus:

$$\bar{c}_{\gamma}^{\uparrow}(\mathbf{x}) = \min_{(\gamma_1,\gamma_2,\dots,\gamma_M)} \bar{c}_{\gamma}^{\uparrow}(\mathbf{x})\Big|_{(\gamma_1,\gamma_2,\dots,\gamma_M)} = \min_{(\gamma_1,\gamma_2,\dots,\gamma_M)} \sum_{i=1}^{M} p_i\bar{c}_{i\gamma_i}^{\uparrow}(x_i) \qquad (24)$$

By combining (21) and (24), the confidence limit $\bar{c}_{\gamma}^{\uparrow}(\mathbf{x})$ is given by:

$$\bar{c}_{\gamma}^{\uparrow}(\mathbf{x}) = \min_{(\gamma_1,\gamma_2,\dots,\gamma_M)} \sum_{i=1}^{M} p_i\bar{c}_i \text{ with the constraints:}$$

$$\sum_{j=0}^{x_i} \binom{n_i}{j}\bar{c}_i^{\,j}(1-\bar{c}_i)^{n_i-j} = 1-\gamma_i \quad \forall i=1,\dots,M$$

From (22), the upper $100\gamma\%$ confidence limit $\bar{c}_{\gamma}^{\uparrow}(\mathbf{x})$ is therefore given by the solution of:

Minimization of $\bar{c} = \mathbf{p}.\bar{\mathbf{c}}^{T}$ under the constraints:

• given by the global confidence:

$$\bar{c} \quad : \quad \prod_{i=1}^{M}\left(1 - \sum_{x_i'=0}^{x_i}\binom{n_i}{x_i'}\bar{c}_i^{\,x_i'}(1-\bar{c}_i)^{n_i-x_i'}\right) = \gamma \qquad (25)$$

• given by the limits of the parameter space:

$$\forall i \in \{1..M\}, \bar{c}_i \in [0,1]$$

---

6 Comparative Examples

In this section, three hypothetical systems are used to compare the various confidence limit estimation techniques defined in Sections 4 and 5. For estimations without the normal distribution approximation, only estimations obtained by the vectorial statistic are presented. Indeed, the vectorial statistic provides a numerical solution for a large range of fault-injection experiments, which is not the case for the estimators $Y_A(\mathbf{X})$ and $Y_W(\mathbf{X})$ [18]. The computational time necessary to solve the maximization problem for both estimators is also higher than that for the vectorial statistic (since the constraint must be approximated).

6.1 System definitions and comparison method

The characteristics of the three example systems are defined in Fig. 3a, 3b and 3c [12]. Each system is partitioned into $M = 50$ classes. The figures show the non-coverage $\bar{c}_i$ and the relative fault/activity occurrence probability p_i of each class as well as the values of the system non-coverage $\bar{c}$, and the *mean* class non-coverage $\bar{\bar{c}} = \frac{1}{M} \sum_{i=1}^{M} \bar{c}_i$.

Each system is also characterized by the correlation factor ρ between the p_i and c_i [12]. The characteristics of the three example systems are quite different and have been purposely chosen to *aggressively* test the coverage estimation techniques in extreme situations. System A (Fig 3a) features a relative homogeneity among the classes regarding the non-coverage, a relative variability of the fault/activity occurrence probabilities p_i and a slight (negative) correlation factor ($\approx$-14%). For system B (Fig. 3b), there is a much greater variability for the non-coverage and occurrence probabilities in each class. Furthermore, the correlation factor is positive and greater than 40%. System C (Fig. 3c) is a near-perfect system with a very low non-coverage. It has quite a high variability over the classes and a large negative correlation between the p_i and c_i ($\approx$-90%).

We compare the various confidence limit estimation techniques by simulating a large number (25,000) of fault-injection campaigns carried out on each of these three systems, with a total sample size (the total number of injected faults in each campaign) varying from 500 to 50,000,000. For each simulated campaign, we draw a random deficiency number (for simple sampling) or deficiency vector (for stratified sampling) using the known overall coverage or class coverages of our hypothetical systems. We then compute the 99% confidence limits that would be obtained with each considered method.

Since we have total knowledge about our three hypothetical systems, we can verify whether the confidence we claim for the various techniques is justified by calculating the proportion of simulated fault-injection campaigns for which the confidence limit statement $\bar{c} < \bar{c}_\gamma^\uparrow(\mathbf{x})$ is true. We call this proportion the *success proportion*. With the prescribed 99% confidence level, the success proportion should also be about 99%. If this is not so for a given system and sample size, then the corresponding method is inadequate for that situation and should not have been used.

To assess the conservatism of the confidence limits for each technique, we would also like to evaluate the expected values of the limits for each total sample size. For all the confidence limits derived from the normal approximation, the expected value of the limit can easily be calculated analytically by taking expectations of the corresponding expressions ((8) for simple sampling, (10) for stratified sampling) and replacing $E\{X\}$ and $E\{X_i\}$ respectively by the known values $\bar{c}$ and $\bar{c}_i$. The expected confidence limits without approximation can be calculated by summing the corresponding confidence limit expressions over the whole sample space weighted by the (known) sample distribution. For simple sampling, we compute the expected limit by summing expression (16) weighted by the (binomial) sample distribution. For stratified sampling,

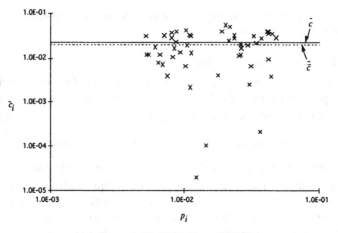

a) System A ($\bar{c}$=2.20E-02, ρ=-13.5%)

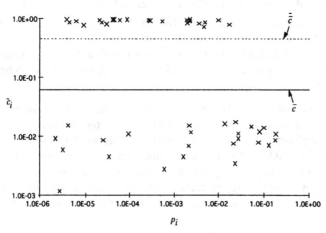

b) System B ($\bar{c}$=6.21E-02, ρ=+41.5%)

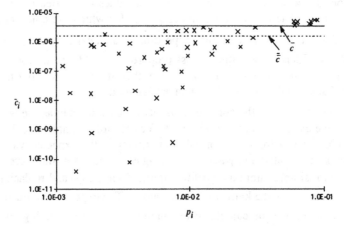

c) System C ($\bar{c}$=3.72E-06, ρ=-89.1%)

Fig. 3 System characteristics

the summation would be much too time-consuming, so we resort to the simulated fault-injection campaigns and use the average of all the simulated confidence limits as an approximation of the expected value.

The results obtained for each system are presented in the tables of Fig. 4a, 4b and 4c. Each estimation method is identified by a mnemonic using the following notation:

Mnemonic	Sampling space	Sample distribution	Statistic	Sample allocation
NA	Non-partitioned	Approximated		
NE	(simple sampling)	Exact		
PAAH		Approximated	naive estimator	(homogeneous)
PAWH	Partitioned	Approximated	stratified estimator	Homogeneous
PAR	(stratified	Approximated	stratified estimator	Representative
PEXH	sampling)	Exact	vector statistic	Homogeneous
PEXR		Exact	vector statistic	Representative

Results are not available for all the cells in the tables of Fig. 4a, 4b and 4c. For all three systems, not all results are given for the exact stratification techniques (rows PEXH and PEXR). Due to the very wide variability of class coverages for system B, the optimization routine[2] failed to find any solution due to numerical problems. For system A, because of the smaller variability of the class coverages, the failure to find a solution with the optimization routine appears for higher total sample sizes. When the routine could find a solution for many, but not all simulated campaigns, the table cells are marked with the sign "°". For systems B and C, results are not given for representative stratification with small total sample sizes since this combination leads to a null allocation ($n_i = 0$) for some classes and is therefore meaningless.

6.2 Simple sampling

6.2.1 Approximated sample distribution

The success proportion for the confidence limit obtained with the normal approximation due to the central limit theorem (row NA) increases with n to a value around the confidence level of $\gamma=0.99$. For systems A and B, this method is justified for quite small sample sizes (i.e., greater than about 5 000). For system C, however, the success proportion starts from a very low value (0.2%) and never quite reaches the assigned 99% confidence level. This underlines the limitation of the normal approximation and illustrates why the exact distribution should be used for systems with very high coverage.

6.2.2 Exact sample distribution

The success proportion for the confidence limit obtained with the exact method (row NE) should be approximately equal to the confidence level. This is indeed the case for systems A and B, even for the very low sample size of 500. For higher sample sizes, both the approximate and exact sample distributions give similar results, with the expected upper confidence limit becoming predictably less and less conservative as the sample size increases.

---

[2] We used the e04vcf routine of the NAG library.

	500	5 000	50 000	500 000	5 000 000	50 000 000
NA	3,73E-02	2,69E-02	2,36E-02	2,25E-02	2,22E-02	2,21E-02
	96,4%	98,4%	98,9%	99,0%	99,1%	99,0%
NE	4,24E-02	2,74E-02	2,36E-02	2,25E-02	2,22E-02	2,22E-02
	99,5%	99,1%	99,0%	99,1%	99,1%	99,0%
PAAH	3,88E-02	2,66E-02	2,27E-02	2,14E-02	2,10E-02	2,09E-02
	96,4%	98,2%	90,7%	0,9%	0,0%	0,0%
PAWH	4,00E-02	2,79E-02	2,39E-02	2,26E-02	2,22E-02	2,21E-02
	94,3%	98,0%	98,4%	98,6%	98,6%	98,6%
PAR	3,74E-02	2,69E-02	2,36E-02	2,25E-02	2,22E-02	2,21E-02
	95,8%	98,4%	98,6%	98,6%	98,6%	98,5%
PEXH	5,88E-01	1,22E-01 [o]	4,18E-02 [o]			
	100,0%	100,0%	100,0%			
PEXR	5,36E-01 [o]	1,22E-01 [o]	4,13E-02 [o]			
	100,0%	100,0%	100,0%			

a) System A ($\bar{c}$=2.20E-02, ρ=-13.5%)

	500	5 000	50 000	500 000	5 000 000	50 000 000
NA	8,72E-02	7,00E-02	6,46E-02	6,29E-02	6,23E-02	6,22E-02
	98,2%	98,6%	98,9%	99,0%	98,9%	99,1%
NE	9,18E-02	7,05E-02	6,46E-02	6,29E-02	6,23E-02	6,23E-02
	99,5%	99,2%	99,0%	99,0%	98,9%	99,1%
PAAH	4,81E-01	4,68E-01	4,63E-01	4,61E-01	4,61E-01	4,61E-01
	100,0%	100,0%	100,0%	100,0%	100,0%	100,0%
PAWH	8,22E-02	6,98E-02	6,46E-02	6,29E-02	6,23E-02	6,22E-02
	73,1%	95,0%	97,9%	98,5%	98,4%	98,6%
PAR					6,22E-02	6,21E-02
					98,6%	98,5%
PEXH						
PEXR						

b) System B ($\bar{c}$=6.21E-02, ρ=+41.5%)

	500	5 000	50 000	500 000	5 000 000	50 000 000
NA	2,05E-04	6,72E-05	2,38E-05	1,01E-05	5,70E-06	4,40E-06
	0,2%	1,9%	17,3%	84,2%	97,7%	98,7%
NE	9,18E-03	9,28E-04	9,96E-05	1,62E-05	6,30E-06	5,00E-06
	100,0%	100,0%	100,0%	100,0%	99,5%	100,0%
PAAH	8,41E-06	1,14E-05	1,06E-05	9,11E-06	5,19E-06	2,79E-06
	0,1%	0,9%	8,2%	53,4%	90,4%	0,5%
PAWH	1,02E-05	1,38E-05	1,28E-05	1,12E-05	7,29E-06	4,89E-06
	0,1%	0,9%	8,2%	48,3%	94,5%	97,7%
PAR		1,24E-05	1,20E-05	9,44E-06	5,71E-06	4,36E-06
		1,9%	17,2%	87,5%	97,7%	98,1%
PEXH	5,42E-01	7,55E-02	7,83E-03	7,94E-04	8,71E-05 [o]	1,51E-05 [o]
	100,0%	100,0%	100,0%	100,0%	100,0%	100,0%
PEXR		7,38E-02	8,39E-03	8,59E-04	9,35E-05 [o]	1,49E-05 [o]
		100,0%	100,0%	100,0%	100,0%	100,0%

c) System C ($\bar{c}$=3.72E-06, ρ=-89.1%)

[o] 23,183 ≤ simulation number ≤ 24,957   No solution obtained   Meaningless sample allocation

Fig. 4 Expected upper 99% confidence limits and success proportions

For system C, however, the success proportion is practically always 100%. This underlines the fact that the confidence limit obtained without approximation is conservative. However, when dealing with highly dependable systems in critical applications, it is better to have a conservative limit with high confidence than a low-confidence and thus often overly-optimistic limit.

6.3 Stratified sampling

6.3.1 Approximated sample distribution

We successively consider the results obtained with the normal approximation for the distribution of the naive and stratified estimators.

Row PAAH of the tables gives the results obtained when the point estimator $Y_A(\mathbf{X})$ is used with a homogeneous distribution. As already discussed in Section 3.2, we call this estimator a naive one since, with any allocation other than a representative one, it leads to a biased estimation. With a homogeneous allocation, the bias depends on the sign of the correlation factor ρ: if ρ is negative (positive) the bias will be optimistic (conservative) [12]. Since system A is negatively correlated, the confidence limit obtained with the normal approximation will be an optimistic limit (row PAAH). Indeed, when the sample size n increases, the expected limit decreases and becomes smaller than the actual non-coverage (2.2E-02). Equivalently, the success proportion decreases to 0. System B is positively correlated, so the confidence limit in this case will be conservative. This is underlined by the fact that, for all sample sizes, the success proportion is equal to 100%. For system C, which is negatively correlated, an interesting phenomenon can be observed. For small sample sizes, the success proportion is very low since the normal approximation for the sample distribution is not valid. As the sample size increases, so does the success proportion. However, for large sample sizes the success proportion again decreases, this time due to the bias in the point estimator due to the negative correlation (note that the expected upper confidence limit becomes less than the actual non-coverage).

The results obtained with the normal approximation for the distribution of the stratified estimator $Y_W(\mathbf{X})$ are given in rows PAWH and PAR, with respectively a homogeneous and a representative sample allocation. For systems A and C, it can be observed that the homogeneous allocation (row PAWH) leads most of the time to a lower success proportion. This is particularly evident for system C and is due to the wide variability of the fault/activity occurrence probabilities for this system. No such conclusion can be drawn for system B since the representative allocations for small sample sizes are meaningless.

In all cases, we observe that success proportions are less than 99%. As was the case for simple sampling, it can be observed that the normal approximation is often unjustified. This is particularly true for system C that is featuring the highest coverage. We also observe, for the cases with a success proportion about 99%, that the anticipated gain in precision procured by the stratified estimator with a representative allocation is small.

6.3.2 Exact sample distribution

The available results with stratified sampling and using the exact distribution of the vectorial statistic are given in rows PEXH and PEXR, respectively for a homogeneous and a representative sample allocation.

As was the case for the exact distribution for simple sampling, the success proportions for system C are 100%, which indicates that the confidence limits are again conservative ones. The degree of conservatism is particularly sensitive to the sample size. For small samples, the stratified sampling leads to results about two orders of magnitude greater than those obtained with the simple sample. Even for large samples, the expected confidence limit is still about three times greater for a stratified sample than for the simple one.

For system A, we only obtained results for $n \leq 50,000$. Unlike the exact distribution for simple sampling, the available success proportions are 100%. As for system C, the confidence limits obtained with a stratified sample are quite conservative ones compared to those with a simple sample. The degree of conservatism depends again on the sample size. For higher values of n on system A, and all values of n on system B, it was not possible to compute a meaningful expected confidence limit and success proportion since the numerical problems mentioned earlier often caused the program to terminate abnormally. Fortunately, however, we do not need to resort to the exact approach for these systems with modest coverage — the confidence limits obtained with the approximated sample distribution are quite valid for even moderate sample sizes.

7 Conclusion

This paper has examined the advantages and disadvantages of simple sampling and stratified sampling when applied to fault-injection for assessing coverage figures of fault-tolerant systems. In particular we have focused on the statistical methods that can be applied to the results of a stratified fault-injection campaign on a system with very high coverage.

Stratification offers several practical advantages. It can be used to re-interpret the results of a fault-injection campaign should it be necessary, for example, to use test data for coverage estimation or should new knowledge be acquired about the actual distribution of real faults. Stratified sampling allows, under certain conditions, for the composition of results of fault-injection experiments. Sometimes, stratification simplifies the fault-injection process, for example for physical fault injection.

Most previous work on stratified sampling has based estimation on the normal approximation of the distribution of a coverage point estimator. However, we have shown that the approximation given by the central limit theorem and leading to a normal distribution is not usually valid for coverage confidence limit estimations. First, most fault tolerance mechanisms are characterised by very high coverage factor values. Second, the number of faults injected during a campaign is often relatively low. Both contribute to the erroneousness of the normal distribution approximation.

For stratified sampling, if the confidence limit estimation cannot be based on a normal distribution, the confidence region theory must be used. Confidence regions obtained by two point estimators and a vectorial statistic have been introduced in this paper. In many cases, the coverage upper confidence limit estimations obtained by using the point estimators are less conservative than those obtained by the vectorial statistic. For the example presented in the introduction, both point estimators lead to a non-coverage upper 99%-confidence limit of 4.7E-04, whereas the vectorial statistic gives 7.6E-04.

For more than three strata, the coverage confidence limit estimations using the point estimators become computationally intractable [18]. So, most of the time, only the vectorial statistic can be applied.

The central limit theorem application leads to the well known result that stratification can reduce estimator variance and thus lead to a better (lower) upper confidence limit estimate. When applying the confidence region theory, this result is no longer correct. Stratification can worsen the coverage confidence limits. Therefore, before starting a fault-injection campaign, the pro and cons of stratified sampling must be carefully analyzed so that the campaign can be planned accordingly.

References

[1] T. F. Arnold, "The Concept of Coverage and its Effect on the Reliability Model of Repairable Systems," *IEEE Trans. on Computers*, vol. C-22, pp. 251-254, 1973.

[2] W. G. Bouricius, W. C. Carter, and P. R. Schneider, "Reliability Modeling Techniques for Self-Repairing Computer Systems", *Proc. 24th National Conference*, pp. 295-309, ACM, 1969.

[3] Z. Segall, D. Vrsalovic, D. Siewiorek, D. Yaskin, J. Kownacki, J. Barton, D. Rancey, A. Robinson, and T. Lin, "FIAT — Fault Injection based Automated Testing Environment", *Proc. 18th Int. Symp. on Fault-Tolerant Computing (FTCS-18)*, pp. 102-107, Tokyo, Japan, IEEE Computer Society Press, 1988.

[4] G. S. Choi, R. K. Iyer, R. Saleh, and V. Carreno, "A Fault Behavior Model for an Avionic Microprocessor: a Case Study," in *Dependable Computing for Critical Applications*, A. Avizienis and J.-C. Laprie, Eds. Vienna, Austria: Springer-Verlag, 1991, pp. 171-195.

[5] R. Chillarege and N. S. Bowen, "Understanding Large System Failures — A Fault Injection Experiment", *Proc. 19th Int. Symp. on Fault-Tolerant Computing (FTCS-19)*, pp. 356-363, Chicago, MI, USA, IEEE Computer Society Press, 1989.

[6] J. Arlat, A. Costes, Y. Crouzet, J.-C. Laprie, and D. Powell, "Fault Injection and Dependability Evaluation of Fault-Tolerant Systems," *IEEE Trans. on Computers*, vol. 42, pp. 913-923, 1993.

[7] U. Gunneflo, J. Karlsson, and J. Torin, "Evaluation of Error Detection Schemes using Fault Injection by Heavy-ion Radiation", *Proc. 19th Int. Symp. Fault-Tolerant Computing (FTCS-19)*, pp. 340-347, Chicago, MI, USA, IEEE Computer Society Press, 1989.

[8] C. J. Walter, "Evaluation and Design of an Ultra-Reliable Distributed Architecture for Fault Tolerance," *IEEE Trans. on Reliability*, vol. 39, pp. 492-499, 1990.

[9] G. A. Kanawati, N. A. Kanawati, and J. A. Abraham, "FERRARI: A Flexible Software-Based Fault and Error Injection System," *IEEE Trans. on Computers*, vol. 44, pp. 248-260, 1995.

[10] V. D. Agrawal, "Sampling Techniques for Determining Fault Coverage in LSI Circuits," *Journal of Digital Systems*, vol. V, pp. 189-201, 1981.

[11] W. Daehn, "Fault Simulation using Small Fault Samples," *Journal of Electronic Testing: Theory and Applications*, vol. 2, pp. 191-203, 1991.

[12] D. Powell, E. Martins, J. Arlat, and Y. Crouzet, "Estimators for Fault Tolerance Coverage Evaluation", *Proc. 23rd Int. Conf. on Fault-Tolerant Computing (FTCS-23)*, pp. 228-237, Toulouse, France, IEEE Computer Society Press, 1993. (An extended version of this paper appears in *IEEE Trans. Computers*, 44 (2), pp.261-274, 1995).

[13] W. Wang, K. S. Trivedi, B. V. Shah, and J. A. Profeta III, "The Impact of Fault Expansion on the Interval Estimate for Fault Detection Coverage", *Proc. 24th Int. Conf. on Fault-Tolerant Computing (FTCS-24)*, pp. 330-337, Austin, TX, USA, IEEE Computer Society Press, 1994.

[14] C. Constantinescu, "Using Multi-Stage & Stratified Sampling for Inferring Fault-Coverage Probabilities," *IEEE Trans. Reliability*, vol. 44, pp. 632-639, 1995.

[15] D. P. Siewiorek and R. S. Swarz, *The Theory and Practice of Reliable System Design*: Digital Press, 1982.

[16] D. A. Rennels and A. Avizienis, "RMS: A Reliability Modeling System for Self-Repairing Computers", *Proc. 3rd Int. Symp. on Fault-Tolerant Computing (FTCS-3)*, pp. 131-135, Palo Alto, CA, USA, IEEE Computer Society Press, 1973.

[17] N. L. Johnson and S. Kotz, *Distributions in Statistics — Discrete Distributions*. New York: John Wiley & Sons, 1969.

[18] M. Cukier, "Estimation of the Coverage of Fault-Tolerant Systems," National Polytechnic Intitute, Toulouse, France, 1996. (in French)

Fault Injection Evaluation of Assigned Signatures in a RISC Processor[1]

Pedro Furtado and Henrique Madeira
University of Coimbra- Portugal
e-mail: pnf @dei.uc.pt

Abstract- This paper proposes a new assigned signature monitoring technique called VASC (Versatile Assigned Signature Checking) and presents a fault injection evaluation of this technique in a modern reduced instruction set processor (RISC). VASC is applied at the machine instructions level and is the very first assigned signature monitoring technique that allows the user to choose block sizes and checking intervals with complete freedom. This feature allows the tuning of the application with the lowest overhead and makes it possible to identify and analyse the relationship between overheads and coverages for different choices of block sizes and checking intervals. Previous works presented assigned signature techniques that were either specific to a Very Large Instruction Word (VLIW) processor or have very high memory and execution time overhead. VASC can be applied to any system with small (and adjustable) execution time and memory overhead. We have measured those overheads in a PowerPC processor and in a Transputer T805 processor, showing that they are completely adjustable. One interesting conclusion is that the best error coverage of the technique does not correspond to the highest amount of control flow checking. The evaluation of the error coverage and latency of VASC, implemented in a PowerPC RISC processor, has been carried out by using the Xception software fault injection tool. The technique accounted for 10 to 16% of the detected errors, but the overall error coverage improvement was relatively small (less than 4%). One reason for this is in the fact that the percentage of control flow errors (the main type of errors detected by VASC) in the PowerPC is relatively low compared to the same percentage in processors with a more complex instruction set, which suggests that assigned signatures are much better suited for systems having variable-sized instructions and less efficient memory access checking.

1.Introduction

Control flow monitoring techniques check the program execution sequence to determine if a legal control flow is being followed. The program control flow can be expressed in a control flow graph (CFG). The CFG shows the legal instruction execution sequence. If instructions are grouped in blocks then a CFG can be built expressing the legal control flow between those blocks - the Block Graph (BG).

Embedded signature monitoring refers to techniques in which a signature is embedded in certain locations in the application program, so that it can be used to determine if an error has occurred. The signature can be an identifier (assigned signatures) or a value obtained through the compacting of the executed code and other

---

[1] This work was supported by Esprit project 6731 - FTMPS "Fault Tolerant Massively Parallel Systems"

relevant signals (derived signatures). Usually, a signature generated at execution time is compared with the embedded one in order to determine if an error has occurred.

Derived signatures [4,5,6,7,12,13,14,15,20] require a signature generator/monitor circuit to compact a signature from the buses signals. These techniques achieve low execution time overhead and have good coverage but require a signature generator/monitor circuit. In modern processors with internal cache, pipeline and often superscalar execution, the signature generator/monitor must be embedded in the processor circuit [11].

There are some other techniques that are not based on signal compacting but use addresses [9], block number of instructions or block cycle count [4, 9]. These techniques also use a signature generator/monitor, even though they do not compact the buses signals.

The aim of the assigned signature techniques is to implement control flow monitoring without having to change the processor hardware. They use a simple identifier assigned to each block in the BG as the signature. The signature for the current block is usually held in a register. All the necessary operations are implemented with regular processor instructions inserted by a signature inserting program or by a modified compiler/linker.

Both derived and assigned signatures techniques are aimed at fast detection of control flow errors within the program code and therefore are complementary of methods that detect different kinds of errors like memory access checking and assertions. The error coverage of the derived signature techniques is very good (99% of control flow errors [5,15,19]) . The coverage of assigned signature techniques is not so good, but the fact that it can be applied to any system makes them a good choice for off-the-shelf control flow monitoring.

This paper presents (and evaluates by fault injection) a technique named Versatile Assigned Signatures Checking - VASC, that can be applied to any system. With this technique, performance overhead is kept at reasonable figures and the user has the flexibility to choose parameters that balance the desired coverage with the performance overhead. To be able to take advantage of processor redundancy or other target system dependent optimisation features there are also some generic parameters that help the algorithm in finding the right place to put the signaturing operations.

The organisation of the paper is as follows: related research is discussed in Section 2. Section 3 presents the algorithm of VASC and the implementation of the technique for two target systems - The transputer and the PowerPC processors. In Section 4 the technique is evaluated. In section 4.1 The execution and memory overheads are measured for the T805 processor and for the PowerPC. Coverage results are assessed using a software fault injector for three applications running in the PowerPC based system. Section 4.2 describes the fault injector tool used in the experiments. In section 4.3 the experimental set-up is presented and in section 4.4 the results are shown. Section 4.5 studies the effect of growing signaturing block sizes and checking intervals on error detection. Finally, Section 5 concludes the paper.

2.Related Research

Assigned signature techniques have been proposed in [8,16,17]. There are two major drawbacks in assigned signature techniques: the performance overhead due to the need of executing extra instructions related to the assigned-signature monitoring and the need of having a register to hold the signature. Architectural redundancy can help solve the performance overhead problem in a few cases.

In [8] the application program was divided into basic blocks consisting of sequences of strictly consecutive instructions not including control flow changing instructions or destinations. In each basic block an entry routine call and an exit routine call was made. This lead to the execution of an excess of an additional set of 13 instructions per basic block. As basic blocks are relatively small the execution time overhead of this technique is very large (88% to 127% in the reported experiments). The technique proposed in [17] has the same basic problems as the one presented in [8].

In [16], two major improvements were introduced in order to eliminate the execution time overhead problem: it was no longer required that blocks should consist of strictly consecutive instructions and the VLIW processor redundancy was used in order to take advantage of execution units vacancies to insert signature operations. This last improvement made it possible to achieve a null performance overhead with the method. However, this technique is limited to a VLIW processor architecture, as signature operations must occupy free resources easily available in this architecture.

Signature placement in superscalar machines can usually be optimised [18,19]. A superscalar machine like the PowerPC can have some resource redundancy useful for the error detection method. But sometimes we can take advantage of other details. For instance, both the performance and memory overhead can be lowered in Transputer based machines due to the variable instruction size (signature handling instructions are small and execute fast in Transputer processors).

Experimental works [3, 11] have shown that the effects of transient faults in a 32-bit RISC are quite different from those in an 8-bit MC6809 CISC processor. In the RISC processor [11] most faults produced data errors (60% data errors, 33% control flow errors), while in the MC6809 [3] most caused control flow errors (77% control flow errors, 18% data errors). This conclusion suggests that control flow error detection techniques, such as the one proposed in this paper, are more adequate to CISC processors. In fact, VASC can be used in both RISC and CISC processors. However, we decided to implement and evaluate VASC in a RISC processor because this type of processor is very commom nowadays. It is worth noting that the evaluation of the VASC coverage obtained this way is conservative.

3.The VASC Technique

3.1 VASC Algorithm

Derived signature techniques logically divide the code into basic blocks [1] or, in more recent approaches, into paths containing a number of sequential blocks and justifying signatures between those blocks [7, 10,15]. Signature justifying happens in most control flow changes, so that the signature is updated to reflect the new sequential block initial signature. Block or path frontiers are usually situated in control flow changing instructions and are used to check the signature, i.e. compare the generated signature with a reference one, which is embedded in the code.

The concept of justifying signatures proposed for derived signature techniques, can also be used in assigned signature techniques. Every time the execution flows from one block to another the signature register must be updated to the new block signature. This operation is called *justifying or tracking operation*. At selected points in the BG the signature register is compared with an embedded reference signature - *verifying or checking operation*. This checking operation must force an exception if there is an error.

The main idea behind VASC is to define logical blocks for control flow checking which are not directly related to the basic blocks structure of the program. This is just the key of having blocks of any size.

In VASC each block can be formed by an arbitrary set of sequential (in dynamic sense) instructions. For instance, a block can include branch instructions, branch destination instructions, subprogram call and return instructions, and loops, provided that any of these instructions can be reached from any other instruction in the block without leaving the block. Each block is given a unique identifier (blockID). One or more checking operations can be inserted at any point inside a block. These checking operations compare the blockID with the current blockID stored in a special location (usually a register). The execution of any instruction in the border of the block (i.e., the instruction executed immediately after an instruction in the border belongs to another block) forces a justifying (or tracking) operation. The task of the justifying operation is to change the blockID stored in the special location to the new block blockID value.

In VASC the user can define two main parameters: *block size* - number of instructions in a block; *check interval* - number of instructions between two checking points. To allow a greater flexibility, block sizes and check intervals are completely independent. Any combination of them can be used.

Some tolerance can be specified by the user for the block size and checking interval to improve the placement of tracking and checking operations. For example, we can define a block size of 10 instructions with a tolerance of 2 instructions, which means that the block sizes can range from 8 to 12 instructions. The improvements depend on the target system.

The algorithm first goes sequentially through the CFG to partition it into blocks. The first instruction begins the first block. All the instructions that could be executed immediately following the current instruction (immediate successors) are also added to the block. Branches and returns from subprograms usually have more than one immediate successor. When the block size is reached a new block is started.

After having generated the block graph, the algorithm assigns unique BlockIDs to the blocks created. Then it goes through the CFG again, this time to insert tracking operations in the block borders and checking operations in regular spaced intervals, given by the checking interval parameter.

We have only imposed one restriction to keep the extra code inserted by VASC small: in a conditional branch and in return from subroutine instructions all possible immediate successor instructions must belong to the same block. Otherwise, we would have to justify to different blockIDs, depending on the destination of the control flow change. This would increase the size of the code inserted by VASC. Figure 1 shows an example of the application of this restriction. In figure 1a) the block size is 4. When the algorithm reaches instruction 2 it is possible to add both immediate successor instructions 3 and 5 to block 1, because the increased size of the block will not exceed the limit established.

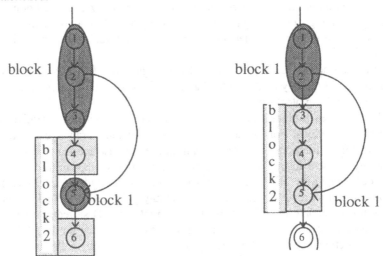

a) Example BG for block size 4   **b) Example BG for block size 3**

(1) - Instruction   ⟶ - valid control flow

Figure 1 - A sample Block Graph

In figure 1 b) the block size is 3. When the algorithm reaches instruction 2 it cannot include both immediate successor instructions 3 and 5 in the same block of the instruction 2 because that would exceed the block size limit of 3.

Any combination of block size and check interval can be used. If the check interval is specified smaller than the block size, then the signature will be checked at least once in each block. If the check interval is specified larger than the block size then a control flow error can lead to the execution of instructions in more than one block before the signature is checked but the error can still be detected, as the signature is not reinitialised in the beginning of a block.

If the block size parameter is specified too large there will be few blocks, which tends to decrease the error detection coverage and to increase latency. On the other hand, a small block size will increase the execution time and the memory overhead.

The tolerance values will be used to search the best position to insert the signature tracking and checking operations. This is a target system dependent optimisation. In superscalar processors, for instance, instruction grouping can be optimised. But in much simpler processors other optimisations can be sought. For instance, the T805 transputer processor uses a three place evaluation stack for almost every operation, working in a push/pop fashion. We have sought program locations where the stack wouldn't be full, in order to be able to operate on the signature without having to temporarily save the top position of the stack.

Figure 2 shows VASC algorithm.

```
FOR each instruction i in the CFG
    IF i belongs to a block B
        current_block -> B
    ELSE
        current_block -> {i}
    ENDIF
    IF number of instructions in current block > DesiredBlockSize
    // here use BlockTolerance parameters to find the best block end
        current_block ->{ }
        // block frontier
    ENDIF
    COUNT n = number of successors of i
    IF
    CurrentBlockSize+n > DesiredBlockSize
        create new block with successors of i
    ELSE current_block=current_block +
                        all successors of i
    ENDIF
ENDFOR
/* eliminate small blocks */
    FOR all instructions i in the CFG
        get a successor s of i
        IF  Size(i's block) + Size(s's block)
                        <DesiredBlkSize + BlockTol
        concatenate i's block with s's block
    ENDIF
    ENDFOR
/* insert tracking and checking operations */
    FOR all instructions in the CFG
        IF block frontier then insert tracking op
        IF check_interval then insert checking op
ENDFOR
```

Figure 2 The signature inserting algorithm

As a summary, the VASC signature generating program executes the following steps:

1. Building the CFG (control flow graph) in memory. This was done by interpretation of the instructions and offsets in the assembly module. A structure node was built in memory for every instruction, carrying all relevant information about it. Pointer arcs were used to make each instruction point to its immediate successor and predecessor instructions in the CFG;

2. Running the signature generating algorithm on the CFG. This creates the *BG* (block graph) in memory, conveniently grouping instructions into blocks. Tolerance values and system dependent information are used at this step to improve signature placement. A second pass of this algorithm eliminates very small blocks by concatenation with neighbour ones;

3. Use the created BG in order to determine the placement of the tracking operations. Every block boundary between two blocks must have a tracking operation that changes the signature key;

4. Determine the placement of the checking operations in regularly spaced intervals, using the checking tolerances and the specific system optimisations to improve its placement;

5. Write the output file with the tracking and the checking operations included.

3.2 Implementation of VASC in Target Processors

The tracking and checking operations consist of regular processor instructions, so this is a system dependent part. During execution, a fast access location must hold the current blockID (signature). Usually a register is used. A least-frequently-used register is chosen to avoid having to save/restore frequently the signature.

The signature handling operations are:

(Rsign: Place that holds the signature)

signature initialisation	tracking operation	checking operation
Put in Rsign the current block ID	Update Rsign to new block ID	Cmp Rsign with reference signature for current block
(beginning of functions)		If different ERROR

Figure 3 - Signature handling operations

VASC has been implemented in two different processor architectures. The PowerPC is a RISC processor with efficient built-in error detection mechanisms, whereas the T805 transputer is a variable-sized instruction processor with inefficient error detection mechanisms.

The Transputer doesn't have general-purpose registers. As mentioned in section 3.1 the instructions operate on an evaluation stack in a push/pop fashion. We keep the signature in the workspace cache because it is a high speed cache, usually used to keep frequently used variables. This cache is accessed using fast access instructions ldl (load from local workspace cache) and stl (store to local workspace cache). The signature handling operations are implemented using the following instructions,

signature initialisation	tracking operation	checking operation
ldc Initial signature	ldl Rsign	ldl Rsign
stl Rsign	adc n	eqc n
(T9000: 1 group)	stl Rsign	cj .ERROR
	(T9000: 2 groups)	(T9000: groupable in 1 group)

Figure 4 - Signature handling operation for the Transputer processors

In the T9000 superscalar processor performance can be further improved by optimising the operations placement in view of better superscalar execution. In that processor, groups of instructions are executed simultaneously. The signature initialisation and the signature checking operations are both groupable in one group, and the signature tracking operation is groupable in two groups, together with other instructions.

In the PowerPC processor we used a register to keep the signature. As we have used a standard compiler (without changes), the implementation of the signature generating program for the PowerPC checks the assembly code of each function to find a free register to store the signature. If there is no free register in one function, the stack is used to store the signature while the register is being used. Figure 5 shows the signature operations for this processor.

signature initialisation sequence	tracking operation	checking operation
addi Rsign,R0,current blck ID	addi Rsign,Rsign,n	cmpi Rsign,current blck ID
		bne ERROR

Figure 5 - Signature handling operations for the PowerPC processor

4. The Evaluation of the VASC Technique

Two different target systems have been used to evaluate the technique: A T805 based Xplorer system and a PowerXplorer system based on PowerPC processors. Both are typical distributed memory parallel systems (each one has four nodes) running the Parix operating system from Parsytec.

The evaluation of the VASC performance and memory overhead has been based on the direct measure of the execution time and size of the code for three different applications. The coverage and latency have been evaluated only in the PowerPC processor by using the Xception fault injection tool [2].

The following test applications have been used:

Dhrystone - statements of C in a distribution considered representative (synthetic benchmark);

Whetstone - similar to Dhrystone, but including floating point operations;

Ising - a parallel simulation of the behaviour of Spin-glass metal. The test program implements a 2-dimensional Ising model. The program has been paralleled in a geographic fashion, mapping different parts of the matrix to different processors. It is a medium sized application;

Matmult - a parallel matrix multiplication program. It calculates the product of two matrices, distributing the work to all nodes;

Sor (Successive Overrelaxation) - a parallel algorithm to solve the Laplace equation over a grid. The algorithm is based on the overrelaxation scheme with red-black ordering.

The performance and memory overhead evaluation have been based on the Dhrystone, Whestone, and Ising programs. The fault injection experiments on the PowerPC based system used Ising, Matmult and Sor programs.

4.1 Performance and Memory Overheads

The VASC technique offers the innovative possibility to choose the most appropriate combination of block sizes and check intervals. Thus, the evaluation should consider different combinations of these two parameters.

Figures 6 and 7 show the overheads in the two systems running Dhrystone and Whetstone for several combinations of block sizes and check intervals (block size/check size). We have chosen block sizes smaller than check intervals because the overhead of the checking operations is greater than the overhead of the tracking. It is worth noting that errors are propagated by tracking operations and will be detected when a checking operation is found.

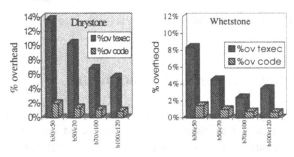

%ovtexec = execution time overhead , %ovcode = code size overhead

Figure 6- Overhead for the Dhrystone and for the Whetstone (T805)

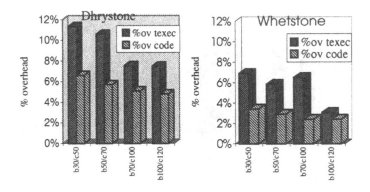

Figure 7- Overhead for the Dhrystone and for the Whetstone (PowerPC)

As expected, both the performance and memory overhead decrease when the block size and the check interval increase. However, some exception to this rule can be observed. For example, in the T805 system the execution time overhead for block size of 100 and check size of 120 increased in relation to that for block size 70 and check size 100. This happened accidentally because our signature placement algorithm doesn't take into account execution profiling information (we didn't choose less-frequently-followed paths in the signatures placement algorithms). For example, even when a large check interval is chosen, a check operation might be inserted in the middle of a loop with many iterations, which causes great performance overhead. Run-time program behaviour as described in [18] could be used to minimise the performance overhead.

In both systems the overheads for Dhrystone are greater than those for the Whetstone. This is because floating-point instructions are slower and larger (size) than the scalar ones. Thus the impact of including the extra instructions (due to VASC) is relatively small.

The code size overhead for the T805 system is much smaller than the PowerPC system. That's because the signature operations instructions in the T805 are small (1 to 2 bytes each, the exact size depending on the offset in the instruction), while in the PowerPC every instruction is 4 bytes long. But, interestingly, the execution time overhead presented the inverse behaviour, being smaller for the PowerPC processor. That's because the signaturing operations work with registers in this processor, while in the T805 they work with a workspace cache position, which has a slower access.

The performance and memory overhead have been analysed for the Ising application in the PowerPC in great detail, using different block sizes and check intervals, as shown in figure 8. This figure shows very clearly that there is great flexibility in choosing the most appropriate parameters for a given application in order to fulfil the overhead requirements.

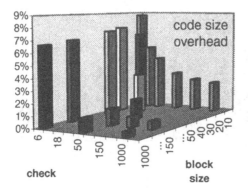

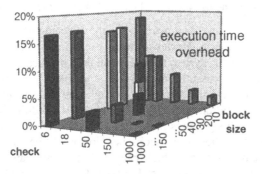

Figure 8- Code size and execution time overheads for the Ising application on the PowerPC

4.2 The Fault Injection Tool

The Xception tool used in the VASC evaluation emulates hardware transient faults in functional units of the processor (and in the memory) [2]. The current version of Xception is targeted for the IBM/Motorola 601 PowerPC processor and runs under the Parix Operating System from Parsytec.

Xception is able to emulate faults in the following functional units: Data Bus, Address Bus, Floating Point Unit (FPU), Integer Unit (IU), General Purpose Registers (GPR), Branch Processing Unit (BPU), Memory Management Unit (MMU), and Main Memory. For instance, to inject a transient fault in the Integer Unit, Xception corrupts the result of the first instruction that uses the Integer Unit after the trigger, like for instance an "add" instruction. For the other functional units similar strategies are followed.

Several kinds of events can trigger the injection of a fault: a specific instruction being fetched, a certain address being used for a load or for a store, or a certain time having elapsed from the start of the program. The faults injected can be bit flips or stuck-at faults, lasting for at least one memory cycle, and can affect one or more bits at a time.

The process of defining the faults to inject can be either manual or automatic. In the latter the user only specifies the range for the fault parameters and the system generates the set of faults by choosing randomly values in the specified range.

Only one fault is injected in each run of the program - after the injection of the fault and the collection of results, the whole system is rebooted for a new injection, in order to guarantee a clean starting state.

When the actual fault injection process starts, the Xception tool runs the application once without fault injection - "*the gold run*" - measuring its execution time and storing the application output results in a reference file. This file is very important, as for each execution of the application with fault injection the output is conveniently compared with that reference to catch undetected errors that corrupted the output. For the applications used the results file consisted of the matrix with the results of the computations. In this phase, the user also specifies a time-out, so that the Xception tool can stop the experiment when it is stalled due to the injected fault.

To inject a fault, Xception loads the description of the fault, programs the processors breakpoint or timer registers according to the fault trigger specified, and lets the system execute until the programmed exception transfers control to the exception handlers to inject the fault. Specific registers or memory contents are then corrupted, before the control is returned to the application.

The results gathered by Xception after each fault are of two kinds: the outcome of the application and the behaviour of the error detection methods (which of them has detected errors and with what latency). Figure 9 shows the most relevant information reported by Xception for each fault.

Injection Status	Information about Fault Activation (injected/ not injected) Address and Opcode of affected instruction
Exit Code	Returned by the application (C exit())
Kernel Error Messages	Error detected and reported by the PARIX kernel
Application output correctness	Result of *byte-to-byte* comparison of program output with reference output
Error detection results	Information on whether the errors have been detected by some Error Detection Mechanism or not
Latency	latency associated with the error detection

Figure 9 - The report on each fault injection in Xception

4.3 Experiments Organisation

For the experiments presented in this paper the fault sets were always defined automatically. The fault parameters have been generated in such a way that all the faults have been injected at a random time during the application execution. Each fault has been injected in one processor chosen at random among the four processors in the target system. The faults caused one or two bit flips associated with a randomly chosen processor functional unit, and lasting for only one instruction cycle.

10000 faults have been injected for each test application to assess the error coverage of VASC and compare with the other error detection mechanisms. Those faults were divided in ten experiments, each consisting of 1000 transient faults.

The processor built-in mechanisms considered are the memory access checking - Data access exception - **DAE**, instruction access exception - **IAE** , and illegal instruction - **II**. The DAE and IAE happen when an effective address cannot be translated in a memory access.

A detailed analysis of the coverage of the error detection methods has been done considering the faults injected in some processor units, based on the set of 10000 injected for the Ising application.

Concerning the impact of the faults and the error detection status the following categories were considered:

1. **detected errors** - When any of the built-in mechanisms or the VASC technique forced an exception reporting a detection. In this case the application is stopped immediately;

2. **undetected (with wrong results)** - faults that produced errors that were not detected by any mechanism and corrupted the application results (detected by the comparison of the results with the gold run results). This is a critical situation as the application has produced wrong results but no error has been detected, i.e., the user will assume that the results are correct;

3. **correct results** - No errors have been detected, the application terminated normally and produced correct results. This means that the errors caused by the fault have been cancelled by the normal program execution or stayed latent during all the execution time;

4. **system hang-up** - Xception had to reboot the target system after the specified time-out because the system stopped responding.

VASC was implemented with a block size of 10 and a check interval of 18 for all the previously stated experiments. We have chosen these values because the execution time and code size overhead is much lower than the approach with a maximum amount of checking (check interval 6, any track size) (Figure 8) and previous experiments have shown that this combination yields good error detection rate for VASC (see section 4.5).

Finally, many combinations of block sizes and check intervals were used to build a graph showing the percentage of error detections that was due to the technique. For these experiments we injected 1000 faults for each combination of block size/check interval considered on the Ising and on the Matmult applications.

In the implementation of the technique only the application source code was signed. This means that the library code that was linked in the linking phase was not signed. Accordingly, errors manifested in that extra code (causing an erroneous control flow change to that extra code) could not be detected by VASC, as no checking operations were performed there. This suggests that the error detection rate could increase if all the executable code was signed. The application object code size was measured to be 28%, 5,7% and 32% of the executable code size for the Ising, the Matmult and the Sor applications respectfully.

4.4 Experimental Results

Figure 10 shows the distribution of error detections between the mechanisms tested.

	Ising (no VASC)	Ising (VASC)	Matmult (no VASC)	Matmult (VASC)	Sor (no VASC)	Sor (VASC)
detection mechanism	% injected errors	% injected errors	% injected errors	% injected errors	% injected errors	% injected errors
VASC	-	6,55±0,54	-	3,91±0,44	-	3,68±0,31
DAE	19,6±0,35	15,7±1,06	16,03±0,72	13,96±0,98	14,93±0,51	14,69±0,64
IAE	13,09±0,42	13,3±0,42	15,01 ±0,85	14,40±0,86	18,32±0,73	17,44±0,82
II	5,0±0,21	6,2±0,3	6,2±0,3	7,11±0,71	8,09±0,43	9,98±0,42
overall detection	37,82±0,59	41,84±0,86	38,38±0,85	42,29±0,92	41,53±0,63	43,28±0,78
undetected	11,32±1,62	7,63±0,92	13,97±0,81	11,53±1,20	7,15±0,98	5,84±0,91
Correct results	49,86±1,85	50,54±0,17	47,65±1,19	42,29±0,92	51,32±1,18	50,88±0,38

*these results are presented with a 95% confidence interval from 10 sets of 1000 faults experiments

Figure 10 - Error distribution for the reference run (no VASC) and with VASC

Memory access checking is responsible for most error detections in the system. The addition of VASC has improved the overall error detections by less than four percent. The percentages of Undetected Errors observed are relatively high for all the applications, which clearly shows that good error detection mechanisms are required to gain confidence in the application results. It should be noted that Undetected Errors mean that the application terminated and everything seemed to be normal (no errors have been reported), but the results delivered to the end user were wrong. The manual observation of the effects of some of these faults (carried out from the information gathered by the Xception on the actual instruction affected by the fault) has shown that most of them correspond to pure data errors which have not affected the program control flow. This fact also explains why VASC only caused a slight improvement on the Undetected Errors.

A high percentage of faults did not affect the application results (Correct Results). This means that the errors have been tolerated in some way (e.g., errors injected in a register that was overwritten afterwards or errors that affected the operands in a comparison without affecting the comparison result) or stayed latent during the whole application execution. It is worth noting that some processor units have fairly high probability to produce this behaviour. For example, faults injected in the general purpose registers are distributed at random and may affect a register that is not being used. On the other hand, faults in the integer unit always affect the results of an integer operation.

Figure 11 shows the distribution of the error detections for the Ising application in some of the most relevant units for a block size of 10 and a check interval of 18. There is a decrease of Undetected Errors in all the functional units considered when VASC is added, which shows that VASC decreases the probabilities of having undetected wrong application results.

Faults injected in the Data Bus and the Integer Unit present higher percentage of Undetected Errors than faults injected in the other processor units. This is consistent with the observation that most errors left undetected are pure data errors (affecting data calculations important for the results or errors that produced a load from the wrong data cell, corrupting the results). These errors must be handled by data verification oriented mechanisms like the ABFTs or assertions. It also should be noted that the target system is based on RISC processors (PowerPC), and faults in these processors cause more data errors (and less control flow errors) than faults in CISC processors, as pointed out in section 2.

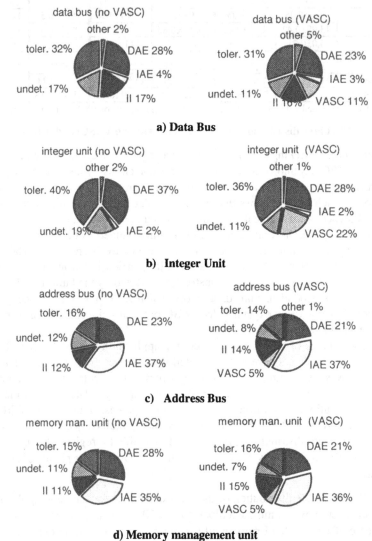

a) **Data Bus**

b) **Integer Unit**

c) **Address Bus**

d) **Memory management unit**

Figure 11- Error coverage of Ising by unit with and without VASC

Figure 12 shows the latencies for the Ising application with and without VASC.

NO	VASC			WITH	VASC		
	Avge latency (µs)	Strd deviation (µs)			Avge (µs)	Std dev (µs)	
DAE	11,19	45,77		DAE	21,66	176,47	
IAE	1,39	0,12		IAE	1,39	0,24	
II	3,70	9,71		II	2,42	6,84	
				VASC	2,15	0,42	

Figure 12 Latency results on Ising (no VASC and with VASC)

The VASC technique presents a much lower latency than the DAE.. We also see that the DAE latency increased with VASC (time between the fault was injected and the moment the error was detected by the mechanism). Errors affecting data accesses can happen either by immediate address modification during the data access (in which case the exception is immediately triggered by a faulty address) or by a fault induced latent error such as a register data pointer which is used some instructions later. It is worth noting that as VASC relies on the addition of extra instruction with no data accesses, the relative percentage of data access instructions will decrease. Therefore, the relative number of occurrences of the fast detection case in the DAE mechanism decreases compared to the latent error case.

4.5 Analysis of the Error Detection Patterns with Growing Block Sizes

We have also analysed the VASC error detection for different block sizes and check intervals (Figure 13), having injected 1000 faults for each pair. The error coverage profile with growing signature block sizes and signature checking intervals is not a strictly descending path. This means that the best VASC error detection coverage is not achieved with the smallest blocks and checking intervals. The explanation for this unexpected result is not totally clear. However, the interaction of VASC with the built-in mechanisms seems to be responsible for that, as small checking intervals correspond to the inclusion of many extra instructions altering the code. Figure 14 shows the observed error detection behaviour of the memory access checking built-in mechanisms and of VASC with different check intervals. IAE doesn't change much, but DAE does.

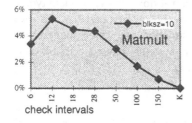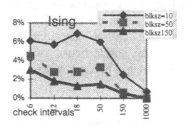

Figure 13 Coverage patterns of VASC with growing checking intervals on Ising and on Matmult

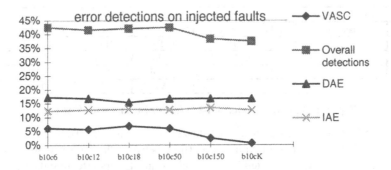

Figure 14 - Error detections for VASC and memory access checking for many check sizes

From figure 13 we can conclude that to obtain good coverage for VASC the check intervals should be less than 50 instructions and the block sizes should be kept small. However, it should be noted that optima found for the VASC error detection coverage does not necessarily correspond to the best overall coverage improvement (VASC + built-in error detection mechanisms).

5. Conclusions

A new assigned signature monitoring technique called VASC (Versatile Assigned Signature Checking) was presented. Unlike many previous signature monitoring techniques, VASC can be used in any existing system without requiring changes in the system or in the compilers. VASC is applied at the machine instructions level and allows the user to choose block sizes and checking intervals with complete freedom. This feature allows the user to balance the memory and performance overhead constraints of the application with the desired error detection coverage. A complete evaluation of VASC was presented in the paper. The performance and memory overhead have been measured for a large range of block sizes and checking intervals for three different applications and in two different systems. The coverage and latency of VASC have been evaluated by fault injection in a parallel system based on PowerPC processors. The technique accounted for 10 to 16% of the detected errors, but the overall error coverage improvement was relatively small (less than 4%). One reason for this is in the fact that the percentage of control flow errors (the main type of errors detected by VASC) in the PowerPC is relatively low compared to the same percentage in processors with a more complex instruction set, which suggests that assigned signatures are much better suited for systems having variable-sized instructions and less efficient memory access checking.

References

[1] A. Aho, R. Sethi, and J. Ulman, "Compilers: principles, techniques, and tools", Addison-Wesley Ed., 1985.

[2] Carreira, J., H. Madeira and João Gabriel Silva "Xception:Software Fault Injection and Monitoring in Processor Functional Units". Procs. 5th Conference on Dependable Computing for Critical Applications, Urbana-Champaign, IL, USA, Sept 27-29,1995.

[3] Gunneflo, U., J. Karsson and J. Torin, "Evaluation of Error Detection Schemes Using Fault Injection by Heavy-ion Radiation", Procs. 19th FTCS, pp.340-347,1989.

[4] Madeira,H., M. Rela,P. Furtado and J. G. Silva "Time Behaviour monitoring as an Error Detection Mechanism". Conf. on Dependable Computing for Critical Applications DCCA-3 Sept- 92

[5] Madeira, H. and J. Gabriel Silva "On-Line Signature Learning and Checking". Conference on Dependable Computing for Critical Applications, Springer-Verlag, J. Meyer and R. Schlichting (eds.) 1992 pp 394-420.

[6] Mahmood, A. and E. McCluskey. Watchdog Processors - Error Coverage and Overhead. Proc. of the 15th Symposium on Fault Tolerant Computing, Ann Arbor, Michigan, USA, June 1985, pp 214-219.

[7] Mahmood, A. and E. McCluskey. Concurrent Error Detection using Watchdog Processors - A Survey. IEEE Trans. on Computers, Vol37, pp160-174, Feb 1988.

[8] Miremadi, G., J. Karlsson,U. Gunneflo, J. Torin, "Two Software Techniques for On-line Error Detection". Procs. of 22th Symp. on Fault Tolerant Computing, 1992.

[9] Miremadi, G., J. Ohlsson, M. Rimém, J. Karlsson, "Use of Time and Address Signatures for Control Flow Checking". Conference on Dependable Computing for Critical Applications (DCCA 5), Urbana-Champaign, USA, Sept. 95, pp 113-124.

[10] Namjoo, M. "Techniques for Concurrent Testing of VLSI Processor Operation". Proceedings of Int. Test Conf., Philadelphia, Nov.15-18 1982, p.461-468.

[11] Ohlssom, J. , M. Rimen,U. Gunneflo, A Study of Transient Fault-Injection into a 32-bit RISC with Built.in Watchdog, Proceedings of the 22th Fault Tolerant Computing Symposium, 1992,pp. 316-325.

[12] Ohlsson, J., M. Rimén, "Implicit Signature Checking" Proc. of 25th Symposium on Fault Tolerant Computing, FTCS-25, Jun 95.

[13] Saxena, N. R. and E. J. McCluskey, " Control Flow Checking Using Watchdog Assists and Extended Precision CheckSums" IEEE Transactions on Computers Vol 39, n°4, April 1990.

[14] Shen, J. P. and M. A. Shuette "On-line self-monitoring using signatured instruction streams", International Test Conference, ITC83,pp 275-282,1983.

[15] Shuette, M. and J. Shen. "Processor Control Flow Monitoring using Signatured Instruction Steams". IEEE Trans. on Computers, Vol 36, pp 264-275, March 1987.

[16] Shuette, M. and J. P. Shen. Exploiting Instruction-level Resource Parallelism for Transparent, Integrated Control-flow Monitoring. Proc.of 21th Symposium on Fault Tolerant Computing, IEEE FTCS 21,318-325, 1991.

[17] Sosnowski, J., "Transient fault tolerance in microprocessor controllers", Hardware and Software for real time process control, J. Zalewski and W. Ehrenberger (eds.), Elsevier Science Publishers B. V. (North Holland), IFIP, 1989, pp. 189-195.

[18] Warter, N. J. and W. W. Hwu, "A software based approach to achieving optimal performance for signature control flow checking", Proceedings of 20th Symposium on Fault Tolerant Computing, FTCS-20, 1991, pp. 442-449.

[19] Wilken, K. and J. P. Shen, "Continous Signature Monitoring: Low-Cost Concurrent Detection of Processor Control Erros", IEEE Transactions on Computer-Aided Design, Vol. 9, No. 6, June 1990, p. 629-641.

[20] Wilken, K. and J. Shen. Continuous Signature Monitoring: Efficient Concurrent Error-detection of Processor Control Errors. IEEE 18th International Test Conference.

An Evaluation of the Error Detection Mechanisms in MARS Using Software-Implemented Fault Injection

Emmerich Fuchs

Daimler-Benz AG, Research and Technology, Berlin in cooperation with
Institut für Technische Informatik, Technische Universität Wien.
E-mail: emmerich@vmars.tuwien.ac.at

Abstract. The concept of fail-silent nodes greatly simplifies the design and safety proof of highly dependable fault-tolerant computer systems. The MAintainable Real-Time System (MARS) is a computer system where the hardware, operating system, and application level error detection mechanisms are designed to ensure the fail silence of nodes with a high probability.

The goal of this paper is two-fold: First, the error detection capabilities of the different mechanisms are evaluated in software-implemented fault injection experiments using the well-known bit-flip fault model. The results show that a fail silence coverage of at least 85% is achievable by the combination of hardware and system level software error detection mechanisms. With the additional use of application level error detection mechanisms a fail silence coverage of 100% was achieved.

Second, the limits of the application level error detection mechanisms are evaluated. In these experiments, the fault model consists of highly improbable residual faults to deliberately force the occurrence of fail silence violations. Despite this worst-case scenario, more than 50% of the presumed undetectable errors were detected by other mechanisms and hence did not lead to fail silence violations.

1 Introduction

The design and implementation of fault-tolerant computer systems often assumes *fail-silent* computers. Traditionally, the fail silence property is implemented using hardware redundancy, usually requiring at least hardware duplication. Some other approaches aim at the realization of the fail silence property without the need for hardware duplication:

Madeira and Silva [MS94] investigated the fail-silent behavior of a computer without hardware or software replication by using only behavior-based error detection mechanisms. Another approach uses a combination of behavior-based error detection mechanisms and two additional error detection layers to implement the fail silence property on simple low-cost controllers [SSMB94]. Yet another software-based approach is the concept of *Virtual Duplex Systems* described by Lovric [Lov94]. This approach uses time redundancy on a single processor and combines compiler generated diversity with design diversity for the implementation of self-checking nodes.

The target of the evaluation described in this paper is the MAintainable Real-Time System (MARS), a fault-tolerant distributed real-time architecture for hard real-time applications. The key concept for the achievement of fault tolerance in MARS is the usage of fail-silent nodes operating in active redundancy. Within the framework of the ESPRIT Basic Research Project *Predictably Dependable Computing Systems* (PDCS), fail-silent processing nodes for the MARS architecture were developed [RS94, RSL95]. The implementation of the fail silence property relies on numerous error detection mechanisms (EDMs) at three levels: the hardware, the system software, and the application software level.

In the successor project PDCS2, the MARS architecture was chosen as the target for the comparison of three different physical fault injection approaches: heavy-ion radiation, electromagnetic interferences, and pin-level fault injection. The fault injection experiments aimed to validate the fail silence assumption and to evaluate the effectiveness and appropriateness of the individual error detection mechanisms[KFA+95].

Due to the limitations inherent to the physical fault injection techniques, e.g., reproducibility, intrusiveness, accessibility, costs, etc., software-implemented fault injection has attracted a number of researchers in the past few years [SVS+88, EL92, KIT93, HRS94, KKA95]. Software-implemented fault injection is seen as the means of overcoming most of the problems associated with physical fault injection; however, confidence has to be established, if—or to what extent—software-implemented fault injection is capable of emulating the consequences of physical faults.

The goal of this paper is two-fold: First, the coverage of the error detection mechanisms on the different levels is evaluated. The following question is discussed: *Are the application level error detection mechanisms necessary to implement fail-silent nodes?* The results of the physical fault injection experiments from the PDCS project and the software-implemented fault injection experiments described in this paper demonstrate that the application level error detection mechanisms are crucial to achieve the goal of fail silence. Based on this result, two specific mechanisms, the message checksums and the double execution feature, are evaluated in more detail.

The second goal of this paper is to evaluate the limits of the application level error detection mechanisms using worst-case fault injection. To this end, error patterns maliciously chosen to circumvent detection by both mentioned application level error detection mechanisms were used in several fault injection experiments. However, experimental results show that despite this worst-case scenario for the error detection mechanisms, less than half of the injected error patterns lead to fail silence violations. Error detection mechanisms at the system software level and additional padding bytes in application output messages are responsible for the improved error detection coverage.

This paper is organized as follows: Section 2 gives a short introduction to the fault tolerance concept of MARS and the error detection mechanisms implemented to achieve fail silence. Section 3 contains a description of the different configurations of the error detection mechanisms and implementation issues of the fault injection tools. Moreover, results from various fault injection experiments with the bit-flip fault model are described. These experiments form the basis for a more detailed evaluation of the application level error detection mechanisms in Section 4, which describes worst-case fault injection experiments investigating the limits of the application level error detection mechanisms. Section 5 discusses the results obtained in the fault injection experiments. The paper concludes with a short summary of the main results in Section 6.

2 Fault Tolerance in MARS

2.1 Fail Silence

The MAintainable Real-Time System (MARS) provides a fault-tolerant distributed platform for hard real-time applications. Fault tolerance in MARS is based on *fail-silent* nodes operating in dual active redundancy and on sending duplicate messages on the two redundant real-time busses [RSL95].

The concept of *fail silence* basically represents the same notion as crash failures [CASD85] or the "halt-on-failure" property of fail-stop processors [SS83]. Fail silence is intended to describe the behavior of a computer that fails "cleanly" by just stopping to send messages in case a failure occurs [PBS+88]. The definition of fail silence used in MARS is nearly equivalent to the notion of fail-silent behavior used in the VOLTAN reliable node architecture [SES+92]:

A node is said to be *fail-silent* if it produces either

- correct messages, which can be verified as such by the non-faulty receivers, or
- it ceases to produce new correct messages, in which case non-faulty receivers can detect any messages it does produce as invalid.

The implementation of fail-silent nodes requires extensive use of error detection mechanisms, which are briefly described next.

2.2 Error Detection Mechanisms

MARS uses three levels of error detection mechanisms (EDMs): the hardware EDMs, the system software EDMs, and the application level EDMs at the highest level.

Hardware: The MARS hardware [RS94] is designed to achieve a high error detection coverage for hardware faults. The hardware EDMs encompass two subclasses; the EDMs of the CPU and the non-maskable interrupts (NMIs) generated by special hardware on the node.

System Level Software: The second level consists of error detection mechanisms implemented by the operating system kernel or special system-tasks [Rei93] and the compiler generated run-time assertions produced by the Modula/R compiler [Vrc94].

Application Level Software: The concept of end-to-end checksums [SRC84] for messages and time redundant (double) execution of tasks [KKG⁺90] are the error detection mechanisms at the highest level.

Because the application level EDMs, i.e., message checksums and double execution, are necessary to achieve fail silence, these mechanisms will be discussed in more detail.

Message Checksums. If application messages should be protected on the entire communication path from a sending application task to a receiving application task, then an application level or end-to-end checksum has to be used. To achieve this, the transmission of application messages in MARS is protected by an end-to-end CRC using the CRC-CCITT generator polynomial[1]. The end-to-end CRC was designed to detect mutilated message contents, out-dated message timestamps, and wrong message types. Therefore, the Modula/R compiler automatically generates code that calculates the CRCs for all messages sent and checks the CRCs for all messages received. For each message sent from an application task, it generates code that calculates a CRC over the message contents, the key of the message, and the invocation time of the task. At the receiving end, the operating system task for message handling checks the CRC and—if no error is detected—writes the message into the message base. To provide protection against errors in the operating system and against faults that occur after the message has been written into the message base, the CRC is checked again at the start of a task receiving the message. If the check fails, an immediate shutdown of the node is performed—since the message has already been checked by the operating system, a failure of the second check reveals an error within the node.

Double Execution of Tasks. The second application level error detection mechanism is the user-transparent double execution of application tasks, which is supported by the Modula/R compiler as follows:

- The compiler produces two assembler output files instead of one. These two files can be linked to form a single executable file that contains two copies of the data space and program code, decreasing the likelihood that a single fault introduces errors into both instances.
- The compiler automatically creates a comparator task. This comparator task is scheduled to run after both instances of the replicated task have terminated. It compares the end-to-end CRCs of the generated messages and performs an immediate shutdown of the node if it detects a mismatch.

Both instances of the task receive identical input messages and therefore produce identical output messages in the fault free case. Any deviation in the

---

[1] $G(x) = x^{16} + x^{12} + x^5 + 1.$

outputs indicates an error and leads to a shutdown of the node. To detect situations in which the comparator task is affected by an error, the CRC creation algorithm is modified as follows: The CRCs for the messages created by each instance of a task are calculated as described above, but are bit-wise negated before being stored at the end of the message. The comparator task compares the negated CRCs and negates them back to the original form. If the comparator task fails to execute for whatever reason, the message does not have a valid CRC and is discarded at the receiving end.

2.3 Error Handling

Whenever an error is detected, the first error handling activity of the node is to save the error information into non-volatile memory. Then it turns itself off. Therefore, all error detection mechanisms described above attempt to establish the fail-silent behavior of a node. On restart the node writes its previously saved error information to a serial port from where it can be read by, e.g., a fault injection experiment supervision program.

3 Software-Implemented Fault Injection

This section covers the implementation of a software-implemented fault injection approach, the experimental setup, and the results from various fault injection experiments with the well known bit-flip fault model.

3.1 Experimental Setup

The experimental hardware and software setup used in the fault injection experiments reported in this paper is the same as within the PDCS2 project, where three physical fault injection techniques were applied in the assessment of the error detection mechanisms of MARS. For a detailed description of the hardware and software setup of the PDCS2 fault injection experiments refer to the paper by Karlsson et al. [KFA+95].

Since the main focus of this paper is an evaluation of the error detection mechanisms in MARS and especially of the application level error detection mechanisms, fault injection experiments with the following three different configurations of these mechanisms were performed.

- All application level EDMs are disabled in the *NO Application level error detection Mechanisms* (NOAM) configuration; i.e., error detection is solely performed by the hardware and system software mechanisms.
- In the *Single Execution plus Message Checksums* (SEMC) configuration, checksums (end-to-end CRC) for application messages are used as an application level error detection mechanism.

– In the *Double Execution plus Message Checksums* (DEMC)[2] configuration, both the time-redundant (double) execution of application tasks and checksums for the application messages are used.

3.2 Effects of the Fault Injection

In principle, fault injection can have four[3] different observable effects on a node under test:

1. An error is detected by one of the error detection mechanisms at the hardware, system software, or application level on the node under test, which leads to the shut down of the node.
2. The node under test fails to deliver the expected application message(s) for one or several application cycles, but no error is detected by the node's EDMs, which points to some kind of failure within the node under test. As a consequence, the node under test is shut down after a pre-specified time interval.
3. The receiver detects a mismatch between the messages of the node under test and the golden node; i.e., a fail silence violation has occurred.
4. The last failure type that only occurred in the software-implemented fault injection experiments is known as no-reply or no-response problem in the literature. The node under test works properly and sends valid output messages in spite of the injected fault(s). After a pre-specified time interval the experimental run is aborted and the node under test is shut down.

Another, undesired effect occurred in a few experimental runs. At node restart no error information was available from the node under test. This may be due to a hardware problem at the serial interface between the node under test and the host computer.

3.3 Technique Selection

Software-implemented fault injection techniques can be distinguished into *pre-runtime* and *runtime* approaches according to time when the actual fault injection is done. In the case of pre-runtime fault injection, all faults are injected before the application is loaded onto the target system. Therefore, there is no need to interfere with the application execution on the target system at runtime. Runtime fault injection on the other hand can be divided into a pre-runtime setup or initialization step and a runtime fault injection step. In the initialization step additional software for the purpose of fault injection is added to the

---

[2] Double execution without message checksums is not supported by the Modula/R compiler; see Section 2.2 for a detailed description.

[3] Failures in the access strategy to the communication medium in the time domain as described by Karlsson et al. [KFA+95] are not considered, because no faults were injected in the communication part of the node. Hence no such errors were detected in the experiments.

target application. In the runtime step, this additional software performs the fault injection. For the fault injection experiments described in this section a pre-runtime approach at the machine code level was selected. The reasons for this selection are the following:

- A pre-runtime technique smoothly integrates with the application development process of MARS, because applications are developed, configured, allocated, and scheduled off-line at a host computer and loaded onto the target system afterwards.
- The intrusiveness is reduced to a minimum, since only faults are injected into the application software. No additional code, which could probably alter the behavior of the application software, is needed; i.e., fault injection is transparent to the application.
- Fault injection at the machine code level is capable of injecting faults which cannot be injected at higher levels.

3.4 Implementation

The pre-runtime software-implemented fault injection on MARS can be basically divided into three steps, which are supported by different tools:

1. In the first (initialization) step, the user, i.e., the person who carries out the fault injection experiments, writes a high-level description of the whole fault injection campaign. This description contains general information about the fault injection location, distribution, the number and type of the faults to inject, and the number of experimental runs to execute.
2. In the second step, the previously written high-level description is read by a conversion tool and is automatically expanded and transformed into a low level experiment description suitable for the actual fault injection. This low level description contains the automatically generated information about location, type, and number of faults to inject for each experimental run.
3. The third or experimental execution step consists of the actual fault injection according to the generated experiment description. The application is loaded onto the MARS cluster and the experimental run is initiated.

During experiment execution, data are collected by a supervision program, which also initiates the next experimental run after one run has been completed. The supervision program writes the data collected from the target system together with status information and timestamps to the host file system for later experiment analysis.

3.5 Experiments

The software-implemented fault injection experiments were carried out for the three configurations of the test application with the pre-runtime technique described above. The main characteristics of the injected faults were the following:

- Faults were either injected into the code or the data segment of the test application.
- The position of a fault within a segment was chosen randomly to achieve a uniform distribution over the whole segment.
- The number of simultaneously injected faults was chosen from one to ten faults per experimental run.
- The faults were single bit-flips.
- The faults were injected permanently into the core image of the test application. The activation of the injected faults, however, is dependent on the program execution paths, which may result in a transient failure behavior.

For every configuration and both segments of the test application, 3000 experimental runs with one to ten simultaneously injected faults were carried out.

3.6 Results

Effectiveness of the Error Detection Mechanisms. Figure 1 shows the experimental results for single random bit-flips in the code and data segment of the test application for the three different configurations of the application level error detection mechanisms. Single bit-flips were chosen because they constitute the most likely fault scenarios, e.g., mostly single bit-flips are generated by heavy-ion radiation [Joh94].

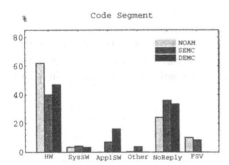 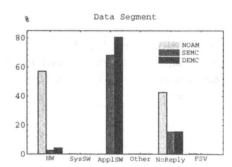

Fig. 1. Relative effectiveness of the error detection mechanisms for single bit-flips in the code and data segment of the test application.

From the experimental data and the bar charts in Fig. 1 the following observations can be made:

- A large percentage of the injected faults is detected by the hardware (HW) EDMs, especially in the NOAM configuration where no additional application level EDMs are available.

- The number of errors detected by the system software (SysSW) EDMs is nearly the same for all three configurations of the test application and shows no significant variation in the number of detected errors when more faults are injected.
- In the double execution configuration, the application level EDMs (ApplSW) close the gap between the 85% fail silence coverage achievable with hardware and system level software mechanisms and the desired 100% fail silence coverage. The main difference between the results for the code and data segment is the amount of errors detected by the application level mechanisms—25% (code segment) vs. 80% (data segment) in the single bit-flip scenario.
- In some other rare cases (Other) the node under test failed to write the previously saved error information to the serial ports upon node restart or the communication unit of the node under test detected an error.
- The SEMC and DEMC configurations exhibit a significantly higher amount of no-replies (NoReply) in the experiments with the code segment, because the application level EDMs introduce additional error check code, which is rarely executed and hence an error may be latent for a long time.
- The last error class constitutes the fail silence violations (FSV). In the case of the single execution configurations a significant portion of the injected faults (10% to 15%) resulted in fail silence violations for the experiments with the code segment. In the experiments with the data segment only 1.5% fail silence violations have been observed. For the double execution configuration—independent of the fault injection location—no fail silence violations were observed.

Application Level EDMs. The experimental results presented above demonstrate that the application level EDMs are necessary to achieve a high error detection coverage. Therefore, these mechanisms will be investigated in more detail, see Fig. 2.

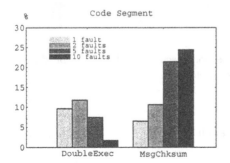 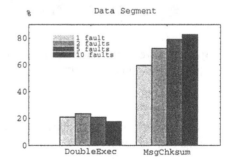

Fig. 2. Percentage of errors detected by the application level error detection mechanisms for different fault scenarios.

It can be observed that the number of detected errors by double execution first increases and then decreases with the number of injected faults, while the percentage of errors detected by message checksums rapidly increases with the number of injected faults. This occurs, because the message checksums are checked at the start of the application and that the double execution check is done after the completion of both application task instances, i.e., the double execution check has a longer latency than the message check.

Fail Silence Violations. In the fault injection experiments with the single execution configurations of the test application, a number of fail silence violations have been observed. Figure 3 compares the amount of fail silence violations in the experiments with the code and data segment of the test application for different fault scenarios.

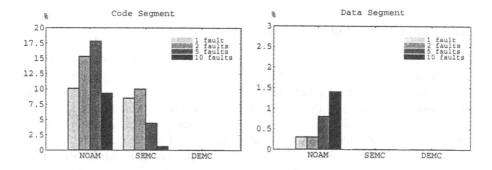

Fig. 3. Percentage of fail silence violations for different fault scenarios.

Comparing the experiments with the code segment of the two single execution configurations, the differences in the number of fail silence violations is rather small for single bit-flips. This observation leads to the conclusion that using message checksums alone is rather ineffective for the prevention of fail silence violations, when single faults are predominant. In contrast to the experiments with the code segment the experiments with the data segment show that all faults injected into the application data were revealed by the message checksums, and hence the message checksum mechanism was sufficient to achieve fail silence.

For the experiments with the text segment the number of fail silence violations first increases with the number of faults and then decreases again when more faults are injected. The cause for this phenomenon is that an increase in the number of injected faults increases both, the probability that the error is detected by one of the mechanisms or that a fail silence violation occurs. For small numbers of injected faults the probability that a fail silence violation occurs is dominant and for higher numbers of injected faults the probability that an error is detected becomes dominant.

For the double execution configuration, however, no fail silence violations have been observed, demonstrating the necessity and effectiveness of this error detection mechanism.

4   A Worst-Case Scenario for the Application Level Error Detection Mechanisms

The results presented in the previous section show that random bit-flips do not generate a significant number of fail silence violations in the configuration where double execution and message checksums are enabled. Since the fail silence property of nodes depends on these two mechanisms, it is important to know what happens when they fail. Therefore another fault injection approach was developed in this section to create a worst-case scenario for the application level error detection mechanisms.

4.1   Worst-Case Fault Injection

Error detection is never perfect, leaving a remote possibility for undetectable or common mode failures. In MARS this possibility is mainly determined by the residual error probability of the end-to-end CRC. CRC-codes have a limited error detection capability that depends on the Hamming distance of the code, the number of check bits, and the error patterns generated by the environment. Error patterns divisible by the generator polynomial are not detectable. Such errors are well known and called *undetectable* or *residual errors* in the literature. Readers interested in a thorough discussion of error correcting or error detecting codes are referred to the book by Peterson and Weldon [PW72].

The basic idea for the worst-case fault injection experiments is to generate and inject such residual errors into the test application to obtain a worst-case scenario for the application level error detection mechanisms.[4]

4.2   Implementation

A mutilation of messages can be achieved by different fault injection techniques, ranging from physical fault injection on the data bus, memory, or the transmission medium to software-implemented fault injection. For the ease of implementation and since the application level EDMs are implemented in software, a software-implemented fault injection approach operating at the same level is the most natural choice. Software-implemented fault injection has the additional advantage that the residual error patterns can be easily generated according to

---

[4] The probability that such a residual error occurs in a real world application is not considered in this paper. Often a residual error probability for CRCs with 16 check bits is pessimistically assumed in the order of 10^{-5} for very high bit error probabilities. In typical environments the residual error probability will be below 10^{-10} [MUK90].

the generator polynomial of the end-to-end CRC. The experiments with residual errors are performed with runtime fault injection, which is implemented as follows:

In a first step, the residual error patterns are generated offline on a host computer from the knowledge about the generator polynomial of the end-to-end CRC.

In a second step, the application software is supplemented with a system level task that performs the fault injection at runtime. The fault injection technique used for the injection of residual errors is based on the concept of *Fault Injection Agents* [HRS94]—additional system level tasks equipped with write permissions on the data space of application tasks and the message base area in memory. This concept is similar to the *Trojan Horses* proposed by Segall et al. [SVS⁺88].

The fault injection agent that was implemented for the experiments is a system task with write permission on the message base (for input messages) and the data segment of the test application (for output messages). Every application task that should be subjected to fault injection is supplemented with a fault injection agent, i.e., the fault injection agent is scheduled before or after the application task depending on the type of message. The input messages are passed to the fault injection agent first, which mutilates the messages. After the fault injection agent has terminated its operation, the application task is started and passed the mutilated input messages. Upon termination of the application task, the output messages are passed to a fault injection agent, and, after the fault injection has been completed, delivered to the message handling subsystem. Following this procedure, fault injection only takes place before or after the execution of application tasks, reducing the intrusiveness of this technique.

The third step consists of the experiment execution during which fault injection is done by the fault injection agents according to error patterns passed in the configuration data upon initialization of the node under test.

4.3 Experiments

The fault injection experiments reported in this section were carried out with the rolling ball test application [KHLS91]. The control task receives two input messages (video and course) and computes an output message (calculation).

Figure 4 shows the message structure of the rolling ball application, where every field in the messages represents one byte. The application variables contained in the messages are two byte quantities and are of four different integer types.[5] Variables of the **speed** type have a range of 3000 (-1500..1500), the **position** and **tangent** type have a range of 4000 (-2000..2000), and the **acceleration** type variables have a range of 26000 (-13000..13000) values. The Modula/R compiler automatically generates code to check these value ranges for all variables in an input message.

---

[5] In Modula/R numeric types such as 'integer' or 'real' are not predefined, instead they have to be defined as ranges.

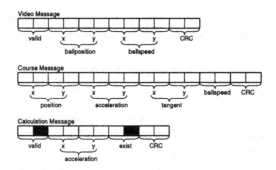

Fig. 4. Message structure of the test application.

In the fault injection experiments, all different residual error patterns of length less than 3 bytes[6] were injected into the application messages. The number of all undetectable errors for a given CRC generator polynomial of degree r up to a given error pattern length n with $r < n$ can be calculated by $\sum_{i=r}^{n-1} 2^{i-r}$, i.e., in our case $\sum_{i=16}^{24-1} 2^{i-16} = 255$.

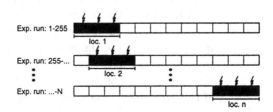

Fig. 5. Fault injection at different locations within messages.

During each experimental run one dedicated error pattern was injected at a given location, e.g., in runs 1–255 the error patterns were injected into location 1, see Fig. 5. After the injection of all 255 error patterns the fault injection location was shifted one byte, and again all patterns were injected at the new location.

4.4 Results

Input Messages. The error detection mechanisms for the video message are quite sensitive to fault injection and only 14% of the injected error patterns lead to fail silence violations.

For the course message type, however, the situation is quite different, resulting in about 47% fail silence violations. Figure 6 shows the number of fail

---

[6] The length of 3 bytes is chosen for pragmatical reasons, because an experimental run lasts for approximately one minute and the injection of all possible residual error patterns less or equal 24 bit into a 10 byte messages requires 2550 runs.

silence violations depending on the fault injection location within the video and course input messages. The small number of fail silence violations for the video message can be explained by the message structure and the value ranges of the variables contained in the message. Since the value range for the variables in the video message uses only 4-6% of the 16-bit integer range, the range checks added by the Modula/R compiler are able to detect all errors which result in variable values outside this range space. An exception is location 10 where the CRC field itself was mutilated, which is not checked by other application level error detection mechanisms.

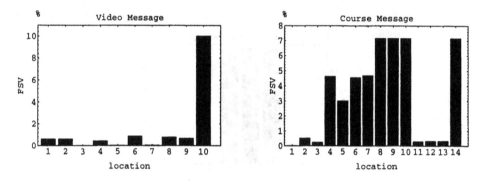

Fig. 6. Location dependence of the fail silence violations for the input messages.

The rather high number of fail silence violations for the course message results from variables of the **acceleration** type which use a large portion of the available range space. Therefore the injected error patterns generate a lot more values within the given range, and hence are undetectable by range checks.

Output Message. For the fault injection experiments on output messages two factors are of importance: the temporal persistence of the injected faults (permanent or transient) and the fault injection location. The calculation output message, as shown in Fig. 4, contains two padding bytes (shaded fields). Fault injection has a different effect if a padding byte is or is not affected by a fault, because the message variables are overwritten with a new value in every application cycle but the padding bytes are initialized only upon application start. The three different effects observed in the fault injection experiments are the following:

1. The temporal persistence, transient or permanent, does not matter if no padding bytes are affected by the fault injection. In this case all injected faults lead to fail silence violations, see locations 3, 4, and 5 in Fig. 7.
2. Permanent faults affecting a padding byte lead to the detection of an error by the double execution mechanism, see locations 1, 2, 6, 7, and 8 in Fig. 7. This happens because the padding bytes are not initialized in every application

cycle. Therefore, some part of the error pattern is incorporated into the end-to-end CRC of one output message instance, leading to a mismatch upon comparison with the CRC of the other message instance.

3. A transient fault affecting a padding byte sometime during experiment execution leads to a single fail silence violation in the current application cycle. In the next application cycle, however, the injected transient fault is partly overwritten by the new output values, the contents of the padding bytes are not changed and incorporated into the end-to-end CRC leading to the detection of an error by double execution.

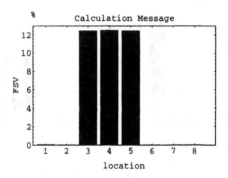

Fig. 7. Location dependence of the fail silence violations in the output message.

Figure 7 shows the results of the fault injection experiments with permanent residual error patterns. In the experiments it was observed that only about 37% of all injected error patterns actually lead to fail silence violations, the rest was detected by double execution.

5   Discussion of the Results

The fault injection experiments with bit-flips in the code segment of the test application show that the hardware mechanisms are predominant in the detection of errors. This observation is consistent with the results from the three physical fault injection techniques where more than 70% of all errors were detected by the hardware mechanisms. For the experiments with the data segment the hardware error detection is significantly lower, in the order of 5%, because only a few data errors can be detected by behavioral EDMs available at the hardware level. The remaining large amount of data errors is detected by application-specific mechanisms such as range checks, plausibility checks on data values, or an end-to-end CRC for messages.

The error detection mechanisms at the system software level detect the smallest amount of the injected faults. These mechanisms showed no significant variation in the number of detected errors for different configurations of the application software and different numbers of injected faults. Comparing physical and software-implemented fault injection, the major part of the errors detected at the system software level is detected by the operating system for the physical fault injection techniques, while for software-implemented fault injection almost all errors were detected by the compiler generated runtime assertions, e.g., range checks for variables.

The experiments with the random bit-flip fault model have demonstrated the need for application level error detection mechanisms. Especially the double execution of application tasks was very useful for the achievement of a high error detection coverage. Comparing the single and double execution configurations, the fail silence coverage increased from approximately 85% in the case of single execution to 100% fail silence coverage with double execution.

Comparing the amount of observed fail-silence violations, software implemented fault injection is far more malicious than the three physical fault injection techniques in the single execution configurations of the test application. For the three physical fault injection techniques, the high hardware error detection coverage effectively prevents the propagation of errors to higher levels and thus the amount of fail-silence violations is also reduced. Errors generated by means of software—especially data errors—are more easily propagated to the application level, where these errors may be either detected by application specific checks or lead to fail-silence violations.

This observation indicates that a simple random bit-flip fault model may be sufficient to emulate the consequences of faults generated by EMI and pin-level fault injection with respect to the evaluation of the fail-silence coverage of processing nodes. But this fault model is not malicious enough to encompass the consequences of internal faults generated by heavy-ion radiation.

The worst-case fault injection experiments, described in the previous section, with residual error patterns affecting output messages showed that the incorporation of padding bytes into the end-to-end CRC significantly enhanced error detection. This occurs due to the implicit assumption that the padding bytes in both message instances have the same contents. If these common data are mutilated in one message instance an error is detected by the double execution comparison. Therefore more than 50% of the injected permanent faults were detected in the experiments and did not lead to fail silence violations.

The interesting case are the transient faults that inevitably lead to a single fail silence violation in the current cycle. In the next cycle however, an error is detected by double execution although the message data are correct. In this case, two scenarios depending on the application requirements can be distinguished. If it is better for an application to continue with its work in the extreme rare case of a fail silence violation, then there is no need to halt and reveal its failure status in the next cycle. The transient fault has already vanished at that time. Therefore the padding bytes should be omitted from the message. In the other case, it may be better for an application to detect the occurrence of a fail silence violation late than to miss it entirely. In this case the interleaving of padding bytes with message data provides an additional means for the improvement of the error detection coverage.

6 Conclusion

This paper reported on an evaluation of the error detection mechanisms in MARS by the use of software-implemented fault injection. A series of fault injection experiments demonstrated that the application level error detection mechanisms are necessary and effective for the implementation of fail-silent processing nodes. Especially the time redundant (double) execution of application tasks increased the observed fail silence coverage from approximately 85% with the single execution configuration to 100%. Moreover, worst-case fault injection experiments with maliciously chosen error patterns were conducted to evaluate the limits of the application level error detection mechanisms. In these experiments more than 50% of the presumed undetectable error patterns were detected by other mechanisms. This increased fail silence coverage provides an additional safety margin in case the application level error detection mechanisms fail.

References

[CASD85] F. Cristian, H. Aghili, R. Strong, and D. Dolev. Atomic broadcast: From simple message diffusion to byzantine agreement. In *Proc. 15th Int. Symposium on Fault-Tolerant Computing*, pages 200–206, Silver Spring, June 1985. IEEE Computer Society.

[EHP94] K. Echtle, D. Hammer, and D. Powell, editors. *Dependable Computing— EDCC-1, First European Dependable Computing Conference*, volume 852 of *Lecture Notes in Computer Science*, Berlin, Germany, Oct. 1994. Springer-Verlag.

[EL92] K. Echtle and M. Leu. The EFA fault injector for fault-tolerant distributed system testing. In *IEEE Workshop on Fault-Tolerant Parallel and Distributed Systems*, pages 28–35, Amherst, Massachusetts, USA, July 1992.

[HRS94] S. Han, H. A. Rosenberg, and K. G. Shin. DOCTOR: An integrateD sOftware fault injeCTiOn enviRonment. In *Third IEEE Int'l Workshop on Integrating Error Models with Fault Injection*, Annapolis, Maryland, USA, April 1994.

[IEE88] IEEE Computer Society. *Proc. 18th Int. Symposium on Fault-Tolerant Computing*, Tokyo, Japan, June 1988.

[Joh94] R. Johansson. On single event upset error manifestation. In Echtle et al. [EHP94], pages 217–231.

[KFA+95] J. Karlsson, P. Folkesson, Jean Arlat, Yves Crouzet, and Günther Leber. Integration and comparison of three physical fault injection techniques. In *Predictably Dependable Computing Systems*, chapter V: Fault Injection, pages 309–329. Springer Verlag, 1995.

[KHLS91] H. Kopetz, P. Holzer, G. Leber, and M. Schindler. The rolling ball on MARS. Research Report 13/91, Institut für Technische Informatik, Technische Universität Wien, Vienna, Austria, Nov. 1991.

[KIT93] W. Kao, R.K. Iyer, and D. Tang. FINE: A fault injection and monitoring environment for tracing the UNIX system behavior under faults. *IEEE Transactions on Software Engineering*, SE-19(11):1105–1118, Nov. 1993.

[KKA95] G. A. Kanawati, N. A. Kanawati, and J. A. Abraham. FERRARI: A flexible software-based fault and error injection system. *IEEE Transactions on Computers*, 44(2):248–260, Feb. 1995.

[KKG+90] H. Kopetz, H. Kantz, G. Grünsteidl, P. Puschner, and J. Reisinger. Tolerating Transient Faults in MARS. In *Proc. 20th Int. Symposium on Fault-Tolerant Computing*, pages 466–473, Newcastle upon Tyne, U.K., June 1990.

[Lov94] T. Lovric. Systematic and design diversity — software techniques for hardware fault detection. In Echtle et al. [EHP94], pages 309–326.

[MS94] H. Madeira and J.G. Silva. Experimental evaluation of the fail-silent behavior in computers without error masking. In *Proc. 24th Int. Symposium on Fault-Tolerant Computing*, pages 350–359, Austin, Texas, USA, June 1994. IEEE Computer Society.

[MUK90] H.-J. Mathony, J. Unruh, and K.-H. Kaiser. On the data integrity in automotive networks. In *Electronic Systems dor Vehicles*, number 819 in VDI Berichte, pages 515–539. VDI Verlag, Düsseldorf, 1990.

[PBS+88] D. Powell, G. Bonn, D. Seaton, P. Verissimo, and F. Waeselynck. The Delta-4 approach to dependability in open distributed computing systems. [IEE88], pages 246–151.

[PW72] W.W. Peterson and E.J. Weldon. *Error-Correcting Codes*. The M.I.T. Press, 1972. (Second Edition).

[Rei93] J. Reisinger. *Konzeption und Analyse eines zeitgesteuerten Betriebssystems für Echtzeitanwendungen*. PhD thesis, Technisch-Naturwissenschaftliche Fakultät, Technische Universität Wien, Wien, Österreich, Juli 1993.

[RS94] J. Reisinger and A. Steininger. The design of a fail-silent processing node for MARS. *Distributed Systems Engineering Journal*, 1994.

[RSL95] J. Reisinger, A. Steininger, and G. Leber. The PDCS implementation of MARS hardware and software. In *Predictably Dependable Computing Systems*, pages 209–224. Springer Verlag, 1995.

[SES+92] S.K. Shrivastava, P.D. Ezhilchelvan, N.A. Speirs, S. Tao, and A. Tully. Principal features of the VOLTAN family of reliable node architectures for distributed systems. *ACM Transactions on Computer Systems*, 41(5):542–549, May 1992.

[SRC84] J. Saltzer, D. Reed, and D. Clark. End-to-end arguments in system design. *ACM Transactions on Computer Systems*, 2(4):277–288, Nov. 1984.

[SS83] R. D. Schlichting and F. B. Schneider. Fail-stop processors: An approach to designing fault-tolerant computing systems. *ACM Transactions on Computer Systems*, 1(3):222–238, Aug. 1983.

[SSMB94] J.G. Silva, L.M. Silva, H. Madeira, and J. Bernardino. A fault-tolerant mechanism for simple controllers. In Echtle et al. [EHP94], pages 39–55.

[SVS+88] Z. Segall, D. Vrsalovic, D. Siewiorek, D. Yaskin, J. Kownacki, J. Barton, D. Rancey, A. Robinson, and T. Lin. FIAT - Fault Injection based Automated Testing environment. [IEE88], pages 102–107.

[Vrc94] A. Vrchoticky. *The Basis for Static Execution Time Prediction*. PhD thesis, Technisch-Naturwissenschaftliche Fakultät, Technische Universität Wien, Vienna, Austria, June 1994.

Session 3

Modeling and Evaluation

Chair: Jean Arlat, LAAS-CNRS, France

Dependability Modeling and Analysis of Complex Control Systems: An Application to Railway Interlocking

Manuela Nelli[1], Andrea Bondavalli[2] and Luca Simoncini[3]

[1] Consorzio Pisa Ricerche, P.zza A. D'Ancona 1, Pisa, Italy
[2] CNUCE Istituto del CNR, Via S. Maria 36, Pisa, Italy
[3] Dept. Information Engineering, University of Pisa, Via Diotisalvi, 2 Pisa, Italy

Abstract. This paper describes the dependability modelling and evaluation of a real complex system, made of redundant replicated hardware and redundant diverse software. It takes into account all aspects of their interactions (including correlation between the diverse software variants) and of the criticality of the several components. Our approach has been to realise the system model in a structured way. This allows to cope with complexity and to focus, where interesting, on specific behaviour for a more detailed analysis. Furthermore each level may be modelled using different methodologies and its evaluation performed with different tools without the need of modifying the general structure of the model. In order to validate the most complex sub-models, we built alternatives using different tools and methodologies; this proved to be very useful since it allowed to find small bugs and imperfections and to gain more confidence that the models represented the real system behaviour. With respect to the real system taken as the example, our analyses, which could not be reported here, allowed to establish the dependability bottlenecks of the current version and to state targets for the several subcomponents such that the system targets could be reached, thus providing hints for next releases or modifications of the system and information to assign targets to the various components of the system.

1 Introduction

Railway station interlocking systems based on microprocessors were developed in all technologically advanced countries and have been used since a few years by those Railway Authorities wishing to have a good cost/benefit ratio. In Europe and in Japan solid state interlocking systems were used in passenger transportation networks with medium/large stations and heavy-medium range traffic; in these applications complex interlocking systems were designed, including central and remote peripheral units, with vital data transmission between them [15], [7], [17], [18], [19], [22], while in the US small systems have been produced since the 80's, usually applied to freight transportation lines [3], [10]. The use of computer controlled interlocking systems, in the place of the usual electro-mechanical systems, introduces non trivial problems in their design and analysis. Most difficult are those parts of the systems delegated to the control of vital functions, where the interactions between the redundant hardware and the application software have a critical impact on system safety. These interactions have an impact on modelling complexity since they induce stochastic dependencies that must be taken into account in modelling the behaviour of components and their interactions. In the literature several papers exist in the field of dependability analysis [1], [20], [5], [4], and some basilar papers exist on the approach to dependability evaluation of combined hardware and software systems [6], [9], [12], [13], [8], but detailed modelling of the interactions between hardware and software components, in particular for critical systems, and the influence of the related dependencies has been treated, at our knowledge, only in [11]. The interest of such modelling lies in the support it may provide in the design phase of a complex system, when decisions have to be taken on possible different structures of the system for matching the dependability requirements imposed by the regulatory authorities. In the design phase it may be cost beneficial to construct different models for the different architectures and the several alternatives can be quantitatively evaluated; in this way sensitivity analysis is possible, to ascertain what are the most important parts of a design on which more resources have to be spent than on others and to identify, in a statistical manner, the dependability levels of the several hardware or software components and the trade-offs between them. This type of analysis, made for an already existing system, as it is the case in this paper, is important for an "a posteriori" dependability evaluation, for pointing out possible design weak points or bottlenecks, for the late validation of the dependability requirements (this can also be useful in certifying phase) and to provide sound hints for next releases or modifications of the systems.

The contribution of this paper is the modelling of a real complex systems, made of redundant replicated hardware and redundant diverse software taking into account all aspects of their interactions (including correlation between the diverse software variants) and of the criticality of the several components. Our approach has been to realise the system model in a structured way. This allows to cope with complexity and to focus, where interesting, on specific behaviour for a more detailed analysis. Structuring in different levels separated by well identified interfaces allows to realise each level with different methodologies and to perform its evaluation with different tools without the need of modifying the general structure of the model. Each level has been subdivided into several sub-levels for a finer analysis of some characteristics. The higher level of the hierarchy is made of the models for the evaluation of the dependability measures of interest (in our case, beside the availability, also reliability and safety measures have been assessed). These models use the values of success or failure probability obtained by the modelling of a mission, which describes the system behaviour on a period of time. The model of a mission uses, in its turn, the values obtained by several different models of a single execution and finally the model of one execution is subdivided into other levels which take into account the specific behaviour of the components of the system. With this structuring, each level is a sort of abstract object, whose implementation details are transparent to the adjacent levels, and therefore can be realised and analysed using the most proper tools and methodologies, which can differ from one level to another. Despite our effort for reducing the complexity of the individual levels with respect to the complexity of the entire system, some complex level remained and has been realised using different methodologies to compare and validate the used model. The paper is organised as follows. Section 2 contains an overview of the Ansaldo TMR MODIAC system; Section 3 defines the meaning of the basic parameters used and describes our assumptions and the modelling approach. Sections 4 and 5 contain a description of the various models for one execution and for the mission respectively. As an example, a few evaluations of the dependability attributes are shown in Section 6 and finally Section 7 concludes this paper.

2 Ansaldo TMR MODIAC System

We analysed the "Apparato Centrale con Calcolatore" (ACC) [15] system nucleus constructed by Ansaldo for their railway station signalling control system, called TMR MODIAC. The system is divided into two parts (Figure 1):

- *SN* -->> is the subsystem which performs vital functions: it comprises the Safety Nucleus and a variable number, depending on the station size, of distributed Trackside Units, which communicate the state of the station to the central computer. After the necessary interactions with the operator, processing and controls, the central computer sends back commands for the signalling system to the Trackside Units.

- *RDT* -->> is a supervisory subsystem that performs Recording, Diagnosis and Telecontrol functions; this subsystem allows continuos monitoring of the system state and events recording; the latter is useful to make estimations and find out less reliable sections.

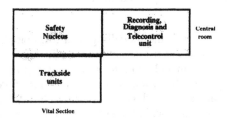

Fig. 1. The TMR MODIAC system

The Safety Nucleus [14] is structured as shown in Figure 2 and is the vital part of the system. Unfortunately the Figure reports the components only, reporting all the data flows among them would have made very difficult to understand the drawing. The nucleus comprises six units with a separated power supply unit. The three Nsi sections represent three computers which are connected in TMR configuration, i.e. working with a "2-out-of-3" majority: three diverse software programs performing iteratively the same tasks, run inside three identical hardware sections. The system is designed to keep on running even after the failure of one section; in such a case the section is excluded and the system uses only two sections with a "2-out-of-2" majority, until the failed section is restored. A section excluded after failing is restored after a few minutes. The Exclusion Logic is a fail-safe circuit whose job is to electrically isolate the section that TMR indicated to be excluded. The activation/de-activation unit is a device that switches on and controls power supply units. The video switching unit controls video images to be transmitted to the monitors of the operator terminal.

The TMR sections carry out the same functions; the hardware, the basic software architecture and the operating environment are exactly the same; while "design diversity" [2] was adopted in the development of software application modules. The following measures were employed to enforce diversity: a) three teams of programmers, b) different programming languages, c) different coding of data and d) different memory locations for data and code. Each section is composed by two physically separated units which carry out different functions in parallel:

- *GIOUL* (operator interface manager and logical unit): executes the actual processing and manages the interactions with the Operator Terminal and the RDT subsystem;

- *GP* (trackside manager): manages the communications with the Trackside Units and modifies, whenever necessary, the commands given by GIOUL.

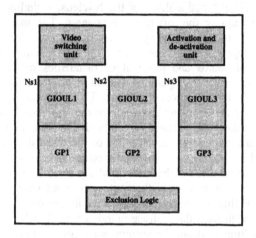

Fig. 2. Structure of the Safety Nucleus

The processing loops last 1 second for GIOUL and 250 msec for GP: this causes the communications between GIOUL and GP belonging to the same TMR section to be performed at every second (GIOUL loop), i.e. once every four loops of GP. Instead the communications between units of the same type (between the three GIOUL units and separately between the three GP units) are carried out at every processing loop. Each TMR (GIOUL and GP separately) unit votes on the state variables and processing results. If it finds any inconsistency between its results and those of the other units and three sections are active, it can recover a presumably correct state and continue processing. If one section disagrees twice in a row it is excluded. No disagreement is tolerated when only two sections are active. Besides voting on software each unit controls communications and tests internal boards functionalities. Based on hardware test results, one section can decide to exclude itself from the system. Diagnostic tests are carried out during the usual unit operation; they are implemented such that they do not modify the operating environment. Each section is also able to detect malfunctions on its databases thus deciding to exclude itself. In addition to these tasks, GIOUL has to manage the communications with the Operator Interface, and to perform tests on keyboard inputs as well. If an error is detected a signal is displayed.

TMR MODIAC is a critical system, meaning that failures or unavailability can have catastrophic consequences, both economical and for human life. The constraints to be satisfied by the system are a probability of catastrophic failure less than or equal to 1E-5 per year according to IEC 1508 (for SIL 4 systems) and no more than 5 minutes down time are allowed over 8600 hours (i.e. availability higher than or equal to 0.999990310078).

3 Assumptions and Modelling Approach

3.1 Assumptions and Basic Parameters

We restricted our modelling effort to the Safety Nucleus, the most relevant part of the system. Our model does not include the RDT subsystem neither the Trackside Units, but represents the overall functionalities of the Nucleus, including the main features and the interactions among the different components. The main components that must be considered in modelling the system are: hardware, software, databases and, only for GIOUL, acceptance test on the input from the Operator Terminal. Hardware aspects cover internal boards and physical characteristics of the communications while software aspects cover the operating system and software modules that are sequentially activated during the processing loops. The databases, whose control represents one of the ways for detecting errors in various modules, cover both hardware and software aspects: database malfunction can be due to either corruption of memory cells or an error of the managing software. One of the tasks that GIOUL has to perform is checking the correctness of the inputs issued by the operator terminal keyboard before transmitting them to the other modules for their processing; this check is very important since it can avoid the system to send wrong commands to the Trackside Units. For this reason the software module performing this check is not considered together with the other software modules of GIOUL. We also made the choice of not modelling in detail the system while an excluded section is restored. More precisely we account for the time required for restoring a section but we neglect the particular configurations that GIOUL and GP can assume during that period.

The definition of the basic events we have considered and the symbols used to denote their probabilities are reported in Table 1. The following assumptions have been made:

1) "Compensation" among errors never happens;

2) The Video Switching, the Activation/de-Activation and the (external fail-safe) Exclusion Logic units are considered reliable;

3) The Diagnostic module, (that exploits majority voting), and Exclusion Management module within GIOUL and GP are considered reliable.

4) Identical erroneous outputs are produced only by correlated errors, while independent errors in the different units are always distinguishable by the voting.

5) Symmetry: the error probabilities of GIOUL and GP are the same for the three sections.

6) Errors affecting different components of the same unit (GIOUL or GP) are statistically independent.

7) The hardware communication resources of the Nucleus are considered together with the other hardware aspects; the software dealing with communications is assumed reliable.

8) During one execution, both GIOUL and GP may suffer from many errors, at most one for each component (software, hardware, databases and acceptance test for GIOUL).

9) The execution of each iteration is statistically independent from the others.

10) GIOUL units receive identical inputs from the keyboard.

Error type (Events)	Symbol (GIOUL)	Symbol (GP)
independent error in a unit caused by an hardware fault	qhl	qhp
an error caused by an hardware fault is not detected by the diagnostics	qhdl	qhdp
spurious error: the diagnostic errs detecting a (non-present) error due to independent hardware fault	qhndl	qhndp
an independent error in a database is detected	qbrl	qbrp
an independent error in a database is not detected	qbnrl	qbnrp
correlated error between three databases	q3bdl	q3bdp
correlated error between two databases	q2bdl	q2bdp
independent software error in a unit	qil	qip
correlated software error between three units	q3vl	q3vp
correlated software error between two units	q2vl	q2vp
independent error of the acceptance test in a unit (it may either accept a wrong input or reject a correct one)	qail	.....
correlated error between the acceptance tests of three units accepting the same wrong input	q3al	......
correlated error between the acceptance tests of two units accepting the same wrong input	q2al	......

Table 1. Basic error types and symbols to denote their probabilities

3.2 Modelling Approach

The model was conceived in a modular and hierarchical fashion, structured in layers. Each layer has been structured for producing some results while hiding implementation details and internal characteristics: output values from one layer may thus be used as parameters of the next higher layer. In this way the entire modelling can be simply handled. Further, different layers can be modelled using different tools and methodologies: this leads to flexible and changeable sub-models so that one can vary the accuracy and detail with which specific aspects can be studied. The specific structure of each sub-model depends both on the system architecture and on the measurements and evaluations to be obtained. The model of the Safety Nucleus of the TMR MODIAC we have built, shown in Figure 3, can be split into two main parts: the first part deals with one execution and computes the probabilities of success or failure; the second one, building on this, allows the evaluations of the dependability attributes for an entire mission.

In the previous section we explained that if a disagreement is found while all three sections are active, GIOUL and GP recover the correct value and participate to the next loop. This holds for one single disagreement: if one section disagrees twice in a row it is excluded at the end of the current loop. Therefore, in order to represent as close as possible the actual system behaviour, we had to make several models to keep memory of previous disagreement of one section at the beginning of the execution.

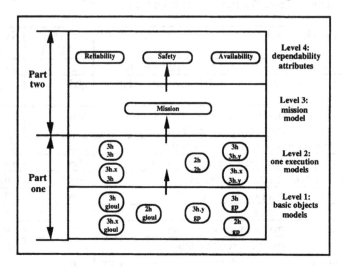

Fig. 3. High level model of the TMR MODIAC

To describe the GIOUL and GP TMR units at level 1 (Figure 3) we defined:

- five sub-models of the behaviour of GP in configurations *3h*, *3h.1*, *3h.2*, *3h.3*, *2h* (*3h.x* means that section x (1, 2 or 3) disagreed during the previous loop);

- five sub-models of the behaviour of GIOUL (*3h, 3h.1, 3h.2, 3h.3, 2h*).

Each of these submodels (as it will be exemplified later) accounts for all the components of GP and GIOUL respectively. Hardware, software (including correlation), databases and (for GIOUL only) acceptance test on the inputs from the operator together with their relationships are considered. Specifically hardware and software aspects cannot be always kept separated because on one side, hardware faults often manifest themselves as software errors and on the other, the methods for software fault tolerance allow to tolerate not only software faults but also hardware faults of the internal boards and of the communication hardware. This explains why GP and GIOUL models do not comprise different separated sub-models each one regarding one single aspect, but are structured as a unique global sub-model in which both interactions and specific aspects are included.

One system execution (level 2) lasts 1 second, it includes one GIOUL (1 second) and four GP (250 msec) iterations and could also be considered as brief one–second mission. Due to the need to keep memory of previous disagreements, 17 different models for one-execution have been defined: one models the system when only two sections are active, while the remaining describe the system with three active sections:

- *3h/3h*: GIOUL and GP are correctly working at the beginning of the execution.

- *3h.x/3h*: the GIOUL of section x (1, 2 or 3) disagreed during the previous loop while GP is correctly working.

- *3h/3h.y*: GIOUL units are correctly working while the GP of section y (1, 2 or 3) disagreed during the previous (GP) execution.

- *3h.x/3h.y*: both the GIOUL of section x and the GP of section y disagreed during the previous loop (x and y can represent the same section or different ones)

- *2h/2h* : execution begins with only two active sections.

Each of the 17 models uses, in different combinations and sequences, the same base objects of level 1 and describes the essential characteristics of the Safety Nucleus. It models the functions of the units as a whole considering their interactions and their peculiar nature. These models are conceived to compute (and to provide to level three) the following probabilities:

- *probability of success of one-execution*; it is the probability that the system performs an entire one second mission correctly. This implies that the system is ready to start the next execution. It is composed by many different success probabilities according to the configuration achieved.

- *probability of safe failure of one-execution*; it is the probability that the system fails during one execution and stops avoiding catastrophic damages (this is ensured by the ACC system that is designed so that it stops when malfunctions occur, forcing devices and subsystems to lock in a safe state).

- *probability of catastrophic failure of one-execution*; it is the probability that the Nucleus, failing, keeps on sending erroneous commands causing serious damages.

The mission model (level 3), considering all the possible system configurations during one execution, describes the system behaviour during time. In particular, this model contains as many states as models defined at level 2 plus the catastrophic and benign failure states. Actually models of level two are used to provide the outgoing probabilities of the corresponding state of the model of level 3. Once that both the single execution and the mission models have been constructed we focused on which kind of measurements are required. For our highly critical system the following dependability attributes have been evaluated: reliability, safety and availability. While reliability and safety can be both obtained by computing the probabilities of catastrophic and safe failure at time t defined as the duration of the mission, availability required the definition of a specific availability model.

4 Models for one Execution

Two methodologies have been adopted built the models for one-execution: Discrete time Markov chains that have been manually drawn and the probability evaluation has been accomplished using "Mathematica"[1], and Stochastic Activity Networks that have been directly solved using the software tool "Ultrasan"[2] . Since Markov chains are often impractical, even if they provide symbolic results, Ultrasan has been adopted in order to avoid building 17 repetitive one-execution models using only Markov chains. Only two models (3h/3h and 2h/2h) have been completely built using Markov chains in order to test and validate the results obtained by Ultrasan. This redundancy in building models has been very useful: some errors occurred during the model developing phase have been detected. Ultrasan has been a good choice, since we could develop one single model that allowed to compute the results for the 17 different scenarios. In fact, by assigning different values to the variables of the model, thus representing different initial markings, we could represent the different states of the system and account for previous failures of the various subcomponents. The model is also able to distinguish the various configurations without having to replicate the unchanged aspects. Only two of the seventeen models were tested using Markov chains but those two models are the most relevant ones and cover all the scenarios that need to be represented. The results obtained by Ultrasan and Markov, using the same values for the parameters, were in agreement. Now we show, as an example, some objects belonging to the two lower levels. First the Markov chains are described and later the Ultrasan model.

As an example of a model of the level 1 (base object level), we report on the left side of Fig. 4 the model of GIOUL TMR in configuration 3h (i.e. that was properly working). All the transition probabilities, not reported here to keep the Figure clear [16], are obtained as combinations of the basic events probabilities reported in Table 1. This Markov chain is organised into five levels plus the final states. Level one involves the hardware aspects, the level two the diagnostic tests carried out on boards and communications channels (hardware). Level three checks databases; level four investigates the behaviour of the acceptance test on the keyboard input whereas level five involves software. It should be noted that the model doesn't represent the timing relations among the various events. The models for other configurations can be obtained by analogy with this. The level upper to this (level 2 of Figure 3) is not concerned with this detailed view, from its perspective it is just necessary to observe that, performing one execution from configuration 3h, the GIOUL TMR can reach all the other GIOUL TMR configurations (success state) or a failure (safe or catastrophic) state. Thus this view can be represented by the Markov chain on the right side of Fig. 4 containing only the initial and the final states of the model on the left and where the transition probabilities are derived by solving the model on the left side of Fig. 4. Once all the models of level 1 have been obtained and the related transition probabilities computed, these objects are composed into the several models for one system execution. Also for this level, only the description of one of the 17 configurations is provided; the remaining 16 can easily be obtained by analogy. This time we proceed in a top-down approach to show our models by showing first what is the viewpoint of the next level, the mission level.

---

[1] Mathematica, vers. 2.2, Wolfram Research, Inc.

[2] Ultrasan, ver. 3.0.1, University of Illinois at Urbana-Champaign: Center for Reliable and High-Performance Computing Coordinated Science Laboratory, 1994.

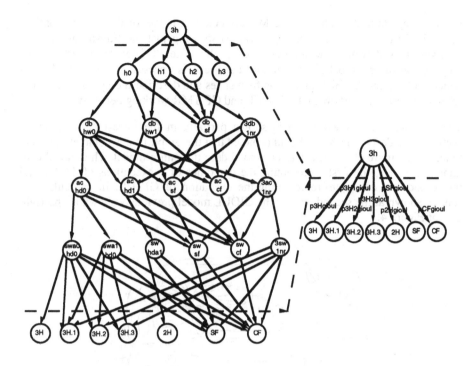

Fig. 4. Detailed and Compact model of GIOUL in configuration 3h

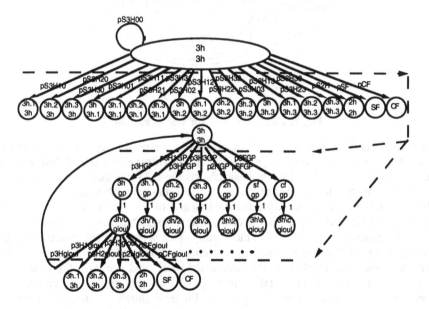

Fig. 5. Compact model of one execution in configuration 3h/3h and its partial

explosion

Figure 5 depicts in its highest part a Markov compact model of the system configuration 3h/3h (i.e. that was properly working) showing just the transitions to other configurations after one execution and their probabilities. Of course, in order to obtain the transition probabilities mentioned above it is necessary to explode the arcs which go from the "3h/3h" state to the final states and describe the system behaviour when one iteration starts with the GIOUL and GP TMR working perfectly.

The first step of this explosion is shown partially in the lowest part of Fig. 5 (between the dashed lines); it should be noted that the graph is not complete in order to leave the figure clear, still it is easy to deduce the entire model. This model contains two levels, the first representing the outcomes of 4 executions of the GP and the second (not complete) representing the execution of GIOUL. In particular, the subtree shown at the second level is the GIOUL model previously shown in the right part of Figure 4.

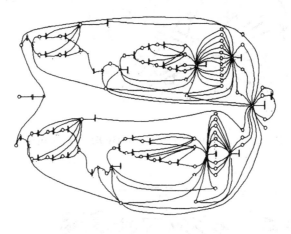

Fig. 6. Ultrasan model for one execution

The system model obtained with Ultrasan allows to represent all the 17 configurations of one execution. Also in modelling using Ultrasan we started following a modular approach, building first the basic objects (level 1) and then putting them together in the system model for one execution. Unfortunately, the valuable possibility offered by Ultrasan to define separated models and to join them into the Ultrasan "Composed Model" is very useful for conceiving a design but slows down the execution of the compound model. In fact the common places between sub-models must be attached to timed transitions, which is wasteful for this model. This causes the increment of the state number in the "Reduced Model" and decreases the evaluation speed. Thus we decided not to take advantage of this opportunity but preferred to speed up the evaluations as much as possible. Figure 6 shows the model that we actually used which was evaluated using the transient solver of Ultrasan. Despite it can just provide an idea of the size and complexity, the existence of two sub-models is visible: the upper part represents one iteration of GP and it is executed four times, the lower part represents one iteration of GIOUL executed once. An additional general problem to describing and understanding the behaviour of models built using Ultrasan derives from the extensive use of C code that is hidden into the gates.

5 Models for the Mission and Wanted Measures

Also the model for a mission has been developed using both Markov chains and SANs. Despite the constant time of one second required for each system execution, modelling a mission using discrete time Markov chains (MC/TD) is not feasible due the following reasons:

1) After the failure of one section, the system can operate with only two active sections (2h/2h), if no failures occur, until the failed section is restored. This usually takes a time interval in the range 5÷45 minutes (15 minutes average) i.e. a much longer time and a very large number n of states "2h/2h";

2) Since the model has to be as general as possible, the time to restore a section should be left as a parameter and this cannot be accomplished using a discrete time model.

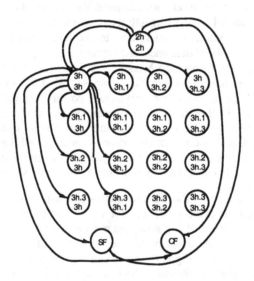

Fig. 7. Partial representation of the MC/TC mission model

For all these reasons continuos time Markov Chains (MC/TC) have been used. The obtained model solves the above problems, but it is approximate. In fact not only it uses exponential distributions in place of the deterministic ones (this is not a problem since we use a very long mission time with respect to the time required from one execution), but the main approximation comes from the fact that the n states "2h/2h" in the hypothetical MC/TD are compressed in only one state "2h/2h". The output rates of this compressed "2h/2h" state approximate the behaviour (averaging both time and probabilities) [16]. The MC/TC model defined is partially depicted in Figure 7 only to give an idea on the state transitions. This model allows to evaluate the probabilities of safe or catastrophic failure of missions of a given duration. The model has been solved obtaining the system of differential equations [21]. The solution was obtained using Mathematica: it provided both symbolic and numerical results. The solutions we have found are complete since they allow to evaluate the probability of safe or catastrophic failure over any given time interval t.

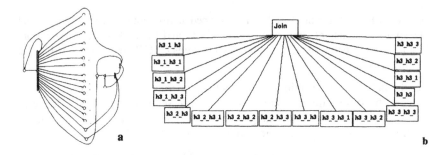

Fig. 8. Ultrasan a) 3h/3h sub-model b) "Composed" mission model

To validate this approximated model we compared the results obtained with those returned by a mission model built using Ultrasan (where time distribution is still exponential). The Ultrasan model is structured into two layers: the lower layer is composed by a number of sub-models each one representing a given system configuration, and an higher level ("Composed Model") that joins the sub-models as required. For the model of a mission we did use the Composed Model without slowing down the execution speed because each sub-model already contained timed transitions at the beginning. In Figure 8a the sub-model representing the configuration "3h/3h" is shown: the other sub-models are very similar. In Figure 8b the "Composed Model" is shown; each box indicates one sub-model of one-execution and the "join" box links them together. Again this drawings are meant just to show the size of the models, to really describe them in details a considerable amount of c code should be shown.

The two mission models (with the Markov chains and with SANs) have been tested against each other on the same input data for variable mission duration up to one year. The results provided are of the same magnitude as soon as t reaches 1000 seconds, and for t from one day up they can be considered identical; as t grows, the number of identical significant digits increases and even exceeds the desired accuracy. While we preferred to use the Ultrasan model to obtain the results for one execution (and used a Markov one to validate it) because of the possibility to represent all the different configurations within a single model, here we have done the opposite: we used the model based on Markov to compute the results and the one based on SANs to validate it. We preferred to use Mathematica and the Markov model to achieve results at a higher speed: only few minutes are required to provide the results for one year missions while our Ultrasan model requires several days.

Once the probabilities of success or failure (safe and catastrophic) in one year have been obtained, it is immediate to find out the reliability and safety measures while to obtain availability measures it is necessary build an availability model which is represented by the continuos Markov Chain (MC/TC) illustrated in Figure 9. When the system is in state F, it is operating and provides a correct service. R and C indicate the repair states: the system is not available following a safe failure (R) or a catastrophic failure (C). The system resuming rates are "m", following a safe failure, and "mm", following a catastrophic failure. "l" indicates the failure transition rate; it should be multiplied for "f", the probability of safe failure, or for "fc", the probability of catastrophic failure. This model may look strange, but it must considered that the system has to manage an entire railway station with several tracks. It must resume working also after a 'catastrophic' failure to manage those parts of the controlled system which have not been affected by the failure.

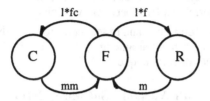

Fig. 9. The availability model

6 Evaluations

Once the models have been realised, the system behaviour can be evaluated, to check for example if the system meets its requirements, and to analyse the sensitivity to the various parameters. There are many input variables for the set of models which can be split in those necessary to the models representing one execution and those for models of the mission. The models of one execution require the probability values of the basic events (described in Table 1) while those related to the mission require i) the results of the evaluation of one execution, ii) the repair time for restoring an excluded section, iii) the mission time, and iv) the recovery time (only for the availability model). To show some examples we assigned "a priori" reasonable values (which are not meant to represent the real situation for the system) to all the parameters and investigated the sensitivity of the dependability measures to just one parameter at a time. Here, due to space limitations, we do not report all our evaluations: i) sensitivity to the main parameters (hardware, software), ii) to the secondary parameters, iii) a specific study on software correlation, and iv) location of dependability bottlenecks [16].

Symbols	Probabilities	Symbols	Probabilities
qhl	8E-5	qhp	2E-5
qhdl	2E-10	qhdp	2E-10
qhndl	3E-12	qhndp	3E-12
qbrl	1E-8	qbrp	1E-8
qbnrl	1E-10	qbnrp	1E-10
qil	1E-5	qip	1E-5
qail	1E-8	.....	.....

Table 2. Values used for GIOUL and GP parameters

The probability values of the basic events (on a period of one hour of observation) are reported in Table 2, while we set the mission duration to one year, the failure rate l (which has to be multiplied by the failure probability) to one per hour, the repair rate following a safe failure, m, to 2 per hour and the repair rate following a catastrophic failure, mm, to 1/2 per hour. In order to reduce the number of parameters in our plots we assumed the probability of software independent faults to be the same for GIOUL and GP: qil = qip = qiv, for the independent errors caused by hardware faults we used qhw, with qhl = .8 qhw and qhp = .2 qhw. Furthermore we decided to link the probability of correlated error between two units (q2c) to that of independent software error (qiv): $q2c = corr\ qiv^2$, and to set "corr" to 100: this corresponds to the assumption of a positive correlation among software errors. The alternative would have been to assign values directly to q2c.

6.1 Measurements with Variable Software Error Probability

Figures 10, 11(a) and 11(b) show the probability of failure, the probability of catastrophic failure and the availability, respectively, on missions of one year, as a function of qiv the probability of software independent error. The range goes from 1E-3 to 1E-6 per hour; curves for different values of the hardware caused error probability per unit are reported.

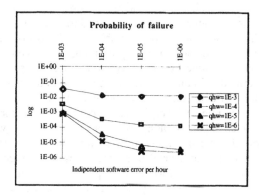

Fig. 10. Failure probability (one year mission)

Observing the shapes of the curves in Figure 10, it is clear that reliability is sensitive to variations of the software error probability if hardware quality is good enough (i.e., 1E-5 to 1E-6), instead it becomes more and more insensitive as the hardware error probability increases. The curves also point out that decreasing the probability of software error over 1E-5 (that is improving the quality of the software) is practically useless without improving the figures related to the other system components as well. In fact, while in the left side of the Figure, from 1E-3 to 1E-5, it can be observed that the reliability improves, it remains approximately constant for the values in the right side. This suggests also the methodology to be used for finding dependability bottlenecks, since in this way it is possible to understand which are the parameters to be improved in order to bring most benefit to the system.

The shape of the curves representing the probability of catastrophic failure, shown in Figure 11(a), appears quite different. Safety is almost a "linear" function of the probability of independent software error: the more the software error probability decreases and the more the safety improves. The same Figure also points out that the safety seems completely insensitive to variations of the hardware error probability: in fact, it is difficult to distinguish among the four curves shown. It should also be noted that the system satisfies its target (that for such systems is usually 1E-5 per year, according to IEC 1508) if independent error probability values are less than or equal to 1E-4.

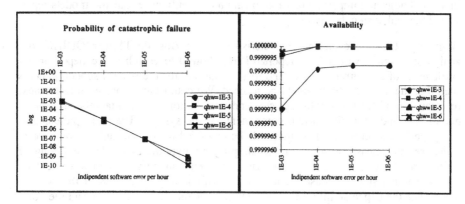

Fig. 11. Catastrophic failure probability (a) and Availability (b) (one year mission)

Figure 11(b) shows the availability, it clearly points out that the availability is very high and almost constant when the software error probability ranges form 1E-4 to 1E-6, while it is a bit worse for higher values. The Figure shows also that there are almost no variations of the availability for values of the hardware error probability equal or better than 1E-4. In any case the system is never affected by availability lacks, since the target (5 minutes unavailability over 8600 hours, i.e. 0.9999903) is satisfied in all the considered range of the software error probability. In short, within our parameters setting, the software must be regarded as a critical factor for safety, while it appears of almost no concern for availability.

7 Conclusions

The present work represents an example that shows how real system models can be built and then studied in order to evaluate their dependability. Of course, conceiving such models is not simple at all, since they usually have to represent complex architectures and account for many different characteristics. Our experience is that this task is made possible when carried out adopting suitable principles. The specifications and all the documentation had to be studied in depth in order to acquire the really important aspects for dependability; later some feasible simplifying hypotheses have been introduced, trying to estimate under which conditions these could be considered valid. Complexity must be reduced as much as possible; our approach has been to build a hierarchical model structured in layers; these layers have been designed keeping in mind the system behaviour and the wanted measures.

Layers can consist of several sub-layers in order to isolate, whenever possible, those components or aspects that must appear to the upper layer as unique objects with their associated probabilities. This further decomposition allows a better analysis of particular system characteristics and reduces the complexity even further. Different modelling approaches and tools can be adopted for the different layers: this gives the flexibility to identify and use the most suitable modelling method and evaluation tool for each level. Last, and very important, in order to validate the most complex models, we built alternatives using different tools and methodologies; this constitutes an example of application of diversity and proved to be very useful since it allowed to find small bugs and imperfections and to gain more confidence that the models represented the real system behaviour.

With respect to the evaluated characteristics of the Ansaldo TMR MODIAC, our analyses, which have not been reported here, allowed to establish the dependability bottlenecks of the current system and to state targets for the several subcomponents such that the system targets could be reached. We could thus provide hints for next releases or modifications of the systems and information to assign targets, and consequently the budget, to the various components of the system. The work presented in this paper constitutes a nucleus that will be expanded in further studies: some directions are, the release of some of the simplifying hypotheses or the modelling of some variation of the system characteristics to better identify directions for next releases. Another step to be also carried on is the modelling of the rest of the system, to evaluate the dependability figures accounting for the Trackside units and the communication network.

References

[1]   J. Arlat, K. Kanoun and J. C. Laprie, "Dependability Modelling and Evaluation of Software Fault-Tolerant Systems," *IEEE Transaction on Computer*, Vol. 39, pp. 504-513, 1990.

[2]   A. Avizienis and J. P. J. Kelly, "Fault Tolerance by Design Diversity: Concepts and Experiments," *IEEE Computer*, Vol. pp. 1984.

[3]   J.B. Balliet and J.R. Hoelscher, "Microprocessor based Interlocking Control - Concept to Application," in *Proc. APTA Rail Transit Conf.*, Miami, Fl., 1986, pp. 13.

[4]   A. Bondavalli, S. Chiaradonna, F. Di Giandomenico and S. La Torre, "Dependability of Iterative Software: a Model for Evaluating the Effects of Input Correlation," in Proc. accepted at *SAFECOMP '95*, Belgirate, Italy, 1995, pp.

[5]   S. Chiaradonna, A. Bondavalli and L. Strigini, "On Performability Modeling and Evaluation of Software Fault Tolerance Structures," in *Proc. EDCC1*, Berlin, Germany, 1994, pp. 97-114.

[6]   A. Costes, C. Landrault and J. C. Laprie, "Reliability and Availability Models for Maintained Systems featuring Hardware Failures and Design Faults," *IEEE Trans. on Computers*, Vol. C-27, pp. 548-60, 1978.

[7] A.H. Cribbens, M.J. Furniss and H.A. Ryland, "The Solid State Interlocking Project," in Proc. *IRSE Symposium "Railway in the Electronic Age"*, London, UK, 1981, pp. 1-5.

[8] F. Di Giandomenico, A. Bondavalli and J. Xu, "Hardware and Software Fault Tolerance: Adaptive Architectures in Distributed Computing Environments," *Esprit BRA 6362 PDCS2* Technical Report, june 26 1995.

[9] J. B. Dugan and M. Lyu, "System-level Reliability and Sensivity Analysis for Three Fault-Tolerant Architectures," in *Proc. 4th IFIP Int. Conference on Dependable Computing for Critical Applications*, San Diego, 1994, pp. 295-307.

[10] E. K. Holt, "The Application of Microprocessors to Interlocking Logic," in *Proc. APTA Rail Transit Conf.*, Miami, Fl., 1986, pp. 13.

[11] K. Kanoun, M. Borrel, T. Morteveille and A. Peytavin, "Modelling the Dependability of CAUTRA, a Subset of the French Air Traffic Control System," LAAS Report, December 1995.

[12] J. C. Laprie, C. Beounes, M. Kaaniche and K. Kanoun, "The Transformation Approach to Modeling and Evaluation of Reliability and Availability Growth of Systems," in *Proc. 20th IEEE Int. Symposium on fault Tolerant Computing, Newcastle*, UK, 1990, pp. 364-71.

[13] J.C. Laprie and K. Kanoun, "X-ware Reliability and Availability modelling," *IEEE Trans. on Software Engineering*, Vol. SE-18, pp. 130-147, 1992.

[14] G. Mongardi, "A.C.C Specifiche Tecniche e Funzionali," Ansaldo Trasporti

[15] G. Mongardi, "Dependable Computing for Railway Control Systems," in *Proc. DCCA-3*, Mondello, Italy, 1993, pp. 255-277.

[16] M. Nelli, "Modellamento e valutazione di attributi della dependability di un sistema critico per l'interlocking ferroviario", Tesi di Laurea, Facolta' di Ingegneria, University of Pisa, Pisa, 1995.

[17] D. Nordenfors and A. Sjoeberg, "Computer Controlled Electronic Interlocking System, ERILOCK 850," *ERICSSON Review*, Vol. 1, pp. 1-12, 1986.

[18] I. Okumura, "Electronic Interlocking to be tried in Japan," *Railway Gazette International*, Vol. 12, pp. 1043-1046, 1980.

[19] H. Strelow and H. Uebel, "Das Sichere Mikrocomputersystem SIMIS," *Signal und Draht*, Vol. 4, pp. 82-86, 1978.

[20] A. T. Tai, A. Avizienis and J. F. Meyer, "Evaluation of fault tolerant software: a performability modeling approach," in "Dependable Computing for Critical Applications 3", C. E. Landwher, B. Randell and L. Simoncini Ed., Springer-Verlag, 1992, pp. 113-135.

[21] K. S. Trivedi, "Probability and Statistics with Reliability, Queuing, and Computer Science Applications," Durham, North Carolina, Prentice-Hall, Inc., Englewood Cliffs, 1982.

[22] G. Wirthumer, "VOTRICS - Fault Tolerant realised in software," in *Proc. SAFECOMP*, Vienna, Austria, 1989, pp. 135-140.

The Effect of Interfailure Time Variability on the Software Reliability Growth Modelling

Peter Popov

Bulgarian Academy of Sciences, Institute of Computer and Communication Systems
Acad. G. Bontchev street, bl.2, 1113 Sofia, Bulgaria
phone: (+359 2) 71 90 97, fax: (+359 2) 72 39 05
e-mail: ptp@sun.iccs.acad.bg

Abstract

This paper deals with the effect of interfailure time variability on the modelling of software reliability growth. Some, primarily mathematical arguments, are outlined that cast a doubt on the commonly adopted concept of failures' occurrence as a Poisson (either homogeneous or non-homogeneous) process. On a contrived (but plausible for the software practice) example the consequences of this assumption, in some cases inappropriate for the software reliability predictions, are illustrated. The idea of "tuning" the reliability growth models based on measurements of the distribution of a single execution time is advocated.

Keywords: *urn model, software reliability growth, Poisson process, software execution time, operational profile.*

1. Introduction

Testing for dependability assessment generally means "statistical testing", i.e., testing software with inputs drawn from the actual input distribution to be expected in operation, and is the only known way of estimating the reliability of individual software products. Concerning the "amount" of testing required in order to achieve a high level of confidence in the reliability of the product, in particular in safety-critical applications, the statistical testing as a procedure of dependability assessment has been for a long time a controversial topic.

The concept of *independent selection of inputs* is the core of statistical testing. Some mathematical arguments against one of the basic assumptions in known reliability growth models are the main scope of this paper. Specifically, the assumption that the interfailure time can conditionally, given a known failure rate, be assumed exponentially distributed. The concept of interfailure time being exponentially distributed, or equivalently (that is more usual in the literature) the concept of failures' occurrence modelled as a Poisson process, has been commonly adopted for a long time and used (sometimes implicitly) in many of the known reliability growth models [Mil86]. In many cases (perhaps in vast majority of cases) one can expect that the variability of the duration of a single software execution (execution time) will be tightly bounded and there will be no reason (at least using the arguments presented in this paper) the known reliability growth modelling to be under doubts. In some cases, however, the variability of the execution time may happen to be so large that the exponential distribution becomes unacceptably inaccurate approximation of the real interfailure time. What seems important is that one *can* check the appropriateness of the assumption of the exponential distribution, and hence whether the known reliability growth models are appropriate, merely measuring the execution time distribution along with the testing and checking whether the variability of the execution time is large enough in order to compromise the exponentiality of the interfailure time.

The first question to answer before going into details is how important the situation with non-exponential interfailure time is. There are, as it seems to me, two kinds of arguments that make the discussion and later the analysis sensible. First, there is some empirical evidence that the distribution of the interfailure time in a system with stable reliability (no fixing of the faults is undertaken) is not exponential, for example the data reported in [TTYL95] representing the interfailure times for Tandem computers. The second sort of evidence is not directly related to the conditional distribution of the interfailure time. Instead, in some cases of applying reliability growth models poor predictability of these has been identified through the u-plot technique [A-GCL86], [BCLS90], [BL92]. These results indicate that there is some inappropriateness between the used models and the failure data. There is a speculative discussion on why different reliability growth models work with different precision when applied to different data, but, to the best of my knowledge, no one has presented some sort of convincing quantitative explanation of this phenomenon. An approach called *recalibration technique* presented by Brocklehurst and Littlewood in numerous of papers, for example in [BL92], is an attempt not to explain why the basic model is inaccurate but just to make use of the observed inaccuracy - the basic model (before the recalibration) is tuned (recalibrated) in a way that makes it explain the past of the failure process better than does the basic model. The recalibration technique is a general statistical procedure relying upon the assumption that the prediction errors are stationary and transforms the predicted distribution (built in the basic reliability growth model) to a new "true" distribution that better fits the collected data. Thus, the recalibration technique is in a sense an attempt to *correct* the (incorrect) assumption built in the basic model. As Littlewood cogently has argued in [Lit80], when the basic assumptions are wrong one can expect the prediction to flaw. The right place for making simplifications at the expense of some loss of accuracy should be the end of the analysis but not in the foundations of the model. This is very much my point in carrying out the analysis in this paper. The approach presented here can be thought of as some alternative of the recalibration technique. One of *the basic assumptions* of reliability growth models - that of the conditional exponential distribution of interfailure times - is subjected to scrutiny in what follows. In contrast, in the recalibration technique the *consequences* of this eventually wrong assumption (and possibly many others) are *compensated*.

In section 2 the basics of the urn model are recalled and how it should be extended when the CPU time scale is used for failure data collection. In section 3 contrived examples demonstrating the consequences of ignoring the variability of the execution time are given. In section 4 a discussion on the potential applications that may require the construction of new reliability growth models is given. Finally, in section 5 conclusions and some suggestions for future research are outlined.

2. Reliability Modelling of Software Executed on Independent Inputs

2.1. Urn Model

The urn model with replacement is an abstraction representing the succession of inputs applied to software as a series of *independently* drawn balls. The model has recently been concisely presented in [Mil92]. In this model the function f and its software implementation F, are considered. f serves as an oracle for F. Assuming that the domain of f is finite black balls are used to signify inputs that reveal failures and white balls to signify inputs not revealing a failure. Conceptually one or several balls represent each input. Testing an input in the domain of F determines whether the balls associated with that input are black or white. For sake of simplicity, in the model the repetition (of drawing the same ball) was adopted that corresponds to picking balls from the urn with replacement. The testing profile is defined as a distribution from which the testing cases are selected. Let $p(x)$ denote the probability that an element x in the domain of F will be randomly selected for a test. Define the indicator function ω so that $\omega(x) = 0$, if x does not reveal a failure. With a negligible error it could be assumed that for each x, $p(x)$ is a rational number. If k is an integer such that $kp(x)$ is an integer for all x in the domain of F, then $kp(x)$ copies of the ball representing x should be put into the urn. Then θ, the true proportion of black balls in the urn, is

$$\theta = \sum_x p(x)\omega(x). \tag{1}$$

Thus only the proportion of the black balls is of interests when one is indifferent between different causes of failures. θ represents the probability of picking at random an input that produces a failure at the program's output. Different probabilities of concern could easily be represented. For example, the probability to observe no failure in a series of t executions would be $(1-\theta)^t$. Similarly the probability to have

r failures in a series of t executions would be $\binom{t}{r}\theta^r(1-\theta)^{t-r}$, etc.

If the software is not subjected to debugging, then θ is constant and observing a series of failures one can with an arbitrary confidence estimate this, which could require an unacceptably huge amount of testing.

If the software undergoes *debugging* then θ tends to decrease with the testing time which is consistently modelled by the urn model - merely some of the black balls representing the inputs making the fixed faults active will now have been replaced by white balls. Thus one could represent the failure activating process while debugging is going on by a succession of urns with decreasing θ ($\theta_1 > \theta_2 > ... > \theta_n$).

Reliability growth models are techniques that provide estimations of θ or other related parameters like mean time between failures, etc. when the debugging is completed based on the observation of a single realisation of the time to a failure for each of the urns. They differ dependent upon the hypothesis about the relationship that exist between θ_1, θ_2, ..., θ_n in respect to the total elapsed time.

A common practice in software reliability engineering is to collect failure data not in runs (number of executions) between failures but instead in *interfailure times* or in numbers of revealed faults (observed failures) in pre-defined time intervals. In what follows the analysis is based on the assumption that the *probability distribution* of the interfailure time at the end of the debugging is of interest. Other parameters could easily be expressed if this is known [MIO87].

The interfailure time is a succession of a *random number, N,* of successful executions and at the end *one* execution producing a failure. N is geometrically distributed with parameter θ. Thus the probability that the interfailure time IF includes exactly n successful executions (and *one failure*) will be:

$$p_n = P(N = n) = (1 - \theta)^n . \theta \tag{2}$$

The expected value of this interval will be

$$E[IF] = \frac{1}{\theta} \, ^1 \tag{3}$$

This explains the terminology used in the literature which refers to θ as the *failure rate* as well as the probability of failure per execution. The first term is related to the reciprocal of $E[IF]$, while the second - to the proportion of the black balls in the urn.

It is worth emphasising that in (2) and (3) the interfailure time is expressed in runs (executions) while the duration of the executions is completely ignored. This differs from most of the approaches used in the reliability growth world recognising the calendar time or the CPU time [MIO87]. If failure data are collected in CPU time scale then the analysis should take into consideration that the execution time is *data dependent* due to executing different branches of the algorithm or arithmetic operations (different branches of the micro-code). The situation becomes even worse when a random number of operations with storage devices are performed during software executions that may include accessing data on disks or communication over a network, etc. Therefore, one faces an uncertainty - that of varying duration of a single software execution. The expected consequences of this for the failure occurrence process will be discussed.

In reliability growth models the *similarity of profiles* is the key condition under which the predictions make sense. The similarity of profiles should include also the similarity of the execution times. This aspect of similarity is not paid special attention. At a very high level of abstraction all time aspects of modelling the operational software reliability are accounted for by the assumption that failures' occurrence could be modelled as a *Poisson process* [MIO87].

The goal of this paper is to discuss in detail whether and when the hypothesis about the failure occurrence process being a Poisson process holds for real systems for which the urn model is applicable and to suggest ways for improving the known reliability growth models.

2.2. The Interfailure Times as a function of θ and the duration of a single execution

Assume a varying duration, L, of a single execution and denote its probability density function (*pdf*) as $l(t)$. The interfailure time IF (measured in CPU time scale) could be

---

[1] In fact in (3) the expected value of the random variable $N+1$ is given.

represented as a renewal process (since independence of successive inputs has been assumed). Denote the duration of consecutive executions none of them producing a failure as L_1, L_2, ..., L_N, respectively, and the duration of the execution producing a failure as L_{N+1}. N, as in 2.1, denotes the number of successful executions between failures and is geometrically distributed with parameter θ. Denote by $E[IF]$, $E[IF^2]$, $E[L]$ and $E[L^2]$ the first two moments of IF and L, respectively.

Obviously,

$$E[IF] = E[L_1 + L_2 + ... + L_{N+1}],$$

that accounting (3) and applying the Wald theorem considering the mean value of a sum of a random number of renewals [Cox55] yields:

$$E[IF] = E[L].E[N+1] = \frac{E[L]}{\theta} \tag{4}$$

Similarly to the previous case the mean time to failure is proportional to the reciprocal of θ and hence θ could again be interpreted as a failure rate.

In the above inference the actual interfailure time is substituted for an interval which includes $n+1$ *identically distributed* intervals. This marginal distribution of the execution time may be different from the conditional distribution of the duration of executions resulting in failures and/or from the conditional distribution of the duration of those executions not resulting in failures. All this however will lead to a negligible bias of the mean value of the interfailure time.

Now the *distribution* of the interfailure time will be analysed. Denote the Laplace transform of $l(t)$ as $L^*(s)$, while the transform of IF (denote its *pdf* as $b(t)$), as $IF^*(s)$. Formally:

$$l(t) \underline{\underline{\Delta}} L^*(s); \qquad\qquad b(t) \underline{\underline{\Delta}} IF^*(s),$$

where $\underline{\underline{\Delta}}$ stands for the operator of Laplace transform of *pdf*. Obviously,

$$IF^*(s) = \sum_{n=0}^{\infty} P_n [L^*(s)]^{n+1} = \sum_{n=0}^{\infty} \theta(1-\theta)^n [L^*(s)]^{n+1} \tag{5}$$

If $|L^*(s)| < 1$, that is always true:

$$IF^*(s) = \sum_{n=0}^{\infty} P_n [L^*(s)]^{n+1} = \frac{\theta.L^*(s)}{1-(1-\theta).L^*(s)}. \tag{6}$$

Following Kleinrock [Kle75, pp. 201-204], the interfailure time could be shown to be exponentially distributed iff the very L is exponentially distributed, i.e. $IF^*(s)$ from

(6) will be $IF^*(s) \equiv IF_{exp}^*(s) = \frac{\theta\lambda}{\theta\lambda + s}$ (exponential distribution with a parameter $\theta\lambda$)

if and only if $L^*(s) \equiv L_{exp}^*(s) = \frac{\lambda}{\lambda + s}$ (exponential distribution with a parameter λ).

It is well-known that the first two moments and the variance of the exponential distribution with a parameter $\theta\lambda$ could be expressed as:

$$E[IF_{exp}] = \frac{1}{\theta\lambda} = \frac{E[L]}{\theta}, \qquad E[IF_{exp}^2] = \frac{2}{(\theta\lambda)^2} = 2\left(\frac{E[L]}{\theta}\right)^2 \text{ and}$$

$$Var(IF_{exp}) = E[IF_{exp}^2] - \left(E[IF_{exp}]\right)^2 = \frac{1}{(\theta\lambda)^2} = \left(\frac{E[L]}{\theta}\right)^2.$$

In other words, $Var(IF_{exp}) = \left(E[IF_{exp}]\right)^2$.

The consequences of this analysis seem important for the practice. Miller has shown [Mil86] that many of the known reliability growth models are special cases of models assuming exponential distribution of the interfailure times. He has given a justification why this assumption could be accepted that is mainly based on the assumption of independent selection of inputs. He also has quoted a case of a diffusion through the input space which had also been proven to lead to an exponential distribution of the interfailure time. Bev Littlewood commenting on the draft of this paper has given an excellent mathematical proof why in *many cases* the exponential distribution may be a *good approximation* for the interfailure time distribution regardless of $l(t)$. This is given in the Appendix. Everything depends on the relationship between three parameters - the first two moments of the execution time and the failure rate θ. When the failure rate approaches 0 (zero) then the interfailure time asymptotically tends to have exponential distribution. The point is that when reliability growth models are applicable the software possesses a *modest failure rate* and the asymptotic result may be inaccurate. This is the main issue of section 3.

2.3. The Effect of Execution Time Variability on the Interfailure Times

Recall (6) from which the first two moments of IF could easily be obtained. It is well known, that:

$$E[IF] = (-1)\frac{dIF^*(s)}{ds}\bigg|_{s=0}, \text{ and } E[IF^2] = \frac{d^2IF^*(s)}{ds^2}\bigg|_{s=0}. \tag{7}$$

Therefore, using $L^*(s)\big|_{s=0} = 1$ the moments of IF could be calculated as follows:

$$E[IF] = \frac{E[L]}{\theta}, \text{ and } \tag{8}$$

$$E[IF^2] = \frac{E[L^2]}{\theta} + \frac{2(1-\theta)(E[L])^2}{\theta^2}. \tag{9}$$

The variance of the interfailure time could easily be expressed through its moments:

$$Var(IF) = E[IF^2] - \left(E[IF]\right)^2 = \frac{E[L^2]}{\theta} + \left(\frac{E[L]}{\theta}\right)^2 - 2\theta\left(\frac{E[L]}{\theta}\right)^2.$$

Let us now compare $Var(IF)$ with $Var(IF_{exp})$ outlined on the previous page. If one assigns $\lambda = \frac{1}{E[L]}$, then the expressions for the first moment of the true distribution and for the exponential approximation are equal - $E[IF] = E[IF_{exp}]$, while variances are different $Var(IF) \neq Var(IF_{exp})$. In the general case the following holds:

$$Var(IF) = \big(E[IF]\big)^2 + Bias\_Var = Var(IF_{exp}) + Bias\_Var, \tag{10}$$

where

$$Bias\_Var = \frac{E[L^2]}{\theta} - \frac{2\big(E[L]\big)^2}{\theta} = \frac{E[L^2] - 2\big(E[L]\big)^2}{\theta} = \frac{Var(L) - \big(E[L]\big)^2}{\theta}. \tag{11}$$

Dependent on the value of Bias_Var, three situations may happen when the exponential approximation of the interfailure time of software with stable reliability is used:

- Bias_Var = 0, the two expressions of the interfailure times (exact and approximated) are indistinguishable in terms of first two moments, and hence variance. Apart from other possible cases this holds for exponentially distributed execution time;
- Bias_Var < 0, the variance of the interfailure time is overestimated when exponential approximation is applied, and finally
- Bias_Var > 0, the variance of the interfailure time is underestimated by using the exponential approximation of the interfailure time instead of exact distribution.

In the last two cases the exponential approximation will cause prediction errors when the maximum likelihood method is used. What seems important is that this error could vary in sign dependent on the moments of the execution time. Thus, being ignorant about the variance of the execution time one makes the prediction model vary arbitrarily in prediction quality - one may get pessimistic, realistic or optimistic predictions.

One may go further and express the ratio:

$$\frac{Var(IF)}{Var(IF_{exp})} = 1 + \theta\left(\frac{Var(L)}{\big(E[L]\big)^2} - 1\right) = 1 + \theta\big(C_L^2 - 1\big), \tag{12}$$

where C_L stands for the coefficient of variation [Lew85] of L.

This is another form of the condition how the variability of the execution time may affect the variability of the interfailure time. When $Var(L)$ is modest compared with $(E[L])^2$ in respect to θ then the exponential approximation of IF is good.

Given the distribution of the execution time could be measured with an arbitrary precision, one may verify, through (12) the quality of the exponential approximation. When the error becomes unacceptable, the exact form for the interfailure time distribution should be used, otherwise the exponential approximation may be expected to give poor results.

2.4. Implications for Software Reliability Growth Modelling

Obviously, the distribution of the execution time may have a crucial effect on the appropriateness of predicting models relying upon the assumption of interfailure time being exponentially distributed. Thus, a phenomenon not being reported so far has been exercised. I wonder if the varying quality of prediction of the known software reliability growth models when applied to different sets of failure data [BL92] is caused by the variability of the execution time! The hypothesis may easily be confirmed if the collected data along with the interfailure times included the execution time distribution. Since this has not been done so far for real software, in the next section, examples based on data collected from simulated systems are given. These confirm that in some cases the assumption of exponential distribution of the interfailure time may indeed be wrong, that causes the reliability growth model to perform poorly. The point that seems important for the practice is, that if one needs to base the future reliability prediction on an accurate model, more efforts should be spend on collecting data needed to *tune* the model. The distribution of the execution time is a candidate in the list of parameters requiring extra measurements.

The recalibration technique [BL92] having been recently developed improves significantly the accuracy of predictions. This is achieved by learning about the biases of the predictions produced by the basic models and then recalibrating these. Such techniques are general in nature and should provide significant improvement in case of any basic model. Investigations are needed in order to compare the quality of predictions using the recalibration together with any basic model and the approach presented here, based on measurement of the execution time distribution. Obviously, recalibration is a *more cost effective approach* than the one presented above because no additional cost should be paid on collecting extra data. It is however difficult to *compare the quality of prediction* of recalibration versus models incorporating the distribution of the execution time without data making this comparison possible.

The analysis presented this far mainly deals with modelling the interfailure time when the software is with *known* probability of failure per execution. In reliability growth models the situation is more complicated. θ is unknown and is modelled as a random variable. Another hypothesis about stochastically non-increasing nature of θ is needed when faults are removed (different urns are modelled). In [Mil92] the *Beta* distribution is argued to be a candidate for expressing our uncertainty about θ.

Constructing a complete software reliability growth model accounting for the distribution of the execution time is beyond the scope of this paper and is an area for future research. Provided the complete reliability growth model is constructed the usual parametric maximum likelihood procedure could be applied to collected data for determining the parameters of the model. The common statistical techniques of validating the prediction quality, like u-plot, or comparison of predictions' quality of the new model with some of the known models (with or without recalibration) using prequential likelihood [BL92], could be performed.

3. Examples

In this section the results of simulation experiments are described that address the effect of execution time variability on the interfailure times' distribution and on the prediction quality of Littlewood-Verrall reliability growth model [Lit80] (LV model). The data used *are not field data* but instead data from simulated systems produced using a pseudo-random number generator.

The reason for choosing LV model is, to some extend of course, a matter of subjective preference, but which is more important is the quality of the model. This model has been proven to perform the best in many comparative studies, most recent

[NL95], [CDLY95]. Another reason for selecting this model is that in it the assumption of conditional exponential distribution of the interfailure time is explicitly asserted (Assumption 1) and this makes it easier to demonstrate the points of this paper.

The technique called u-plot [A-GCL86] was used to verify the prediction accuracy in experiments. The technique is intended to illustrate when the prediction is poor and in this sense the good u-plot is only a *necessary* condition for an accurate prediction. In general, a good u-plot does not guarantee a good prediction (the good u-plot does not constitute a *sufficient* condition for an accurate prediction). However, for the purposes of this study (to demonstrate the negative effect of the increasing variance of the software execution time upon the prediction quality) the u-plot technique is appropriate.

3.1. System with stable reliability

In the first experiment the probability of failure per execution has been assumed known $\theta = 0.001$. Three different execution times have been used for the systems being simulated:

- exponentially distributed with a rate $\lambda = 1$, referred to as System 1 in the following text,
- uniformly distributed in the range (0.01, 1.99) with a mean value = 1, referred to as System 2, and
- with "bimodal" distribution: $p(L = l) = \begin{cases} C, for\ l = a, C < 1, \\ 1 - C\ for\ l = b, \\ 0, elsewhere. \end{cases}$

    where a, b and C had been chosen in such a way that the mean of the execution time was 1. A series of experiments was carried out with $a = 0.01$ and various bs for $C = 0.9, 0.95, 0.98, 0.99, 0.995, 0.998$ and 0.999, referred to as System 3 - System 9. Corresponding bs are listed in Table 1.

The "bimodal" distribution allows the variance of the execution time to be easily changed and thus the effect of this upon the interfailure time explored. This kind of distribution seems to be typical for many database applications. For example, a sort of this distribution was observed in a variety of systems reported in [Pop96].

In case of any of the selected distributions a sample of 1000 realisations of the time to next failure was generated using a pseudo-random number generator. The sample was checked using the *chi-square goodness-of-fit test* (with varying degree of freedom 12 - 30) against two hypotheses about its distribution: the exponential distribution (with a parameter derived as a reciprocal of the sample mean value, 1 / $E[IF]$) and against the "true" distribution of the interfailure times depending on the distribution of the execution time. The goodness-of-fit tests' results served as indicators, on the one hand, of the systematic error one implicitly accepts assuming the interfailure time being exponentially distributed and, on the other hand, of the potential benefits of using the "true" distribution of interfailure times in reliability growth modelling (instead of the wrong exponential hypothesis). The cells (intervals) for the chi-square tests were chosen following the general rule: the frequency for each cell to be at least 5 [Mann92, p.551] (in all reported cases the frequencies were ≥ 8). The results of these experiments are summarised in Table 1. In case of the "bimodal" distribution of the execution time the interfailure time distribution was determined by generating a very large sample of actual interfailure times (the sample size was much larger than 1000 realisations) and this pattern sample was used to calculate the expected frequencies for the chi-square goodness-of-fit testing.

System id	Exponential	Uniform	"Bimodal"						
	System 1	System 2	System 3	System 4	System 5	System 6	System 7	System 8	System 9
C	-	-	0.9	0.95	0.98	0.99	0.995	0.998	0.999
b (a = 0.01)	-	-	9.91	19.81	49.51	99.1	198.01	495.01	990.01
$E[L]$	1	1	1	1	1	1	1	1	1
$Var(L)$	1	0.33	8.82	18.62	49.02	98.2	195	490	980.1
$E[IF]$	980.8	997.9	1006.8	1006.2	1009.8	1017.2	999.7	1013.5	1001.1
$Var(IF)$	1071210	916501.4	1043877	1057013	1061740	1135673	1269848	1605949	1605949
$Var(IF_{exp})$	961969	995345	1013646	1012376	1019761	1034610	999468	1027172	1002241
Degree of freedom	18	18	18	21	21	21	14	14	14
α_{exp}	0.63	0.62	0.13	0.103	0.035	3.55E-26	0	0	0
α_{true}	Not evaluated	Not evaluated	Not evaluated	0.389	0.768	0.129	0.467	0.842	0.738

Table 1. In the table parameters of the execution times' distribution for System 1 - System 9 and estimations of some parameters for the generated samples of interfailure times are given. The last two rows of the table represent the level of significance (α_{exp} and α_{true}) using which the chi-square goodness-of-fit test does not reject the hypotheses "sample being exponentially distributed" and "sample having the "true" distribution", respectively. The "true" distribution was represented by a sample much larger than 1000 realisations that was derived from the corresponding "bimodal" distribution.

In order to avoid any confusion regarding the parameters α_{exp} and α_{true} their calculations will be clarified. Let us consider, for example, System 7 for which $\alpha_{exp} = 0$ and $\alpha_{true} = 0.467$. The sample of the generated 1000 interfailure times for this system was divided into 15 cells (intervals) each containing more than 10 interfailure times (the *observed* frequencies of the cells were > 10). Thus the degree of freedom was 14. For the hypothesis "sample has the "true" distribution" the much larger sample of interfailure times was used for determining the *expected* frequencies of the cells. The calculated chi-square statistic was $\chi^2 = 13.7737$. From the chi-square distribution tables [Mann92, p.744] for a degree of freedom 14 and a significance level $\alpha = 0.1$ the critical value of χ^2 is 21.064. Similarly, for $\alpha = 0.9$ the critical χ^2 value is 7.790. Thus, the calculated value 13.7737 indicates that there is no evidence to reject the hypothesis using 10% (0.1) significance level and that the hypothesis should be rejected using 90% (0.9) significance level. The value $\alpha_{true} = 0.467$ (46.7%) (that is put in Table 1) has been calculated using the build-in function CHIDIST(χ^2 ,degree_of_freedom) of Microsoft EXCEL 5.0 that allows to calculate the significance level for which the *critical value* of the chi-square test becomes equal to the *calculated chi-square test statistic* (for the chosen cells and degree of freedom). This value (α_{true}) is the upper bound of the significance level using which the test does not provide sufficient evidence for rejecting the tested hypothesis. Therefore, using any significance level, that is lower than the determined α_{true} the test does not reject the hypothesis. The significance level α_{exp} is similarly calculated. The difference is that now the expected frequencies for the selected cells are directly calculated using the corresponding exponential distribution (with a parameter calculated as a reciprocal of the mean value of the generated interfailure times) and the sample size (1000). Generally, if the calculated values for α_{exp} and α_{true} are beyond 0.1 the corresponding hypothesis ("the sample being exponentially distributed" or "the sample having "true" distribution", respectively) can hardly be rejected. If, on the contrary, either value (α_{exp} or α_{true}) is very close to 0, then the hypothesis about the corresponding distribution of the sample should be rejected.

Clearly, for the first two distributions of the execution times, System 1 and System 2, the hypothesis of the exponential distribution of the time to failure holds at a very high level of significance. In the third case, with the increase of C the hypothesis becomes less likely and for $C \geq 0.99$ it obviously should be rejected. Note that in this case $Var(IF)$ becomes significantly biased from the value of $Var(IF_{exp})$ one could expect under the assumption of IF being exponentially distributed (shaded cells in Table 1). For these cases from the figures in Table 1 and from the Appendix it follows that IF can hardly be assumed exponential. Thus, the theory is in a good accordance with the experiment. Not surprisingly, in all experienced cases, $\alpha_{exp} < \alpha_{true}$ and for all calculated α_{true}'s they were strongly beyond 0.1.

The lesson to be learned from this (although contrived) example is that the large variability of the execution time may indeed discredit the assumption of the time to failure being exponentially distributed.

3.2. System with growing reliability

The second group of examples deals with reliability growth of the *simulated* systems described in section 3.1. The difference is that now the systems have been subjected to debugging and hence their reliability has been growing with the time. The simulated systems contained 300 "bugs" with probabilities of being activated (and producing a failure) coming from a uniform distribution. Initially, in the systems all bugs were active. Then randomly these were fixed, thus the overall rate of failure declined. The history of such "debugging" (reliability growth) was saved in a file and later used (*the same reliability growth* was in place) for generating failure data for systems with different execution times (as shown in Table 1). The simulation exercise comprises *two groups of cases* - with initial rates of failure θ (resulting from all 300 bugs being active) equal to 0.01 and 0.001. The debugging time was set equal to 50000 and 300000 time units for each of groups, respectively. At the end of the testing the achieved failure rates were of order 10^{-4}, values quite reasonable for real software. Failure data were collected and then the LV model applied for reliability prediction. Figures 1 - 4 depict the u-plots for the first group (tested for 50 000 time units), while the u-plots for the second group of cases are not shown because of space limitations. The particular testing cases and the results of model's parameters fitting are summarised in Table 2.

	u-plot on	Initial θ	Testing time	LV - model best fitting parameters			
				α	b_1	b_2	chi-square goodness-of-fit test significance level
System 3	Fig. 1	0.01	50 000	8.976	483.66	13.505	0.1262
System 4	Fig. 2	0.01	50 000	8.862	419.77	13.218	0.521
System 5	Fig. 3	0.01	50 000	4.624	210.93	6.483	3.479E-18
System 6	Fig. 4	0.01	50 000	0.247	0.5753	0.0038	3.21E-43
System 1		0.001	300 000	345.196	295185.3	4081.53	0.415
System 6	Not	0.001	300 000	22.005	15702.31	255.29	0.974
System 7	shown	0.001	300 000	13.617	9145.82	156.01	0.930
System 8		0.001	300 000	5.3246	3057.87	57.017	1.233E-13

Table 2. Each row of the table represents a summary of results with a particular system. In the first column a reference of the execution time distribution is given in accordance with Table 1. In the second column a reference to the figure representing the u-plot of that particular system is given. In the third and fourth columns probabilities of failure per execution, θ, before the testing and the testing duration, respectively, are given. Next three columns represent the LV model parameters determined maximising the likelihood of the model on the observed failure data. Finally, in the last column the chi-square goodness-of-fit test significance level for not rejecting the hypothesis "the u's of the sample of failure data being uniformly distributed" for the best-fitting parameters is given. This has been calculated in a manner similar to the calculation of α_{exp} and α_{true}, used in Table 1.

3.2.1 *Group 1* of simulated systems (initial $\theta = 0.01$, testing duration 50 000 time units)

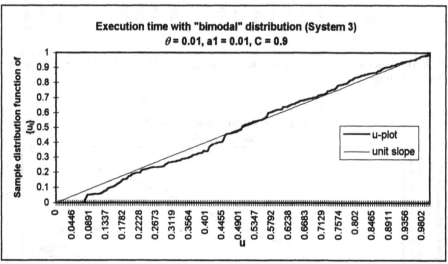

Fig. 1. The u-plot of System 3. 203 failures were observed and the residual failure rate at the end of the testing was 0.001729.

The comparison of the u-plots shown on Fig. 1 - 4 indicates the tendency of worsening the prediction quality when the variance of the execution time increases. For small values of this variance (corresponding to values of C = 0.9 and 0.95) the u-plots are close to the unit-slope and the chi-square goodness-of-fit test does not give an evidence for rejecting the uniform distribution of u's using significance level of up to 12%. For highly variable execution times (C = 0.98 and 0.99), however, the u-plots tend to be significantly biased from the unit slope. The chi-square goodness-of-fit test of u's being uniformly distributed fails (the uniformity should be rejected) using any reasonable level of significance. For the last tested case ("bimodal" distribution with C = 0.99) the prediction is extremely poor - for the calculated best fitting parameters of the model (α, b_1 and b_2 in Table 2) the expected value of the time to failure becomes infinite!

Thus this group of experiments confirms the hypothesis that the execution time variability has a crucial effect on the predictive accuracy of the reliability growth model.

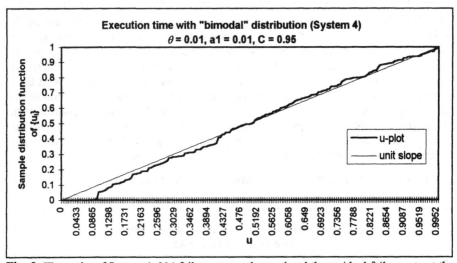

Fig. 2. The u-plot of System 4. 214 failures were observed and the residual failure rate at the end of the testing was 0.001419.

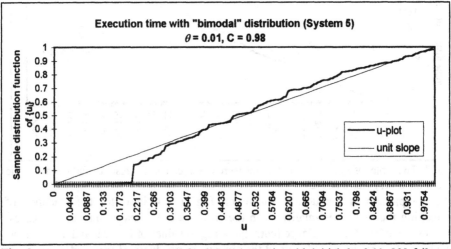

Fig. 3. The u-plot of System 5, tested for 50000 time units with initial $\theta = 0.01$. 203 failures were observed and the residual failure rate at the end of the testing was 0.001729.

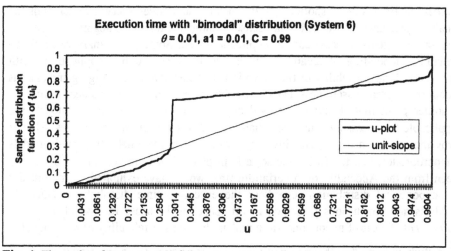

Fig. 4. The u-plot of System 6. 210 failures were observed and the residual failure rate at the end of the testing was 0.00158584.

***3.2.2. Group 2** of simulated systems (initial θ = 0.001, testing duration 300 000 time units)*

The u-plots of systems belonging to the second group, although not shown, have indicated the same tendency (as that observed in section 3.2.1) of worsening the quality of prediction when the variability of the execution time, and hence of the variability of the interfailure time, increases.

The observations, as it seems to me, support the conclusion that the inaccuracy of predictions has something to do with the variability of the execution time!

4. Discussion

Historically software reliability predictions have been very often used for telecommunications software [MIO87]. Although the CPU time scale has been recognised as the right scale to be used for collecting failure data very often the calendar time scale has been used even recently [KMS91]. For such (telecommunications) software tested in a real environment, the intervals between executions depend not on the software execution time, but instead on producing demands by the customers (calls). It has been noticed that the demands could well be modelled as a Poisson process. If the processing of a demand is much shorter than the average interval between demands then the interfailure time (in the calendar time scale) depends on the demands' inter-arrival times but not on the duration of demand's processing (software execution time). Thus, the influence of the execution time variability is immaterial. Since the demands' inter-arrival times come from the exponential distribution the interfailure time, as shown in section 2, will also be exponentially distributed. Thus, the conclusion to be outlined here is that applications like telecommunications software, especially when calendar time scale is in place, are excellent examples for using the existing reliability growth models.

If neither the times between external demands are exponentially distributed nor the processing time is much shorter than the mean time between successive demands the analysis presented above will make sense. Candidates for this category of cases are data-base systems, process-control applications, etc. Some preliminary research on reliability modelling of database software and process control applications with inherently large variability of the execution time has given encouraging indications about the approach usefulness. Hope to be able to report on this in the near future.

Another point that should be stressed again is that reliability growth models are applicable for accessing a modest reliability, i.e. θ takes on *modest* values. That is why the execution time variability may make the known reliability growth models inappropriate when the CPU time scale is in place. If θ were very small, as can be seen from the Appendix, the interfailure time would have exhibited asymptotically an exponential distribution regardless the execution time distribution. Thus the analysis and conclusions presented in this paper make sense in case of a *modest failure rate* that is of major concern in real applications of reliability growth models.

The study presented in this paper in no way is an attempt to underestimate the work done recently on recalibrating the basic reliability growth models. The tools like u-plot and, in particular the prequential likelihood, are very generic and allow the quality of reliability growth models to be objectively checked. The approach [A-GCL86] to consider any prediction system as a *triad* of a model, inference procedure and prediction making use of the observed biases, noises, etc., is very deep in nature. The current state of knowledge in the area is such that often allows to get accurate predictions of software reliability even starting off with an imprecise basic model. Why then should one care much about the quality of the basic model? First of all, the success of the recalibration technique on the known failure data was not absolute! Conceptually, recalibration is a legal transformation only if the predictions of the basic model exhibit a stationary bias with the u-transforms of the collected failure data. The success in ("blindly" [BCLS90]) using the recalibration technique even when such stationary bias is absent is a luck rather than a rule. There have been cases [BL92] when even with the powerful recalibration technique the goal of getting accurate predictions had remained unattainable. The intention of this study was to show *one* of the possible sources that makes the basic models inaccurate. In this sense the study gives directions for improvement of the basic models through incorporating the knowledge of the execution time variability, that does not seem to be difficult to measure objectively. Intuitively, one can expect that eliminating some of the sources of predictions' inaccuracy (those due to execution time variability) the ability of the triad to cope with other sources of prediction inaccuracy will be enlarged. Clearly, such an (eventual) improvement of the basic model will be bought at some price. The tester should pay for collecting more data (necessary for estimating the execution time distribution). Therefore the trade-off between the expected improvement of the prediction quality and the price to be paid for getting information about the execution time variability should be explored.

5. Conclusions

In this paper some issues in modelling reliability of software systems executed on independently drawn inputs have been addressed. The influence of the execution time variability upon the interfailure time distribution is stressed. It has been argued that the ignorance of this effect may be the explanation of the unstable quality of predictions of some known reliability growth models when applied to different failure data. Illustrative examples are given that explain the idea. Some speculative discussion on how realistic it may be for real software systems to expect execution times with large variability is also given.

Although mathematical arguments are strong additional investigations are needed to deeper understand the influence of the execution time variability upon the predicting quality of software reliability growth models. Since documented failure data do not provide information about the distribution of the execution time it was impossible to check whether precise knowledge of this will help improve predicting quality. I dare hope that software developers will be encouraged to collect the lacking data trying to make use of the theoretical results presented in this paper. This was the motivation to carry out the research and to present the results to the interested audience. The next step in this direction would be to develop a reliability growth model incorporating the precise knowledge of the execution time and a tool facilitating the usage of the approach.

Acknowledgement

I would like to thank Professor Bev Littlewood, from the Centre for Software Reliability, City University, London, for the helpful comments of the drafts of the paper and also for the inference included in the Appendix that helped clarify the idea presented here. I would also like to thank the anonymous reviewers for the insightful comments.

References

[A-GCL86] Abdel-Ghaly, A.A., Chan, P. Y., Littlewood, B. "Evaluation of Competing Software Reliability Predictions", IEEE Trans. Software Eng., Vol. SE - 12, Sept. 1986, pp. 950 - 967.

[BCLS90] Brocklehurst, S., Chan, P.Y., Littlewood, B., Snell, J. "Recalibrating Software Reliability Models", IEEE Trans. Software Eng., Vol. 16, No. 4, April 1990, pp. 458 - 469.

[BL92] Brocklehurst, S. and B. Littlewood, "New Ways to Get Accurate Reliability Measures", IEEE Software (special issue on Reliability Measurement), July 1992, pp. 34-42

[CDLY95] Carman, D. W., Dolinsky, A. A., Lyu, M. R., and Yu, J. S., "Software Reliability Engineering Study of a Large-Scale Telecommunications Software Systems", Proc. ISSRE'95 Int. Symp. on Software Reliability Eng., 24 - 27 Oct., 1995, Toulouse, France, pp. 350 - 359.

[Cox55] Cox, D. R., "Renewal Theory", London: Methuen & Co. Ltd, 1955.

[Kle75] Kleinrock, L., "Queuing Systems. Volume 1: Theory", 1975, Wiley & Sons, 741 p.

[KMS91] Kanoun, K., Martini, M. R. B., Souza, J. M. "A Method for Software Reliability Analysis and Prediction Application to TROPICO-R Switching System", IEEE Trans. Software Engineering, Vol. 17, No. 4, April 1991, pp. 334 - 344.

[Lew85] Lew, A., "Computer Science: A Mathematical Introduction", Prentice-Hall Int. Series in Computer Science, C.A.R. Hoare Series Editor, 1985, 421 p.

[Lit80] Littlewood, B. "Theories of Software Reliability: How Good Are They and How Can They Be Improved?", IEEE Trans. Software Eng., Vol. SE-6, Sept. 1980, pp. 489-500.

[Mann92] Mann, P. S., "Introductory Statistics", John Willey & Sons, 1992, 774 p.

[Mil86] Miller, D. R. "Exponential Order Statistic Models of Software Reliability Growth", IEEE Trans. Software Engineering, Vol. SE-12, No. 1, January 1986, pp. 12 - 24.

[Mil92] Miller, K. W., Morrel L. J., Noonan R. E., Park, S. K., Nicol, D. M., Murrill, B. W., and Voas, J. M. "Estimating the Probability of Failure When Testing Reveals No Failures", IEEE Trans. Software Eng., Vol. 18, No. 1, pp. 33 - 43, January, 1992.

[MIO87] Musa, J. D., Iannino, A., and Okumoto, K. "Software Reliability. Measurement, Prediction, Application", McGraw Hill, 1987.

[NL95] Nikora, A. P. and Lyu, M. L., "An Experiment in Determining Software Reliability Model Applicability", Proc. ISSRE'95 Int. Symp. on Software Reliability Eng., 24 - 27 Oct., 1995, Toulouse, France, pp. 304 - 313.

[Pop96] Popov, P., "Design for changeability - a remedy against uncertain requirements", 13th Annual CSR Workshop "Design for Protecting the User", Burgenstock, Switzerland, 11-13 Sept., 1996, accepted for presentation.

[TIYL95] Thakur, A., Iyer, R. K., Young, L., and Lee, I. "Analysis of Failures in the Tandem NonStop-UX Operating System", Proc. ISSRE'95 Int. Symp. on Software Reliability Eng., 24 - 27 Oct., 1995, Toulouse, France, pp. 40 - 49.

Appendix

This is the inference given by Bev Littlewood showing if and when the conditional distribution of the time-to-failure given a known θ could be assumed exponential.

Recall the Laplace transform of the interfailure time given by formula (6) of the main text. Obviously, the following holds [Kle75, Appendix 2]:

$$IF^*(s) = E\left(e^{-sIF}\right) = \frac{\theta L^*(s)}{1-(1-\theta)L^*(s)}.$$

Consider normalised IF: $IFN = \dfrac{IF}{E[IF]}$.

$$\therefore IFN^*(s) = E\left(e^{-s\left[\frac{IF}{E[IF]}\right]}\right) = E\left(e^{-\frac{s}{E[IF]}IF}\right) = IF^*\left(\frac{s}{E[IF]}\right) = \frac{\theta L^*\left(\frac{s}{E[IF]}\right)}{1-(1-\theta)L^*\left(\frac{s}{E[IF]}\right)}.$$

But $E[IF] = \dfrac{E[L]}{\theta}$.

$$\therefore IFN^*(s) = \frac{\theta L^*\left(\dfrac{s\theta}{\mathrm{E}[L]}\right)}{1-(1-\theta)L^*\left(\dfrac{s\theta}{\mathrm{E}[L]}\right)} . \; \text{Now}$$

$$L^*\left(\frac{s\theta}{\mathrm{E}[L]}\right) = 1 - \mathrm{E}(L) \cdot \frac{s\theta}{\mathrm{E}[L]} + \mathrm{E}[L^2]\left(\frac{s\theta}{\mathrm{E}[L]}\right)^2 \cdot \frac{1}{2} + \dots$$

So,

$$IFN^*(s) = \frac{\theta\left[1 - \mathrm{E}[L]\dfrac{s\theta}{\mathrm{E}[L]} + \mathrm{E}[L^2]\left(\dfrac{s\theta}{\mathrm{E}[L]}\right)^2 \cdot \dfrac{1}{2} + \dots\right]}{1-(1-\theta)\left[1 - \mathrm{E}[L]\dfrac{s\theta}{\mathrm{E}[L]} + \mathrm{E}[L^2]\left(\dfrac{s\theta}{\mathrm{E}[L]}\right)^2 \cdot \dfrac{1}{2} + \dots\right]} =$$

$$= \frac{\theta\left[1 - \mathrm{E}[L]\dfrac{s\theta}{\mathrm{E}[L]} + \mathrm{E}[L^2]\left(\dfrac{s\theta}{\mathrm{E}[L]}\right)^2 \cdot \dfrac{1}{2} + \dots\right]}{\theta\left[1 - \mathrm{E}[L]\dfrac{s\theta}{\mathrm{E}[L]} + \dots\right] + \mathrm{E}[L]\dfrac{s\theta}{\mathrm{E}[L]} - \mathrm{E}[L^2]\left(\dfrac{s\theta}{\mathrm{E}[L]}\right)^2 \cdot \dfrac{1}{2} + \dots} =$$

$$= \frac{1 - s\theta + \dots}{1 - s\theta + \dots + s - \mathrm{E}[L^2]\left(\dfrac{s\theta}{\mathrm{E}[L]}\right)^2 \cdot \dfrac{1}{\theta} \cdot \dfrac{1}{2} + \dots}$$

that approaches $\dfrac{1}{1+s}$ as $\theta \to 0$, i.e. the distribution of *IFN* is *asymptotically* exponential.

Clearly, if IFN is exponential, it follows that *IF* is exponential.

QED.

For modest $\theta = [10^{-3}, \dots, 10^{-4}]$

$$IFN^*(s) \approx \frac{1}{1 + s - \dfrac{\theta}{2}\dfrac{\mathrm{E}[L^2]}{(\mathrm{E}[L])^2}s^2} = \frac{1}{1 + s - \dfrac{\theta}{2}\left(1 + \dfrac{Var[L]}{(\mathrm{E}[L])^2}\right)s^2} .$$

Thus, it becomes clear that for the range of θ that is of interest for software reliability predictions, only first two moments of the execution time distribution may affect the exponentiality of *IFN* and hence *IF*.

Dependability Evaluation of a Computing System for Traction Control of Electrical Locomotives

Silke Draber, Bernhard Eschermann
ABB Corporate Research
CH-5405 Baden
email: silke.draber@chcrc.abb.ch

Abstract. This article presents the dependability analysis of a computing system controlling the traction system and especially the semiconductor current-converters of a modern electric locomotive. Following special aspects of this application are taken into account: different degrees of performance reduction, lurking errors, periodic tests, short repair times. The dependability evaluation started from a simple "symptomatic model" showing the stages of performance degradation. It turned out to be a very helpful visualisation aid when discussing the failure modes with the experts for the components concerned. The detailed knowledge about hardware failures and their effects was collected in one large FMEA-table. For the subsequent mathematical analysis an elaborate "FMEA-oriented Markov model" was automatically constructed from the FMEA-table. This approach proved to be efficient and straightforward, giving clear results and hints on which components have most influence on MTTF, which must possibly be redesigned or planned redundantly. The customer's special requirements could be taken into account by arbitrarily varying the sets of up- and down-states. The approach is assumed to be applicable to many similar problems of dependability evaluation.

Keywords: Reliability Analysis, Dependability Analysis, FMEA, Markov Models, Performance Degradation, Locomotive

1 Introduction

A large number of articles in the field of dependability analysis deals with the distribution of up and down times in repairable technical systems (Csenki, 1994; Zhao, 1994; Sericola, 1994; Laprie, Beounes, Kaâniche and Kanoun, 1990). Not only Markov models but also Semi-Markov models, fault trees (Barlow et al., 1975) or extended stochastic Petri nets (Dugan et al., 1984) are applied in order to characterise the dependability. Basic quantities describing dependability (Laprie, 1985) are the mean time to failure from a special starting condition or the asymptotic value of the point availability. More advanced analysis deals with distributions of the time to first failure or interval availability.

In many of the systems studied there is a fixed a priori definition of up and down states, or, in other words, components may either be fully redundant or not (Csenki, 1994; Cai, 1994). In contrast, this article deals with a system exhibiting a behaviour known as "graceful degradation" in case of failures. It consists of several identical components which are not fully redundant in the following sense: Full performance requires all of the components working, but if some of the components are down, the whole system is still able to fulfil its task, but with reduced performance.

The system considered in this article is an electric locomotive with two nearly independent three-phase-current motor groups, each of them being fed by a number of computer-controlled current-converters (see section 2). The system performance can be degraded slightly by a failure of one current-converter or substantially by the failure of a motor group. Depending on the application or the customer's point of view, these stages of reduced performance may be counted as up or down states. Example given: What might be considered as an acceptable performance reduction for a locomotive pulling a few passenger coaches in flat country can be classified as a complete failure if the same locomotive is used in a long cargo train climbing a mountain.

This article is structured as follows. After providing an overview over the computer-controlled power system of the locomotive in section 2, a symptomatic model describing the different stages of performance reduction is introduced in section 3. Section 4 shows the FMEA-table composed of the information about component failures. Section 5 explains how this FMEA-table can be transferred into a Markov model which is then used (section 6) to calculate the desired dependability figures: MTTF, asymptotic availability, distribution of the failures among the different types of reduced performance, and sensitivity of the MTTF to changes in the primary component failure rates.

2 The Traction System of the Electrical Locomotive

The mechanical traction elements of the locomotive studied are the same as those of the Re 4/4 type 460 developed by ABB and SLM. They consist of two bogies (undercarriages) one at the front, one at the rear end of the locomotive, each with four wheels on two axles (see Fig. 1).

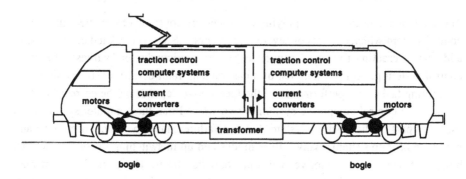

Fig. 1. Side view of locomotive.

Each of the four axles of the locomotive is driven by one three-phase induction motor (asynchronous motor). The required variable frequency voltage supply for the motors is generated in two independent groups of power electronics devices, one group for each bogie. The circuit diagram in Fig.2 shows these two groups which first convert the AC line voltage (16.66 Hz) into DC voltage before then converting it into the three-phase stator voltage with variable frequency. The frequency variation is a prerequisite for employing induction motors in this variable-speed framework of train traction. The two motors of one bogie which are fed by a common current-converter are called "motorgroup" (MG).

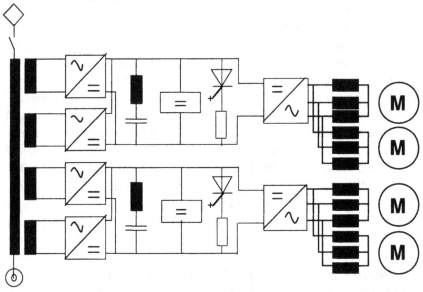

Fig. 2. Main power circuit diagram with two independent current-converters (frequency converters). From left to right: Main circuit breaker switch, line-side transformer, AC-DC converter, DC-Link with L-C-bandstop filter (33.3 Hz), main DC capacitor, overvoltage protection, DC-AC converter for the three motor windings.

The semiconductor inverters supplying one bogie are controlled by an electronic drive control system which consists of several processors, ASICs, and related electronics. In addition to creating the firing sequence for the semiconductor "valves", the drive control system performs a long list of measurement, fault detection, supervision, and monitoring tasks. The performance of the locomotive depends on the correct function of the drive control computing system in two ways. First, the computer system is an essential part of the traction system. Since a failure cannot be compensated by any hardware backup system, many failure modes end up in switching off one of the two bogies, leaving the locomotive with only half its power. The control system may also trip the locomotive's main power switch so that it is completely stopped. Second, – and even more severe – a malfunction of the drive control computer may partly destroy the power electronic devices. These aspects underline how important dependability of the computing system is in this application, which in turn explains the efforts made in designing a highly dependable system and in analysing and evaluating its dependability.

3 Symptomatic Model

A computing system consists of hardware (e.g. AD converters) and software. The dependability evaluation in this study is restricted to hardware faults and the failures occurring as a consequence. Software faults are not considered. This does not mean that the investigated dependability were independent of the software. In contrast, the response to several hardware faults is to a great extent determined by the software design. Fault detection and diagnosis algorithms, application of periodic tests, reconfiguration and use of redundant sensors – All these are software issues but important keys for tolerance against hardware faults.

The central milestone in the dependability evaluation project was the creation of a complete list of component failures, failure modes and possible effects including realistic estimates of corresponding failure rates, probabilities, response and repair times. Interviewing the hardware and software designers, the FMEA-table grew line by line, each line corresponding to a new failure mode. For each failure mode we had to ask the same questions: What is the primary failure rate? What are the possible pathways of performance degradation in response to the failure mode considered? What are the rates and probabilities describing the transitions between the different degrees of performance reduction and subsequent repair? If the fault does not have immediate consequences, what are the test and repair periods involved before the fault is diagnosed and removed? And how about the risk to encounter a more serious failure as long as the lurking error is not repaired?

In order to visualise the generally possible pathways through the stages of reduced performance and lurking errors, we soon began to use a simple "symptomatic model".

The "symptomatic model" consists of symptom-descriptions as nodes and arrows in between showing possible degradation/diagnosis/repair transitions. In such a kind of model it is very easy to follow the system response to one single failure. The hardware or software expert can easily tell which path of symptoms is walked through, where different system responses are possible from an intermediate failure state, i.e. specified by a probability to go this or that way. Failures with immediate consequences or dormant failures can be specified.

For increased clarity the long-lasting states (OK, dormant error, state of reduced performance) are drawn as rectangles whereas the intermediate short-living states are drawn as ovals. Further, to prevent ambiguities and to ease notation in the FMEA-table, every transition arrow is identified by a unique symbol. In the FMEA-table the symbols are used as synonyms for the corresponding rate constants (arrows emanating from long-lasting rectangles) or transition probabilities (arrows emanating from intermediate ovals).

Since the symptomatic model resembles a Markov scheme, one gets used to loosely speaking of "states" instead of nodes or classes. Indeed, under the condition that only one certain failure mode is considered, the symptomatic model comes close to a Markov model. Similarities and differences are discussed in further detail below.

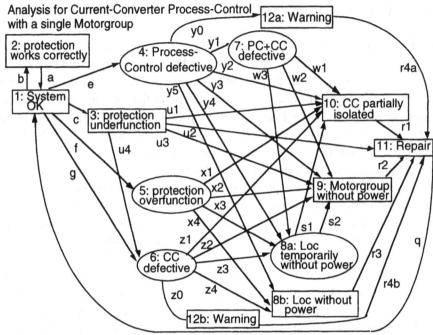

Analysis for Current-Converter Process-Control with a single Motorgroup

Fig. 3. Symptomatic model. This model shows the possible reactions of the system following a component failure. Rectangular boxes indicating a state with a lifetime longer than 0, oval boxes indicating a state with a lifetime equalling 0. The *protection underfunction* may belong to both types due to the fact that an underfunction can be detected immediately or not. (PC=Process Control; CC=Current-Converter)

In case of the electric locomotive the symptomatic model (Fig.3) consists of:

1) the OK-state

2) a state in which the system is (partly) shut off due to correct protection against external disturbances. Of course the availability of the total system (the train) is reduced, but this is out of consideration as well as other external influences for example: a passenger uses the emergency brake, mains pollution, or the bogie of a passenger coach is severely damaged. Because only the system consisting of current-converter and its process control is considered, state 2 is not taken into account in the following. It is viewed as correct function according to specification.

3) a lurking error with still full motor power but with protection underfunction, i.e. a higher risk of suffering from external line disturbances.

4) a defect of the process control computing system which is an intermediate (short-living) state resulting either in a diagnostic warning (12a), a partial current-converter isolation (10), an isolation of one motor group (one bogie without power, 9), a temporary (8a) or persistent (8b) trip of the main circuit breaker (see Fig.2) or a destruction of the semiconductor current-converters (7) as the most serious consequence of a computing system fault.

5) a short-living state of protection overfunction resulting in switching off a part of the system although such "protection" would not have been necessary.

6) a short-living state of a current-converter defect.

In the case of a spontaneous current-converter defect (6) or a current-converter defect caused by a failure of the control system, the further reaction depends on the type of defect and the functionality of the control system that is still available. In the best case only a part of the current-converter is affected and can be isolated (10), otherwise the complete motor group has to be taken out of operation (9). Another possible effect is that the main circuit breaker is tripped (8a + 8b). Some faults (8a) can be handled by isolating a part of the current-converter or a motor group and powering the locomotive again. But some (8b) are so serious that the main circuit breaker must stay open and another locomotive has to come and tow the inoperable one away.

All the long-living ("final") states of degraded performance (8b, 9, 10) shown as rectangles in Fig. 3 are going to be repaired (11) after the locomotive has been taken out of service. During repair time a full check of the system is performed which allows to assume that repair always brings the system back into the OK-state.

The symptomatic model as described above is the answer of a very important question in practical application of reliability analysis. How to define a workable "user-model" permitting easy, clear and consistent specification of system structure, failures, failure modes and effects.

A Markov model is the type of stochastic model most commonly used in the mathematical calculation of dependability figures. But it is by no means suited as user model. It consists of too many states because a Markov model has to keep track of the different failure modes by assigning different states to them. By definition of a Markov model it is not allowed to subsume different failure modes under one state if the future development, at least for instance the repair time required, depends on what failure mode has occurred. Every new FMEA-line will give rise to several new states in the Markov model, growing soon beyond what can be treated manually. Such large Markov models should better be created from a workable user model by means of a program, as described in section 5.

Several authors favour Petri nets as "user model" (see Geist and Trivedi, 1990). Petri nets have one big advantage over state-oriented models. They allow to follow the propagation of two or more failures in the system simultaneously. A second fault is represented by a second token travelling through the net. Another minor advantage of timed stochastic Petri nets over Markov models is the possibility to specify immediate transitions and "timed" transitions together. There are powerful toolkits available for transforming the user-specified Petri net model into a Markov or related type of model which then allows evaluation of MTTF, availability etc.

For the traction system treated in this application example, we found that Petri net models were still too complicated for interviewing the experts of the different parts of the hard- and software. If one is not used to thinking in Petri net models, it is not quite easy to tell what kind of token-passing sequences may occur in reality.

On the other hand, the simultaneous-failure feature of the Petri net was not required in this case. We account for simultaneous (or near-coincident) failures by the following strategy: The symptomatic model describes the consequences of a single primary failure, only. This single-failure treatment is extended on the level of the symptomatic model by considering the manifestation of a lurking underfunction (transition u_4 in Fig.3). Combinations of independent failures are taken into account in a later stage of the analysis when creating the Markov model from the symptomatic model (see section 5). From every long-lasting failure-state which does not lead to immediate performance degradation (compare 3, 12a, 12b in Fig.3), the occurrence of a second failure with immediate consequences is explicitly considered. After that the lurking error is neglected. This is justified by the assumption that any repair will lead to detection and repair of all dormant failures, too.

4 FMEA-table

The experts of the process control computing system and those of the current-converter hardware were interviewed to collect all possible failure modes, their probabilities, and their effects in a FMEA-table. At the end, the FMEA-table consisted of 83 lines concerning the computing system and 30 lines concerning the current-converter. The numerical values for the rate constants were taken from three different sources: The specifications of the ASIC suppliers, experimental results of hardware tests, and an ABB-internal catalogue of hardware failure rates for commonly used electronic devices and circuits. The rate constants for detecting faults by means of periodic tests were taken to be the inverse of the typical test interval, e.g. one week. The rate constants r_i for going into repair after a failure has occurred were taken to be the inverse of the mean remaining mission time, i.e. eight hours for a typical 16-h-service. The rate constants q of repair are taken to be the inverse of the repair time for the affected devices. Due to spare part management these times are decreased to the order of one hour. Note that rates r and q are not necessarily unique within one FMEA line if a dormant fault may either lead to a severe failure or may be detected and repaired before. In such FMEA lines the two different pathways have to be carefully distinguished.

As example for computing system failures, Fig.4 shows three FMEA-lines:

FMEA line 1.2.3 describes the effects of a protection underfunction caused by an AD-converter fault. After entering this state 3 via path c, the underfunction may either be detected by ADC fault detection procedure and repaired at next maintenance stop (path u_2, q) or the protection fails to prevent a current-converter damage by external disturbances in the meantime (path u_4, z_2, r_2, q).

FMEA line 1.2.5 gives an example of a fault in the computing system, which by means of redundant lay-out does not have any consequences except for a warning (path e, y_0, r_{4a}, q).

FMEA line 1.9.9 is an example of protection overfunction.

FMEA line	component	failure mode	effect	testing procedure	path(es) in symptomatic model
1.2.3	ADC for drive-side voltage measurement	incorrect digital value, protection underfunction with the possibility to manifest before being detected	no protection against potential damage of CC by external disturbances (no direct effect on availability); but if the actually not protected part of the Current Converter will suffer from a secondary failure, this will result in shutting off one motor group and lead to a longer repair-time.	offset test performed periodically (every 24 hours)	$c = 7.3 \cdot 10^{-4}$ tu^{-1}, $u_2 = 1/24$h, $q = 1/T_{rep} = 1/1$h (detection of lurking error by means of a periodic test and subsequent repair) or c, $u_4 = 2.1 \cdot 10^{-2}$ tu^{-1}, $z_2=1$ (i.e. $z_1=z_3=z_4=0$), $r_2 = 1/8$h, $q = 1/T_{rep} = 1/1.05$h (manifestation of lurking error with transition rate u_4 before test and repair)
1.2.5	ADC for DC-link voltage measurement	incorrect digital value	none (applying 3 redundant sensors)	plausibility test performed every week	$e = 1.2 \cdot 10^{-3}$ tu^{-1}, $y_0 = 1/168$h ($y_1, y_2, y_3, y_4, y_5 =0$), $r_{4a} = 1/8$h, $q = 1/T_{rep} = 1/1$h
1.9.9	drive-side comparators	upper threshold too low	protection overfunction: protection triggers even in normal operation, shutting off one motor group	threshold test off-line (every 24 hours)	$f = 5.8 \cdot 10^{-4}$ tu^{-4}, $x_3 = 1$ ($x_1, x_2, x_4=0$), $s_2 = 1$, $s_1 = 0$, $r_2 = 1/8$h, $q = 1/T_{rep} = 1/1$h

Fig. 4. Three exemplary lines out of the FMEA table. For the meaning of the transition rates and transition probabilities in the last column compare the symptomatic model (Fig.3). Some of the rates are confidential and therefore given in "time units" tu.

5 FMEA-oriented Markov Model

After finishing the FMEA-table the dependability figures (MTTF, down-time per year, ...) were to be calculated.

As stated above, the Markov model, which is to be used for the mathematical analysis, has to distinguish between failure modes, i.e. associate the states of reduced performance to the lines of the FMEA-table in an unequivocal way. Such a model was constructed by means of a special MATLAB program. Starting with only one state, the OK state, it scans through the FMEA lines one by one and introduces as many additional states as needed. For line 1.2.5 (compare Fig.4) for instance, one needs to introduce one intermediate state (see state 4 in the symptomatic model), one long-lasting state (12a), and one repair state (11) between the general OK-state. These states are shown in the middle of Fig.5.

To give a better impression of how the program works, one could roughly say that for every line of the FMEA-table a corresponding little symptomatic model is placed between the OK-boxes at the left and at the right in Fig.5.

In addition, the program also accounts for the transition rates from the long-lasting states with full performance (near the left OK-box in Fig.5) to any other failure state. Two of these transitions can be found in Fig.5. For all other states – except OK and long-lasting with full power – the lifetime is quite short, i.e. if the system is not OK, it will be repaired relatively quickly. This argument suggests that the approximation made by a single-failure assumption is not very heavy and its effect is probably limited, i.e. it is not necessary to take another failure into account after a first failure has happened, because the time between occurrence of the failure and subsequent transition into the OK state is very short compared with the failure rate constants.

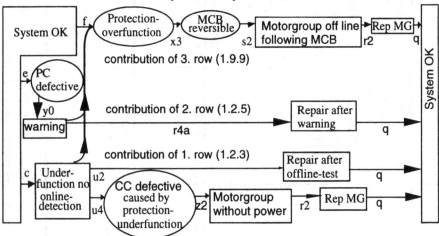

Fig.5. The translation into a Markov representation. The drawing shows only those few states corresponding to the three exemplary FMEA-lines of Fig.4. For reasons of a clear arrangement, the OK-state (being only one general state) is depicted at the left and at the right. In the full Markov model used for calculation there are not only 3 but 113 distinct transitions emanating from the OK state on the left-hand-side. (MCB: Main Circuit Breaker; MG: Motor Group)

A final optimisation step of the program concerns the intermediate (oval) states with zero lifetime. They are removed from the Markov model by adequately multiplying the transition probabilities with the incoming rate constants.

After transforming all 113 lines, the FMEA-oriented Markov model consisted of 253 states where the intermediate states had already been replaced by substituting effective rate constants instead.

6 Calculation of the Different Dependability Figures

Once the FMEA-oriented Markov model is constructed, all kinds of dependability-characterising quantities can be evaluated and analysed. In case of the traction control computing system for the locomotive, the following analyses were carried out:

A) The probabilities of passing through the six principal branches of the symptomatic model were calculated:
1. main circuit-breaker persistently opened (locomotive totally powerless),
2. one motor group (one bogie) without power after shortly triggering the main circuit-breaker,
3. one motor group (one bogie) powerless without triggering the main circuit-breaker,
4. CC partially isolated after shortly triggering the main circuit-breaker,
5. CC partially isolated without triggering the main circuit-breaker,
6. failure without power reduction and subsequent repair.

final state before repair	1.MCB persist-ently open	2. MG down after MCB open	3. MG down	4. CC part. down after MCB open	5. CC par-tially down	6. only a warning with full power
1) probability	$5 \cdot 10^{-7}$	0.2945	0.3627	0.0197	0.2121	0.1110
2) time to final state in tu	$1.5 \cdot 10^{7}$	26.0	21.1	388.7	36.1	68.9

Fig.6. 1) Probabilities of passing through the six principal branches of the symptomatic model, conditioned on leaving the OK state. The sum of the six probabilities is 1.0.
2) Time to reach a final state before repair is needed in time units (tu). A time unit can be assumed to be approximately one year.

In addition the mean time to any of the final states before repair (including the warning-state) is determined 7.653 time units.

B) The reliability in terms of MTTF was calculated by means of solving the integral equations (*compare* Birolini, 1991) for starting in the OK-state. Like in the following analyses C and D, the MTTF depends on the customer's point of view, i.e. which of the six symptomatic scenarios above is considered as up and which as down for the customer's special application.
One customer M may require more than the power from one remaining motorgroup and therefore count the final states 3, 2, and 1 with one powerless motorgroup as down. With this definition, the MTTF is 11.6 time units.

Another customer L, operating only light-weight trains may view only the totally powerless locomotive as down. From this point of view the MTTF is remarkably longer: $1.65 \cdot 10^7$ time units.

C) The availability, or rather the unavailability to be more specific, is calculated by solving the Markov model for the steady-state probabilities of the down states. Since the real values of unavailability cannot be given here because they are confidential, let us assume that the "time units" introduced in the FMEA table were exactly one year, just to have an illustrative example. For the customer L with the light-weight trains, the steady-state unavailability is $6.4 \cdot 10^{-11}$, i.e. $5.6 \cdot 10^{-7}$ hours down-time per year.

The customer M with higher requirements has to expect an unavailability of $8.6 \cdot 10^{-5}$ or 0.75 hours down-time per year.

D) The sensitivity of the MTTFs to changes in the primary failure rates of the components. In contrast to analysing the sensitivity by studying the derivatives with respect to the rates by means of Monte-Carlo simulations (Haverkort and Meeuwissen, 1995) the following numerical approach was used: For all the primary failure rate constants (c, e, f, g) a modified Markov model with 10% reduction of the rate was created and the MTTF equations were solved for each of these modified models. The increase of MTTF upon 10% reduction of the primary rate constant is a sensitivity measure, which allows immediate conclusions about where an improvement could be rewarding. The table below shows the sensitivity results for the both customer requirements and for the three FMEA-lines introduced in Figures 4 and 5. The additional results of lines 4.1.1 and 1.2.1 are the most sensitive for each requirement. They are given for comparison here.

FMEA-line	MTTF increase on 10% reduction of rate constant	
	customer M	customer L
1.2.3	$1.4 \cdot 10^{-6}$ time units	10.1 time units
1.2.5	0	109 time units
1.9.9	$5.7 \cdot 10^{-4}$ time units	1.55 time units
4.1.1	0.20 time units	
1.2.1		$1.20 \cdot 10^6$ time units

Fig.7. Exemplary results of the sensitivity analysis.

The sensitivity analysis in this case shows that improving the fault-tolerance in one of the three exemplary FMEA-lines, for instance increasing the frequency of the offset test in line 1.2.3, would have nearly no impact on the MTTF, because the MTTF is dominated by other faults.

7 Conclusion

For the purpose of analysing the dependability of a computing system controlling the current-converters in a modern electric locomotive, the applied concept proved to be very powerful: A simple and small symptom-oriented model of degradation was used in the phase of interviewing experts and establishing the FMEA-table. For the subsequent analysis a failure-mode-oriented Markov model with a larger number of states is constructed rendering much more clarity, hints on which components have most influence on MTTF, which must possibly be redesigned or planned redundantly. The customer's special application could be taken into account by arbitrarily varying the sets of up- and down-states.

The only drawback of the FMEA-oriented model, the larger number of states (253 in the case presented here) is not a problem with today's powerful numerical tools.

Acknowledgement

The authors wish to thank the "Perseus"-team, especially Daniel Meier and Jörg Bellingen, and the "Camilla"-team, especially Gernot Enzensberger and Roland Manser, for many helpful discussions.

References

Barlow, R.E., J.E. Fussell, N.D. Singpurwalla, eds., (1975). *Reliability and Fault Tree Analysis, Theoretical and Applied Aspects of System Reliability and Safety Assessment.* Society for Industrial and Applied Mathematics (SIAM), Philadelphia.

Birolini, A. (1991). *Qualität und Zuverlässigkeit technischer Systeme.* 3rd edition. Springer, Berlin.

Cai, J. (1994). Reliability of a large consecutive-k-out-of-r-from-n:F system with unequal component-reliability. *IEEE Trans. on Reliability* **43**: 107-111.

Csenski, A. (1994). The number of working periods of a repairable Markov system during a finite time interval. *IEEE Trans. on Reliability* **43**: 163-169.

Dungan, J.B., K.S. Trivedi, R.M. Geist, N. Victor. (1984). Extended stochastic Petri nets: Applications and Analysis. In: *Performance 84,* E. Gelenbe, ed., Elsevier, Amsterdam.

Geist, R.M., K.S. Trivedi. (1990). Reliability estimation of fault-tolerant systems: Tools and techniques, *IEEE Computer,* Vol. 23, 52-62.

Haverkort, B.R., A.M.H. Meeuwissen (1995). Sensitivity & uncertainty analysis of Markov-reward models. *IEEE Trans. on Reliability* **44**: 147-154.

Kim, K., K.S. Park. (1994). Phased-mission system reliability under Markov environment. *IEEE Trans. on Reliability* **43**: 301-309.

Laprie, J.-C. (ed.) (1992). Dependable computing and fault tolerant systems (Vol.5); Dependability: Basic Concepts and terminology. Springer, Wien, New York.

Laprie, J.C., C. Beounes, M. Kaâniche K. Kanoun (1990). The transformation approach to the modelling and evaluation of the reliability and availability growth. *Proc. 20th IEEE Int. Symp. Fault-Tolerant Computing.* pp. 364-371.

Sericola, B. (1994). Interval-availability distribution of 2-state systems with exponential failures and phase type repairs. *IEEE Trans. on Reliability* **43**: 335-343.

Zhao, M. (1994). Availability for repairable components and series systems. *IEEE Trans. on Reliability* **43**: 329-334.

Dependability Models of RAID Using Stochastic Activity Networks

Vicente Santonja, Marina Alonso, Javier Molero,
Juan J. Serrano, Pedro Gil and Rafael Ors

Departamento de Ingeniería de Sistemas, Computadores y Automática
Universitat Politècnica de València.
Apdo. 22012   46071 València. Spain

Abstract. The development of CTMCs to model RAIDs with a general failure-repair process seems a complex task. The introduction of a technique with higher modeling level, that facilitates the description of the failure-repair processes is essential to deepen in the dependability analysis of these systems.

In this paper, different dependability models of RAID level 5 are presented. The chosen technique is an extension of timed Petri nets known as Stochastic Activity Networks (SAN). As will be shown, it is relatively simple to describe a SAN equivalent to the developed CTMC. This model will be called the basic model. Furthermore, the flexibility introduced by these nets, through the cases associated with its timed activities and the input and output gates, allows an extension of the basic SAN model in order to obtain more accurate results or to adapt it to a new specification of the system operation. Thus, the basic model will be modified to represent the repair process with detail, differentiating its two phases: replacement and reconstruction. Also, the influence of a limited number of on-line spares on the reliability of the system will be considered. Thereinafter, using the structure of the basic model, a SAN of a RAID with a higher protection level (RAID level 6) is presented.

1   Introduction

Redundancy techniques were introduced initially in disk arrays to equal their reliability with a single conventional disk. However, recent studies and the accumulated experience demonstrate that these techniques are adapted to build secondary storage subsystems with very high availability at a reasonable cost. As the use of RAIDs is becoming more generalized, the reliable storage of large quantities of information depends, mainly, on their correct behavior. Thus, the detailed analysis of their dependability is becoming increasingly urgent and necessary.

In this paper, different dependability models of redundant arrays of inexpensive disks (RAIDs) are presented. The modeling task begins using continuous time Markov chains (CTMC). Several authors agree to apply this technique to accomplish this kind of analysis [1, 2, 3]. Some assumptions of the model and a careful analysis of the system symmetries to be modeled will allow us to develop a CTMC with a moderate number of states. Specifically, a CTMC of a RAID level 5 with orthogonal organization is designed. In order to simplify the model, it is assumed that there is a large number of on-line spare disks in such a way that the disk repair time is reduced to the duration of the reconstruction process of its information, since replacement time is negligible.

The development of CTMCs to model RAIDs with a more general failure-repair process seems to be a complex task. The introduction of a technique with higher modeling level, that facilitates the description of the failure-repair processes, including all the dependencies that are generated in these processes, is essential to study in depth the RAID dependability.

In this work the chosen technique is an extension of timed Petri nets known as Stochastic Activity Networks (SAN) [4, 5]. As will be shown, it is relatively simple to describe a SAN equivalent to the developed CTMC. This model will be called the basic model. Furthermore, the flexibility introduced by these nets, through the cases associated with its timed activities and the input and output gates, allows an extension of the basic SAN model to obtain more accurate results or to adapt it to a new specification of the system operation. Thus, the basic model will be modified to represent the repair process with detail, differentiating its two phases: replacement and reconstruction. Also, the influence of a limited number of on-line spares on the system reliability will be considered. Thereinafter, using the structure of the basic model, a SAN of a RAID with a higher protection level (RAID level 6) is presented.

This work presents a set of models that serve as a test bench to study various configurations of RAIDs and different maintenance policies evaluating their impact on the system dependability.

Throughout the paper, it will be assumed that a RAID is composed by $G \times N$ disks, this is, the disks are organized in G parity groups of N disks each one.

The rest of the paper is organized as follows. In Sect. 2, a short overview of previous work in the area is presented. In Sect. 3 y 4 the failure and recovery processes in a RAID are analyzed. Section 5 reviews *UltraSAN* tool that has been used in the modeling and evaluation of different RAID organizations. The two following sections are devoted to the dependability analysis of the orthogonal organization in RAIDs level 5 and 6, using Markov models and stochastic activity networks. Finally, Sect. 8 presents the conclusions.

2 Related Work

The interest on reaching a high dependability and to develop models and techniques to evaluate this characteristic is closely bound to the development of RAID systems. In the early papers by the RAID team of Berkeley [6, 7], the MTTF of a RAID is evaluated, under the assumption that only disks can fail (other components of the RAID are safe).

The influence of the support hardware —controllers, power supplies, SCSI host bus adapters (HBA), cooling equipment and cabling— on RAID dependability is investigated in [8]. To avoid that one of these components may become a single point failure, an *orthogonal organization* is proposed in [8]. In this organization, the set of disks sharing the same support hardware components —disks connected through a common bus to the same controller, with the same cooling system and power supply— is orthogonal to the parity group. This organization is shown in Fig. 1. As we can see, the disks are organized in a two dimensional grid with each row representing a parity group and each column can be denoted as a *support hardware group* or a *string*. The failure of one support component may render a single disk in each parity group inaccessible, but this is recoverable. Hence, using the redundancy stored in the disks it is possible to survive the failure of a support component. As soon as the component is repaired, the information of its drives —which is lost or out-of-date— must be rebuilt and, meanwhile, the requests addressed to the unavailable disks can be served by on-the-fly reconstructions.

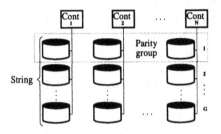

Fig. 1. *A RAID with orthogonal organization.*

Gibson [1] presents a comprehensive study of RAIDs dependability. His analysis, based on analytical models, Markov chains and simulation, focuses on the orthogonal organization. Markov models are based on the assumption that time to failure of a disk group is exponentially distributed. Some measures of the reliability improvements that can be obtained with the use of on-line spare disks are also derived. He shows how the inclusion of a small pool of on-line spares is enough to obtain substantial benefits. Moreover, a RAID with parity based redundancy and on-line spares can get higher reliability at lower cost than a mirrored disk array with the same amount of user data.

Malhotra [2] derives approximated dependability measures of orthogonal RAID using continuous time Markov chains. In his models, imperfect coverage and various failure modes are included.

It has been pointed out in [9] that the three following factors have a major influence on RAID dependability. First, parity inconsistencies may follow a system crash due to an interrupted write operation that has updated parity but not data or vice versa. If a disk fails, inconsistencies may hinder the reconstruction process. Second, common or correlated failure modes can appear due to environmental factors, organization of the RAID or manufacture defects. And third, uncorrectable bit errors may occur during the reconstruction of a disk, precluding the reconstruction for completing successfully.

Aside from the orthogonal organization, the dependability studies are restricted to an approximate derivation of the MTTDL [10].

3   The Failure Process of The RAID

Whenever a disk fails, the surviving disks within its parity group increase their load by a factor γ, since they must serve their own requests plus the requests directed to the failed disk. Depending on the size of those requests, the load in each surviving disk increases up to 100% servicing on-the-fly reconstructions and even more during the reconstruction onto a replacement. The increased workload in the system could lead to further degradation of system reliability. According to [3, 11] the failure rate of the overloaded disks, λ_s, can be obtained from $\lambda_s = \gamma^\alpha \lambda_d$, where λ_d is the disk failure rate and $\alpha \approx 1$.

In addition to disk unit failures, we must consider operation failures caused by uncorrectable bit errors in read requests. If, after a sequence of retries, it is not possible to read the contents of a bit, the error is declared unrecoverable. Then the sector can be reconstructed from the redundant data in the array into a free sector of the affected disk [1, 2, 8]. This sector reconstruction takes place in a very short time and will not be considered in our models. However, when an error of this kind occurs during the reconstruction process that follows a disk failure, the consequences are catastrophic [9], since neither the reconstruction can progress nor the error recovery is possible. Let p_b be the probability of an unrecoverable bit error. The probability of reading the entire disk without error is $P_{\text{Disk}} = (1 - p_b)^B$, where B is the disk capacity in bits. The probability of successfully performing a reconstruction without the occurrence of an error of this kind, in a RAID level 5, is $P_R = P_{\text{Disk}}^{N-1}$.

In the following models, we will assume that the computer has the appropriated mechanisms to handle the parity inconsistencies resulting after system crashes during write operations. In order to avoid this problem, information concerning the consistent/inconsistent state of each parity sector must be logged into nonvolatile storage before executing each write operation. So after a system crash the interrupted write can be consistently repeated [9].

A realistic model of the RAID behavior must take into account that other components in the RAID, the components of the support hardware, can fail too. As has been seen, the orthogonal organization helps to tolerate this kind of failures. It will be assumed that the lifetime of the support components in a string, as a whole, have an exponential distribution with rate λ_c.

4   The Repair Process of The RAID

The repair of a failed disk in a RAID is a two-step process: disk replacement and data reconstruction. The length of the first step depends on the availability of spare disks. According to the maintenance policy, it ranges from minutes to days. During this time the system is vulnerable and is exposed to a second failure that would lead to the data loss. Replacement time can be greatly reduced by using on-line spare disks. These are electrically connected disks that come into service automatically when one disk fails.

Reconstruction time is highly variable and depends on many factors. If reconstruction is considered a priority process —over users requests— and the controllers and other related components have enough bandwidth, reconstruction of a disk can take place in a few minutes [12]. But this figure can be considered rather optimistic. The components implied in the process are not designed usually with enough bandwidth. Moreover, in some applications the delay experienced by the users may be unacceptable. Continuous-operation systems like on-line transaction processing (OLTP) systems, for example, mandate a minimum acceptable level of responsiveness (the TPC-A benchmark requires that 90% of all transactions complete under two seconds) [13]. So it is necessary to service user requests while rebuilding is going on. Both rebuilding and users requests compete for service resulting in a trade-off between reliability and performance. All these facts considerably increase the reconstruction time.

According to the repair sequence just described, the repair time distribution has two components. The first is a time with almost deterministic distribution that corresponds to the replacement time. The second, with exponential distribution, is the reconstruction time that can present higher variability, depending on the load that the RAID sustains while the reconstruction takes place. In spite of these peculiarities of the repair time that hinder the development of markovian dependability models, in [1, 14] it is shown, using simulation results, that the exponential distribution is a good approximation for the repair times (the authors detect an error close to 5%). In our models we will consider that the repair time is exponentially distributed with rate μ_d. When there are on-line spare disks, the replacement time can be neglected. In this case, the repair time is limited to the reconstruction time. The repair rate of the support components in a string is μ_c.

5   Evaluation Methodology

Section 6 begins the dependability modeling of disk arrays using continuous time Markov chains. The CTMCs are built enumerating all the states that the system reaches as a consequence of the fault occurrence and the corresponding repair actions, and indicating how the system transits from one state to another. Though it is possible to develop manually CTMCs for simple systems, when the complexity increases, the modeling task by means of CTMC becomes intractable. In this paper, two non-excluding approximations are taken: the symmetries of the system are exploited in order to design a CTMC with the smaller possible size, and on the other hand, when the system complexity requires it, we will resort to the stochastic activity nets. The use of SANs allows a much simpler way to describe the system behavior. From the SAN specification it is possible to automatically generate the equivalent CTMC.

Stochastic activity networks, developed by Meyer and Sanders [15, 16, 17], are an extension of the timed Petri nets. A team directed by Sanders, initially in the University of Arizona and currently in the University of Illinois at Urbana-Champaign, has developed a tool for the specification and solution of SAN known as *UltraSAN* [4].

SAN are comprised of *places, activities, input gates* and *output gates*. The places can hold *tokens*. The number of tokens in each place of the net defines the *marking* of the SAN. There are two types of activities. The *timed* activities represent those actions that take place in the system and whose duration has a relevant effect on its behavior. An *activity time distribution*, possibly marking dependent, is associated to each timed activity. The *instantaneous* activities, on the other hand, have so small duration that it can be neglected without affecting to the performance indices given by the SAN.

The marking of the SAN changes when an activity *completes*. So that an activity could complete, it must be previously *enabled*. After its completion, the marking of the SAN is modified to reflect the new state of the system. The possibility that after the completion of an activity the system could progress toward different states is modeled in SANs by mean of *cases*. Each case of an activity has a discrete probability distribution associated that can be marking dependent.

Input and output gates connect places and activities. They offer the necessary flexibility to specify under which marking each activity is enabled and the changes on the marking due to an activity completion. Input gates consist of a *predicate* and a *function*. Output gates only have a function. The predicate of an input gate is a boolean expression of its input places; when the value of the predicate is true, it is said that the input gate holds. A line from a place to an activity represents an *implicit* input gate. This gate holds when there is at least one token in its input place. A user defined input gate replaces this default predicate. An activity is enabled when all its input gates holds. When an activity completes, the functions of its input gates are executed first and, then, the functions of its output gates. The function associated with the implicit output gate consists in removing a mark from its input place. The implicit output gate is represented with a line from an activity to a place and its function is to add a mark to its output place. An output gate defined by the user replaces this default function. Input and output functions are specified using statements of the C programming language.

6 RAID Level 5 Dependability Models

In this section, CMTC and SAN based models of RAID level 5 are presented. Section 6.1 presents a basic model. Sections 6.2 and 6.3 modify this basic model to remove the on-line spare disks or include a limited number of them, respectively.

6.1 RAID Level 5 Basic Model

The support hardware components whose failure will be considered in the following dependability models are the controllers and the cables that link disks

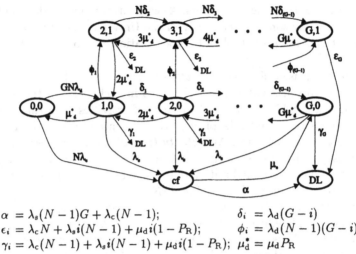

$$\alpha = \lambda_s(N-1)G + \lambda_c(N-1); \qquad\qquad \delta_i = \lambda_d(G-i)$$
$$\epsilon_i = \lambda_c N + \lambda_s i(N-1) + \mu_d i(1-P_R); \qquad \phi_i = \lambda_d(N-1)(G-i)$$
$$\gamma_i = \lambda_c(N-1) + \lambda_s i(N-1) + \mu_d i(1-P_R); \quad \mu_d^* = \mu_d P_R$$

Fig. 2. *Markov model of an orthogonal RAID.*

to controllers. Failures in the power supply are ignored as they can be easily avoided using an uninterruptable power supply (UPS).

The failure of a support component renders the data of a string inaccessible during a period time. After this period, these data are obsolete, since the attention to user requests has continued (in particular write operations) while the repair of the failed component lasts. Later, the information in all the disks at the column affected by the failure must be reconstructed.

Model Based on CTMC. For the sake of brevity, we will refer with the term *controller* to the set comprised of a controller and cables. The system operation is now more complex since there are different causes that can lead to the data loss in the RAID:

1. A disk failure followed by another disk failure in the same group.
2. A disk failure followed by a controller failure in a different string.
3. A controller failure followed by a disk failure in a different string.
4. A controller failure followed by another controller failure.

The Fig. 2 shows the Markov model of an orthogonal RAID with $G \times N$ disks corresponding to that behavior. The model size is $2G+2$ states. The state of the disk array is represented by (i, a), where $i \in (0, \ldots, G)$ is the number of failed disks. The system tolerates up to G disk failures as long as they occur in different parity groups. The second element, $a \in (0, 1)$, has the value 0 when all the failed disks are aligned in the same column; otherwise, $a = 1$. When the failed disks are on the same column, the failure of a controller causes the RAID failure (state DL) with probability $1/N$ or it is tolerated with probability $1 - 1/N$. In the case of non-aligned failed disks ($a = 1$), the failure of a controller leads necessarily (with probability 1) to the RAID failure.

When a controller fails, the system transits to state cf. After the repair or replacement of the controller, the content of the disks of its *string* has become out of date. So, all the disks in the string should be submitted to a reconstruction process of their information. This process takes place concurrently in each parity group.

To simplify the model, we assume that, among the two components of the disk repair time, replacement and reconstruction, the first can be neglected. This assumption implies that whenever a disk fails, on-line spare disks are available.

A pessimistic assumption has been made in the model. When there are some non-aligned failed disks —states $(i, 1)$— the disk repair is done following an order that keeps the non-alignment until the penultimate failed disk is repaired. As the non-alignment of the disks exposes the system to a controller failure that would lead to the RAID failure, this repairing strategy is pessimistic.

Model Based on SAN. An accurate CTMC model of the system operation that considers separately the replacement and reconstruction times presents high complexity and large size. To make the modeling and analysis of these systems easier, it is necessary to resort to higher level techniques that offer a much more concise description of system behavior. In this section we present a model based on stochastic activity networks.

As a starting point, an orthogonal RAID that verifies the same assumptions made in the CTMC in Fig. 2 is modeled using SAN. In particular, we will assume that there are infinite on-line spare disks and, thus, the repair time is equal to the reconstruction time. This *basic model* will be modified in subsequent sections to limit the size of the on-line spare pool.

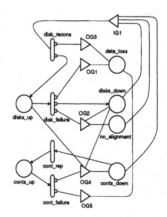

Fig. 3. *SAN model of a RAID level 5 with orthogonal organization and infinite on-line spares.*

The stochastic activity network of the basic model, shown in the Fig. 3, contains the following places:

disks_up Initially it contains $D = G \times N$ tokens, corresponding to the failure-free disks.

disks_down Contains the disks that after the failure have been replaced and are in the reconstruction process.

conts_up Initially it contains N tokens corresponding to the controllers (support hardware) of each one of the N columns (*strings*).

conts_down Initially it is empty. It can contain one token representing the system with a failed controller.

no_alignment The concept of *alignment* is used to refer to the concentration of failed disks in just one column. This *state information* is introduced in the model because it is necessary to decide if the failure of a controller will lead or not to the RAID failure. When the failed disks are aligned in a column, the failure of the controller corresponding to this *string* will be tolerated, while the failure of any other controller will produce the data loss. If the failed disks are not aligned, the failure of any controller induces, immediately, the RAID failure. Initially this place is empty. When the number of failed disks is greater or equal to two, this place can contain a token indicating that the failures are not aligned.

data_loss When a token appears in this place the RAID has failed, losing the information that it contained.

Actions considered in the model are represented by *activities*. The time distribution associated with each activity appears in Table 1 in the Appendix. The meaning of the activities is the following:

disk_failure Failure of a disk. This activity contains three cases corresponding to the following situations[1]: 1. The disk failure leads to the failure of the RAID. 2. The disk failure is tolerated and it is the first failure or it is aligned with the other existing failed disks. 3. The disk failure is tolerated. It produces non-alignment.

disk_recons Reconstruction of a disk. It has two cases: 1. The reconstruction fails due to an irrecoverable error in the reading of a bit. 2. The reconstruction completes successfully.

cont_failure Failure of a controller. It has the following cases: 1. If there are not failed disks, the failure is tolerated. If the there are failed disks, these should be aligned and the failure will be tolerated as long as the just failed controller belongs to the same string as the failed disks. 2. Otherwise the failure of the controller leads to data loss.

cont_rep Repair of a controller.

Probabilities associated with these activity cases are specified according to *UltraSAN* rules, in Table 2 in the Appendix.

The goal of the output gates OG1, OG3 and OG5, described in Table 3, is to carry the SAN to a predetermined marking (a token in the place data_loss and

---

[1] The enumeration order corresponds to the graphic representation, numbering the cases from top to bottom.

no tokens in the other places) when data loss is reached. In this way, we avoid that a same state —RAID failure— would be represented by different markings, thus, achieving an important reduction in the reachability space. According to SAN definition, a connection from these three gates to each one of the places in the network must exist in Fig. 3, since the functions associated with these gates modify the marking in all places. However, only the connection with the place data_loss has been drawn in order to increase the graph clarity. Functions of gates OG2 and OG4 can be easily deduced from their definition in Table 3.

Input gate IG1 defines the conditions that must hold to make possible disk reconstruction. Specifically, when there is a failed controller, disk reconstruction is not possible. The function associated with this gate defines the marking changes that must be done after a disk repair (completion of the activity disk_recons).

Note that, again, a pessimistic assumption has been made. We assume that until the penultimate disk is not repaired the token in no_alignment (if any) can not be removed.

The CTMC generated by this SAN model is exactly the same as the one obtained in the previous section (Fig. 2). Thus, the number of generated states is $2G + 2$.

Numerical Results. Using these two equivalent models, some numerical results are presented. Figure 4 plots the 10-years reliability for a set of systems with different number of disks and variable configuration. The parameters used in this and the following graphics are: $P_{\text{Disk}} = 0.9996$, $\lambda_c = \lambda_d = 1/150000 \text{ hours}^{-1}$, $\lambda_s = 2\lambda_d$, $\mu_c = \mu_d = 1/24 \text{ hours}^{-1}$. The reduction in system reliability as the size of the parity group and the number of groups increase is shown in this figure.

Figure 5 displays the reliability corresponding to the different orthogonal configurations that can be build with a fixed number of disks. Considering only the cost of the disks, all the configurations compared in this graph have the same cost. As expected, the configuration devoting a greater number of disks to parity, 50×2, has the highest reliability. Actually it is a RAID level 1. Figure 6 shows a similar result, but now with a fixed number of data disks, that is, all the configurations have the same user capacity. Again, the reliability depends on the proportion of data and parity disks. Repair times of disks and controllers also have a decisive influence in the RAID reliability. System vulnerability depends on the length of these processes, as we can see in Fig. 7.

6.2 RAID Level 5 Without On-Line Spares

From the model in Fig. 3 it is easy to design a new model where the actions of replacement and reconstruction of a disk are considered separately. This is essential when there are not on-line spares. In that case, replacement time can not be neglected. To take into account this new system behavior, we make some minor modifications in the model: a new place, disk_in_rec, and two new activities, disk_rec_fail and disk_replace, are added to the SAN model of RAID level 5, as Fig. 8 shows.

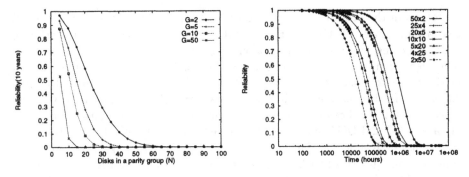

Fig. 4. *10-years reliability of different G × N RAID configurations.*

Fig. 5. *Reliability of different fixed cost RAIDs. Number of disks in the RAID: 100.*

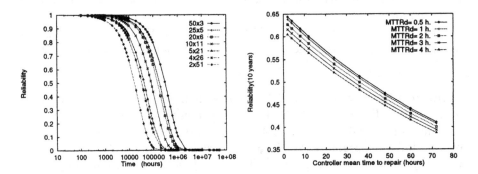

Fig. 6. *Reliability of different fixed capacity RAIDs. Capacity: 100 data disks.*

Fig. 7. *10-years reliability of a RAID 10 × 10 as a function of disk and controller repair times.*

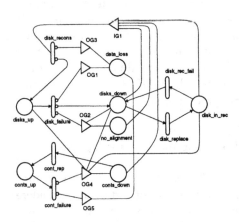

Fig. 8. *SAN model of a RAID level 5 with orthogonal organization without on-line spares.*

The only differences between this model and the previous one come from two places:

disk_in_rec Contains as many tokens as disks have been replaced and are undergoing the reconstruction process of its information.

disks_down This place was in the previous model but here it represents disks waiting to be replaced,

and two activities:

disk_replace A failed disk is replaced and the new disk undergoes reconstruction phase. The activity time is exponentially distributed with a marking dependent rate $\mu_{rpl}*$MARK(disks_down).

disk_rec_fail A disk that was undergoing reconstruction fails. The activity time has a exponential distribution with rate λ_d*MARK(disk_in_rec).

Probabilities associated with the cases of each activity in this new SAN model can be obtained substituting, in Table 2, the number of tokens in the place disks_down by the sum of tokens in the places disks_down and disk_in_rec. Input and output gate definitions are similar to those defined in Table 3, and some minor changes can be easily deduced from Fig. 8.

6.3 RAID Level 5 With On-Line Spares

It is possible to introduce the effect of a limited pool of on-line spare disks in the previous model. The modifications that must be introduced in the SAN model in the Fig. 8 are shown in Fig. 9.

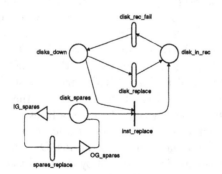

Fig. 9. *Modification to be made in the previous models to consider a limited pool of on-line spare disks.*

The instantaneous activity inst_replace determines that while there are available on-line spare disks, the replacement phase is immediate; when spares are exhausted the delay experimented in this phase is fixed by the timed activity disk_replace.

The predicate associated with the input gate IG_spares defines when new spares should be reordered to refill the spare pool. When IG_spares holds, activity spares_replace is enabled. Its completion time is determined by the maintenance policy and the disk delivery time. Finally, the functions associated with gates IG_spares and OG_spares will update the marking in the place disk_spares after the replacement.

Thus, using the SAN flexibility, it is easy to test different reorder policies of spare disks and to evaluate their impact on the system reliability. This can be done simply by changing the definition of IG_spares and OG_spares without modifying the SAN structure. For example, it could be decided that certain quantity of new spares should be reordered when the number of spares falls under a given threshold.

7 RAID Level 6 Dependability Model

The model of the RAID level 6, shown in Fig. 10, has a structure similar to the previous SAN models though with some differences reflecting the capacity of this organization to tolerate double disk failures within a same parity group. The place disks_down has been substituted by the places row1 and row2 which marking correspond to the number of parity groups in which there is a simple or double disk failure respectively.

Again, we suppose that there are infinite on-line spare disks. Thus, the repair time is reduced to the reconstruction time. Reconstructions are represented in the SAN through the activities row1_repair and row2_repair. The reconstruction of two failed disks in a parity group can fail due to an irrecoverable error in the reading of the $N - 2$ surviving disks in the group. The possibility that the reconstruction is successfully completed or fails is modeled through the two cases of the activity row2_repair. However, during the repair of a single failure, if an irrecoverable reading error occurs in one of the disks that participates in the reconstruction, the redundancy included in a RAID level 6 permits an on-the-fly regeneration of the information, so that the reconstruction process could continue without additional problems. This regeneration is accomplished in a negligible time, therefore it will not be considered in the SAN model. Activity row1_repair models the reconstruction of single failures.

As in the previous models, the concept of *alignment* is used to refer to the grouping of failed disks around some few columns. Once again, the introduction of this information in the model is justified by the need to decide if the failure of a controller leads or not to the RAID failure. When the failed disks are grouped around 1 or 2 columns, the failure of the one of their controllers is tolerated, while the failure of any other controller leads to the data loss.

For a RAID level 6, the relevant fact that must be considered in the model is the alignment that could exist between the double failures (parity groups with 2 failed disks). Specifically:

- If there is not any parity group with two failed disks (see Fig. 11A) the failure of any controller can be tolerated. The failure of a controller will lead, in the

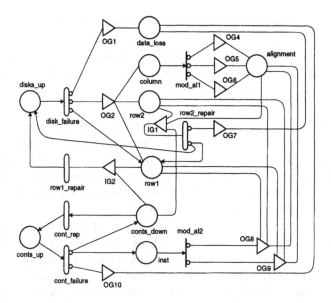

Fig. 10. *SAN model of a RAID level 6 with orthogonal organization.*

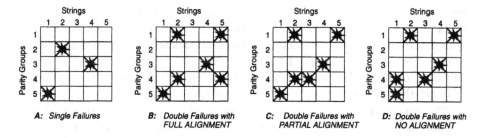

Fig. 11. *Failures distribution in a RAID level 6.*

worst case, to the existence of two failed (or inaccessible) disk within the same group; this situation can be tolerated in a RAID level 6.

- If there is only one group with two failed disks, the controller failure is tolerated with probability $2/N$. This is because there are N controllers and only the failure of one of the two which are in the same column as the failed disks is tolerated. Therefore, the failure of a controller will lead to data loss with probability $1 - 2/N$.
- If there are several groups with double disk failure the situation is more complex. In this case the concept of alignment plays an important role. We review the different cases:
  - If double failures are *fully aligned* (see Fig. 11B) the situation is the same as in the previous point.
  - If the double failures are *partially aligned* (see Fig. 11C) only the failure of the controller associated to the column with multiple failures is tolerated.

Thus, the conditional probability of tolerating the failure of a controller is $1/N$.

- If there is no *alignment* (see Fig. 11D) between the double failures, the controller failure will lead necessarily to the data loss, since a triple failure will appear in one or more groups.

It is important to emphasize that the existence of single failures in other groups does not modify in any way the behavior just described, since these groups can always tolerate the failure of an additional disk. Summarizing, the information that should be stored in the model must be enough to distinguish between the three previous cases, that is, if the double failures (when they exist) are fully aligned, partially aligned or non-aligned.

To register this information, the place alignment has been included in the model. This place can contain 0, 1 or 2 tokens corresponding to the three afore-mentioned possibilities. The updating of place alignment marking after the failure/repair of a disk/controller, is a complex task. Specifically, in the case of disks failures, the maintenance of the place alignment has been assigned to the instantaneous activity mod_al1. Thus, the definition of disk_failure is simplified. The three cases of this activity only decide if the failure of the disk leads to data loss (case 1), generates a double failure (case 2) or a simple failure (case 3). Since the alignment only can be altered by the occurrence of a new double failure, only in the case 2 a token is located in the place column which immediately after enables the activity mod_al1. This activity decides (probabilistically) how the new double failure affects the alignment level. The output gates OG4, OG5 and OG6 are the responsible of updating the marking of alignment.

The role of the instantaneous activity mod_al2 is similar: together with the output gates OG8 and OG9, it is entrusted with updating the alignment after a controller failure. This activity decides if the controller failure will increase or not the alignment level. Again, upon moving this decision to mod_al1 the definition of cont_failure has been simplified as now it only must decide, through its two cases, if the controller failure can be or not tolerated.

In the disk repair process a pessimistic assumption has been made: it is supposed that only when the number of double failures falls to one, the tokens of the place alignment (if any) are removed.

Output gates OG1, OG7 and OG10 are included to carry the system to the failure marking. As in previous models, for the sake of clarity, the connections of these gates with each one of the places in the SAN have not been drawn. The size of the Markov chain generated by this SAN is $2 + (G + 1)(3G + 2)/2$.

In [18] there is a detailed specification of input/output gate functions and a description of the probabilities associated with the activity cases.

Figures 12 and 13 show some numerical results obtained from the SAN resolution. It can be observed that RAID level 6 presents a high reliability within its useful lifetime, estimated in 10 years as a maximum. During this period of time, the probability of a data loss is very small even for extremely high disk reconstruction and controller repair times.

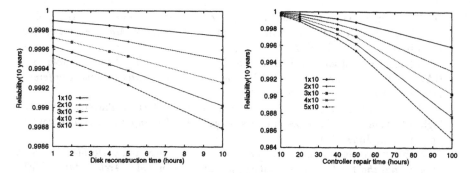

Fig. 12. *10-years reliability for various configurations G × N of RAID level 6 as a function of disk reconstruction time.*

Fig. 13. *10-years reliability for various configurations G × N of RAID level 6 as a function of the mean time to repair a controller*

8 Conclusions

This paper shows that Markov chains have a limited applicability to model the dependability of disk arrays, due to large number of states that are generated even for moderate size systems. As alternative to this modeling technique, the stochastic activity networks present a more appropriated solution. Their higher expressive power and their flexibility make of SANs a suitable tool to model this kind of systems.

In this work, it has been shown how from a RAID level 5 basic model, it is possible to undertake various modifications with relative ease. These modifications can help in the study of various replacement policies. Also the general structure of the SAN model corresponding to the RAID level 5 has been extended to build a dependability model for the RAID level 6.

References

1. G. A. Gibson, *Redundant Disk Arrays: Reliable, Parallel Secondary Storage*. MIT Press, 1992.
2. M. Malhotra, *Specification and Solution of Dependability Models of Fault-Tolerant Systems*. PhD thesis, Duke University, May 1993.
3. R. Geist and K. S. Trivedi, "An analytic treatment of the reliability and performance of mirrored disk subsystems," in *FTCS-23*, pp. 442–450, June 1993.
4. Centre for Reliable and High-Performance Computing. Coordinated Science Laboratory. University of Illinois at Urbana-Champaign, *UltraSAN. Users's Manual. Version 3.0.* 1995.
5. W. Sanders, W. Obal II, M. Qureshi, and F. Widjanarko, "UltraSAN version 3: architecture, features and implementation," Tech. Rep. 95S02, Center for Reliable and High-Performance Computing. Coordinated Science Laboratory. University of Illinois at Urbana-Champaign, 1995.
6. R. H. Katz, G. A. Gibson, and D. A. Patterson, "Disk system architectures for high performance computing," *Proc. IEEE*, vol. 77, pp. 1842–1858, Dec. 1989.

7. D. A. Patterson, G. Gibson, and R. H. Katz, "A case for redundant arrays of inexpensive disks (RAID)," in *In International Conference on Management of Data (SIGMOD). ACM.*, (N. Y. ACM, ed.), pp. 109–116, June 1988.

8. M. Schulze, G. Gibson, R. H. Katz, and D. A. Patterson, "How reliable is a RAID?," in *Procedures of the IEEE Computer Society International Conference (COMPCON)*, pp. 118–123, Spring 1989.

9. P. M. Chen, E. K. Lee, G. A. Gibson, R. H. Katz, and D. A. Patterson, "RAID: high-performance, reliable secondary storage," *ACM Computing Surveys*, vol. 26, pp. 145–185, June 1994.

10. S. W. Ng, "Crosshatch disk array for improved reliability and performance," in *In Proceedings the 1994 International Symposium on Computer Architecture*, (IEEE, ed.), (New York), 1994.

11. R. K. Iyer, D. J. Rosetti, and M. C. Hsueh, "Measurement and modeling of computer reliability as affected by system activity," *ACM Transactions on Computer Systems*, vol. 4, pp. 214–237, 1986.

12. H. M. Sierra, *An Introduction to Direct Access Storage Devices.* Academic Press, 1990.

13. M. Holland, G. A. Gibson, and D. P. Siewiorek, "Fast, on-line failure recovery in redundant disk arrays," in *Proceedings of the 23rd International Symposium on Fault Tolerant Computing*, (Washington, D.C.), pp. 422–431, IEEE Computer Society, 1993.

14. G. A. Gibson and D. A. Patterson, "Designing disk arrays for high data reliability," *Journal of Parallel and Distributed Computing*, vol. 17, pp. 4–27, Jan. 1993.

15. J. Meyer, A. Movaghar, and W. Sanders, "Stochastic activity networks: structure, behavior and application," in *Proceedings of the International Conference on Timed Petri Nets*, (Torino, Italy), pp. 106–115, July 1985.

16. J. Meyer and W. Sanders, "Specification and construction of performability models," in *Proceedings of the Second International Workshop on Performability Modeling of Computer and Communication Systems*, (Mont Saint-Michel, France), pp. 28–30, June 1993.

17. W. Sanders and J. Meyer, "Reduced base model construction methods for stochastic activity networks," *IEEE Journal on Selected Areas in Communications*, vol. 9, pp. 25–36, Jan. 1991.

18. V. Santonja, *Evaluación y modelado de prestaciones y garantía de funcionamiento en matrices redundantes de discos (RAID).* PhD thesis, Universitat Politècnica de València, Jul 1996.

9 Appendix

The specification of a SAN is composed by a graphic representation and different tables that define the activities and gates included in the models. In this appendix we include the tables of the SANs that have been used in the paper[2].

---

[2] All tables shown in this appendix use the notation specified by the tool *UltraSAN*. However, the syntax has been simplified in some aspects to improve their legibility. The function MARK() returns the number of tokens in a place.

Table 1. Activity Time Distributions for the SAN Model of a RAID level 5

Activity	Distribution	Activity	Distribution
disk_failure	$\exp(\lambda_d*\text{MARK}(\text{disks\_up}))$	disk_recons	$\exp(\mu_{reco}*\text{MARK}(\text{disks\_down}))$
cont_failure	$\exp(\lambda_c*\text{MARK}(\text{conts\_up}))$	cont_rep	$\exp(\mu_c)$

Table 2. Activity Case Probabilities for the SAN Model of a RAID level 5

cont_failure

1 if (MARK(disks_down) ==0) return(1.0);
 if ((MARK(no_alignment) >0) || (MARK(conts_down) >0)) return(0.0);
 return(1/N);

2 if (MARK(disks_down) ==0) return(0.0);
 if ((MARK(no_alignment) >0) || (MARK(conts_down) >0)) return(1.0);
 return(1-1/N);

disk_failure
1 if (MARK(disks_down) ==0) return(0.0); if (MARK(disks_down) ==G) return(1.0);   return(MARK(disks_down)*(N-1)/MARK(disks_up));
2 if (MARK(disks_down) ==0) return(1.0); if (MARK(disks_down) ==G) return(0.0);   return((1−(MARK(disks_down)*(N-1)/MARK(disks_up)))/N);
3 if (MARK(disks_down) ==0) return(0.0); if (MARK(disks_down) ==G) return(0.0);   return((1−(MARK(disks_down) * (N-1)/MARK(disks_up))) * (1−1/N));

disk_recons
1 return(1.0−pow(P_{Disk}, $N-1$));
2 return(pow(P_{Disk}, $N-1$));

Table 3. Input and Output Gate Definitions for the SAN Model of a RAID level 5

Gate	Definition
IG1	*Predicate* (MARK(disks_down) >0) && (MARK(conts_down) ==0) *Function* MARK(disks_down) − −; if (MARK(disks_down) == 1) MARK(no_alignment) =0;

Gate	Definition	Gate	Definition
OG1	MARK(disks_up) =0;	OG2	MARK(no_alignment) =1;
OG3	MARK(conts_up) =0;		MARK(disks_down) + +;
OG5	MARK(data_loss) =1;		
	MARK(disks_down) =0;	OG4	MARK(disks_down) =G;
	MARK(no_alignment) =0;		MARK(conts_down) =1;
	MARK(conts_down) =0;		MARK(disks_up) =D−G;

Session 4

Fault Tolerant Design

Chair: Bjarne E. Helvik, SINTEF Telecom and Informatics, Norway

Compiler Assisted Self-Checking of Structural Integrity Using Return Address Hashing

Uwe Wildner

Max-Planck-Society
Fault-Tolerant Computing Group at the University of Potsdam
PO Box 60 15 53, 14415 Potsdam, Germany
e-mail: uwe@techno.de
URL: http://www.techno.de/~uwe

Abstract. A software-based approach to control-flow checking is presented. The method uses the control flow graph of a program to construct a state machine which is embedded into the program using a modified GNU C-compiler. Using the return address register as the state variable of the FSM no data overhead occurs. Employing a Compiler for the embedding of the redundant code into the program permits the exploitation of delay slots and jump optimizations for modern RISC processors. The method is evaluated on a SPARC processor using software-implemented control-flow error injection and the SPECint92 benchmark suite. The average temporal overhead is below 20% and the errors violating the fail-silent model can be reduced by a factor of 6 down to 0.3%.

1 Introduction

The increasing complexity of modern computer systems also accounts for an increased vulnerability to transient hardware faults. The costs caused by computer failure are increasing with the share of work transferred to powerful computing systems. In this context dependability features are gaining importance in the computer industry.

Dependability can be achieved with a number of different approaches. However, they all comprise a mean of fault and error detection to be able to distinguish correct from erroneous behavior.

Fault detection can be achieved by two main approaches, one is the *duplication* of the system or parts thereof and subsequent comparison, the other is the *monitoring* of observable features of the system by relatively simple devices. The former approach is currently used in the industry for dependable computer systems like the TANDEM computers. However, its overhead is at least 100% for the duplication plus some more for the comparator devices. In the academic field the monitoring approach is pursued more vigorously to reduce the costly overhead.

Observable features to be monitored by a checker include timely execution of certain instructions monitored by a watchdog timer, memory access behavior monitored by a memory management unit, control flow behavior monitored by a signature checker (i.e. watchdog processor), and coding methods monitored by a decoding circuit. This paper presents a software implemented method of monitoring the control-flow behavior of an application.

The monitoring of control-flow behavior as an indicator of error-free execution has been widely used in the literature. In the mid-seventies the theoretical basis to control flow has firstly been presented [KY75]. The used approach of checking the processing sequence history is a method of *assigned signature checking*.

Using watchdog processors to monitor control-flow behavior has become very popular in the field in the eighties [MM88]. The watchdog monitors the instruction stream fetched by the main processor and derives signatures from the instructions controlled by precalculated and stored signatures. Errors are detected by a deviation of the new calculated signature from the precalculated one. This is called *derived signature checking*. In the following years a number of improvements have been made to the method by reducing the overhead caused by the inserted signatures or by changing the coding to improve latency and coverage.

In recent years the costs of special hardware and off-the-shelf hardware started to diverge rapidly. From this a demand for software solutions to replace special hardware solutions has risen. In addition the observability of the control flow by monitoring its external bus interface has decreased due to prefetching and caching on the processor chip which makes the monitoring of the control flow by software methods executing on-chip even more attractive.

Compiler Assisted Self-Checking (CASC) is a pure software approach to assigned signature control flow checking. It obviates the need for a separate watchdog processor since the checker is a separate program embedded into the code of the executing application and executed by the main processor. The efficiency of this method is based on the mapping of a malicious fault-class to other fault-classes which are readily detected by hardware checkers inherent to modern computer systems. Using this method is as easy as the recompilation of the application with a special compiler, a rather uncostly procedure.

Embedding the control flow checker into the program code can cover only control-flow errors inside the program code segment of an application. However, these control flow errors (CFE) constitute the malicious class of CFEs. All other CFEs leaving the program code segment, except some very rare cases, will be caught by the checking circuits inherent to modern computer systems. Those checkers are a prerequisite for this method, though. Fortunately, all modern computer architectures comprise the concept of virtual memory[i]. A memory management unit which is capable of detecting memory access violations is a required part of such a system. In addition, a check for valid instruction codes is performed by the instruction decoder of such processors providing for additional means to catch errors caused by control flow deviations.

The remainder of this papers is organized as follows. In Section 2 the different approaches to signature based control flow checking are reviewed and the related work on software based methods is presented. In Section 3 the new method of software based control flow checking is introduced. This comprises the theoretical framework as well as implementation issues. The evaluation system used for this work is presented in Section 4. The definition of the used fault model and an introduction to the employed software-implemented fault injector is found there as well as a description of the experimental setup and the used benchmark applications. The experimental results can be found in Section 5. They comprise temporal and spatial overhead figures as well as coverage figures obtained from a large number of fault injection experiments. Concluding remarks are given in Section 6.

---

i. Let this be the definition of a *modern computer system*.

2 Related Research

2.1 The early days

Already in the mid-seventies a theoretical framework for control flow checking has been presented in [KY75]. The work introduced a first model of control flow, a fault model for CFEs and a fault detection method. However, the underlying system model is hardly applicable to modern systems.

The *relay-runner* scheme in [YC75] is an approach to self-checking software with some similarities to the CASC approach. The scheme uses a signature to identify the previously executed code block. In the next block the signature is checked against the set of valid predecessor signatures. With this approach the signature has to be checked in each block, whereas CASC is capable of propagating the sequencing information throughout the program, thereby making checks at each block optional.

Another approach to self-checking software is presented in [YC80]. It uses a path table which includes path predicates and signatures for each block. This approach is a superset of CASC but incurs an overhead higher by an order of magnitude to CASC.

2.2 Structural Integrity Checking (SIC)

In [Lu82] the basic idea of assigned signature checking is presented. A preprocessor is applied to the source code of a program and two programs are generated. The original application is enhanced with instructions to transfer the signatures to a watchdog processor and a second program is generated for the watchdog processors for the checking of the signature sequences. This can be modeled as two automata, one emits signatures according to a context-free grammar and the other accepts them. A similar approach has been used for CASC.

2.3 Path Signature Analysis (PSA)

The method presented in [Nam82] is based on derived signature checking. The instruction stream is partitioned into blocks and encoded at compile time. The signatures computed from the instruction blocks are added to the beginning of a block. At run time the signature is fetched by a watchdog processor while the main processor executes a *nop*. In parallel to the execution of the block the watchdog then recomputes the signature and compares it at the end of the block to the stored one. An improvement to PSA called *Generalized PSA* has been devised in [Nam82]. In order to reduce the number of embedded signatures those are calculated for paths instead of blocks. The program is split into path sets where each path in the set starts at the same node at which the signature is embedded. Since the signatures of all paths cannot be equal, *justifying signatures* are inserted into some paths to provide for this.

2.4 Signatured Instruction Streams (SIS)

A scheme similar to PSA has been introduced by [SS83]. The main difference is in the placement of the signatures at the end of the instruction block. If the block ends in a branch instruction the signature is encoded into the branch address to reduce the memory overhead. This is called Branch Address Hashing (BAH).

2.5 Continuous Signature Monitoring (CSM)

A further improvement to the signature methods is presented in [WS90]. Here, the focus is shifted on the placement of the justifying signatures. For example, the delay slot of a branch instruction is a perfect candidate. The execution profile of a program can be used to select locations which are executed less frequent than others, thereby reducing the temporal overhead. The profiling approach to produce weighed control flow graphs has also been used for an $O(n^2)$ algorithm in [WH90]. In addition, CSM also comprises horizontal signatures. The horizontal signature bits for each instruction are calculated from all the instructions in the block up to the current instruction. This method provides for constant memory overhead and low latency but lower coverage and is therefore combined with vertical signatures. In [Wil93] an optimal graph-theoretic approach for the placement of signatures is presented which overcomes the limitations of the previous approaches in an $O(n)$ algorithm.

2.6 Available Resource-Driven Control-Flow Monitoring (ARC)

ARC [SS91] is a software based approach to integrated control-flow monitoring. The idle resources of a VLIW processor are used to execute the Monitoring Computation (MC) in parallel to the Application Computation (AC). The resource use of the MC can be tailored to the existence of idle resources in a Multiflow TRACE VLIW processor. The MC consists of a tracking task and a checking task. The tracking task stores a key in a register which is updated in each block of the program. The blocks are determined by the availability of idle resources to execute the tracking instruction. Similarly, whenever resource usage permits, a checking instruction is executed to compare the key with the one assigned to the current block.

2.7 Block Signature Self-Checking (BSSC)

This software based approach, firstly presented in [MKGT92], splits the program graph into basic blocks and adds a signature, the address of the current basic block, to their ends. At the beginning of a block in the entry routine the signature is saved in a static variable. At the end of the basic block in the exit routine it is compared to the stored address. This way all CFEs leaving a block and entering another one are detected.

In [MT95] the method is enhanced as follows. In order to make the code position independent the signature added to the block is equal to the size of the current block. The entry routine checks the correctness of a key in the static variable and then stores the current address there. In the exit routine the sum of the stored value (the address of the entry point) and the signature (the size of the block) is compared to the current address (the exit point). This way a correct entrance to the block is checked. Thereafter, the key for the next block is stored in the static variable and the return address is modified to skip the signature and resume execution.

2.8 Extended Structural Integrity Checking

This software-based approach presented in [MH91] and applied in [SH95] also constructs a control flow graph for each function to check for CFEs. The C code preprocessor analyses the source code statements and modifies the source. At the beginning of each function the code to initialize the signature variable and the adjacency matrix of the functions CFG^i is inserted. Using the signature value and the block number the adjacency matrix is accessed in each block to check the correct sequence of blocks. Then, the signature is updated and operation continued.

3 The CASC Approach

The CASC Method uses the control flow graph of each function in a program to construct a tracing function, a finite state machine (FSM). The additional code is embedded into the original program by an enhanced GNU C-compiler on a per function basis. The state transitions are placed between the basic blocks such that the state variable contains the code assigned to the current block. Each state machine provides for a reference to the correct control flow throughout the execution of the current function.

The novel idea of this approach is the use of the return address storage, usually a register for RISC processors, for tracing the valid control flow. The state variable of the FSM is stored into the return address storage as an offset to the original return address. Upon function entry the FSM is initialized and the return address invalidated. Just before the return from the function the valid return address is recovered from the state variable of the FSM. Any disturbance of the state variable due to a CFE will cause an invalid return address being used for the return. Due to the construction of the state codes of the FSM invalid *misaligned* values are found there during execution of the function. Only during function *calls* and *returns* the return address values are valid. Thus, most invalid values are *misaligned*.

This approach provides for the mapping of most control flow errors to alignment errors, employing the built-in error detection mechanisms of the processor whenever an invalid return address is used. If the wrong address is not misaligned the execution continues at the wrong target address. Depending on the data found there, either an illegal instruction exception is thrown immediately or the program crashes with additional latency. However, there is no way to continue the program properly after a state machine has been corrupted except the very unlikely case of compensating errors or aliasing effects.

To minimize the execution overhead a compiler is used to perform the code integration in order to exploit the delayed branch and jump optimizations in later optimization phases. In addition, the compiler based approach has proven to be highly portable. The resulting self-checking program runs without any special treatment on the target system but provides for better error behavior than a program compiled without the checking code.

3.1 Construction of the State Machine

Definition: A *control flow graph* CFG is a tuple (V,E,S,F) consisting of a set V of vertices and a set $E \subseteq V \times V$ of directed edges. The vertices correspond to the processor instructions and the edges to the flow of control between the instructions. S and F are the entry and exit vertices of the graph.

Definition: The RFG $= (V, E, S, F)$ is the *reduced flow graph* constructed from a CFG by grouping the *basic blocks* [ASU86] or branch-free intervals to single vertices.

Definition: A path of length n within a CFG is a sequence of nodes $(v_i)_{i=0...n-1}$ with $\forall i=0...n-2: (v_i,v_{i+1}) \in E$.

The only difference between the CFG and the RFG is in the sequences of linear connected vertices in CFG constituting a single vertex in RFG. They are homomorphic by construction.

Function calls are treated as normal statements, thus they are omitted from the CFG since a separate CFG is built for each function. Therefore, a complete program graph consists of a set of CFG^i, one for each function of the program.

For a software-implemented solution to signature checking the RFG is used instead of the CFG to reduce overhead. The tuple (V,E,S,F) of the RFG^i of each function is used to define the structure of a finite state machine FSM^i for the function. Some additional properties of the FSM^i are needed in order to use it for the CASC method:

1. The same odd code gets assigned to all states contained in S and F. This way, the state variable can be used to invalidate and recover the return address.

2. All other states get assigned a distinct odd number. Hence, the return address is invalidated during execution of the function since these codes are used as offsets from the return address producing a misaligned address.

3. A simple operation is needed for the transition function to minimize the overhead. The addition executes in one cycle and is sufficient for this purpose.

4. The codes used for the states have to be chosen such that each state transition operation fits into a single instruction.

The state assignment has some effects on CASC since it influences the effect of a CFE when the invalid return address is used by the processor. A rubber band algorithm has been used to generate the state assignment. It generates an initial unique assignment. Then the values are pulled as far apart as possible while trying to avoiding duplication of state codes.

3.2 Implementation

In order to implement CASC a GNU C-compiler version 2.5.7 has been enhanced. Specifying an additional compiler flag on the command line causes the compiler to execute an additional pass before the *Delayed Branch Scheduling* pass and modify the pro- and epilogues of the function:

- The prologue is changed to offset the return address to an invalid value in the first statement.

- The epilogue is changed to return correctly despite the changed return address.

- The additional compiler pass generates a new RFG from the function and performs the necessary state assignment.

- Since each transition is related to a single edge in the RFG the code has to be manipulated to guarantee that only single flows of control are passing through the

---

i. The FSM can also be seen as an acceptor which accepts strings belonging to $L(RG^i)$ the language defined by the grammar RG homomorphic to RFG^i.

transition statements. Depending on the complexity of the program this can be a costly procedure.

- The FSM transition statements are inserted along the edges of the RFG using the internal RTL[i] representation of the program.

The changed RTL code is then processed further by some other optimization passes and finally converted into assembler code.

To implement the FSM = (X, Z, f) two mappings are needed. One to assign codes to the states of the FSM and the basic blocks, and another to determine the input values for the state transition function. In order to minimize the spatial overhead the state transition function f should fit into a single instruction. The SPARC has an immediate addition statement with space for a 12 Bit wide integer constant. This is the candidate for the transition function: `add   %i7,%i7,x`

The limitation of the input values $x \in X$ to 12 Bit incurs a maximum difference of $-2^{12} \leq x \leq 2^{12}$-1 between the codes assigned to adjacent states. This is the limiting factor for the rubber band algorithm mentioned before.

3.3 Delayed Branches

To follow the RFG of a function the FSM instructions need to be placed at the edges of the control flow graph. The delay slot after branches in modern RISC processors is a perfect candidate for the placement of those instructions. Due to the ability to tie the execution of the delay slot to the condition of the branch, it is also tied to the edge of the CFG belonging to the branch. On the first look this seems not extremely beneficial, but taking a closer look it can be seen that the splitting of execution paths in order to assign FSM instruction to single edges can be a quite costly procedure. Without the delay slot every branch which shares its target with another branch has to be redirected. This accounts for at least another cycle, maybe even more, since the redirected branch might not be able to fill its delay slot. The exploitation of the delayed branches is a special feature of the CASC approach.

3.4 Return Address Hashing

Using a separate state machine for each function introduces a vulnerable point to the system. Since the state variable of the FSM is saved and restored during a function call we have to avoid to restore an error free FSM after an error occurred. If this could be done by just executing a simple *return* statement, the coverage would suffer since *return* statements are quite frequent.

The solution to this problem is to use the return address storage as the state variable of the FSM. The state codes are used as offsets from the original return address RA. The FSM is encoded such that its entry and exit states are coded as INITVAL, a fixed odd value, and all other states as distinct odd values. The function prologue and epilogue are changed by offsetting the return address by INITVAL immediately upon function entry. The return statement is changed to return to the value in the state variable less INITVAL. This way upon entering a new function the return address is imme-

---

i. The Register Transfer Language is the machine independent internal representation of a program in the GNU compiler.

diately invalidated. Only upon error-free execution until the end of the function by executing all the FSM instructions in the correct sequence the return address is restored to RA + INITVAL. Together with the changed return instruction the function can return to the caller. The remaining control faults escaping this technique are the correct entry to a wrong subroutine and the aliased faults with the appropriate probability. Since each basic block contains instructions changing the return address any other control fault will be catastrophic, however, maybe with some latency. In analogy to the watchdog based signature technique [SS83] we call this *return address hashing* as the signature is encoded in the return address.

3.5 Effects of Control Faults

Any control fault causing a deviation from the CFG used for the construction of the FSM changes the sequence of signatures (=states) produced by the FSM during the execution of the function. Consequently, the state of the FSM differs from the state related to the basic block (=vertex of the RFG) erroneously entered. Except for aliasing effects, the lost synchronization between FSM and application program code will be propagated until the next return instruction changes the current context. Then, the current FSM is left and execution continues one level up using the saved state code of the previous FSM. Hence, the state of the FSM has only to be checked before the context change which is achieved by using the state code of the FSM as the return address.

In Fig. 1 a simple example of a control flow error within a function is shown. The probability of not detecting such an error is:

$p(\text{undetected}) = 1/2^n * 1/N_{blocks} + p(\text{escape}).$

For the used pseudo-random signatures the probability of equal signatures is $1/2^n$ for n used bits in the signature. However, this formula applies only to functions with more than 2^n basic blocks and to the interprocedural CFEs. Within the same function the state assignment can avoid assigning duplicates for up to 2^n signatures which should be enough for any structured program[i]. The interesting probability is the escape probability. At the very beginning of a function the stack frame is set up. This single instruction cannot be protected by the method without changing the function call mechanism. Thus, a CFE can escape if a wrong function is entered exactly at its correct entry point:

$p(\text{escape}) \approx N_{entry} / \text{laddress spacel}.$

However, this should be sufficiently low to be negligible.

From the construction of the FSM above it should be clear that entering a basic block from a wrong function caused by a control fault has the same effect as entering it from an invalid basic block. The state code of the FSM is wrong and therefore the correct return address cannot be recovered from it.

3.6 Mapping of Control Flow Errors

If the used processor architecture has an aligned instruction format, the same technique also permits to completely omit the checking instructions at the exit point of a function. The embedded state machine can be constructed such that the value of the

---

i. The effect of assigned duplicates only occurs after assigning all 2^n distinct codes. For the SPARC this are at least 4096 codes or distinct basic blocks and this can be extended further.

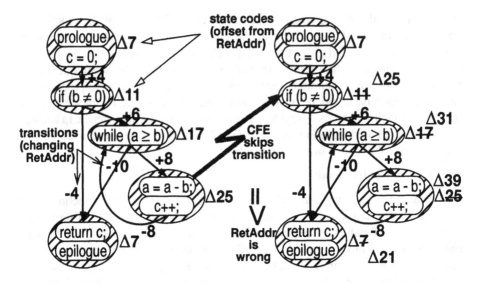

Fig. 1 **Example of a simple CFE**
The shown control fault causes a deviation of the control flow from the state (Δ25) to the state (Δ11) skipping the following state transition (RA-=8). The state machine continues with an incorrect value in the state variable (Δ25 instead of Δ11). Since the erroneous state is propagated until the next *return instruction* we will find the value Δ21 instead of Δ7 before the epilogue. The epilogue subtracts 7 from the return address while returning in order to return to the original address. Using the resulting RA+14 for the return will cause a misalignment exception since the address is not on the 4 Byte boundary required for the instruction fetch.

state variable which is the return address will contain a misaligned value virtually anytime. Thus, any control fault will be mapped to an alignment error as soon as the state variable is reused as an instruction address. This obviates the need for checking instructions before the value is used for the return statement. In addition, the register to save the correct return address can be left out as well, hence eliminating any run-time data storage overhead.

4 The Evaluation System

The evaluation system comprises a set of benchmarks, namely the SPECint92 benchmark suite and a fault injection tool. The fault injection tool is based on software-implemented fault injection and has been integrated into the SPECint92 suite to provide for automatic data collection. A definition of the employed fault class is given, followed by a description of the fault injector. Thereafter, the employed benchmark programs and the performed experiments are described.

4.1 Fault Model

Definition: A *control flow error* is the deviation of the control flow of a program from the set of paths as defined by the control flow graph. That is the processor is executing a path which either contains an edge not belonging to the CFG or a node

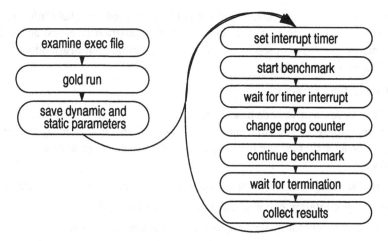

Fig. 2 **The Fault Injection Loop**

not belonging to the CFG:

$$P = (v_i)_{i=0...n-1} \text{ with } \exists\, i = 0...n-2: ((v_i,v_{i+1}) \notin E\ ) \vee (v_i \notin V)$$

This is not an entirely representative model of control faults but a practical one as it can be simulated easily in software. The processor is stopped at an instant t_{int} during program execution and the program counter PC is set to an equally random selected address in the accessible address space different from the correct next instruction. The correct next instruction is the one found in the PC when the process is stopped. The accessible address space is determined by the memory management unit and very work-load dependent. However, this restriction is necessary since pointing the PC to inaccessible memory will inhibit the restart of the benchmark process. This mapping to the instruction level is not identical to the definition above. The main effect is a limitation of the injected control faults to the ones which produce a valid address in the PC. However, this definition is sufficiently close to it for our purposes, since we keep most interesting errors in our model, namely the ones of this model violating the fail-silent model. The interested reader is referred to [Wil96].

Like all other assigned signature methods operating on the basic block level [MKGT92][SH95] the fine grained control flow deviations not leaving a basic block cannot be detected. This fault class comprises PC stuck, increment and instruction fetch address line faults. The address line faults causing the fetch of a single wrong instruction are not simulated. The minor PC deviations are probably underrepresented in the fault model assuming equiprobability since they might occur more frequent than other control faults. The obtained results have to be considered keeping this in mind.

4.2 Software Implemented Control Flow Error Injection

Software Implemented Fault Injection has been widely used before and proven quite useful [KKA92][CMS95][SH95]. In Fig. 2 the basic algorithm of the fault injector is shown. The tool can be used as a simple command line prefix for any program. Similar to some other approaches it is based on the UNIX *ptrace* mechanism to change the core image of running processes [KKA92]. There is no interaction with the execution of the program under test.

The examination of the executable and the gold run is used to collect information about the error-free outputs as well as execution time, program size, and accessible memory. This information is used to provide for an equal random distribution of the injected CFEs in time and space.

4.3 SPECint92 Benchmarks

To provide a representative code base for the experiments the SPECint92 benchmark suite has been employed. The suite consists of 6 benchmarks compiled by the SPEC Corp. to provide a useful measure for computing performance of workstations. The six benchmarks are

1. **espresso:** An optimizer for combinational circuits optimizing a few circuits.

2. **xlisp:** A lisp interpreter computing the eight queens problem

3. **eqntott:** A solver for linear equations solving a number of those.

4. **compress:** A Lempel-Ziv compression algorithm using random text with a determined character frequency as input and vice versa.

5. **sc:** A spreadsheet calculator calculating interest rates.

6. **gcc:** The GNU C-compiler version 1.39 compiling its own sources.

These benchmarks comprise many thousand lines of C code and where compiled properly with the CASC compiler.

4.4 Experimental Setup

In order to provide reproducible results the SPEC benchmark suite was modified as little as possible. Only an additional Vendor Wrapper for the used compiler options has been added and an additional target has been inserted into the Makefile. The inserted target just prefixes the command line for the benchmark execution with the fault injector command. This way the original user interface for the SPECint92 suite could be maintained.

The suite has been executed 3 times to measure overhead and fault coverage figures:

- with standard options in the following called Reference

- using CASC and Return Address Hashing without checking instructions, in the following called *RA-Hashing*. Since no explicit checking instructions are employed the overhead is less than the next alternative.

- using CASC without RA-Hashing but with checking instructions to compare the state variable with its stored value at the end of a function before each *return* instruction in the following called *Check-Insn*. Since an additional register is needed to keep the state of the FSM the incurred overhead is expected to be higher. This approach is similar to other software based checking methods.

5 Experimental Results

In Fig. 3 the relative overhead figures of the SPECint92 benchmark suite are shown. The code size and the execution times of the programs using CASC RA-Hashing and

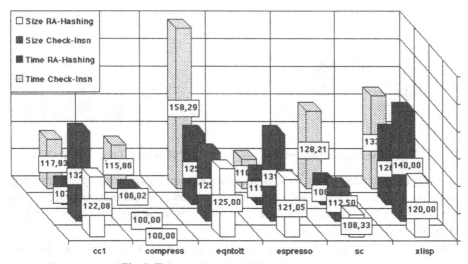

Fig. 3 **Temporal and Spatial Overhead (%)**

CASC with checking instructions are shown. The absolute numbers for the overheads are listed in Table 1. The dependency on the work-load is obvious. The *eqntott* benchmark has a remarkably higher temporal overhead. This is due to the high number of conditional branches, which account for a relatively low basic block size. This is valid also for the *xlisp* interpreter and the spreadsheet calculator *sc* . The complexity of the CFG can be used as a measure for the overhead. In contrast, the *compress* benchmark comprises more complex computations and, therefore, has a simpler CFG and a moderate overhead. However, the average overhead for the execution time is below 15% for CASC RA-Hashing and 26% for CASC Check-Insn. These numbers relate perfectly to an average basic block size of about 5 instructions plus the additional FSM instruction.

Table 1 SPARC 10/51 Overhead Figures

	Method	ccl	compress	eqntott	espresso	sc	xlisp
size of text segment (in Bytes)	Reference	630784	16384	32768	155648	196608	81920
	RA-Hashing	770048	16384	40960	188416	212992	98304
	Check-Insn	835584	16384	40960	204800	221184	114688
execution times (in sec)	Reference	101.5	68.1	19.9	45.8	95.0	161.8
	RA-Hashing	109.0	72.2	25.0	51.0	103.1	204.2
	Check-Insn	119.7	78.9	31.5	50.7	121.8	216.5
SPECint92	Reference	53.79	40.68	55.28	49.56	47.68	38.38
	RA-Hashing	50.09	38.37	44.00	44.51	43.94	30.41
	Check-Insn	45.61	35.11	34.92	44.77	37.19	28.68

5.1 Fault Coverage

The 3 pie charts in Fig. 4, Fig. 6 and Fig. 8 show the average error distribution per experiment type. The aim of the CASC approach is the reduction of the CFEs violating

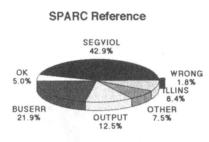

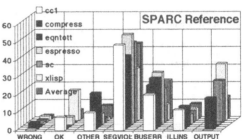

Fig. 4 **Averages of Reference**   Fig. 5 **Reference Error Distribution**

the *fail-silent* model. Those errors are minor enough to keep the system running, avoiding all system checks and error indication. However, the outputs produced are erroneous and can't be recognized as such. This most malicious fault class is termed *WRONG* in the following figures.

Of course, the majority of errors are caught by the system checks. These are the common memory bounds violation *SEGmentationVIOLation*, the alignment errors *BUSERRor*, and the processor check *ILLegalINStruction*. Another class are the tolerated errors and the ones which did not become effective, called *OK*. *OUTPUT* is an error which is identified by inspection of the output file. Executions producing output files containing an error indication from the application program belong to this class, i.e. the lisp interpreter has an elaborated error handling mechanism cleanly exiting the program. A deviation of the size of the output file by a factor ≥ 2 to the reference file is also considered fail-silent since any inspection of the output file will reveal the error. *FSM* is the fault class discovered by the checking instructions of CASC Check-Insn and *OTHER* comprise the remaining faults such as program *aborts*, program *exits* with error code or time-outs.

The pie charts document the change of the error distribution in the average for the SPECint92 suite. The malicious error class WRONG could be reduced from 1.81% down to 0.29% for CASC RA-Hashing and 0.89% for CASC Check-Insn. This is a reduction of such errors by a factor of 6 and 2, respectively. In the total coverage this is only an additional percent, but for the confidence into the results this is a remarkable increase. Even with less extra instructions not contributing to the result, the coverage of the RA-Hashing method increased in comparison to the Check-Insn method. Hence, a real reduction of fail-silent violations can be concluded.

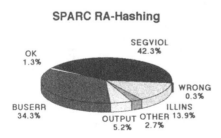

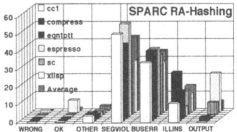

Fig. 6 **Averages of CASC RA-Hashing**   Fig. 7 **Error Distribution of RA-Hashing**

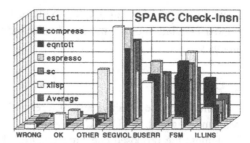

Fig. 8 Averages of CASC with Checking Instructions (no RA-Hashing)   **Fig. 9 Error Distribution of CASC Check-Insn**

The increase in coverage of the RA-Hashing method can be explained by the reduction of unprotected locations in the instruction sequence, where a jump can escape the error detection. Changing the return address upon function entry has shown to be a quite safe way to avoid incorrect continuation of a program.

The checking instructions in CASC Check-Insn could catch 23% of the injected control flow errors in the average, a result mainly showing the effect of the error injection method. As mentioned before the fault class used for the experiments is only the special class of CFEs causing a jump to an accessible address in the address space. How much those errors contribute to the class of *real* errors can only be guessed.

In Fig. 6 the increase of alignment errors (BUSERR) in comparison to the reference in Fig. 4 can be noticed. This shows the partially successful effect of the error mapping introduced in Section 3. About 10% of the errors are mapped to alignment errors due to the misaligned values placed in the return address, thereby reducing latency. However, the error mapping into the alignment errors is not as complete as one might expect, some errors were instead mapped to memory bounds violations and illegal instructions. This can be related to the fact that the FSM coding cannot guarantee a misaligned value in the return address in the erroneous case. There is always a portion of control faults which cause valid but wrong addresses to be used for the return. In those cases the program crash might be delayed. The heavy dependence on the code structure is remarkable and obvious (see Fig. 5, Fig. 7 and Fig. 9). The complexity of the CFG[i] of a program relates clearly to the overhead. Also some program features like *setjmp/longjmp* for the programming of error handling has an distinctive effect on the coverage (*xlisp*). Absolute figures including 95% confidence intervals are given in the appendix.

5.2 Latency

Table 2 SPARC 10/51 Latency Figures (msec)

ccl	compress	eqntott	espresso	sc	xlisp
21.2 ±9.3	17.6 ±10.4	19.3 ±11.2	13.6 ±7.9	24.5 ±13.5	22.7 ±10.4

The SPARC processor does not provide support for a trace mode. The alternative is a single step mode by replacing each instruction with a software interrupt in turn. Due to the high number of experiments this solution was not practicable. Therefore, the latency measurements are limited to the resolution of the system clock. However, the standard deviation of the measured values is too high to use the numbers for detailed analysis.

6 Conclusion

In this paper the effectiveness of a refined software-based control flow method has been investigated. A GNU C compiler for a SPARC processor has been devised to implement the proposed checking schemes. It could be shown that by employing an elaborated scheme integrated into a compiler, exploiting additional optimizations, like delay slots and jump optimization, a software-based method can yield satisfying results regarding the overhead and coverage figures given the appropriate work-load. The percentage of terminations without error indication could be decreased significantly by a factor of up to 6 through the application of self-checking code. This could be achieved by just using a simple compiler switch during the compilation of the benchmarks.

Especially regarding the increasing difficulty of monitoring a processor from the outside due to the transfer of the memory hierarchy on the chip, a compiler based method might provide an interesting alternative to the watchdog based approaches.

To further investigate the properties of this approach a compiler for the INTEL x86 and the PowerPC is currently under development. As well, more elaborate fault injection schemes are projected to investigate the effectiveness of the method in more detail.

7 References

[ASU86] A. V. Aho, R. Sethi and J. D. Ullman: *"Compilers - Principles, Techniques, and Tools"*, Addison-Wesley, 1986

[CMS95] J. Carreira, H. Madeira, and J. G. Silva: "Xception: Software Fault Injection and Monitoring in Processor Functional Units", *5th Intern. Conference on Dependable Computing for Critical Applications*, p. 135-149

[CS90] Edward W. Czeck, Daniel P. Siewiorek: "Effects of Transient Gate-Level Faults on Program Behavior", *20th International Symposium on Fault-Tolerant Computing*, p. 236-243

[GKT89] Ulf Gunneflo, Johann Karlsson, Jan Torin: "Evaluation of Error Detection Schemes Using Fault Injection by Heavy-Ion Radiation", *19th International Symposium on Fault-Tolerant Computing*, p. 340-347

[KKA92] G. A. Kanawati, N. A. Kanawati, and J. A. Abraham: "FERRARI: A Tool for The Validation of System Dependability Properties", *22th International Symposium on Fault-Tolerant Computing*, p. 336 - 344

[KY75] J.R.Kane and Stephen S.Yau: "Concurrent Software Fault Detection", *IEEE Transactions on Software Engineering* SE 1(1):87-99, March 1975

[Lu82] David Jun Lu: "Watchdog Processors and Structural Integrity Checking", *IEEE Transactions on Computers*, C-31(7): 681-685, July 1982

[MH91] E. Michel and W. Hohl: "Concurrent Error Detection Using Watchdog Processors in the Multiprocssor System MEMSY", *Fault Tolerant Computing Systems. Informatik Fachberichte 283*, p. 54 - 64

[MKGT92] G. Miremadi, J. Karlsson, U. Gunneflo, and J. Torin: "Two Software Techniques for On-line Error Detection", *22th International Symposium on Fault-Tolerant Computing*, p. 328-335

[MM88] Aamer Mahmood and E.J. McCluskey: "Concurrent Error Detection Using Watchdog Processors - A Survey", *IEEE Transactions on Computers*, C-37(2): 160-174, February 1988

[MT95] Ghassem Miremadi and Jan Torin: "Effects of Physical Injection of Transient Faults on Control Flow and Evaluation of Some Software-Implemented Error Detection Techniques", *4th International Conference on Dependable Computing for Critical Applications*, p. 435 - 457

[Nam82] M. Namjoo: "Techniques for Concurrent Testing of VLSI Processor Operation", 1982 *International Test Conference*, p.461-468

[SH95] Volkmar Sieh and Joachim Hönig: "Software Based Concurrent Control Flow Checking", *Internal Report 10/95, IMMD III, University of Erlangen-Nürnberg*, Dec.1995

[SM89] Nirmal R. Saxena and Ed. J. McCluskey: "Control-Flow Checking Using Watchdog assists and extended-precision checksums", *19th International Symposium on Fault-Tolerant Computing*, p. 428-435

[SS83] Michael A. Schuette and John P. Shen: "On-line self monitoring using signatured instruction streams", *13th International Test Conference*, p. 275-282

[SS91] Michael A. Schuette and John P. Shen: "Exploiting Instruction-level Resource Parallelism for Transparent, Integrated Control-Flow Monitoring", *21th International Symposium on Fault-Tolerant Computing*, p. 318-325

[SSSZ86] M.A. Schuette, J.P. Shen, D.P. Siewiorek and Y.X. Zhu: "Experimental Evaluation of Two Concurrent Error Detection Schemes", *16th International Symposium on Fault-Tolerant Computing*, p. 138-143

[WH90] Nancy J. Warter and Wen-Mei W. Hwu: "A Software Based Approach to Achieving Optimal Performance for Signature Control Flow Checking", *20th International Symposium on Fault-Tolerant Computing*, p. 442-449

[Wil93] Kent D. Wilken: "An Optimal Graph-Construction Approach to Placing Program Signatures for Signature Monitoring", *IEEE Transactions on Computers*, C-42(11): 1372-1380, November 1993

[Wil96] Uwe Wildner: "Software Implemented Control Flow Error Injection" *Tech. Report MPI-96-601*, Max-Planck-Working Group on Fault Tolerant Computing, Jan. 1996, *http://www.mpag-inf.uni-potsdam.de/reports/MPI-I-96-601.ps.gz*

[WS90] Kent Wilken and John Paul Shen: "Continuous Signature Monitoring: Low-Cost Concurrent Detection of Processor Control Errors", *IEEE Transactions on Computer-Aided Design of Integrated Circuits*, 9(6):629-641, June 1990

[YC75] Stephen. S. Yau an R. C. Cheung: "Design of Self-Checking Software", *International Conference on Reliable Software*, March 1975

[YC80] Stephen S. Yau and Fu-Chung Chen: "An Approach to Concurrent Control Flow Checking", *IEEE Transactions on Software Engineering* SE 6(2):126-137, March 1980

8 Appendix

In the following three tables the measured means and the corresponding 95% confidence intervals are given. Some of the experiments have been carried out frequent enough such that the distribution stabilized quite well.

Table 3 Average Error Distribution & Confidence Intervals for the Reference

	OK	WRONG	OTHER	SEG VIOL	BUS ERR	ILLINS	OUTPUT
ccl	7.62±0.16	0.73±0.09	10.34±0.18	48.87±0.27	20.61±0.22	11.83±0.18	0
compress	0.28±0.25	3.36±1.23	4.84±0.43	41.08±0.99	24.87±0.80	8.04±0.52	17.54±1.43
eqntott	0	1.11±0.06	19.18±0.27	40.47±0.31	27.71±0.30	11.53±0.20	0
espresso	4.41±0.26	1.37±0.18	6.37±0.43	51.38±0.65	29.82±0.60	5.82±0.32	0.84±0.12
sc	0.05±0.04	1.75±0.47	2.52±0.16	45.83±0.38	19.28±0.31	6.48±0.19	24.08±0.54
xlisp	17.39±1.27	2.53±0.82	1.77±0.46	29.76±1.07	9.23±0.75	6.98±0.59	32.33±1.22
Average	4.96	1.81	7.50	42.90	21.92	8.47	12.46

Table 4 Averages Error Distribution & Confidence Intervals for CASC RA-Hashing

	OK	WRONG	OTHER	SEGVIOL	BUSERR	ILLINS	OUTPUT
ccl	0.3±0.04	0.02±0.01	3.8±0.18	50.63±0.44	34.24±0.44	11.0±0.33	0
compress	0	0.00±0.01	4.33±0.23	34.78±0.83	31.33±0.92	27.49±1.30	2.07±0.17
eqntott	0	0.29±0.09	2.69±0.22	42.56±0.75	38.70±0.65	15.66±0.71	0.10±0.05
espresso	0.2±0.11	0.02±0.02	2.37±0.37	53.02±0.87	38.82±0.85	5.48±0.39	0.09±0.04
sc	0	0.25±0.23	2.34±0.42	43.36±0.99	33.95±1.05	13.31±0.67	6.80±0.87
xlisp	7.06±2.10	1.15±0.55	0.82±0.76	29.47±2.20	28.47±2.42	10.65±2.25	22.38±2.48
Average	1.26	0.29	2.72	42.30	34.2517	13.93	5.24

Table 5 Averages Error Distribution & Confidence Intervals for CASC Check-Insn

	OK	WRONG	OTHER	SEGVIOL	BUSERR	FSM	ILLINS
ccl	7.12±0.06	2.27±0.04	4.81±0.05	48.60±0.11	22.2±0.10	5.11±0.05	9.88±0.07
compress	0.14±0.21	0.14±0.12	4.80±0.71	29.47±1.19	17.8±0.88	24.44±.40	23.18±1.76
eqntott	0	0.12±0.01	1.79±0.06	35.75±0.22	23.62±0.19	29.92±0.19	8.80±0.12
espresso	0.23±0.02	0.09±0.01	1.78±0.06	44.46±0.20	29.12±0.19	20.03±.17	4.28±0.08
sc	0.00±0.005	1.01±0.11	2.95±0.22	37.30±0.62	21.89±.49	27.03±0.54	9.80±0.47
xlisp	3.91±0.32	1.72±1.32	23.48±1.32	22.40±0.64	10.24±0.42	31.59±0.71	6.65±0.39
Average	1.90	0.89	6.60	36.33	20.81	23.02	10.43

Single Source Fault-Tolerant Broadcasting for Two-Dimensional Meshes Without Virtual Channels

D. R. Avresky and Chris M. Cunningham*

Texas A&M University Department of Computer Science, College Station, TX, USA

Abstract. In this paper, the authors propose a fault-tolerant single source broadcast algorithm for wormhole routed two-dimensional meshes that utilizes neighbor status information to dynamically construct a broadcast spanning tree when up to $N-1$ faults are present in an $N \times N$ two-dimensional mesh. Correctness proofs for the proposed broadcasting algorithm are presented and the algorithm is also proven to be livelock- and deadlock-free. The proposed Virtual Source Broadcast (VSB) algorithm can be implemented alone without requiring any virtual channels. However, supporting simultaneous unicast and broadcast messages will require two additional virtual channels per physical link in addition to the virtual channels required for the unicast algorithm. The paper also compares the proposed VSB algorithm with broadcasting techniques that have been proposed by other authors.

1 Introduction

Many authors have proposed multicasting and broadcasting algorithms for wormhole routed two-dimensional meshes. All of these algorithms can be classified as either multiple source or single source and either tree based or hamiltonian path based. In [7] and [4], the concept of multidestination worms was introduced for tree-based broadcasting and multicasting in mesh networks utilizing wormhole routing. A multidestination worm is a sequence of flits that travels from the source through all destination routers, with the flits being copied and sent to each host node as they pass through the router. Hence, by carefully planning the path a message will travel, only one sequence of flits is needed for multicasting or broadcasting. Store-and-forward-based multicasting and broadcasting, on the other hand, require each node along the path from the source to the destinations to completely consume and then retransmit the message. Both approaches require careful implementation if deadlock and livelock are to be prevented.

In [2], two single source multicast and broadcast routing algorithms for wormhole routed two-dimensional meshes were presented. The Hierarchical Leader scheme (HL) [2] hierarchically groups the destinations such that the total number of unicast multidestination worms is minimized. The destinations are first grouped into disjoint subsets; each subset is then assigned a leader. The source

---

* Now with Omnes, 5599 San Felipe, Houston, TX, USA

then sends a copy of the broadcast or multicast message to each leader. The leaders then either repeat this process, or generate a single multidestination worm that visits each member of the leaders subset. The Multiphase Greedy Scheme (MG) [2] sends a copy of the broadcast or multicast message to each node in the source row that has a destination in its column. These nodes in turn send multidestination worms throughout the columns to the destination nodes.

The column-path [8], dual-path [6], and multipath [6] each use Hamiltonian paths to accomplish multicasting and broadcasting in a two-dimensional mesh. The column-path strategy is similar to the MG algorithm, however, multiple sources are supported through the use of two consumption channels at each node, where consumption channels may be virtual channels that are multiplexed over the link between the router and the host node. The dual-path algorithm partitions the destinations into two disjoint subsets such that one multidestination worm is introduced into each subset. Similarly, the multipath algorithms allows for as many as four subsets and hence at most four multidestination worms.

The double-channel algorithm presented in [11] divides the mesh into four channel-disjoint networks - upper right, upper left, lower right and lower left. Multidestination worms travel away from the source toward the corners of the mesh, traversing unvisited nodes that are in the destination list for the corresponding submesh.

A turn model based approach to multicasting is presented in [9]. Like other path based methods, the west-first method requires the source to construct a path that traverses each destination node exactly once. As the name implies, deadlock is prevented by forcing the message to travel west before any other direction. Since the message is not allowed to travel west more than once, the authors assert that the method is deadlock free. However, this method requires a spare row and column to achieve fault-tolerance. Such a high price is unacceptable for massively parallel systems with thousands of nodes.

The trip-based multicasting model for wormhole-routed networks, presented in [10], requires two virtual channels per physical unidirectional channel and provides fault-tolerant multisource multicasting. Like the Hamiltonian path methods, trip-based multicasting also requires the source node to sort and divide the destination nodes into disjoint sets - in this case two sets are required. An independent worm is generated at the source for each destination set. These worms then travel through the network - avoiding at most f faults in an $N \times N$ two-dimensional mesh. Since this method allows nodes to be visited more than once, nodes must be given an additional "virtual label" each time they are visited by the same message.

While all of these methods address one or more aspects of multicasting and broadcasting in a wormhole routed two-dimensional mesh, none of them provides a complete solution to the problem. For this reason, the authors are proposing a new single source fault-tolerant broadcasting and multicasting algorithm for wormhole routed two-dimensional meshes.

In [3], broadcast and multicast routing based on trees is deemed unsuitable because "it produces many headers for each message." The authors instead conclude that deadlock freedom can be obtained even if cycles are permitted, and by allowing cycles the message headers can be simplified. The broadcast and multicast algorithm presented here refutes this "unsuitability" assertion and demonstrates the effectiveness of combining a fault-tolerant unicast algorithm with a spanning tree based broadcast and multicast routing algorithm to provide reliable broadcast and multicast services in an $N \times N$ two-dimensional mesh with up to $N - 1$ faulty nodes.

2 Definitions for Fault-Tolerant Routing

In [5], the use of safe, unsafe, and faulty states to assist nodes in making dynamic routing decisions in a hypercube was proposed. Such multistate, virtual-channel adaptive routing schemes require each node of the network to check its neighbors' status regularly. Whenever a neighbor's status changes, the locally executed routing algorithm uses the new status information to determine the best link for forwarding messages. In [1], This idea has been used to produce a fault-tolerant wormhole routing algorithm (NAFTA) that can successfully route unicast messages for up to $N - 1$ faults in an $N \times N$ two-dimensional mesh. NAFTA eliminates the need for global network information by allowing each node in the network to obtain the current status of each of its neighboring nodes. Therefore, let us consider the following nine status definitions:

(1) **Row Fault** indicates that a faulty node exists in the row; (2) **Column Fault** indicates that a faulty node exists in the column; (3) **Dead End North** means that once a north-bound packet is passed to the node, it cannot travel east or west. A node is dead end north if it satisfies any of the following two conditions: (a) For any northern perimeter node, if the node's status is row fault, then the node's status is also dead end north. (b) For any nonperimeter node, if the node's status is row fault and the northern neighbor's status is dead end north. (4) **Dead End South**, (5) **Dead End East**, and (6) **Dead End West** are all simply rotations of the definition for dead end north, where Dead End East and West require the definition of Column Fault instead of row fault; (7) A node is **Faulty** if an "I'm Alive" message has not been received within a specified time interval; (8) A node is **Unsafe** if either of the following conditions are met: (1) A node is row fault and the status of either the northern or southern neighbor is faulty or unsafe. (2) A node is either dead end east or dead end west and is also row fault. Unsafe nodes are functionally equivalent to faulty nodes because they are not allowed to participate in any computations or message passing activities between safe nodes. (9) A **Safe** node is neither faulty nor unsafe - only safe nodes are allowed to participate in communication and computation activities;

An example of how NAFTA uses these nine state definitions, consider Figure 1 – our node references are always row major. Nodes (2,8) and (3,8) are marked Unsafe because each fulfills the requirements set forth in Case 2 of the definition of an Unsafe node. Nodes (2,2) and (3,6) are marked unsafe because they fulfill the requirements set forth in Case 1 of the definition of an Unsafe node.

Now, let us assume that node (7,1) must send a message to node (3,5). NAFTA begins by routing the message toward Column 5, and then north toward Row 3. Unfortunately, node (5,5) is faulty. Since neither node (6,4) nor (6,6) is in a Dead End state, NAFTA arbitrarily chooses node (6,6) as the next hop. Node (6,6) then directs the message north toward the destination row. Since node (4,5) is in the destination column and is safe, the message is directed west toward the destination column to node (4,5), and then north to node (3,5) - the destination.

As an example of how the Dead End East status is used to make routing decisions, assume that node (1,4) must send a message to node (6,8). NAFTA once again begins by directing the message toward the destination column. When node (1,7) receives the message, it checks the status byte for node (1,8) and discovers that node (1,8) is Dead End East. Therefore, the message is routed south toward the destination row. Once the message reaches node (6,7), it is safe to send the message on a one-way trip east because the destination is in Row 6 and east of node (6,7). Notice that NAFTA was able to avoid using Column 8 for its south bound routing and, hence, maintain a minimum length path.

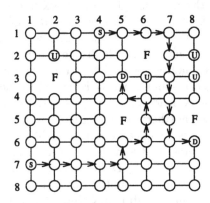

Fig. 1. Example of Routing Within a Faulty Mesh.

3 Single Source Fault-Tolerant Broadcasting Without Virtual Channels

Single source Broadcasting in a two-dimensional mesh can be accomplished by constructing a spanning tree composed of multidestination, unidirectional worms, such that every destination node is visited exactly once and all branches of the tree contain the shortest disjoint paths from the source to the destinations. As Figure 4a shows, one popular method of building a single-source broadcast spanning tree within a mesh is to allow the column of the source to act as the "trunk" of the tree, while the rows form the branches. Because this method produces the shortest disjoint paths from the source to all destinations, the efficiency of the broadcast is maximized. Unfortunately this method requires the broadcast message to pass through every node in the source node's row and column, hence the source must reside in a fault free row and column. This restriction can be overcome if NAFTA's nine state definitions are used to construct the broadcast spanning tree.

NAFTA's nine state definitions can be used to dynamically divide the mesh into, at most, five disjoint regions, where each region contains a "virtual source" for the broadcast message. By dynamically modifying the header flits at intermediate nodes, routing decisions within each region can be made relative to the corresponding virtual source instead of the real source. Figure 2 shows "C" based pseudocode for the virtual source broadcasting algorithm (VSB) that is invoked at the source, while Figure 3 shows the broadcasting algorithm that is invoked by the intermediate nodes. We will let $H_{(x,y)}$ denote a header flit with a source node $n_{(x,y)}$ that resides in row x and column y. Whenever a source node is row fault or column fault a "?" will be used to indicate that a virtual source is required. Intermediate nodes will use the status definitions to replace the "?" symbols with a new virtual source row and/or column value.

VSB SOURCE ALGORITHM:

```
No transmissions to nodes that are Faulty, Unsafe, or non-existent.
BEGIN
x=current row
y=current column
H(Sr,Sc) = outgoing header flit with source id n(Sr,Sc).
if(current node is RF) Sr =? else Sr = x
if(current node is CF) Sc =? else Sc = y
if (current node is RF){
        if(southern neighbor ≠ DES){
            send H(Sr,Sc) south
            send H(x,Sc) north}
        else if(northern neighbor ≠ DEN){
            send H(Sr,Sc) north
            send H(x,Sc) south}}
else if(current node is DEE){
        send H(x,y) east
        send H(Sr,Sc) west
        if ((northern neighbor = RF) or (Sc = y)) send H(x,Sc) north
        if ((southern neighbor = RF) or (Sc = y)) send H(x,Sc) south}
else {
        send H(x,y) west
        send H(Sr,Sc) east
        if ((northern neighbor = RF) or (Sc = y)) send H(x,Sc) north
        if ((southern neighbor = RF) or (Sc = y)) send H(x,Sc) south}
END
```

Fig. 2. The Virtual Source Broadcast Algorithm Executed at the source node.

Figure 4b shows how a mesh can be dynamically divided into, at most, five disjoint regions, each with its own virtual source. Because the source, $n_{(2,4)}$, is both row fault and column fault, virtual sources are necessary. The dead end north status of the source node forces the source algorithm to send the special

VSB INTERMEDIATE ALGORITHM

```
No transmissions to nodes that are Faulty, Unsafe, or non-existent.
BEGIN
x=current row
y=current column
H(Sr,Sc) = incomming header flit with source id n(Sr,Sc).
if((Sr =?) and (current node not RF)) Sr = x
if((Sc =?) and (current node not CF)) Sc = y
if((incoming link = east) or ((Sc = y) and (current node not RF) and (incoming link ≠ west))) send H(Sr,Sc) west
if((incoming link = west) or ((Sc = y) and (current node not RF) and (incoming link ≠ east))) send H(Sr,Sc) east
if((incoming link = north) and (Sc = y)) send H(Sr,Sc) south
else if((incoming link ≠ south) and (((southern neighbor = RF) and (x ≥ Sr)) or (Sc = y))
    send H(Sr,Sc) south
if((incoming link = south) and (Sc = y)) send H(Sr,Sc) north
else if((incomming link ≠ north) and (((northern neighbor = RF) and (x ≤ Sr)) or (Sc = y))
    send H(Sr,Sc) north
if((incoming link = north) or (incoming link = south)){
    if((Sr = x) and (Sc =?)){
        if(eastern neighbor ≠ DEE){
            send H(Sr,Sc) east
            send H(x,y) west}
        else{
            send H(Sr,Sc) west
            send H(x,y) east}}
    else if((Sc = y) and (current node ≠ RF)){
        send H(Sr,Sc) west
        send H(Sr,Sc) east}}
END
```

Fig. 3. The Virtual Source Broadcast Algorithm Executed at the intermediate nodes.

header southward into a fault free row. Once a fault-free row is reached, $n_{(3,4)}$ in this case, the first virtual source is detected and the "?" symbol corresponding to the source row is changed to a "3". The VSB algorithm now searches for a fault free column by sending a "?" symbol in the column position to node $n_{(3,5)}$, where $n_{(3,5)}$ is designated as a virtual source.

Theorem 1: The (VSB) algorithm (shown in Figures 2 and 3) will divide a mesh into no more than five disjoint sets of destination nodes.

Proof: For a given $N \times N$ two-dimensional mesh M, we will designate a single broadcast source $n_{(x,y)} \in S$, where S is the set of all safe nodes in M and $n_{(x,y)}$ resides in row x and column y. Let $H_{(x,y)}$ denote a header flit with a source of $n_{(x,y)}$. From the definitions of row fault and column fault we can construct $(C \cup R) \subset S$, where $\forall n_{(p,q)} \in S$, $n_{(p,q)} \in R \implies n_{(p,q)}$ is in a faulty row, and $n_{(p,q)} \in C \implies n_{(p,q)}$ is in a faulty column. Therefore, we know that exactly one of the following four assertions must be true about $n_{(x,y)}$: 1) $n_{(x,y)} \in S \cap (R^c \cap C^c)$; 2) $n_{(x,y)} \in R \cap C^c$; 3) $n_{(x,y)} \in C \cap R^c$; 4) $n_{(x,y)} \in C \cap R$.

Let rows e and f be defined as perimeter rows, such that row e is the northern perimeter when row f is the southern perimeter and vice versa. Let columns g and h be defined as perimeter columns, such that column g is the western perimeter when column h is the eastern perimeter and vice versa. Let k be the fault free row closest to row x within rows x through e; let l be the fault-free row closest to row x within rows x through f; let m be the fault-free row closest to row l within rows l through f; let b be the fault-free column closest to column y within columns y through h.

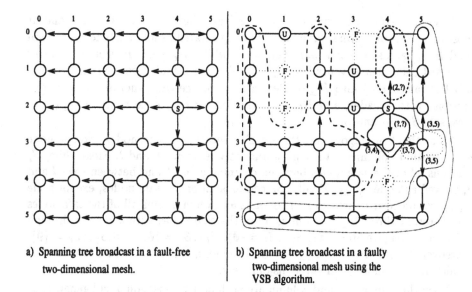

a) Spanning tree broadcast in a fault-free
two-dimensional mesh.

b) Spanning tree broadcast in a faulty
two-dimensional mesh using the
VSB algorithm.

Fig. 4. Example of a VSB Single-Source Broadcast in a Faulty and Fault-Free Mesh.

Let us also construct $(S_1 \cup S_2 \cup S_3 \cup S_4 \cup S_5 \cup S_6 \cup S_7 \cup S_8 \cup \{n_{(x,y)}\}) = S$, where $\forall n_{(p,q)} \in S,$: $n_{(p,q)} \in S_1 \iff n_{(p,q)}$ receives $H_{(x,?)}$; $n_{(p,q)} \in S_2 \iff n_{(p,q)}$ receives $H_{(?,?)}$; $n_{(p,q)} \in S_3 \iff n_{(p,q)}$ receives $H_{(l,y)}$; $n_{(p,q)} \in S_4 \iff n_{(p,q)}$ receives $H_{(l,?)}$; $n_{(p,q)} \in S_5 \iff n_{(p,q)}$ receives $H_{(l,b)}$; $n_{(p,q)} \in S_6 \iff n_{(p,q)}$ receives $H_{(?,y)}$; $n_{(p,q)} \in S_7 \iff n_{(p,q)}$ receives $H_{(x,y)}$; $n_{(p,q)} \in S_8 \iff n_{(p,q)}$ receives $H_{(x,b)}$.

Consider assertion 1: When the source resides in a fault free row and column, the only header that is received by the destination nodes is $H_{(x,y)}$. Hence, the VSB algorithm produces exactly one set of destination nodes: $S_7 \cup \{n_{(x,y)}\} = S$.

Now consider assertion 2: When row x is faulty but column y is fault-free, at most three sets of destination nodes will be generated as follows: The source node will not send a copy of the message across the faulty row, hence one header must be sent north, and one south. Therefore, $H_{(x,y)}$ will be sent in one direction, while $H_{(?,y)}$ will be sent in the other. Eventually, $H_{(?,y)}$ will reach a fault-free row where it will be transformed into $H_{(l,y)}$.

Because the source can generate at most two versions of the header, and $H_{(?,y)}$ is transformed only once at node $n_{(l,y)}$, we have the sets S_6, S_7, and S_3.

From the VSB algorithm, the set S_7 contains all safe nodes between rows x and e in column y and all of the safe nodes within rows k through e. Meanwhile, S_6 contains all of the safe nodes between rows x and l in column y plus node $n_{(l,y)}$. Finally, S_3 contains all of the safe nodes, except $n_{(l,y)}$, within rows l through f, as well as all of the safe nodes not in column y between rows k and l. Hence, as Figure 5a shows, $S_6 \cap S_7 = \{\emptyset\}$, $S_7 \cap S_3 = \{\emptyset\}$, and $S_6 \cap S_3 = \{\emptyset\}$. Moreover, $S_6 \cup S_7 \cup S_3 \cup \{n_{(x,y)}\} = S$. Therefore, when assertion 2 is true, S is divided into no more than three disjoint sets.

When assertion 3 is true, column y is faulty but row x is fault-free and at most three sets of destination nodes will be generated as follows: The source will send $H_{(x,y)}$ across row x toward column g, while $H_{(x,?)}$ will be sent across row x toward column h. Eventually, $H_{(x,?)}$ will reach a fault-free column where it will be transformed into $H_{(x,b)}$. Because the source can generate at most two versions of the header, and $H_{(x,?)}$ is transformed only once at node $n_{(x,b)}$, we have sets S_1, S_7, and S_8.

From the VSB algorithm, the set S_7 contains all safe nodes, except node $n_{(x,y)}$, within columns y through g and between rows k and l. Meanwhile, S_1 contains all of the safe nodes between columns y and b and between rows l and k, as well as node $n_{(x,b)}$. Finally, S_8 contains all of the safe nodes, except node $n_{(x,b)}$, within rows l through k in columns b through h, plus all of the safe nodes within rows l through f, as well as all of the safe nodes within rows k through e. Hence, as Figure 5b shows, $S_1 \cap S_7 = \{\emptyset\}$, $S_7 \cap S_8 = \{\emptyset\}$, and $S_1 \cap S_8 = \{\emptyset\}$. Moreover, $S_1 \cup S_7 \cup S_8 \cup \{n_{(x,y)}\} = S$. Therefore, when assertion 3 is true, S is divided into no more than three disjoint sets.

When the source row and column are both faulty, assertion 4 will generate at most five sets of destination nodes as follows: The source will send $H_{(?,?)}$ through column y toward row f, and $H_{(x,?)}$ through column y toward row e. eventually, $H_{(?,?)}$ will reach the fault free row l. Node $n_{(l,y)}$ will generate $H_{(l,y)}$ and $H_{(l,?)}$. $H_{(l,y)}$ will be sent across row l toward column g, while $H_{(l,?)}$ will be sent across row l toward column h. Eventually, $H_{(l,?)}$ will reach a fault free column where it will be transformed into $H_{(l,b)}$. Hence the source node and node $n_{(l,y)}$ can each generate at most two unique versions of the header and $H_{(l,?)}$ is transformed only once at node $n_{(l,b)}$, we have sets S_1, S_2, S_3, S_4, and S_5.

From the VSB algorithm, the set S_1 contains all safe nodes that are between rows x and k in column y. The set S_2 contains all safe nodes, except $n_{(x,y)}$, within rows x through l in column y. S_3 contains all the safe nodes between rows l and m in column y, plus all the safe nodes between rows k and m between columns y and g, plus all the safe nodes within column g between rows k and m. Set S_4 contains all of the safe nodes between columns y and b and between rows k and m, as well as node $n_{(l,b)}$. S_5 contains all the safe nodes, except $n_{(l,b)}$, in rows k through m, within columns b through h, plus all the safe nodes within rows m through f and rows k through e. Hence, as Figure 5c shows, $S_1 \cap S_2 = \{\emptyset\}$, $S_1 \cap S_3 = \{\emptyset\}$, $S_1 \cap S_4 = \{\emptyset\}$, $S_1 \cap S_5 = \{\emptyset\}$, $S_2 \cap S_3 = \{\emptyset\}$, $S_2 \cap S_4 = \{\emptyset\}$, $S_2 \cap S_5 = \{\emptyset\}$, $S_3 \cap S_4 = \{\emptyset\}$, $S_3 \cap S_5 = \{\emptyset\}$, and $S_4 \cap S_5 = \{\emptyset\}$. Moreover, $S_1 \cup S_2 \cup S_3 \cup S_4 \cup S_5 \cup \{n_{(x,y)}\} = S$. Therefore, when assertion 4 is true, S is divided into no more than five disjoint sets.

Since every source node must satisfy exactly one of the assertions, and no assertion generates more than five disjoint sets, the VSB algorithm will divide a mesh into no more than five disjoint sets of destination nodes.

■

Theorem 2: The VSB algorithm will cause every safe node of each of the previously defined eight potential subsets of destination nodes to receive exactly one copy of a broadcast message.

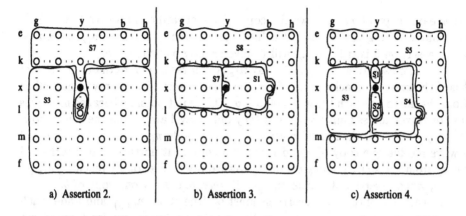

a) Assertion 2.   b) Assertion 3.   c) Assertion 4.

Fig. 5. Examples of VSB Broadcasts regions generated under when assertions 2, 3, and 4 from Theorem 1 are true.

Proof by contradiction: For a given $N \times N$ two-dimensional mesh M, we will assume that a destination node $n_{(x,y)} \in S$ does not receive exactly one copy of a header flit for a broadcast message b. When the number of faulty nodes is within the range $0 \leq f < N$, we know that exactly one of the following four assertions must be true about $n_{(x,y)}$: 1) $n_{(x,y)} \in S \cap (R^c \cap C^c)$; 2) $n_{(x,y)} \in R \cap C^c$; 3) $n_{(x,y)} \in C \cap R^c$. 4) $n_{(x,y)} \in C \cap R$.

Consider assertion 1. The only way $n_{(x,y)}$ will receive more than one copy of b is if the message is traveling across row x and the message also reaches $n_{(x,y)}$ from the north or south through column y. If the message reaches $n_{(x,y)}$ from the north or south, then $n_{(x,y)}$ must reside within the source column. If $n_{(x,y)}$ resides within the source column, it is not possible for $n_{(x,y)}$ to receive more than one copy of b because messages are only allowed to travel away from the source column along fault-free rows. Hence, it is not possible for $n_{(x,y)}$ to receive more than one copy of b. If $n_{(x,y)} \in S \cap (R^c \cap C^c)$, then there must also exist a node $n_{(x,z)} \in S$ that will always receive one copy of b and forward a copy of it eastward and westward along row x, eventually reaching $n_{(x,y)}$. Hence, when assertion 1 is true, $n_{(x,y)}$ will receive exactly one copy of b.

Consider assertion 2. The only way $n_{(x,y)}$ will receive more than one copy of b is if the message reaches $n_{(x,y)}$ from the north and south through column y. Since messages are only allowed to enter a faulty row from either the north or the south, it is not possible for $n_{(x,y)}$ to receive more than one copy of b. If $n_{(x,y)} \in R \cap C^c$, then there must also exist a node $n_{(z,y)} \in R^c$ that will always receive one copy of b and forward a copy of it northward or southward (away from the source) along column y toward row x, eventually reaching $n_{(x,y)}$. Hence, when assertion 2 is true, $n_{(x,y)}$ will receive exactly one copy of b.

Consider assertion 3. The only way $n_{(x,y)}$ will receive more than one copy of b is if the message reaches $n_{(x,y)}$ from the east and west through row x. This is not possible because messages only travel away from the source column. If $n_{(x,y)} \in C \cap R^c$, then there must also exist a node $n_{(x,z)} \in C^c$ that will always receive one copy of b and forward a copy of it eastward or westward (away from the source) along row x toward column y, eventually reaching $n_{(x,y)}$. Hence, when assertion 3 is true, $n_{(x,y)}$ will receive exactly one copy of b.

Consider assertion 4. The only way $n_{(x,y)}$ will receive more than one copy of b is if the message reaches $n_{(x,y)}$ from the east or west through row x as well as from the north or south through column y. This is not possible because messages do not travel across faulty rows, and they only travel away from the source row. If $n_{(x,y)} \in C \cap R$, then there must also exist a node $n_{(x,y)} \in R^c \cap S$ that will always receive one copy of b and forward a copy of it northward or southward (away from the source) along column y toward row x, eventually reaching $n_{(x,y)}$. Hence, when assertion 3 is true, $n_{(x,y)}$ will receive exactly one copy of b.

At least one of the four assertions must be true about $n_{(x,y)}$, and under each of the assertions, $n_{(x,y)}$ receives exactly one copy a header flit for a broadcast message b, this contradicts our assumption that $n_{(x,y)}$ does not receive exactly one copy of a header flit for a broadcast message b. ∎

Theorem 3: The (VSB) algorithm will cause every safe node in the mesh to receive exactly one copy of the broadcast message.
Proof: We have already seen that the safe nodes in the mesh can be divided into no more than five subsets. Furthermore, it has been shown that every destination node within each subset will be visited exactly once. Since the subsets are also disjoint, every destination node in the mesh will receive exactly one copy of the broadcast message. ∎

Theorem 4: The (VSB) algorithm is deadlock and livelock free.
Proof: We have already seen that every safe node in M is visited exactly once. Hence cyclic dependencies cannot exist within the broadcast virtual network. Since the VSB algorithm cannot generate cyclic dependencies, VSB is deadlock free. Moreover, because backtracking is not allowed VSB is also livelock-free. ∎

3.1 Supporting Simultaneous Unicast and Broadcast Traffic

The VSB algorithm can be implemented alone without requiring any additional virtual channels. The authors have shown in [1] that NAFTA uses four virtual channels per physical link to create two independent virtual networks. Therefore, the easiest way to implement VSB is to simply add two more virtual channels per physical link to create a third independent broadcast virtual network. Because the broadcast virtual network is independent of the unicast routing strategy deadlock freedom is assured. As an example of simultaneous unicasting and broadcasting, consider the faulty mesh in Figure 6. The solid arrows show the path taken by the broadcast message with source B_s (1,1). The nodes labeled VS_1 and VS_2 are the virtual sources for the broadcast. The dotted lines indicate the path taken by a unicast message as it uses NAFTA to avoid faulty and unsafe nodes while traveling from node S1 (4,0) to D1 (0,5) and the dashed lines show the path taken from node S2 (5,0) to D2 (0,2).

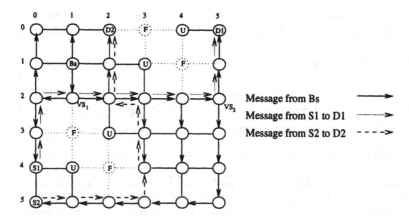

Fig. 6. Example of Unicast and Single-Source Broadcast traffic in a Faulty Mesh.

4 Conclusions and Future Work

In Table 1 the VSB algorithm is compared with other recent work in the area of broadcasting and multicasting in wormhole routed two-dimensional mesh networks. While other authors have proposed broadcast and multicast algorithms that require the source node to build and sort complex lists of destinations, VSB uses simple headers and allows intermediate nodes to reliably participate in the broadcast. Table 1 also shows us that while the MG and HL methods also provide fault-tolerance, they still require global fault knowledge, hence scalability is a serious problem for such methods. If the routers contain the logic to modify the VSB header flits, the full potential of wormhole routing can be exploited to minimize the time required to perform the broadcast.

The main advantage of VSB is its distributed parallel nature and use of local state information. The VSB algorithm does not require the source node to maintain global network information, nor does it need to build and sort complex lists of destination nodes. Future work will include extensions for three-dimensional meshes and tori, as well as a more detailed analysis of the VSB algorithm for real mathematical applications.

References

1. C. M. Cunningham and D. R. Avresky. Fault-tolerant adaptive routing for two-dimensional meshes. In *Proceedings of the First Internationl Symposium on High Performance Computing Architecture*, Raleigh, North Carolina, U.S.A., January 1995.
2. S. Singhal D. K. Panda and P. Prabhakaran. Multidestination message passing mechanism conforming to base wormhole routing scheme. In *Proceedings of the Parallel Computer Routing and Communication Workshop, Lecture Notes on Computer Science*, pages 131–145, 1994.

Performance Measure	VSB	Column Path Path [8]	Double Channel [11]	Dual Path [11]	Multi Path [11]	MG [2]	HL [2]	Trip-Based [10]
Additional Virtual Channels/Link	0^3	0	2	0	0	0	0	4
Additional Consumption Channels	0^3	2	0	$0/2$ [1]	$0/2$ [1]	3	3	2
Multiple Sources	No	Yes	No	No/Yes [1]	No/Yes [1]	No	No	Yes
Faults Tolerated	N-1	0	0	0	0	Varies [2]	Varies [2]	???
Basic Strategy	Spanning Tree	Hamiltonian Path	Tree	Hamiltonian Path	Hamiltonian Path	Tree	Hamiltonian Path	Trip

[1] For Dualpath and Multipath, only single source multicasting and broadcasting is supported with 0 additional consumption channels [11]. However, with 2 additional consumption channels multiple sources can be supported [8].
[2] For the HL and MG algorithms, fault-tolerance is determined by the fault-tolerant abilities of the unicast algorithms upon which the HL and MG strategies rely.
[3] For simultaneous unicasts using NAFTA and a single source broadcast using VSB, 6 virtual channels are required for each physical link.

Table 1. FTSTBM Versus Other Broadcast and Multicast Wormhole Routing Algorithms.

3. J. Duato. A theory of deadlock-free adaptive multicast routing in wormhole networks. *IEEE Transactions on Parallel and Distributed Systems*, 6(9):976–987, September 1995.

4. P. K. McKinley H. Xu and L. M. Ni. A scalable multicast service for mesh networks. In *Frontiers of Massively Parallel Computation*, pages 156–163. IEEE, 1992.

5. T. C. Lee and J. P. Hayes. A fault-tolerant communication scheme for hypercube computers. *IEEE Transactions on Computers*, 41(10):1242–1255, October 1992.

6. X. Lin and L. M. Ni. Deadlock-free multicast wormhole routing in multicomputer networks. *Computer Architecture News*, 19(13):116–125, 1991.

7. A. Esfahanian P. K. McKinley, H. Xu and L. M. Ni. Unicast-based multicast communication in wormhole-routed networks. In *Proceedings of the International Conference on Parallel Processing*, volume 2, pages 10–18, 1992.

8. S. Chalasani R. V. Boppana and C. S. Raghavendra. On multicast wormhole routing in multicomputer networks. *Computer Architecture News*, 21(2):722–729, May 1994.

9. F. N. Sibai and S. D. Kulkarni. Performance of multicast wormhole routing algorithms in fault-tolerant 2d meshes. In *22nd Annual International Symposium on Computer Architecture*, pages 610–613, August 1994.

10. Y. Tseng and D. K. Panda. A trip-based multicasting model for wormhole-routed networks. In *Parallel Processing Symposium*, pages 276–283, 1993.

11. P. K. McKinley X. Lin and L. M. Ni. Deadlock-free multicast wormhole routing in 2-d mesh multicomputers. *IEEE Transactions on Parallel and Distributed Systems*, 5(8):793–803, August 1994.

Industrial Track paper

On-line Testing of an Off-the-shelf Microprocessor Board for Safety-critical Applications[1]

F. Corno*, M. Damiani***, L. Impagliazzo**, P. Prinetto*,
M. Rebaudengo*, G. Sartore****, M. Sonza Reorda*

*	******
Politecnico di Torino	CRIS
Dipartimento di Automatica e Informatica	Centro Ricerche Innovative per il Sud
Torino, Italy	Napoli, Italy
***	********
Università di Padova	Ansaldo Trasporti
Dip. Elettronica e Informatica	
Padova, Italy	Genova, Italy

Abstract

The paper describes the strategy adopted to implement on-line test procedures for a commercial microprocessor board used in an automated light-metro control system. Special care has been devoted to chose the most effective test strategy for memory elements, processors, and caches, while guaranteeing a minimum impact on the normal behavior of the whole system. Implementation of the described techniques will significantly improve the system ability to safely react to possible faults. This will be quantitatively determined in the subsequent dependability evaluation phase.

1. Introduction

The control systems of many safety-critical applications are currently undergoing the transition from electro-mechanical to electronic devices. Examples are the control systems used in nuclear plants, planes, and rail-ways. A major problem with the new systems is how to ensure a given threshold of reliability, and in particular how to guarantee that the occurrence probability of unsafe situations is lower than a given accepted value.

These systems are often composed of several parts, some designed specifically for this kind of applications, and some others sold by third parties. In both cases,

---

[1]Contact Person: Paolo PRINETTO, Politecnico di Torino, Dip. di Automatica e Informatica, Corso Duca degli Abruzzi 24, I-10129 Torino, Italy, tel. +39 11 564 7007, fax +39 11 564 7099, E-mail Paolo.Prinetto@polito.it

particular care must be devoted to the evaluation of the reliability degree of the parts, and to the development of techniques to possibly improve it. The latter objective can be achieved in different ways:

- by introducing hardware redundancy
- by introducing information redundancy in the transmission and processing phases
- by developing on-line test procedures which continuously check the correct behavior of the hardware.

A mix of the different approaches is normally adopted when large systems are considered.

This paper focuses on the development of the on-line test procedures for a commercial microprocessor board used in an automated light-metro system. The procedures aim at detecting possible faults in the board and signaling this to the outside, so that the board can be disabled within a maximum time since the fault occurrence, thus improving the system reliability.

The main contribution of this paper is in the description of an on-line test strategy which is compatible with the normal behavior of the board. Moreover, the impact of test procedures on the software development and maintenance phases has been taken into account to limit the costs.

The paper is organized as follow: Section 2 briefly describes the system from the hardware and software point of view; Section 3 outlines the test strategy adopted for each component. Section 4 draws some conclusions.

2. System Description

The addressed board is produced by Motorola under the code MVME162 [Moto94a] [Moto94b]. It includes (Fig. 1) a 25 MHz 68LC040 microprocessor, 8MB of DRAM, 512 KB of SRAM, and some ASICs devoted to different tasks (interface towards the VMEbus, memory management and Watchdog Timer, peripheral interface). The board also supports up to four IndustryPack modules. In our configuration, three IP-COMM302 modules [Gree94] are installed, each managing three serial lines. Each IP-COMM302 module includes a 68302 processor, a 512 KB SRAM, and a Xilinx interface towards the MVME162 board (Fig. 2). The 68040 processor exchanges information with the three IP-COMM modules by accessing to their local memory.

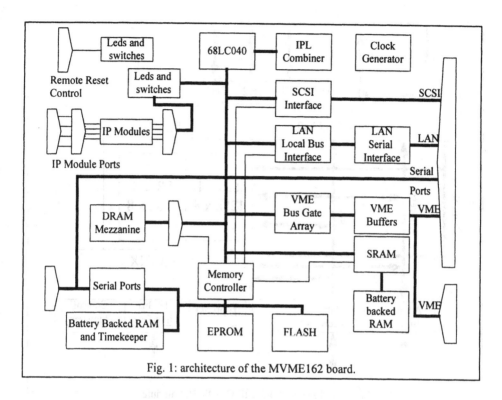

Fig. 1: architecture of the MVME162 board.

The board runs two layers of software:
- the *Operating System* layer, which is in charge of system management (memory mapping, process activation, etc.)
- the *Application* layer, which includes the processes performing the specific tasks the board is used for.

All the software but a very small bootstrap piece of code, written in a local ROM, is loaded in the DRAM during the bootstrap phase through the VMEbus from an external memory board.

The system iterates through cycles, which include an operating period (300ms), when input, processing, and output tasks are activated, and an idle period (50ms), when the system does not perform any operation. As the railways system time constraints are relatively loose, the interrupt mechanism is not used, and all tasks, including those devoted to I/O operations, are managed through polling. Security is also enhanced by this mechanism since the polling loop also acts as an implicit watchdog.

Safety is first guaranteed in the system by *hardware redundancy* (in terms of both MVME162 boards and transmission lines) [Mong92] and *software redundancy* (in terms of redundant information in the transmission and processing phases). Additionally, the on-line test procedures described in this paper have been added to the Operating System layer in order to detect possible faults in the board.

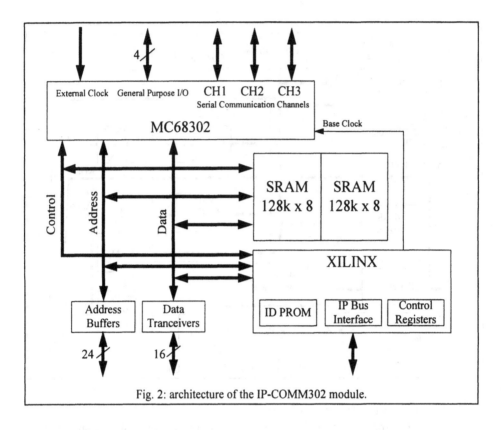

Fig. 2: architecture of the IP-COMM302 module.

3. Test Strategy

When developing the test strategy for the MVME162 board, we started from the observation that the memory elements (both memory chips and memory elements inside other components, e.g., registers and caches in the microprocessor) are the most critical components from the point of view of the reliability [Moto94d].

Moreover, the addressed faults are both permanent and transient faults; the latter ones are particularly important when affecting high-density memory components [CaWi87].

The test procedures for each component have been developed following several different approaches:

- when *memory chips* are considered, specific algorithms have been exploited, taken from the literature [Goor91]
- for *microprocessors*, two approaches have been combined: from one hand, the test code developed by Motorola for the 68K core and based on the knowledge of the core structure has been adopted; some changes have been introduced to transform this code into separate on-line test procedures. On the other hand, a functional approach has been followed, based on the

method described in [BrAb84], and a set of test procedures implementing this approach is currently under development

- for the *other components*, no structural knowledge is available, and the only viable solution is based on developing test procedures exciting the functionality of each component.

Since we are dealing with an on-line test strategy, an additional constraint is that the test procedure activation must not interfere with the normal behavior of the board, unless a fault is detected.

Table 1 provides a summary of the characteristics (in terms of number of assembly code lines and time for execution) of the implemented test procedures. The memory occupation of the assembly code for the whole test set amounts to less than 30KByte, and since the procedures are activated alternatively, the memory for data storage is shared. The code is executed at the processor speed of 25MHz; the average rate of execution is less than the nominal one for the 68040 processor since caches need to be disabled during the execution of memory testing procedures.

Procedure	#Lines	Time
RAM	70	30ms/KByte
ROM	220	15ms/KByte
CPU - addressing modes	480	250 µs
CPU - microcode	1,750	170 µs
CPU - registers	200	300 µs
CPU - cache	1,800	23 ms
TOTAL	4,520	

Table 1: Characteristics of the test procedures.

The following paragraphs analyze more in detail the strategy adopted for each of the component types.

3.1. RAM Testing

The test strategy we adopted for RAMs had to take into account the constraints on time and space imposed by the system characteristics: as stopping the system for a long period is also not allowed, solutions like *Transparent Testing* [Nico92] could not been adopted, as they can not be interrupted before they reach their conclusion.

The adopted solution is based on the *March* algorithm proposed in [NTAb78], and extended to general memories in [CPSB95]. This algorithm guarantees that all the permanent stuck-at faults in the decoding circuitry, and all the permanent stuck-at, transition, and coupling faults in the memory matrix are detected; the algorithm complexity is $O(30 \cdot n \cdot (\lceil log_2 m \rceil + 1))$, where n is the number of words in the memory, and m the bit width of each word.

The algorithm does not make any assumption on the physical structure of the memory; therefore, its adoption makes our approach independent on the type and organization of the chip modules on the board.

The adopted algorithm destroys the previous contents of the memory. Moreover, it can not be interrupted nor suspended, unless no other accesses to the memory are made until its re-activation.

As a consequence, we have been forced to limit the use of the memory for functional purposes to one half of the available size. At each moment, one half of the memory is used for normal purposes, while the other half is under test. The test procedure is activated during the idle periods of the processor, and suspended when these periods end. When the procedure finishes testing one half of the memory, the two halves are swapped (i.e., useful data are copied from one half to the other), and the test starts on the other half. Swapping is made easier by the presence of a programmable Memory Management Unit.

3.2. ROM Testing

The procedure devoted to testing the ROM memory, as well as any part of the RAM memory which only contains fixed data (e.g., the code, or configuration data), is based on computing a signature of the memory content and then comparing it with the expected signature, stored at the end of the memory itself. Signature computation is performed by resorting to a primitive polynomial of degree $n=64$, thus guaranteeing an aliasing probability of the order of $O(2^{-n})$ [BMSa87].

If aliasing effects are neglected, the procedure is able to detect any permanent or temporary fault in the memory and in the decoding circuitry.

3.3. CPU Testing

The 68040 CPU is one of the most complex components on the MVME162 board, and due to its internal structure different test strategies are needed. Due to the inaccessibility of CPU pins during on-line testing, and to the lack of any detailed knowledge about the internal structure of the microprocessor, a functional test is needed.

In our case some procedures were made available by Motorola for testing the 68020 core (registers, addressing modes, and microprogrammed control unit), which are based on the designers knowledge. The validity of the same code on the 68040 processor is not proven, since the internal structure is different, but one can argue that it provides a good functional fault coverage. In particular, all instruction groups are tested, as well as registers and functional units.

In order to use these procedures we had to modify them in order to face the following issues:
- the test procedures were written for a bootstrap test, not an on-line one: we thus had to add initial and final parts, aimed at saving and restoring the

content of registers and memory areas whose content is modified by the procedures

- the correct execution of instructions is verified by checking the results they compute and comparing the computed result with the expected one. A critical point is therefore the correct execution of the compare instruction itself and the subsequent conditional branch to an error routine. Since the original code did not take this criticality into account, the direction of the conditional branches has been adjusted so that, even if the comparison or the branch fail, then the error code is guaranteed to be executed
- new procedures were added to test the cache control and the memory management unit instructions of the 68040 that were not in the 68020
- the test procedures were written for a microprocessor hosted by a generic board, and some parts could not run on our system (e.g., the one for testing the Memory Management Unit).

With the above procedure, an acceptable coverage of the processor can be attained; however, no quantitative data can be provided to measure the test effectiveness. To complement the test provided by Motorola in order to be able to measure the effective fault coverage and to have means to identify ways to improve it in the critical areas, we developed additional procedures. They are especially aimed at testing the CPU components that other procedures don't cover. In particular, they can be classified as follows:

- procedures for testing *register files, data transfers, and instruction set*: they are currently being developed resorting to the functional approach described in [BrAb84] and further developed in [vGVe92]. The main advantage of this approach is that it guarantees (at least from a functional point of view) that a given fault coverage is reached. The S-graph for the 68040 processor has been built, consisting of about 60 nodes and taking into account about 100 combinations of instructions and addressing modes. Some parts of the CPU model have been simplified, such as caches, since in our approach they are already tested through different methodologies. We are now deriving assembly code to implement the various tests
- procedures for testing the *cache*: due to the many problems they pose, they are separately described in Section 3.3.1
- procedures for testing the *Memory Management Unit* (MMU), which in our system is just used during memory testing to swap the different memory banks. As a consequence, we devoted special attention to testing the sequence of operations used in bank switching.

Note that the test of the Floating Point Unit has not been considered, as this is not present on the CPU version mounted on our board.

The Operating System activates the above procedures during the processor idle times; as a consequence, the procedure execution time is shorter than that of a minimum-length idle period.

3.3.1. Cache Testing

The 68040 processor is equipped with two separate caches, devoted to data and instructions, respectively. The main characteristics of each cache are as follows:
- 8Kbyte of static RAM, organized as 256 lines of 16 bytes each
- four-way set associative; there are then 64 sets of four lines each
- random replacement on cache miss
- physical addressing.

Each cache line is equipped with a 22-bit tag. For each cache, the input address is the output of an on-chip Memory Management Unit. The tag field then records a physical address of the line in main memory. To support copyback, each long word of each line in the data cache is equipped with a dirty bit. Special instructions allow the dynamic selection of the write policy and the separate enabling/disabling of each cache. The input address is the output of the on-chip MMU, and it represents a physical address in main memory. Block replacement within a set is controlled by a two-bit random generator. There is no control to this part of the block selection logic.

The main idea beyond the test strategy adopted for caches is to exploit the same algorithms used for RAMs: however, cache associativity, the block replacement logic, and the type of addressing introduce nontrivial observability and controllability problems. A good systematic approach to the general problem of testing cache memories taking into account the mentioned problems is in [Sosn95].

Hereafter, we report the design choices for the test routines and the basic motivations behind each choice.

The data cache consists of:
- Four memory arrays (data, tag, dirty bits, valid bits) and decoding logic
- Tag comparators and hit/miss generation logic
- Block replacement logic
- Cache control register.

The instruction cache misses the dirty bit array. Each functional block is tested separately.

Memory arrays are tested using march tests [Goor91]. We chose *March C-* because it was the most accurate test (from fault coverage standpoint) that could be fit within the allotted time. Moreover, it seems to be best suited in practice for static memory arrays.

In practice, however, to test the various arrays we had to modify March C-, sometimes substantially:
- The data cache memory array can be fully tested by a straightforward implementation of March C-.
- For the valid bit array, implementation of March C- presents difficulties, because the block replacement logic is not directly controllable. It is then impossible to validate/invalidate the lines of a set in a well-defined order. We have thus introduced a modified March C- which achieves the same coverage as a regular March C-, with a small CPU time penalty.
- The implementation of March C- for the dirty bit array is likewise difficult, as read and write operations can not be directly implemented: any write operation corresponds to reading the word (so that it is loaded into cache)

and modifying it (so that the dirty bit is modified); any read operation corresponds to verifying that the dirty bit has the right value by checking whether the corresponding line is flushed. Because a substantial fraction of the code is executed with the data cache disabled, procedure is CPU time demanding.

- Because of the physical addressing, the tag arrays can only contain the (very limited) range of physical addresses, and it is therefore in general impossible to test them completely. In particular, it is impossible to set arbitrarily the most significant bits of the tags. In the case of the MVME162 board, however, we were able to circumvent this problem because of the additional memory management capabilities provided by the MCchip memory manager.

- The instruction cache data array is probably the most lengthy and difficult object to test, first because its contents cannot be arbitrary (they must be instructions), and second because modifying a cache location bit-by-bit implies finding a complex sequence of instructions with adjacent encodings to be loaded always in the same location. Moreover, as the verification of a cache location is the execution of its content, we must be sure that the presence of a fault always impacts the end result of the test procedure (e.g., a register content). In practice, we could not fit the execution of one such complex code within the allotted time, and had to shorten the test slightly. The test covers all stuck-ats, all disjoint transition faults, and all disjoint inversion coupling faults, provided the two cells do not belong to the same word. This test is completed by a second routine, covering all decoder faults.

3.4. IP modules

Most of the devices hosted by the IP modules (68302 microprocessor and RAM memory) are very similar to those existing on the MVME162 board, and slightly different versions of the procedures for RAM and CPU testing described for the MVME162 board are used for testing the corresponding components on the IP-modules. However, some additional issues had to be considered.

A first problem is how to activate the test of the IP-COMM, and how to gather the results. In our approach, the activation of the local test procedures is autonomously done by the 68302 processor exploiting its own idle periods: the result of each test is stored in a pre-defined memory area, which is periodically read and checked for correctness by the 68040 processor. Both the result and the last activation time are stored, so that it is possible to easily detect any situation in which no more tests are activated, due to some fault inside the IP-COMM module.

Second, the same approach used for the MVME162 board memory is exploited for the IP-COMM memory. However, RAM testing is made more difficult by the lack of a Memory Management Unit on the IP-COMM module. Swapping the contents of two memory modules thus requires the relocation of the addresses of data and code, which is too expensive. We thus decided to split the memory in two parts: at any moment, one is under test, while the other is used for normal functions. Both parts contain a copy of the code and of the static data; however, the two copies are slightly different, as any address has been suitably relocated to work on the local data. The swap of the two parts can be easily done by just copying the dynamic data from one part to the other, and then forcing the processor to fetch instructions from the other part of the memory. The test procedure adopted for the RAM is again based on the algorithm described in [NTAb78]. Memory positions containing constant information (code and static data) are tested through the computation of the signature.

Third, the test of the interface devices between the IP module and the MVME162 board has to be based only on functional information, as structural ones are missing. Moreover, any attempt to test the programming facilities of the interface requires resetting the IP module itself, which is not allowed during the board functioning. The only viable solution we devised is thus based on exciting the functions performed by these devices during the internal memory test procedures.

Some of the test procedures for the 68302 processor have been taken from the ones developed by Motorola [GoLa93]. They have been modified according to the same criteria described for the testing of the 68040 processor.

3.5. ASICs

Several ASICs are hosted by the MVME162 board to perform specific operations, such as system bus arbitration, memory access management, VME bus and IP-COMM interface. Their testing is made critical by the lack of any structural information about them.

As a consequence, procedures for testing these components have been developed following two avenues of attack:
- some specific procedures taken from the diagnostic code developed by Motorola [Moto94c] for the MVME162 board have been first exploited; they have been modified according to the same strategy described for the test procedures of the 68040 processor
- additional test procedures aimed at verifying that each component correctly performs its task have been developed; however, these have mainly been integrated into the test procedures for other components: for example, testing the ASIC in charge of memory management is done by adding some new parts to the test procedure for RAM memory, aiming at verifying that the error detection logic existing in the ASIC properly works.

4. Conclusions

The paper describes the strategy adopted for developing the on-line procedures for testing a commercial microprocessor board used in a safety-critical environment, where the achievement of fault-tolerance and safety target is a key point in the design process.

The board components can be grouped in three categories:

- *memories*, which are known to be particularly critical from the reliability point of view, as their high integration level makes faults more frequent; algorithms have been adopted, able to cover a great percent of permanent faults; exploiting them for on-line testing requires a careful design of system software
- *microprocessors*, which include different types of components, such as irregular combinational logic (e.g., arithmetic-logic units), caches, registers, and control units; therefore, specific test procedures must be developed, resorting to the most advanced techniques so far proposed; where no other approaches are possible, pure functional testing can be exploited; eventually, existing test procedures developed by the manufacturer can be transformed into on-line test procedures
- ASICs, which can only be tested on a functional basis.

A critical issue when developing such a kind of test procedures is the evaluation of the attained fault coverage; the availability of more efficient fault simulators and of powerful description languages (e.g., VHDL [IEEE88]) makes now possible to perform this task by modeling the system and simulating it in the presence of faults. Work is currently being done in this direction to evaluate the effectiveness of the described approach.

As the system software becomes available, we are also evaluating whether its idle times allow the execution of the test procedures with a frequency sufficient to guarantee that the target maximum latency is respected.

It is our belief that the results of this work will be of great help in the subsequent phase, aimed at evaluating the reliability of the whole system resorting to fault injection techniques [ClPr95].

5. References

[BMSa87]   P.H. Bardell, W.H. McAnney, J. Savir: *Built-In Test for VLSI*, John Wiley & Sons, 1987

[BrAb84]   D. Brahme, J.A. Abraham: *Functional Testing of Microprocessors*, IEEE Trans. on Computers, Vol. C-33, June 1984, pp. 475-485

[CaWi87]   P.M. Carter, B.R. Wilkins: *Influences on Soft Error Rates in Static RAM's*, IEEE Journal of Solid-State Circuits, Vol. SC-22, No. 3, June 1987

[ClPr95]   J.A. Clark, D.K. Pradhan: *Fault Injection: A Method for Validating Computer-System Dependability*, IEEE Computer, June 1995, pp. 47-56

[CPSB95]   P. Camurati, P. Prinetto, M. Sonza Reorda, S. Barbagallo, A. Burri, D. Medina: *Industrial BIST of embedded RAMS*, IEEE Design and Test, Fall 1995, pp. 86-95

[GoLa93]   K. Godfrey, G. Lawton, *MC68302 Confidence Test Software*, AN469/D, Motorola Semiconductor Application Note, 1993

[Goor91]   A.J. van de Goor: *Testing Semiconductor Memories: Theory and Practice*, John Wiley and Sons, 1991

[Gree94]   GreenSpring Computers, *IP-COMM302 User Manual*, Menlo Park, CA (USA), 1994

[IEEE88]   IEEE, *IEEE standard VHDL language reference manual*, IEEE Computer Science Series, March 1988

[Mong92]   G. Mongardi, *Dependable Computing for Railway Control Systems*, DCCA-3 Conf., Palermo (Italy), 1992

[Moto94a]   Motorola Inc., *MVME162 Embedded Controller User's Manual - MVME162/D1*, 1994

[Moto94b]   Motorola Inc., *MVME162 Embedded Controller Programmer's Reference Manual - MVME162PG*, 1994

[Moto94c]   Motorola Inc.: *162Bug^{TM} Debugging Package User's Manual - MVME162BUG/D1A2*, 1994

[Moto94d]   Motorola Inc.: Microprocessor and Memory Technology Group, *Reliability and Quality Report*, BR1100/D, Rev. 14

[Nico92]   M. Nicolaidis: *Transparent BIST for RAMS*, Proc. Int. Test Conf., 1992, pp. 598-607

[NTAb78]   R. Nair, S.M. Thatte, J.A. Abraham: *Efficient algorithms for testing semiconductors random access memories*, IEEE Trans. on Computers, Vol. C-27, June 1978, pp. 572-576

[Sosn95]   J. Sosnowski: *In system testing of cache memories*, IEEE Int. Test Conf., 1995, pp. 384-393

[vGVe92]   A.J. van de Goor, T.J.W. Verhallen: *Functional Testing of Current Microprocessors (applied to the Intel i860^{TM})*, IEEE Int. Test Conf., 1992, pp. 684-695

Session 5

Basic Hardware Models

Chair: Karl E. Grosspietsch, GMD, Germany

The Logic Threshold Based Voting: A Model for Local Feedback Bridging Fault

M. Renovell, P. Huc and Y. Bertrand

Laboratoire d'Informatique, Robotique et Microélectronique de Montpellier (LIRMM) UMR 9928 CNRS
Université de Montpellier II : Sciences et Techniques du Languedoc
161 rue ADA 34392 Montpellier Cédex 5 FRANCE
Tel: (33)67418523 Fax:(33)67418500 Email: renovell@lirmm.fr

Abstract

In order to simulate the effects of a bridging fault it is necessary to accurately determine the intermediate voltage of the shorted nodes and compare it to the logic threshold voltage of the driven gates. This paper presents a model called "the Logic Threshold Based voting model" which can be used to determine if a bridging fault with local feedback gives an intermediate voltage which is higher or lower than a given threshold voltage. The approach is extremely faster than the previous ones since no SPICE simulation is required.
Keywords: Test, Fault Modelling, Bridging Fault.

1. Introduction

Inductive fault analysis has shown that the most commonly occurring type of failure resulting from fabrication defects, modeled as dust particles of various sizes on photomasks, is a short between physically adjacent lines, giving rise to a Bridging Fault [1,2,3]. As classicaly invoked, the difficulty of BFs comes from the fact that they exhibit intermediate voltages V_{br} in CMOS circuits. In order to determine the logic interpretation of the bridged nodes, the intermediate voltage V_{br} must be compared to the logic threshold V_T of the driven gates as illustrated in figure 1. The logic thresholds of the driven gates are assumed to be known and so, the key point consists in accurately determining the intermediate voltage V_{br}.

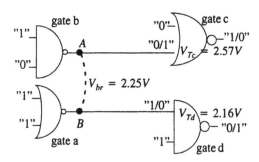

Figure 1: Example of inter–gate BF

The most recent model for intergate BFs is the voting model [4–10] and its refined versions such as the biased voting model [11]. These models try to evaluate if the intermediate voltage V_{br} created by the BF is smaller or higher than the logic threshold V_T of the driven gates by using a set of pre–simulations (SPICE) whose results are stored in tables. These models easily work on BFs with no Local Feedback but require a lot of additionnal tables and CPU time for Local Feedback BFs (LFBF).

A LFBF appears when one of the gates is both a driving and a driven gate (gate b) as illustrated in figure 2. In such situation, a bridge exists from output to input of a single gate. From layout extraction, it can be observed that LFBFs are very numerous. For some benchmark circuits, we have found up to 10% of LFBFs. The previous remarks clearly indicate a need for defining a model for Local Feedback Bridging Faults.

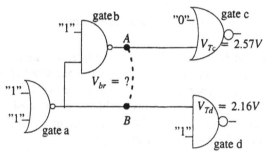

Figure 2: Local Feedback BF

In this paper a new model called the Logic Threshold Based voting model is proposed for the LFBFs. It is demonstrated that the LTB voting model allows to determine if a particular LFBF gives an intermediate voltage which is higher or lower than a given threshold voltage. According to the input stimuli, the LTB voting model can be used directly or indirectly.

In section 2 different definitions are given and the direct application of the LTB voting model is presented. The LFBF simulation principle using the LTB voting model is illustrated.

In section 3, the indirect application of the LTB voting model is presented using the simple inverter case. It is next extended to the general case of NOR, NAND,.. gates.

2. Direct Logic Threshold Based Voting

In case of a BF without LF as represented in figure 1, the gates are classified into driving gates (a and b) and driven gates (c and d). In case of a LFBF as represented in figure 2, the gates are differently classified. Gate (a) is a driving gate and gates (c and d) are driven gates, but gate (b) is called the "balancing" gate. In figure 3, the LFBF of figure 2 has been differently represented in order to illustrate the different gate classes.

In presence of a LFBF, the driving gate and the balancing gate create the intermediate voltage V_{br}. Each driven gates simply "observe" and logically "interpret" V_{br}, the interpretation being dependent on its logic threshold. The logic thresholds of the gates are assumed to be known and the key point consists in determining the intermediate voltage V_{br} created by the driving and the balancing gates.

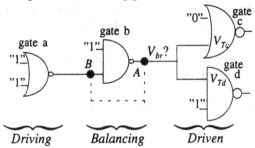

Figure 3: Gate Classification

The LTB voting model allows to determine the intermediate potential created by a driving and a balancing gate in a very simple and efficient way. Let us first assume that the balancing gate (b) is not connected to the driving gate (a) as illustrated in figure 4.a. In such condition, the bridged input–output exhibits an intermediate potential which exactly corresponds to the logic threshold of the bridged input V_{Tb}. In such conditions, V_{br} is equal to the logic threshold V_{Tb} of the gate b input.

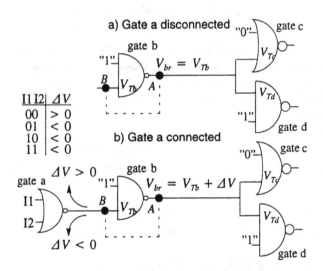

Figure 4: The Logic Threshold Based Voting

Of course the actual intermediate voltage V_{br} is not equal to V_{Tb} because the driving gate (a) is connected to the balancing gate (b). The driving gate (a) produces an additionnal voltage noted ΔV according to its input combination: $V_{br} = V_{Tb} + \Delta V$. An input combination which try to set the gate (a) output to '1' increases V_{br} inducing a positive ΔV. On the contrary, an input combination which try to set the gate (a) output to '0' decreases V_{br} inducing a negative ΔV.

Using the LTB voting model, any LFBF produces an intermediate voltage given by $V_{br} = V_{Ti} + \Delta V$ where V_{Ti} is the logic threshold of the balancing gate (i) and ΔV the additionnal voltage produced by the driving gate. The LTB voting model in its simplest form can yet be used for LFBF simulation: The logic threshold of the balancing gate V_{Tb} is simply compared to the logic thresholds of the driven gates V_{Tc} and V_{Td}. According to the different logic thresholds and to the gate (a) input, four different cases may occur as illustrated below for the driven gate c:

1: $V_{Tb} > V_{Tc}$ and $\Delta V > 0 \Rightarrow V_{br} > V_{Tc} \Rightarrow node = 1$
2: $V_{Tb} > V_{Tc}$ and $\Delta V < 0 \Rightarrow V_{br}$?
3: $V_{Tb} < V_{Tc}$ and $\Delta V > 0 \Rightarrow V_{br}$?
4: $V_{Tb} < V_{Tc}$ and $\Delta V < 0 \Rightarrow V_{br} < V_{Tc} \Rightarrow node = 0$

For 2 among 4 cases (cases 1 and 4), the LTB voting model allows to directly determine if the intermediate voltage is higher or lower than the logic threshold of the driven gate. It must be noted that this direct LTB voting model needs no computation since the logic thresholds of all gate inputs are known.

3. Indirect Logic Threshold Based Voting

As presented in the previous section, the intermediate voltage produced by a LFBF is given by $V_{br} = V_{Tb} + \Delta V$. Note that V_{Tb} is known but not ΔV. The direct LTB voting model can not be used in case 2 and 3. For these two cases, the additionnal voltage ΔV must be accurately determined. The indirect LTB model allows to determine the additionnal voltage and consequently the intermediate voltage of the LFBF.

In order to clearly illustrate the indirect LTB voting model, we consider first a LFBF affecting simple inverters as illustrated in figure 5. Figure 5.a represents the disconnected and the connected balancing gate and figure 5.b gives the transistor representation.

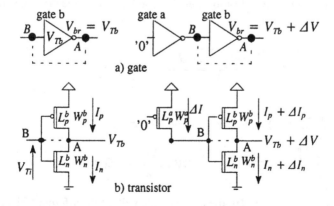

a) gate

b) transistor

Figure 5: LFBF between inverters

In our model, we consider that a current $I_p = I_n$ flows through the disconnected balancing gate producing the intermediate voltage $V_{br} = V_{Tb}$. This current is illustrated in figure 5.b. When the driving gate is connected to the balancing gate, an additionnal current ΔI produces an additionnal voltage ΔV. The global structure produces an intermediate voltage: $V_{br} = V_{Tb} + \Delta V$ as illustrated in figure 5.b for a '0' at the driving gate input and a positive ΔV. From figure 5.b we can write the following equations:

$$\Delta I + \Delta I_p = \Delta I_n \quad (1)$$

$$\Delta I_p = \frac{\beta_p^b}{2}[\Delta V^2 - 2A\Delta V] \quad (2)$$

$$\Delta I_n = \frac{\beta_n^b}{2}[\Delta V^2 + 2B\Delta V] \quad (3)$$

$$\Delta I = \beta_p^a[C(D - \Delta V) - \frac{(D - \Delta V)^2}{2}] \quad (4)$$

with $A = Vdd{-}VTO_p{-}V_{Tb}$ $B = V_{Tb}{-}VTO_n$
   $C = Vdd - VTO_p$ $D = Vdd - V_{Tb}$

$$\beta_p^b = \mu_p Cox\frac{W_p^b}{L_p^b} \quad \beta_n^b = \mu_n Cox\frac{W_n^b}{L_n^b} \quad \beta_p^a = \mu_p Cox\frac{W_p^a}{L_p^a}$$

Substituting equations (2), (3) and (4) into equation (1) and isolating ΔV gives:

$$\Delta V = \frac{K_1 {+}\sqrt{K_1^2 + 2K_2K_3}}{K_2} \quad (5)$$

with $K_1 = -\frac{B^2}{A} - B - \frac{\beta_p^a}{\beta_n^b}E$ $E = V_{Tb}{-}VTO_p$

$K_2 = 1 - \frac{B^2}{A^2} + \frac{\beta_p^a}{\beta_n^b}$ $K_3 = \frac{\beta_p^a}{\beta_n^b}[CD - \frac{D^2}{2}]$

Of course, the same demonstration can be made for a '1' at the driving gate input and a negative ΔV :

$$\Delta V = \frac{K_4 \sqrt{K_4^2 + 2K_5K_6}}{K_5} \quad (6)$$

with $K_4 = \frac{\beta_p^b}{\beta_n^a}(\frac{A^2}{B} + A) + F$ $F = Vdd{-}VTO_n{-}V_{Tb}$

$K_5 = 1 + \frac{\beta_p^b}{\beta_n^a}(1 - \frac{A^2}{B^2})$ $K_6 = GV_{Tb}{-}\frac{V_{Tb}^2}{2}$ $G = Vdd - VTO_n$

In order to validate our model, the intermediate voltage of different LFBFs have been computed using the LTB voting model and compared to the results of SPICE simulations. The validation is made for different transistor sizes, figure 6 gives the characteristics V_{br} versus W_p and V_{br} versus W_n. It clearly appears in figure 6 that the two characteristics are exactly superimposed demonstrating the accuracy of the LTB voting model.

Using the direct and indirect LTB voting model, the fault simulation procedure for any LFBF can be described by the following pseudo–algorithm:

For each input vector
    For each LFBF
        If $V_{Tb} > V_{Tc}$ & $\Delta V > 0$ (case 1) then
            $V_{br} > V_{Tc}$ *direct LTB voting*
        If $V_{Tb} < V_{Tc}$ & $\Delta V < 0$ (case 4) then
            $V_{br} < V_{Tc}$ *direct LTB voting*
        If $V_{Tb} > V_{Tc}$ & $\Delta V < 0$ (case 2) then
            compute ΔV using equation (6)
            compute $V_{br} = V_{Tb} + \Delta V$
            compare V_{br} to V_{Tc} *indirect LTB voting*
        If $V_{Tb} < V_{Tc}$ & $\Delta V > 0$ (case 3) then
            compute ΔV using equation (5)
            compute $V_{br} = V_{Tb} + \Delta V$
            compare V_{br} to V_{Tc} *indirect LTB voting*
    end
end

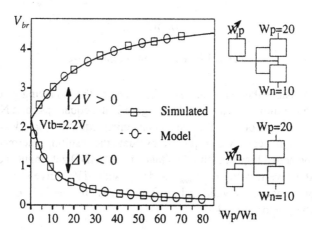

Figure 6: Model validation

4. Indirect LTB Voting for Complex Gates

As presented in the previous section, the intermediate voltage produced by a LFBF is given by $V_{br} = V_{Tb} + \Delta V$. The direct LTB voting model can be used in case 1 and 4 and the indirect LTB model allows to determine the additionnal voltage and consequently the intermediate voltage of the LFBF in case 2 and 3. Note that this model needs neither SPICE simulation nor precomputed and stored values.

The indirect LTB voting model has been introduced in the previous section with simple inverters. In this section, it is extended to more complex gates such as NOR, NAND... Figure 7 gives an example of LFBF between a NOR and a NAND gate. The NOR gate is the driving gate and the NAND the balancing gate.

Let us first consider the driving gate. The type of the driving gate does not modify the previous demonstration, only the β^a parameters must be adapted in equation (5) or (6). For any parallel network, the resulting β^a parameter is equal to the sum of the β^a of the different transistors. And, for any serial network, the resulting β^a parameter can be computed using the equation proposed in [12–13].

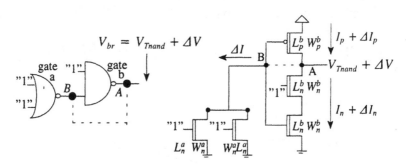

Figure 7: LFBF between complex gates

Let us now consider the balancing gate. The type of the balancing gate modifies the previous demonstration. As an example in figure 7, the equations for a NAND gate are very complex and it is not easy to obtain a convenient equation for ΔV similar to equation (5) or (6). In this case, we propose to evaluate the resulting intermediate potential by summing the actual logic threshold voltage of the NAND gate input and the value ΔV obtained for the inverter: $V_{br} = V_{Tnand} + \Delta V_{inv}$ with ΔV_{inv} given by equation (5) or (6). This approximation is validated in figure 8 where the SPICE simulations are compared to the proposed model.

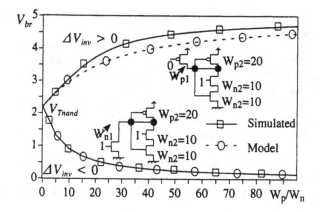

Figure 8: LTB model accuracy

The characteristics of figure 8 show that the accuracy of the model is very acceptable. And so, the indirect LTB voting model can be used for LFBF simulation. This model requires neither SPICE simulation nor pre–computed value stored in tables.

5. Conclusion

This work introduces a novel model called the "Logic Threshold Based" (LTB) voting model which can be used for Local Feedback Bridging Faults (LFBF) simulation. When using the proposed model, the usual comparison between the intermediate potential of the bridging fault and the logic threshold of the driven gates is very simple and very fast. It is demonstrated that the intermediate voltage is given by:

$$V_{br} = V_{Tb} + \Delta V$$

where V_{Tb} is the logic threshold of the balancing gate i.e. the gate with the input–output bridge, and ΔV is the additionnal voltage produced by the driving gate.

For 2 among 4 cases the direct LTB voting model allows to directly compared the intermediate potential and the logic threshold of the driven gates without any computation.

For the 2 remaining cases, the indirect LTB voting model allows to easily compute the intermediate voltage using a simple equation (equation 5 or 6). As a consequence no SPICE simulation is required to determine the intermediate voltage of the bridged nodes.

It should be recalled that the proposed model allows to model Local Feedback bridging faults with the accuracy of SPICE simulations and a negligible effort since neither pre–simulation nor iterative procedure are required, compared to previously published methods.

6. References

[1] W. Maly, "Realistic Fault Modeling for VLSI Testing", in Proceeding of Design Automation Conference, pp. 173–180, 1987.

[2] F. J. Ferguson and J. P. Shen, "A CMOS Fault Extractor for Inductive Fault Analysis", IEEE Transactions on CAD, vol. 7, pp. 1181–1194, Nov. 1988.

[3] J. M. Soden and C. F. Hawkins, "Electrical Properties and Detection Methods for CMOS ICs Defects", in Proc. of IEEE European Test Conference, pp. 159–167, 1989.

[4] S.D. Millman and J. McCluskey, "Detecting Bridging Faults With Stuck–at Test Sets", Proc. Int. Test Conf., pp. 773–783, Washington, DC, USA, Sept. 12–14, 1988.

[5] M. Abramovici, "A Practical Approach to Fault Simulation and Test Generation for Bridging Fault", IEEE Trans. Comput., C–34, No. 7, pp. 658–663, July 1985.

[6] T. Storey & W. Maly, "CMOS Bridging Fault Detection", Proc. Int. Test Conf., pp. 842–851, 1990.

[7] J.M. Acken & S.D. Millman, "Accurate Modelling and Simulation of Bridging Faults", Proc. Custom Integrated Circuits Conf., pp. 17.4.1–17.4.4, 1991.

[8] G.S. Greenstein & J.H. Patel, "E–PROOFS: A CMOS Bridging Fault Simulator", Proc. Int. Conf. on CAD, pp. 268–271, 1992.

[9] J.M. Acken & S.D. Millman, "Fault Model Evolution for Diagnosis: Accuracy vs Precision", Proc. Custom Integrated Circuits Conf., pp. 13.4.1–13.4.4, 1992.

[10] J. Rearick & J.H. Patel, "Fast and Accurate CMOS Bridging Fault Simulation", Proc. Int. Test Conf., pp. 54–62, 1993.

[11] P.C. Maxwell and R.C. Aitken, "Biased Voting: A Method for Simulating CMOS Bridging Faults in the Presence of Variable Gate logic Threshold", Proc. Int. Test Conf., pp. 63–72, 1993.

[12] M. Renovell, P. Huc, Y. Bertrand "A Unified Model for Intergate and Intragate CMOS Bridging Fault: The Configuration Ratio", Proc. Asian Test Symposium, 15–17 Nov., Nara, Japan, pp. 486–495, 1994.

[13] M. Renovell, P. Huc, Y. Bertrand " The configuration ratio : a model for simulating CMOS intra–gate bridge with variable logic thresholds ", First European Dependable Computing Conference, Berlin Germany, pp 165–177, Oct. 1994.

This work has been partially supported by the EEC under contract ARCHIMEDES (ESPRIT III BRA no. 7107).

On the Yield of VLSI Processors with On-Chip CPU Cache

D. Nikolos & H. T. Vergos

Department of Computer Engineering and Informatics,
University of Patras, 26500 Rio, Patras, Greece

e-mail : nikolosd@cti.gr
vergos@cti.gr

Abstract

Yield enhancement through the acceptance of partially good chips is a well-known technique [1-3]. In this paper we derive a yield model for single-chip VLSI processors with a partially good on-chip cache. Also, we investigate how the yield enhancement of VLSI processors with on-chip CPU cache relates with the number of acceptable faulty cache blocks, the percentage of the cache area with respect to the whole chip area and various manufacturing process parameters as defect densities and the fault clustering parameter.

Indexing terms- On-chip CPU caches, Partially good chips, Yield Enhancement, Fault Tolerance.

1 Introduction

All the recently developed high-performance single-chip VLSI processors incorporate one or more on-chip CPU caches [4-6]. The area occupied by these on-chip caches is already a great percentage of the total chip area and is expected to become greater in the near future. Cache memory can be thought as a "redundant" resource in the sense that the correctness of the processor operation does not depend on the presence of the cache. A processor can still operate correctly, although with degraded performance, in the absence of an architecturally invisible cache memory. Thus to enhance the yield of single-chip VLSI processors with on-chip CPU caches the acceptance of partially good chips (chips with the faulty cache blocks disabled) has been proposed and the way that the number of faulty cache blocks affects the miss ratio of the cache for various cache sizes and organizations has been investigated [7, 8].

To the best of our knowledge no yield expression has been given for predicting the yield of VLSI processors with a partially good on-chip cache. The yield expressions derived for partially good memories [2, 3] can not be used in this case. In this paper we derive a yield model for single-chip VLSI processors with a partially good single level on-chip CPU cache. Using this model we investigate how does the yield (denoted hereafter as Y) of the partially good chips relate to the number of acceptable faulty cache blocks and the percentage of the chip area occupied by the cache. During the manufacture of VLSI processors with on-chip cache, chips with up to R faulty cache blocks can be accepted as good for yield enhancement. The value of R will depend on the required yield and the maximum cache performance degradation that can be accepted.

Given the required yield, the yield expression derived in this paper can be used to determine the value of R.

2 Yield model and discussion

It has been generally accepted [9, 10] that the Poisson distribution can not be used to adequately model the manufacturing defects, due to that in practice defects are clustered rather than evenly distributed throughout the wafer. Defect clustering can be modeled by assuming that the number of defects per area unit is Poisson distributed, with the parameter λ being a random variable :

$$\text{Prob } \{ X = x \} = \frac{e^{-\lambda} \lambda^x}{x!} \tag{1}$$

The fact that λ is a random variable and not a constant, leads to increased clustering, no matter what distribution it follows.

One choice often made [9, 10] of a distribution function for λ is the Gamma distribution with two parameters, α and β :

$$f(\lambda) = \frac{1}{\beta^\alpha \Gamma(\alpha)} \lambda^{\alpha-1} e^{-\frac{\lambda}{\beta}} \tag{2}$$

Averaging λ in (1) with respect to (2), results in the defects per unit area being distributed according to the negative binomial distribution :

$$\text{Prob } \{ X = x \} = \frac{\Gamma(x+\alpha)}{x! \Gamma(\alpha)} \frac{\gamma^x}{(1+\gamma)^{\alpha+x}}$$

One of the most useful properties of the Poisson distribution, which the negative binomial one lacks, is the statistical independence between defects in disjoint areas. For overcoming this difficulty and calculate the yield when the negative binomial distribution is assumed, we follow a method based on the well-known total probability theorem. That is, we assume Poisson distribution for the defects, utilizing the independence property of this distribution to calculate the yield for a fixed λ value. By averaging the result over all values of λ, using the Gamma density function, we obtain the yield for the negative binomial model [9, 10].

In our case, that is, processors with on-chip cache, we firstly consider statistical independence between defects in three disjoint areas, the data part of the cache, the tag part of the cache and the rest part of the chip (processor and the cache support circuit). We then average the result over all values of λ (number of defects), using the Gamma distribution function. A chip is unusable when the processor and/or the cache support circuits are not fault free. On the contrary, the chip operates correctly even if some of the tags and /or the data blocks are faulty. Thus, chips with faults in the processor and/or the cache support circuits are discarded while those with fault free processor and cache support circuits and some faulty tags and/or data blocks are accepted as good.

Let N denote the number of cache blocks. Then the yield can be expressed as a probability as follows :

Y = Prob {at least M out of the N cache blocks are operational and the rest chip is fault free}

= Prob {at most R, $R=N-M$, cache blocks are not operational and the rest chip is fault free}

$$= \sum_{i=0}^{R} \alpha_{i,N}, \tag{3}$$

where $\alpha_{i,N}$ = Prob { exactly i cache blocks are not operational and the rest chip is fault free}.

i cache blocks are not operational means that s tags and q data blocks are not operational. We have to note here that a tag corresponds to just one data block. Let t be the number of faulty tags that correspond to faulty data blocks. Then $0 \leq t \leq \min\{s, q\}$ and $s + q - t = i$. The assumption that the s tags and the q data blocks belong to different cache blocks, that is, t=0, inserts a very small error for small values of R. The yield expression that will be derived making the above assumption will give smaller values for the yield of the chips with partially good cache than what if we do not make this assumption. It is evident that this assumption does not affect the perfect chip yield. As perfect chips we call the chips that are fault free. Making the above assumption we get :

$$\alpha_{i,N} = \sum_{s=0}^{i} \text{Prob \{ exactly } s \text{ tags and } q = i - s \text{ data blocks are not operational while the}$$

$$\text{rest chip is fault free \}} = \sum_{s=0}^{i} \beta_{s,q}. \tag{4}$$

We consider that the faults occurring in different modules are independent (as in the case where the faults follow the Poisson distribution). We then have :

$$\beta_{s,q} = c \, d_s \, g_q \tag{5}$$

where : c = Prob { the processor and the rest support circuit is fault free }
d_s = Prob { exactly s tags of the cache tag part are faulty } and
g_q = Prob { exactly q blocks of the cache data part are faulty }.

Following Poisson distribution for the defects we have

$$c = e^{-\lambda_{ck}} \tag{6}$$

where λ_{ck} is the number of defects in the processor and the rest support circuits.

In the case of the tag part of the cache memory the identical modules are the tags. Considering the area requirements of a tag, which are very small (in the order of the area occupied by a few static RAM cells), it is evident that the probability of a single fault to affect more than one tags is greater than the probability of a tag to contain any number, greater than one, of faults. In our analysis we consider that one fault affects one tag. In the case that one fault affects two or more tags, we consider that two or more faults have occurred. Assuming Poisson distribution for the defects of the tag memory, we get :

$$d_s = \frac{e^{-\lambda_{tag}} \lambda_{tag}^s}{s\,!} \tag{7}$$

where λ_{tag} is the number of defects in the tag part of the cache.

In the case of the data part of the cache memory the identical modules are the blocks which usually consist of 8, 16 or 32 bytes. Because of the large area of the block, with respect to the area of spot defects, we consider that a module may have any number of faults. If the faults occurring in different modules are independent using binomial distribution we can get

$$g_q = \binom{N}{q} y^{N-q} \left(1 - y\right)^q \tag{8}$$

where y is the yield of a single data block, given by $y = e^{-\lambda_{block}}$ and λ_{block} is the number of defects per block. By expanding $(1-y)^q$ into the following binomial series we get

$$(1-y)^q = \sum_{k=0}^{q}(-1)^k \binom{q}{k} y^k$$

and by substituting this in (8) we get

$$g_q = \binom{N}{q} \sum_{k=0}^{q}(-1)^k \binom{q}{k} e^{-(N-q+k)\lambda_{block}} \tag{9}$$

Therefore, from (5), (6), (7) and (9) we have :

$$\beta_{s,q} = e^{-\lambda_{ck}} \frac{e^{-\lambda_{tag}} \lambda_{tag}^s}{s!} \binom{N}{q} \sum_{k=0}^{q}(-1)^k \binom{q}{k} e^{-(N-q+k)\lambda_{block}}$$

We next have to apply the compounding procedure [9, 10] in order to calculate the yield when clustering of faults is allowed. We should not however, perform three separate compounding steps (for the two types of modules and the support circuits) since the clustering of faults in one type of circuits is not independent of the clustering in the other two. Therefore we must perform a single compounding step using the average number of faults in the complete chip, i.e. $\lambda = \lambda_{ck} + \lambda_{tag} + N \lambda_{block}$

To simplify the integration which contains different multiples of λ we define:

$$\delta_1 = \frac{\lambda_{ck}}{\lambda}, \quad \delta_2 = \frac{\lambda_{tag}}{\lambda}, \quad \delta_3 = \frac{N\lambda_{block}}{\lambda}$$

Note that δ_1, δ_2 and δ_3 are constants which mainly depend on the ratio of the corresponding chip areas to the area of the whole chip. The exponential term now becomes :

$$e^{-\lambda_{ck}-\lambda_{tag}-(N-q+k)\lambda_{block}} = e^{-\left[\delta_1+\delta_2+(N-q+k)\delta_3/N\right]\lambda}$$

Then considering as compounder the Gamma distribution with two parameters α and β, relation (2), we get :

$$\beta_{s,q} = \binom{N}{q} \sum_{k=0}^{q}(-1)^k \binom{q}{k} \int_0^{\infty} e^{-\left[\delta_1+\delta_2+(N-q+k)\delta_3/N\right]\lambda} \frac{(\delta_2\lambda)^s}{s!} f(\lambda)\, d\lambda$$

After the evaluation of the integral (hints are provided in the Appendix) we get :

$$\beta_{s,q} = \binom{N}{q} \sum_{k=0}^{q}(-1)^k \binom{q}{k} \frac{\Gamma(\alpha+s)}{s!\,\Gamma(\alpha)} \left(\frac{\delta_2\bar{\lambda}}{\alpha}\right)^s \left(1+\frac{\left[\delta_1+\delta_2+(N-q+k)\delta_3/N\right]\bar{\lambda}}{\alpha}\right)^{-\alpha-s} \tag{10}$$

Finally, we define $\quad \delta_1\bar{\lambda} = \bar{\lambda}_{ck}, \quad \delta_2\bar{\lambda} = \bar{\lambda}_{tag}, \quad \delta_3\bar{\lambda} = N\bar{\lambda}_{block} \tag{11}$

Combining (3), (4), (10) and (11) we get the following yield expression for processors with a single level of partially good cache memory, when at most R cache faulty blocks are acceptable:

$$Y=\sum_{i=0}^{R}\sum_{s=0}^{i}\left\{\binom{N}{i-s}\sum_{k=0}^{i-s}(-1)^{k}\binom{i-s}{k}\frac{\Gamma(\alpha+s)}{s!\,\Gamma(\alpha)}\left(\frac{\bar{\lambda}_{tag}}{\alpha}\right)^{s}\left[1+\frac{\bar{\lambda}_{ck}+\bar{\lambda}_{tag}+(N+k+s-i)\bar{\lambda}_{block}}{\alpha}\right]^{-\alpha-s}\right\}$$

Note that in the above expression α is the defect clustering parameter and $\bar{\lambda}_{ck} = A_{ck} D_{ck}$, $\bar{\lambda}_{tag} = A_{tag} D_{tag}$ and $\bar{\lambda}_{block} = A_{block} D_{data}$, where A and D stand for the area and the defect density in the corresponding parts of the chip.

It is evident that the derived expression for the yield can be applied independently of the cache organization, direct mapped, set associative or fully associative. Having obtained an expression for the yield we can study how the yield depends on various parameters as the acceptable number R of faulty cache blocks, the percentage of the cache area with respect to the whole chip area, the values of D_{ck}, D_{tag}, D_{data}, as well as, the fault clustering parameter α.

We have to note, that any yield enhancement technique that is used for the on-chip cache of VLSI processor chips, requires some extra implementation area. This extra implementation area should be kept as small as possible, because any additional area may be the cause for increased number of defects per chip and may result in perfect chip yield loss. Moreover, when the area of a chip increases the number of chips per wafer tends to decrease. Therefore we have to consider the effective yield, which is the chip yield multiplied by the area increase factor, as a most suitable metric rather than the yield itself. For applying the faulty block disabling technique an additional bit (availability bit) should be added in each tag of the cache, whose value denotes whether the corresponding block is faulty or not.

In figures 1 to 8 we present the effective yield of VLSI processor chips with on-chip cache, as a function of the number of acceptable cache faulty blocks. We consider four different direct-mapped caches (8 and 32 Kbytes with block size equal to either 8 or 32 bytes), two different amounts of silicon area occupied by the processor core, 35 and 50 mm^2, and an implementation technology with minimum feature size of 1.0 micron. We assume that the fault clustering parameter α is equal to 2, and D_{ck}, D_{tag} and D_{data} are varied from 0.02 up to 0.05/mm^2. The yield model presented in this paper can be applied equally well no matter which layout organization for the on-chip cache is followed. For the examples presented in figures 1 to 8 we considered the layout organization that leads to the best cache access time (as computed by the model presented in [11]). For estimating the area that the on-chip cache occupies we used the area model presented in [12]. The choice D_{ck}=0.02 and $D_{tag} = D_{data} = 0.05$/mm^2 is based on the fact that cache arrays are fabricated with the tightest feature and scaling rules available in a given technology which means that caches are more susceptible to faults [13, 14]. Only experimental data obtained by monitoring wafers can show which values of D_{ck}, D_{tag} and D_{data} should be used in the yield expression.

From the curves presented in these figures we conclude that :

• The effective yield increases significantly with the number of acceptable cache faulty blocks until we reach a value beyond which the effective yield is practically constant. The effective yield enhancement is greater for the small values of D and even greater for $D_{ck} < D_{tag} = D_{data}$. We can also see that the maximum effective yield is achieved by accepting a small number of faulty cache blocks, so there is no need to accept chips with a large number of faulty blocks and hence a significantly degraded cache performance.

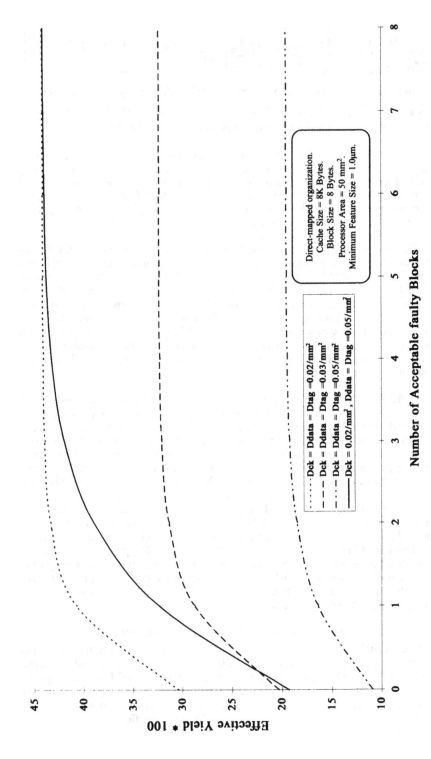

Figure 1. The effective yield versus the number of acceptable faulty blocks.

220

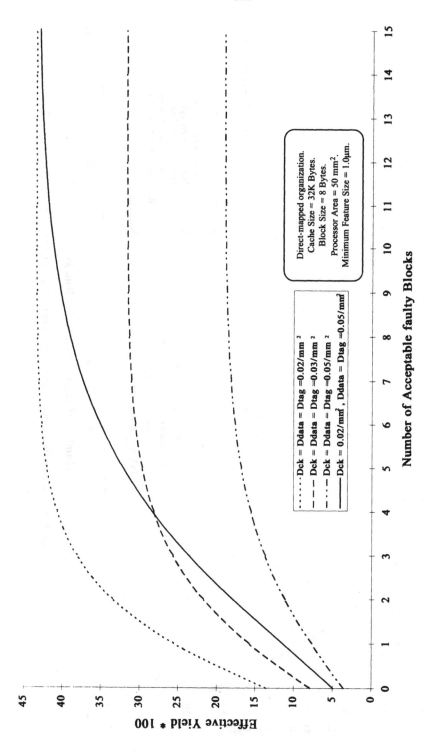

Figure 2. The effective yield versus the number of acceptable faulty blocks.

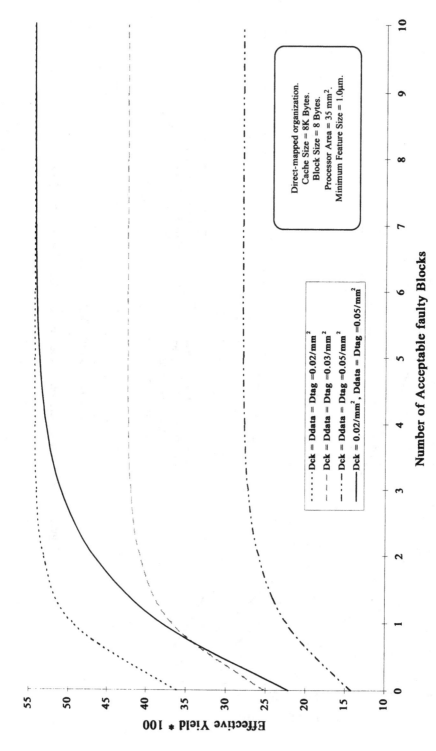

Figure 3. The effective yield versus the number of acceptable faulty blocks.

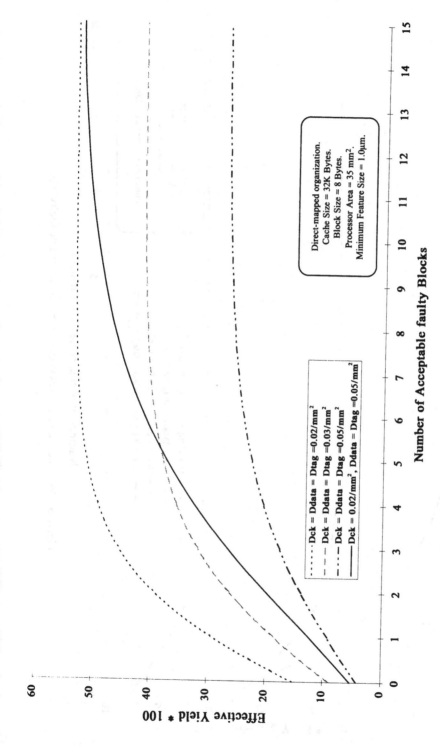

Figure 4. The effective yield versus the number of acceptable faulty blocks.

223

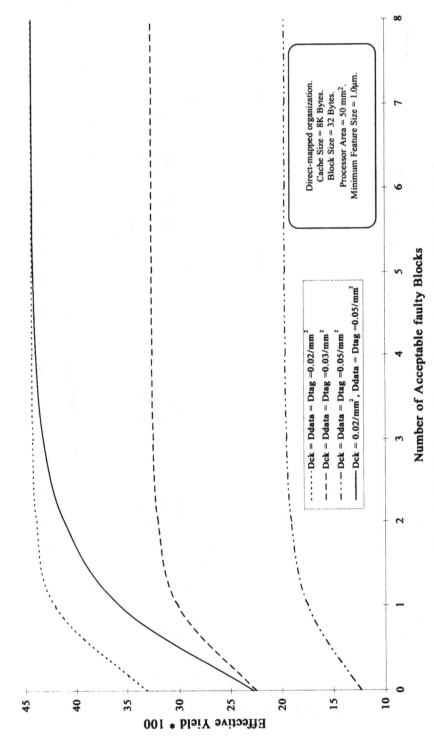

Figure 5. The effective yield versus the number of acceptable faulty blocks.

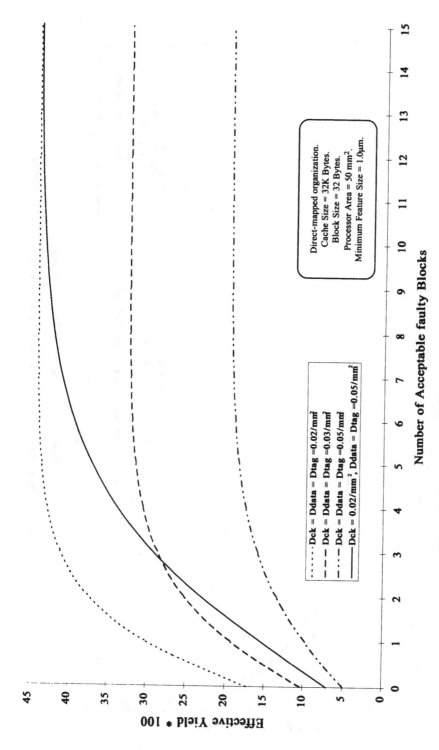

Figure 6. The effective yield versus the number of acceptable faulty blocks.

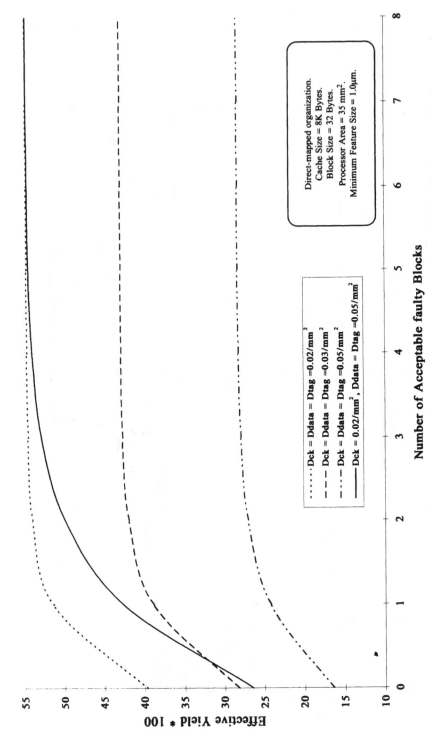

Figure 7. The effective yield versus the number of acceptable faulty blocks.

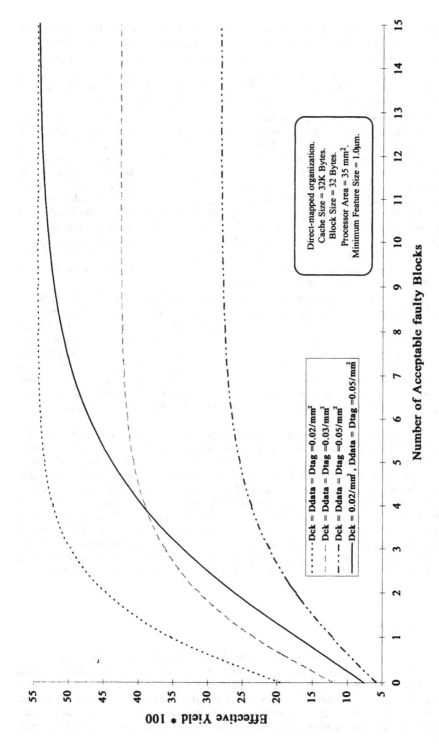

Figure 8. The effective yield versus the number of acceptable faulty blocks.

- The number of the faulty cache blocks that should be accepted for reaching the maximum effective yield, increases as the percentage of the total chip area devoted to the on-chip cache increases. For example, this can be observed by keeping the processor area constant and comparing figures 1 and 2 (in which the on-chip cache occupies approximately 38% and 70.5% respectively) or figures 3 and 4 (the area percentage occupied by the on-chip cache is 47% and 77% respectively).

- As it was expected keeping constant all other parameters, the perfect yield of the chips depends heavily on the cache size (that is, the area occupied by the cache). For example from figures 1 and 2 we can see that for $D_{ck} = D_{tag} = D_{data} = 0.02/mm^2$ and processor area 50 mm^2 the perfect chip yield is 30.39% and 13.54% for chips with caches of size 8K and 32K Bytes respectively. However as the number of the accepted faulty cache blocks increases the yield of the chips with partially good caches approaches almost the same value Y_a independently of the cache size. As larger is the cache size, so greater is the number of the faulty cache blocks that should be accepted as good in order to approach the value Y_a. For example from figure 1 and 2 we can see that the yield of the chips with $D_{ck} = D_{tag} = D_{data} = 0.02/mm^2$, area processor equal to 50 mm^2 and cache capacity equal to 8K and 32K Bytes is almost equal to 44% when the number of the accepted faulty cache blocks is greater than or equal to 3 and 8 respectively.

- When the block size increases, for constant cache size the number of cache blocks as well as the number of tags decreases. Thus, the tag memory occupies less area when we move to larger block sizes and the yield of the perfect chips is increased. This can be observed by comparing figures 1 to 4 with figures 5 to 8 for equal values of the defect densities. The maximum value though that can be achieved for the effective yield by the acceptance of processors with partially good on-chip cache does not depend very strongly on the block size. Moving to larger block sizes can only achieve a marginal better maximum effective yield value, only when the cache area is a great percentage of the total chip area, as observed by the curves of figures 1-8.

As we have mentioned earlier, every yield enhancement technique for processors with on-chip cache requires some extra implementation area. The extra area requirements for implementing the availability bit for the faulty block disabling technique, is small enough, as verified by the values presented in Table I. This Table presents the effective yield of several perfect processor chips with various on-chip caches, when either no yield enhancement technique is used (denoted by "Without redundancy") or the faulty block disabling technique is used, as well as, the percentage of effective yield lost because of the additional implementation area, for several cases of defect densities in the three disjoint areas of the chip. As we can see from Table I, the perfect chip yield loss due to the extra implementation area of the faulty block disabling technique is usually negligible, (less than 1%), while the maximum value is 2,05%.

3 Conclusion

In this paper a yield model for single-chip VLSI processors with partially good on-chip cache was derived. Using this model we have shown that accepting as good chips with a relatively small number of faulty cache blocks we achieve a significant increase of the yield. We have also shown how the yield depends on various parameters as the percentage of the cache area with respect to the whole chip area, the cache block size and various manufacturing process parameters as defect densities and the fault clustering parameter.

Appendix

$$\left(\frac{d}{dz}\right)^s \int\limits_0^\infty e^{-z\lambda} f(\lambda)d\lambda = (-1)^s \int\limits_0^\infty e^{-z\lambda} \lambda^s f(\lambda)d\lambda.$$

Then taking into account that $\displaystyle\int\limits_0^\infty e^{-z\lambda} f(\lambda)d\lambda = \left(1+\frac{z\overline{\lambda}}{\alpha}\right)^{-\alpha}$ and

$$\left(\frac{d}{dz}\right)^s \left(1+\frac{z\overline{\lambda}}{\alpha}\right)^{-\alpha} = (-1)^s \alpha(\alpha+1)(\alpha+2)...(\alpha+s-1)\left(\frac{\overline{\lambda}}{\alpha}\right)^s \left(1+\frac{z\overline{\lambda}}{\alpha}\right)^{-\alpha-s}$$

we get $\displaystyle\int\limits_0^\infty e^{-z\lambda} \lambda^s f(\lambda)d\lambda = \frac{\Gamma(\alpha+s)}{\Gamma(\alpha)}\left(\frac{\overline{\lambda}}{\alpha}\right)^s \left(1+\frac{z\overline{\lambda}}{\alpha}\right)^{-\alpha-s}$.

Acknowledgment - The authors would like to thank Prof. G. Moustakides for his help in the evaluation of the above integral.

References

[1] Koren I. and Singh A.D., "Fault Tolerance in VLSI Circuits", IEEE Computer, pp. 73-83, July 1990.

[2] Stapper C. H., Mc Laren A. N. and Dreckmann M., "Yield Model for Productivity Optimization of VLSI Memory Chips with redundancy and Partially Good Product", IBM Journal of Research and Development, Vol. 20, 1980, pp. 398-409.

[3] Stapper C. H., "Block Alignment : A Method for Increasing the Yield of Memory Chips that are Partially Good", Defect and Fault Tolerance in VLSI Systems, I. Koren (ed.), pp. 243-255, New York : Plenum, 1989.

[4] " PowerPC 601 - RISC Microprocessor User's Manual" Motorola Semiconductor Ttechnical Data Book, Motorola 1993.

[5] Miraburi S. at. al., " The MIPS R4000 Processor", IEEE Micro, April 1992, pp. 10-22.

[6] Edmodson J. H. et. al., " Superscalar Instruction Execution in the 21164 Alpha Microprocessor", IEEE Micro, April 1995, pp. 33-43.

[7] Sohi G., "Cache Memory Organization to Enhance the Yield of High-Performance VLSI Processors", IEEE Transactions on Computers, vol. 38, no. 4, pp. 484-492, April 1989.

[8] Pour A. F. and Hill M. D., "Performance Implications of Tolerating Cache Faults", IEEE Transactions on Computers, vol. 42, no. 3, pp. 257-267, March 1993.

[9] Koren I., Koren Z. and Pradhan D. K., "Designing Interconnection Buses in VLSI and WSI for Maximum Yield and Minimum Delay", IEEE Journal of Solid-State Circuits, Vol. 23, No. 3, pp. 859-865, June 1988.

[10] Koren I. and Stapper C. H., "Yield Models for Defect-Tolerant VLSI Circuits: A review", Defect and Fault Tolerance in VLSI Systems, Vol. 1, Koren, ed., Plenum, New York, pp. 1-21, 1989 .

[11] Wilton S. J. E. and Jouppi N. P., "An Enhanced Access and Cycle Time Model for On-Chip Caches", DEC Western Research Lab, Tech Report 93/5.

[12] Mulder J. M., Quach N. T. and Flynn M. J., "An Area Model for On-Chip Memories and its Application", IEEE J. of Solid-State Circuits, 26, 2, pp. 98-106, Feb. 1991.

[13] Gallup M. G., et. al., "Testability Features of the 68040", in Proc. of International Test Conference, Washington DC, USA, 10 - 14 September, 1990, pp. 749-757.

[14] Saxena N. R., et. al., "Fault-Tolerant Features in the HaL Memory Management Unit", IEEE Transactions on Computers, Vol. 44, No. 2, pp. 170-179, February 1995.

TABLE I

PERFECT CHIP YIELD		$D_{ck} = D_{tag} = D_{data} = 0.02/mm^2$	$D_{ck} = D_{tag} = D_{data} = 0.03/mm^2$	$D_{ck} = D_{tag} = D_{data} = 0.05/mm^2$	$D_{ck} = 0.02, D_{tag} = D_{data} = 0.05/mm^2$
8KB Cache, Block Size = 8 Bytes, Processor Area = 35 mm^2	Without redundancy (Y_1)	36,402	25,349	14,309	22,301
	With Block Disabling (Y_2)	36,090	25,109	14,156	22,128
	(Y_1-Y_2) / Y_1	0,85 %	0,94 %	0,50 %	0,77 %
8KB Cache, Block Size = 8 Bytes, Processor Area = 50 mm^2	Without redundancy (Y_1)	30,610	20,453	10,974	19,448
	With Block Disabling (Y_2)	30,385	20,286	10,875	19,319
	(Y_1-Y_2) / Y_1	0,73 %	0,81 %	0,90 %	0,66 %
8KB Cache, Block Size = 32 Bytes, Processor Area = 35 mm^2	Without redundancy (Y_1)	39,700	28,274	16,420	26,523
	With Block Disabling (Y_2)	39,604	28,198	16,371	26,464
	(Y_1-Y_2) / Y_1	0,24 %	0,27 %	0,29 %	0,22 %
8KB Cache, Block Size = 32 Bytes, Processor Area = 50 mm^2	Without redundancy (Y_1)	33,139	22,554	12,374	22,855
	With Block Disabling (Y_2)	33,072	22,503	12,343	22,812
	(Y_1-Y_2) / Y_1	0,20 %	0,22 %	0,25 %	0,19 %
32KB Cache, Block Size = 8 Bytes, Processor Area = 35 mm^2	Without redundancy (Y_1)	15,434	9,082	4,227	5,315
	With Block Disabling (Y_2)	15,159	8,902	4,140	5,242
	(Y_1-Y_2) / Y_1	1,78 %	1,91 %	2,05 %	1,37 %
32KB Cache, Block Size = 8 Bytes, Processor Area = 50 mm^2	Without redundancy (Y_1)	13,764	7,965	3,644	4,965
	With Block Disabling (Y_2)	13,536	7,824	3,574	4,902
	(Y_1-Y_2) / Y_1	1,65 %	1,77 %	1,92 %	1,26 %
32KB Cache, Block Size = 32 Bytes, Processor Area = 35 mm^2	Without redundancy (Y_1)	19,608	11,994	5,818	7,632
	With Block Disabling (Y_2)	19,505	11,925	5,782	7,600
	(Y_1-Y_2) / Y_1	0,52 %	0,57 %	0,62 %	0,42 %
32KB Cache, Block Size = 32 Bytes, Processor Area = 50 mm^2	Without redundancy (Y_1)	17,242	10,322	4,893	7,037
	With Block Disabling (Y_2)	17,158	10,269	4,865	7,01
	(Y_1-Y_2) / Y_1	0,49 %	0,51 %	0,57 %	0,38 %

Session 6

Testing

Chair: Jan Hlavicka, Czech Technical University, Czech Republic

Design of Dependable Hardware: What BIST Is Most Efficient?

Andrzej Kraśniewski

Warsaw University of Technology
Institute of Telecommunications
Nowowiejska 15/19, 00-665 Warszawa, Poland

Abstract. We show that self-testability is an essential feature of VLSI circuits used as components of dependable systems. We discuss one of the key problems associated with designing self-testable circuits - the selection of BIST (built-in self-test) technique. Specifically, we present advantages and disadvantages of two basic strategies that can be applied when designing a VLSI chip: using one universal BIST technique vs. using several dedicated BIST techniques for a single chip design. As a good candidate for a universal BIST technique, having a potential to effectively and efficiently support the design of a large class of VLSI circuits, we advise the CSTP (Circular Self-Test Path) technique. The applicability of the CSTP is illustrated with an example of self-testable design of a bit-slice processor 2901, a circuit of diversified internal structure comprising various types of functional blocks (ALU, two-port RAM, registers, latches, random logic, multiplexer-based shifters). The design characteristics and the results of simulation experiments carried out for this circuit show that the proposed solution offers high quality testing at acceptable BIST implementation costs.

1 Introduction

Designing highly dependable computer-based systems requires special approach to the design of hardware components. There are basically two ways to enhance hardware dependability:

- using dependable (possibly, fault-free) components,
- providing fault-tolerance.

Basic components of today's computer systems are digital VLSI circuits. The quality of VLSI circuits supplied by the manufacturer can be represented by the defect level (called also reject ratio), which is defined as a fraction of chips that passed all phases of the manufacturing testing, but are actually defective. The defect level is commonly given in parts (defective parts) per million, or ppm. The defect level for today's complex chips is in the range of 50-200 ppm, but the system reliability requirements will soon make such values unacceptable. The Semiconductor Research Corporation, for example, aims at the defect level in the range of 1 ppm for 10^7-transistor chips by the end of the century [20]. The defect level for a particular type of component depends on the quality of manufacturing process (manufacturing yield) and the quality of testing. As it is not reasonable to expect that the manufacturing yield for state-of-the-art chips will significantly increase in the near future, high quality testing is the key to satisfying reliability requirements for VLSI components.

For a complex VLSI circuit, the costs of development and execution of the test procedure as a percentage of total costs of circuit design and manufacturing are steadily increasing. This creates a particularly difficult problem for ASICs (application specific integrated circuits) where high costs of the test development are distributed over a relatively small number of fabricated chips. Thus, for such circuits the costs of testing can account for as much as 50-55% of total design and manufacturing costs [7, 22]. The development of a test procedure can take as much as 25-50% of the total design development time [4]. It is claimed that effective testing of complex ASICs expected to appear on the marketplace in 1998 may require a $10,000,000 tester [23].

Overcoming tremendous problems associated with testing of complex VLSI circuits requires methods and techniques that differ from the ones used in the 1970's and early 1980's. In the 1990's design-for-testability approach has become a common practice. In particular, built-in self-test (BIST) techniques that support the design of self-testable components are gaining increasingly more attention [8].

Traditionally, BIST techniques are intended to support off-line testing and do not aim at concurrent fault detection which can be performed using self-checking circuits. Nevertheless, self-testability is a very desirable feature of components of fault-tolerant systems. Self-testable chips make it significantly easier to provide self-testability at higher levels of system integration (multichip modules, printed circuit boards, ...). This provision is of primary importance for the following reasons:

- periodic testing of the system or its individual components can be performed; it can take the form of:
  - periodic maintenance test (self-test),
  - concurrent testing by interleaving test cycles with operational cycles during normal system operation,
  - concurrent testing of temporarily idle components during normal system operation.
- recovery mechanisms are made more effective; in particular, BIST is very helpful in the following situations:
  - identification of whether an error has been caused by a permanent or by a transient fault,
  - diagnostics, i.e., identification of the smallest replaceable component of the system that contains the fault.

Finally, it is worth noting that BIST can be combined with self-checking to take advantage of each other and to support both off-line testing and on-line fault detection in a cost efficient way [14].

The above discussion clearly shows that self-testability is an essential design objective for hardware components of highly dependable systems. In this paper, we discuss one of the key problems associated with designing self-testable circuits - the selection of BIST technique. Being more specific, we address the following question: Is it better to apply a single BIST technique to the entire chip logic or to use a mixture of BIST techniques, each dedicated to a particular type of functional block? In the next section, the arguments in favor and against each of these two general strategies are brought. In Section 3, we present the CSTP (Circular Self-Test Path) technique which, we believe, is universal enough to be applied to a large class of VLSI chip architectures. Section 4 contains experimental results that demonstrate the effectiveness of the CSTP as a universal BIST technique. In Section 5 the presented results are summarized and general conclusions are drawn.

2 One Universal or Several Dedicated BIST Techniques?

With numerous BIST techniques available, there are basically two design strategies to make a complex VLSI circuit, containing a wide variety of functional blocks, self-testable:

- using one universal BIST technique,
- using several dedicated BIST techniques for individual chip modules.

Most universal BIST techniques are based on the concept of using an LFSR (Linear Feedback Shift Register) for test pattern generation, and a MISR (Multiple-Input Signature Register) for test response compaction. The representative examples of such techniques are STUMPS, LOCST, and the techniques based on using the BILBO modules [1, 2].

The major advantage of universal techniques is simplicity of design procedures. Also, the implementation cost, in terms of extra logic required, can usually be made acceptable because of the relatively simple test control logic and a possibility to share test-dedicated logic (such as BILBO registers) among different functional modules included in the chip.

The major problem with the universal techniques lies in that they are not particularly suitable for regular structures, such as RAMs or PLAs, typically encountered in today's VLSI circuits. Standard BIST components must usually be augmented with dedicated logic (to accommodate specific test requirements, such as the need for RAM initialization) which adds to the circuit complexity. Even with such extensions, universal self-test schemes do not guarantee sufficient quality of fault detection within reasonable test time limits. Besides, application of the same test methodology to all the chip components quite often results in a situation when some portions of the chip (containing difficult-to-test faults) are undertested, whereas other parts are overtested.

An alternative to using a single universal BIST technique is to rely on a mixture of BIST methods. Numerous dedicated BIST techniques have been developed to support testing of embedded ROMs, RAMs, PLAs, or ALUs [1, 2]. Some of them use LFSRs or MISRs, the modules typically encountered in universal solutions, but dedicated logic is always a significant part of the test-supporting circuitry.

With regard to test quality and test application time for a particular module, dedicated techniques are more effective than universal ones. Furthermore, a large variety of available methods allow the VLSI designer to trade-off test quality with implementation costs for a particular module on the chip.

Using a mixture of BIST schemes on a single chip containing different types of functional blocks can, however, lead to large implementation costs (large logic overhead). The reasons for this are as follows:

- since each functional block requires specific test-dedicated logic (especially, specific test pattern generator), sharing such resources among different blocks is unlikely;
- an essential component of BIST logic is a test controller which initializes the test-dedicated logic, switches operation modes of the test pattern generators at appropriate times, etc.; each of the different BIST techniques used requires individual test control logic;

- extra logic is required to create interfaces between possibly incompatible test schemes; such interfaces are necessary, for example, to combine the results of testing different functional blocks into a single faulty/fault-free signal for the chip;
- relatively complex test control scheme may require several external test control lines (extra pins).

With the apparent shortcomings of both the above described major strategies for design of self-testable circuits, it appears that there is no single methodology, i.e., no single BIST technique or a simple combination of techniques, which could effectively and efficiently support the whole spectrum of architectures encountered in today's VLSI chips. Recent studies indicate, however, that the circular self-test techniques, such as the Circular Self-Test Path (CSTP) [10, 11, 15] and Circular BIST [18, 21] are likely to emerge as a universal BIST solution for a relatively large class of VLSI circuits.

3 Emerging Solution - CSTP

The CSTP (Circular Self-Test Path) technique was originally proposed for circuits composed of arbitrarily connected combinational modules and registers [10, 11]. In what follows, we recall the principles of the CSTP assuming its application to such a circuit.

In a circuit designed according to the CSTP methodology, selected registers (individual flip-flops are considered one-bit registers) are arranged to form one long circular shift register, referred to as the circular self-test path. Each flip-flop (register cell) included in the circular path is augmented with an XOR gate and a simple logic that selects the operation mode of the cell. In the normal mode of circuit operation, each cell of the circular path serves as a conventional D flip-flops. In the test mode, however, the modulo 2 sum of the functional input (data input) and the output of the preceding cell is loaded into the flip-flip. Thus, the circular path provides the circuit with test patterns and, simultaneously, compacts the circuit responses as illustrated in Fig. 1. A pass/fail decision is made by comparing the signature, i.e. the stream of bits that appear at the preselected output of the circuit, driven by the circular path cell, within a specified time interval at the end of the test session, with that expected from a fault-free circuit.

The CSTP technique was shown to offer a number of attractive features [11]. In particular:

- the testing is performed at the normal operation speed of the circuit, which makes it possible to detect a large percentage of timing-related faults,
- the silicon area overhead is substantially lower than that required by the other BIST techniques,
- the whole circuit is tested in one test session, which means that the complexity of a test controller and the number of external test control signals (pins) is minimized,
- as the circular path may include an arbitrarily selected set of circuit registers (flip-flops), the circuitry overhead can be traded-off with the test quality.

In a short time after its introduction, the circular self-test proved to be successful in engineering practice. In particular, it was applied, in conjunction with an appropriate

RAM-dedicated self-test technique, to several VLSI chips designed and manufactured at AT&T [21]. Later, it was successfully implemented in other industrial ASICs where it also was combined with dedicated test techniques [5, 9].

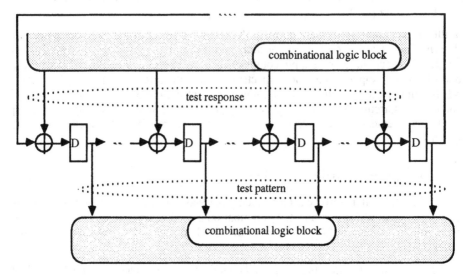

Fig. 1. Circular self-test path in the self-test mode

The recent studies have revealed that the CSTP technique assures a high level of fault detection not only for the type of circuits it was originally intended to support, but also for many different regular-structure modules. It provides embedded RAMs of up to several Mbits of capacity with a very high quality of fault detection, much higher than offered by the BIST schemes based on deterministic test patterns [12]; this clearly demonstrates a suitability of the CSTP for design of self-testable embedded ROMs. The CSTP technique is also suitable and effective for testing large PLAs [16]. Other reported results indicate that the CSTP technique is quite effective in detection of delay faults [17].

In all the above mentioned studies, circuits of simple internal structure were examined. In the next section of this paper, we show that the CSTP can be effectively applied, in terms of both implementation costs and fault detection quality, to a circuit with quite a diversified internal structure (containing various types of functional blocks). We present the results of a design and simulation experiment with a self-testable version of a bit-slice processor 2901 [3]. Despite relatively small size (measured by the number of gates), the 2901 circuit has a diversified internal structure containing typical blocks that occur in today's ASICs: ALU, two-port RAM, memory elements of various type (edge-triggered registers and latches), combinational circuitry (control logic), multiplexer-based shifters. On the other hand, small size of the circuit makes it possible to design and compare several self-testable versions of the circuit and to run, for each version, a large number of simulation experiments which is necessary to examine various aspects of the alternative solutions.

4 Experimental Results

A straightforward application of the CSTP technique to the 2901 circuit results in the design shown in Fig. 2 [13]. In this design, CSTP cells are included on all the primary inputs and outputs of the circuit, and in addition, on the data input of the RAM. In addition, register Q and latches placed on the outputs of the RAM are converted into CSTP cells. The circular path is appropriately arranged to adjust to the specific clocking scheme of the 2901 circuit where the two clock edges are used to control different memory elements.

Besides the design of Fig. 2, hereafter referred to as version 1, two other schemes have been examined. Version 2 differs from version 1 in that the CSTP cells are not included on the data input of the RAM. Version 3 differs from version 2 in the way the circular path is routed: a sequence of flip-flops added on the inputs of the circuit (I8-I0, ADDRA, ADDRB, D3-D0, CN, OE') is split into two parts, one of which is included in the path between the register Q and the flag register.

The overhead associated with the BIST logic, measured in the percentage of extra gates, is approximately 35%. It must, however, be observed that the overhead given in relative numbers (percentage of extra gates, silicon area overhead) is much larger for circuits containing small functional blocks, such as the circuit under examination, than circuits with large blocks; this is especially true for regular-structure components, such as PLAs or RAMs, for which the relative overhead decreases several times as we move from small arrays to large arrays. Therefore, an overhead of no more than 20% can be expected for large chips, which could be acceptable for many ASICs.

Another way of looking at the estimated logic overhead of 35% is to compare the solution based on the CSTP technique with some alternative design. We have estimated the logic overhead for a BIST solution in which a dedicated BIST technique described in [19] is applied for RAM, and LFSRs and MISRs are used for testing the remaining portions of the circuit. It turns out that the overhead for this solution exceeds 70%, i.e., is approximately twice as large as for the design based on the CSTP technique.

An assessment of test quality for CSTP-based circuits that include embedded RAM blocks is a non-trivial task. As the conventional stuck-at fault model is not adequate for RAMs, two different fault models must be handled simultaneously when a sequence of consecutive states of the circular path is derived. To deal with this problem, a dedicated tool has been developed that combines conventional fault simulation procedure with a special procedure for analysis of detectability of RAM faults. This tool produces separate fault detection statistics for the RAM modules and for the remaining part of the circuit. In what follows, we present the results of a comprehensive series of experiments performed using this tool.

For the main part of the circuit (all the circuitry except the RAM module), the single stuck-at model has been assumed and the experimental results indicate that:

- the fault coverage is little dependent on the circular path design (version of the circuit): an inclusion of an extra CSTP segment on the input of the RAM has little impact on the coverage; splitting the input segments of the CSTP slightly improves the coverage for certain range of test times;

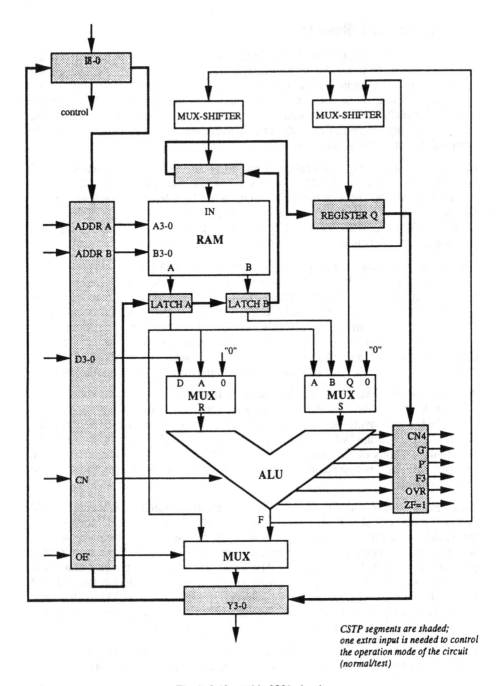

*CSTP segments are shaded;
one extra input is needed to control
the operation mode of the circuit
(normal/test)*

Fig. 2. Self-testable 2901 circuit

- the impact of the initial state of the CSTP and the initial state of the RAM on the fault coverage can be characterized as follows:
  - for short test times the coverage is sensitive to the initial state of the CSTP: all-zeroes or all-ones initial state is the worst, whereas random initialization is effective; for longer test times (more than 64 clock cycles which corresponds to the fault coverage of about 90%), the impact of the initialization is becoming negligible;
  - the initial state of the RAM has little impact on the fault coverage; only in the case when the initial state of the CSTP is all-zeroes, a large number of 1's in the RAM positively affects the efficiency of testing for short test times.

Typical experimental results that illustrate the above statements on the impact of the initial state of the CSTP and the initial state of the RAM on the fault coverage are shown in Fig. 3.

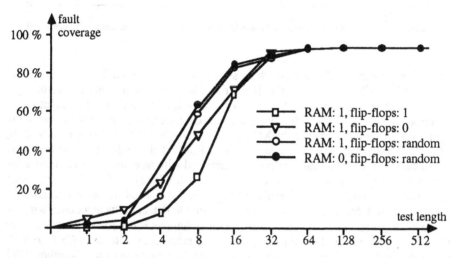

Fig. 3. Impact of RAM and CSTP flip-flops initialization on test effectiveness

In Table 1 we show the fault coverage as a function of the test length, obtained for three differently defined sets of faults [13]: (a) the set of faults that includes only faults in the functional portions of the 2901 circuit (no faults in the CSTP logic), (b) the set of faults that includes faults in the 2901 circuitry and CSTP flip-flops (no faults in multiplexers that select whether the circuit is in normal operation mode or in test mode), and (c) the set of faults that includes all possible faults in the circuit.

It can be observed that the faults in the functional portions of the 2901 circuit (except the RAM module) and the CSTP flip-flops are tested very efficiently - the coverage exceeding 99.9% is obtained after just 256 clock cycles. Low coverage of faults in the remaining part of the BIST logic, indicated by the entries in the last column of Table 1, is due to the fact that the mode control logic has a number of stuck-at faults that cannot be detected during the self-test session regardless of the sequence of patterns generated by the CSTP.

Table 1. Fault coverage in the 2901 circuit (without the RAM module)

test length [clock cycles]	fault coverage [%]		
	2901 logic	2901 logic and CSTP flip-flops	2901 logic and entire BIST logic
4	29.21	23.49	22.69
8	53.90	54.81	51.34
16	74.21	80.37	74.45
32	95.35	97.40	90.35
64	99.32	99.62	92.23
128	99.66	99.81	92.53
256	99.93	99.96	92.64
512	99.93	99.96	92.64

This effect is explained in Fig. 4 which shows the gate-level model of a multiplexer included in a CSTP cell. The multiplexer is controlled by the mode control input TEST which selects whether the input of the flip-flop is driven by the output of the functional circuitry (or the primary input of the circuit), as it is in the normal mode of operation, or by the output of the XOR gate included in the CSTP cell, as it is in the self-test mode. It can be easily seen that with TEST = 1 the faults shown in Fig. 4 are not testable. These untestable faults can be detected with an extra test performed using externally supplied test patterns or by running extra "quasi self-test" sessions with appropriate segments of the circular path put in the normal mode of operation. It should be noted that the need for such extra testing to detect faults associated with the mode control logic is not specific to the CSTP technique; it is necessary regardless of the BIST technique applied. Furthermore, as the mode control logic in CSTP cells is extremely simple, the extra testing for the CSTP is simpler than for the other BIST techniques.

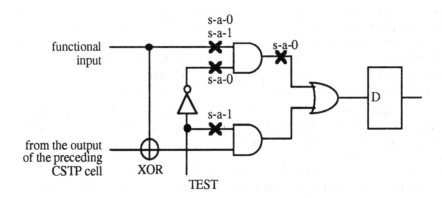

Fig. 4. Untestable faults in the mode control logic of the CSTP cell

The above presented results on the coverage of faults in the CSTP-based design have been compared with those obtained for the earlier mentioned alternative design in which LFSRs and MISRs are used for testing all the 2901 logic except for the RAM. The shape of the fault coverage curve for both designs is very similar. In particular, for the LFSR- and MISR-based design it takes approximately 200 clock cycles (depending on the initial state of the BIST logic) to obtain the fault coverage of 99.9% in the 2901 logic (cf. column "2901 logic" in Table 1). Clearly, the problem of low coverage of faults in the entire circuit due to undetectable faults in the mode control logic is also observed in the LFSR- and MISR-based solution; in fact, the fault coverage for this design is even lower than for the CSTP-based design.

As alluded to earlier, to estimate the effectiveness of testing embedded RAMs, a simple stuck-at fault model is not sufficient. Therefore, the "weighted" fault coverage is used as a measure of the quality of RAM testing. Such a measure takes into account several classes of faults representing possible physical defects and their relative frequency of occurrence. For the experiments with the 2901 circuit, we assume the following fault model:

stuck-at faults	87.5%
static 2-coupling faults	1.5%
unidirectional 2-coupling faults	3.0%
other (unknown) faults	8.0%

The above statistics are based on the quantitative fault model representing physical defects in memories undergoing logic testing (self-test) proposed in [12], derived from the results of studies on modeling faults in RAMs carried out at Philips [6]. The group of unknown faults represents defects identified by the Inductive Fault Analysis or observed in the manufactured RAM chips, but not represented by the fault model developed in [6]. Characteristics of the group of unknown faults similar to those described in [12] have been assumed when calculating the weighted fault coverage.

The results of experimental study based on the above described fault model indicate that:

- the coverage of faults is little dependent on the circular path design (version of the circuit);
- the coverage of faults in both sections of the two-port RAM, RAMA (RAM port addressed by address A) and RAMB (RAM port addressed by address B), is comparable;
- the impact of the initial state of the CSTP and the initial state of the RAM on the fault coverage can be characterized as follows:
  - the initial state of the CSTP has little impact on the fault coverage,
  - the initial state of the RAM has some impact on the fault coverage; generally a large number of 1's in the RAM positively affects the efficiency of testing for short test times.

To illustrate these results, in Table 2 we show the weighted fault coverage as a function of the test length for version 1 of the circuit with the CSTP flip-flops initialized to 1, for two different initial states of the RAM: all-zeroes and all-ones.

The results in Table 2 show that the faults in the RAM are tested very efficiently - the coverage exceeding 99.8% is obtained after just 2048 clock cycles.

Table 2. Weighted fault coverage for the RAM module

test length [clock cycles]	fault coverage [%]	
	RAM initialized to all-ones	RAM initialized to all-zeroes
16	28.48	24.13
32	53.33	44.38
64	82.31	52.14
128	93.69	75.74
256	96.80	89.03
512	99.22	97.08
1024	99.74	99.48
2048	99.98	99.83

Regarding the compaction of the test responses, the following conclusions have been drawn based on the experimental results:

- for the two examined values of the length of signature, 16 bits and 32 bits, no difference in the quality of testing has been observed which indicates that the 16-bit signature adequately represents the result of the self-test session;
- error masking (aliasing) is only important for very short test sessions; for a reasonable length of the test session (128 clock cycles or more), no aliasing has been observed.

The above results on the coverage of RAM faults in the CSTP-based design have been compared with those obtained for the earlier considered alternative design in which the dedicated BIST technique described in [19] is applied for the RAM. For this alternative design it takes 4352 clock cycles to execute the RAM test procedure. For the RAM fault model assumed in [19], the coverage of 100% is obtained after that time. However, assuming the fault model described earlier in this section, the coverage offered by the dedicated test procedure does not exceed 99.5% - a significantly lower value than obtained for the CSTP-based design.

5 Conclusion

We show that self-testability is an essential feature of VLSI circuits used as components of dependable systems. We discuss one of the key problems associated with designing self-testable circuits - the selection of BIST (built-in self-test) technique. Specifically, we present advantages and disadvantages of two basic strategies that can be applied when designing a VLSI chip: using one universal BIST technique vs. using several dedicated BIST techniques for a single chip design.

As a good candidate for a universal BIST technique, having a potential to effectively and efficiently support the design of a large class of VLSI circuits, we advise the CSTP (Circular Self-Test Path) technique. The applicability of the CSTP is illustrated with an example of self-testable design of a bit-slice processor 2901. This example shows that the CSTP technique can be successfully applied to design a self-testable circuit of a diversified internal structure that comprises various types of functional blocks. The design characteristics and the results of simulation experiments carried out for this circuit show that the proposed self-test solution is well balanced, i.e., the quality of testing for individual components of the circuit is comparable, and overall offers high quality testing at acceptable BIST implementation costs.

Acknowledgment

The author is grateful to Sławomir Pilarski who supported the development of the CSTP analysis tools and to Krzysztof Gaj who developed the RAM fault simulator. The contribution of Grzegorz Jankowski who adjusted the simulator and performed the experiments described in this paper is also gratefully acknowledged.

References

1. M. Abramovici, M. A. Breuer, A. D. Friedman, "Digital Systems Testing and Testable Design," Computer Science Press, 1995.
2. V. D. Agrawal, C. R. Kime, K. K. Saluja, "A Tutorial on Built-In Self-Test: Part 2 - Applications", IEEE Design & Test of Computers, pp. 69-77, June 1993.
3. Advanced Micro Devices, "The Am Family Data Book with Related Support Circuits", 1978.
4. S. Chandra et al., "CrossCheck: An Innovative Testability Solution", IEEE Design & Test of Computers, pp. 56-68, June 1993.
5. F. Corno, P. Prinetto, M. Sonza Reorda, "An Experimental Analysis of the Effectiveness of the Circular Self-Test Path Technique", Proc. EURO-DAC'94, pp. 246-251, 1994.
6. R. Dekker, F. Beenker, L. Thijssen, "Realistic Built-In Self-Test for Static RAMs", Proc. IEEE International Test Conf., pp. 343-352, 1988.
7. C. Dislis, I. D. Dear, A. P. Ambler, "The Economics of Chip Level Testing and DFT", Test Synthesis Seminar - Digest of Papers, paper 2.1, International Test Conf., 1994.
8. "The Challanges of Self-Test", IEEE Design & Test of Computers, pp. 46-56, Feb. 1990.
9. R. Gage, "Structured CBIST in ASICs", Proc. IEEE International Test Conf., pp. 332-338, 1993.
10. A. Kraśniewski, S. Pilarski, "Circular Self-Test Path: A Low Cost BIST Technique", Proc. 24th ACM/IEEE Design Automation Conf., pp. 407-415, 1987.
11. A. Kraśniewski, S. Pilarski, "Circular Self-Test Path: A Low Cost BIST Technique for VLSI Circuits", IEEE Trans. on CAD, vol. CAD-8, pp. 46-55, 1989.
12. A. Kraśniewski, S. Pilarski, "High Quality Testing of Embedded RAMs Using Circular Self-Test Path", Proc. IEEE International Test Conf., pp. 652-661, Baltimore, Sept. 1992.

13. A. Kraśniewski, "Circular Self-Test Path as a Universal BIST Technique", Proc. Workshop on Design Methodologies in Microelectronics, pp. 256-263, Smolenice Castle, Slovakia, 1995.
14. M. Nicolaidis, "A Unified Built-In Self-Test Scheme: UBIST", Proc. 18th Int. Symp. on Fault-Tolerant Computing, pp. 157-163, 1988.
15. S. Pilarski, A. Kraśniewski, T. Kameda, "Estimating Testing Effectiveness of the Circular Self-Test Path Technique", IEEE Trans. on CAD, pp. 1301-1316, Oct. 1992.
16. A. Pierzyńska, S. Pilarski, "Built-In Self-Test Strategy for Large Embedded PLAs", Proc. 10th IEEE VLSI Test Symp., pp. 73-78, 1992.
17. S. Pilarski, A. Pierzyńska, "BIST and Delay Fault Detection", Proc. IEEE International Test Conf., pp. 236-242, 1993.
18. M. M. Pradhan, E. J. O'Brien, S. L. Lam, J. Beausang, "Circular BIST with Partial Scan", Proc. IEEE International Test Conf., pp. 719-729, 1988.
19. K. K. Saluja, S. H. Sng, K. Kinoshita, "Built-In Self-Testing RAM: A Practical Alternative", IEEE Design & Test of Computers, pp. 42-51, Feb. 1987.
20. "Guidelines for Research Proposals", Semiconductor Reseach Corporation, Aug. 1985.
21. C. E. Stroud, "Automated BIST for Sequential Logic Synthesis", IEEE Design & Test of Computers, pp. 22-32, Dec. 1988.
22. B. Tuck, "High-density ASICs force focus on testability", Computer Design, pp. 59-66, April 1, 1991.
23. D. L. Wheater et al., "ASIC Test Cost/Strategy Trade-offs", Proc. International Test Conf., pp. 93-102, 1994.

Pseudorandom Testing of Microprocessors at Instruction/Data Flow Level

Janusz Sosnowski, A. Kuśmierczyk
Institute of Computer Science, Warsaw University of Technology,
ul. Nowowiejska 15/19, Warsaw 00-665, Poland, Email: jss@ii.pw.edu.pl

A universal approach to testing microprocessors is described. It is based on a test program with pseudorandom stream of instructions and data. An original software generator of such programs has been presented. Theoretical studies and many simulation experiments show that the proposed approach has similar properties to pseudorandom testing at the circuit level and covers a lot of fault models.

1. Introduction

Efficient microprocessor testing is a crucial point in digital system diagnostics. Recent achievements in BIST techniques improve processor testability features. Nevertheless they do not cover all microprocessor blocks and many fault models, so still there is a strong need for good test programs. Many papers has been devoted to microprocessor test methodology. A large part of them related to the deterministic approach based on functional testing [1,7,17,21]. Due to microprocessor complexity the deterministic test pattern generation process is strongly handicapped. Beyond the complexity of this process there are still some problems not satisfactorily resolved in this process namely coverage of sophisticated fault models (e.g. delay, pattern sensitivity, coupling faults) and unanticipated faults. Moreover for the end user the detailed information on the microprocessor structure is not available. To overcome these problems we can use pseudorandom (PSR) tests.

The PSR test approach attracted many researchers and valuable publications in this area appeared [3-5,18-20,23-25]. They cover mostly the problem of random testing effectiveness for general combinational circuitry, RAMs and to some extent microprocessors. Some experiments with PSR tests at the circuit input/output level showed [12,19] that the required test length was about 10 times larger than that for deterministic tests (100% error coverage for single stuck-at faults or exhaustive tests). The PSR tests for RAMs need 5-10 times more test vectors than deterministic tests oriented towards basic faults. For sophisticated fault models PSR tests are more effective. Moreover they cover simultaneously different classes of faults (including unanticipated fault models) and can be easily implemented without the knowledge of the structure of the tested circuitry. PSR tests at the instruction/data flow level (pseudorandom stream of instructions and data) applied to simple microprocessors assured higher error coverage than deterministic tests [11,24] (in [11] for the same test length). In [11,24] the authors gave also a theoretical estimation of PSR test length in function of the assumed error coverage. For Intel 8080 and Motorola 6800 processors PSR tests comprising several millions of instructions cover 99.9% of faults. These results encouraged us to develop pseudorandom test programs.

The published approaches to random testing assumed the use of special external testers (they are quite complex for microprocessors). These testers generate random instructions, random data and random control signals and analyze processor responses. In this paper we present a new approach which bases on the idea of generating pseudorandom test sequences with the use of a special program. In the paper we show that the generated stream of instructions and data produces (in a large extent) pseudorandom stimuli, at the circuit level, for various processor logical blocks. Hence good results with pseudorandom tests at the circuit level (largely used in BISTs [10,12,16]) can be considered as the good prognostic for the instruction/data flow level approach. However, we must be conscious of faults which are not sensitive (difficult to detect) to PSR tests. The presented approach is very attractive from the practical point of view. Nevertheless it faces more problems (related to test controllability and observability) than in the case of using external testers. To evaluate the effectiveness of this approach we performed many simulation experiments. As opposed to experiments developed by other authors (insertion of a limited number of faults) our original experiments allow us to evaluate the testability features of various processor blocks for pseudorandom test programs. This analysis is very useful to asses test effectiveness and identify functions which should be checked with supplementary deterministic tests. It also gives some hints on how to optimize PSR tests. Some ideas of improving PSR test effectiveness with additional hardware has also been outlined.

2. Generation of PSR Test Program

The basic idea of the test is to generate a pseudorandom test program and execute it in the system environment. Each program generation is unique and defined by the test generator parameters (seed constant, test length and some other optional specifications). In the testing process we can use either the generated test program or only its generator. The first approach needs more memory, however is faster than the second one. In the sequel we discuss only the second approach as the most general (it can be easily reduced to the first one). The test result is verified by checking some signatures calculated as a function of register states, RAM contents and exception situations. The test generator has a modular structure which assures high flexibility in implementing various test strategies (needed in experiments on test efficiency and program optimization). The test generator (TPG) comprises the following modules: pseudorandom pattern generator (PG), code composer (CC), test controller (TC) and supplementary modules (SM). Developing the test generator for Intel processors we admitted some optional solutions which were useful to study test complexity and effectiveness (helpful in designing such generators for other processors).

In the basic mode the test controller initiates generation of a testing subsequence TSS_i specified by the seed constant, sequence length and optionally generator type. This subsequence is created by the code composer in cooperation with PG module. Then the generated subsequence is executed. Before this the test controller allocates RAM areas for the TSS_i subsequence, initiates processor registers and RAM (data, stack areas for this subsequence, unused RAM areas etc). After the execution of the test subsequence TSS_i the test controller updates test signatures and initiates generation of the next subsequence TSS_{i+1} etc. The number of generated subsequences is specified as a parameter for the test generator. The memory map of the system is illustrated in fig.1. It is important to note that the position of the TSS_i area can be different for each generation, moreover this area can be composed of different segments scattered in the memory space. RAM allocation to subsequences TSS_i is assured by TC module with appropriate setting of segment register states (pseudorandom and fixed schemes can be used).

To assure a unique test result the processor registers and RAM memory have to be initialized to a specified state (e.g. pseudorandom codes) before the execution of the test subsequence. We have also introduced an option which allows to use the final state of subsequence TSS_i as the initial state for the next subsequence TSS_{i+1}. Flexible programming of the test environment and schemes is useful for some experimental studies e.g. RAM and register initialization with a pseudorandom or fixed pattern.

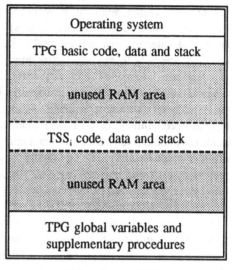

Fig.1. **System memory mapping.**

For Intel 80x86 processors the test subsequences are generated by the code composer which requests bytes from the pattern generator and composes subsequence TSS_i. The number of created instructions is specified by the parameter $T_{SL(i)}$ (it can be also fixed for all subsequences) which specifies the maximal length of the subsequence (in bytes). In the basic test program it is assumed that $T_{SL(i)} < 64$-kbytes. The first received byte is considered as the first opcode byte of the microprocessor, then if the opcode is valid subsequent instruction bytes are generated. Invalid and critical opcodes (10-20%) are either discarded or replaced with other codes (two optional versions). Depending upon the instruction format resulting from the first byte other bytes are requested and an instruction is composed. Some relations between bytes are also considered (e.g. the prefix REP can be followed by a few opcodes). Each generated instruction is stored in the instruction list. Generating subsequent instructions we have to take into account the existing context of instructions. Due to this some specific instructions will be added or modified. Other code transformations involving more changes may be also useful. Hence the code generator is two-pass. In other processors with opcode bits dispersed in the word (e.g. 32 bits) it is more natural to generate whole words assuring equal probability of 0s and 1s for each bit. This allows to cover all combinations of characteristic instruction fields (opcode, address mode, register specifications etc) if they are short enough. In case of long opcode fields (with many invalid codes) we can select pseudorandomly the test values from a table comprising allowable codes.

The software generation of the test instruction sequence is more complicated than in the case of external testers, this results from the fact that the generated instruction sequence will be loaded into the system RAM as the program code for the execution. So data addresses and branch instructions must be appropriately adapted to the system physical capabilities. Moreover we have some limitations to assure program controllability and unique results (this also holds for external testers). Hence some critical instructions are skipped (e.g. invalid, halt, input, output, load status word), instructions loading segment registers are dealt with a special care (e.g. preceded by PUSH and followed by POP instructions), subroutine call and return instructions are correlated, interrupt instructions lead to well specified handling routines etc. Similar problem arises with system instructions (related to cache, memory management, privilege adjustment etc). Various possibilities to deal with branch instructions can be programmed (e.g. branches with severely limited target addresses, partially limited target addresses with loop collision avoidance etc.). Moreover it is possible to define different probabilities of generated codes (e.g. using transcoding table). In the basic mode only some fixed subroutines and interrupt handling routines are provided (stored in the supplementary area). Optionally it is possible to insert pseudorandomly some critical instructions into the generated subsequence assuring deterministic program flow.

In microprocessors with segmented memory and 16-bit address offset it is quite easy to assure conformity of the generated addresses with the physical system memory space (e.g. by controlling segment register states). In system using 32-bit address offset and virtual memory this problem is more intricate for instruction codes with register or indirect addressing modes. The simplest solution is to skip this address mode (and add deterministic procedures for testing it) or to limit it to some specified registers (with controlled states) or to modify (if needed) the states of registers used in addressing. In some microprocessors we may have other dependencies. For example in RISC processors there is data dependency related to the situation where a result from a previous operation may be required as an operand before it has been written into register file (due to the pipeline delay in result write-back). If this is not assured by the hardware (e.g. scoreboarding circuitry) then it must be resolved in software. In pseudorandom testing this dependency has to be taken into account only if it leads to nondeterministic results. The effect of delaying jumps and branches is not critical in PSR testing.

For each generated PSR test sequence we have to define the reference signatures which represent the test result. We have analyzed several possibilities of verifying test results. Each executed subsequence TSS_i produces specific states of processor registers, RAM areas and exceptions (e.g. program interrupts, division by 0). All this can be considered as the test response (result). An important thing is to find a compact and representative form of the test result which differentiates an erroneous from the correct test program execution. If an error occurs it may influence the processor control logic, processor data path, test sequence code, RAM etc. Erroneous states may appear during instruction execution and result either in disturbance of the program flow or the state of the processor or RAM. Subsequent instructions basing on this erroneous state may generate subsequent erroneous states etc. On the other hand subsequent instructions may overwrite wrong results generated by previous instructions (we studied this in simulation experiments, section 3). For each test subsequence TSS_i the test control module stores, in a reserved RAM area, the final state of processor registers and a signature calculated over final states of RAM (TSS_i area, unused areas etc). Moreover the number of correct and non correct exceptions, generated during TSS_i execution, is also stored as the test result. It is also possible to generate a signature calculated from processor states taken during the test subsequence execution (the CC module can optionally insert signature update procedures into the generated subsequence every specified number of instructions). Intermediate updating of RAM signature during the test subsequence practically is not needed if the number of performed RAM write operations is relatively low (so that the probability of overwriting the same RAM cell is low). In processors with on-chip local memories (e.g. caches) the state of these resources constitutes also the test result. For a big number of generated test subsequences instead of storing separate test results for each subsequence the test control module delivers a single compact signature (updated on each subsequence execution). Having initiated the execution of a test subsequence the test control module waits to regain the control (RET instruction). If it does not happen before a specified timeout an error is detected. The calculated signatures are compared with the reference ones.

We introduced many options to the test generator in order to check the influence of different strategies on test effectiveness (sections 3 and 4). The universal test generator was developed as about 20kB program. It can be reduced significantly (down to 10kB) if some options are eliminated or more restrictions on the generated test are imposed. The test generator complexity increases with the instruction and other structural dependencies of the processor. In most applications memory requirements (relatively low) for the test generator are not important. In some cases more critical can be the test generation time. Depending upon the developed test generator we need execution of 100 - 400 instructions to generate one instruction of the test. If the test generation time is critical we can use previously generated tests (however in this case we have to store quite long test sequences in the system).

The developed approach assures quite good test controllability, however due to the test program executed in the real system it is a little bit lower than in the case of external tester. Test observability is also comparable to that of external testers. It is only lowered in a negligible range by overwriting the same memory cells during the test execution. The probability of this effect is very low, moreover it decreases with more frequent calculation of signatures (at the cost of some increase in execution time). The test effectiveness is studied in the next sections.

The presented test can be significantly improved by adding simple supplementary circuits. The easiest to implement is to add a parallel signature analyzer to the system bus (e.g. TI chip SN74ACT8994). This improves test observability and eliminates subprograms needed for calculating RAM signatures. Significant improvement of the test observability is to design processors with on-chip signature analyzers monitoring internal bus (data path). Hardware implementation of the test generator is more complex due to code dependencies and other limitations (this could be alleviated if the processor designer took into account the problem of pseudorandom testing). The on-chip test generator can be located at the level of the data bus. External test generator is also possible. However the problem is to assure no performance degradation of the system. As compared with the software implementation of the test generator, the hardware approach is less susceptible to various system restrictions (e.g. branch addressing). Nevertheless in systems with on-chip memory management circuitry address restrictions hold also for external tester. This problem can be alleviated with a test mode which assures hardware suppression of generated addresses to an acceptable space area. Other dependency problems can be eliminated designing processors with deterministic behavior for any instruction/data flow. Making internal structure of the processor susceptible to PSR testing is also advantageous.

3. Simulation Experiments

To study the effectiveness of the random test programs we have developed some tools for performing various simulation experiments. These experiments were aimed at the analysis of dynamic changes of the processor internal states, propagation of these changes to the RAM, signature analysis, checking profiles of generated test stimuli for selected functional blocks, fault insertion experiments etc. For the simulation experiments we used an extended test pattern generator (MTPG - it runs on IBM PC) which generates the same test sequences as described in section 2 and in addition it produces various files comprising simulation images (e.g register states for each generated instruction). The MTPG program (described in [25]) cooperates with other software modules used to find different simulation statistics, insert faults etc.

We have performed a lot of simulations for various options of the test pattern generator. Here we give some illustrative results for test sequences compatible with Intel 286 processor instruction set. The performed experiments allowed us to define some measures which, in our opinion, are useful to characterize and optimize the generated tests (e.g. distribution of instruction codes and register states, test controllability and observability factors). The distribution of generated instruction opcodes was almost uniform, however this leads to different probabilities of various instruction classes (the most probable are MOV instructions - 15%). An important issue in PSR tests is to assure pseudorandom distribution of register states during the test. Let us assume equal probability $(p(R_i))$ of generating any state, in register R_i, by any instruction (from the considered test of length T_L) which loads this register. In this case we can calculate the number of different states $S(R_i)$ assumed by the specified register (R_i), during the test execution, from the following formula (derived in appendix 1):

$$S(R_i) = \alpha_i[1 - \exp(-\lambda_i T_L)] \tag{1}$$

where $\lambda_i = 1/(\alpha_i f_i)$, α_i is the number of possible states $(p(R_i)=1/\alpha_i)$ for register R_i and f_i is an average distance between subsequent state changes of the register R_i in the test

Fig.2. Cardinality of different states assumed by register AX during a PSR test sequence.

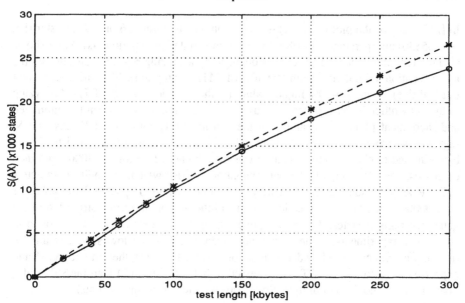

Fig.3. Distribution of register states for a pseudorandom test sequence: a) register AX - case 1, b) register AX - case 2, c) register AX - case 3, d) register CX.

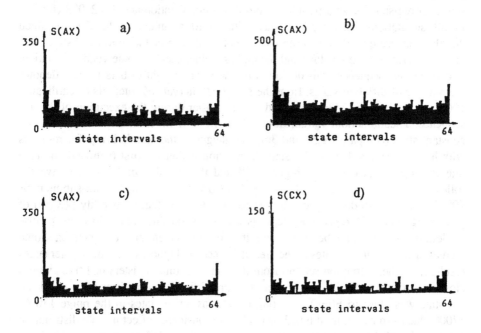

sequence, T_L is the total test length i.e. the sum of all $T_{SL(i)}$ related to the generated subsequences.

In fig.2 we give the plot of S(AX) derived from (1) assuming 16 bit AX register (i.e. $\alpha_i = 65536$) and parameter $f_{AX}=8.8$ bytes (from simulation experiments). Fig.2 shows also the real plot of S(AX) which was obtained by analyzing register states during the test execution (simulation with the use of MTPG program). The theoretical plot (dashed line) assumes 6-10% higher values (in the considered range of T_L). Analyzing in this way other 16 bit registers we have got similar relations between the simulated and theoretical plots. For example in the considered T_L range for BX, CX and SI registers we have got lower values up to 15-20%. In the case of flag register FL (7 bits admitted to change) this deviation was even higher (25% for $T_L=40000$ and then decreases, $f_{Fl}=4.4$). To get better approximation of $S(R_i)$ we could modify parameters f_i. For example assuming $f_{AX} = 9.3$ we get 0% deviation up to $T_L=10000$ and 4.4% for $T_L=300000$. The reason for this deviation is a little bit non uniform distribution of the generated register states. This is illustrated in fig.3. Parameters f_i has been found in simulation experiments, some values are given in tab.1 (the lowest values are for instruction pointer - $f_{IP}=1$ and accumulator - AX). However they are rounded and expressed in instructions. If T_L is expressed in bytes (as in fig.2) then the value of f_i given in tab.1 should be multiplied by 2 (average length of instructions).

Fig.3 gives the distribution of AX register (accumulator) states for 3 generated test sequences: with pseudorandom initialization of RAM and $T_L=21093$ instructions (fig.3a) or $T_L=42186$ (fig.3b), with RAM initiated to 0 (fig.3c) and the distribution of states for register CX with pseudorandom RAM initialization and $T_L=21093$ (fig.3d). In all simulations each register was initiated to a unique code. The obtained distributions are quite close to the ideal theoretical case of the uniform distribution, only in the range of low values and the highest values there is some visible deviation. For longer test sequences this deviation is lower. The height of bars in fig.3 denotes the number of different states, from the specified interval (65 intervals of cardinality 1000 and the last one 1536), assigned to the register during the execution of the test sequence. Pseudorandom initialization of RAM is a little bit better than a fixed constant state (compare fig.3a and 3c). The height of the bars is lower for registers with higher f_i ($f_{AX} = 4$, $f_{CX}=12$). State distribution within the first (similarly the last) interval is also not even. For register AX and the situation of fig.3a we have the following values of S(AX): 92, 82, 49, 8, 6, 17, 15, 19, 4, 9 collected for subintervals 100, 200, 300,..., 1000, respectively. These results show that probability $p(R_i(v))$ of generating state v in register R_i depends a little bit on this value. So more precise modelling of $S(R_i)$ can be done with the formula given in the appendix. Some increased probability of states in the area of lowest and highest values of register states results from the instruction set and from the fact that some registers had fixed values close to zero (CS, DS, ES segment registers), modification of register SP is restricted (its state was close to FFFF). The flag register assumed states in the range 13000-17000, due to some not used bits. Practically the considered effect in state distribution can be reduced if for every test subsequence we will use different states of the above mentioned registers. However this effect is not so critical.

Tab.1. **Selected statistic parameters for test sequences comprising about 21k instructions (1 and 2 refer to two different seed numbers used in the test generator).**

Statistic parameter		Processor register						
		BP	AX	BX	CX	DX	SI	DI
$\Delta_{0,1}$	L	-6%	-8%	-8%	-6%	-6%	-10%	-6%
	H	12%	10%	5%	7%	7%	9%	3%
$\Delta_{7,8}$	L	-2%	-2%	-2%	-3%	-3%	-3%	-6%
	H	3%	3%	1%	9%	2%	3%	9%
$\Delta_{14,15}$	L	-3%	-3%	-3%	-4%	-6%	-1%	-1%
	H	3%	9%	6%	10%	4%	1%	2%
f_i	1	39	4	13	12	12	15	12
	2	35	4	14	12	12	15	13
g_i	1	1992	496	1285	991	1469	1321	1198
	2	1732	629	1182	1262	1658	1108	1129

Tab.2. **Number of 0-1 state changes on i-th bit of register R_j detected during the execution of a PSR test with 4028 instructions .**

i	0	1	2	3	4	5	6	7	8	9	10	11	12	13	14	15
AX	205	220	194	191	194	164	173	180	146	131	132	121	117	127	111	119
BX	64	52	42	41	38	34	34	34	48	42	40	44	35	39	38	34
SI	109	57	37	27	27	21	18	22	24	21	24	26	23	19	19	14

Tab.3. **Hamming distance between subsequent register states (PSR test of 4028 instructions).**

i	0	1	2	.	.	.	.	6	7	.	.	.	.	.	.	15	16
AX	3001	102	111	127	154	101	108	90	83	71	50	22	8	0	2	0	1
BX	3745	52	32	26	30	31	27	23	29	16	13	5	4	0	1	0	0
DI	3692	133	59	27	12	18	21	17	18	8	13	4	3	2	0	0	1

To study the process of register state generation we performed simulation experiments for various initial states of RAM and processor. In the worst case, i.e. 0 state of registers (except SP) and RAM cells, we observed small decrease in $S(R_j)$, some increase in f_i and larger number (g_i) of situations with the same state in more than one register (g_i was more than two times greater for some registers than for pseudorandom initialization shown in tab.1). We have checked also state distribution at the bit level within specified registers and specified pairs of registers. In a test sequence of $T_L=21093$ instructions, for all general purpose registers, the probability of 0 state at the bit positions 0, 7 and 15 was in the range 51-55%, 54-58% and 55-60%, respectively. State correlation between subsequent bits of the same register are shown in tab.1. This table gives deviation range (L - lower, H - higher) of state distribution from the optimal case i.e. 25% (equal probability of all sates on two considered bits). The presented deviation ranges relate to bit pairs: 0,1 ($\Delta_{0,1}$); 7,8 ($\Delta_{7,8}$) and 14,15 ($\Delta_{14,15}$). These results proved low correlation between bit states. However we observed higher probability of state 00 (deviation from 0-12% over all registers). For IP register almost uniform distribution was observed. Similar simulations we performed for various test seeds, initial states etc. The results were very close to those presented here (they differed up to 10%). So we can state that the generated test sequences well randomize states of registers and RAM. This is a good prognostic for assuring high test controllability of other data processing blocks in the processor. However more detailed analysis showed also some anomalies in the frequency of state changes on different bit positions of registers. A sample of results is given in tab. 2.

Analyzing the test controllability it is also important to check the distribution of the Hamming distance between subsequent test stimuli. In tab.3 we give some selected results related to the Hamming distance between subsequent states (corresponding to two subsequent program test instructions) of some registers. For the specified distance i from 0 (no change) to 16 (all bits changed) tab.3 gives the number of instructions for which the state of the considered register changed on i positions (after instruction execution). Similar results has been obtained for subsequent test stimuli of selected functional blocks e.g. ALU. They proved relatively good randomization of delivered test patterns.

Correlation between the same bit position (k) in different registers (R_i, R_j) is illustrated in tab.4 (considered bit pair states $R_i(k)$, $R_j(k)$). Here we also give only the deviation range from the optimal value i.e. 25%. We also analyzed the correlation of states between different registers. For the test sequence of 21093 instructions (with pseudorandom initialization) we found that during the execution of 15138 instructions all registers comprised different patterns, in 5236 cases a single pair of registers comprised the same pattern. The same pattern was in 3, 4, 5, 6 and 7 registers within 139, 556, 7, 14 and 3 instructions respectively. For other tests results were similar. Even in the case of registers (except SP) and RAM initialized to 0 after 60 instructions distinct states appeared in all registers. This confirms good capabilities of filling register state space by the pseudorandom programs.

Tab.4. State distribution of k-th bit in two registers (deviation from optimum 25%).

Reg. R_i-R_j	deviation on k-th bit [%]			deviation of bit states over all k [%]			
	k=0	k=7	k=15	00	01	10	11
AX-BX AX-SI	-2; 5 -5; 5	-1; 3 -3; 3	-3; 5 -3; 4	3; 5 3; 4	3; 0 -5; 1	-2; 0 -2; 5	-3; -2 -3

Tab.5. Numbers of not detected transient faults per 200 inserted faults in each experiment (27 experiments).

Code area	16-bit faults			single bit faults		
	AX	CX	DI	AX	CX	DI
A	11; 9	7; 6	9; 7	56	44	47
B	12; 12	8; 4	9; 9	50	39	46
C	9, 8	5; 5	6; 5	64	51	43

In other experiments we checked the distribution of argument values for logic and arithmetic operations, distribution of referenced register and memory addresses, distribution of used addressing modes, distribution of invoked machine cycles etc. The obtained results confirmed a close to uniform distribution. So we can state that the basic processor functional blocks are sensitized with almost random patterns. However the number of different patterns for each of these blocks may be different for the same test sequence. It can be assumed that it is described also by similar equation to (1). However for most blocks we achieved exhaustive test patterns (e.g. memory addressing controller, register file, instruction sequencer, BIU, control ROM, instruction prefetch buffer and pipeline). We refer to this problem in the next section.

The described experiments confirmed good test controllability. Another important parameter influencing test effectiveness is its observability. Analyzing test observability we performed a series of simulation experiments. The simplest experiments derived the frequency of storing the states of processor registers (including combined states resulting from various operations) in the memory and the frequency of using some registers as the argument address modifiers etc. More complex experiments allowed to find the frequency of situations such that a register is initiated to some value and the same value (not disturbed) is stored in some memory cell (after some delay). For registers AX this happened about 200 times per 10k executed instructions, for other basic registers it is about 100/10k. So the direct register controllability and observability (at the data bus level) is relatively low. It is higher if we take into account the influence of the register state on other registers, data and control flow within the testing sequence. For example registers influencing memory addressing are observable indirectly in the image of RAM and program flow. We performed a series of experiments to check RAM changes during the test execution. This gives a more general measure of test result observability. For a pseudorandom test sequence of about 10k instructions we found that within the processor data segment (64kbytes) about 1200 bytes were changed (by about 800 instructions with memory write cycles). In the extension segment 840 bytes were changed (by string operation instructions). For the stack segment 400 bytes with pseudorandom addresses were changed with about 200 move instructions and 2000 bytes located at the top of the segment were changed due to push instructions. In the program pushing on the stack operations override a little bit the number of pop operations. So resuming we can observe that for the test sequence, composed of 1k instructions, we have about 360 bytes in RAM comprising test response. With the increase of the test length the probability of overwriting test results increases so it is recommended to calculate test signatures (from all memory segments) periodically e.g. every single test subsequence.

The most sophisticated experiments involved fault injection. Faults were injected at the functional level. We took into account two classes of faults: transient and permanent. Permanent fault effects were regenerated for each instruction execution (e.g. stuck-at fault of the register decoder resulting in not selecting some register, stuck-at faults in register bits, opcodes). Transient fault effects were produced only for one instruction (e.g. a bit change in a register). The test observability for permanent faults was very good (all faults resulted in wrong signature even within a single test subsequence). Experiments with transient faults characterize test observability. These faults were injected into the register file by changing a single or multiple bits. In each experiment only one fault was injected. Some results are given in tab.5. which shows the number of not detected transient faults (single or 16 bit) inserted into a specified register and test code area (A, B and C correspond to initial, middle and final area of the test, respectively). The 16-bit faults were inserted into two tests (about 20k instructions each) generated for different seed numbers. Each entry in the table corresponds to 200 fault injections. The percentage of not detected single and 16-bit transient faults is in the range 19-32% and 2.5-6%, respectively. In the case of flag register (FL) 27-30% 16-bit faults were not detected. Practically for all detected faults RAM signature was not correct. Detection based only on the state of registers is poorer. Inserting faults into IP register or test codes (equivalent to instruction register disturbance) resulted in test suspension (detected with timeout) or wrong signature. Test suspension was found in 60-70%, 50-60% and 10-30% cases of inserted faults in IP, the first opcode byte and other bytes, respectively. Resuming we can state that transient fault coverage is in the range 70-100%. This can also be considered as some measure of test observability (lower bound). Direct test observability is characterized by the fraction of instructions (in the test) which comprise write cycles (<20%). It is lower than transient fault coverage. This observation confirms us that the register file performs to some extent the function of signature generator. This is a good prognostic for high effectiveness of PSR tests also for processors with large number of registers and caches (where the percentage of RAM write cycles is low).

4. Error Coverage Problems

Various approaches to the evaluation of error coverage of the pseudorandom tests were presented in the literature [2-5,9,13,14,18,19,25]. Some of them relied on simulation experiments others based on some theoretical analysis. Simulation experiments were performed either with the use of known faulty elements ([24] with limited number of faults < 100) or with fault models (e.g. at the gate level) injected in the circuit model [11] (several thousands of faults). Simulation experiments with microprocessors proved good error coverage for random testing performed with external testers. However one may consider that the limited number of injected faults is not sufficient. On the other hand the theoretical studies also proved high error coverage for random tests applied to microprocessors and various logical circuits. Moreover they gave some estimations of the expected error coverage (E) in function of the number of test vectors (L). For 8-bit ALU 181 and E=99% we need L=150 pseudorandom vectors [19], for a block composed of 8x8 multiplier combined with 16-bit ALU in TMS32010 processor we need L=4000 vectors [10]. Knowing parameter L_i for the i-th functional block of the microprocessor we can find the required length (T_L) of the instruction sequence in the test from the following formula:

$$L_i = d_i(T_L)/\beta_i \qquad (2)$$

where $d_i(T_L)$ is the number of different test stimuli for the checked i-th circuit in the test of length T_L, β_i is the observability factor defined as the ratio of the number of applied stimuli (to the considered circuit) to the number of observable output results (i.e. stored in the memory or in other registers if their states propagate to the data, address and control lines of the processor). This can be estimated by transient fault coverage factor (section 3). If L_i is given for random vector sequence (with repetitions) then in (2) we replace $d_i(T_L)$ with T_L/γ_i, where γ_i is the average distance (expressed in instructions) between subsequent test stimuli of the circuit.

All the parameters needed in (2) can be derived in the simulation experiments. For example to detect active pattern sensitive faults in the processor register file we need L=20000 pseudorandom vectors (E=99.9%) [6]. In generated tests we have got $d_i(T_L)=0.5T_L$ for the register file, so for $\beta_i=0.6$ we get $T_L > 67000$ instructions. If the parameter L_i is not known (or not precise enough) then we can use another general estimation. Let β_i and δ_i denote the observability and controllability ($\delta_i = d_i(T_L)/T_L$) factors for the i-th functional block in the microprocessor. Next let us assume that a single test stimuli for the considered block detects any fault (from some specified class) with probability p_i. The error coverage (E) can be estimated as:

$$E = (1 - p_i)^{L(i)} \qquad (3)$$

where $L(i) = T_L\beta_i\delta_i$. Hence for a given E we can find the required test length T_L:

$$T_L = \log(1-E)/[\beta_i\delta_i\log(1-p_i)] \qquad (4)$$

Assuming the hypothesis that during the random test sequence the testing stimuli generated for the considered functional block are pseudorandom (simulation experiments confirm this assumption) we can use the presented estimation. For E=0.99 we obtain several millions of instructions (assuming the same p_i as in [11]). The presented estimations are useful if the generated stimuli for processor blocks is pseudorandom. Some deviation found in simulation experiments may increase the calculated test length by about 20%. In advanced processors it will be difficult to assure good controllability of complex blocks (e.g. multipliers, coprocessors). In this case hierarchical PSR tests should be used: a general test and specialized tests targeted for specific blocks or functions.

It is worth noting that during the test sequence some functional blocks are tested in parallel (e.g. instruction sequencer, bus interface unit, addressing circuitry and additionally for some instructions ALU, register file). So estimating the length of the test we can take into account the maximal value obtained for the set of all functional blocks. Finding the required test length from (4) we can take parameter p_i as the probability of detecting most difficult fault [24]. However for many circuits this seems to be not reasonable, because some most difficult-to-detect-faults can be detected easily using additionally simple deterministic test patterns.

PSR tests assure for most internal processor lines 0 or 1 state with probability close to 0.5 (low correlation). So these test can be considered as similar to CSTP approach [12]. So they assure exhaustive generation of v-bit test patterns on inputs of internal processor blocks if $T_L > 8 \cdot 2^v f_i$. As compared with CSTP PSR programs need more clock cycles (however no hardware is required). Pseudorandom tests are quite effective in detecting sophisticated faults, e.g. various delay faults, because they cover practically all possible pairs of instruction codes, addressing modes etc executed in succession. The path delay fault coverage strongly depends upon the ability of the generator to provide pairs of uncorrelated patterns [15]. Moreover PSR tests cover all k sequences of any m classes of instructions or addressing modes if $m^k << T_L$ (in many cases m < 10). Similarly PSR test effectiveness is quite high for PSF faults and various interactions between different functional blocks.

PSR tests are not effective in testing some processor blocks which are designed taking into account specific properties of the real programs e.g. space and time locality of program/data in caches and memory management circuitry, repetition of branch execution in loops (branch target cache). We improve test effectiveness for these blocks by partitioning PSR sequences into segments (comparable with cache sizes) and executing them twice. This also allows to check other processor blocks at higher speed (resulting from cache hits during the second execution). Nevertheless we use additional deterministic test procedures based on well known algorithms (e.g. [7,21]) to check the above mentioned blocks. Similarly we deal with testing some critical instructions. Hence having analyzed the effectiveness of the derived pseudorandom test (with the help of introduced simulation tools) we can optimize them and add some deterministic test procedures or specialized pseudorandom tests (in the developed test the multiplier/divider circuitry is checked with an additional sequence comprising multiply/divide instructions with pseudorandom arguments).

5. Conclusion

A new approach to testing microprocessors and experimental results has been presented. It was found that this approach is very effective not only in detecting basic stuck-at faults but also complex faults such as: bridging, coupling, pattern sensitivity and block interaction disturbances. Moreover it covers unanticipated models of faults. For many of these faults nothing can be said about deterministic test coverage, whereas probability of detecting them using pseudorandom tests increases with the test length. There are some faults difficult to be detected with pseudorandom sequences due to the low number of fault sensitizing vectors or due to program context limitations (e.g. testing segment registers, system level instructions, caches). So it is reasonable to support random testing with some deterministic test procedures. To evaluate the effectiveness of random testing we developed a set of special programs for analyzing test controllability and observability. It was shown that the test effectiveness (lower test length, higher error coverage) can be improved with some simple signature monitors. In this case it approaches to the capabilities of the cyclic self-test-path (CSTP - [12,15]), however at lower hardware cost. PSR testing seems to be useful also in the design process of new chips. Having generated long PSR tests we are able to detect design faults. For example if we generate test responses at some functional level, we can verify logical and electrical models or prototype chips of the designed circuit.

References

[1] D. Brahme, J.A. Abraham, Functional testing of microprocessors, IEEE Transactions on Computers, C-33, No.6, June 1984, pp.475-485.

[2] C.K. Chin, E.J. McCluskey, Test length for pseudorandom testing, IEEE Transactions on Computers, vol.C-36, No.2, February, 1987, pp.252-256.

[3] R. David, J. Brzozowski, Random test length for bounded faults in RAMs, Proc. European Test Conf. 1993,149-158.

[4] R. David, A. Fuentes, B. Courtois, Random pattern testing versus deterministic testing of RAMs, IEEE Transactions on Computers, C-38, May 1989, pp.637-650.

[5] X. Fedi, R. David, Experimental results from random testing of microprocessor, IEEE Int. Symp. FTCS-14, 1984, pp.225-230.

[6] A.J. van de Goor, Testing semiconductor memories, John Wiley & Sons, 1991.

[7] A.J.van de Goor, Th.J.W. Verhallen, Functional testing of current microprocessors, Proc. IEEE Int. Test Conf., 1992, pp.684-695.

[8] Ch.L. Hudson, G.D. Paterson, Parallel self-test with pseudorandom test patterns, Proc. IEEE Int. Test Conf., 1987, pp.954-963.

[9] M. Jacomino, R. David, A new approach of test confidence estimation, Proc. IEEE FTCS-19, 1989, pp.307-314.

[10] K. Kim, S. H. Dong, J. G. Tront, On using signature registers and pseudorandom pattern generator in built-in-self-test, IEEE Transactions of Computer Aided Design, No.8, August 1988, pp.919-928

[11] H. P. Kluge, Microprocessor testing by Instruction Sequences derived from random patterns, Proc. IEEE Int. Test Conf., 1988, pp.73-80.

[12] A. Kraśniewski, S. Pilarski, Circular self-test-path: a low cost BIST technique for VLSI circuits, IEEE Transactions on Computer Aided Design, vol.8, No.4, 1989, pp.46-55.

[13] Y.K. Malaiya, S. Yang, The coverage problem for random testing. Proc. of IEEE Int. Test Conf., 1984, pp.237-245.

[14] E.J. McCluskey, Probability models for pseudorandom test sequences, IEEE Transactions on Computer Aided Design, vol.7, No.1, January, 1988, pp.68-74.

[15] S. Pilarski, A. Pierzyńska, BIST and delay fault detection, Pro. of IEEE Int. Test Conf., 1993, pp.236-242.

[16] I.M. Ratiu, H.B. Bakoglu, Pseudorandom built-in self-test methodology and implementation for IBM RISC system/6000 processor, IBM J. Res. Develop. vol.34, No.1 January 1990, pp.78-84.

[17] J. Salinas, F. Lombardi, A data path approach for testing microprocessors with a fault bound, Microprocessors and Microsystems, vol.16, No.10, 1992, pp.529-539.

[18] S. Sastry. A. Majumder, Test efficiency of random self-test of sequential circuits, IEEE Transactions on Computer Aided Design, vol.10, No.3, March 1991, pp.390-398.

[19] J. Savir, P.H. Bardel, On random pattern test length, IEEE Transactions on Computers, vol. C-36, No.3, March 1987, pp.332-343.

[20] H. D. Schnurmann, E. Lindbloom, R. Carpenter, The weighed random test pattern generator, IEEE Transactions on Computers, vol. c-24, No.7,July, 1975, pp.695-700.

[21] J. Sosnowski, In system testing of cache memories, Proceedings of IEEE Int. Test Conf., 1995, pp.384-393

[22] P. Thevenod Fosse, R. David, Random testing of the data processing section of a microprocessor, Proc. IEEE FTCS-11, 1981.

[23] P. Thevenod Fosse, R. David, Random testing of the control section of a microprocessor, Proc. IEEE FTCS-13, 1983, pp.366-373.

[24] K. D. Wagner, C. K. Chin, E. J. McCluskey, Pseudorandom testing, IEEE Transactions on Computers, vol. C-36, No.3, March 1987, pp.332-343.

[25] J. Sosnowski, A. Kuśmierczyk, Pseudorandom vs deterministic testing of Intel 80x86 processors, Proceedings of 22nd EUROMICRO conference, IEEE Computer Society, 1996 (to appear).

Acknowledgement: This work was supported by grant KBN 8 S503 010 06.

Appendix. 1 Analytical estimation of register state distribution during the test.

Let N_k be the number of different patterns among k patterns generated by the test sequence. We define two probabilities:

$p_r(l) = prob(N_k=l)$ - probability that l patterns are different within the k generated patterns,

$u_k(l) = prob(N_k=l \mid N_{k-1}=l-1)$ - conditional probability that k-th generated pattern is not included in previously generated k-1 patterns (l-1 of these patterns are different).

The expected value of N_k can be calculated as follows:

$$E[N_1] = 1, \quad E[N_k] = \sum_{l=1}^{k} l p_k(l) \quad \text{for } k>1 \tag{A1}$$

Taking into account the following relations:

$$p_k(l) = p_{k-1}(l-1)u_k(l) + p_{k-1}(l)[1 - u_k(l+1)] \quad \text{for } 2 \leq l < k \text{ and } 2 \leq k$$
$$p_k(1) = p_{k-1}(1)[1 - u_k(2)] \quad \text{for } l=1 \text{ and } 2 \leq k$$
$$p_k(k) = p_{k-1}(k-1)u_k(k) \quad \text{for } l=k, \ 2 \leq k$$

we transform (A1) into:

$$E[N_k] = p_{k-1}(1)[1-u_k(2)] + \sum_{l=2}^{k-1} l\{p_{k-1}(l-1)u_k(l) + p_{k-1}(l)[1-u_k(l+1)]\} + kp_{k-1}(k-1)u_k(k) =$$
$$= p_{k-1}(1)[1-u_k(2)] + A + B - C + kp_{k-1}(k-1)u_k(k) \tag{A2}$$

where terms A, B and C are defined as follows:

$$A = \sum_{l=2}^{k-1} l\{p_{k-1}(l-1)u_k(l)\} = \sum_{l=3}^{k-1} l\{p_{k-1}(l-1)u_k(l)\} + 2u_k(2)p_{k-1}(1) \tag{A3}$$

$$B = \sum_{l=2}^{k-1} l p_{k-1}(l) = \sum_{l=1}^{k-1} l p_{k-1}(l) - p_{k-1}(1) = E[N_{k-1}] - p_{k-1}(1) \tag{A4}$$

$$C = \sum_{l=2}^{k-1} l\{p_{k-1}(l)u_k(l+1)\} = \sum_{l=3}^{k-1}(l-1)\{p_{k-1}(l-1)u_k(l)\} + (k-1)u_k(k)p_{k-1}(k-1) \tag{A5}$$

hence we get:

$$E[N_k] = E[N_{k-1}] + \sum_{l=2}^{k} p_{k-1}(l-1)u_k(l) = E[N_{k-1}] + \sum_{l=1}^{k-1} p_{k-1}(l)u_k(l+1) \tag{A6}$$

The final result in fact is intuitively obvious.

Assuming all register states as equiprobable, the probability of a transition from a given state to any state is equal to $1/2^n$ (where n is the number of register bits). The probability that the k-th pattern is included in the previously generated patterns (there are l different patterns) is $l/2^n$. Thus $u_k(l+1)=1-l/2^n$. Hence the expected value of N_k can be found as:

$$E[N_k] = E[N_{k-1}] + (1/2^n)\sum_{l=1}^{k-1} l p_{k-1}(l) + \sum_{l=1}^{k-1} p_{k-1}(l) = E[N_{k-1}] - (1/2_n)E[N_{k-1}] + 1 =$$

$$= 1 + E[N_{k-1}](1 - 1/2^n) \qquad (A7)$$

So:

$$E[N_2] = 1 + (1 - 1/2^n)$$
$$E[N_3] = 1 + \{1 + (1 - 1/2^n)\}(1 - 1/2^n) = 1 + (1 - 1/2^n) + (1 - 1/2^n)^2$$
....
$$E[N_k] = 1 + (1 - 1/2^n) + (1 - 1/2^n)^2 + ... + (1 - 1/2^n)^{k-1} \qquad (A8)$$

The final formula is the sum of geometric series terms, so we have:

$$E[N_k] = \{1 - (1 - 1/2^n)^k\}/\{1 - (1 - 1/2^n)\} = = 2^n[1 - (1 - 1/2^n)^k] =$$
$$= 2^n\{1 - [(1 - 1/2^n)^{2^n}]^{k/2^n}\} \qquad (A9)$$

taking into account that $(1 - 1/m)^m \rightarrow \exp(-1)$ for $m \rightarrow \infty$ we obtain:

$$E[N_k] = 2^n[1 - \exp(-k/2^n)] \text{ for } 2^n >> 1 \qquad (A10)$$

Equations (A6) and (A10) can be used to estimate the distribution of register states during PSR test sequence. In (A10) 2^n refers to the number of all possible states of the considered register R_i (we will denote it as α_i). A little more complex is specification of parameter k. Practically it denotes the number of generated patterns in the experiment, for the considered register. We should notice that during the PSR test sequence only some fraction of generated instructions results in storing some generated pattern into the considered register. Average distance between such instructions we denote $f(R_i)$ ($1/f(R_i)$ is the fraction of such instructions in the test sequence). So we can substitute for k the following value $T_L/f(R_i)$ (where T_L is the length of test sequence in instructions). In the developed simulation experiments we analyzed also average distance (f_i) between subsequent state changes for register R_i. This parameter can be considered as a good approximation of $f(R_i)$. In practice f_i is lower then $f(R_i)$ by less then 1%. This results from the fact that f_i does not take into account instructions loading the same state (i.e. equal to its previous state) to the considered register (e.g. MOV R_i R_i, or loading the state from some other register, memory cell or the operation result if they are the same as the state of the considered register). These situations are of low probability (as found in simulation experiments). Hence we get equation (1): $S(R_i) = \alpha_i(1-\exp(-\lambda_i T_L))$, where $\lambda_i = 1/(\alpha_i f_i)$. In the case of non uniform generation of register states we should use equation (A6).

Multi-Level Test Generation and Fault Diagnosis for Finite State Machines

R. Ubar, M. Brik

Tallinn Technical University
Ehitajate tee 5, EE0026, Tallinn, ESTONIA
raiub@pld.ttu.ee

Abstract. *In this paper, a new multi-level technique, based on alternative graphs, with uniform procedures at each level for test generation, fault simulation and fault diagnosis in finite state machines (FSM) is presented. For the description of function (behavior), structure and faults in FSM, three levels are used: functional (state transition diagrams), logical (signal path) and gate levels. In test generation, simultaneously all levels are used. Faults from different classes are inserted and activated at different levels by uniform procedures. State initialization and fault propagation are carried out only at the functional level. Backtracking will not cross level borders, hence, the high efficiency of test generation can be reached. Fault diagnosis is carried out using top-down technique, keeping the complexity of candidate fault sets in each level as low as possible.*

1. Introduction

Due to increasing complexity of VLSI circuits, testing has become a bottleneck in VLSI development, especially in case of sequential circuits [1-4]. The difficulty in generating tests for finite state machines (FSM) lies basically in 1) setting the states of memory flip-flops into a certain combination, so that the fault under test was activated, and, 2) propagating the fault effect to the primary outputs. The longer the length of the shortest input sequence needed, the more difficult it is to find an input sequence to test the circuit. Checking experiments [1] as an approach to create tests is shown to be impractical because of the long test sequence it produces. Deterministic structural approaches [2] are ineffective because of no *a priori* knowledge of the test length is available: a large amount of effort may be wasted in trying to find short sequence tests for faults that require long ones. Random testing [3] can be very time consuming for "hard" faults that have only few long test sequences. Functional approaches based on branch testing [4] are more efficient than structural approaches, however the fault coverage remains open.

Previous work in the area of the diagnosis of digital systems has come from both artificial intelligence (AI) and non-AI based approaches. AI-approaches, rule-based [5] and reasoning from first principles [6] are time-consuming. In [7] VHDL descriptions for fault diagnosis and in [8] new functional fault models based on VHDL were introduced. The disadvantages of VHDL approaches are in the diversity of fault models and in the difficulty to use other fault analysis methods than direct fault simulation. The most traditional non-AI based diagnosis conception is using fault dictionaries [9]. However, because a complete fault simulation for producing dictionaries is practically impossible, this approach cannot be adequate. The post-test fault simulation to diagnose faults in structured designs [10] is more efficient, however, problems will arise in multiple fault cases. Dedicated diagnosis methods for multiple faults are usually developed for unilevel (gate-level) descriptions [11], because of the good mathematical tools for fault analysis available. For multi-level diagnosis, a comprehensive theoretical apparatus is lacking.

The problems of fault diagnosis and test generation as, correspondingly, direct and reverse mathematical tasks have been regarded soundly only at the logical level using Boolean differential calculus. For multi-level problem solution, different languages and tools for different levels, or heuristical AI-approaches have been proposed, which all together are difficult to use for mixed level representations, especially when the level borders are to be crossed.

In this paper, we introduce alternative graphs (AG) [12] as a uniform mathematical model for systematic multi-level solution of test generation and fault diagnosis tasks in finite state machines. For describing the function (behavior), structure and faults in FSMs, three levels are used: functional (state transition diagrams), logical or signal-path and gate levels. For all these levels, a uniform model of FSM in the form of AGs is proposed. The uniformity of the model allows to use the same technique for all levels. Different fault classes have been proposed, which traditionally are specified at different FSM representation levels, e.g. gate-level stuck-at faults, STD-level transition (branch) faults etc. In this paper, the faults are activated on the level where they are specified. State initialization and fault propagation are carried out only at the functional level. Inconsistencies in signal assignment are solved inside the level they were assigned and backtracking will not cross the level borders. This helps to reduce search area during test generation. Fault diagnosis will be carried out using top-down technology, keeping the complexity of candidate fault sets in each level as low as possible. It is shown that the fault localization and test generation can be defined and solved on AGs as the direct and reverse mathematical problems, correspondingly. Hence, the same multi-level conception proposed in the paper can be utilized for solving both problems by using the same processing tools developed for AGs.

In the next section we first introduce the alternative graph model and show how STD and gate-level descriptions of FSMs can be substituted in a uniform way by AGs. The classification of faults in FSMs and representation of these fault classes on AGs is discussed in Section 3. Section 4 describes the multi-level test generation technique developed on the basis of AGs. Hierarchical fault diagnosis approach with an example is presented in Section 5. Finally, some experimental data are presented in Section 6.

2. Representation of finite-state machines by alternative graphs

2.1. Finite state machine. To simplify further considerations, let us assume some restrictions about the class of FSMs considered without loss of generality of the approach. We assume the FSM is a synchronous and free of races under simple design rules Moore machine. We also assume there is a reset state, all other states are reachable from the reset state, and memory elements such as D flip-flops are identified and represented as logical primitives to facilitate loop cutting and representing the FSM as an iterative array of combinational circuits. A FSM is traditionally represented by its state transition diagram (STD) which is a graph $G(V,B,X(B),Y(V))$ where V is the set of vertices corresponding to the set of states of the FSM, B is a set of branches (edges) in G and a branch $b = (v_i, v_j) \in B$ joins $v_i \in V$ to $v_j \in V$ if there is a primary input that causes the FSM to evolve from state v_i to state v_j, $X(B)$ is a set of labels attached to each branch, each label carrying the information of the value of the input that caused that transition, and $Y(V)$ is a set of output labels attached to each vertice, each label carrying the information of the value of the output signal generated in that state. In general, the $X(B)$ labels are Boolean expressions.

2.2. Alternative graphs and Boolean functions. Alternative graphs [12] will be used here as means for representing multi-valued digital functions. Consider at first a special case of Boolean functions. An AG that represents a Boolean function (binary decision diagram [13]) is a directed noncyclic graph with single root node, where all nonterminal nodes are labelled by (inverted or not inverted) Boolean variables (arguments of the function) and have always exactly two successor-nodes whereas all terminal nodes are labelled by constants 0 or 1. For all nonterminal nodes, an one-to-one correspondence exists between the values of the label variable of the node and the successors of the node. This correspondence is determined by the Boolean function inherent to the graph.

Let us denote by $x(m)$ the *node variable* which labels the node m. We say that a value of the node variable *activates* the node output branch. According to the value of $x(m)$ one of two output branches of m can be activated. *A path in an AG is called activated* if all the branches that form this path are activated. The AG *is called activated to the value 0 (or 1)* if there exists an activated path which includes both the root node and the terminal node labelled by the constant 0 (or 1). Alternative graph G_y with nodes labelled by variables $x_1, x_2, ..., x_n$, represents the Boolean function $y = f(X) = f(x_1, x_2, ..., x_n)$, if for each pattern of X the AG will be activated to the value which is equal to y. Consider a digital system as a network of components each of which described by one or more Boolean functions. Consequently, a digital system, particularly, a combinatorial circuit can be represented by a system of AGs.

2.3. Alternative graphs and FSMs. There are two ways of representing FSMs: 1) structural way - by a circuit which can be decomposed into combinational and memory parts, and 2) functional way - by STDs. In the first case, there is no principal difference in using AGs for representing FSMs compared to the case of combinational circuits. The output and transition functions of the FSM are Boolean and therefore can be represented by AGs for Boolean functions (or similar BDDs [13, 22]). For the second case, we use integer variables for representing inputs, outputs and internal states of the FSM. A FSM is represented by AGs for describing, correspondingly, the transition and output behaviors of the machine. By introducing complex variables and representing the FSM by a single complex function $q.y = f(q',x)$, where state variable q and output variable y are concatenated, we can represent a FSM by a single AG. As an example, in Fig.1 two representations of a FSM by a STD and by an AG are depicted. AG represents the complex behavior function of the FSM $q.y = F(q', Res, x_1, x_2)$ where q.y is the concatenation of the integer state variable q (with possible values 1,2,3,4,5,6 for representing states) and the binary output variable y. The input of the FSM is structured and represented by three

Boolean variables Res, x_1 and x_2. By q' we denote the previous state variable. Terminal nodes of the AG are labelled by complex (concatenated) constants which represent the new state of the FSM and the value of the output variable y at the new state. To be able formally to model the faulty behavior of the FSM, we have to specify in AGs if possible also the behavior of FSM at illegal states denoted by q = *. In the example in Fig.1, for illegal states, it has been assumed that y = 0.

Two extreme cases can be considered in representing FSMs by AGs: 1) the case of abstract FSM, where we have only three abstract variables for representing the input, output and internal states of the automata and, correspondingly, two AGs for representing the transition and output functions, and, 2) the case where the input, output and internal states of the FSM are binary coded and we can represent it by a set of Boolean output and transition functions. Mixed cases can be placed between these two extremes. By introducing complex variables (e.g. microinstruction words consisting of fields), and representing the FSM by a single complex function q.y = f(q',x), where state variable q and output variable y are concatenated, we can represent a FSM by a single AG.

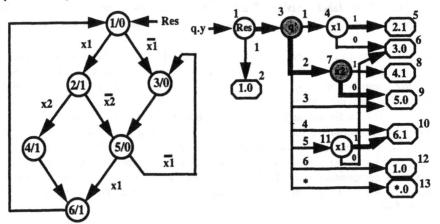

Fig.1 FSM representations by a STD and a functional level AG.

As an example, in Fig.1 two representations of a FSM by a state transition diagram and by an alternative graph are depicted. The AG represents the complex behavior function of the FSM q.y = F(q', Res, x_1, x_2) where q.y is the concatenation of the integer state variable q (with possible values 1,2,3,4,5,6 for representing states) and the binary output variable y. Input of the FSM is structured and represented by three Boolean variables Res, x_1 and x_2. By q' we denote the previous state variable. Terminal nodes of the AG are labelled by complex (concatenated) constants which represent the new state of the FSM and the value of the output variable y at the new state. To be able formally to model the faulty behavior of the FSM, we have to specify in AGs also the behavior of the FSM at illegal states, denoted by q = *. In the example, for illegal states it has been assumed that y = 0.

The are two properties of AGs that essentially differ them from STD-s which, however, may be not noticed at a glance on the example:

-similarity in representation with Boolean AGs (BDDs) that allows to generalize methods developed for the logical level as well to the higher functional (state transition) level;

-in AGs, only one model in the form of graphs is used whereas STDs consist in two models - graphs for representing transitions between states and Boolean expressions to determine the branching conditions.

3. Fault model

3.1. Fault model in alternative graphs. Each path in an AG describes the behavior of the system represented by the AG in a specific mode of operation. The faults having effect on the behavior can be associated with nodes along the given path. A fault causes an incorrect leaving the path activated by a test. From this point of view we introduce the following abstract fault model for nodes m with label variables $z(m)$ in AG-representations of FSMs:

1) the output branch for $z(m)=i$ of a node m is always activated (notation for the fault: $z(m)/-> i$),

2) the branch for $z(m)=i$ of a node m is broken ($z(m)/ i -> *$), and

3) instead of the given branch for $z(m) = i$ of a node m, another branch for $z(m)=j$ is activated ($z(m)/ i -> j$).

Different fault models for different representation levels of FSMs can be replaced on AGs by this uniform node fault model. The physical meaning of faults associated with a particular node depends on the "structural meaning" [12] of the node. For example, the fault model for nodes labelled by Boolean variables $z \in \{0,1\}$ correponds to the stuck-at fault model $z/0$ ($z/1$) in gate-level representations. On the other side, the fault model for nodes labelled by integer variables can represent widely spread functional faults for decoders, multiplexers, instruction decoding units of microprocessors [21], case constructions in procedural or behavioral models of systems [8] etc.

From above it follows that the fault model defined on AGs can be regarded as a generalization of the classical gate-level stuck-at fault model for more higher level representations of digital systems. The stuck-at fault model is defined for *Boolean variables (literals)*, the generalized new fault model is defined for *nodes of AGs*. As the nodes with Boolean labels represent only a special class of nodes in AGs, the logical level stuck-at fault model represents also only a special class of faults in AGs. In the following we consider how the different fault classes in finite state machines can be represented uniformly using alternative graphs.

3.2. Fault classes for finite state machines. Any irredundant structural fault in the implementation of the FSM will cause some changes in its STD. One or multiple transitions will be corrupted. So, a test sequence that detects all multiple transition faults will detect all irredundant permanent physical defects. However, the analysis of multiple transition faults is too complex, therefore usually a single transition fault will be considered. In the following, we try to find relationships between structural and functional level faults, to analyse how different single structural fault types affect the behavior of the

FSM, are they manifesting himself as single or multiple transition faults, and how test sequences can be generated for them.

The faults of the FSM circuitry can be divided into the following fault classes: 1) single transition faults (class a) - faults that effect on a single transition condition only; 2) input faults (class b) - faults that effect on the input of the FSM; 3) state faults (class c) - faults that effect on the state of the FSM.

We shall show in, the following that a single fault in a FSM, represented by an iterative array of identical combinational circuits, can manifest himself in a test sequence in different ways: *as a single fault both* in each time frame and, under special restrictions, also in the whole array (transition faults), or *as a multiple fault* both in each time frame and in the whole array (input and state faults). From the different complexity of faults, it follows that the faults are to be processed during test generation by different strategies, e.g. to be processed at different FSM representation levels. Using AGs, it will be possible to process the faults at different FSM levels by uniform algorithms.

3.3. Representing transition faults on gate-level AGs. The class *of transition faults* (not to mix up with functional faults related to branches in STDs, as used in [4]) is related exclusively to the circuitry which calculates the transition condition effect, provided that all condition signals are fault free. These faults are difficult to define at the functional level because of the implementation dependency. Assume that all the next state circuits for different flip-flops are disjoint. If it is not the case, the faults in joint parts of the logic shared for different flip-flops should be handled in the same way as the input and state faults. It is easy to notice that in the assumed case the transition faults influence always on a single transition condition only and therefore, they cannot mask themselves as long the same transition will not repeated. It means that as long not yet tested loops are not containing in test sequences, the faults of type (a) manifest himself as single faults in the whole iterative array related to the test sequence. This property gives the possibility to carry out the test synthesis on different levels without crossing the level borders if backtracking is needed. Particularly, the fault activization procedure will be carried out on the gate level where these faults are specified, whereas the signal justification (state initialization) and the fault propagation procedures can be carried out on the functional STD level. Transition faults can be concisely represented in structural AGs of the next-state logic.

3.4. Representing transition faults on signal-path-level AGs. Generation of a compressed structural AG-model for a given gate-level digital circuit is based on the superposition of AGs [12]). AGs for logical gates are assumed to be given as a source library. Starting from the gate-level AG-description and using iteratively graph superposition, we can produce a more concise higher level representation of the circuit. As a result of this procedure, we create structural AGs (SAG) which have the following property [12]: each node in a SAG represents a signal path in the corresponding gate-level circuit. To avoid repeating in the AG-model same subgraphs, it is recommendable to create separate AGs for tree-like subcircuits. In this case, the number of all nodes in the set of AGs will be equal to the number of paths in all tree-like subnetworks of the circuit, and one to one correspondence will exist between paths in these subnetworks and nodes in AGs. Hence, using the concept of SAGs, it is possible to rise from the gate-level descriptions of digital circuits to higher level structural descriptions without of loosing accuracy of representing gate-level stuck-at faults. The task of simulating structural stuck-at-faults in a given path of a circuit can be substituted by the task of simulating faults at a node in the corresponding SAG.

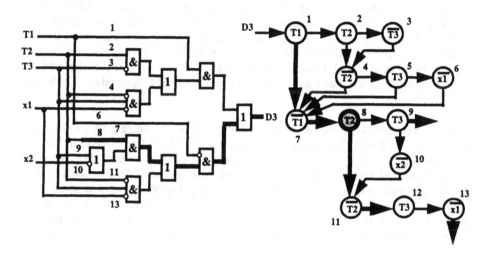

Fig.2. Representing a gate-level structure by a structural AG

An example of a SAG for a combinational circuit is depicted in Fig.2. The nodes of AG are labelled by input variables of the circuit. For simplicity, the values of variables on branches are omitted (by convention, the right-hand branch corresponds to 1 and the lower-hand branch to 0). Also, terminal nodes with constants 0 and 1 are omitted (leaving the AG to the right corresponds to y=1, and down to y=0). To each node in the AG, a path in the circuit corresponds (the correspondence is shown by numbers). For example, a node 8 (bold circle) in the AG represents the bold path from the input branch 8 up to the output of the circuit. The node variables are inverted if the number of invertors in the corresponding path is odd. The set of stuck-at-1 faults along this path in the circuit is represented in the AG by only one representative fault $T_2/1$ (T_2 stuck-at-1, i.e. the branch from the node 8 constantly activated to the right direction). The activated paths in the AG (shown by bold arrows) represent the situation when the fault $T_2/1$ is activated (the test pattern 0011x (T1,T2,T3, x1,x2), where x denotes an arbitrary value).

3.5. Representing input and state faults of FSMs in functional level AGs. *Input faults* (b) in FSMs are related to the input lines of the FSM and, in general case, they affect upon more than one transition conditions during the test sequence. Hence, a single structural fault manifests himself as a multiple fault in the iterative array representation of a FSM, which results in difficulties of test generation at the structural level. From the other point of view, input faults are easily to be specified, activated and propagated at the functional level. Hence, in test generation for input faults of the FSM, the functional FSM representation in the form of STD is more preferred than the complex gate level model.

State faults (c) in FSMs are related to the memory flip-flops and, at the functional level, they could be related also to the state decoder, if the latter is a part of the next-state logic or if it is used for implementing output functions. For flip-flops, the stuck-at-0 (1) fault model can be used. For the state decoder, at the functional level, a more general functional fault model is used: stuck-at-0 (1) on outputs and faults "instead of given output another output or a set of outputs is active". The state faults (flip-flop faults) affect upon more than one transition conditions and represent also the multiple fault case for the iterative combinational array model. Hence, to simplify the test generation, it is recommendable to define and process these faults only at the functional level FSM representation in the form of STD.

For representing the input (b) and state (c) faults in FSMs, alternative graphs will be used, which represent directly the state transition diagram of the FSM (see example in Fig.1). If decoders are used in a FSM for decoding input and/or internal states, then in the AG model, nodes with integer variables will represent these decoders. The functional faults of a decoder (stuck-at-0 (1), "instead of the given output another output is active") are represented by analogical faults at the corresponding node in the AG (compare to the fault model for nodes of AGs in Section 3.1). The structural bit-level stuck-at faults of functional integer variables are not difficult to insert if the tests for them are generated.

From above, it follows that for efficient test generation, a multi-level approach is advisable, where different faults will be at different levels processed. Traditionally for different levels, different languages, fault models and test generation algorithms are used. Introducing AGs as a model for FSMs allows to remove this drawback.

4. Test sequence generation

4.1. Test generation for FSMs by pipelining partial test sequences.
The test sequence for a single fault consists of three subsequences: initialization sequence, activation sequence and fault propagation sequence. The *initialization sequence* brings the FSM from current state to the state needed for activation the fault, the *activation sequence* contains only one input pattern needed additionally for activation the fault and the *fault propagation sequence* is the state-pair differentiating sequence that differentiates the good destination state from faulty ones and, thus, propagates the fault effect to the output. From the Section 3, it follows that all these subsequences can be carried out at the functional level, except only the fault activation stage for transition faults in the current time frame, which has to be processed at the structural level. However, for transition faults, after they are activated at the lower structural level, the results can be easily transformed as well into the functional level by specifying the internal and input states needed for fault activation.

Test sequences for different faults will be automatically pipelined (overlapped) if we organize the test procedure by moving along paths in the STD rather than by generating tests for different faults separately (Fig.3). The necessary but not sufficient condition to create a test is traversing a set of paths that contains all branches in the STD. If not all faults are yet tested by this sequence, we have to find a set of branches needed for activating the remaining faults, and to traverse a new set of paths that contain all these branches. This procedure has to be repeated until all the faults in FSM will have a test sequence.

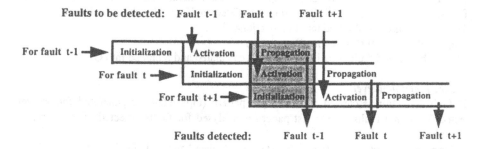

Fig.3. Pipelining test sequences for different faults

In this procedure described, at each current step we have the following information: 1)the current state q' reached by traversing the STD, and 2) the list $Q'(q') = \{q_k'(F)\}$ of faulty states q_k' for faults $f \in F$ activated, but not yet detected, and propagated up to this step (for all $q_k' : y(q_k') = y(q')$ is valid); the faults f are needed to be indicated at the related faulty state only if they manifest himself as multiple faults.

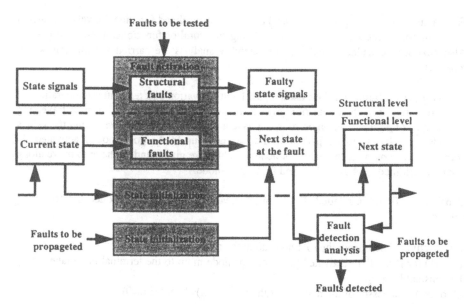

Fig.4. Test generation for the current time frame (current state of the FSM)

The operations to be carried out at the current step of the test generation procedure are the following (see also Fig.4):

- at the structural level
1) the current state q is decoded into state signals of flip-flops T_i;
2) fault activation is carried out and input pattern is generated for not yet tested structural faults, or the test pattern is analysed for faults detected, if it is already available;
3) the results are transformed into the functional level
- input pattern is transformed into input state;
- for each detected fault, a faulty next state is calculated and included into Q;

- at the functional level,
1) fault activation is carried out and input pattern (input state) is generated for not yet tested functional faults, or the test pattern is analysed for faults detected, if it is already available);
2) for each detected fault, a faulty next state is calculated and included into Q;
3) the next state q for the current q' is calculated;
4) for all current faulty states $q_k' \in Q'$, faulty next states are calculated and included into the list Q;
5) for all faulty next states $q_k \in Q'$, the following analysis is carried out:
- if $y(q_k) \neq y(q)$ then the faults related to q_k, are detected;
  q_k is excluded from the list Q;
- if $y(q_k) = y(q)$ then the faults related to q_k, are not detected and they are propagated into the next time frame.

Fault activation (or test pattern analysis) at both, structural and functional levels are carried out by uniform procedures using corresponding structural or functional alternative graphs. Also next state calculation and fault detectability analysis are carried out on AGs which represent STDs.

4.2. Test generation for FSMs using AGs. Fault activation and test pattern generation on AGs are based on path activization procedures. Fault analysis is based on path traversing procedures. *In path activation* on AGs, we have a goal-node and we have to find the values of node-variables, so that a path from the root-node up to the goal-node is activated. *In path traversing on AGs,* the values of node-variables are given, and we have to move along a path determined by these values and find a goal-node.

Consider, at first, AGs labelled only by Boolean variables and introduce the following notations:

l(m) - activated path from the root node up to the node m;
l(m, =1) (or l(m, =0)) - activated path from the node m up to the terminal node labelled by the constant 1 (or 0);
m^1 (or m^0) - successor of the node m for the value z(m)=1 (or z(m)=0).

To activate a fault (generate a test for a fault) $z(m)/e$ ($z(m)$ stuck-at-e), $e \in \{0,1\}$ at a node m, means to activate simultaneously two nonoverlapping paths: $l(m).l(m^{-e}, = -e)$ and $l(m^e, =e)$ at the value $z(m) = -e$. For example, in Fig.2, for testing a fault $T_2/1$ at the node 8, we can activate paths $l(m).l(m0, =0) = (1, 7, 8)$. $(11,12,13, =0)$, and $l(m^1, =1) = (9, =1)$, which gives the test pattern 0011x (T1,T2,T3,x1,x2). Activated paths in Fig.2 are depicted by bold arrows.

To analyse a test pattern for faults detected, means:
1) to find an activated by the pattern path l with a terminal node m^T where $z(m^T) = e$,
2) for all nodes $m_k \in l$, find the value $e_k = z(m_k^T)$ where m_k^T is the terminal node of the path $l(m_k^{-e}, m_k^T)$ activated by the same pattern;
3) for all nodes $m_k \in l$, the given pattern detects the fault $z(m_k /-e$ if $e_k \neq e$ is valid.

As an example, in Fig.2, by the test pattern 0011x (T1, T2, T3, x1, x2), a path $l = (1,7,8,11,12,13)$ is activated. The condition (3) is valid only for nodes 8 and 13. So, by this pattern, the faults $T_2/1$ and $\neg x1/1$ are detected.

In the general case of AGs labelled by integer variables, test generation is based on the same path activization principles. Denote by $l(m^i, m^{T,i})$ - activated path from the node m_i up to a terminal node $m^{T,i}$ (m^i is the successor of the node m for the value $z(m)=i$).

To activate a fault (generate a test for a fault) $z(m)/i \rightarrow j$ ($z(m)=j$ instead of $z(m)=i$), means to activate simultaneously nonoverlapping paths $l(m)$ and $l(m^k, m^{T,k})$ where $k = i, j$, so that $z(m^{T,i}) \neq z(m^{T,j})$.

For example, in Fig.1, to activate the fault $q'/2 \rightarrow 5$ to output y, two test patterns are possible: 2010 (q', Res, x1, x2) or 2001. Here, in terminal nodes, for comparison, only y is considered. By the first pattern 2010, the following three paths for testing the node m = 3 (i = 2, j = 5) are activated: $l(3) = (1,3), l(7, =0) = (7, 9, =0)$ and $l(11, =1) = l(11,10, =1)$. As an example of the test pattern analysis, consider again a pattern 2010 that activates a path $l= (1, 3, 7, 9)$ on the AG in Fig.2 (shown by bold arrows). The condition (3) of the fault detection is valid only for the node 7 and for the values 1, and 4 of the variable q' in the node 3 (shown by bold circles). Hence, the following faults are detected by this pattern: $q'/2 \rightarrow 1, q'/2 \rightarrow 4, x2/1$.

4.3. Complexity of test generation. Using the described multi-level approach, it is possible to reduce the complexity of test generation and the complexity of discovering redundant faults nearly to the complexity of solving the same tasks for combinational circuits. Test generation for transition faults in gate-level next-state logic will be carried out, actually, in only a single time frame - a pattern will be generated on structural AGs, which specifies a state needed for testing the given fault. If the state is reachable, then the fault can be tested. On the contrary, if the state is not reachable, the fault is redundant and not testable. The reachability of states can be determined on the functional level, using AGs that correspond to STDs.

As an example, when trying to generate a test sequence for a fault ¬T3/1 at the node 3 in the graph D_3 in Fig.2, it is needed only to try to test this node in D3. Activating the path $1(3) = (1,2,3)$, the only possible path to reach the node 3, it cames out that a state $q = 7$ (Tl=l, T2=1,T3=1) is needed to test the given fault. On the other side, at the functional level, it is easy to see that this state is not reachable. Hence, without trying to create any sequence longer than l, it was possible to show that the fault ¬T3/1 is redundant and not testable.

5. Fault diagnosis

5.1. Hierarchical fault diagnosis in FSM-s. In the following, the diagnosis methodology which operates on the observed erroneous behavior and the structure of the FSM will be considered. By examining the error and the structure of the FSM, possible sources of the error can be determined. There is a definite flow of signals from inputs to the outputs in the system. In this flow, an effect-cause relationship can be created in the form of diagnostic trees, where each node except leaves represents a signal error (an effect) and the successors of this node represent the possible causes of this error. Based on this tree, guided signal probing in the faulty system can be carried out.

To increase the efficiency of the diagnostic procedure (to reduce the number of signals to be probed), a hierarchical multi-level analysis and signal probing can be carried out. At first, faulty subcircuit will be localized at the higher functional level. This result can be achieved by a fault localization procedure organized on the basis of a higher level diagnostic tree (DT). A subcircuit will be qualified as faulty if he has a faulty output signal y and all input signals - successors of y in the DT - are correct. Next, the lower level description of the subcircuit will be taken, the corresponding lower level DT will be created and fault diagnosis based on this DT will be carried out. In this procedure, if possible, the results from the higher level diagnosis (for example, the information of correctness of certain input signals) can be exploited. Using AGs for describing FSMs at different levels, uniform procedures for creating and minimizing DTs at different FSM representation levels can be developed.

5.2. Fault backtracking on alternative graphs. Each path in an AG describes the behavior of the circuit in a specific mode of operation. The faults having effect on the behavior are related to nodes along the given path. A fault causes an incorrect leaving the path activated by a test. Hence, if we have activated a path in an AG by a test pattern which has failed then all faults related to nodes of the path can be regarded as fault candidates for the diagnosis procedure.

If an erroneous signal is detected in an output y of the circuit then by fault backtracking procedure, a set of candidate faults which can explain the misbehavior of y will be created. This set will be represented in the form of diagnostic tree (DT) with the root labelled by the failed output y. In this procedure, at first, in the graph G_y the path activated by failed test pattern will be determined. All the nodes of this path will be put into DT as successors of the root node. For each successor with a label x that corresponds to an internal node of the circuit and is represented by another graph G_x, again an activated path will be

276

repeated recursively until all the leaves in DT are labelled by input variables. The number of nodes in DT found in this way is generally less than the number of nodes contained in the whole traceback cone [14] in the corresponding circuit. Using special analysis procedures in AGs, the number of nodes in the DT can be sometimes further reduced [14].

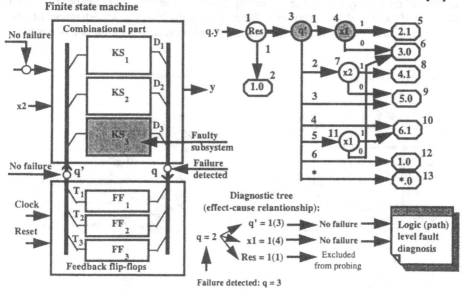

Fig.5. Fault diagnosis in FSM at the functional (STG) level

Let l be a path activated in the given AG by a failed test pattern, M(l) the set of nodes which are passed by l and m^T the terminal node reached by l. The following rules can be used for further reducing nodes in the diagnostic tree:

1) *Rule 1* (for all level AGs): if by the test pattern analysis procedure described in Section 4.2, a detectable fault at a node m ∈ M(l) is found, then the node m remains in the DT; all other nodes will be excluded from probing. However, the use of the Rule 1, in general case, is thoroughly justified only under single fault consumption.

2) *Rule 2* (for AGs only, synthesized by the superposition procedure from the gate-level circuit [14]): only these nodes m ∈ M(l) are consistent to explain the fault and have to remain in the DT, for which $z(m) = z(m^T)$ holds. The Rule 2 is less restrictive and it is valid also for the multiple fault cases.

5.3. Example. Consider a FSM represented in Fig.5 as a higher level structure, consisting of three next-state calculation blocks KSi, i=1,2,3 and a feedback register of three flip-flops. The behavior of the FSM is described by the functional AG in Fig.5 which represents the STD of the FSM. By bold arrows in the AG, an activated path is depicted which corresponds to the test pattern 101x (q', Res, xl, x2) at which an error in the value of q was detected. The path passes nodes 1,3,4, all of which will be included into the DT

(Fig.5). However, the subsequent analysis (Rule 1) shows that only changes at nodes 3 (q'=5) and 4 (xl=0) can explain the faulty behavior q=3 of the FSM. Hence, additional signal probing is needed to observe the real values of q' and x1. Suppose, both signals are correct. From this it follows that the combinational part of the FSM has to be faulty because it has a faulty output and correct input signals. The conclusion has been made on the basis of functional level diagnosis. Descending to the bit-level, we determine that the 3rd bit in the state code is faulty which means that the next-state logic block KS$_3$ has to be faulty.

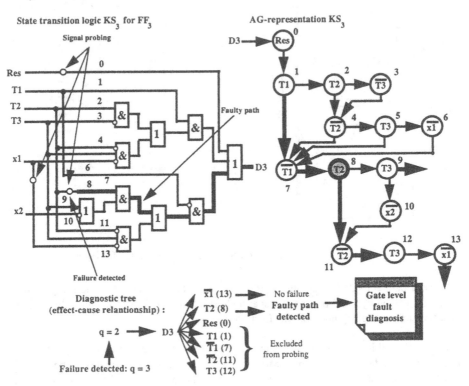

Fig.6. Fault diagnosis in FSM at the logic (path) level

Consider now the gate-level implementation of the block KS$_3$ (Fig.6) and the AG-model, synthesized from the circuit by the superposition procedure [12]. By bold arrows in the AG, an activated path is depicted which corresponds to the test pattern 00101x (T_1,T_2,T_3,Res,x_1,x_2) at which an error in the value of D$_3$ was detected. The path passes nodes 0,1,7,8,11,12,13, all of which will be included into the DT (Fig.6). However, the subsequent analysis (Rule 1) shows that only changes at nodes 0 (Res = 1), 8 (T$_2$ = 1) and 13 (x_1 = 0) can explain the faulty behavior q = 3 of the FSM. Using the result from higher level analysis that faults at the input Res cannot explain the failure, only nodes 8 and 13 remain to probe. Using the less restrictive Rule 2 for the multiple fault case, we find that also the node 1 has to be probed as a potential fault source.

6. Experimental results

A multi-level test generation system CPTEST [15], was implemented in C++ at the Tallinn Technical University. The system is considered as a part of a hierarchical ATPG to be developed in the framework of the EC-sponsored Copernicus JEP 9624 FUTEG (Functional Test Generation) international project [16-18]. The finite state machines considered as examples for experimental research are those of MCNC benchmarks for test synthesis. For our experiments, the gate-level implementations were synthesized by Synopsys. No control was exercised on this tool, and binary state coding was applied. Test generation results for 15 FSM's in Table 1 are described in Table 2. For each example in Table 1, the numbers of inputs (*Inp*), outputs (*Out*) and transitions (*Tran*) are given.

In Table 2, on the left side the length of test sequence (number of patterns) needed in order to have traversed throughout all branches in STG each at least once (*Test length*), the fault coverage achieved by traversing all branches (*Coverage*), and the time required for that (*Time*) on a PC 486 66MHz are shown for each example.

On the right side of Table 2, the length of test sequences (*Test length*), the total number of gate-level faults (*Total faults*) in FSM, the number of inserted (activated) faults (*Ins faults*), the number of detected faults (*Detected faults*), the fault coverage achieved (*Coverage*), and the time required (*Time*) are given. In the present version of CPTEST, for searching the target state (when activating a target fault), and for searching the state where the activated fault can be detected, the random path traversing technique is used. Also, in this version nonefficient traversing cycles which do not increase the fault coverage are not excluded from the total test sequence. A deterministic technique is currently under development which is expected to increase the efficiency of the tool in reducing dramatically the test length, test generation time and increasing the fault coverage.

Table 1. Characteristics of MCNC benchmark FSMs

FSM	States	Inp	Out	Tran
lion9	9	25	2	1
bbara	10	4	2	60
cse	16	7	7	91
sand	32	11	9	184
planet	48	7	19	115
vtiidec	5	11	32	77
mc	4	3	5	10
dk15	4	3	5	32
lion	4	2	1	11
tav	4	4	4	49
log	17	9	24	29
s27	6	4	1	34
beecount	7	3	4	28
bbsse	16	7	7	56
mul8x8*	8	4	13	21

* The circuit is not MCNC Benchmark

Table 2. Test generation results for MCNC benchmarks

FSM	Test length	Total faults	Ins. faults	Detected faults	Coverage, %	Time, min
lion9	37	112	112	112	100.00	0.00,45
bbara	144	202	194	193	95.54	0.03,18
cse	615	540	538	527	98.70	0.43,44
sand	767	1140	1119	1119	98.16	1.22,09
planet	900	1070	1058	1058	98.88	1.22,07
vtiidec	823	210	207	207	98.57	0.12,58
mc	14	74	74	74	100.00	0.00,14
dk15	67	92	92	85	92.39	0.01,10
lion	20	58	58	58	100.00	0.00,15
tav	14	34	34	34	100.00	0.00.09
log	399	378	367	367	97.09	0.40,70
s27	48	60	60	60	100.00	0.00,36
beecount	150	126	126	120	95.24	0.02,70
bbsse	867	456	451	438	96.05	0.47,12
mul8x8	313	94	94	93	98.94	0.01,76

The results of the experiments listed in Table 2 can be compared with published results [19,20] of using different approaches and the same benchmarks described in Table 3. In our approach, no modifications of gate-level circuits produced by Synopsys have been made to improve the testability as, for example, in [19].

Table 3. Comparison with other ATPGs

FSM	HITEC [19]			STED [20]			CHE90 [4]		
	No. of vectors	Cover %	Time, s (Sparc2)	No. of vectors	Cover %	Time, s (on VAX 11/8800)	No. of vectors	Cover %	Time, s Sun 4/260
lion9	38	97,3	8.63	-	-	-	-	-	-
bbara	96	82.0	89.33	-	-	-	241	100.0	2
cse	349	100.0	23.48	397	100.0	29.5	880	97.86	45
sand	52	45.2	1339.9	722	99.43	7.7min	809	97.74	202
planet	91	64.5	917.7	1046	100.0	5.8min	600	98.26	35
mc	38	100.0	0.37	-	-	-	-	-	-
dk15	53	100.0	0.73	-	-	-	146	100.0	0.2
lion	47	100.0	0.45	-	-	-	-	-	-
tav	26	100.0	0.27	-	-	-	-	-	-
bbsse	255	100.0	18.38	-	-	-	-	-	-
s27	40	100.0	0.27	-	-	-	-	-	-
beec.	85	100.0	1.40	-	-	-	-	-	-

7. Conclusions

In this paper, we have introduced alternative graphs as a mathematical model for systematic multi-level solution of test generation and fault diagnosis in finite state machines. For the description of functions, structure and faults in FSM, three levels are used: functional level (state transition diagrams), logical or signal-path level and gate level. For all these levels, uniform description language, uniform fault model and uniform procedures for test synthesis and analysis were developed. This uniformity allows easily to move and carry partial results from level to level when solving the tasks mentioned. From the more general point of view, the uniformity of the model allows to generalize methods, developed earlier for the logical level, to the higher functional (state transition) level as well. For example, the fault model defined on AGs can be regarded as a generalization of the classical gate-level stuck-at fault model for more higher level representations of digital systems.

In test generation, simultaneously all levels are used. One part of faults (gate-level stuck-at faults) are specified at the gate level, however, for further processing, the gate level fault model is replaced by a more concise signal-path fault model. Another part of faults (functional faults) are specified at the functional level. State initialization and fault propagation procedures are carried out only at the functional level. The test generation approach proposed allows to solve the inconsistencies of signals by backtracking at the level where signals were assigned without crossing level borders. This helps dramatically to reduce the search area during test generation, e.g. for gate-level faults, the complexity of test generation for sequential circuits is reduced nearly to the complexity the combinational parts have.

Fault diagnosis will be carried out using top-down technology, keeping the complexity of candidate fault sets in each level as low as possible. A new minimization technique for reducing the fault canditates list general for all description levels of FSMs was proposed. The technique is uniform for all levels and is consistent to the multiple fault case whereas the fault class considered is general, not restricted to only the traditional stuck-at fault model.

Acknowledgements

The European Community (under Copernicus JEP 6575) and the Estonian Science Foundation (under Grants 1850 and 2104) have supported this work.

References

[1] Hennie F.C. Fault detecting experiments for sequential circuits. *Proc. of 5th Symp. on Switching Circuit Theory and Logical Design,* Princeton, N.J., Nov,1964, pp.95-110.
[2] Ghosh A., Devadas S., Newton A.R. Sequential logic testing and verification. *Kluwer Acad. Publish.*, 1992, 214 p.

[3] Agrawal W.D. When to use random testing. *IEEE Trans. on Computers,* vol. C-27, Nov.1978, pp.1054-1055.

[4] Cheng K.-T., Jou J.-Y. Functional test generation for FSMs. IEEE *Int. Test Conference.* 1990, pp.162-168.

[5] Grillmeyer O., Wilkinson A.J. The design and construction of a rule base and an inference engine for test system diagnosis. *IEEE Int. Test Conf.,* 1985, pp.857-867.

[6] Davis R. Diagnostic reasoning based on structure and behavior. *Artificial Intelli-gence* 24 (1984) 347-410.

[7] Pitchumani V., Mayor P., Radia N. Fault diagnosis using functional fault model for VHDL descriptions. *IEEE Int. Test Conf.* Nashville, Oct., 1991, . pp.327-337.

[8] Ward, P.C., Armstrong, J.R. (1990). Behavioral fault simulation in VHDL. 27th *ACM/IEEE Design Automation* Conference,1990, pp.587-593.

[9] Ramamoorthy C.V. A structural theory of machine diagnosis. *Proceedings of Spring Joint Computer* Conference,1967, pp.743-756.

[10] Waicukauski J.A., Gupta V.P., Patel S.T. Diagnosis of BIST failures by PPSFP simulation. *18th IEEE International Test Conference,* Washington, Sep.1987,pp.480-484.

[11] Rajski J. GEMINI - a logic system for fault diagnosis based on set functions. *18th Int. Symposium on Fault Tolerant Computing,* Tokyo,1988, June,pp.292-297.

[12] Ubar R. Test Synthesis with alternative graphs. IEEE Design & Test of Computers. Spring 1996, pp.48-57.

[13] Bryant R.E. Graph-based Algorithms for Boolean Function Manipulation. *IEEE Trans. Computers,* Vol. C-35, No. 8, Aug. 1986, pp.667-690.

[14] Ubar R., Evartson T. Optimization of fault localization procedures in computer : hardware. In *"CAD in electronical and computer engineering ",* Part I., Vilnius, Lithuania, 1981, pp.175-184 (in Russian).

[15] Brik M., Ubar R. Hierarchical test generation for finite state machines. *Proc. of the 4th Baltic Electronics Conference.* Tallinn, October 1994, pp.319-324.

[16] Sallay B., Petri A., Tilly K., Pataricza A. High Level Test Pattern Generation for VHDL Circuits. *IEEE European Test Workshop,* Montpellier, France, June 12-14, 1996, pp. 201-205.

[17] Gramatova E., Cibakova T., Bezakova J. Test Pattern Generation Algorithms on Functional/Behavioral Level. Tech. Rep. FUTEG-4/1995.

[18] Gulbins M., Straube B. Applying Behavioral Level Test Generation to High-Level Design Validation. *The European Design & Test Conference,* Paris, March 11-14, 1996, p. 613.

[19] Niermann T.M., Patel J.H. HITEC: A test generation package for sequential circuits. *Proc. European Design Automation Conference,*1991, pp.214-218.

[20] Ghosh A., Devadas S., Newton A.R. Test generation and verification for highly sequential circuits. *IEEE Trans. on CAD,* Vol.10, No.S, May 1991.

[21] Thatte S.M., Abraham J.A. Test Generation for Microprocessors, *IEEE Trans. Computers,* Vol.29, 1980, pp.429-441.

[22] Minato S. Binary Decision Diagrams and Applications for VLSI CAD. Kluwer Academic Publish., 1996, 141 p.

Session 7

Verification

Chair: Ernst Schmitter, Siemens AG, Germany

Dynamic Testing
from Bounded Data Type Specifications

Agnès Arnould[1], Pascale Le Gall[2], and Bruno Marre[1]

[1] L.R.I, URA CNRS 410, Université de Paris-Sud, bât. 490, 91405 Orsay Cedex,
France. E-mail: {arnould, marre}@lri.lri.fr
[2] L.a.M.I., Université d'Évry, Cours Monseigneur Roméro, 91025 Evry Cedex,
France. E-mail: legall@lami.univ-evry.fr

Abstract. Due to practical limitations in software and hardware, data
type implementations are always bounded. Such limitations are a frequent source of faults which are difficult to find out. As soon as boundaries are clearly identified in a specification, functional testing should be
able to address any boundary fault.
We propose to enrich a data type specification formalism, namely algebraic specifications, allowing a natural description of data type boundaries. This enhancement allows us to adapt the existing testing theory,
the method and the tool, initially dedicated to functional testing from
unbounded data type specifications.
Several examples of test data selection with the LOFT tool, from two
bounded data type specifications, will illustrate the benefit of our approach: an assisted test selection process, formally defined in a functional
testing theory, allowing adequate coverage of both data types bounds and
the definition domain of the specified operations.

Keywords. functional testing, software verification, formal specifications, bounded data types, test data set selection.

1 Introduction

Functional testing is widely recognized as a major activity during software verification. It is primarily based on practical expertise and in-depth knowledge of
the software being verified. Theoretical works carried out in the late 80's and
early 90's have showed that functional testing can rely on a formal framework.
For instance, in the area of protocol verification, conformance testing from LO-
TOS specifications and finite transition systems have been studied extensively
[19, 6, 17]. Model-based specifications (Z, VDM) have also been studied as formal bases for test data selection [21, 8]. Functional testing can be based on
algebraic specifications [3, 9]. It is then possible to assist the test data selection
process with tools like ASTOOT [9] or LOFT [15].

Nevertheless, due to practical limitations in software and hardware, data type
implementations are always bounded. Such limitations are a frequent source of
faults which are difficult to find out. As soon as boundaries are clearly identified

in a specification, functional testing should be able to address any boundary fault. The previously cited formalisms (Z, VDM or B) allow to describe our *bounded world* either by using predefined bounded data types, or by adding specialized preconditions devoted to restrict the operation domains. However, the definition of systematic testing criteria well suited to bound coverage becomes difficult when bounds are not explicitly characterized.

From a theoretical perspective, the testing theory defined in Orsay and Evry [3, 11, 14] does not point to any intractable limitation. The real problem comes from the non existence of an appropriate description mechanism for the specification of bounds. We propose the enrichment of a data type specification formalism, namely algebraic specifications, allowing a natural description of data types bounds. This enhancement is done in order to preserve as much as possible the original semantics. Such a semantical preservation allows us to adapt the existing test theory, the method and the tool initially dedicated to functional testing from unbounded data type specifications.

In section two, we informally introduce the basic concepts underlying our functional testing theory. We show how practical considerations such as test selection, test submission and test decision are taken into account when functional testing is done with respect to a formal specification. In section three, we describe our specification formalism dedicated to bounded data type descriptions. Bounded data type specifications are classical algebraic specifications provided with a constraints language allowing to characterize bounds w.r.t. measures defined on terms. In section four, the general concepts of our testing theory are illustrated on the case of bounded data types specifications. The characterization of a *complete test data set* is given, and test selection strategies devoted to ensure bound coverage and domain coverage are proposed. These test selection strategies ensure the coverage of sub-domains built by case analysis on bound and operation definitions. In section five, several examples of test data selection with the LOFT tool illustrate the benefits of our approach.

2 Dynamic testing from formal specifications

This presentation is based on previous works done in Orsay and Evry [2, 3, 11] and specifically on the theory presented in [14].

We consider a rather classical framework of algebraic specifications. A formal specification SP contains a signature Σ which defines the specified operations. The set of all models (all the program behaviors) on Σ is denoted $Mod(\Sigma)$. The set of all formulas, denoted by $Sen(\Sigma)$, represents all the possible properties on computations. For example, these formulas may contain logical connectives as $\wedge$ or $\Longrightarrow$ and predicates as equality. For each formula ϕ in $Sen(\Sigma)$, for each model M in $Mod(\Sigma)$, $M \models \phi$ denotes ϕ is satisfied in M. The model semantics of SP are given by a set $Mod(SP)$ of all models of $Mod(\Sigma)$ satisfying SP. Each specification formalism provides an inference system ($\vdash$). The proof semantics are given by the set $Th(SP)$ of formulas inferred from SP. Moreover, the inference system is supposed to be correct and complete:

$$\forall \varphi \in Sen(\Sigma), \ (\varphi \in Th(SP)) \iff (\forall M \in Mod(SP), M \models \varphi)$$

Similarly to other approaches of dynamic testing, testing with respect to a formal specification consists in the three following steps:

- selection of some values from the set of all possible input values with respect to some criteria;
- execution of some program functions with the selected input values;
- verification that the program results match the results expected from the specification; this verification step, often named the **oracle step**, requires some predicates, e.g. equality predicates of the programming language;

Most of the time, all the input and output values can be denoted by ground terms built from well formed combinations of the operations exported by the program. Moreover, tests can be denoted by formulas built over operations, logical connectives and formal predicates corresponding to the concrete predicates used in the verification step. The testing activity does not consider the program alone, but considers the program within the context of a programming language and a test driver. In the sequel, P denotes both the program and its instrumentation.

So, any functional test may be denoted by a formula. Such a point of view is rather common (see for example [3]). The converse is false for two reasons. First, any test should be interpretable by the program P as being true or false. By stating this, we discard formulas for which the program does not provide enough observations. The set of all **observable formulas** will be denoted Obs and the notation $P \rightsquigarrow \phi$ means that P interprets as true the observable formula ϕ. Secondly, a formula which is not true in every correct implementation (model) could reject a correct program. Such a formula is **biased** w.r.t. SP. The set $Th(SP)$ of the formulas which are true for all the models of SP (i.e. unbiased w.r.t. SP) are the **consequences** of SP.

Finally, a **test** for P w.r.t. SP is defined as a formula being both observable for P and unbiased w.r.t. SP. $T(SP) = Obs \cap Th(SP)$ denotes the set of all tests w.r.t. SP. A **test data set** is any subset of $T(SP)$ and is said to be in **success** (resp. **failure**) for P if all of its tests are interpreted as true for P (resp. one of its tests is interpreted as false). Since the only way to check program correctness with black-box testing is to interpret observable formulas, a program P is **correct w.r.t.** SP if and only if P behaves as at least one model of SP w.r.t. observable formulas:

$$\exists M \in Mod(SP), (\forall \phi \in Obs, P \rightsquigarrow \phi \iff M \models \phi)$$

Our definition of tests assumes a **testability hypothesis** on P: P exports all the operations of the signature[1] of SP, and the behavior of P through the interpretation of observable formulas is consistent (when a test set Φ is successful for P, then necessarily all the observable consequences of Φ should be in success).

---

[1] It would be possible to consider that some operations are hidden or renamed, but for the sake of simplicity, we prefer to assume that the signatures of P and SP are identical.

Test data sets can be compared by their ability to reject programs. Any test data set rejecting the same programs as $T(SP)$ is said to be **complete**. By definition of $T(SP)$, all the correct programs are successful for any complete test data set. Complete test data sets are the most efficient ones because any other test data set rejects less incorrect programs.

The challenge of testing is to manage the infinite (or too large) size of complete test data sets by using appropriate criteria. In our framework, such criteria are formalized by the notion of **selection hypotheses** [2, 3, 14]. Once the program successfully achieved some tests representative of a given property (denoted by a formula), then it is assumed that the program satisfies all the instances of this formula. Selection hypotheses allow to discard some formulas of $T(SP)$ which become redundant w.r.t. the selection hypothesis.

3 Bounded data type specifications

3.1 Using bounding constraints

Intuitively, a bounded data type can be seen as an unbounded data type in which the number of applications of some operations is bounded. We choose to specify the "unbounded" view of the data type and to define some constraints to limit the application of operations building bounded data type values. Thus, our specifications have two parts.

Firstly, unbounded data types are specified through algebraic specifications (with total functions) using positive conditional equational formulas [10]. Among the data type operations, **constructor operations** (also called generators) are distinguished. The unbounded data type specification (Σ, Ax) constitutes the **Ideal** part of the bounded data type specification. The model semantics of the ideal part are defined as usual by the set $Mod_I((\Sigma, Ax))$ of all the finitely generated models[2] which satisfy all the axioms of Ax. And the proof semantics $Th_I((\Sigma, Ax))$ is defined as the set of all formulas inferred from Ax with the usual conditional positive inference system.

Secondly, data type bounds are specified through constraints on constructor terms. The aim is to interpret any bound on a data type (i.e. a number of constructor applications) into a decidable constraint language. Our choice for this language is the one of Presburger arithmetic over natural numbers [18] that only contains first order formulas over the operations 0, 1, +, the predicate[3] $\leq$, and a set of variables. The satisfiability of a constraint (i.e. any first order formula of this language) is decidable. Data type constructor terms are measured by means of **sort measures** which are inductively defined w.r.t. constructors, other measures on component sorts, and Presburger arithmetic operations. **Bounding constraints** are formulas built over Presburger arithmetic and sort measures.

---

[2] A finitely generated Σ-algebra (model) is a multi-sorted algebra (a set of values for each sort, and an operation over the corresponding sets for each Σ-operation) such that each value can be denoted by a combination of Σ-operations.

[3] We also obtain by combination the functions maximum, multiplication by a constant ... and the predicates $=$, $> ...$

The definitions of sort measures and bounding constraints appear in the **Bound** part of a specification.

Definition 3.1. A bounded data type specification $SP = (\Sigma, Ax, \mathcal{M}, \mathcal{C})$ is defined by:

- the ideal part of SP, (Σ, Ax) which consists in a classical signature with constructors $\Sigma = (S, \Omega, F)$, (S is a set of sort names, F is a set of operation names with arity in S, and $\Omega \subset F$ is the set of constructors), and in a set Ax of positive conditional equational formulas over Σ and variables sorted in S (universally quantified);
- the bound part of SP, $(\mathcal{M}, \mathcal{C})$ which consists in a S-indexed set of sort measures $\mathcal{M} = (\mathcal{M}_s)_{s \in S}$ and in a S-indexed set of bounding constraints $\mathcal{C} = (C_s)_{s \in S}$. Each set $\mathcal{M}_s$ is a set of measures for the sort s, $\mu_s : (T_\Omega)_s \rightarrow \mathbb{N}$. Each measure μ_s is inductively defined on constructor terms. A bounding constraint C_s is a formula expressed in the constraint language (0, 1, $+$, $\leq$, $\wedge$, $\vee$, ...) enriched by measures on typed variables ranging in T_Ω.

T_Σ (resp. T_Ω) denotes the set of ground terms built over F (resp. Ω).

3.2 A simple example

Let us consider the specification of bounded natural numbers given in Figure 1.

Spec : Nat

Ideal

Use : Bool   **Axioms** :

Sort : Nat $lt(n, 0) = false$

Generators : $lt(0, succ(n)) = true$

   $0 : \rightarrow Nat$ $lt(succ(n), succ(m)) = lt(n, m)$

   $succ_- : Nat \rightarrow Nat$ $lt(n, m) = true \Rightarrow le(n, m) = true$

Operations : $le(n, n) = true$

   $lt_-\,_- : Nat \times Nat \rightarrow Bool$ $lt(m, n) = true \Rightarrow le(n, m) = false$

   $le_-\,_- : Nat \times Nat \rightarrow Bool$

   $add_-\,_- : Nat \times Nat \rightarrow Nat$ $add(0, n) = n$

   $sub_-\,_- : Nat \times Nat \rightarrow Nat$ $add(succ(n), m) = succ(add(n, m))$

Variables : $sub(n, 0) = n$

   $n, m : Nat$ $sub(succ(n), succ(m)) = sub(n, m)$

Bound

$\alpha : (T_\Omega)_{Nat} \rightarrow \mathbb{N}$

   $0 \qquad \mapsto 0$ $C_{Nat}(n) = \alpha(n) \leq 8$

   $succ(n) \mapsto \alpha(n) + 1$

Figure 1. Specification of natural numbers bounded by 8

The ideal part of the Nat specification defines two constructors 0 and *succ*. Moreover, the ideal part also imports a Bool specification not given here. The bound part of the Nat specification defines a measure α which counts the number of applications of the $succ$ operation. The bounding constraint C_{Nat} on Nat limits to 8 the measure of each bounded natural number[4]. Only the constructor terms of the form $succ^i(0)$ with $i \in [0, 8]$ satisfy C_{Nat}.

Definition 3.2. Let $SP = (\Sigma, Ax, \mathcal{M}, \mathcal{C})$ be a bounded data type specification.

We note $\mathcal{C}(T_\Omega)$ the set of ground constructor terms u, every sub-term u' of which satisfying $C_{s'}$, where s' is the sort of u'. A term t in T_Σ is said to be **below bounds** if and only if for each of its sub-terms t', there exists a term u in $\mathcal{C}(T_\Omega)$ such that $Ax \vdash t' = u$.

A ground formula is **below bounds** if and only if all its terms are below bounds. We note $Below$ the subset of Σ-formulas which are below bounds.

The terms $t_1 : add(succ^3(0), succ^2(0))$, and $t_2 : sub(succ^7(0), succ(0))$ are two examples of terms below bounds because all their strict sub-terms are ground constructor terms satisfying C_{Nat} and because one can infer $Ax \vdash t_1 = succ^5(0)$, $Ax \vdash t_2 = succ^6(0)$ where $succ^5(0)$ and $succ^6(0)$ satisfy C_{Nat}.

On the contrary, $t_3 : add(succ^4(0), succ^6(0))$, $t_4 : sub(succ^9(0), succ^2(0))$ and $t_5 : sub(0, succ(0))$ are terms **beyond bounds**. These cases depict three different ways for a term of not being below bounds. t_3 obviously corresponds to a bound overtaking. For t_4, the first argument of sub is already beyond bounds. And, t_5 corresponds to an under specified case of the operation sub, which cannot be identified with any term below bounds.

Thus, terms beyond bounds are not only terms the measures of which are too big, but also terms that cannot be proved equal to any ground constructor term. The semantics of a bounded specification are defined in order to allow any behavior (even a non terminating computation) for the terms beyond bounds.

Definition 3.3. Let $SP = (\Sigma, Ax, \mathcal{M}, \mathcal{C})$ be a bounded data type specification.
The **proof semantics** is $Th_B(SP) = Th_I(Below \cap Th_I((\Sigma, Ax)))$
The **model semantics** $Mod_B(SP)$ is defined by the set:
$\{B \in Mod(\Sigma) \mid \exists A \in Mod_I((\Sigma, Ax)), \forall \phi \in Below, (A \models \phi \iff B \models \phi)\}$

The proof semantics is derived from the restriction on formulas below bounds of the proof semantics of the ideal part. The model semantics is defined through formulas below bounds using an observational approach [20].

Intuitively, the set $Th_B(SP)$ of bounded consequences of SP is exactly the set of properties (below and beyond bounds) shared by all the models of SP:

Proposition 3.4. *Let $SP = (\Sigma, Ax, \mathcal{M}, \mathcal{C})$ be a bounded data type specification.*
$$\forall \varphi \in Sen(\Sigma), \varphi \in Th_B(SP) \iff (\forall M \in Mod_B(SP), M \models \varphi)$$

Proof. The left to right implication is a direct consequence of the definition of $Mod_B(SP)$. The right to left implication is proved by contradiction for a particular model of SP (see [1] for a detailed proof).

---

[4] All the bound values chosen in this paper are kept voluntary small in order to make easier term reading.

Spec : Tree
Ideal

Use : Nat

Sort : $Tree$

Generators :

$empty : \to Tree, \quad cons\_\_\_ : Tree \times Nat \times Tree \to Nat$

Operations :

$root\_ : Tree \to Nat, \quad left\_ : Tree \to Tree, \quad right\_ : Tree \to Tree$

$isempty\_ : Tree \to Bool, \quad lmost\_ : Tree \to Nat, \quad rmost\_ : Tree \to Nat$

$isbst\_ : Tree \to Bool$

Variables :

$n, m : Nat, \quad T, L, R : Tree$

Axioms :

$root(cons(L, n, R)) = n$

$left(cons(L, n, R)) = L$

$right(cons(L, n, R)) = R$

$isempty(empty) = true$

$isempty(cons(L, n, R)) = false$

$lmost(cons(empty, n, R)) = n$

$lmost(cons(cons(L, n, R), m, T)) = lmost(cons(L, n, R))$

$rmost(cons(L, n, empty)) = n$

$rmost(cons(T, m, cons(L, n, R))) = rmost(cons(L, n, R))$

$isbst(empty) = true$

$isbst(cons(empty, n, empty)) = true$

$isempty(L) = false$

$\quad \Rightarrow isbst(cons(L, n, empty)) = and(le(rmost(L), n), isbst(L))$

$isempty(R) = false$

$\quad \Rightarrow isbst(cons(empty, n, R)) = and(le(n, lmost(R)), isbst(R))$

$isempty(L) = false \wedge isempty(R) = false \Rightarrow isbst(cons(L, n, R))$

$\quad = and(and(le(rmost(L), n), le(n, lmost(R))), and(isbst(L), isbst(R)))$

Bound

$\nu : (T_\Omega)_{Tree} \quad \to \mathbb{N} \qquad\qquad \gamma : (T_\Omega)_{Tree} \quad \to \mathbb{N}$

$empty \quad\quad \mapsto 0 \qquad\qquad\qquad empty \quad\quad \mapsto 0$

$cons(L, n, R) \mapsto \nu(L) + \nu(R) + 1 \quad\quad cons(L, n, R) \mapsto \gamma(L) + \gamma(R) + \alpha(n)$

$$C_{Tree}(T) \equiv \nu(T) \le 9 \wedge \gamma(T) \le 15$$

Figure 2. Specification of bounded binary trees

Thanks to this proposition, there exists a **correct and complete calculus** for bounded data type specifications (its inference symbol is denoted $\vdash_B$). A formula φ can be inferred from Ax using the $\vdash_B$ inference system: $Ax \vdash_B \varphi$, if and only if $\varphi \in Th_B(SP)$.

3.3 A second example

Let us consider a second example (cf. figure 2) with more elaborated bound definitions. The ideal part of Tree specifies binary trees of natural numbers. The operations *root, left* and *right* allow respectively to access the root, the left sub-tree and the right sub-tree of a binary tree. The boolean function *isempty* checks whether a binary tree is empty, and *isbst* checks whether a binary tree is a binary search tree. The operations *lmost* and *rmost* compute respectively the left-most node and the right-most node of a binary tree.

The bound part defines two measures on binary trees, ν counts the number of nodes in a binary tree, and γ sums the α measures of the natural numbers occurring in a binary tree (α is inherited from the Nat specification). The bounding constraint C_{Tree} limits both the number of nodes to 9 and the cumulative size of the nodes of a binary tree to 15. The operations *root, left, right, lmost* and *rmost* are under specified, similarly to the *sub* operation of the specification Nat.

This example clearly shows that our formalism makes it possible to specify bounded data types in a concise, structured and elegant way.

3.4 Related works

Our formalism can be compared to other algebraic approaches dedicated to the more general problem of exception specification [12, 5, 4]. These works either do not allow to specify bounded data types or mutually specify bounds and other operations in such a way that specifications are sometimes difficult both to write and understand.

In other formal specification methods such as model approaches (Z, B, VDM), bounded data types may be specified either by using predefined bounded data types or by restricting the definition domain of operations (by adding specialized preconditions). Thus, bounds are implicitly defined by predicates and state invariants. Since such domain restrictions are not decidable, proof obligations increase in complexity. Moreover, the implicit aspect of bound definitions makes it difficult to define systematic testing criteria well suited to bound coverage.

4 Testing from bounded data type specifications

In Section 2, we gave the general notions of our dynamic testing framework. We now describe these notions more precisely for bounded data type specifications.

4.1 A complete test data set

Let $SP = (\Sigma, Ax, \mathcal{M}, \mathcal{C})$ be a bounded data type specification and let P be a program under test with respect to SP. We assume that constructors are free, more precisely, for all Ω-sentences φ, if $\varphi \in Th_B(SP)$, then φ is a tautology ($\emptyset \vdash \varphi$). This restriction is mainly introduced to simplify this presentation[5].

First, the testability hypothesis on P includes the following points:

1. P is assumed to export all the operations of Σ;
2. a subset S_{Obs} of the set of sorts S is distinguished in order to characterize the set Obs of all observable formulas[6] in P. The set Obs is the set of all ground positive conditional formulas built over equality predicates in observable sort;
3. the behavior of P through the interpretation of Obs is consistent:
$$\forall \Phi \subset Obs, (\forall \phi \in \Phi, P \rightsquigarrow \phi) \implies (\forall \psi \in Th(\Phi) \cap Obs, P \rightsquigarrow \psi).$$

Intuitively, this testability hypothesis means that the program P implements all the operations of the specification and that the observations on P provided by the observable formulas are reliable. This last point can be ensured by taking for S_{Obs} the set of types providing an equality which behaves like a congruence relation. For example, it is the case when operations ranging on observable types have a functional behavior, i.e. do not corrupt any kind of program global state.

A test is any observable consequence of SP, thus a test belongs to $T(SP) = Th_B(SP) \cap Obs$. By definition, $T(SP)$ is a complete test data set, but it contains many redundant tests. We define now a complete test data set T_0 which somehow represents usual test practices. The key idea is that any n-ary operation should be tested for all n-tuples of possible values denoted by ground constructor terms. The expected result for each n-tuple argument, also denoted by a ground constructor term, is deduced from the specification.

Definition 4.1. The test data set T_0 is defined as follows. $T_0 = \bigcup_{f \in F - \Omega} T_0(f)$ where $T_0(f)$ is the set of tests for $f : s_1 \ldots s_n \to s$ defined as follows:

- if s is an observable sort, $T_0(f) = \{f(u_1, \ldots u_n) = v \mid \forall i \in 1..n,$
$u_i \in (\mathcal{C}(T_\Omega))_{s_i}, v \in (\mathcal{C}(T_\Omega))_s, Ax \vdash f(u_1, \ldots u_n) = v\}$
- otherwise, $T_0(f) = \{c[f(u_1, \ldots u_n)] = c[v] \mid \forall i \in 1..n,$
$u_i \in (\mathcal{C}(T_\Omega))_{s_i}, v \in (\mathcal{C}(T_\Omega))_s, Ax \vdash f(u_1, \ldots u_n) = v, c[.] \in Min_s \}$

where Min_s is the set of minimal observable contexts over the sort s. An observable context is a term of observable sort with only one variable occurrence of non observable sort. It is minimal if it does not contain any observable sub-context.

By definition, any formula $f(u_1, \ldots u_n) = v$ occuring in the definition of $T_0(f)$ is below bounds because the terms $u_1, \ldots u_n, v$ are below bounds and $Ax \vdash f(u_1, \ldots u_n) = v$.

Two terms of non observable sort can be considered as denoting the same value in P as soon as they cannot be distinguished by any observation. This explains why in T_0, any non observable equality is surrounded by all the minimal observable contexts. These equalities surrounded by contexts are the only test beyond bounds. They allow to reject programs dealing with values higher than the bounds in an incoherent way.

---

[5] In the case of non free constructors, Ω-sentences should be added in the set of tests.

[6] Such kind of hypotheses are also used for unbounded data type specification [3].

Proposition 4.2. T_0 *is a complete test data set for SP.*

The proof (given in [1]) of this proposition is based on a proof on the shape of proofs built from the rules of $\vdash$ [10].

$D(f)$ denotes the set of tuples $(u_1, ..., u_n)$ occurring in the definition of $T_0(f)$, and we call it the **domain of** f **below bounds**. Similarly, we call **graph of** f **below bounds**, denoted $G(f)$, the set of tuples $(u_1, ..., u_n, v)$ occurring in the definition of $T_0(f)$.

4.2 Selection of minimal observable contexts

For each $T_0(f)$, we have to select a finite set of minimal observable contexts through which equality between non observable terms will be exercised. Any finite subset of Min_s (definition 4.1) is convenient, even if it contains observable contexts leading to values beyond bounds. This selection may be done following a random strategy or in a uniform way for each sort [2].

Due to the lack of place, we do not detail this selection of a finite subset of Min_s. For a detailed description of this selection, the reader can consult [2, 1].

4.3 Selection of tuples in $G(f)$

In order to get a fine coverage of $G(f)$, $G(f)$ is split up into smaller sub-graphs. This step is common to almost every test data selection method, either structural or functional, and is often guided by some coverage criteria. As soon as the decomposition of $G(f)$ leads to sufficiently small sub-graphs, we arbitrary select one tuple $(u_1, ..., u_n, v)$ belonging to each sub-graph in order to build the test $f(u_1, ..., u_n) = v$. This selection strategy corresponds to the assumption of a uniformity hypothesis on each sub-graph. More precisely, let g be a sub-graph of $G(f)$ a uniformity hypothesis on sub-graph g is defined as follows: as soon as $P \rightsquigarrow f(u_1, ..., u_n) = v$ for a tuple $(u_1, ..., u_n, v)$ in g, then P is assumed to verify $P \rightsquigarrow f(u'_1, ..., u'_n) = v'$ for all tuples $(u'_1, ..., u'_n, v')$ in g.

Now, let us detail our process of decomposition into sub-graphs. This decomposition can be done in two ways.

The first decomposition technic consists in splitting up $G(f)$ by **unfolding** the definition of f w.r.t. the axioms of the ideal part. This case analysis technique was initially introduced for splitting up into sub-graphs the (unbounded) graph of an operation in classical positive conditional specifications [3]. It amounts to apply equal by equal replacements from the axioms defining an operation f. This unfolding process can be iterated on the operations occurring in the axioms, until to reach a fine coverage of $D(f)$.

The second decomposition technique, called **bound splitting**, splits up $G(f)$ w.r.t. its bounding constraint (i.e. C_s). For example, when bounding constraints are conjunctions of inequalities, the graph of an operation $f : s_1 \ldots s_n \to s_{n+1}$ is included in a parallelepiped of as many dimensions as the sum of the number of measures for every sort in the operation arity. More precisely, if each sort constraint $C_{s_i}(u)$ is written $\bigwedge_{j=1..k_i} \mu^j_{s_i}(u) \leq c^j_{s_i}$, then the dimension of the parallelepiped is $\sum_{i=1..n+1} k_i$, its side lengths being respectively equal to the

$c_{s_i}^j$, constants. The bound splitting decomposition technique amounts to identify geometric sub-graphs in such a parallelepiped, such as edges, vertices and faces corresponding to the highest possible values of $C_{s_i}(u)$.

Bound splitting allows us to select tests just on bounds and strictly below bounds. This bound splitting technique is similar to classical boundary analysis [13, 22]. We will show (in the next section) how the unfolding of a bounding constraint can be used for the prototyping of a bound splitting strategy.

These two decomposition techniques can be composed together to reach a finer splitting of $G(f)$. The selection strategies corresponding to these decomposition techniques and to uniformity hypotheses are implemented with LOFT.

5 Examples of test data selection with LOFT

5.1 Using LOFT for bounded data type specifications

LOFT (LOgic for Functions and Testing) is a tool for assisted test data selection from classical positive conditional algebraic specifications [15]. It is based on an equational resolution procedure (conditional narrowing) with some control mechanisms similar to the ones used in logic programming languages like PROLOG II or NU-PROLOG.

Let us introduce the basic LOFT concepts that will be used for our experiments. The unfolding strategy is implemented by a controlled version of the resolution procedure (via the **unfold_std** command). It is applied to graphs described by conjunctions of equations, and controlled through an argument list of operations that should not be unfolded (resolved) during the resolution of the graph expression. This controlled resolution returns sub-graphs expressed by pairs of substitutions and constraints (constraints are conjunctions of equations involving operations that are not unfolded). It is possible to specify an arbitrary number of unfolding steps for each operation. For the implementation of uniformity selection strategies on a sub-graph, we select the first solution of some equational goal (expressing the sub-graph) computed with a random choice strategy for the choice of the axiom to be applied. This particular axiom selection rule makes it possible to compute answers of an equational goal in a non deterministic order. This strategy is activated in LOFT by the **?** command. These strategies have already been demonstrated on real case studies [16, 7] from classical unbounded specifications. We will use them without giving detailed explanations.

The LOFT resolution procedure is correct and complete w.r.t. the classical inference system of the ideal part of a specification ($\vdash$). In particular, LOFT is correct and complete w.r.t. the set of all formulas $f(u_1, \ldots u_n) = v$ inferred from Ax occurring in $T_0(f)$ (see Definition 4.1) with $u_1, \ldots u_n, v$ in T_Ω. Since we can check whether these formulas $f(u_1, \ldots u_n) = v$ are below bounds, we can use the resolution procedure of LOFT for bounded data type specifications. For this checking, we choose to define a boolean function **bound(_)** for each sort s which algebraically specifies the bounding constraints of sort s[7]. Such boolean

---

[7] The algebraic axiomatization of the bound boolean functions is straightforward, they

functions will be used in LOFT queries in order to limit the proof tree built during resolution, ensuring that the returned answers satisfy their associated bounding constraints. Of course, this is not the most efficient resolution procedure for the bound part of a specification. However, this allowed us to easily experiment and study test data selection from bounded data type specifications. Such a simulation cannot be done for every bound part of a specification. Indeed, LOFT requires that the rules defining sort measures and **bound** boolean functions constitute a ground convergent rewriting system [15] (i.e. a confluent and terminating rewriting system). Furthermore, the **bound** functions will be used for the implementation of the **bound splitting strategy**. The key idea is to use the classical unfolding strategy on comparison operations involved in **bound** function definitions.

5.2 Selection from the Nat specification

Let us consider the Nat specification (see figure 1). As an illustration of the bound splitting decomposition technique, we split up $G(add)$. $G(add)$ is included in a cube of side length equal to 8:

$$\{(x, y, z) \in (T_\Omega)^3 \mid \alpha(x) \leq 8, \ \alpha(y) \leq 8, \ \alpha(z) \leq 8\}$$

Figure 3(a) gives a graphical representation of $G(add)$. It is represented by the triangular face inscribed in the dashed cube of side length 8.

The following LOFT query points out the bounding constraints involved in $G(add)$. The unfold_std command asks for the unfolding of the definition of the bound function, without unfolding the α measure, the $\leq$ boolean function occurring in the bounding constraint definition, and the add function[8].

```
unfold_std([#('add:nat,nat->nat', 0), #('bound:nat->bool', 1),
     #('≤:nat,nat->bool', 0), #('α:nat->nat', 0)],
     add(X,Y)=Z, bound(X)=true, bound(Y)=true, bound(Z)=true).

REMAINING CONSTRAINTS = { add(X,Y) = Z, α(X) = _v0, ≤(_v0,8) = true,
     α(Y) = _v1, ≤(_v1,8) = true, α(Z) = _v2,≤(_v2,8) = true }
```

Now, let us split up the cube embodying $G(add)$ w.r.t. $\alpha(z) \leq 8$. We first consider the face (the right-most dashed face of figure 3(b)):

$$\{(x, y, z) \in (T_\Omega)^3 \mid \alpha(x) \leq 8, \ \alpha(y) \leq 8, \ \alpha(z) = 8\}$$

and then, the smaller parallelepiped (the left-most dashed parallelepiped of figure 3(b)):

$$\{(x, y, z) \in (T_\Omega)^3 \mid \alpha(x) \leq 8, \ \alpha(y) \leq 8, \ \alpha(z) < 8\}$$

---

are nothing else but the sort bounding constraints defined over sort measures and arithmetic operations, sort measures being axiomatized by the direct translation of their rules.

[8] The "#(op-name, number)" directives mean that at most "number" unfolding steps are allowed for the operation "op-name"

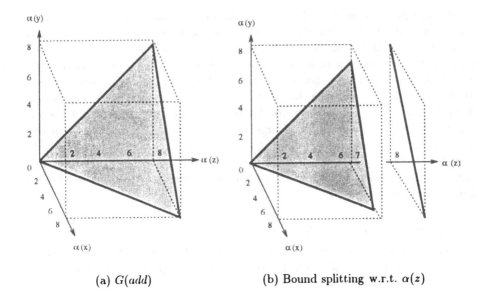

(a) $G(add)$ (b) Bound splitting w.r.t. $\alpha(z)$

Figure 3. $add(x, y) = z$

$G(add)$ is thus split up into two sub-graphs represented in figure 3(b) by a bold vertex and a bold triangular face.

This bound splitting can be done in LOFT by unfolding the equation **bound(Z) = true**. The following query asks for the unfolding of the **bound** operation (only in the second **unfold_std** command for the sub-goal **bound(Z) = true**), without unfolding the α measure and the $<$ operation used in the definition of $\leq$. The first **unfold_std** command only keeps as constraints its goal arguments.

```
unfold_std([#('bound:nat->bool', 0), #('add:nat,nat->nat', 0)],
    add(X,Y) = Z, bound(X) = true, bound(Y) = true),
unfold_std([#('bound:nat->bool', 1), #('α:nat->nat', 0),
    #('<:nat,nat->bool', 0)], bound(Z) = true).
```

We get the following answers, which characterize the two $G(add)$ sub-graphs corresponding to $\alpha(z) = 8$ and $\alpha(z) < 8$:

```
REMAINING CONSTRAINTS = { add(X,Y) = Z, bound(X) = true, bound(Y) = true,
    α(Z) = 8 }
```

```
REMAINING CONSTRAINTS = { add(X,Y) = Z, bound(X) = true, bound(Y) = true,
    α(Z) = _v0, <(_v0,8) = true }
```

Let us generalize this bound splitting to the three faces $\alpha(x) = 8$, $\alpha(y) = 8$ and $\alpha(z) = 8$. This is done by the following query:

```
unfold_std([#('add:nat,nat->nat', 0)], add(X,Y) = Z),
```

```
unfold_std([#('bound:nat->bool', 1), #('α:nat->nat', 0),
    #('<:nat,nat->bool', 0)],
    bound(X) = true, bound(Y) = true, bound(Z) = true).
```

As in the previous query, the operation $\leq$ occurring in bounding constraint definition is unfolded, while the α measure, the **add** operation and the $<$ boolean function are not unfolded. This allows to split up each $\leq$ occurrence in two cases (the equal and strictly less cases). Thus, $G(add)$ is split up into 8 sub-graphs (2^3 cases).

```
REMAINING CONSTRAINTS = { add(X,Y) = Z, α(X) = 8, α(Y) = 8, α(Z) = 8 }
REMAINING CONSTRAINTS = { add(X,Y) = Z, α(X) = 8, α(Y) = 8, α(Z) = _v0,
    <(_v0,8) = true }
REMAINING CONSTRAINTS = { add(X,Y) = Z, α(X) = 8, α(Y) = _v0,
    <(_v0,8) = true, α(Z) = 8 }
REMAINING CONSTRAINTS = { add(X,Y) = Z, α(X) = 8, α(Y) = _v0,
    <(_v0,8) = true, α(Z) = _v1, <(_v1,8) = true }
REMAINING CONSTRAINTS = { add(X,Y) = Z, α(X) = _v0, <(_v0,8) = true,
    α(Y) = 8, α(Z) = 8 }
REMAINING CONSTRAINTS = { add(X,Y) = Z, α(X) = _v0, <(_v0,8) = true,
    α(Y) = 8, α(Z) = _v1, <(_v1,8) = true }
REMAINING CONSTRAINTS = { add(X,Y) = Z, α(X) = _v0, <(_v0,8) = true,
    α(Y) = _v1, <(_v1,8) = true, α(Z) = 8 }
REMAINING CONSTRAINTS = { add(X,Y) = Z, α(X) = _v0, <(_v0,8) = true,
    α(Y) = _v1, <(_v1,8) = true, α(Z) = _v2, <(_v2,8) = true }
```

Only four of these 8 sub-graphs are not empty. The strategy of applying a uniformity hypothesis in each of the sub-graphs previously computed is implemented in the following query where the **?** command asks for one solution of each sub-graph.

```
unfold_std([#('add:nat,nat->nat', 0)], add(X,Y) = Z,
unfold_std([#('bound:nat->bool', 1), #('α:nat->nat', 0),
    #('<:nat,nat->bool', 0)],
    bound(X) = true, bound(Y) = true, bound(Z) = true), ?.
```

```
FINAL BINDING: X = 8, Y = 0, Z = 8    FINAL BINDING: X = 0, Y = 8, Z = 8
FINAL BINDING: X = 2, Y = 6, Z = 8    FINAL BINDING: X = 0, Y = 1, Z = 1
```

from these four test scenarios it is obvious to build these four test formulas:

$$add(8,0) = 8 \quad add(0,8) = 8 \quad add(2,6) = 8 \quad add(0,1) = 1$$

5.3 Selection from the Tree specification

Let us consider the more elaborate specification of Tree. We will select test formulas for the operation *isbst*. In order to ensure the selection of binary search trees, we first split up $G(isbst)$ into the two sub-graphs $G_{true}(isbst)$ and $G_{false}(isbst)$ corresponding to the truth values of *isbst*.

In the sequel we will only detail the selection of test cases for $G_{true}(isbst)$. The following query points out the bounding constraints involved in the definition of the bound operation for $G_{true}(isbst)$:

```
unfold_std([#('isbst:tree->bool', 0), #('bound:tree->bool', 1),
    #('boundaux:tree->bool', 0), #('≤:nat,nat->bool', 0),
    #('ν:tree->nat', 0), #('γ:tree->nat', 0)],
    isbst(T) = true, bound(T) = true).

REMAINING CONSTRAINTS = { isbst(T:tree) = true, ν(T:tree) = _v0:nat,
    ≤(_v0:nat,sucf(9)) = true, boundaux(T:tree) = true,
    γ(T:tree) = _v1:nat, ≤(_v1:nat,sucf(15)) = true }
```

The auxiliary operation boundaux (occurring both in the query and the answer) is used in the definition of bound in order to check that strict sub-terms of a tree also satisfy their associated bounding constraints.

Now we split up $G_{true}(isbst)$ by unfolding the isbst operation, the and operation (defined by its truth table), and the ≤ operation (defined w.r.t. <).

```
unfold_std([#('bound:tree->bool', 0)], bound(T) = true),
unfold_std([#('isbst:tree->bool', 1), #('lmost:tree->nat', 0),
    #('rmost:tree->nat', 0), #('and:bool,bool->bool', 1),
    #('≤:nat,nat->bool', 1), #('<:nat,nat->bool', 0)], isbst(T) = true).

FINAL BINDING: T = empty
REMAINING CONSTRAINTS = { bound(empty) = true }

FINAL BINDING: T = cons(empty,_v0,empty)
REMAINING CONSTRAINTS = { bound(cons(empty,_v0,empty)) = true }

FINAL BINDING: T = cons(cons(_v0,_v1,_v2),_v3,empty)
REMAINING CONSTRAINTS = { bound(cons(cons(_v0,_v1,_v2),_v3,empty)) = true,
    rmost(cons(_v0,_v1,_v2)) = _v3, isbst(cons(_v0,_v1,_v2)) = true }

FINAL BINDING: T = cons(cons(_v0,_v1,_v2),_v3,empty)
REMAINING CONSTRAINTS = { bound(cons(cons(_v0,_v1,_v2),_v3,empty)) = true,
    rmost(cons(_v0,_v1,_v2)) = _v4, <(_v4,_v3) = true,
    isbst(cons(_v0,_v1,_v2)) = true }
```

⋮

Due to lack of place we only give the first 4 answers among 10. These 10 sub-graphs correspond to the following cases: the first two cases come from the first two axioms defining isbst; the two following cases come from the unfolding of the ≤ operation in the third axiom of isbst; they correspond to the "=" and "<" cases; the two following cases come from the unfolding of ≤ in the fourth axiom of isbst; and the last four cases come from the unfolding of the two occurrences of ≤ in the fifth axiom of isbst.

Now let us illustrate the bound splitting of $G_{true}(isbst)$ w.r.t. its bounding constraints. It leads to 4 sub-graphs:

```
unfold_std([#('isbst:tree->bool',0)], isbst(T) = true),
unfold_std([#('bound:tree->bool',1),#('boundaux:tree->bool',0),
```

```
#('γ:tree->nat',0),#('ν:tree->nat',0),#('<:nat,nat->bool', 0)],
bound(T) = true).
```

REMAINING CONSTRAINTS = { isbst(T) = true, ν(T) = 9, boundaux(T) = true,
γ(T) = 15 }

REMAINING CONSTRAINTS = { isbst(T) = true, ν(T) = 9, boundaux(T) = true,
γ(T) = _v0, <(_v0, 15) = true }

REMAINING CONSTRAINTS = { isbst(T) = true, ν(T) = _v0, <(_v0, 9) = true,
boundaux(T) = true, γ(T) = 15 }

REMAINING CONSTRAINTS = { isbst(T) = true, ν(T) = _v0, <(_v0, 9) = true,
boundaux(T) = true, γ(T) = _v1, <(_v1, 15) = true }

We can compose the previous unfolding strategy with the bound splitting strategy. Then, we assume uniformity hypotheses on each computed sub-graph. The whole selection strategy (i.e. unfolding, bound splitting and uniformity on each sub-graph) can be implemented at once in the following LOFT query:

```
unfold_std([#('isbst:tree->bool', 1), #('lmost:tree->nat', 0),
    #('rmost:tree->nat', 0), #('and:bool,bool->bool', 1),
    #('≤:nat,nat->bool', 1), #('<:nat,nat->bool', 0)], isbst(T) = true),
unfold_std([#('bound:tree->bool', 1), #('boundaux:tree->bool',
    0), #('γ:tree->nat', 0), #('ν:tree->nat', 0),
    #('<:nat,nat->bool', 0)], bound(T) = true), ?.
```

We give only the 4 answers (among 34 no empty sub-graphs) corresponding to the 4 bound splitting sub-graphs coming from the first case of the third axiom of isbst (i.e. the third sub-graph computed when unfolding isbst):

```
T = cons(cons(cons(empty,0,empty), 1, cons(cons(cons(empty,2,empty),
2,empty), 2, cons(empty,2, cons(empty,2, cons(empty,2,empty))))), 2,empty)

T = cons(cons(cons(empty,1,empty), 1, cons(empty, 1, cons(cons(empty, 1,
cons(cons(empty,2,empty), 2, empty)), 2, cons(empty,2,empty)))), 2, empty)

T = cons(cons(empty, 2, cons(empty, 2, cons(cons(empty,3,empty), 4,
empty))), 4, empty)

T = cons(cons(cons(empty,0,empty), 1, empty), 1, empty)
```

Even if there exist more efficient resolution procedures for Presburger arithmetic, the example of bounded binary search trees clearly shows the ability of the LOFT tool to handle complex symbolic constraints. In order to address real sized bounds, (e.g. 2^{32} bits integers) it would be more convenient to use dedicated solvers (finite domain solvers, rational solvers ...). The integration of such solvers is planned in the next LOFT generation. However, the example of binary search trees, while being rather academic, is somehow close to the upper bound of complexity for symbolic constraint problems. This research area is very active, many theoretical and practical results let us hope that new automatic proof techniques will be helpful for test data selection of huge data.

6 Conclusion

This paper presents an application of algebraic specifications to describe data types bounds and to define a black box testing theory for bounded data types. Thus, it is possible to select from specification test data sets devoted to bound coverage. We follow three main directions:

- the definition of a specification formalism devoted to the description of bounded data types. We have introduced an intuitive notion of bounds which can be seen as a simple counting of operation applications;
- the characterization of a complete test data set including all the observable requirements of a bounded data type specification. Its definition is justified by the definition of program correctness coming from the underlying testing theory. Furthermore, this test data set copes with usual test practices;
- the definition of selection strategies ensuring the coverage of data type bounds and operation domains. These strategies are expressed by means of selection hypotheses which link the selected test data set with the original complete test data set.

Furthermore, this selection process is assisted. This has been illustrated on several examples of test data selection with the LOFT tool. These results should be confirmed on real sized case studies. For this purpose, the study of more efficient solvers for bounding constraints may be necessary.

Our approach allows to describe bounds explicitly and to clearly distinguish them from other restrictions on operation domains. The use of sort measures for the specification of bounds makes it possible to define naturally bound neighborhoods and adequate test criteria. None of existing formalisms (algebraic: [5, 4] or model-based: Z, VDM, B) give such facilities for describing and testing bounds. We think that the work reported here can be applied to other specification formalisms. The key idea is to enrich the considered specification formalism with bound description while preserving as much as possible the original semantics.

Acknowledgments: we would like to thank Frédéric Voisin, Marc Aiguier, and Marie-Claude Gaudel for a careful reading of the draft version of this article. We are particularly indebted to Marie-Claude Gaudel for numerous discussions about the notion of bound. This work has been partly supported by the French "GDR de programmation."

References

1. A. Arnould, P. Le Gall, and B. Marre. Dynamic testing from bounded data type specifications. Technical report, L.R.I, Université Paris-Sud, 1996.
2. G. Bernot. Testing against formal specifications: a theoretical view. In *TAP-SOFT'91*, LNCS 494, pages 99–119, Brighton UK, 1991. Springer Verlag.
3. G. Bernot, M.C. Gaudel, and B. Marre. Software testing based on formal specifications: a theory and a tool. *Software Engineering Journal*, 6(6):387–405, 1991.
4. G. Bernot, P. Le Gall, and M. Aiguier. Label algebras and exception handling. *Journal of Science of Computer Programming*, 23:227–286, 1994.

5. M. Breu. Bounded implementation of algebraic specifications. In *Recent Trends in Data Type Specification*, LNCS 655, pages 181–198, Dourdan, France, 1991. Springer Verlag.

6. E. Brinksma. *A theory for the derivation of tests*. 8th International Conference on Protocol Specification, Testing and Verification, North-Holland, 1988.

7. P. Dauchy, M.-C. Gaudel, and B. Marre. Using algebraic specifications in software testing: a case study on the software of an automatic subway. *Journal of Systems and Software*, 21(3):229–244, 1993.

8. J. Dick and A. Faivre. Automating the generation and sequencing of test cases from model-based specifications. In *FME'93*, LNCS 670, pages 268–284. Springer-Verlag, 1993.

9. R.K. Dong and P.G. Frankl. The astoot approach to testing object-oriented programs. *ACM Transactions on Software Engineering and Methodology*, 3(2), 1994.

10. H. Ehrig and B. Mahr. *Fundamentals of algebraic specification*. EATCS Monographs on Theoretical Computer Science, 6, 1985.

11. M.C. Gaudel. Testing can be formal, too. In *TAPSOFT'95*, LNCS 915, Aarhus, Denmark, 1995. Springer Verlag.

12. M. Gogolla, K. Drosten, U. Lipeck, and H. Ehrig. *Algebraic and operational semantics of specification allowing exceptions and errors*. Theorical Computer Science 34, p. 289-313, 1984.

13. B. Jeng and E.J. Weyuker. A simplified domain-testing strategy. *ACM Transactions on Software Engineering and Methodology*, 3(3):254–270, July 1994.

14. P. Le Gall and A. Arnould. Formal specification and test: correctness and oracle. In *Recent Trends in Data Type Specification, Oslo, Norway*, LNCS, 1996.

15. B. Marre. *Toward automatic test data set selection using Algebraic Specifications and Logic Programming*. ICLP'91, Paris, 25-28, MIT Press, 1991.

16. B. Marre, P. Thevenod-Fosse, H. Waeselynck, P. Le Gall, and Y. Crouset. *An Experimental Evaluation of Formal Testing and Statistical Testing*. SAFECOMP'92, Switzerland, Ed. Heinz H. Frey, Pergamon Press, 1992.

17. D.H. Pitt and Freestone D. The derivation of conformance tests from lotos specifications. *IEEE Transactions on Software Engineering*, 16(12):1337–1343, 1990.

18. M. Presburger. Über die Vollständingen einer gewissen Systems der Arithmetik ganzer Zahlen, in welchem die Addition als einzige Operation hervortritt. In *Comptes Rendus du premier Congrès des Mathématiciens des Pays slaves*, Warszawa, 1929.

19. Dssouli R. and Bochmann G. Conformance testing with multiple observers. In *In Protocol Specification Testing and Verification, North-Holland*, pages 217–229, 1987.

20. D. Sannella and A. Tarlecki. Toward formal development of programs from algebraic specification: implementation revisited. *Acta Informatica*, 25:233–281, 1988.

21. P. Stocks and D.A. Carrington. Test template: A specification-based testing framework. In *15th ICSE*, pages 405–414, 1993.

22. L.J. White and I.A. Perrera. An alternative measure for error analysis of the domain testing strategy. In *Workshop on Software Testing*, IEEE Computer Society Order 723, 1986.

A Theory of Specification-Based Testing for Object-Oriented Software

Stéphane Barbey, Didier Buchs and Cécile Péraire

Swiss Federal Institute of Technology
Software Engineering Laboratory
1015 Lausanne Ecublens
Switzerland

email: {Stephane.Barbey, Didier.Buchs, Cecile.Peraire} @ di.epfl.ch
phone: +41 (21) 693.52.43 - fax: +41 (21) 693.50.79

ABSTRACT The current strategies for testing object-oriented software all lack the formal basis which is necessary to perform this task efficiently. We propose the adaptation to object-oriented software of an existing theory of testing for stateless *ADTs*, to find errors in a class by checking that its implementation meets its specification. We present shortly in an informal way an object-oriented language, *CO-OPN/2*, in which language we will write the specification. We introduce a notion of test that takes into account the possible and impossible sequences of call of class methods. We examine the black-box test procedure, and give techniques to select a finite and pertinent test set from an exhaustive test set, including all the possible behaviors of the class under test, by applying test reduction hypothesis. We also study the construction of an oracle, the procedure that analyses the results of the tests, adapted to object-oriented software.

KEYWORDS object-orientation, testing, black-box testing strategy, formal methods, validation and verification, test and evaluation.

1 Introduction

Object-oriented methods are now used for all kinds of software developments. Although some people have assumed that object-orientedness leads by itself to quality, experience has proved that object-oriented software cannot escape to a validation and verification process. One way to verify that a program meets its specification is testing.

In this paper, we will focus on specification-based (also known as black-box) testing. This kind of testing is usually a three steps process. It starts with a given requirement, to find faults in a program by comparing it against a specification. It is decomposed in a *test selection step*, in which the test cases that will validate or not the requirement are generated, a *test execution step*, in which the test cases are executed and results of the execution collected, and a *test satisfaction step*, in which the results obtained during the test execution phase are compared to the expected results. This last step is commonly performed through the help of an oracle [12]. The results of this comparison give the result of the requirement, 'yes' if it is validated, 'no' it is not, and 'undecided' if the oracle is unable to analyse the result, or if the test execution did not return a result. If the answer is 'no', then the test set has found errors in the program —the goal of testing—, and the programmer can correct the implementation to remove them. Of course, the main problem is to build a test set that has enough significance to find a maximal number of errors, so that a 'yes' answer gives confidence to the programmer that the program meets its specification.

It has been argued, for example by [11], that testing object-oriented software is very similar to testing traditional software, or that it is even simplified, and that it does not require specific strategies. (By traditional software development, we understand functional decomposition development.) However, testing must take into account the specifics of the object-oriented developments methods, and of the structure of object-oriented software. Traditional strategies need adaptation to be fit for object-oriented systems. Several strategies for testing object-oriented software have already been proposed. However, those strategies lack the theoretical basis necessary to ensure the quality of the development, and especially the meaning of the 'yes' answer. In this paper, we propose a generalization and an adaptation to object-oriented software of the Bernot, Gaudel, and Marre theory of testing (called *BGM* theory), described in [3]. This theory considers testing of abstract data types. We enhance it to meet the specifics of object-oriented systems. This theory is formally defined and we will keep this rigor in our adaptation. An other advantage of this theory is that it is fit for automatization. A tool, called *LOFT* [9], has already been implemented for algebraic specifications and an adaptation of *LOFT* to the presented theory is planned.

The structure of the paper is the following. In section 2, we present the syntax and the semantics of a concurrent object-oriented specification language, called *CO-OPN/2* (Concurrent Object-Oriented Petri Nets), using a small but significant example: a phonecard system. In section 3, we propose a theory of specification-based testing for object-oriented software, introducing for each step of the test procedure both the general theory of testing and the adaptation to the particular case of object-oriented systems.

2 Specifying Object Systems

Although the theory presented in this paper does not require the specification of the software under test to be written using a formal specification language, the use of such a language is beneficial to ensure the consistency and the completeness of the specification. In this section, we will briefly present a concurrent object-oriented specification language, called *CO-OPN/2*. Interested readers will find more complete information in [4] and [5].

CO-OPN/2 (Concurrent Object-Oriented Petri Nets) is a formalism developed for the specification and design of large object-oriented concurrent systems. Such a system consists of a possibly large amount of entities, that communicate with each other by sending messages, or, in our (concurrency-friendly) terminology, by triggering parameterized events. The events to which an object can react are also called its methods. The behavior of the system is expressed with a Petri net, and the semantics of this system is given through a transition system.

Some objects in the system are active objects. The synchronization on the active objects is specified by means of synchronization expressions that appear in the axioms of the classes. To communicate with an instance of a class (an object), i.e. to send it a message, a client object must synchronize itself with that object by means of triggering one of its external events.

2.1 Architecture of a *CO-OPN/2* Specification

A *CO-OPN/2* specification consists of a collection of two different kinds of modelling entities: algebraic abstract data types (*ADTs*) and classes. Two different kinds of sorts, algebraic sorts and class' type sorts (later simply called types), are defined in those entities.

- Algebraic sorts are defined together with related operations, called functions, in *ADT* modules. A variable of an algebraic sort has no identity. Algebraic sorts are used to specify values such as the primitive sorts (integer, boolean, enumeration types, etc.) or purely functional sorts (stacks, etc.).

- Each class' type sort and its bound operations —its methods— are defined in one class module. Such a module corresponds to the notion of encapsulated entity that holds an internal state and provide the outside with various methods. A class module is a template from which objects can be instantiated, and that contains a type definition, whose variables will have an identity, defined by an object identifier algebra. Class types are used to define the classes in an object-oriented system.

To illustrate our theory, we introduce a small but significant example: a simplified phonecard system. This example models the behavior of a telephone machine that can be used with a phonecard. Each phonecard includes an identification code (the *ADT* Pin), that is also known to the user, and requested by the telephone machine when the user tries to make a phone call and to pay with the card. The remaining balance is also written on the card. We model this system using several *ADTs* (Pin, Money, Bool and Nat) and two classes (PhoneCard and Telephone).

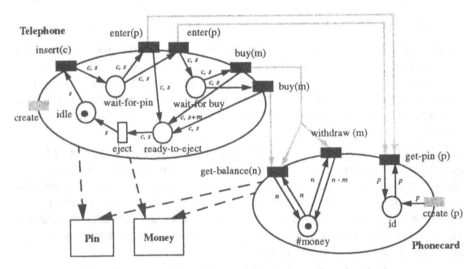

Fig. 1. The classes and their internal description and synchronizations

In figure 1, we give a partial representation of the classes, their synchronizations and their clientship relations with abstract data types. Inside each oval, representing an encapsulated class, one Petri net describes the behavior of the considered class. This Petri net represents the state of the objects through the places (circles) and the object methods through the external transitions (black rectangles). Internal transitions (the usual transitions of Petri nets) describe the internal invisible behavior (white rectangles) hidden in the semantics. Creation transitions appear as grey rectangles. Synchronizations between transitions are drawn using grey arrows.

2.2 The Syntax of a *CO-OPN/2* Specification

Every modelling entity (*ADT* or class) has a *header* (which holds the module name and the information related to genericity or inheritance), an *interface* (corresponding to the visible part of a module; it includes the information on the components of the module that are accessible to its clients) and a *body* (that describes the local aspects of the module, such as the behavior of its operations, by means of axioms).

In our example, the balance (*ADT* Money) as well as the personal identification number (*ADT* Pin) are static objects and then are correctly modelled as abstract data types (see figure 2). The *ADTs* Bool and Nat are standard data types axiomatized as usual. Since the *ADT* Money is defined to model balance, it seems natural to describe this type as a renamed copy of the *ADT* Nat. It inherits all the operations of Nat. The *ADT* Pin is defined with two generators to create new pins and one operation to compare two pins in order to validate the access to a phonecard.

```
ADT Pin;
    Interface
        Use Bool;
        Sorts pin;
        Generators
            first-pin : -> pin;
            new-pin _ : pin -> pin;
        Operations
            _=_ : pin pin -> bool;
    Body
        Axioms
            (new-pin n = new-pin m) = (n = m);
            (new-pin n = first-pin) = false;
            (first-pin = new-pin m) = false;
            (first-pin = first-pin) = true;
        Where n, m : pin;
End Pin;

ADT Money as Nat;
    Renaming nat -> money;
End Money;
```

Fig. 2. The *ADTs* Pin and Money

Cooperation between objects is performed by means of a synchronization mechanism, i.e. each event may request synchronization with the method of one or of a group of partners using a synchronization expression. Three synchronization operators are defined: "*//*" for simultaneity, "*..*" for sequence, and "*+*" for alternative. The syntax of the behavioral axiom that includes synchronization is

[Condition =>] Event [**with** SynchroExpression] : Precondition -> Postcondition

in which

- Condition is a condition on the algebraic values, expressed with a conjunction of equalities between algebraic terms.
- Event is an internal transition name or a method with term parameters.
- SynchroExpression is the (optional) expression described above, in which the keyword **with** plays the role of an abstraction operator.

- Precondition and Postcondition correspond respectively to what is consumed and to what is produced at the different places within the net (in arcs and out arcs in the net).

For instance, the figure 3 shows the textual description of the class Phonecard. (The graphical representation in figure 1 is equivalent to that textual representation). The state of a phonecard is described by the place #money, which stores the money still available on the card, and id, which stores the associated pin-code. The balance is initialized (keyword **Initial**) to a constant value 20 for each new card. Four methods are exported by this class: to create the phonecard (create), to get the pin (get-pin), to access the balance (get-balance), and to reduce it (withdraw). Since it is a throw-away card, it is not possible to reload it. In the field **Axioms**, the behavior of the methods is given by Petri net causal relations. Since the places are independently accessed through the methods, simultaneous access can be performed on the pin and on the balance. However, it is not possible to simultaneously read the balance and withdraw it because get-balance and withdraw used the same critical resource #money.

```
Class PhoneCard;
    Interface
        Use Pin, Money;
        Type phonecard;
        Creation
            create _ : pin;
        Methods
            get-pin _ : pin;
            get-balance _ : money;
            withdraw _ : money;
    Body
        Places
            #money : money;
            id : pin;
        Initial
            #money 20;
        Axioms
            create p : -> id p;
            get-pin p : id p -> id p;
            get-balance n : #money n -> #money n;
            n >= m => withdraw m : #money n -> #money n - m;
        Where n,m:money; p:pin;
End PhoneCard;
```

Fig. 3. Textual specification of the class Phonecard

The class Telephone (figure 4) specifies the behavior of the automaton which accepts a card, waits for and checks a pin number, and, as long as the pin is correct, reduces the balance of the card of a given amount corresponding to the price of a phone call. These operations are events corresponding to the methods insert, enter and buy, which can be activated sequentially. The places of the class are used to describe the state of the telephone. In this state figures the money already collected by the telephone, and, when a card is in the machine, a reference to this card. These data are also used to sequentialize the events which are possibly activated. The internal transition eject is automatically activated if an error occurs, or when the process is finished. Its effects are not directly observable, but correspond to the rejection of the card. In the class header, the field Object allows the definition of statically created objects, in our example an object called cabin, which can be referenced as an object of the class.

```
Class Telephone;
    Interface
        Use Pin, Money, PhoneCard;
        Type telephone; Object cabin : telephone;
        Creation
            create;
        Methods
            insert _ : phonecard;
            enter _ : pin;
            buy _ : money;
    Body
        Places
            idle : money;
            wait-for-pin: phonecard money;
            wait-for-buy: phonecard money;
            ready-to-eject: phonecard money;
        Initial idle 0;
        Transition eject;
        Axioms
            insert c: idle s -> wait-for-pin c s;
            (pp = p) = true => enter p With c.get-pin pp :
                            wait-for-pin c s -> wait-for-buy c s;
            (pp = p) = false => enter p With c.get-pin pp :
                            wait-for-pin c s -> ready-to-eject c s;
            (m > b) = true => buy m With c.get-balance b :
                            wait-for-buy c s -> ready-to-eject c s;
            (m > b) = false => buy m With c.get-balance b .. c.withdraw(m):
                            wait-for-buy c s -> ready-to-eject c s+m;
            eject: ready-to-eject c s -> idle s;
        Where s, m, b: money; c: phonecard; p, pp : pin;
End Telephone;
```

Fig. 4. Textual specification of the class Telephone

2.3 The Semantics of a *CO-OPN/2* Specification

In a *CO-OPN/2* specification, all the possible behaviors can be modelled by a labelled transition system. A labelled transition system $G = < Q, E, \rightarrow, I > \in \Gamma$ (where Γ is the class of all transition systems) is such that:

- Q: set of states (built over the local state of each object)
- E: set of events (built from objects creations, calls of methods and algebraic terms)
- $\rightarrow \subseteq Q \times E \times Q$: transition relationship (noted: $q \xrightarrow{e} q'$)
- $I \in Q$: a non-empty initial state

These models are built for *CO-OPN/2* using inference rules which are not given here due to the lack of space, interested readers should find the detailed descriptions in [4] and [5]. We will see (cf. full agreement theorem) that a labelled transition system must be image-finite, this will be a hypothesis of the testing procedure:

- A state $q \in Q$ is image-finite, if $\{q' \in Q \mid q \xrightarrow{e} q'\}$ is finite for each $e \in E$.
- G is image-finite, if all the reachable states of G are image-finite.

A program $P \in PROG$ (*PROG*: the class of all programs) is said to have the same semantics as a specification $SP \in SPEC$ (*SPEC*: the class of all specifications), if P satisfies to a satisfaction relationship $\models$. This relationship is defined with regard to the bisimulation equivalence ($\leftrightarrow$) which identifies systems with a similar arborescent structure. By bisimulation we understand *strong* bisimulation which is the adequate equivalence relationship for CO-OPN/2, because the semantics of CO-OPN/2 hide the internal transitions. Readers interested in the bisimulation equivalence relationship should refer to [10]. We often use in the next definitions the function $EVENT(X)$ which returns all the events of a system X expressed in a considered language.

Definition: Satisfaction relationship $\models$

Let $P \in PROG$ a program, $SP \in SPEC$ its CO-OPN/2 specification, $G(P) = <Q_1, EVENT(P), \rightarrow_1, I_1>$ and $G(SP) = <Q_2, EVENT(SP), \rightarrow_2, I_2>$ two labelled transition systems modeling P and SP, where the sets of events $EVENT(P)$ and $EVENT(SP)$ are the same. Assuming P and SP have a similar signature, the satisfaction relationship $\models \subseteq PROG \times SPEC$ is such that:

$$(P \models SP) \Leftrightarrow (G(P) \underset{}{\leftrightarrow} G(SP)).$$

The test procedure is based on the knowledge of the properties of the specification language, which must be theoretically well founded. Usually, specification languages have a notion of formula representing the properties that all the desired implementation satisfy. In practice it is not necessary to have the same language to express the specification properties and the tests. The most interesting solution is to have a specification language well adapted to the expression of properties from an user point of view, and an other language to describe test cases that can be easily applied to an oracle; as long as there is a full agreement between these two languages.

If the specification language is CO-OPN/2, the tests could be expressed with the *HML* Logic (or with any other logic compatible with $\models$), introduced by Hennessy-Milner in [7], because, in the context of image-finite labelled transition systems, it exists a full agreement between the bisimulation equivalence ($\leftrightarrow$) and the *HML* equivalence ($\sim_{HML}$). Hence the following *HML* definitions and full agreement theorem:

Definition: Syntax of HML

The HML_{SP} language is defined for a specification $SP \in SPEC$ as follows:

- $T \in HML_{SP}$
- $f \in HML_{SP} \Rightarrow (\neg f) \in HML_{SP}$
- $f, g \in HML_{SP} \, P \Rightarrow (f \wedge g) \in HML_{SP}$
- $f \in HML_{SP} \Rightarrow (<e> f) \in HML_{SP}$ where $e \in EVENT(SP)$

Definition: Semantics of HML

Given $SP \in SPEC$ a specification, $G = <Q, EVENT(SP), \rightarrow, I>$ a labelled transition system with same events as the specification, and $q \in Q$. The satisfaction relationship $\models_{HML_{SP}} \subseteq \Gamma \times Q \times HML_{SP}$ is defined as follows:

- $G, q \models_{HML_{SP}} T$
- $G, q \models_{HML_{SP}} (\neg f) \Leftrightarrow G, q \not\models_{HML_{SP}} f$
- $G, q \models_{HML_{SP}} (f \wedge g) \Leftrightarrow G, q \models_{HML_{SP}} f$ and $G, q \models_{HML_{SP}} g$
- $G, q \models_{HML_{SP}} (<e> f) \Leftrightarrow$ it exists $e \in EVENT(SP)$ such that $q \xrightarrow{e} q'$
  with $G, q' \models_{HML_{SP}} f$

Let $f \in HML_{SP}$ a formula, we write $G \models_{HML_{SP}} f$ when $G, I \models_{HML_{SP}} f$.

Definition: *HML* Equivalence

Given $SP \in SPEC$ a specification, $G_1 = <Q_1, EVENT(SP), \rightarrow_1, I_1>$ and $G_2 = <Q_2, EVENT(SP), \rightarrow_2, I_2>$ two labelled transition systems, the HML_{SP} equivalence relationship $(\sim_{HML_{SP}})$ is such that:

$$(\forall f \in HML_{SP}, G_1 \vDash_{HML_{SP}} f \Leftrightarrow G_2 \vDash_{HML_{SP}} f) \Leftrightarrow (G_1 \sim_{HML_{SP}} G_2).$$

Theorem: Full Agreement

Given $SP \in SPEC$ a specification, $G_1 = <Q_1, EVENT(SP), \rightarrow_1, I_1>$ and $G_2 = <Q_2, EVENT(SP), \rightarrow_2, I_2>$ two image-finite labelled transition systems, we have:

$$(G_1 \leftrightarrows G_2) \Leftrightarrow (G_1 \sim_{HML_{SP}} G_2).$$

An advantage of this approach is to have an observational description of the valid implementation through the tests. One test is a formula which is valid or not in the specification and that must be experimented in the program i.e. correct implementation behaves similarly on the tests. Other approaches can be taken, depending on the hypothesis we have select about the valid implementation, for instance traces are used as test patterns for ASTOOT [6].

3 The Theory of Testing

The "black box" test method is an approach to find errors in a program by validating its functionalities, without analysing the details of its code, but by using the specification of the system. The goal is to answer the question: *"Does a program satisfy the requirements of its specification?"*, or, in accordance to the goal of testing, to find if a program does not satisfy its specification. We will study in the following the relationships between the specification of a system and its realizations. Through the help of the oracle (formally denoted by $\vDash_O$) we will decide if the tests that are produced by the examination of the specification are successful or not. The final result will be that the program is acceptable or not for the given specification.

3.1 The Test Procedure

The strategy used to answer to this former question is to select, from the specification, the services required from the system. For each service, the specification allows the selection of a number of scenarios for the program under test. The set of all these scenarios makes up what we call the test set. The test procedure is as follows:

Given:

- *SPEC*: class of all specifications written in the specification language considered,
- *PROG*: class of all programs expressed in the language used for the implementation,
- *TEST*: class of all test sets that can be written,
- $\vDash$: satisfaction relationship on $PROG \times SPEC$, expressing the validity of the program with respect to the specification,
- $\vDash_O$: satisfaction relationship on $PROG \times TEST$, deciding if the tests are successful or not for the program under test.

311

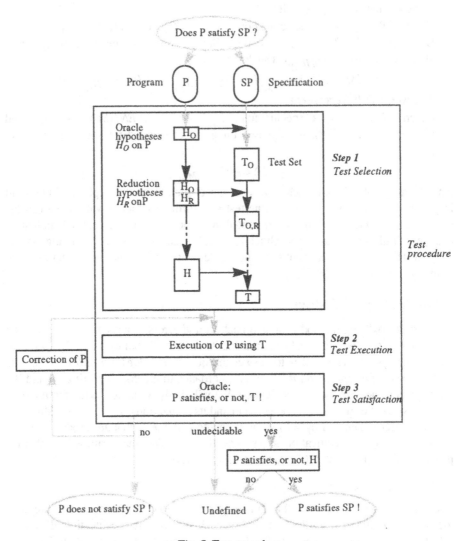

Fig. 5. Test procedure

Step 1 Selection of a test set $T_{SP, H}$ from a specification *SP* of the system and from a set of hypotheses *H* on the program under test *P*.

$$T_{SP, H} \in TEST, SP \in SPEC, P \in PROG.$$

Step 2 Execution of the program under test *P* using the test set $T_{SP, H}$.

Step 3 Analysis of the results obtained during the execution of the program *P*.

If the test set is successful ($P \models_O T_{SP, H}$), then the test procedure is finished. In addition, if *P* verifies the hypotheses *H*, then the program satisfies the requirements of the specification ($P \models SP$). If the test set is not successful, then the program contains faults or omissions, and it is possible to return to the second step of the test procedure after having corrected *P*. Note that the test procedure itself is successful if the test set helped finding as many errors as possible, i.e. if the test set is unsuccessful. The efficiency of the test set, i.e. its aptitude to detect errors, must be aligned to some quality criteria. For instance, the realization of an aerospace system requires a higher level of quality than the realization of a computer aided design system.

The test procedure is shown on figure 5. These steps are discussed in more detail by the following text. To implement the procedure of the "black box" test method it is necessary to answer the following questions:

- *"How should we select a test set?"*,
- *"How should we determine the success or the failure of a selected test set?"*.

The test set selection method is based on the existence of decision criteria for the success or failure of a test. To answer the previous questions, it is necessary to start with the second question, assuming that a test set has been selected during the first step of the test procedure. Beforehand, we will particularize the theory of testing to the particular case of object oriented systems.

3.1.1 A Theory for Testing Object-Oriented Software

In the object-oriented context, an elementary test for a program under test $P \in PROG$ and a specification $SP \in SPEC$ can be defined as a couple <*Formula, Result*> where:

- *Formula*: (ground) temporal logic formula, such that *Formula* belongs to HML_{SP}.
- *Result* $\in$ {*true, false*}: boolean value showing whether the expected result of the evaluation of *Formula* (from a given initial state) is *true* or *false*.

A test <*Formula, Result*> is successful if *Result* is *true* and *Formula* is valid in the (image-finite) labelled transition system modeling the expected behavior of *P*, or if *Result* is *false* and *Formula* is not valid in the (image-finite) labelled transition system modeling the expected behavior of *P*. In all other cases, a test <*Formula, Result*> is a fails. It is important to note that the test definition will allow the test procedure to verify that a non-acceptable scenario cannot be produced by the program (ex: make a call even though the identification code of the phonecard is wrong).

Formula can be expressed with the *HML* logic. For example, given *G* the labelled transition system modeling the telephone in figure 1 and a phonecard referenced by the name card and containing the pincode 1234 obtained with the following creation sequence <card.create 1234> (1234 is the decimal representation of new-pin applied 1234 times to first-pin) and the initial balance 20, we have:

$$G \models_{HML_{Telephone}} \text{<cabin.create> <cabin.insert card> <cabin.enter 1234> <cabin.buy 12> } T$$

because making a call is possible when the identification code is right.

$$G \not\models_{HML_{Telephone}} \text{<cabin.create> <cabin.insert card> <cabin.enter 4321> <cabin.buy 12> } T$$

because making a call is impossible when the identification code is wrong.

3.2 The Oracle

Once a test set has been selected, it is used during the execution of the program under test. Then the results collected from this execution must be analyzed. It is the role of the oracle to perform the analysis, i.e. to decide the success or the failure of the test set.

Definition: Oracle

The oracle $O = <\vDash_O, Dom_O>$ is a partial decision predicate of a formula in a program P. For each test $\phi \in TEST$ belonging to the oracle domain Dom_O, the satisfaction relationship $\vDash_O$ on $PROG \times TEST$ allows the oracle to decide:

- If ϕ is successful in P ($P \vDash_O \phi$).
- If the answer is undefined (for instance, a deadlock situation which prevents the normal termination of P).

The oracle is constituted of a collection of equivalence relationships which compare similar elements of the scenario derived from the specification to the program under test; these elements are said to be observable. The problem is that the oracle is not always able to compare all the necessary elements to determinate the success or failure of a test; these elements are said to be non-observable. This problem is solved using the oracle hypotheses H_O which are part of the possible hypotheses and collect all power limiting constraints imposed by the realization of the oracle:

Definition: Oracle Hypotheses

The oracle hypotheses H_O are defined as follows:

- When a test $\phi \in TEST$ is observable ($\phi \in Dom_O$) for a program P, the oracle knows how to decide the success or the failure of ϕ:

$$(P \text{ satisfies } H_O) \Rightarrow ((P \vDash_O \phi) \vee (\neg (P \vDash_O \phi))).$$

- When a test ϕ is non-observable for a program P ($\phi \in Dom_O$), the oracle has a set C of criterion c_i allowing to observe ϕ:

$$(P \text{ satisfies } H_O \wedge P \vDash_O (\wedge_{c_i \in C} c_i (\phi))) \Rightarrow (P \vDash_O \phi).$$

It seems rational to put the oracle hypotheses H_O, which assure the observability of the system, at the beginning of the selection test set procedure (see figure 5).

The oracle evaluation is performed using the equality for functional approaches and traces for concurrency or state based approaches. For object oriented languages, and for *CO-OPN/2*, the oracle must handle formulae such as process logic or traces of method calls, to take into account the state of the objects.

3.2.1 Oracle for Object Specifications

In the case of object systems, the observation criteria of a test formula expressed using *HML* logic, which is operational by nature, can be (with a simple oracle) the paths of the formula. A path is a subformula without *And* operators. These paths are submitted to the program under test that accepts or rejects them. Acceptation or rejection are compared to the expected behavior expressed in the test by the boolean value *Result* attached to the logical formula. If they correspond, the test is successful, otherwise it reveals an error. A more sophisticated oracle should introduce state memorization to compute the *And HML* operator. This is an intrusive way of implementing the oracle. See [8] for an explanation of the *CO-OPN/2* operational semantics.

Definition: Satisfaction relationship $\models_O$

Let $P \in PROG$ a program, $SP \in SPEC$ a specification, $G(P) = <Q, EVENT(P), \rightarrow, I>$ a labelled transition system modeling the expected behavior of P such that $EVENT(SP) = EVENT(P)$, $T_{SP, H} \in TEST$ a test set, $Formula \in HML_{SP}$ and $Result \in \{true, false\}$. The satisfaction relationship $\models_O \subseteq PROG \times TEST$ is such that:

$$(P \models_O T_{SP, H}) \Leftrightarrow$$

$$(\forall <Formula, Result> \in T_{SP, H} ((G(P) \models_{HML_{SP}} Formula \text{ and } Result = true) \text{ or}$$

$$(G(P) \not\models_{HML_{SP}} Formula \text{ and } Result = false)))$$.

An oracle hypothesis of H is that the labelled transition system modelling the expected behavior of P is image-finite. This property is necessary to state the theorem of correspondence between the test satisfaction and the specification validity. Moreover, another necessary oracle hypothesis is the assumption of a bounded and fair non-deterministic call of methods. It involves making a limited number of applications of the same test.

3.3 The Test Set Selection Problem

Assuming that we have an oracle O that ensures the observability of the system with the oracle hypotheses H_O, the first task of the test procedure consists of selecting, from the specification, a test set that allows the exhaustive validation of each service required from the system. This is theoretically achieved by selecting an exhaustive test set which contains all the test that are required by the specification. However the exhaustive test set selected is generally infinite, and it is necessary to apply a number of reduction hypotheses H_R to the behavior of the program to obtain a finite test set of "reasonable" size. Therefore, we proceed by successive reductions of the number of tests (see figure 5). Thus, when the test set is successful, the program is correct on condition that it satisfies the oracle and the reduction hypotheses. The test set quality is therefore function of the number of oracle and reduction hypotheses satisfied by the program under test. The idea of the test set selection procedure is to find $T_{SP, H}$ such that:

$$(P \text{ satisfies } H) \Rightarrow (P \models_O T_{SP, H} \Leftrightarrow P \models SP).$$

The equivalence relationship is satisfied when the test set $T_{SP, H}$ is pertinent, i.e. valid (any incorrect program is discarded) and unbiased (it rejects no correct program):

Definition: Pertinent Test Set

Given H hypotheses, $P \in PROG$ and a specification $SP \in SPEC$. The test set $T_{SP, H} \subseteq TEST$ is pertinent iff:

- $T_{SP, H}$ is valid: $(P \text{ satisfies } H) \Rightarrow (P \models_O T_{SP, H} \Rightarrow P \models SP)$.
- $T_{SP, H}$ is unbiased: $(P \text{ satisfies } H) \Rightarrow (P \models SP \Rightarrow P \models_O T_{SP, H})$.

A pertinent test set $T_{SP, H}$ can be used to test a program P only if $T_{SP, H}$ has a "reasonable" finite size. For that purpose we build a test context, called practicable because it can be effectively applied to the oracle, using reduction hypotheses. Beforehand, we will particularize the theory of testing to the particular case of object oriented systems.

3.3.1 The Test Selection for Object Oriented Specifications

In this section, we give the relationship between the two satisfaction relationships ($\models$ and $\models_O$) by using a corollary of the full agreement theorem (see section 2.3). For that purpose, we define the exhaustive test set.

Definition: Exhaustive Test Set

Given $SP \in SPEC$ a specification, $G(SP) = < Q, EVENT(SP), \rightarrow, I>$ an image-finite labelled transition system representing the semantics of the object system specification SP and H_O the oracle hypotheses. An exhaustive test set $EXHAUST_{SP, Ho} \subseteq TEST$ is such that:

$EXHAUST_{SP, Ho} = \{<Formula, Result> \in HML_{SP} \times \{true, false\} \mid$

$\qquad (G(SP) \models_{HML_{SP}} Formula$ and $Result = true)$ or

$\qquad (G(SP) \not\models_{HML_{SP}} Formula$ and $Result = false)\}.$

Corollary of the full Agreement Theorem:

Let $P \in PROG$ an object-oriented system under test, $SP \in SPEC$ its specification, and $EXHAUST_{SP, Ho}$ an exhaustive test set obtained from SP and from a set of hypotheses H_O on P. We have:

$$(P \text{ satisfies } H_O) \Rightarrow (P \models SP \Leftrightarrow P \models_O EXHAUST_{SP, Ho}).$$

The figure 6 summarizes the correspondences between the different theoretical relationships, on which the test process is built, introduced in this paper.

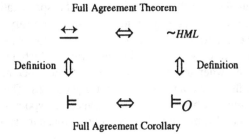

Fig. 6. Full agreement theorem and its corollary

For the example of the telephone cabin and the phonecard card containing the pincode 1234 and the initial balance 20, the exhaustive test set contains tests such as:

`<<cabin.create> <cabin.insert card> <cabin.enter 1234> <cabin.buy 12>` $T, true>$

`<<cabin.create> <cabin.insert card> <cabin.enter 4321> <cabin.buy 12>` $T, false>(1)$

`<<cabin.create> <cabin.insert card> <cabin.enter 1234> <cabin.buy 12>`
`<cabin.insert card> <cabin.enter 1234> <cabin.buy 6>` $T, true>$

The two first tests correspond to an excerpt of the possible combinations of events applied in one single cycle of telephone usage, whereas the third corresponds to successive uses of the cabin. We can also give more sophisticated tests, including the $\wedge$ (and) and $\neg$ (negative) operators, such as:

<<cabin.create> <cabin.insert card> <cabin.enter 4321> ¬(<cabin.buy 12> T), *true*>

<<cabin.create> <cabin.insert card> (<cabin.enter 1234> <cabin.buy 12> T) ∧
(<cabin.enter 4321> <cabin.buy 12> T), *false*>

The last test is redundant with respect the test (1). In the following section, we will explain how to avoid such redundancy, while keeping the pertinence of the test set, by reducing the exhaustive test set using adequate strategies.

3.4 Construction of a Practicable Test Context and Reduction Hypotheses

We express in this section how to iteratively reduce a test set, in order to reach a test set that reflects the expected behaviors that are crucial for the validation of an implementation with respect to its specification. The definition of a practicable test context is the following:

Definition: Practicable Test Context

Given a specification $SP \in SPEC$. A test context $(H, T_{SP, H})_O$ is defined by a set of hypotheses H on a program under test P, a test set $T_{SP, H} \subseteq TEST$ and an oracle O.

$(H, T_{SP, H})_O$ is practicable iff:

- $T_{SP, H}$ is pertinent and has a "reasonable" finite size.
- $O = < \vDash_O, Dom_O>$ is defined for each element of $T_{SP, H}$ $(T_{SP, H} \subseteq Dom_O)$.

To simplify, $(H, T_{SP, H})_O$ is noted $(H, T)_O$ in the rest of the paper.

The selection of a pertinent test set $T_{SP, H}$ of "reasonable" size is made by successive refinements of an initial test context $(H_0, T^0)_O$ which has a pertinent test set $T^0{}_{SP, H_0}$ until the obtention of a practicable test context $(H, T)_O$:

$$(H_0, T^0)_O \leq ... \leq (H_i, T^i)_O \leq (H_j, T^j)_O \leq ... \leq (H, T)_O.$$

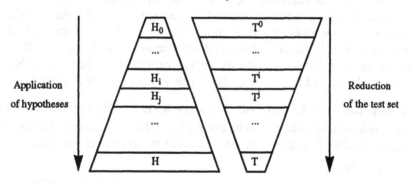

Fig. 7. Iterative refinement of the test context

At each step, the preorder refinement context $(H_i, T^i)_O \leq (H_j, T^j)_O$ is such that:

- The hypotheses H_j are stronger than the hypotheses H_i: $H_j \Rightarrow H_i$.
- The test set $T^j{}_{SP, H_j}$ is included in the test set $T^i{}_{SP, H_i}$: $T^j{}_{SP, H_j} \subseteq T^i{}_{SP, H_i}$.
- If P satisfies H_j then $(H_j, T^j)_O$ does not detect more errors than $(H_i, T^i)_O$:
  $$(P \text{ satisfies } H_j) \Rightarrow (P \vDash_O T^i{}_{SP, H_i} \Rightarrow P \vDash_O T^j{}_{SP, H_j}).$$
- If P satisfies H_j then $(H_j, T^j)_O$ detects as many errors than $(H_i, T^i)_O$:
  $$(P \text{ satisfies } H_j) \Rightarrow (P \vDash_O T^j{}_{SP, H_j} \Rightarrow P \vDash_O T^i{}_{SP, H_i}).$$

Therefore, we have the following theorem:

Theorem:

Given specification $SP \in SPEC$. Given two test contexts $(H_i, T^i)_O$ and $(H_j, T^j)_O$ such that $(H_i, T^i)_O \leq (H_j, T^j)_O$. If T^i_{SP, H_i} is pertinent then T^j_{SP, H_j} is pertinent.

A test is a formula with or without universally quantified variables. The reduction hypotheses act on tests with variables, replacing theses variables to reduce the formula complexity. Thus we define $Var(\phi)$: the set of variables of a formula ϕ.

3.4.1 The Uniformity Hypotheses

The uniformity hypotheses, which are very strong, stipulate that if a test of a formula ϕ, with $v \in Var(\phi)$, is successful for a given value of v, then it is successful for all possible values of v. For instance, in the case of a stack, if a test is successful for a stack which has a top element of 2, then it is successful for all possible values of the top element. Since the uniformity hypothesis is very strong, it is usually not applied alone to the sort under test, but to the sorts imported into the specification, which we suppose being already tested. Uniformity hypotheses can be combined with domain decomposition.

3.4.2 The Regularity Hypotheses

The regularity hypotheses stipulate that if a test of a formula ϕ, containing a term t, is successful for all terms t which have a complexity less or equal than a bound k, then it is successful for all possible complexities of t. For instance, in the case of an unbounded stack, if a test is successful for all stacks of a size smaller or equal to 20, then it is successful for all possible stack sizes.

In our case, if an uniformity hypothesis or a regularity hypothesis is applied on a pertinent test set, then the new test set obtained is pertinent too. Note that those two hypotheses correspond (possibly in a more formal way) to usual test practices. In further works, we will study the *HML* formula domain decomposition, and we will explore other interesting reduction hypotheses, such as incremental hypotheses, to build the test set of a descendant class upon the test set already selected for its parents.

3.4.3 Application of the Test Reduction Hypotheses for Object-Oriented Systems

The test reduction hypotheses can be applied to all three dimensions of a test: object management, *HML* formulae selection, algebraic term parameters selection.

- Object management

For the object management mechanism (class operations), both the regularity and the uniformity hypothesis can be used depending on the confidence on the underlying object management system which creates, destroys and modifies objects. If the system is supposed to work properly, stronger hypothesis may be chosen such as the uniformity hypothesis on the class type under test. Otherwise, if the system can have unexpected behavior depending on the number of objects, hypothesis such as the regularity must be applied.

For instance we can apply uniformity on the class Telephone, assuming that we have a phonecard referenced by card containing the pincode (new-pin first-pin) (obtained with the following creation sequence <card.create new-pin first-pin>) and the initial balance 20. This will produce the test set:

T_1 = {<<cabin.create> *f, result>* |
    f ∈ $HML_{TELEPHONE}$, *result* ∈ {*true, false*} such that (s.t.) the test is valid}

Other test sets shall be applied using the regularity hypothesis if the number of telephone machine could produce wrong behavior.

- *HML* formulae

For *HML* formulae, the regularity hypothesis can be applied to reduce the size of the formulae to be tested, and the uniformity hypothesis can be applied on formulae of a given size in order to reduce the number of tests. Moreover, we can apply a reduction technique based on the semantics of tests, since some tests imply other tests. For instance redundant tests such as *<f, true>* and *<¬(f), false>* are equivalent and can be reduced to one test.

For instance, T_1 can be reduced by applying an uniformity hypothesis on the variable *f* producing the test set T_2 (resp. T_3):

T_2 = {<<cabin.create> <cabin.insert card> <cabin.enter *pin_1*> <cabin.buy *amount_1*>
    <cabin.insert card> <cabin.enter *pin_2*> <cabin.buy *amount_2*> *T, result>* |
    pin_1, pin_2 ∈ pin, *amount_1, amount_2* ∈ money, *result* ∈ {*true, false*} s.t. the test is valid}

T_3 = {<<cabin.create> <cabin.insert card> (<cabin.enter *pin_1*> <cabin.buy *amount_1*> *T*) ∧
    (<cabin.enter *pin_2*> <cabin.buy *amount_2*> *T*), *result>* |
    pin_1, pin_2 ∈ pin, *amount_1, amount_2* ∈ money, *result* ∈ {*true, false*} s.t. the test is valid}

T_3 (of complexity 6) covers all tests (of complexity 4) of the following pattern:

T_4 = {<<cabin.create> <cabin.insert card> <cabin.enter *p*> <cabin.buy *amount*> *T, result>* |
    p ∈ pin, *amount* ∈ money, *result* ∈ {*true, false*} s.t. the test is valid}

which can be suppressed from the test set.

From T_1, a regularity hypothesis of complexity 2 can also be applied on the variable *f* producing the test pattern T_5.

T_5 = {<<cabin.create> <cabin.insert card> *T, result>*,
    <<cabin.create> <cabin.enter *pin*> *T, result>*,
    <<cabin.create> <cabin.buy *amount*> *T, result>*,
    <<cabin.create> <cabin.insert card> <cabin.insert card> *T, result>*,
    <<cabin.create> <cabin.insert card> <cabin.enter *pin*> *T, result>*,
    <<cabin.create> <cabin.insert card> <cabin.buy *amount*> *T, result>*, ... |
    pin ∈ pin, *amount* ∈ money, *result* ∈ {*true, false*} s.t. the test is valid}

- Algebraic term

Starting with a test set generated by the previous selection procedure we apply on the algebraic variables the regularity or the uniformity hypothesis and we fix the correct value of *result*, depending on the semantics of the specification. For instance if we chose the test set T_4, we can apply a regularity hypothesis of complexity 3 on the variable *p*, leading to the test set T_6:

T_6 = {<<cabin.create> <cabin.insert card> <cabin.enter first-pin> <cabin.buy *amount*> *T, result>*,
<<cabin.create> <cabin.insert card> <cabin.enter new-pin first-pin> <cabin.buy *amount*> *T, result>*,
<<cabin.create> <cabin.insert card> <cabin.enter new-pin new-pin first-pin> <cabin.buy *amount*> *T,
result>* | *amount* ∈ money, *result* ∈ {*true, false*} s.t. the test is valid}

An uniformity hypothesis can be applied on this test for the variables *amount*, the new test T_7 includes now only ground term formulae.

T_7 = {<<cabin.create> <cabin.insert card> <cabin.enter first-pin> <cabin.buy 15> T, *result*>,
<<cabin.create> <cabin.insert card> <cabin.enter new-pin first-pin> <cabin.buy 10> T, *result*>,
<<cabin.create> <cabin.insert card> <cabin.enter new-pin new-pin first-pin> <cabin.buy 22> T, *result*> | *result* $\in$ {*true, false*} s.t. the test is valid}

Then *result* can be evaluated in order to select a valid test set:

T_8 = {<<cabin.create> <cabin.insert card> <cabin.enter first-pin> <cabin.buy 15> T, *false*>,
<<cabin.create> <cabin.insert card> <cabin.enter new-pin first-pin> <cabin.buy 10> T, *true*>,
<<cabin.create> <cabin.insert card><cabin.enter new-pin new-pin first-pin> <cabin.buy 22> T, *false*>}

It must be noted that we have essentially tested in T_8 the correctness of the pin usage.

4 Conclusion

In this paper we have presented a generalization and an adaptation of the Bernot, Gaudel, and Marre theory of testing to object oriented software. The key points of the adaptation of the *BGM* method to the object oriented software is that we generalize this theory to systems where the specification and the test sets are given in a different language. Thus we are able to give some formal definitions of the test sets that can be used for systems having persistent states through the use of the *HML* temporal logic. It is also shown that these tests are fully compatible with the program satisfaction notions based on bisimulation. We illustrate our definitions through the Telephone example, a simple but sufficiently complete specification used to show the different kind of application of the reduction hypothesis on either object management mechanism, the event call part or the algebraic level of elements composing the *CO-OPN/2* specification.

Although our theory solve the most common problems of testing object-oriented software, it does not deal with some aspects of this paradigm, namely polymorphism and inheritance. Moreover, the presented strategy does not discuss the operational techniques for the reduction of the test set. Those aspects are not part of this paper and can be partly found in [2] and [1]. However, the test selection principles presented above have been designed to be incorporated as specific logical rules in *LOFT*. *LOFT* is an equational logic programming environment. Its purpose is to generate tests sets from algebraic specifications. We intend to extend this tool to handle object-oriented specifications, by coding the *HML* semantics rules and the *CO-OPN/2* class semantics into equational logic.

This paper proposes the first theoretical step in the direction of a complete practical methodology which will be enriched in the direction of concrete oracle construction, inheritance and operational techniques.

5 Acknowledgments

The authors would like to thank the anonymous referees and Pascal Racloz for their helpful comments. This work has been supported partially by the Esprit Long Term Research Project 20072 "Design for Validation" (DeVa) with the financial support of the OFES (Office Fédéral pour l'Education et de la Science), and by the Swiss National Science Foundation project 21-36038.92 "Research in Object-Oriented Software Development".

6 References

[1] Stéphane Barbey, Manuel Ammann, and Alfred Strohmeier. Open issues in testing object-oriented software. In Karol Frühauf, editor, *ECSQ '94 (European Conference on Software Quality)*, pages 257–267, Basel, Switzerland, October 17-20 1994. vdf Hochschulverlag AG an der ETH Zürich. Also available as Technical Report (EPFL-DI-LGL No 94/45).

[2] Stéphane Barbey, Didier Buchs, and Cécile Péraire. A theory of specification-based testing for object-oriented software. Technical Report 96/163, EPFL-DI-LGL, January 1996.

[3] Gilles Bernot, Marie-Claude Gaudel, and Bruno Marre. Software testing based on formal specifications: a theory and a tool. *IEE Software Engineering Journal*, 6(6):387–405, November 1991.

[4] Olivier Biberstein and Didier Buchs. Structured algebraic nets with object-orientation. In *Workshop on Object-Oriented Programming and Models of Concurrency '95*, Turin, June 1995.

[5] Didier Buchs and Nicolas Guelfi. A concurrent object-oriented Petri nets approach for system specification. In M. Silva, editor, *12th International Conference on Application and Theory of Petri Nets*, pages 432–454, Aahrus, Denmark, June 1991.

[6] Roong-Ko Doong and Phyllis G. Frankl. The ASTOOT approach to testing object-oriented programs. *ACM Transactions on Software Engineering and Methodology*, 3(2):101–130, April 1994.

[7] Matthew Hennessy and Robin Milner. Algebraic laws for nondeterminism and concurrency. *Journal of the ACM*, 32(1):137–161, January 1985.

[8] Jarle Hulaas. An evolutive distributed algebraic petri nets simulator. In A. Javor, A. Lehmann, and I. Molnar, editors, *Modelling and Simulation 1996*, pages 348–352, Budapest, Hungary, June 2-6 1996. 10th European Simulation Multiconference ESM96, Society for Computer Simulation International.

[9] Bruno Marre. *Sélection automatique de jeux de tests à partir de spécifications algébriques en utilisant la programmation logique*. PhD thesis, LRI, Université de Paris XI, Orsay, France, January 1991.

[10] Robin Milner. *Communication and Concurrency*. Prentice Hall, 1989.

[11] James Rumbaugh, Michael Blaha, William Premerlani, Frederick Eddy, and William Lorensen. *Object-Oriented Modeling and Design*. Prentice Hall, 1991.

[12] Elaine J. Weyuker. The oracle assumption of program testing. In *13th International Conference on System Sciences*, pages 44–49, Hawaii, USA, 1980.

Industrial Track paper

Proving Safety Properties for Embedded Control Systems

Cinzia Bernardeschi[1], Alessandro Fantechi[2], Stefania Gnesi[3] and Giorgio Mongardi[4]

[1] Dipartimento di Ingegneria dell'Informazione, Università di Pisa, Italy
[2] Dipartimento di Sistemi e Informatica, Università di Firenze, Italy
[3] IEI - C.N.R., Pisa, Italy
[4] Ansaldo Trasporti, Genova, Italy

Abstract. It is well-known that a fundamental problem in embedded control systems is the verification of the safety requirements. Formal methods and related support tools can successfully be applied in the formal proof that a system is safe. However, the complexity of real systems is such that automated tools often fail to formally validate such systems. A typical case is when "state explosion" problems arise.

In this paper, we show some "abstraction techniques" to make the problem of safety requirements validation tractable by current tools. These abstraction techniques have been defined inside a verification methodology that has been tested on the specification of a railway computer based interlocking signalling control system. The conditions under which this methodology can be applied to systems in different application areas are finally discussed.

1 Introduction

Safety is usually defined as the property of a system of not being subject to specific dangerous failures, such as those that may hurt human beings. According to Laprie [17], safety is the property of a system "to be dependable with respect to the non occurrence of catastrophic failures". Safety measures are often stated in quantitative terms: we want the probability of a serious accident to be lower than some acceptable threshold. Starting from the study of the critical issues of the system, we usually derive the constraints necessary to guarantee a safe behavior of the system, called the safety constraints. A system will be developed applying strategies to guarantee the safety constraints to be satisfied along the system life. Verification is the activity that aims to check that the actual behavior of the system respects the safety constraints.

Formal methods may be used to specify and model the behavior of a system at different levels of abstraction, and to mathematically verify that the system design and implementation satisfy system properties [2]. A variety of methodologies and techniques have recently been developed for this purpose. Moreover, the use of formal methods is increasingly required by the international standards and guidelines for the development of safety critical computer-controlled systems.

For example, the CENELEC SC9XA/WG1 European Standard [9] highly recommends the use of formal techniques in the software requirements specification and in the design and the validation of software. Formal methods have been a topic of research for many years and the question now is whether these methods can be effectively used in industrial applications. Tool support is necessary for a full industrialization process and there is a clear need for improved integration of formal method techniques with other software engineering practices.

A special class of embedded systems is that of railway control systems. In the development of railway control systems, efforts in introducing formal methods have been recently carried out. We can recall the experience made by MATRA Transport and the Paris Rapid Transit Authority that started working on the development of a computerized signalling system for commuter trains in Paris [10]. This experience is often cited as one of the most successful cases of application of formal methods in the development of industrial safety critical software. Other interesting cases are the one of the formal specification and verification of a Distributed Control of Track Vehicles [14], the one related to the British Rail's Solid State Interlocking [5] and the approach followed in [15].

To evaluate the introduction of formal methods in the development of software for railway critical applications, Ansaldo Trasporti became interested in the possibility of the application of a formal approach to a class of systems whose behaviour does not depend on heavy amounts of data. It was thus decided to conduct a pilot project with the aim of assessing the formal specification and verification methods and tools to evaluate their potential advantages in reducing the cost and the time of the validation. In this pilot project [1] the formal specification of a railway interlocking signalling control system was given using both process algebra and finite state automaton formalisms [16, 20]. Model checking techniques [7, 11] were then used to verify the safety constraints, which were expressed as temporal logic formulae [18, 12, 13], on the finite state model of the behavior of the system. The generation of this model and the verification of the properties of the system was obtained through the use of the tools in the JACK environment [3]. The outcomes of this pilot project have shown that the application of formal validation methodologies is feasible and well accepted in this industrial context. However, the main problem encountered inside the project was that of the capacity of tools, in terms of number of states which can be handled.

In this paper we concentrate on the techniques that have made possible to solve the state explosion problems that have affected this project, as often happens when dealing with real systems. We then give some evaluations about the effort required by the approach and we show how the same approach can be used on other systems in different application areas, by discussing the characteristics that a system should have to be successfully tractable within this approach.

2   An overview of the experience

The object of the experience, reported with more details in [1], was the Computer Based Interlocking system (CBI), that is the part of the application software responsible for the interlocking of the equipment of a signalling system developed at Ansaldo Trasporti. The interlocking signalling system is a distributed system in which each node is responsible for the interlocking logic of a set of track units. Each node can control a line section with complex railway stations, a line section with small stations or a complete low traffic line with simple interlocking logic. The CBI is the core of the node and it can be configured according to the railway plant topology application requirements. The interlocking system has been validated with traditional methods (static analysis and simulation, Decision Tables, testing) [21], and this experience addressed a re–validation of the system using formal verification methods.

This experience was particularly devoted to examine the interlocking logic of two different entities, namely the Level Crossing Control (LCC) and the Shunting Route mechanism (SH_ROUTE). The LCC represents the level crossing physical entity, while the SH_ROUTE represents a logical entity in charge of building the route for a train. This entity will require the closure of a level crossing before letting the train to proceed as well as the opening of it after the train has left the level crossing, see Fig. 1.

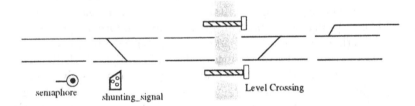

Fig. 1. Interlocking a level crossing with a shunting route mechanism

The state of the system is represented by variables corresponding to the physical or to the logical entities. *Operations* act on variables: they are specified by a list of verifications on some variables and a list of value assignments to other variables (operation's output). The control of each physical/logical entity (the level-crossing and the shunting route mechanism in our example) is realised by the set of operations related to the entity. In particular, each of such entities can be seen as a collection of *operations*, that describe the behavior of the entity, *variables* that are used to store global information about the entity, and *attributes*, that are statical configuration parameters for the entity itself. The system operates manually or automatically. Examples of operations are the Manual Closure/Open Request or the Automatic Closure/Open Request. An operation typically modifies the value of variables; the modification of the value of a variable may trigger the execution of other, internal, operations. The

Automatic Closure Request operation, for example, triggers the internal Doing Closure Operation, which in its turn, triggers the internal Verify Closure Operation. The shunting route process, in order to create a path for a train, must book the segments of track calling the Automatic Closure Operation for each LCC on each line segment. The system may need to control several identical entities; for example several pairs of interacting LCC and SH_ROUTE entities may be present. This requires different instances of the variables related to these entities, and will require different instances of the operations to be run for each of these entities.

Due to the structure of the specification, the most difficult task in the use of traditional validation methods, is tracing the interactions between the control of different entities. Therefore, a possible intervention area for the fruitful use of formal verification methods was identified in the analysis of the interactions between different entities.

The formalization of the CBI system started from the industrial semi-formal specification, through the use of the tools in the JACK environment [3]. JACK [2] provides an automatic support both in specification and in verification.

In the first part of the formalization work, the formal specifications of the level-crossing LCC and of the shunting route SH_ROUTE of the CBI were developed. The formalization of these entities takes care in particular of the interaction between them. In the original industrial specification, which is the subject of our validation, the main concern is related to the states: there are *passive entities* (i.e., state *variables*) and *active entities* (i.e, those entities activated by state changes and which execute *operations*).

Variables in the original specification are mapped onto processes in the process algebra specification language CCS/MEIJE [4, 20]. In CCS/MEIJE a system consists of a set of communicating processes; each process executes input or output actions (denoted by the suffix "?" or the suffix "!" respectively) and synchronizes with other processes to execute its activities. A process corresponding to a variable has a different state for each value which the variable can assume; the actions possible for such a process are the writing and reading of each value. Operations are instead formalized using a graphical representation by means of automata which model their state changes, by a one-to-one transformation from the state-machine structure of the operations to the corresponding automata. The process algebra formalism and the graphical representation of automata, summing up, permitted formal specifications sufficiently adherent to the semi-formal original one to be written. Each formal specification previously generated (for both operations and variables) is then graphically represented by a box with name equal to the name of the specification and ports corresponding to the actions of the specification itself. Boxes are then composed together by linking ports

---

[2] Detailed information about JACK and its component tools are available at http://repl.iei.pi.cnr.it/Projects/JACK

related to actions on which the entities must synchronize. In Fig. 2 the graphical representation, called network, related to the interactions of the "lcc_state" and "command_state" variables and to the Automatic Closure Request operation is reported. According to the figure, the "lcc_state", for example, must synchronize with the Automatic Closure Request operation when executing the action ""s_wait_the_timer". Starting from the network describing the whole system, the global automaton of the system is finally generated.

Our formal verification language was the temporal logic ACTL that stands for "Action-based Computation Tree logic" [12]. This logic is a branching time logic, that is particularly suitable to express properties of systems that perform actions in the time. Each safety requirement that we wanted to verify on the CBI system was formalized into ACTL formulae. These safety requirements are then checked against the global model associated with the composition of the LCC and SH_ROUTE entities.

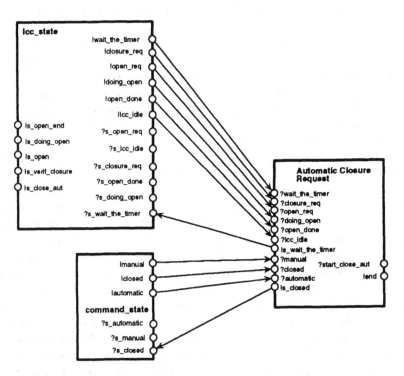

Fig. 2. Graphical composition of command_state variable, lcc_state variable and the Automatic Closure Request operation.

3   Abstraction Techniques for the CBI system

The main drawback of this approach lies in the generation of the global model of the CBI. The system is in fact composed by a large number of entities, each modeled by a set of processes, one for each variable and one for each operation, and the number of states of the global automaton of the system grows exponentially with the number of processes composed together. This problem, known as the "state explosion problem", makes it often impossible to deal with a complete system composed of several entities. In the pilot project we dealt with, some safety preserving abstraction techniques were used. A particular technique used in the composition of LCC and SH_ROUTE was to make a "zoom" on those parts of the system which are directly responsible for the satisfaction of a safety requirement.

To make this technique applicable, we performed the following steps:

1. The system is specified as a collection of separate subsystems, using process algebra terms and their underlying models (as we did for the Level Crossing Control and the Shunting Route Control subsystems);
2. The safety requirements are expressed as temporal logic formulae;
3. The safety requirements are analyzed to enlight the subsystems directly involved in their satisfiability; typically, only few subsystems are engaged in the definition of a single requirement. Moreover, the system can be composed of a replication of subsystems of the same type. In this case safety requirements can be factorized following this replication (this is what we did, considering only a pair of LCC and SH_ROUTE subsystems. The safety requirements considered are valid for any pair of interacting LCC and SH_ROUTE entities in the system);
4. An abstract version of the global system was obtained composing together the related subsystems, after that suitable "abstraction techniques" are applied, which allow to throw away all the uninteresting details of the system with respect to the safety property to be checked. These parts of the system ignored become a "free" external environment. Any possible behavior is simulated by such an environment.
5. Any formula produced in step 2) is then verified on the corresponding abstract model, using model checking tools.

We now discuss the three main abstraction criteria we adopted in the CBI validation, showing informally why they preserve the safety properties.

3.1   Global Environment

The CBI system is able to interact with the human operator at a control post. Moreover the LCC subsystem is able to interact with the SH_ROUTE subsystem. The human operator and the instances of the SH_ROUTE process which require operations at that level crossing form the external environment of the LCC. We refer to the set of processes able to interact with a given process as the global environment of the process.

In absence of any further specification of the global environment, operations at the interface of the LCC, for example the Manual Closure Request, are free to be executed at any moment. This is quite rare in reality, since human operators interact with the system according to a predefined protocol. However, abstracting from this protocol, allows an abstract system model which includes all possible behaviors of the system to be obtained.

A safety property is an expression of the fact that nothing bad happens in the system. We can say that a safety property implies that hazardous states of the system are never reached. Validity of the safety property is checked on the model of the abstract model of a system. If the property is checked true on the abstract model, then the property is also true on the real system. On the other hand, if the property is checked false then nothing can be said about the satisfaction of that property by the real system.

A property that is not maintained by this abstraction criterion is deadlock freedom. If the abstract model of the system does not deadlock, we are not sure that the real system (that is, the system considering a particular interaction protocol) is free of deadlock. Note that deadlock is a good solution to realize a safety strategy: in the case in which we can no more guarantee a safe behavior of the system we accept that the system stops.

3.2 Testing signal values

When a subsystem must sequentially test several signals coming from the external environment in order to proceed and the failure of anyone of these tests leads to the failure of the operation, the following abstraction technique can be defined. If the different signals are generated by entities which have not been specified, because they belong to the free global environment of the previous section, the actions corresponding to single operations of testing may be modeled as a non-deterministic choice between the success and the failure of the sequence of tests.

Let us consider, as an example, the case in which a system executes sequentially a test on three different signals represented by the automaton in Fig. 3 (a). The failure of any test leads to the same state C; the success of all the tests leads to the state B. Applying the above abstraction technique, we generate the abstract automaton in Fig. 3 (b), in which the sequential tests are substituted by a simple abstract test which can fail, leading to the state C, otherwise leading to the success state B.

This abstraction technique was used both for LCC and SH_ROUTE subsystems any time actions related to entities like the "switch lock" entity, which has not been modeled in the specification, were met. We note that this abstraction technique does not limit the possibility of later refinements of the specification. Suppose that, as the work proceeds, we detect the need of including the detailed specification of a real entity in the model of the system. Since the specification is a process and the real entity is modeled as a process itself, the problem can be solved by defining a simple process P which is in charge of handling the interaction between the two processes (the process corresponding to the specification and the process corresponding to the real entity) by using the actions: "ver_signals" and "not_ver_signals".

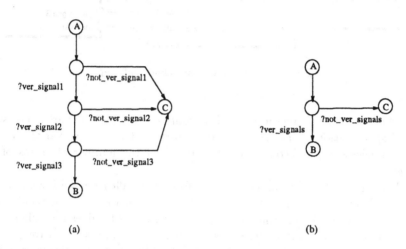

(a)   (b)

Fig. 3. (a) A fragment of a general operation (b) The fragment after the application of the abstraction technique.

Let us assume we add the entities related to the previous signals 1, 2 and 3 and let E be the box containing the specification of the behavior of such entities, while S represents the net corresponding to the specification of the system. We obtain the net shown in Fig. 4.

We note that, since the module P is strictly synchronized with the other processes of the specification, the price we pay in terms of number of states with respect to the solution which directly includes the entity in the specification is limited.

Safety requirements are preserved by this kind of abstraction because all the possible behaviors of the system are implicitly expressed by taking into account the non-deterministic choice between the success or the failure of the test shown in Fig. 3 (b).

3.3 Static configuration parameters

The original semi-formal specification of the LCC takes into account some *attributes* that can be considered as static configuration parameters and describe the particular type of level crossing entity that is controlled; a typical attribute

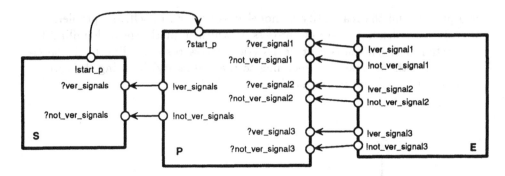

Fig. 4. The net after the refinement step.

says whether the level crossing is on the mainline or on a parking area. The semi-formal specification considers these attributes as if they were variables. This would unnecessarily contribute to the growth of the number of states of the model.

Therefore, in the development of the formal specification we have not considered all the attributes, but rather we have modeled just the particular configuration of level crossing that we were interested in. This does not rule out the possibility of proving safety properties: after all, taking into account the possible attribute combinations, there are at most eight different configurations of a level crossing. If we want to prove that a safety property is satisfied in all possible configurations, we just repeat (at most eight times) the generation of the model and the verification of the safety properties.

4   Conclusions

The purpose of the pilot project was to assess the use of formal methods and associated tools inside the Ansaldo development methodology. In particular, it was recognized that the introduction of formal methods could be fruitful in the validation of the interactions between system components. In this respect, the result of this project was positive. Indeed some safety requirements, that guarantee the correct behavior of the interactions between the interlocking logic components, were satisfied by the associated global model.

One of the expected critical point of the introduction of formal methods inside the industrial methodology was the passage from the semi-formal specification of the interlocking logic to its formal description. Indeed, the translation from the original, semi–formal level crossing control specification to its formal specification was made initially with some difficulties, mainly due to the use of two different languages: railway and formalist. These initial communication problems between the two groups involved in the project (the industrial staff and the academic group) disappeared once the two groups became acquainted

Table 1. Project scheduling

Phase		man days
1.Translation from	LCC, 1st version	24
the semi-formal specification	LCC, 2nd version	4
to the formal specification	LCC, 3rd version	10
	SH_ROUTE	8
2. Global model generation		12
3. Verification of safety requirements		6
Final Revision, including refinements of SH_ROUTE specification		10
Organization, documentation, meetings		12
	Total	86

with each other languages and techniques. The second process (i.e., the shunting route) was thus much quicker to formalize. This is evident considering the resulting project schedule shown in Table 1.

The other main interest of this project was the application of tools to support the formal specification and verification process. Previously, JACK was successfully tested on small case studies. The experience reported in this paper was the first industrial use of this environment.

The assessment of the used methods and tools has revealed the following good scores:

- The verification tools have been effectively usable for the verification of the required safety characteristics.
- Due to the good user-interface of JACK the tools are usable also by industrial staff, not particularly trained in formal methods.
- The specification method that underlies the use of JACK, that is the use of finite-state models, has proved from one side viable in this domain of application, in which the amount of data on which the model is based is very limited; from the other side, it has been well-accepted by the industrial staff, already trained to think in terms of automata.
- Abstraction techniques were used with success; in fact any single safety requirement was related to few subsystems, each of which can be modeled with a reduced number of states. Since the number of states of the global model is limited by the product of the number of states of the component subsystems, we produced submodels in a size range well accepted by verification tools. This was possible because the modeled CBI system has the following characteristics:
  - The system is composed of a number of subsystems, each devoted to the control of a physical or logical entity (such as level crossing, pointworks or shunting route control). The interactions among entities develop along

the spatial contiguity of the controlled physical entities. So, the satisfaction of a safety requirement will interest only adjacent subsystems.

- Each subsystem can be modeled with a reduced number of states. In fact, this happens if the space of data values is restricted. A subsystem is related to the different states that the controlled physical entity can assume, and such entities exhibit a discrete behavior, rather than a continuous behavior which requires a large amount of different values to be represented.

We claim that this approach can be successfully applied to all those complex systems that share the above two characteristics. Further work in this direction will concentrate on the generalization of the application of our formal validation approach to other classes of systems, and on the comparison and integration of this approach with other methods based on the use of abstraction techniques to reduce the number of states of the system on which to apply model checking algorithms [8, 19].

Anyway, stronger tool support is needed; the capacity of the tools, in terms of number of states that can be handled, has proved to be still low. This was due to the actual memory limitation of the hardware used in this experiment and to the explicit representation of the state space of the global model used by AMC .

In this respect, a new version of the AMC model checker based on Binary Decision Diagrams (BDDs) is planned to join the JACK environment quite soon, in order to be able to handle larger specifications. In fact, verification tools based on the representation of the automata by means of BDDs are able to deal with automata with a number of states several order of magnitude larger than other representations [6].

References

1. A. Anselmi, C. Bernardeschi, A. Fantechi, S. Gnesi, S. Larosa, G. Mongardi, F. Torielli. An experience in formal verification of safety properties of a railway signalling control system, in *Proceedings of the SAFECOMP'95 Conference*, Belgirate, Springer - Verlag, 1995, pp. 474-488.
2. Bowen, J.P., Hinchey, M.G, Seven More Myths of Formal Methods, *IEEE Software*,12, July 1995, pp. 34-41.
3. A. Bouali, S. Gnesi, S. Larosa. The integration Project for the JACK Environment. *Bulletin of the EATCS*, n.54, October 1994, pp.207-223.
4. Boudol, G Notes on Algebraic Calculi of Processes. *Notes on Algebraic Calculi of Processes*, NATO ASI Series F13, 1985.
5. G. Bruns. A Case Study in safety Critical Design. *Workshop on Computer Aided Verification*, Lecture Notes in Computer Science 663, Springer-Verlag, 1992, pp. 213-224.
6. J. R. Burch, E.M. Clarke, K. L. McMillan, D. L. Dill, L. J. Hwang. Symbolic model checking: 10^{20} states and beyond. *Information and Computation* 98(2), June 1992, pp. 142-270.

7. E.M. Clarke, E.A. Emerson, A.P. Sistla. Automatic Verification of Finite State Concurrent Systems using Temporal Logic Specifications. *ACM Transaction on Programming Languages and Systems*, vol.8, n. 2, 1986, pp. 244-263.

8. E.M. Clarke, O. Grumberg, D.E. Long. Model Checking and Abstraction. *ACM Toplas* 16(5), 1994, pp. 1512-1542.

9. Railway Applications: Software for Railway Control and Protection Systems. CEN-ELEC draft CLC/SC9XA/WG1 (sec) 78, February 1994.

10. C. Da Silva, B. Dehbonei, F. Mejia. Formal Specification in the Development of Industrial Applications: Subway Speed Control System. *Formal Description Techniques*, V (C-10) M. Diaz and R. Groz (Editors) Elsevier Science Publishers B, V, (North-Holland), 1993.

11. R. De Nicola, A. Fantechi, S. Gnesi, G. Ristori. An Action-based Framework for Verifying Logical and Behavioural Properties of Concurrent Systems. *Computer Networks and ISDN Systems*, vol. 25 (7), Elsevier Science Publishers B.V. (North-Holland), 1993, pp. 761-778.

12. R. De Nicola, F.W. Vaandrager. Actions versus State Based Logics for Transition Systems. In *Proc. Ecole de Printemps on Semantics of Concurrency*, Lecture Notes in Computer Science vol. 469, Springer, Berlin, 1990, pp. 407-419.

13. E.A. Emerson, J.Y. Halpern. Decision procedures and expressiveness in the temporal logic of branching time. *Journal of computer and system sciences*, **30**, pp. 1-24.

14. S. Fisher, A. Scholz, D. Taubner. Verification in Process Algebra of the Distributed Control of Track Vehicles - A Case Study. *Journal of Formal Methods in System Design*, Kluwer Academic Publishers, February 1994.

15. V. Hartonas-Garmhausen, T. Kurfess, E.M. Clarke, D. Long. Automatic verification of Industrial Designs. *Workshop on Industrial-Strength Formal Specification Techniques*, Boca Raton, Florida, April 1995.

16. C.A.R. Hoare. *Communicating Sequential Processes* Prentice Hall Int., London, 1985.

17. J.C. Laprie (Ed.). *Dependability: Basic Concepts and Terminology*. Dependable Computing and Fault-Tolerant Systems, vol. 5, Springer-Verlag, 1992.

18. Z. Manna, A. Pnueli. The Temporal Logic of Reactive and Concurrent Systems - Specification. Springer-Verlag, 1992.

19. K.L. McMillan. Symbolic Model Checking: An approach to the State Explosion Problem. Kluwer Academic Publisher, 1993.

20. R. Milner. Communication and Concurrency. Prentice Hall, 1989.

21. G. Mongardi. Dependable Computing for Railway Control Systems, in *Dependable Computing for Critical Applications 3*, Dependable Computing and Fault-Tolerant Systems 8, Springer-Verlag, 1992, pp. 255-277.

Session 8

Replication and Distribution

Chair: Gilles Muller, IRISA, France

Enhancing Dependability of Cooperative Applications in Partitionable Environments *

François J.N. Cosquer[1], Pedro Antunes[1] and Paulo Veríssimo[2]

[1] IST***-INESC[†]
[2] FC/UL[‡]

Abstract. *This paper presents a pragmatic approach to providing partition processing system support for cooperative applications. A method for specifying and programming application-level partition processing strategies is described. The system support is based on a partition typing mechanism which allows the application programmer to model the relative importance of partitions. This is combined with a split/merge rules configuration table through which the partition processing strategy is defined. In the context of cooperative application semantics, our approach combines the correctness of the pessimistic, and the availability of the optimistic approaches for data management in partitionable environments. The paper focuses on the practical issues linked with, firstly, the specification, and secondly, the support at runtime, of the partition processing strategies. This approach is relevant in the context of large-scale asynchronous distributed systems such as the Internet, which, as a result of current technology and topology, are inevitably prone to partitions. Examples are given, illustrating how the partition support is used and combined with new feedback techniques in order to implement more robust cooperative environments.*

Keywords: *Fault-Tolerance, Cooperative Applications, Tool, Configuration, Interconnected Networks.*

1 Motivation

The growth of interconnected networks has enabled the development of a wide range of distributed applications. Among the most promising are those dealing with multi-user collaboration, usually referred to as Computer Supported Cooperative Work (CSCW) or groupware. Cooperative applications include tools as varied as shared-drawing, concurrent engineering, teleconferencing, etc. These

* This work was partially supported by the CEC, through Esprit Project BR 6360 Broadcast and CaberNet, Basic Research Network of Excellence 6361 in Distributed Computing Systems. E-mail of the authors: fjnc@inesc.pt, paa@inesc.pt, pjv@di.fc.ul.pt.
*** Instituto Superior Técnico - Technical University of Lisboa.
† Instituto de Engenharia de Sistemas e Computadores, R. Alves Redol, 9 - 6° - 1000 Lisboa - Portugal, Tel.+351-1-3100000.
‡ Faculdade de Ciências da Universidade de Lisboa, C5 Campo Grande, 1700 Lisboa - Portugal.

cooperative tools have a multitude of application fields including education, business, medicine, etc.

Cooperative applications represent a high demand for large-scale distributed systems because they lessen the need for a collection of people to commute to a single location. Furthermore, the widespread existence of simple cooperative tools has broken the physical distance barrier and enabled daily interactions over large distances. However, large-scale communication infrastructures suffer from problems inherent to the nature of the current technology, topology, and, of course, sheer dimension and distance. One obvious problem is that they are prone to partitioning, meaning that sites may occasionally be unable to communicate with each other. Furthermore, inaccurate failure detection due to the high variance and unpredictability of communication delays may also lead to what are known as "virtual partitions"[1].

These problems not only represent an obstacle to the development of new cooperative applications, but also, to a wider use of existing applications. The symptoms they generate burn down to one factor: dependability impairments. In fact, network partitioning hinders the correct execution of any application that shares state, be it messages or data. The major sources of unreliability are: blocking upon partitions, and/or inconsistency upon uncontrolled mergers.

Surprisingly, having surveyed a number of groupware applications and platforms[2], we have found little or no concern for scaling and fault-tolerance issues in general. Most applications are based on the "absence of partitions" assumption[1] which, we believe, is not justified when targeting current asynchronous distributed systems. There exist a number of partition processing techniques which have been developed for database and filesystem applications[3, 4]. Such techniques address data consistency and availability issues. Two extreme approaches for these techniques are the *pessimistic* approach and the *optimistic* approach. The former trades availability for correctness while the latter allows availability of data but might have to resolve conflicts upon reconnection.

These techniques in their current form do not solve all problems of collaboration-oriented applications. Cooperative applications require a notion of what is usually referred to as *collaboration awareness* at all levels, hence the need for a notion of partition at the programming level. *Partition support*, as used in this text, means preserving the notions of control, coordination and cooperation.

In [5], we have pointed out the role of the functionality provided by group-oriented systems and the requirements of groupware applications. Early group-oriented systems, like Isis[6], only allow a majority partition to make progress, minority partitions having to abort. Recent membership protocols are promising because they integrate the notion of multiple partitions [7, 8].

Another motivation for our work came from connectivity statistics of the Internet, the largest distributed computing infrastructure today. It was observed on some links that 95% of partitions do not last on average more than a few minutes[6], a duration which is too high to be ignored and too low to reschedule the cooperative session taking place.

---

[6] From monthly statistics reports of the T3 backbone in 1994.

The above considerations have led us to believe that dependability of cooperative applications would highly benefit from the underlying system support if the latter could:

- Allow multiple partitions to operate simultaneously.
- Control progress in each partition, according to a correctness specification.
- Provide connectivity feedback clues to users.

The first two objectives are normally antagonistic: they correspond respectively to the aforementioned optimistic and pessimistic policies. The paper describes an approach for attaining both objectives and thus, contributes to bridging the gap between application requirements and current limitations of large-scale asynchronous computing systems.

In a brief explanation, we abandon the primary-partition paradigm, whose liveness— and thus availability— can be compromised in a large-scale setting, since several partitions form many often, not rarely none of them being primary. In that sense, our approach could be termed optimistic. However, we exploit the conjunction of two attributes, namely: the low rate of conflict occurrence due to collaboration awareness superimposed on raw data operations; and the assumption of short-lived connectivity disruptions. In consequence, we are capable of defining a semantics that yields the global correctness typical of pessimistic approaches, whereas we achieve a virtually non-blocking operation, as seen in optimistic approaches. In that sense, we termed our approach *pragmatic* partition processing. At runtime, the user is aware of the occurrence of partitioning. However, the system support allows seamless transitions between the various connectivity situations. By allowing multiple partitions to operate simultaneously, the system support enables applications to proceed during transient disruptions in connectivity according to the specified semantics. The third objective, of connectivity feedback, is achieved through the instrumentation (e.g. failure detection) we put in place to help materialize our pragmatic semantics. The interested reader will find a more detailed description in [9]. We believe this work to be an innovative experiment in distributed applications in general, and in groupware system support in particular.

The paper is organized as follows. Section 2 briefly presents the membership problem and how partitions are dealt with in group-oriented systems. Section 3 presents NAVCOOP, a groupware platform which constitutes the framework for the work presented in this paper. It describes PSS, the Partition Support Service, the NAVCOOP module which implements the partition processing support. Section 4 illustrates the applications and our current experience with PSS. Section 5 presents the concluding remarks.

2 Group-Oriented Systems and Partitions

Group-oriented systems can be seen as providing two main services:

- a *membership service* which maintains consistent information, called the *view*, about which processes are involved in a distributed computation at any given time. The membership protocol forces the system to conform with connectivity information provided by what is referred to as the *Failure Detector* (FD).

- a *multicast service* which provides various semantics of group communication, such as for example, causal and total ordered multicast[10, 11].

A particular combination of the two services implements what is usually known as Virtual Synchrony (VS)[6]. However, group-oriented systems suffer from the fact that failure detectors (FD) are unreliable due to asynchronism in the underlying system (a result whose foundation lies in the FLP impossibility result[12]). In practice, this has been partially overcome by early systems such as Isis, whose FD is tuned to make few mistakes in Local Area Network (LAN) environments. However, such systems can still partition in case of erroneous suspicions or broken communication links: they implement what is known as the primary partition strategy. The system identifies at most one partition where some pre-defined condition holds (usually, the majority of processes) and prevents progress in any other partition by forcing processes to leave the system.

The primary partition offers a simple, yet efficient, solution to a wide range of distributed applications[13]. This is especially true in LAN environments because partitions are rare events. However, the primary partition approach implements a behavior which does not satisfy the initial requirements presented in Section 1. For example, the system might block as long as the majority condition is not satisfied. Furthermore, the system forces members of minority partitions to quit the application.

Recently, new membership protocols have been developed which take into consideration the problems associated with large-scale distributed systems. This means that the membership service will deliver (concurrent) views in different partitions. In[7], a protocol which allows multiple partitions to operate simultaneously offers a service referred to as *strong-partial membership*. Informally, this means that the service guarantees that, at any time in the system, concurrent views are non-intersecting. Partial membership services are being implemented in group-oriented systems like Horus[14], Totem[15] and Transis[16]. Finally, [17] proposes a fully configurable membership protocol. The customized membership service is built by composing separate modules, each implementing some abstract property.

Some systems try to preserve the consistency properties of virtual synchrony at low level, across partitions. This is the case with the work on extended virtual synchrony[18]. Our research effort on groupware support has been directed towards relying on a *partial membership service* at the communication level, ensuring virtual synchrony as the baseline communication paradigm. Consistency in the presence of partitions is achieved by supplying a semantics of partition to the programmer.

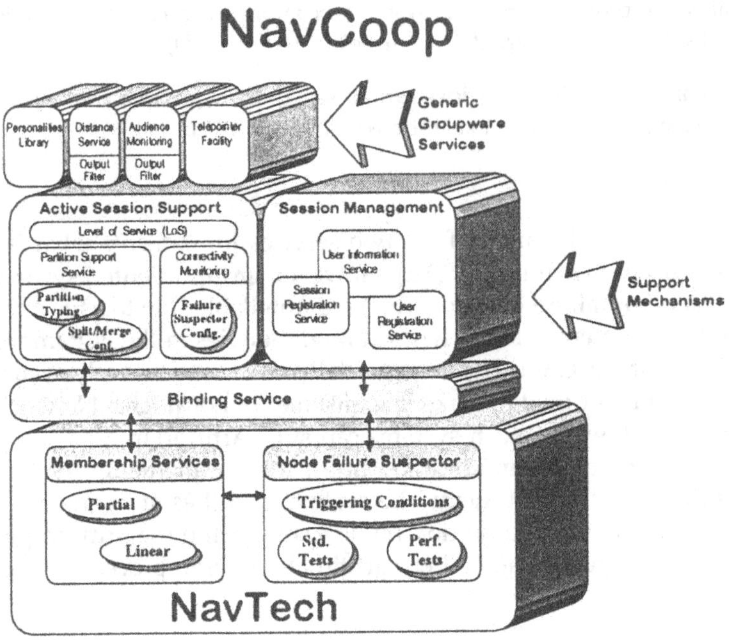

NavCoop

NavTech

Fig. 1. NAVCOOP functional architecture

3 The NAVCOOP Partition Support Service

3.1 NAVCOOP Overview

NAVCOOP is a groupware platform developed at INESC which is intended to provide support mechanisms and a set of generic groupware services dedicated to large-scale networks.

NAVCOOP is based on a group-oriented communication architecture as shown in Figure 1. An earlier phase of our work emphasized the need for configurable failure suspectors[9]. More recently, efforts have been devoted to programming and runtime support mechanisms for partition processing. PSS, Partition Support Service, is the NAVCOOP module which provides support for partition processing. PSS is based on two concepts: partition levels and the associated split/merge rules configuration interface.

3.2 Terminology and System Considerations

In order to avoid possible confusions, we clarify below the key concepts involved with the Partition Support Service.

- *Group and sub-group*: a group is a set of participants involved in a computation. A sub-group is a sub-set of the participants in a group originated by

the splitting of a group (typically due to a partition). The semantics chosen
for the membership service implies that concurrent sub-groups are disjoint.
- *Partition:* designates a system event that leads to the splitting of a group in
two or more sub-groups.

PSS is based on the following assumptions about the underlying system.

- *Fault-coverage:* the targeted fault-coverage of PSS are link failures. Links may
  fail by not delivering data (omission failure). The intention is to cover temporary disruption in connectivity between nodes (i.e. recoverable). Process
  crashes may be masked using traditional redundancy techniques[19, 20].
- *Dynamic join and leave operations:* the underlying group-communication sub-
  system allows voluntary "join and leave" operations. The system also differentiates those operations from failure suspicions which lead to the splitting
  of the group of processes involved in a computation into sub-groups.

3.3 Levels and Typing

Users interested in participating in a cooperative application first have to register their intention. The list of registered users will be the basis for partition
processing support. It is referred to as the *initial* group as it corresponds to a
partition-free set-up.

The NAVCOOP PSS implements *levels*. The levels, $[1, 2, ..., n]$, reflect the relative importance of the group/sub-groups. Level 1 corresponds to the *initial*
group, level 2 to the second most important, and so forth. The depth, n, is dic-
tated by the needs of the application, as will become clearer ahead. Each level
is specified by means of type and composition definitions:

Level(l, ⟨ *type, composition* ⟩) - specification of the *type* and *composition* of
the group/sub-group of level l.

Typing applies the idea of social role or *role*, a concept found in cooperative applications to model the relative importance of each user. The role is
materialized by two variables: the *identity* of a participant, and its *weight*[7]. In
PSS, weight values reflect the importance of users, both during the normal operation of a cooperative session, and during partitions. Identities are used to
designate group/sub-groups containing given participants. The *composition* of
a group/sub-group $\mathcal{G}$ is defined by its m participants p_i, and the sum of the individual weights $w(p_i)$. The total sum of weights in the *initial* group is referred to
as $\mathcal{W}_{ini}$. The three resulting *type* and *composition* specifications are listed below.

- **Quorum group/sub-group:** specifies that a group/sub-group comprises a
  known sum of weights. A group/sub-group $\mathcal{G}$ is defined as a quorum Q
  group/sub-group iff $[\sum_{i=1}^{m} w(p_i) > Q]$. Q is a pre-defined value.
- **Designated group/sub-group:** specifies that a group/sub-group comprises
  a set of known user(s). A group/sub-group $\mathcal{G}$ is defined as a designated

---

[7] Weights have also been proposed in [21] for maintaining replicated data.

D group/sub-group iff $[D \subseteq \mathcal{G}]$. D is a pre-defined set of participants $\{p_j, ..., p_u\}$.

- **Combined group/sub-group**: specifies that a group/sub-group comprises a known sum of weights Q and a set of designated user(s) D. A group/sub-group $\mathcal{G}$ is defined as a combined $Q - D$ group/sub-group iff $[\sum_{i=1}^{m} w(p_i) > Q \wedge D \subseteq \mathcal{G}]$. Q is a pre-defined value. D is a pre-defined set of participants $\{p_j, ..., p_u\}$.

Formally speaking, the importance of group/sub-groups, expressed by the levels, is translated into progress specifications:

Progress$(l, \langle$ *progress* $\rangle)$ - specification of the *progress* of participants in a level l group/sub-group.

The main idea behind decreasing importance is to capture a degradation of the level of activity a participant is allowed to have, as it gets further away from the initial group of participants. In classical approaches, progress specifications are essentially binary: simply allowing all reads and writes (as in a primary partition), or blocking all activity (as in a minority partition). With the mechanisms we introduced however, we can define richer semantics, such as proceeding *up-to* a certain application phase, or execute *only* a subset of actions.

As soon as the application starts running, the Level(l) is evaluated in increasing order of l ($1 \rightarrow$n), to determine which level does a given group/sub-group belong to. Registered users start in the level corresponding to their current connectivity, obeying the relevant semantics Progress(l).

It is up to the application programmer to define the level depth n, and to make the several Level(l) and Progress(l) specifications. These mechanisms are complemented by a configuration interface called the split/merge rules table, which allows the programmer to specify how the application should respond to a partition event at runtime.

3.4 Split/Merge rules configuration table

When the application is running, the group communication subsystem forwards *views* to the NavCoop platform from which the new level is evaluated. The NavCoop level event can be described as one of the following:

$E_{downgrade(k)}$: The current level was decremented by k levels.
$E_{upgrade(k)}$:   The current level was incremented by k levels.

To each of those events corresponds an application level rule referred to as *split/merge rule*. The application programmer defines the code corresponding to each rule as a way to implement the desired behavior. The split/merge functions are presented in Table 1. The number of rules to be defined for a level depth of n is $n * (n - 1)$. This number might appear high at first glance, but in practice a number of the functions will be identical and/or share code. In any case, there will always be a tradeoff involved between the programming complexity of the support, and the functionality enhancement provided to the users at runtime. However, the services provided by a groupware platform such as NAVCOOP may drastically simplify the application programmer's task in what concerns dependability in face of partitions.

Levels	Transition event	
	$E_{downgrade(k)}$	$E_{upgrade(k)}$
1	func($split_{1\to2}$) func($split_{1\to3}$) . func($split_{1\to n}$)	not applicable
2	func($split_{2\to3}$) . func($split_{2\to n}$)	func($merge_{2\to1}$)
.	.	.
n	not applicable	func($merge_{n\to1}$) func($merge_{n\to2}$) . func($merge_{n\to n}$)

Table 1. Split and Merge rules table

3.5 Current Status

NAVCOOP is based on the NAVTECH communication subsystem. Following the xAMp protocol suite[22], NAVTECH is a new group-oriented communication subsystem developed at INESC which is intended to support the development of reliable applications over large-scale networks[23].

The current prototype of NAVCOOP was developed using Horus-based virtual synchrony[14], NAVTECH configurable failure suspector and abstract network layer. NAVCOOP is implemented in C, uses the OSF Motif toolkit, and runs over a network of UNIX workstations. NAVCOOP mechanisms and the Horus/NAVTECH protocols run in the same Unix process.

4 Applications and Experience

Terminology. This work bearing relationship with two research fields that use the same words with different meanings, we are left in the uncomfortable position of having to make a differentiation. Since we have already used "synchronous" and "asynchronous" with the traditional meaning taken in the distributed systems community— whether time bounds exist and are known, or otherwise— we will adopt other terms for synchronous and asynchronous co-operation as used by the CSCW community. Without any attempt to create a new terminology, we will use in this paper "synchronized" and "non-synchronized", when referring to operations performed simultaneously (i.e at the same time) or independently (i.e at different time) by users.

We present below two examples which illustrate the benefits of the NAV-COOP PSS. The first example illustrates how well-accepted groupware artifacts used for synchronized cooperation can be modified for providing a partition-resilient behavior. The second example briefly relates our experience with a "same time/different place" Group Decision Support System showing how partition support can be integrated in already existing applications.

4.1 Telepointer facility

When designing the NAVCOOP generic services (see Figure 1), we studied and experimented the way of incorporating feedback in various building blocks. In order to further improve the level of support at runtime, we explored how connectivity and partition level information could be integrated in existing artifacts. The idea consisted of combining the typing information provided by the PSS with standard cooperative modules using new feedback techniques for improving group awareness. To illustrate our claim we have selected here a mechanism frequently used during synchronized cooperative sessions: the *telepointer*, which is used for gesture support.

A telepointer is a shared graphical entity which is manipulated by one participant at a time in order to point or get attention to a specific area or item of the shared workspace. Telepointer facilities are usually provided by many synchronized cooperative applications. The telepointer usually assumes that position, movements and timing of the telepointer are shared by all users. The aim is to make the telepointing mechanism rich enough to express a user's intentions to the whole group.

The basic design problem we address concerns the implementation of a WYSIWIS paradigm (What You See Is What I See) in presence of long com-munication delays which may eventually lead to partition. Traditional straight-forward implementations suffer from the underlying system limitations. The contradiction between users' expectations and system limitations results in lost of shared context and ambiguity.

The principles adopted for the telepointer are illustrated in Figure 2 consist of the following three steps.

1. The first step avoids flooding the network with too many messages. The telepointer movement is recorded until the user stops. The recorded movement is then dis-tributed to other participants in one single message.
2. In the second step, when each participant's shared space receives a recording, it executes a playback, i.e., replays the movement. Furthermore it broadcasts an ac-knowledgement message to the group informing that the operation is completed.
3. In the third step, we use the count of feedback messages from the group participants to inform the telepointer's user of the current shared context. The feedback infor-

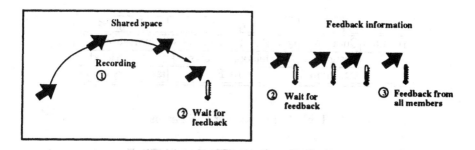

Fig. 2. The Telepointer

mation is displayed using a meter located next to the telepointer (see right part of Figure 2).

After recording a gesture, the user should refrain from moving the telepointer until knowing that all participants have replayed the gesture. This information is provided by the meter icon. After the meter goes full, the user is sure that all participants have seen the telepointer movement. This functionality was implemented using the communication service with acknowledged message deliveries.

The design problem related to partitions is to define which degree of telepointer semantics it is possible to sustain during a partition. Our strategy is to proceed with telepointer usage *but* to inform users that not all members will be aware of the recorded gestures. The functionality of the telepointer is maintained in partition mode but the participants are notified that not all original group members are participating. We have defined a generic scenario in which there exists a unique *major* sub-group and possibly many *minor* sub-groups.

1. A *major* sub-group holds the telepointer owner and therefore sustains the telepointer semantics to reachable members;
2. A *minor* sub-group which does not hold the telepointer owner. A *temporary* telepointer owner is designated in order to preserve *localized* telepointer semantics.

The corresponding levels were defined using PSS and are given in Table 2. Recall that levels are evaluated in increasing order $[1 \rightarrow n]$. The default policy based on this information allows each sub-group to possess its own telepointer so as to preserve animation during partition mode. The users are immediately aware of the situation by seeing a shadowed telepointer. This is illustrated in the top half of Figure 3. This Figure also shows that the telepointer is displayed differently to owners/not owners. Also note that, if excluded participants have not crashed, they also have created their sub-group and entered into partition mode. It was decided to implement three different graphical aspects for telepointer owner depending on the level (black for *initial,* black shaded grey for *major* and grey shaded black for *minor*). For not owners, the telepointers is displayed in white for the *initial* group and shaded grey in both the *major* and *minor* sub-groups.

Level	Type	Composition	Progress
1-initial	Quorum	$Q = W_{ini}$ (all reg. users)	unrestricted
2	Designated	$D =\{$telepointer owner$\}$	unrestricted
3	Designated	TRUE	temporary owner

Table 2. Telepointer PSS Levels

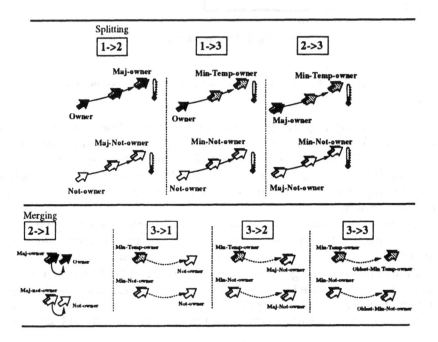

Fig. 3. Partition mode feedback

When participants who were excluded from the *major* sub-group become reachable again, the system will terminate the partition mode associated with the *minor* sub-group. The system merges and eliminates any condition local to *minor* sub-groups. We defined in Table 3 the different merge functions that may occur. We detail below the various merge cases (see bottom half of Figure 3.

- 2 → 1: corresponds to the *major* sub-group merging back to the *initial* group.
  - The owner: the telepointer owner is a user in the major sub-group and the system decides that it will continue to own it. The telepointer regains its original graphical aspect and remain in same location.
  - Not owner: for all other users who are not owner of the telepointer, the telepointer just regain its graphical aspect.
- 3 → 1: corresponds to a *minor* sub-group merging back to the *initial* group.
  - The owner: the temporary telepointer owner of the *minor* sub-group looses its privilege and the graphical aspect is changed back to a not owner telepointer.

If the temporary telepointer had been used it moves (animation) to the new owner's telepointer location.

- Not owner: the telepointer just regain its original graphical aspect with a possible animation back to the new owner's telepointer location.

- 3 → 2: corresponds to a *minor* sub-group merging to the *major* sub-group.

  - The telepointer owner: the telepointer was owned by a user in a *minor* sub-group. The system will give the telepointer to the owner in the *major* sub-group. The telepointer changes its aspect and moves (animation) to the other participant's telepointer location.
  - Not owner: the telepointer keep the same graphical aspect with a possible animation to the current *major* sub-group owner position.

- 3 → 3: corresponds to 2 *minor* sub-groups merging.

  - The telepointer owner: The system will give the telepointer to the oldest owner of the 2 *minor* sub-groups.
  - Not owner: the telepointer keeps the same graphical aspect with a possible animation to the current selected sub-group owner position.

	Transition event	
Levels	$E_{downgrade(k)}$	$E_{upgrade(k)}$
1	$\text{func}(split_{1 \to 2})$ { Shadow telepointer() } $\text{func}(split_{1 \to 3})$ { Designate temporary owner() Owner record, others playback() Shadow telepointer() }	
2	$\text{func}(split_{2 \to 3})$ { Designate temporary owner() Owner record, others playback() Shadow telepointer() }	$\text{func}(merge_{2 \to 1})$ { Owner record, others playback() Remove shadow() }
3		$\text{func}(merge_{3 \to 1})$ { Disable temporary owner() Move to owner's position() Remove shadow() } $\text{func}(merge_{3 \to 2})$ { Disable temporary owner() Move to owner's position() Remove shadow() } $\text{func}(merge_{3 \to 3})$ { Change temporary owner() Move to owner's position() }

Table 3. Split and Merge rules table

In our telepointer implementation, users are aware of how a synchronized operation is being carried out. This functionality is complemented by the audience monitoring service which informs the participant of the current composition of his/her group/sub-group.

4.2 The NGTool Experiment

Application Overview NGTool is a Group Decision Support System (GDSS) which runs on Unix workstations over the Internet and uses X Windows and the OSF Motif toolkit. The NGTool supports same time/different place meetings. The tool provides synchronized operations over a display space shared by 5/6 users, one of which known as the *moderator*. The functionality of the NGTool is described in [24, 25]. The NGTool was ported to the NAVCOOP PSS as depicted in Figure 4. We will illustrate the implemented functionality for a particular meeting situation.

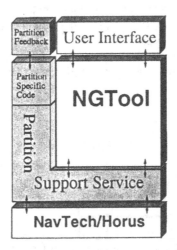

Fig. 4. Porting NGTool to NAVCOOP

Figure 5 shows screen dumps of the NGTool of two users, a participant on the left and the moderator on the right, in the phase when they are generating and proposing ideas. The ideas are generated (i.e. written down on a text field) in a private space which is on the screen's left hand side. Ideas are represented by a small electric lamp. To propose an idea to the participants of the meeting, the user must drag the idea from the private space to the shared space: the screen's right hand side. To mediate this operation the NGTool provides a graphical entity named teleassistant ("switched-on" electric lamp). The teleassistant controls concurrent accesses to the shared space and coordinates the actions of the moderator and other users. Since the teleassistant provides feedback to all users over these events, it is a natural origin for delivering information about partitions.

Adding Partition Functionality When defining the partition processing strategy, a preliminary study led us to consider the following aspects:

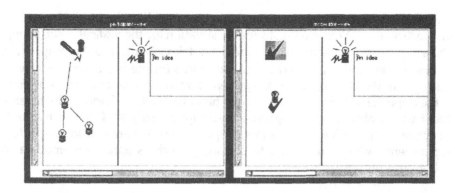

Fig. 5. The NGTool windows

- *Relative importance of sub-groups:* due to the moderated aspect of the NGTool session it was decided to discriminate two types of sub-groups. Those are referred to as *moderated* and *non-moderated* depending on whether the sub-group includes the moderator.
- *Temporal factor:* we identified two cases depending on the time-frame of the connectivity disruption. This is because the NGTool session goes through different phases. As we will discuss below this has consequences on the merging phase and rules definition.

The NGTool was modified such that when a partition occurs both individual and group work can proceed. We describe here the strategy adopted during the phase of generating and proposing ideas. As explained in Section 3, the first task is to define the levels (see Table 4). This definition means that the application will only differentiate two kinds of progress depending on the presence of the moderator. The NGTool designer made this decision since the application is strongly coordinated by the moderator. This results in the fact that moderated sub-group will always have higher privileges than non-moderated sub-groups.

Level	Type	Composition	Progress
1-initial	Quorum	$Q = W_{ini}$ (all reg. users)	unrestricted
2 *(moderated)*	Designated	$D =\{$moderator$\}$	unrestricted
3 *(non-moderated)*	Designated	TRUE	same phase

Table 4. NGTool PSS Partitions Levels

When a partition occurs, the sub-group which includes the moderator is allowed to proceed work as if no partition had occurred, i.e. users can generate and propose ideas. However, this sub-group is visually informed of the partition occurrence, in order to be aware that not all of the original members are participating. Figure 6 illustrates the situation for the *moderated* sub-group, showing a small two-hands icon under the teleassistant. A sub-group which looses moderation is allowed to generate ideas (in the users' private spaces) The graphical partition feedback representation in the *non-moderated* sub-group is the opposite of the *moderated* i.e. grey hand with white shadow. However in order to comply with the original (non-computerized) NGT semantics, users in *non-moderated* sub-groups cannot propose ideas. We are considering future experiments with more optimistic semantics, such as letting non-moderated sub-groups propose ideas.

Fig. 6. Partition feedback

When the system merges, it is assumed that the moderated sub-group has several ideas in its shared space which are not available to the previously disconnected, non-moderated sub-groups. The merge function must therefore re-synchronize the shared space by delivering the missing ideas to the non-moderated sub-groups.

However, the temporal factor aspect influences the merge functions since the NGTool phase may have changed during the occurrence of the partition. Being isolated from the moderator of the session, members of the non-moderated sub-group(s) cannot change session phase. This means that it is possible that a merge occurs between a *moderated* sub-group and a *non-moderated* sub-group which are not in the same NGTool phase. As a result, the NGTool defined two types of merges depending on the phases of the session of the various sub-groups merging. PSS does not provide support for this kind of conditional merge function (referred to as temporal factor) but only level transition function definition. Therefore, the functionality was implemented as part of the application. This resulted in the configuration presented in Table 5.

The main benefits of using the NavCoop platform for the development of the NGTool come from the approach to *pragmatic* partition processing support. Although levels and split/merge rules must be defined accordingly to the particular semantics of the application, NavCoop PSS allows tackling the problem associated with partitions in a structured and manageable way.

Levels	Transition event	
	$E_{downgrade(k)}$	$E_{upgrade(k)}$
1	$func(split_{1\rightarrow2})$ { Show moderated partition icon() } $func(split_{1\rightarrow3})$ { Disable public teleassistant() Show non-moderated partition icon() }	
2	$func(split_{2\rightarrow3})$ { Disable public teleassistant() Show non-moderated partition icon() }	$func(merge_{2\rightarrow1})$ { Remove partition icon() }
3		$func(merge_{3\rightarrow1})$ { Enable public teleassistant() Check phase changes () Re-synchronize shared space() Remove partition icon() } $func(merge_{3\rightarrow2})$ { Enable public teleassistant() Check phase changes () Re-synchronize shared space() Show moderated partition icon() }

Table 5. Split and Merge rules configuration table

5 Concluding Remarks

The paper presented a method for defining, what we refer to as, *pragmatic* partition processing strategies, exhibiting the correctness of pessimistic, and the availability of optimistic approaches to the management of partitionable applications. Based on a typing mechanism which is combined with a split/merge configuration table, the Partition Support Service has been integrated in the NAVCOOP groupware platform.

The pragmatic partition support approach provides a concrete answer to application designers for tackling situations of temporary deviations from normal operation due to connectivity problems. It is known that these phenomena contribute to the lack of dependability of distributed applications, and of cooperative applications in particular. Observed application blocking and data inconsistency are current symptoms, and they should be addressed by adequate measures to tolerate partition faults. We proposed reconfiguration mechanisms to overcome the transient faults caused by partitions, based on the semantics of cooperative applications, namely, the social roles played by the participants. We believe these results to be innovative, with regard to approaches taken in other fields of work, such as distributed databases. The latter depended on lower level data operation semantics, and were thus less flexible, leading to the pessimistic versus optimistic dichotomy.

Our method forces/helps the application designers to carefully define the importance of participants taking part in a cooperative activity. The configuration process is intended to provide a solution for closely modeling the real-life cooperative activity. The benefits of this approach were illustrated by examples. At the implementation level, this work constitutes an experiment in using group communication systems services for supporting cooperative applications. Our experience shows how partial membership services can be used to enhance cooperative applications support.

Further work is underway to validate our initial results. We need to ensure that the complexity inherent to the various configurations proposed can be partially hidden from the application programmer. For example, we aim at simplifying the rules generation by making this process partially automatic. Overlooking this issue could be detrimental to the use of groupware support technologies.

Acknowledgements: The authors would like to thank Jorge Frazão and Nuno Guimarães, who, besides the authors, contributed to the two demos where the NGTool and NAVCOOP support were demonstrated; Broadcast Open Workshop (Grenoble, July, 1995) and the Cyted-Ritos International Workshop on Groupware (Lisboa, September, 1995). We are also grateful to Carlos Almeida, André Zúquete, David Matos, Susan Tinniswood, Alexandre Lefebvre and Luís Rodrigues for commenting on early versions of this document.

References

1. Aleta Ricciardi, Andre Schiper, and Kenneth Birman. Understanding Partitions and the No Partition Assumption. In *Proceedings of the 4th Workshop on Future Trends of Distributed Computing Systems*, pages 354–360, September 1993.
2. François J.N. Cosquer and Paulo Veríssimo. Survey of Selected Groupware Applications and Supporting Platforms. Technical Report 2nd Year - Vol. 1, BROADCAST, Rua Alves Redol 9-6°, 1000 Lisboa, Portugal, September 1994. (Also available as INESC Report RT-21-94).
3. Hector Garcia-Molina Susan B. Davidson and Dale Skeen. Consistency in partitioned networks. *Computing Surveys*, 17(3):341–370, September 1985.
4. James J. Kistler and M. Satyanarayanan. Disconnected Operation in the Coda File System. *ACM Transactions on Computer Systems*, 10(1):3–25, February 1992.
5. François J.N. Cosquer and Paulo Veríssimo. The Impact of Group Communication Paradigms in Groupware Support. In *Proceedings of the 5th Workshop on Future Trends of Distributed Computing Systems*, Cheju Island,, August 1995.
6. Kenneth P. Birman and Thomas A. Joseph. Exploiting Virtual Synchrony in Distributed Systems. In *11th Symposium on Operating Systems Principles*, pages 123–138, November 1987.
7. A. Shiper and A. Ricciardi. Virtually Synchronous Communication based on a weak failure suspector. In *Proceedings of the 23rd Int. Conf. on Fault Tolerant Computing Systems*, June 1993.
8. Danny Dolev, Dalia Malki, and Ray Strong. An Asynchronous Membership Protocol that Tolerates Partition. Technical report, Institute of Computer Science, The Hebrew University of Jerusalem, Israel, 1995.
9. François J.N. Cosquer, Luís Rodrigues, and Paulo Veríssimo. Using Tailored Failure Suspectors to Support Distributed Cooperative Applications. In *Proceedings of the 7th International Conference on Parallel and Distributed Computing and Systems*, Washington D.C., October 1995.

10. Luís Rodrigues and Paulo Veríssimo. Causal Separators for Large-Scale Multicast Communication. In *Proceedings of the 15th International Conference on Distributed Computing Systems*, June 1995.

11. L. Rodrigues, H. Fonseca, and P. Veríssimo. Totally ordered multicast in large-scale systems. In *Proceedings of the 16th International Conference on Distributed Computing Systems*, pages 503–510, Hong Kong, May 1996. IEEE.

12. M. J. Fischer, N. A. Lynch, and M. S. Paterson. Impossibility of Distributed Consensus with One Faulty Process. *Journal of the Association for Computing Machinery*, 32(2):374–382, April 1985.

13. Kenneth P. Birman and Robbert van Renesse. *Reliable Distributed Computing with the Isis Toolkit*. IEEE Computer Society Press, 1994.

14. R. van Renesse, Ken Birman, Robert Cooper, Brad Glade, and Patrick Stephenson. The Horus System. Technical report, Cornell University, July 1993.

15. Y Amir, L. Moser, P. Melliar-Smith, D. Agarwal, and P. Ciarfella. Fast Message Ordering and Membership Using a Logical Token-Passing Ring. In *Proceedings of the 13th International Conference on Distributed Computing Systems*, pages 551–560, Pittsburgh, Pennsylvania, USA, May 1993.

16. Danny Dolev, Dalia Malki, and Ray Strong. A Framework for Partitionable Membership Service. Technical Report CS95-4, The Hebrew University of Jerusalem, Jerusalem, Israel, 1995.

17. Matti A. Hiltunen and Richard D. Schlichting. A Configurable Membership Service. Technical Report TR 94-37, University of Arizona, Tucson, AZ 85721, December 1994.

18. L.E. Moser, Y. Amir, P.M. Melliar-Smith, and D.A. Argawal. Extended Virtual Synchrony. In *Proceedings of the 14th International Conference on Distributed Computing Systems*, pages 56–65, Poland, June 1994.

19. Flaviu Cristian. Understanding fault-tolerant distributed systems. *Communications of the ACM*, 34(2):56–78, February 1991.

20. D. Powell, editor. *Delta-4 - A Generic Architecture for Dependable Distributed Computing*. ESPRIT Research Reports. Springer Verlag, 1991.

21. David K. Gifford. Weighted Voting for Replicated Data. In *Proceeding of the Symposium on Operating Systems Principles (SOSP)*, pages 150–163, 1979.

22. Luís Rodrigues and Paulo Veríssimo. xAMp: a Multi-primitive Group Communications Service. In *11th Symposium on Reliable Distributed Systems*, pages 112–121, October 1992.

23. Paulo Veríssimo and Luís Rodrigues. The NavTech Large-Scale Distributed Computing Platform. Technical Report RT-95, Broadcast Project, INESC, Rua Alves Redol 9-6°, 1000 Lisboa, Portugal (in preparation).

24. Pedro Antunes and Nuno Guimarães. Structuring Elements for Group Interation. In *Second Conference on Concurrent Engineering, Research and Applications (CE95)*, Washington D.C., August 1995.

25. P. Antunes and N. Guimaraes. NGTool - exploring mechanisms of support to interaction. In *First CYTED-RITOS International Workshop on Groupware CRIWG '5*, Lisboa, Portugal, August 1995. CYTED-RITOS.

Efficient Message Logging
for Uncoordinated Checkpointing Protocols

Achour Mostefaoui and Michel Raynal

IRISA, Campus de Beaulieu
35042 Rennes Cedex, France.
{mostefaoui,raynal}irisa.fr

Abstract. A message is *in-transit* with respect to a global state if its sending is recorded in this global state, while its receipt is not. Checkpointing algorithms have to log such in-transit messages in order to restore the state of channels when a computation has to be resumed from a consistent global state after a failure has occurred. Coordinated checkpointing algorithms log those in-transit messages exactly on stable storage. Because of their lack of synchronization, uncoordinated checkpointing algorithms conservatively log more messages.

This paper presents an uncoordinated checkpointing protocol that logs all in-transit messages and the smallest possible number of non in-transit messages. As a consequence, the protocol saves stable storage space and enables quicker recoveries. An appropriate tracking of message causal dependencies constitutes the core of the protocol.

keywords: Distributed Systems, Backward Recovery, Consistent Global Checkpoints, Optimistic Sender-Based Logging.

1 Introduction

Checkpointing and backward recovery are well-known techniques for providing fault-tolerance in asynchronous systems. During the execution of an application a checkpointing algorithm computes and saves global checkpoints (global states) of the computation on stable storage. When a fault occurs, a backward recovery algorithm restores the computation in the most up to date global checkpoint from which this computation can be resumed.

A global checkpoint is composed of two parts: (1) a local checkpoint (local state) for each application process, and (2) a set of messages (channel state) for each communication channel. Informally, a global checkpoint is consistent if the computation could have passed through it.

A lot of checkpointing algorithms have been defined. They can be divided into two classes according to the way local checkpoints are determined. In the class of *coordinated* algorithms [5, 9, 17], the determination of local checkpoints and the computation of corresponding channel states are synchronized in such a way that the resulting global checkpoints are always consistent.

The main disadvantage of this approach is the added synchronization requiring control messages that can slow down or even freeze the computation for a given duration [9]. Its main advantage is that the last global checkpoint computed (as it is consistent) is the only one that has to be kept in stable storage. Moreover, when a fault occurs, the only work of a backward recovery algorithm consists in installing this global checkpoint and resuming the computation from it.

In the class of *uncoordinated* checkpointing algorithms [2, 6, 7, 8, 19, 21], processes save local checkpoints on stable storage in an independent way. Furthermore, they also log messages on stable storage so that channel states can be determined. When a failure occurs, it is up to the backward recovery algorithm to compute a consistent global state from local checkpoints [18] and messages saved on stable storage. The message logging technique is called *sender-based* (respt. *receiver-based*) if messages are logged by their senders (respt. receivers). Two logging techniques are possible. In the case of *pessimistic* logging, messages are logged on stable storage at the time they are sent (respt. received). This can incur high overhead in failure-free executions as each sending (respt. receiving) entails an additional input/output. This is why optimistic message logging techniques have been developed. In that case, when a message is sent (respt. received), it is saved on a volatile log and this log is saved on stable storage when the process takes a local checkpoint (as all messages are saved, the stable storage contains all in-transit messages).

In this paper we are interested in uncoordinated checkpointing algorithms with optimistic sender-based message logging. We develop a technique allowing a process to save the smallest possible number of volatile log messages on stable storage. This subset is consistent in the sense that it includes all the messages which are in-transit with respect to any consistent global checkpoint from which the computation could be resumed.

This paper is composed of two main parts. Section 2 introduces the model of distributed computations and formally defines the consistency of a global checkpoint. Section 3 presents the checkpointing algorithm.

2 Consistent Global Checkpoints

2.1 Distributed Computations

A distributed program is made up of n sequential local programs which, when executed, can communicate and synchronize only by exchanging messages. A distributed computation describes the execution of a distributed program. The execution of a local program gives rise to a sequential process. Let $P_1, P_2, \ldots, P_n$ be this finite set of processes. We assume that, at run-time, each ordered pair of communicating processes (P_i, P_j) is connected by a reliable and FIFO channel c_{ij} through which P_i can send messages to P_j. Message transmission delays are finite but unpredictable. Process speeds are positive but arbitrary. In other words, the underlying computation model is asynchronous. Processes can fail by crashing, i.e. halting prematurely. The local program associated with P_i can include send, receive and internal statements; some statements can be non-deterministic[1].

Execution of an internal, send or receive statement produces an internal, send or receive event. Let e_i^x be the xth event produced by process P_i. The sequence $h_i = e_i^1 e_i^2 \dots e_i^x \dots$ constitutes the history of P_i. h_i^x denotes the partial history $e_i^1 \dots e_i^x$ of process P_i.

Let H be the set of events produced by a distributed computation. This set is structured as a partial order by Lamport's causal precedence relation [10], denoted "$\rightarrow$" and defined as follows:

$e_i^x \rightarrow e_j^y$ if, and only if:

1. $i = j$ and $x \leq y$, or
2. e_i^x is the sending of a message whose receiving is e_j^y, or
3. $\exists e_k^z : e_i^x \rightarrow e_k^z$ and $e_k^z \rightarrow e_j^y$ (transitive closure).

The partial order $\widehat{H} = (H, \rightarrow)$ constitutes a model of the distributed execution it is associated with.

2.2 Local States and Local Checkpoints

Let σ_i^0 be the initial state of process P_i. Event e_i^x entails P_i's local state change from σ_i^{x-1} to σ_i^x: σ_i^x is the local state of P_i resulting from its local history h_i^x; we say that e_i^y *belongs to* σ_i^x if $y \leq x$. Figure 1 depicts a distributed computation where events are denoted by black points and local states by (white or grey) rectangular boxes.

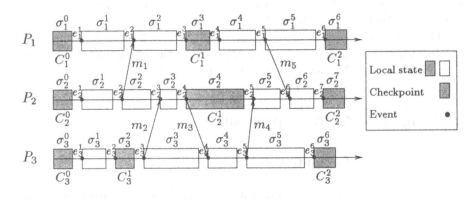

Fig. 1. Local states of a distributed computation.

Let Σ be the set of all local states associated with a distributed computation $\widehat{H}$. Lamport's precedence relation can be extended to local states in the following way:

---

[1] When the only non-deterministic statements are *"receive"* statements, the program is *piece-wise* deterministic. If statements other than *"receive"* are non-deterministic the program is *fully* non-deterministic.

$$\sigma_i^x \to \sigma_j^y \Leftrightarrow e_i^{x+1} \to e_j^y$$

Local states not related by "$\to$" are said to be *concurrent*, (denoted $\|$); more formally:

$$\sigma_i^x \| \sigma_j^y \Leftrightarrow \neg(\sigma_i^x \to \sigma_j^y) \text{ and } \neg(\sigma_j^y \to \sigma_i^x)$$

In Figure 1, we have $\sigma_3^2 \to \sigma_2^4$ and $\sigma_1^3 \| \sigma_3^6$.

A local checkpoint of process P_i is a local state of P_i saved on stable storage. So, the set of all local checkpoints is thus a subset of Σ. C_i^t will denote the t-th local checkpoint of P_i; it corresponds to some local state σ_i^x with $t \leq x$. We assume that each process takes an initial local checkpoint C_i^0 corresponding to σ_i^0. Grey rectangular boxes on Figure 1 depict local states that correspond to local checkpoints.

Determining which local states of a process are selected as local checkpoints, and consequently which are not, is the job of a checkpointing algorithm superimposed on the computation. When this algorithm defines the current local state of a process P_i as a local checkpoint, it saves it on stable storage, and P_i is said to "take a checkpoint".

2.3 In-transit Messages

A message m is *in-transit* with respect to an ordered pair (C_i^s, C_j^t) if its sending event belongs to C_i^s while its receiving event does not belong to C_j^t. In Figure 1, m_4 is in transit with respect to (C_3^2, C_2^1). In-transit messages actually constitute channel states which have to be considered to define consistency of global checkpoints.

2.4 Consistent Global Checkpoints

Informally, a consistent global checkpoint is a global state of a computation through which this computation could have passed. It consists of: (1) a set of concurrent local checkpoints (one per process), and (2) for each channel c_{ij}, the sequence[2] of messages that are in transit with respect to the ordered pair of local checkpoints of P_i and P_j. Formally, let C_i be a local checkpoint of process P_i and c_s_{ij} a state of the channel c_{ij}, i.e. a sequence of messages sent by P_i to P_j. A global checkpoint G is defined as:

$$G = \cup_i \{C_i\} \cup_{i,j} \{c\_s_{ij}\}$$

G is *consistent* if for any ordered pair (P_i, P_j):

- $\neg(C_i \to C_j)$ (C_j does not depend on C_i).

---

[2] As we consider FIFO channels, their states are sequences of messages. If channels were not FIFO, their states would be sets of messages.

- c_s_{ij} is the sequence of messages in transit with respect to (C_i, C_j).

As an example, let us consider Figure 1. C_3^1 and C_2^1 cannot belong to a same consistent global checkpoint as $C_3^1 \to C_2^1$. C_1^1, C_2^1 and C_3^2 can belong to a same consistent global checkpoint when considering all channel states empty except $c\_s_{32} = \{m_4\}$.

This consistency definition is the classic one used to define global checkpoints. The algorithms described in [5, 9] are classic examples of coordinated checkpointing algorithms. Due to the synchronization they use to define local checkpoints and associated channels states, coordinated checkpointing algorithms ensure the a priori consistency of the global checkpoints they determine.

3 Efficient Optimistic Sender-Based Message Logging

Uncoordinated checkpointing algorithms replace the previous a priori synchronization by tracking dependence on local checkpoints and by logging enough messages so that all in-transit messages can be retrieved to determine correct channel states. In the rest of this paper, we are interested in optimistic sender-based message logging.

3.1 Optimistic Sender-Based Logging

The principle of optimistic sender-based message logging is illustrated on Figure 2. When a message is sent, it is momentarily logged by its sender on a volatile log. More precisely, when P_i takes a local checkpoint C_i^x, (1) it saves C_i^x and the current content of the volatile log on the stable storage and (2) it re-initializes the volatile log to empty. Then P_i logs on its volatile log all the messages it sends till its next local checkpoint C_i^{x+1} (m_1, m_2 and m_3 in the example depicted in Figure 2). In this way, messages are saved on stable storage "by batch" and not independently. This decreases the volume of input/output and, consequently, the overhead associated with message logging.

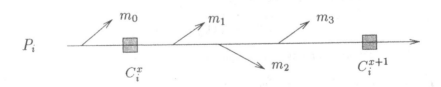

Fig. 2. Sender-based message logging.

3.2 To Log or not to Log on Stable Storage?

The question we want to answer is the following one: "given a message m stored in its volatile log, should P_i log it on stable storage when it takes its next local checkpoint C_i^{next} ?" Basically, a message has not to be saved on stable storage if it cannot be in transit in any consistent global checkpoint. To answer the previous question more precisely, let us consider the message m in Figures 3.a and 3.b; C_j^{last} denotes the last local checkpoint taken by P_j before receiving m.

In Figure 3.a, C_j^{last} and C_i^{next} are concurrent and can therefore belong to a same consistent global checkpoint in which $c\_s_{ij} = \{m\}$. In this case, m, kept in the volatile log of P_i, must be saved on stable storage when C_i^{next} is taken. In that way, this in-transit message can be retrieved if a consistent global checkpoint including C_j^{last} and C_i^{next} has to be restored.

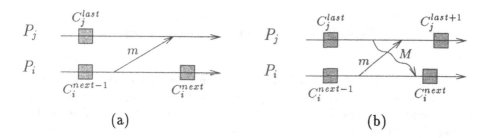

Fig. 3. To log or not to log.

Let us now consider Figure 3.b where M denotes a causal chain[3] of messages starting after C_j^{last} and arriving at P_i before C_i^{next}. We have then $C_j^{last} \to C_i^{next}$ from which we conclude that C_j^{last} and C_i^{next} cannot belong to the same consistent global checkpoint.

Let C_j^{last+1} be the first local checkpoint taken by P_j after receiving m. When considering any global checkpoint including C_i^x and C_j^y:

- if $x \leq next - 1$ and $y \leq last$: m has been neither sent nor received.
- if $x \geq next$ and $y \geq last + 1$: m has been sent and received.

As, additionally, $C_j^{last} \to C_i^{next}$ (because of M) and $C_i^{next-1} \to C_j^{last+1}$ (because of m), we can conclude that m cannot be in transit in any consistent global checkpoint. It follows that m need not be logged in stable storage when P_i takes C_i^{next}.

Figure 3.b exhibits the pattern of local checkpoints and message exchanges in which a message m has not to be logged on stable storage. The problem is now

---

[3] A causal chain of messages is characterized by the following property: every message of the chain (but the first one) is received, according to "$\to$", before the sending of the next one.

to answer the following question: "how can a process P_i know that a message m it sent to P_j will never be in transit with respect to any pair of local checkpoints (C_i^s, C_j^t)?" The only way[4] for P_i to learn this is on receiving a message piggybacking the information "m has been received by P_j". This situation is described in Figure 4 where the causal chain M conveys this information to P_i. On the contrary, in Figure 3.b, the chain M missed the information "P_j receives m".

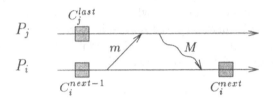

Fig. 4. P_i can decide not to log on stable storage.

The uncoordinated checkpointing algorithm described in the next section exploits the flow of messages exchanged by a distributed computation to convey control information used to reduce the number of messages logged on stable storage by their senders.

3.3   A Checkpointing Algorithm

We assume an uncoordinated checkpointing algorithm[5] that uses an optimistic sender-based message logging strategy. We augment it, according to the previous discussion (Section 3.2), in order to reduce the number of messages transferred from a volatile log to stable storage.

Let CKT_i be the checkpointing algorithm associated with P_i. CKT_i is augmented with the following data structures:

- vol_log_i: a volatile log initialized to empty.
- $sn_i[1..n]$: an array of sequence number generators.
  $sn_i[j] = \alpha \Leftrightarrow P_i$ sent α messages to P_j.
- $known\_rec_i[1..n, 1..n]$: a matrix of sequence numbers.
  $known\_rec_i[j, k] = \beta \Leftrightarrow P_i$ knows P_j has received β messages from P_k.

These three data structures are managed[6] and used by CKT_i. The following

---

[4] Remember we are in the context of uncoordinated checkpointing algorithms and, consequently, no additional control messages are used to convey control information.

[5] The most encountered uncoordinated checkpointing algorithm is the periodic one: at regular time intervals, each process individually takes local checkpoints.

[6] If we suppose processes do not send messages to themselves, entries $known\_rec_i[x, x]$ remain equal to zero. These entries can therefore be used to store the array sn_i and consequently save space.

one is managed by CKT_i but used (with the previous ones) only by the recovery algorithm (Section 3.4) to compute a set of concurrent local checkpoints.

— $ckpt\_ts_i[1..n]$: a vector clock for local checkpoints.
$ckpt\_ts_i[j] = \gamma \Leftrightarrow CKT_i$ knows P_j has taken γ local checkpoints.

Vector $ckpt\_ts_i$ is a vector clock [11] representing P_i's knowledge of the number of local checkpoints taken by each process.

When P_i sends or receives a message or when it takes a local checkpoint, CKT_i is required to execute the following statements atomically:

when P_i **sends** m **to** P_j
begin $sn_i[j] := sn_i[j] + 1;$
    append $(m, sn_i[j], j)$ **to** $vol\_log_i;$
    send $(m, known\_rec_i, ckpt\_ts_i)$ **to** P_j
end
when P_i **receives** (m, k_r, c_ts) **from** P_j
begin deliver m **to** $P_j;$
    $known\_rec_i[i, j] := known\_rec_i[i, j] + 1;$
    $\forall(x, y) : known\_rec_i[x, y] := \max(known\_rec_i[x, y], k\_r[x, y]);$
    $\forall x : ckpt\_ts_i[x] := \max(ckpt\_ts_i[x], c\_ts[x])$
end
when a local checkpoint is taken by P_i
begin $ckpt\_ts_i[i] := ckpt\_ts_i[i] + 1;$
    let $x = ckpt\_ts_i[i];$
    let $C_i^x = P_i$'s current local state; /* last local checkpoint */
    $\forall(m, sn_m, dest_m) \in vol\_log_i :$
        do if $sn_m \leq known\_rec_i[dest_m, i]$
            then suppress $(m, sn_m, dest_m)$ **from** vol_log_i
            fi
        od
    save on stable storage $(C_i^x, vol\_log_i, ckpt\_ts_i, known\_rec_i[i, *], sn_i);$
/* $known\_rec_i[i, *]$ is a vector whose value is the i-th line of the matrix $known\_rec_i$ */
    $vol\_log_i := \emptyset$
end

3.4 A Recovery Algorithm

A recovery algorithm, similar to the one described in [21], can be associated with the previous checkpointing algorithm. Upon a fault occurrence, the recovery algorithm executes the following steps.

1. First, non-faulty processes are required to take a local checkpoint (this allows as much correct computation as possible to be saved).
2. Then, the most recent set of n concurrent local checkpoints is determined. This determination is done in the following way:

- construct a set $\{C_1, C_2, \ldots, C_n\}$ by taking the last local checkpoint C_i of each process P_i; let c_ts_i be its timestamp (value of $ckpt\_ts_i$ when C_i is saved on stable storage)[7].
- **while** $\exists(i, j) : C_i \to C_j$
  do let C_j' be the first predecessor of C_j such that $\neg(C_i \to C_j')$
  $\quad C_j := C_j'$
  od

The set $\{C_1, \ldots, C_i, \ldots, C_n\}$ obtained contains the latest local local checkpoints which are concurrent.

3. The state of each channel c_{ij} (messages in transit with respect to the ordered pair (C_i, C_j)) is extracted from the stable storage of P_i in the following way. Let SQ_i^j and KR_j^i be the values of $sn_i[j]$ and $known\_rec_j[j, i]$ saved on stable storage with C_i and C_j, respectively. As channels are FIFO, messages sent by P_i to P_j which are in transit with respect to (C_i, C_j) have sequence numbers x such that $KR_j^i < x \leq SQ_i^j$ (Figure 5).

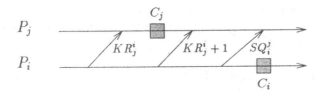

Fig. 5. Determining in-transit messages.

This set of messages is contained in P_i's stable storage (see the discussion of Section 3.2) from which they can be extracted to constitute a consistent global checkpoint.

3.5   Discussion

Unlike coordinated checkpointing algorithms, "pure" uncoordinated checkpointing algorithm cannot a priori prevent the occurrence of the *domino effect* [13] when a fault occurs. In the worst case, it is not possible to construct a set of n concurrent local checkpoints distinct from the initial set of local checkpoints. To prevent the occurrence of the domino effect, uncoordinated checkpointing algorithms can be made "adaptive": in that case, processes are required to take additional local checkpoints so that any local checkpoint belongs to at least one set of n concurrent local checkpoints. Contrary to coordinated algorithms, the implementation of this "adaptiveness" does not require the addition of control

---

[7] Due to the vector clock properties, we have: $C_i \to C_j \Leftrightarrow \forall x : c\_ts_i[x] \leq c\_ts_j[x]$ and $c\_ts_i \neq c\_ts_j$.

messages. [1, 3, 16] present such "adaptive" uncoordinated checkpointing algorithms.

Remarks: About strategies for preventing the domino effect.
In [12] Netzer and Xu state and prove a necessary and sufficient condition for a local checkpoint to be useless; a local checkpoint is *useless* if it cannot belong to any consistent global checkpoint. Useless local checkpoints are *the* cause of domino effects. In [4] we formally studied the modeling of consistent global checkpoints and the domino effect in distributed systems. We extended the following result due to Russell [16] (this result states a sufficient condition to eliminate the domino effect).

- Russell's adaptive algorithm. Let P_i be a process and $ckpt_i, receive_i$ and $send_i$ denote the event "P_i takes a local checkpoint", "P_i receives a message" and "P_i sends a message", respectively. If, for any P_i, the sequence of events produced by P_i obeys the following (regular language) pattern:

$$(ckpt_i \ receive_i^* \ send_i^*)^*$$

then no local checkpoint will be useless, and consequently the domino effect can not occur. It follows that the domino effect will be prevented by forcing each process P_i to take an additional local checkpoint between each sequence of $send_i$ events and each sequence of $receive_i$ events.
- Russell's adaptive algorithm follows (in some sense) a "brute force" strategy as the decision to force a process P_i to take an additional local checkpoint is only based on P_i's local behaviour.
A more sophisticated algorithm preventing the domino effect is presented in [3]. This adaptive algorithm uses global information (piggybacked by application messages) to force processes to take "as few as possible" additional local checkpoints in order no local checkpoint be useless. When there is no look-ahead on the future of the execution (a realistic assumption!) this algorithm is nearly optimal with respect to the number of additional local ckeckpoints that are taken.

End of remarks

Local checkpoints and messages logged on stable storage constitute a space overhead. A space reclamation algorithm is described in [22]. Basically, as soon as a consistent global checkpoint has been determined, all local checkpoints and messages that belong to its "past" can be discarded.

Sender-based message logging algorithms have been investigated for a long time [7, 19]. They usually either consider executions of piece-wise deterministic distributed programs [6, 8, 19] or log all messages. In the context of receiver-based message logging, [21] characterizes a particular set of messages that are not in transit with respect to any pair of local checkpoints; [23] adapts [21] to the case of sender-based logging. Expressed in our framework, [23] actually considers causal chains composed of only one message; this reduces the size of control information carried by messages but increases the number of messages that are logged on stable storage though they can not belong to a consistent global checkpoint.

A cost of the algorithm we presented lies in the matrix $known\_rec_i$, messages have to piggyback. Actually only entries of the matrix corresponding to edges of the communication graph have to be considered. In the case this graph is a directed ring, the matrix shrinks and becomes a vector. Matrices with similar semantics are used (1) in [20] to solve the distributed dictionary problem and (2) in [14] to implement causal message delivery in point-to-point communication networks. As shown in [15] the size of such matrices can be reduced by appropriate techniques when considering the actual communication graph.

4 Conclusion

This paper has studied the logging of messages in the context of optimistic sender-based uncoordinated checkpointing algorithms. A global checkpoint is consistent if it is composed of a set of n concurrent local checkpoints and a set of channel states recording all messages sent but not received (*in-transit* messages) with respect to these local checkpoints.

Coordinated checkpointing algorithms log those messages exactly. Because of their lack of synchronization, uncoordinated algorithms can be more efficient in failure-free computation but conservatively log more messages. This paper has presented a general technique to reduce the number of messages logged by uncoordinated checkpointing algorithms. An appropriate tracking of the causal dependencies of the underlying computation message exchanges constitutes the core of the protocol.

Acknowledgement

The authors want to thank the referees whose comments about the domino effect helped improve the presentation.

References

1. A. Acharya, B.R. Badrinath, Checkpointing Distributed Applications on Mobile Computers, *Proc. 3rd Int. Conf. on Par. and Dist. Information Systems*, 1994.
2. L. Alvisi, K. Marzullo, Message Logging: Pessimistic, Optimistic, and Causal, *Proc. 15th IEEE Int. Conf. on Distributed Computing Systems*, 1995, pp. 229-236.
3. R. Baldoni, J. M. Hélary, A. Mostefaoui, M. Raynal, Consistent Checkpointing in Distributed systems, INRIA *Research Report* 2564, June 1995, 25 p.
4. R. Baldoni, J. Brzezinski, J.M. Hélary, A. Mostefaoui, M. Raynal, Characterization of Consistent Checkpoints in Large Scale Distributed Systems. *Proc. 6th IEEE Int. Workshop on Future Trends of Dist. Comp. Sys.*, Korea, pp. 314–323, August 1995.
5. K.M. Chandy, L. Lamport, Distributed Snapshots: Determining Global States of Distributed Systems, *ACM Trans. on Comp. Sys.*, Vol. 3(1), 1985, pp. 63-75.
6. E.N. Elnozahy, W. Zwaenepoel, Manetho: Transparent Rollback-Recovery with Low Overhead, Limited Rollback and Fast Output Commit, *IEEE Trans. on Computers*, Vol. 41(5), 1992, pp. 526-531.
7. D.B. Johnson, W. Zwaenepoel, Sender-Based Message Logging, *Proc. 17th IEEE Conf. on Fault-Tolerant Computing Systems*, 1987, pp. 14-19.

8. D.B. Johnson, W. Zwaenepoel, Recovery in Distributed Systems Using Optimistic Message Logging and Checkpointing, *Journal of Algorithms*, Vol. 11(3), 1990, pp. 462-491.

9. R. Koo, S. Toueg, Checkpointing and Rollback-Recovery for Distributed Systems, *IEEE Trans. on Software Engineering*, Vol. 13(1), 1987, pp. 23-31.

10. L. Lamport, Time, Clocks and the Ordering of Events in a Distributed System, *Communications of the ACM*, Vol. 21(7), 1978, pp. 558-565.

11. F. Mattern, Virtual Time and Global States of Distributed Systems. In Cosnard, Quinton, Raynal, and Robert, Editors, *Proc. Int. Workshop on Dist. Alg.*, France, October 1988, pp. 215-226, 1989.

12. R.H.B. Netzer, J. Xu, Necessary and Sufficient Conditions for Consistent Global Snapshots, *IEEE Trans. on Parallel and Distributed Systems*, Vol. 6(2), 1995, pp. 165-169.

13. B. Randell, System Structure for Software Fault-Tolerance, *IEEE Trans. on Software Engineering*, Vol. 1(2), 1975, pp. 220-232.

14. M. Raynal, A. Schiper, S. Toueg, The Causal Ordering Abstraction and a Simple Way to Implement it, *Inf. Processing Letters*, Vol. 39, 1991, pp. 343-350.

15. F. Ruget, Cheaper Matrix Clocks, *Proc. 8th Int. Workshop on Distributed Algorithms*, Springer Verlag, LNCS 857, pp. 340-354, 1994.

16. D.L. Russell, State Restoration in Systems of Communicating Processes, *IEEE Trans. on Software Engineering*, Vol. 6, 1980, pp. 183-194.

17. L.M. Silva, J.G. Silva, Global Checkpointing for Distributed Programs, *Proc. 11th IEEE Symp. on Reliable Distributed Systems*, Houston, TX, 1992, pp. 155-162.

18. M. Singhal, F. Mattern, An Optimality Proof for Asynchronous Recovery Algorithms in Distributed Systems, *Inf. Processing Letters*, Vol. 55, 1995, pp. 117-121.

19. R.E. Strom, S. Yemini, Optimistic Recovery in Distributed Systems, *ACM Transactions on Computer Systems*, Vol. 3(3), 1985, pp. 204-226.

20. G.T. Wuu, A.J. Bernstein, Efficient Solutions to the Replicated Log and Dictionary Problems, *Proc. 3rd ACM Symp. on Principles of Dist. Comp.*, 1984, pp. 233-242.

21. Y.M. Wang, W.K. Fuchs, Optimistic Message Logging for Independent Checkpointing in Message-Passing Systems, *Proc. 11th IEEE Symp. Reliable Distributed Systems*, 1992, pp. 147-154.

22. Y.M. Wang, P.Y. Chung, I.J. Lin, W.K. Fuchs, Checkpointing Space Reclamation for Uncoordinated Checkpointing in Message-Passing Systems, *IEEE Trans. on Parallel and Distributed Systems*, Vol. 6(5), 1995, pp. 546-554.

23. J. Xu, R.H.B. Netzer, M. Mackey, Sender-Based Message Logging for Reducing Rollback Propagation, *Proc. 7th IEEE Symp. on Parallel and Distributed Processing*, 1995, pp. 602-609, San Antonio.

Atomic Updates of Replicated Data [*]

Rachid Guerraoui   Rui Oliveira   André Schiper

Département d'Informatique
Ecole Polytechnique Fédérale de Lausanne
1015 Lausanne, Switzerland

Abstract. Although several replication strategies have been described and compared in the literature, very few work has been published on the underlying protocols needed to support these strategies. In fact, the classical transactional protocols that are usually assumed are not fault-tolerant, and thus create a window of vulnerability for the "fault-tolerant" strategies they intend to support. In this paper, we point out this issue for "quorum voting" replication strategies. We describe a fault-tolerant protocol that enables to adequately support these strategies. We present some performance figures showing that, in addition to its higher resilience, our protocol provides better performance than the other possible alternatives.

1 Introduction

When compared to hardware-based techniques, replication is considered as a software-based cheap way of ensuring fault-tolerance. Fault-tolerance of data objects can be increased by replication. If an object is replicated on several sites, it can still be available despite failures. However, concurrent updates on different replicas of the same object may lead to inconsistent states. A replicated database is considered correct if it behaves as if each object has only one copy, as far as the user can tell. This property is called *one-copy equivalence* [1].

A great effort has been put on finding strategies that ensure *one-copy equivalence*. These strategies are usually classified according to their trade-off between consistency and fault-tolerance [4]. However, when focusing on the strategies, the necessary underlying support protocols are usually overlooked. It is often implicitly assumed that the underlying protocol does not condition the characteristics of the strategy. Nevertheless, the fact that the strategy is tightly dependent on system services such as reliable communication, commit protocols, and concurrency control, contradicts this assumption [5].

In this paper, we focus on *quorum voting* replication strategies, which was shown to preserve fault-tolerance and consistency despite unreliable failure detections [7]. For the sake of simplicity of the presentation, but without loss of generality, we will consider the simplest version of quorum voting strategies,

[*] Research supported by the "Fonds national suisse" under contract number 21-43196.95

that is, *majority voting with a single object and a static configuration*. We first point out the fact that the classical transactional protocols, usually assumed to support replication strategies, are blocking, i.e. are not fault-tolerant. Then we show that existing non-blocking alternatives, actually suffer from *unilateral abort* or *missing opportunities* drawbacks, i.e. abort transactions unnecessarily in the case of false failure suspicions.

The protocol we present, called *Replica Majority Commit (RMC)*, is intended to be used at the commit time of transactions updating replicated objects. RMC can be viewed as a variation of a decentralized *three phase commit* protocol [13], dedicated to update replicated objects. RMC preserves the fault-tolerance of the *majority voting* replication strategy, and exploits all commit opportunities of the transactions. Furthermore, as shown by the performance figures we present, RMC provides better performance than the other alternatives.

We give a precise characterization of the correctness of RMC by showing that safety (consistency) is never violated, and liveness (fault-tolerance) is ensured as long as (i) a majority of replica managers are correct, and (ii) the failure detector is of class $\diamond S$ [2]. The assumption that a majority of replica managers are correct is necessary for any non-blocking commit protocols assuming unreliable failure detectors [2], and is also necessary for the liveness of the majority voting strategy itself. Failure detectors of class $\diamond S$ are those which ensure that (1) eventually every process that crashes is suspected by all correct processes, and (2) eventually some correct process is never suspected by any correct process. Such failure detectors are unreliable in the sense that they can make an infinity of false failure suspicions. It has been shown that such failure detectors are the weakest ones that allow to solve consensus-like problems [3].

The rest of the paper is organized as follows. The next section discusses related work and gives an intuitive idea of the characteristics of our RMC protocol. Section 3 describes our model of an asynchronous system augmented with unreliable failure detectors, and defines the problem to be solved in a precise way. In Section 4, we present the RMC protocol and we prove its correctness. In Section 5, we give some performance figures and compare RCM with the other possible alternatives. In Section 6, we discuss extensions of RMC to more general quorum voting replication strategies. Finally, Section 7 summarizes the main contributions of this paper.

2 Related work and motivation

2.1 Replication strategies

A replication strategy can be viewed as a rule on the way data objects can be accessed, i.e. read and written. The *available* copy strategy ensures *one-copy equivalence* by a "read one/write all" rule: a read operation can be performed on any available copy while a write operation must be performed on all available copies [1]. Whenever a copy crashes, it is removed from the set of available copies. A major limitation of this strategy is that it is based on the assumption of reliable failure detectors (which never make false suspicions), and thus exclude the possibility of partitions [2]. As shown in [1], unreliable failure detections can lead to the reading of old and inconsistent replicas. The *quorum voting* strategies overcome this limitation. The basic idea was initially introduced by Gifford [7]: it consists in assigning votes to every replica, and defining read quorums and write quorums, for each object, such that: (1) read quorums and write quorums intersect, and (2) two write quorums intersect.

In this paper we discuss the underlying protocol needed for updating data objects, according to a quorum voting strategy. As we will show in Section 2.2, choosing a protocol which preserves the fault-tolerance of the strategy, and exploits all the commit opportunities, is not straightforward. For the sake of simplicity of the presentation, we will consider the simplest version of quorum voting strategies, that is, the *majority voting strategy with a single object and a static configuration*. In other words, we assume that a single object is accessed, a quorum is simply defined by a majority (i.e. weights are all 1), and the set of replicas on which a majority must be reached is statically defined. In Section 6, we will consider more general models.

2.2 Issues in supporting a "majority voting" replication strategy

The blocking problem: Replication strategies, such as majority voting, usually assume an underlying transactional system. They rely on traditional transactional protocols, such as *two phase locking* to ensure serialisability, and *two phase commit* (2PC) to ensure failure atomicity [9]. A locking protocol introduces a window of vulnerability as it is not itself fault-tolerant. Indeed, a locking protocol can block all replica managers if the holder of the lock crashes. A way to circumvent the blocking issue of locking is to use an optimistic technique where concurrency control conflicts are resolved at commit time (within the atomic commitment protocol). That is, no locking is issued during a transaction execution. At the time of commit, if a replica manager had a concurrency control conflict, it refuses to commit the transaction. In this case, both the serializability and failure atomicity of the transaction rely on the atomic commitment protocol. Nevertheless, the atomic commitment protocol that is generally used, namely 2PC, is not fault-tolerant, as it leads to block all replica managers, if the coordinator crashes while the replica managers are waiting for a decision [1].

The unilateral abort problem: An alternative non-blocking atomic commitment protocol is the three phase commit (3PC) [12]. It has been shown in [13, 8], that 3PC can be designed for systems with unreliable failure detectors and can be resilient to a minority of crash failures. Nevertheless, a careful look at 3PC reveals its limitation in the context of replication. Indeed, the *unilateral abort* aspect of 3PC leads a transaction to be aborted even if a single replica manager crashes. More precisely, 3PC leads a transaction to be aborted, if any replica

---

[2] As failure detections are usually implemented using time-outs, a partition (caused by a communication failure) may lead to falsely suspect a correct process.

crashes in the first step of the protocol. This is in contradiction with the aim of a majority voting strategy, which is precisely to enable data object updates (i.e. commit), despite the crash of a minority of replica managers.

The missing opportunities problem: A way to circumvent the unilateral abort problem is to use nested transactions prior to the execution of 3PC [6]. In this model, access to replicas is done on-line using nested transactions. A nested transaction can abort whereas its parent transaction can commit. If a majority of nested transactions commit, the parent transaction can commit. The commit protocol involves then only the replicas on which nested transactions have suceeded. However, the commit protocol should involve a strict majority of the replicas otherwise the *unilateral abort* problem remains. Choosing a strict majority from the set of successful nested transactions introduces however a subtle problem of *missing opportunities*. If one of the chosen replicas crashes, the transaction is aborted even if any of the discarded replicas is correct. As an example, suppose an initial set of five replica managers $\{p_1, p_2, p_3, p_4, p_5\}$, the nested transactions on the first four replicas commit (p_5 aborts or crashes) and the commit protocol is started over, say $\{p_1, p_2, p_4\}$, as they are a strict majority of the initial set. If then one of the replica managers crashes, for instance p_4, the transaction aborts. Given that p_3 is correct, the opportunity of commit by choosing $\{p_1, p_2, p_3\}$ is missed. This phenomena can occur with unreliable failure detectors, since they can make false suspicions and afterwards reconsider them.

The RMC protocol: Basically, the intuitive idea underlying our RMC (Replica Majority Commit) protocol, is that it enables to reach commit eventhough a minority of replica crashes. RMC avoids both the *unilateral abort* and the *missing opportunities* drawbacks of the alternatives discussed above. RMC can be viewed as a variation of a 3PC protocol (more precisely of a decentralized version of 3PC [13]), integrating nested transactions. This integration leads to use the same messages and the same communication steps for different purposes, and hence leads to better performance than the alternatives we have discussed above (see Section 5).

3 Model and problems

3.1 System Model

We consider a distributed system composed of a finite set of processes. Processes fail by crashing; we do not consider Byzantine failures. A *correct* process is a process that does not fail. The processes are completely connected through a set of channels. Communication is by message passing, *asynchronous* and *eventually reliable*. Asynchrony means that there is no bound on communication delays. An eventually reliable channel ensures that a message sent by a process p_i to a process p_j is eventually received by p_j, if p_i and p_j are correct. This assumption does not exclude communication link failures, if we require that any link failure is eventually repaired.

We assume that our asynchronous system is augmented with a failure detector [2]. A failure detector can be viewed as a distributed oracle. Each process has access to a local failure detector module. This module maintains a list of processes that it currently *suspects* to have crashed. We do not make any assumption on how a failure detector is implemented. It can for example simply be based on time-outs, and failure detector modules can consult each other before suspecting a process. Failure detectors are abstractly characterized by their *completeness* and *accuracy* properties. In the following, we consider failure detectors of the class $\Diamond S$ (*Eventually Strong*) [2]. These failure detectors guarantee (1) *strong completeness*, i.e eventually every process that crashes is permanently suspected by every correct process, and (2) *eventual weak accuracy*, i.e eventually some correct process is never suspected by any correct process. Notice that failure detectors of class $\Diamond S$ are unreliable as they can make mistakes, i.e false failure suspicions. The fundamental characteristic of $\Diamond S$ is that it is the *weakest* class of failure detectors that allow to solve consensus-like problems [3].

3.2   The majority voting replication strategy

In the majority voting replication strategy, to read or write a logical object, a transaction must access some majority of the replicas.

To ensure that each read returns the last written value (one-copy equivalence), every replica is assigned a version number which is incremented every time the replica is written. To read a logical object, a transaction accesses some majority of the replicas, chooses one with the highest version number, and returns the replica's value. To write a logical object, a transaction must also access a majority of replicas. To calculate the version of the write, the transaction chooses a replica with the highest version number and increments it. After the write, all replicas in the accessed majority are updated with this new version number.

The above version management is done on every write access and need to be embedded in the replica update protocol. Read accesses, on the other hand, have no effect on the update protocol. Due to the common need to always choose a replica with the highest version number, some optimizations can be envisioned for read/write transactions [1]. However this is not our goal here, and in the following, we concentrate solely on write-only transactions.

3.3   The update majority problem

Here we precisely define the problem to be solved when updating a replicated object according to majority voting strategy. We call this problem the *update majority* problem, and we show later that our RMC protocol (Section 4.4) solves exactly this problem.

The problem consists for a set of replica managers to agree on an outcome of a transaction. The outcome depends on the votes *(yes* or *no)* provided by the replica managers. Each vote reflects the ability of the replica manager to perform the updates. A replica manager will vote *no* if it detects a local concurrency control conflict. The outcome can be either *(commit,number)* or *abort*. The meaning of a *(commit,number)* outcome is that the replica managers have agreed to commit the transaction, and the new version number is *number*. This can be the case only if a majority of replica managers vote *yes*. The meaning of an *abort* outcome is that a majority of *yes* could not be obtained. This can be the case for example if some replica managers that vote *yes* are suspected to have crashed. In order to exclude trivial situations where replica managers always decide *abort*, and to exclude *unilateral abort* and *missing opportunities* situations, we require the transaction to be committed if there is a majority of replica managers which vote *yes*, and do not suspect each others.

We define the update majority problem by the following properties:

1. *Uniform-agreement:* no two replica managers decide differently.
2. *Non-blocking:* every correct replica manager that starts the protocol eventually decides.
3. *Uniform-validity:* (i) the decision can be *(commit,number)* only if a majority of replica managers has voted *yes*, and *number* is the highest version number plus 1; (ii) the decision must be *(commit,number)* if there is a majority of replica managers which vote *yes*, and do not suspect each others.

The *uniform-agreement* property is a safety property, whereas the *non-blocking* property is a liveness property. The *uniform-validity* property can be viewed both as a liveness and as a safety property, as it defines conditions under which the replicas can/must be updated.

4 The Replica Majority Commit protocol

In this section we describe the *Replica Majority Commit* protocol, or simply *RMC*, and we show how it solves the update majority problem above. First we give a global overview of RMC (Section 4.1), then we describe it in detail (Sections 4.2 and 4.3), and finally we prove its correctness (Section 4.4).

4.1 Overview of RMC

The structure of RMC is similar to that of the *decentralized three phase commit (D3PC)* protocol of Skeen [13]. Basically, a set of processes (replica managers) decide either to commit or abort a transaction by exchanging their votes in a decentralized fashion. There are however two major differences between the two protocols:

1. The first difference is in the way of deciding to commit or to abort a transaction: RMC requires a majority to vote *yes*, whereas *D3PC* requires all to vote *yes*. Hence no *unilateral abort* is permitted with RMC.

2. The second difference is that RMC integrates the version number management of the majority voting replication strategy. In RMC, whenever the replica managers decide to commit a transaction, they also decide on a new version number.

To reach *commit*, the RMC protocol needs three communication steps. Figure 1 illustrates these steps with the set of replica managers $\{p_1, p_2, p_3, p_4, p_5\}$ (as in the example of Section 2.2). For this simple description, we assume that (1) the coordinator is p_1, (2) replica managers p_4 and p_5 crash before sending their votes, and (3) the replica managers in $M = \{p_1, p_2, p_3\}$ (3.1) are correct, (3.2) they vote *yes*, and (3.3) they do not suspect each others.

In step 1, the coordinator p_1 asks all replica managers to vote. When receiving this "request to vote" message, every replica manager sends its vote, together with its version number, to all the replica managers. In step 2, every replica manager in M receives *yes* votes from all members of M, and sends a *commit* proposal to all replica managers. In step 3, every replica manager that receives a *commit* proposal from all members of M decides *commit* [3]. Note that, because we assume unreliable failure detectors, messages are always sent to all replica managers (including suspected ones). In Figure 1 for example, the messages are also sent to p_4 and p_5.

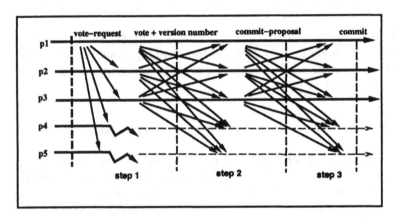

Fig. 1. Communication steps in RMC: coordinator is p_1

Negative votes and failure suspicions can prevent from reaching the *commit* decision. If a replica manager cannot collect *yes* votes from a majority in step 2, it invokes a termination protocol by proposing to abort the transaction. If a replica manager cannot collect *commit-proposals* from a majority in step 3, it invokes the termination protocol by proposing to commit the transaction. The termination protocol guarantees that replica managers agree on the same decision, which must be *commit* if a majority has proposed *commit*.

---

[3] Hence *commit* is decided despite the crash of p_4 and p_5.

In the following, we describe the RMC protocol in more details. We assume the existence of a termination protocol invoked in the case of failure suspicions. We will discuss the termination protocol in Section 4.3.

4.2 Description of RMC

The detailed RMC protocol is given by the function $RMC()$ in Figure 2. This function is periodically called by every correct replica manager p_i, to receive and perform updates. The termination protocol is encapsulated inside the function $Termination()$, which takes as argument either $(commit, number)$ or $abort$, and returns either of these values. While executing the RMC protocol, every replica manager p_i is informed by its local failure detector module of crash suspicions: the notation $p_j \in \mathcal{D}_i$ (eg. line 9) indicates that process p_i suspects process p_j. Every replica manager p_i maintains a number, $number_i$, which indicates the version number of the replica handled by the replica manager. This number is updated whenever the replica manager updates a transaction. Finally, every replica manager p_i has a vote, $vote_i$, reflecting the ability of p_i to commit the transaction. We do not discuss here how the vote is determined, e.g. the vote can be *"no"* if the replica manager has detected a concurrency control conflict, and *"yes"* otherwise.

The function $RMC()$ triggers two concurrent tasks, noted *Task 1* (lines 1 to 29) and *Task 2* (lines 30 to 33), and terminates by the execution of a **"return v"** statement, where v is either $(commit, number)$ or $abort$ (lines 17, 25, 29, and 33). When p_i executes **return** v, it *decides* on the outcome v of the transaction.

- *Task 2* is a decision task. It waits for a decision message $(p_j, decide, outcome)$, and forwards the *outcome* to the other replica managers (line 31). This ensures that if one correct replica manager decides on an outcome, then all the correct replica managers also decide on the outcome.

- *Task 1* executes the main protocol, i.e. step 1, step 2 and step 3 below.
  1. **Step 1** (lines 1-5): At line 2, the coordinator sends the *voteRequest* message to all. From there on, the protocol is decentralized: there is no coordinator. A replica manager p_i that receives the message *(coord,step1,voteRequest)* starts the protocol and forwards this message to all. This ensures that if one correct replica manager starts the protocol, every correct replica manager also starts the protocol (despite the failure of the coordinator). Then p_i sends its vote, together with its version number, to all replica managers, and moves to step 2 (line 6).
  2. **Step 2** (lines 6-17): Every replica manager p_i that starts step 2, waits until (i) it receives votes from $\lceil (n+1)/2 \rceil$ participants (i.e. a majority), and (ii) it receives *votes* from, or it suspects, each of the rest ($\lceil (n-1)/2 \rceil$) of the replica managers (lines 6-9). (1) If p_i has not received a majority of *yes* votes, p_i sends a *"startconsensus"* notification to all and starts the termination protocol by invoking the *Termination* function with *abort*

```
function RMC()

cobegin
 ‖   /* Task 1 */                                                      /* Step 1 */
1    if p_i = coord then   /* Only the coordinator executes: */
2        send(coord, step1, voteRequest) to all replica managers ;

3    when [received(coord, step1, voteRequest)]   /* Starting the protocol */
4        send(coord, step1, voteRequest) to all replica managers ;
5        send(p_i, step2, (vote_i, number_i)) to all replica managers ;

6    for k = 1 to ⌈(n + 1)/2⌉                                          /* Step 2 */
7        wait until [for some p_j: received(p_j, step2, (vote_j, number_j))] ;
8    for k = 1 to ⌈(n − 1)/2⌉
9        wait until [for some p_j: received(p_j, step2, (vote_j, number_j)) or p_j ∈ 𝒟_{p_i}] ;
10   if (for ⌈(n + 1)/2⌉ replica managers p_j: received(p_j, step2, (yes, number_j))) then
11       number := largest number_j such that received(p_j, step2, (yes, number_j)) ;
12       send(p_i, step3, (commit, number)) to all replica managers ;
13   else
14       send(p_i, startCons) to all replica managers ;
15       outcome := Termination(abort) ;   /* Termination protocol */
16       if outcome = (commit, number) then number_i := number ;
17       return outcome ;   /* End of the protocol */

18   for k = 1 to ⌈(n + 1)/2⌉                                          /* Step 3 */
19       wait until [for some p_j: received(p_j, step3, (commit, number))
                               or received(p_j, startCons)] ;
20   for k = 1 to ⌈(n − 1)/2⌉
21       wait until [for some p_j: received(p_j, step3, (commit, number))
                               or received(p_j, startCons) or p_j ∈ 𝒟_i] ;
22   if (for ⌈(n + 1)/2⌉ replica managers p_j: received(p_j, step3, (commit, number))) then
23       send(p_i, decide, (commit, number)) to all replica managers ;
24       number_i := number ;
25       return (commit, number) ;   /* End of the protocol */
26   send(p_i, startCons) to all replica managers ;
27   outcome := Termination((commit,number)) ;   /* Termination protocol */
28   if outcome = (commit, number) then number_i := number ;
29   return outcome ;   /* End of the protocol */

 ‖   /* Task 2 */
30   wait until [for some p_j: received(p_j, decide, outcome)] ;
31   send(p_i, decide, outcome) to all replica managers ;
32   if outcome = (commit, number) then number_i := number ;
33   return outcome ;   /* End of the protocol */
coend
```

Fig. 2. The RMC protocol (executed by a replica manager p_i)

as initial value. The value returned by *Termination* is the value decided by p_i. (2) If p_i has received a majority of *yes* votes, p_i defines the new version number as the maximum of the numbers received, sends this number together with a *commit* notification to all (line 12), and moves to step 3 (line 18).

3. **Step 3** (lines 18-29): Every replica manager p_i that starts step 3, waits until: (i) it receives *commit* proposals or "*startconsensus*" notifications from $\lceil (n+1)/2 \rceil$ participants, and (ii) it receives a *commit* proposal or a "*startconsensus*" notification from, or it suspects, each of the rest ($\lceil (n-1)/2 \rceil$) of the replica managers. (1) If p_i has not received a majority of *commit* proposals, p_i sends a "*startconsensus*" notification to all and starts the termination protocol by invoking the *Termination* function with ⟨*commit, number*⟩ as initial value. The value returned by *Termination* is the value decided by p_i. (2) If p_i has received a majority of *commit* proposals, p_i informs all about its *commit* decision, updates its version number and decides ⟨*commit, number*⟩.

4.3 The termination protocol

Up to now, we have assumed the existence of a termination protocol which is used to handle "bad terminations". In this section we discuss such a protocol. The problem that must be solved by the termination protocol is the *majority consensus* problem which we have introduced in [8]. This problem is actually a variation of the well known *uniform consensus* problem [2].

In both problems, a set of processes (resp. replica managers) propose, each an initial binary value 0 or 1 (resp. *abort* or ⟨*commit, number*⟩) , and must decide on a common final binary value 0 or 1 (resp. *abort* or ⟨*commit, number*⟩). The uniform consensus problem is defined by the following properties: (1) *agreement*: no two processes decide differently; (2) *non-blocking*: every correct process eventually decides; (3) *uniform-validity*: the value decided must be one of the initial values proposed; The majority consensus problem is defined by (1) the *agreement* and (2) the *non-blocking* properties of uniform consensus, and also the following (3) *majority-validity* property: (i) 1 can only be decided if at least one process has proposed 1 as initial value, and (ii) 0 can only be decided if at least a majority of the processes have proposed 0 as initial value.

Rather than presenting a complete majority consensus protocol, we adopt a modular approach and we show how to obtain such a protocol from any uniform consensus protocol.

In the following, we present a simple algorithm that transforms any uniform consensus protocol into a majority consensus protocol, to be used as a termination for our RMC protocol. The transformation below can thus be applied for example to the Chandra-Toueg protocol described in [2], which solves uniform consensus, given that there is a majority of correct processes and the failure detector is of class $\Diamond \mathcal{S}$.

Consider a function *UnifConsensus*() that solves the uniform consensus problem. This function, which can be called by every process p_i, takes a binary value as argument (the initial value), and returns a binary value (the decision value of uniform consensus). Using $UnifConsensus()$, a solution to the majority consensus problem can be obtained as follows:

1. Every replica manager p_i broadcasts its initial value to all replica managers;
2. If the initial value of p_i is 1, p_i calls $UnifConsensus(1)$ and decides on the returned value;
3. If the initial value of p_i is 0, p_i waits until it receives initial values from a majority of replica managers. If one of these values is 1, p_i calls $UnifConsensus(1)$ and decides on the returned value. If all received values are 0, p_i calls $UnifConsensus(0)$ and decides on the returned value.

Proposition. *If there is a majority of correct processes, then any uniform consensus protocol, together with the above transformation, solves solves the majority consensus problem.*

PROOF. The *uniform-agreement* and *non-blocking* properties of majority consensus are trivially ensured by the *uniform-agreement* and *non-blocking* properties of uniform consensus. The *majority-validity* property of majority consensus is satisfied since, (i) by the *uniform-validity* property of uniform consensus, 1 can only be decided if 1 has been proposed, and (ii) if less than a majority of initial values are 0, then every process will call $UnifConsensus(1)$. By the *uniform-validity* property of uniform consensus, no correct process decides 0. □

We thus assume in the following that the termination protocol used in RMC is a majority consensus protocol. Hence the termination protocol, invoked through function *Termination* in Figure 2, satisfies the *agreement*, *non-blocking*, and *majority-validity* properties above.

4.4 Correctness of RMC

We show in the following that our RMC protocol solves the update majority problem (defined in Section 3.3), assuming any failure detector of class $\diamond S$, and a majority of replica managers are correct. We introduce a lemma for each property of the update majority problem.

Lemma 1. *(uniform-agreement) No two replica managers decide differently.*

PROOF. A replica manager decides *abort* (resp. *(commit,number)*) in Task 2 only if some replica manager has decided *abort* (resp. *(commit,number)*) in Task 1 (either at line 17, 25 or 29). We show in the following that if two replica managers decide in Task 1, they decide the same outcome. Assume that some replica manager p_i decides *(commit,number)* at line 25. This means that p_i has received a majority of *(commit,number)* messages (line 22), which implies that less than a half of the replica managers have started *Termination* with *abort* as initial value (line 15). By the *majority-validity* property of *Termination*, no replica manager can thus decide *abort* (either at line 17 or 29). If no replica manager decides at line 25, then every replica manager that decides, decides through *Termination* (either at line 17 or 29). By the *agreement* property of *Termination*, no two replica managers decide differently. □

Lemma 2. *(non-blocking) If a majority of replica managers are correct, and the failure detector is of class $\Diamond S$, then every replica manager that starts the protocol eventually decides.*

PROOF. Assume that some correct replica manager starts the protocol. By the eventually reliable channel assumption, if any correct replica manager receives the *voteRequest* message at line 3 (i.e starts the protocol), every correct replica manager also receives the *voteRequest* message (and starts the protocol). Also by the reliable channel assumption, if some correct replica manager decides either at line 25, or in Task 2, every correct replica manager eventually receives the decision message and decides (in Task 2). Assume in the following that no correct replica manager decides either at line 25, or in Task 2. By (1) the assumption of a majority of correct replica managers, (2) the *strong completeness* property of $\Diamond S$, and (3) the assumption of eventually reliable channels, no correct replica manager remains blocked forever either at line 7 or 9. Hence every replica manager either starts *Termination* (line 15) or proceeds to step 3. In a similar way, by (1) the assumption of a majority of correct replica managers, (2) the *strong completeness* property of $\Diamond S$, and (3) the assumption of eventually reliable channels, no correct replica manager remains blocked forever either at line 19 or 21. As we assume that no replica manager decides at line 25, thus every correct replica manager starts *Termination*. By the *non-blocking* property of *Termination*, every correct replica manager eventually decides. □

Lemma 3. *(uniform-Validity) (i) the decision can be (commit,number) only if a majority of replica managers have voted yes, and number is the highest version number plus 1; (ii) the decision must be (commit,number), if there is a majority of replica managers which vote yes and do not suspect each others.*

PROOF. (i) A replica manager can decide *(commit,number)* either in Task 1 or in Task 2. To decide *(commit,number)* in Task 2, at least one replica manager must have decided *(commit,number)* in Task 1. Let p_i be a replica manager that decides *(commit,number)* in Task 1: p_i can do so either at line 17, 25, or 29. To decide *(commit,number)* at line 17, p_i must have got *(commit,number)* as the result of *Termination* at line 15. By the *majority-validity* property of *Termination*, some participant p_j must have started *Termination* with *commit* as its initial value, i.e at line 27. For any p_i to reach any of the lines 25, 27 or 29, p_i must have received a *yes* vote from a majority or replica managers (line 10). By construction, if *(commit,number)* is decided, then *number* is the higher version number plus 1. (ii) A replica manager cannot reach any decision unless a majority of replica managers have started the protocol. As a majority of replica managers are correct, then at least some correct replica manager must have started the protocol. This implies that all correct replica managers also start the protocol.

As a majority of correct replica managers vote *yes* and are not suspected, then these replica managers send *yes* messages to all at line 12. Consequently, at least some correct replica manager receives these (*commit, number*) messages at line line 22, sends its decision to all and decides (*commit, number*). Hence (by Lemma 1), every correct replica manager decides (*commit, number*) and no replica manager decides *abort*. □

By Lemma 1, Lemma 2, and Lemma 3, we have:

Proposition. *If there is majority of correct replica managers, and the failure detector is of class $\Diamond S$, then the RMC protocol (figure 2) solves the update majority problem.*

5 Evaluation of RMC

In this section, we compare the performances of RMC with other alternatives: that is 2PC (two phase commit) [9], 3PC (three phase commit) [12] and D3PC (decentralized three phase commit) [13], considering a system with n replica managers. The 2PC algorithm is used as a reference but cannot really be viewed as an alternative as it is not fault-tolerant. We do not consider here MD3PC (modular decentralized three phase commit) [8] as it actually is an optimization of D3PC, and the optimization could also be applied to our RMC protocol. For 2PC, 3PC and D3PC, we also consider their extensions with nested transactions [6].

We compare the protocols only for the case where *commit* is directly decided, i.e. without passing through the termination protocol. This corresponds to the most frequent case. The table in Figure 3 recalls the resilience characteristics of each protocol (Section 2), and shows, for each protocol, the number of communication steps and the number of messages, required to reach commit. To reach commit, 2PC, D3PC, and RMC, require 3 communication steps, whereas 3PC needs 5 communication steps. When nested transactions are used, two additional communication steps are required. When establishing the number of messages, we distinguish two cases: (a) using point-to-point communication, and (b) using broadcast communication (broadcast network). For instance, with point-to-point communications, $2PC$ requires $3n$ messages, and when used together with nested transactions, $5n$ messages are required.

The tables in Figure 4 compare the performances of the protocols, (a) using point-to-point communication, and (b) using broadcast communication. The measures have been obtained on FDDI (100Mb/s), with SPARC20 machines (running Solaris 2.3), using the UDP transport protocol. Different replica managers were located on different machines.

Protocol	Resilience	Number of steps	Number of messages point–to–point communication	Number of messages broadcast communication
2PC	*blocking unilateral abort*	*3*	*3n*	*n+2*
2PC + N	*blocking missing opportunities*	*5*	*5n*	*2n+3*
3PC	*non–blocking unilateral abort*	*5*	*5n*	*2n+3*
3PC + N	*non–blocking missing opportunities*	*7*	*7n*	*3n+4*
D3PC	*non–blocking unilateral abort*	*3*	*n(2n+1)*	*2n+1*
D3PC + N	*non–blocking missing opportunities*	*5*	*n(2n+3)*	*3n+2*
RMC	*non–blocking*	*3*	*n(2n+1)*	*2n+1*

Fig. 3. Steps and messages for direct *commit*

The measures convey an average time to commit a transaction. More precisely, every replica manager was, in its turn, the initiator of a transaction. Whenever a replica manager commits a transaction and is the new coordinator, it starts a new RMC protocol. The figures show that both with point to point communications and with broadcast communications, RMC provides better performances than other non-blocking alternatives. Furthermore, with broadcast communications, the price to pay for having a non-blocking protocol like RMC is not very high, when compared to 2PC (which is blocking). The reason why RMC provides sensibly better performances than D3PC, although the same number of communication steps and messages are required, is that with RMC, a replica manager needs only a majority of *yes* votes to move to step 3, whereas in D3PC, all *yes* votes must be received. Hence, beside the fact that RMC does not suffer from the unilateral abort and missing opportunities drawbacks of other protocols, RMC provides better performances.

6 Extensions of RMC

For the sake of clarity of presentation and better focus on the more relevant issues, we have considered some model simplifications in the protocol. More precisely, we considered the simplest version of quorum consensus strategies, that is, the majority strategy with static configurations. Furthermore, we considered transactions accessing single objects. In the following we show how RMC can be easily extended to cover more general models.

(a) point–to–point communication

Protocol	3 managers	6 managers	9 managers	12 managers
2PC	4.4 ms. ± 0.0	6.5 ms. ± 0.0	10.1 ms. ± 0.1	12 ms. ± 0.1
2PC + N	7 ms. ± 0.0	11 ms. ± 0.0	18 ms. ± 0.1	20 ms. ± 0.1
3PC	7.5 ms. ± 0.0	11.4 ms. ± 0.0	17.7 ms. ± 0.1	21.2 ms. ± 0.2
3PC + N	9 ms. ± 0.0	14 ms. ± 0.0	21 ms. ± 0.2	25 ms. ± 0.2
D3PC	5.4 ms. ± 0.0	10 ms. ± 0.0	17 ms. ± 0.1	22 ms. ± 0.2
D3PC + N	8.5 ms. ± 0.0	13 ms. ± 0.0	20 ms. ± 0.2	26 ms. ± 0.2
RMC	5.4 ms. ± 0.0	10 ms. ± 0.0	16 ms. ± 0.0	20 ms. ± 0.1

(b) broadcast communication

Protocol	3 managers	6 managers	9 managers	12 managers
2PC	5ms ± 0.0	7.5 ms. ± 0.0	10 ms. ± 0.1	12.3 ms. ± 0.1
2PC + N	8ms. ± 0.0	12 ms. ± 0.0	16ms. ± 0.1	15 ms. ± 0.1
3PC	8ms. ± 0.0	11.8 ms ± 0.0	16 ms. ± 0.1	21 ms. ± 0.2
3PC + N	10ms. ± 0.0	14 ms. ± 0.0	19ms. ± 0.2	25ms. ± 0.2
D3PC	5.2 ms. ± 0.0	8 ms. ± 0.0	12 ms. ± 0.1	17.5 ms. ± 0.2
D3PC + N	7ms. ± 0.0	10ms. ± 0.0	15ms. ± 0.2	20ms. ± 0.2
RMC	5.2 ms. ± 0.0	8 ms. ± 0.0	11 ms. ± 0.0	17 ms. ± 0.1

Fig. 4. Time to commit a transaction.

6.1 Quorum consensus

In a general quorum strategy [7], quorum conditions are (1) read quorums and
write quorums intersect, and (2) two write quorums intersect. A strict majority
is the smallest permitted write quorum. Read fault-tolerance can be increased by
reducing the size of read quorums. Our protocol can be easily tuned to accommodate different quorums. To do this, the required number of "good" messages at
decision stages of the algorithm must be changed accordingly. Also the *majority-
validity* property of our *Termination* protocol needs to take the write quorum
size in consideration. The size of the write quorum establishes a trade-off with
the resilience of the protocol. Assuming a set of n physical replicas of an object
the resilience is given by $n - WriteQuorum$. This trade-off fault-tolerance with
resilience of the protocol.

6.2 Dynamic configuration

With a static configuration, replica crashes compromise the liveness of the system. To cope with this problem and tolerate failures, dynamic adjust of quorums

is usually adopted [10]. To ensure consistency, it is required that any update quorum includes a majority of the replicas from the last one.

Since each quorum depends on the set of replicas that participated in the last commit, the system must keep track of this set. To achieve this, along with its version number, each replica also holds the set of replicas that composed its versioned update.

6.3 Multiple objects

In order to handle multiple-object transactions, the algorithm must involve all the logical objects accessed by the transaction. This means that to commit, the transaction has to aggregate in a logical *"and"*, the commitment of each object's majority of replicas. The coordinator, for each accessed object, requests its replicas to vote and thus to start RMC. The outcome of RMC can be commit only if for every object's replica set, the outcome is commit. In the algorithm of figure 2 this can be obtained by: in line 5 broadcast a vote from the replica of each involved object, waiting for the votes for each object by repeating the loops of lines 6 to 9 and 18 to 21; both decisions at lines 10 and 22 depends on the the majorities for each object; and *Termination* is invoked for each of the objects (lines 15 and 27) returning the logical *"and"* of their outcomes.

7 Concluding remarks

To ensure mutual consistency replica management must prevent concurrent updates of the replicas. The replication strategy is said to preserve *one-copy equivalence*. Quorum strategies are appealing as they enable to cope with unreliable failure detections. However, the proposals of such strategies often overlook the necessary underlying protocols.

The contribution of this paper is two-fold. First, we pointed out the inadequacy of traditional transactional protocols to support quorum replication strategies. We argued on their intrinsic lack of fault-tolerance compromising the supported strategies. Second, we presented a protocol, named RMC, which can be used with a simple transaction model and can be viewed as integrating nested transactions inside an atomic commitment protocol. RMC ensures the promised fault-tolerance of quorum strategies and still provides performant figures. The protocol relies on a canonical asynchronous system augmented with unreliable failure detectors. An interesting characteristic of the protocol is that it "accommodates" wrong suspicions therefore exploiting commitment opportunities.

With the adequate adaptations, RMC is clearly suited for any optimized quorum strategy (eg. voting with witnesses [11] or voting with ghosts [14]).

References

1. P.A. Bernstein, V. Hadzilacos, and N. Goodman. *Concurrency Control and Recovery in Database Systems*. Addison Wesley. 1987.
2. T. Chandra and S. Toueg. Unreliable failure detectors for reliable distributed systems. Journal of the ACM, 34(1), pp 225-267, March 1996. A preliminary version appeared in *Proceedings of the 10th ACM Symposium on Principles of Distributed Computing*, pp 325-340. ACM Press. August 1991.
3. T. Chandra, V. Hadzilacos and S. Toueg. The weakest failure detector for solving consensus. Journal of the ACM, 43(4), July 1996. A preliminary version appeared in *Proceedings of the 11th ACM Symposium on Principles of Distributed Computing*, pp 147-159. ACM Press. August 1992.
4. S. Ceri, M. Houstsma, A. Keller and P. Samarati. A Classification of Update Methods for Replicated Databases. Technical Report CS-TR-91-1392, Department of Computer Science, Stanford Univ, 1991.
5. S-W. Chen and C. Pu. A Structural Classification of Integrated Replica Control Mechanisms. Technical Report CUCS-006-92, Department of Computer Science, Columbia University, 1992.
6. K. Goldman and N. Lynch. Quorum Consensus in Nested Transaction Systems. In *ACM Transactions on Database Systems* 19 (4), pp 537-587. December 1994.
7. D. K. Gifford. Wheighted Voting for Replicated Data. In *Proceeding of the 7th ACM Symposium on Operating System Principles*, pp 150-161. ACM Press. 1979.
8. R. Guerraoui, M. Larrea and A. Schiper. Reducing the Cost of Non-Blocking in Atomic Commitment. *Proceedings of the 16th IEEE International Conference on Distributed Computing Systems*, pp 691-697, May 1996.
9. J. Gray. Notes on Database Operating Systems. In *Operating Systems: An Advanced Course*, pp 10-17. Lecture Notes in Computer Science (60), Springer Verlag. 1978.
10. S. Jajodia and D. Mutchler. Dynamic voting algorithms for maintainning the consistency of replicated databases. In *ACM Transactions on Database Systems* 15, pp 230-280. June 1990.
11. J.-F. Pâris. Voting with Witnesses: A Consistency Scheme for Replicated Files. In *Proceedings of the 6th IEEE International Conference on Distributed Computing Systems*, pp 606-612. 1986.
12. D. Skeen. NonBlocking Commit Protocols. In *Proceedings of the ACM SIGMOD International Conference on Management of Data*, pp 133-142. ACM Press. 1981.
13. D. Skeen. A Quorum-Based Commit Protocol. In *Proceedings of the Berkeley Workshop on Distributed Data Management and Computer Networks* (6), pp 69-80. February 1982.
14. R. van Renesse and A. Tanenbaum. Voting with Ghosts. In *Proceedings of the 8th IEEE International Conference on Distributed Computing Systems*, pp 456-462. June 1988.

Session 9

System Level Diagnosis

Chair: Henryk Krawczyk, Technical University of Gdansk, Poland

Removal of All Faulty Nodes from a Fault-Tolerant Service by Means of Distributed Diagnosis with Imperfect Fault Coverage

André Postma, Gerie Hartman, Thijs Krol

University of Twente, Department of Computer Science, P.O.Box 217, NL7500 AE Enschede, the Netherlands
email: postma@cs.utwente.nl, krol@cs.utwente.nl

Abstract. In general, offering a fault-tolerant service boils down to the execution of replicas of a service process on different nodes in a distributed system. The service is fault-tolerant in such a way, that, even if some of the nodes on which a replica of the service resides, behave maliciously, the service is still performed correctly. To be able to guarantee the correctness of a fault-tolerant service despite the presence of maliciously functioning nodes, it is of key importance that all faulty nodes are timely removed from this service. Faulty nodes are detected by tests performed by the nodes offering the service. In practice, tests always have an imperfect fault coverage. In this paper, a distributed diagnosis algorithm with imperfect tests is described, by means of which all detectably faulty nodes are removed from a fault-tolerant service. This may, however, inevitably, imply the removal of a number of correctly functioning nodes from the service too. The maximum number of correctly functioning nodes removed from the service by the algorithm is calculated. Finally, the minimally required number of nodes needed in a fault-tolerant service to perform this diagnosis algorithm is given.

1. Introduction

Reliable computer systems have become indispensable in today's society. The services provided by these systems are usually implemented in a fault-tolerant way as a set of replicated processes, where every replica of a process runs on a different node. These fault-tolerant services satisfy their specification as long as the number of nodes that concurrently fail is less than a certain predefined maximum. To avoid inconsistency within such a fault-tolerant service, it is highly important that faulty nodes are excluded from the fault-tolerant service as soon as possible.

System-level fault diagnosis algorithms are a convenient way to determine faulty nodes within a set of nodes on which a fault-tolerant service resides. After the basic work by Preparata, Metze and Chien [1], called the PMC model, a vast amount of system-level fault diagnosis algorithms have appeared in literature. In [2], several extensions to the PMC model are given.

Many diagnosis algorithms assume permanently faulty nodes and tests having a 100% fault coverage [1,4,5,10]. In reality, tests do not have a 100% fault coverage. Therefore, in literature, algorithms have appeared that use a probabilistic technique to cope with imperfect tests [3,7,11,12]. On basis of the test results, these so-called probabilistic diagnosis algorithms find the set of faulty nodes that is most likely to have produced the test results. As the number of nodes in the system grows to infinity the percentage of correct diagnoses approaches 100%. Adaptations to the probabilistic algorithms described in [6,8,9] assume a restricted fault model. For every possible set of test results within such a restricted fault model, we know the corresponding set of faulty nodes.

To achieve a sufficiently high reliability, it may be necessary to exclude all faulty nodes from a fault-tolerant service. If the service nodes suffer from Byzantine failures and the performed tests do not have a 100% fault coverage, the algorithms mentioned above are not applicable.

This paper describes a new system-level distributed diagnosis algorithm, by means of which all faulty nodes are removed from the system, and which is based on the assumptions that nodes may fail in an arbitrary way and that tests need not have a 100% fault coverage. Byzantine faults can be handled by having a worst case approach in a distributed environment. In the cases in which the test results are indeterminate, all possibly faulty nodes are excluded from the service. This implies that in some cases, a number of correctly functioning nodes must also be excluded from the service.

In the following section, we will describe our new diagnosis algorithm. Then, we will calculate the maximum number of correctly functioning nodes that may be removed by the algorithm. Finally, we calculate the minimum number of nodes needed in order to be able to perform the described diagnosis algorithm as a function of the maximum number of faulty nodes that is tolerated.

2. A distributed diagnosis algorithm with imperfect tests

In this section, we will describe our distributed diagnosis algorithm with imperfect tests. This algorithm is performed in every node of the fault-tolerant service. All nodes together form the set $\mathcal{N}$ of nodes. At the start of the algorithm, it is assumed that every node in $\mathcal{N}$ has tested every other node in $\mathcal{N}$, and that these test results are available in every node. We assume that the test results have been distributed among the nodes by means of interactive consistency processes, so that every node has its own copy of the test results before the start of the algorithm[1].

The test results can be denoted in a matrix $\mathcal{M}$, in which the row indices represent the testing nodes and the column indices represent the tested nodes. An entry $\mathcal{M}_{i,j}$ (with $i,j \in \mathcal{N}$) of the matrix represents a test result and can have the value C or F. $\mathcal{M}_{i,j} = C$ indicates that the test was successful and j (the tested node) is considered correct by i (the testing node). $\mathcal{M}_{i,j} = F$ indicates that the test failed, and j (the tested node) is considered faulty by i (the testing node).

---

1. If, due to link failures the system is split into disjoint parts, the test results can not be obtained, and the diagnosis algorithm can not be executed. It is impossible to simply assume that a node from which no test results are obtained is faulty (resp. correct). Then, e.g. assumption A1 (resp. A2)as formulated in 2.1. may not hold.

On basis of the test results, the algorithm creates two sets of nodes, a so-called *correct-set* C, which contains identifiers of correctly functioning nodes only, and a *fault-set* $\mathcal{F}$, which contains the identifiers of the other nodes, being all the faulty nodes and possibly some correctly functioning nodes also. The correct-set and fault-set are created using a number of *reduction rules*, given in 2.2. These rules follow from the assumptions stated in 2.1. After execution of our diagnosis algorithm, all nodes from set $\mathcal{N}$ are either in the correct-set C or the fault-set $\mathcal{F}$. Then, all nodes in the fault-set $\mathcal{F}$ are removed from the service. Since we know that all remaining nodes in the service are functioning correctly, we can now, one by one, adopt new correct nodes in the service, if each remaining node in the service agrees upon the correctness of the new nodes (by testing them).

2.1. Assumptions

We assume a completely connected network of nodes with perfect communication links. In practice, the effect of a link failure is indistinguishable from a failure in the sending node. For simplicity, we assume that every communication failure is caused by a node failure, and assume that link failures do not occur. We assume that in the network, at most T nodes are faulty during an execution of the diagnosis algorithm. Faulty nodes may exhibit Byzantine failures, i.e. they may fail in an arbitrary way. For a node $n \in \mathcal{N}$, the predicate *faulty(n)* means that n is faulty, whereas *correct(n)* means that n is correct. The assumptions concerning the nodes and their test results, are:

A1. $\forall\, a,b \in \mathcal{N}:(correct(a) \wedge correct(b)) \Rightarrow \mathcal{M}_{a,b} = C$
         i.e. if a node a and b are both correct, then a has a positive test result for b

A2. $\forall\, a \in \mathcal{N}: faulty(a) \Rightarrow (\exists\, b \in \mathcal{N}: correct(b) \wedge (\mathcal{M}_{a,b} = F \vee \mathcal{M}_{b,a} = F))$
         i.e. if a node a is faulty, there exists a correct node for which a has negative test results or there exists a correct node which has negative test results for a.

A3. $\forall\, a \in \mathcal{N}: (faulty(a) \Rightarrow \neg\, correct(a)) \wedge (correct(a) \Rightarrow \neg\, faulty(a))$
         i.e. a node is either faulty or correct

A4. $\forall\, a,b \in \mathcal{N}: (\mathcal{M}_{a,b} = F \Rightarrow \neg\, (\mathcal{M}_{a,b} = C)) \wedge (\mathcal{M}_{a,b} = C \Rightarrow \neg\, (\mathcal{M}_{a,b} = F))$
         i.e. test results are either positive or negative

A5. $|\{ a \in \mathcal{N}: faulty(a)\}| \leq T$
         i.e. the number of faulty nodes is less than or equal to T

A2 expresses our assumption that faulty nodes exhibit detectably faulty behaviour, i.e. it is impossible that a faulty node n has positive test results for every correct node, and every correct node has positive test results for n.

2.2. Reduction rules

Using the assumptions given in 2.1., for a given set of test results of a set $\mathcal{N}$ of nodes, we are able to determine for a number of nodes of $\mathcal{N}$ whether they should be put in the correct-set C or in the fault-set $\mathcal{F}$. This is done by a repeated application of the following reduction rules on the nodes in set $\mathcal{N}$ until no more nodes can be classified anymore.

The reduction rules are as follows:

R1. $\forall\, n \in \mathcal{N} - \mathcal{F} - C : (\mathcal{M}_{n,n} = F \Rightarrow n \in \mathcal{F})$

i.e. if a node has negative test results for itself, it is put in the fault-set.

R2. $\forall\, n \in \mathcal{N} - \mathcal{F} - C : |\{\, i \in \mathcal{N} - \mathcal{F} \mid \mathcal{M}_{i,n} = F \vee \mathcal{M}_{n,i} = F \,\}| > (T - |\mathcal{F}|) \Rightarrow n \in \mathcal{F}$

i.e. if the number of nodes that are not in the fault-set and for which a node n has negative test results or which have negative test results for n exceeds T minus the number of nodes in $\mathcal{F}$, then n is put in the fault-set.

R3. $\forall\, n \in \mathcal{N} - \mathcal{F} - C : (\forall\, m \in \mathcal{N} - \mathcal{F} : \mathcal{M}_{m,n} = C \wedge \mathcal{M}_{n,m} = C) \Rightarrow n \in C$

i.e. if all nodes that are not in the fault-set have positive test results for a certain node n, and n has positive test results for all nodes not in the fault-set, we assume that this node n is correct, and it is put in the correct-set.

If a node n is correct and $\mathcal{M}_{n,m} = F$ or $\mathcal{M}_{m,n} = F$, by assumption A1, node m is assumed to be faulty. For a node n we define its set of suspicious nodes as the set of nodes which is assumed to be faulty, if n is correct. Thus, for every node $n \in \mathcal{N}'$, with $\mathcal{N}' = \mathcal{N} - \mathcal{F} - C$, the set $S(n, \mathcal{N}')$ of suspicious nodes is defined as follows:

$$S(n, \mathcal{N}') = \{\, m \in \mathcal{N}' \mid \mathcal{M}_{m,n} = F \vee \mathcal{M}_{n,m} = F \,\}$$

For a set $X \subset \mathcal{N}'$, the set $S(X, \mathcal{N}')$ of suspicious nodes for set X is defined as follows:

$$S(X, \mathcal{N}') = \bigcup_{i \in X} S(i, \mathcal{N}')$$

We will define a *presupposed correct-set for a node n within set $\mathcal{N}'$* as a set of nodes which, if we assume these nodes correct, results in a consistent solution (i.e. a classification of all nodes which satisfies all assumptions stated in 2.1). For a presupposed correct-set P for n within $\mathcal{N}'$, we require that

$$(n \in P) \wedge (S(P, \mathcal{N}') \cap P = \varnothing)$$

Clearly, for certain $n \in \mathcal{N}'$, more than one presupposed correct-set may exist. Therefore, we define the set $PS(n, \mathcal{N}')$ of all presupposed correct-sets of n within $\mathcal{N}'$ as follows:

$$PS(n, \mathcal{N}') = \{\, P \mid n \in P \wedge (S(P, \mathcal{N}') \cap P = \varnothing)\,\}$$

Now, we are able to formulate reduction rule R4:

R4. $\forall\, n \in \mathcal{N} - \mathcal{F} - C : (\neg (\exists\, P \in PS(n, \mathcal{N} - \mathcal{F} - C) : |\mathcal{N} - \mathcal{F} - C - P| \leq T - |\mathcal{F}|)) \Rightarrow$
               $n \in \mathcal{F}$

i.e. if for a certain node n no presupposed correct-set P can be found, such that the number of nodes in $\mathcal{N} - \mathcal{F} - C - P$ is less than or equal to $T - |\mathcal{F}|$, then n is put in the fault-set.

By repeated application of reduction rules R1 through R4 we can classify several nodes from $\mathcal{N}$ either in the fault-set or the correct-set. In Appendix 1, we prove that the predicates:

$$\forall\, n \in \mathcal{F} : faulty(n)$$
$$\forall\, n \in C : correct(n)$$

are invariant under application of the reduction rules R1 through R4. This means that, by the reduction rules only faulty nodes are put in the fault-set and only correct nodes are put in the correct-set.

Provided that reduction rule R1 is first applied repeatedly, the other reduction rules may be applied in any order. Furthermore, the rules are consistent, i.e. it is impossible to classify a node both in the fault-set and in the correct-set. A proof of this can be found in Appendix 2.

If for a remaining set of nodes none of the reduction rules above can be applied anymore, then the remaining nodes satisfy the conjunction of the negations of the premises of the reduction rules. The remaining nodes form a set $\mathcal{N}' = \mathcal{N} - \mathcal{F} - C$ of nodes with so-called *indeterminate test results*. The nodes in $\mathcal{N}'$ satisfy:

$$\forall\, n \in \mathcal{N}': \quad ((\mathcal{M}_{n,n} = C) \wedge (|\{i \in \mathcal{N} - \mathcal{F} |\, \mathcal{M}_{i,n} = F \vee \mathcal{M}_{n,i} = F\}| \leq (T - |\mathcal{F}|) \wedge$$
$$(\exists\, m \in \mathcal{N}': \mathcal{M}_{m,n} = F \vee \mathcal{M}_{n,m} = F) \wedge$$
$$(\exists\, \mathcal{P} \in \mathcal{PS}(n, \mathcal{N}'): |\mathcal{N}' - \mathcal{P}| \leq T - |\mathcal{F}|))$$

Notice that, if $\mathcal{N}'$ is non-empty, one or more nodes in $\mathcal{N}'$ must be faulty. This can be seen as follows. From the definition of indeterminate test results given above, we conclude that every node in $\mathcal{N}'$ has negative test results for another node in $\mathcal{N}'$, or there is another node in $\mathcal{N}'$ which has negative test results for it (viz. $\forall\, n \in \mathcal{N}': (\exists\, m \in \mathcal{N}': \mathcal{M}_{m,n} = F \vee \mathcal{M}_{n,m} = F)))$. Let a and b be nodes in $\mathcal{N}'$. Assume that node a has negative test results for node b. Then, by assumption A1, either node a or node b must be faulty.

In order to exclude all faulty nodes from the fault-tolerant service, all nodes from $\mathcal{N}'$ are put in the fault-set $\mathcal{F}$. Then, all nodes from $\mathcal{N}$ have been classified and the algorithm ends. Since $\mathcal{N}$ contains a finite number of nodes, the algorithm always ends.

We will illustrate the definition of indeterminate test results by means of an example:

Example 1
Assume a set $\mathcal{N}$ contains two nodes 1 and 2. Assume furthermore that the maximum number of faulty nodes $T = 1$. Node 1 has negative test results for node 2 and positive test results for itself. Node 2 has negative test results for node 1 and positive test results for itself. For this example, matrix $\mathcal{M}$ is defined as follows:

$$\mathcal{M} = \begin{bmatrix} C & F \\ F & C \end{bmatrix}$$

Reduction rule R1 through R4 can not be applied to these test results. The test results of node 1 and node 2 are indeterminate. So node 1 and 2 are put in the fault-set and the algorithm ends. ❏

We will now explain the use of the reduction rules by means of three examples.

Example 2

Assume a service contains four nodes 1,2,3, and 4. Assume furthermore that $T = 2$. The test results of the nodes 1,2,3, and 4 are given in the matrix below. The algorithm

$$\mathcal{M} = \begin{bmatrix} C & F & F & C \\ C & C & C & C \\ C & C & C & F \\ F & C & C & C \end{bmatrix}$$

proceeds as follows. Initially, $\mathcal{F} = \varnothing$ and $C = \varnothing$. Reduction rule R2 can be applied to node 1. Since $\mathcal{M}_{1,2} = \mathcal{M}_{1,3} = \mathcal{M}_{4,1} = F$, node 1 can be put in the fault-set. Then we apply reduction rule R3 to put node 2 in the correct-set. Now, we can not apply reduction rules anymore. so node 3 and 4 are put in the fault-set. Notice that node 2 is assumed to be correct, although node 2 has a positive test result for nodes 1, 3, and 4. This is possible, since we assumed that tests do not have a perfect coverage. Notice that it is possible that by application of the diagnosis algorithm one or more correctly functioning nodes are put in the fault-set (In this example, finally, $\mathcal{F} = \{1,3,4\}$ while $T = 2$). ❑

Example 3:

Assume a service contains five nodes 1,2,3,4, and 5. Assume furthermore that $T = 2$.

$$\mathcal{M} = \begin{bmatrix} C & C & C & F & C \\ F & F & F & C & C \\ C & F & C & C & C \\ F & C & C & C & C \\ C & F & C & C & C \end{bmatrix}$$

The test results for the nodes are given in the matrix above. By applying reduction rule R1, node 2 is put in the fault set. It is not possible to apply rule R2 to the remaining test results. By rule R3, node 3 and 5 are put in the correct-set. The remaining nodes (node 1 and 4) show indeterminate test results. Both node 1 and node 4 are put in the fault-set. Thus, our algorithm concludes with $\mathcal{F}$ consisting of node 1,2, and 4, and C consisting of node 3 and 5. ❑

Example 4:

Assume a service contains five nodes 1,2,3,4, and 5. Assume furthermore that $T = 2$.

$$\mathcal{M} = \begin{bmatrix} C & F & F & C & C \\ F & C & C & C & C \\ F & C & C & C & C \\ C & C & C & C & F \\ C & C & C & F & C \end{bmatrix}$$

The test results for the nodes are given in the matrix above. Reduction rule R1 through R3 can not be applied to these results. We can, however, apply reduction rule R4 to node 1. The possible presupposed correct-sets for node 1 are $\{1,4\}$ and $\{1,5\}$. Both have a number of suspicious nodes greater than T, so node 1 must be put in the fault-set. By reduction rule R3, then, node 2 and 3 can be put in the correct-set. Node 4 and 5 have indeterminate test results, therefore, they are both put in the fault-set and the algorithm ends with $\mathcal{F}$ consisting of node 1,4, and 5, and C consisting of node 2 and 3. ❏

3. Determining the maximum number of correct nodes removed from the service by the diagnosis algorithm

Putting all nodes from $\mathcal{N}'$ in the fault-set may result in the removal of correct nodes from a service. In this section, we will derive an upper bound for the number of correct nodes that may be removed from a service by using the above-described diagnosis algorithm. We first give some definitions we will use in the sequel.

N	the total number of nodes in the service.
T	the maximum number of faulty nodes in the service
S	the actual number of faulty nodes ($S \leq T$)
b	the number of faulty nodes detected by application of reduction rule R1 through R4
a	the number of correct nodes detected by application of reduction rule R1 through R4

We will denote $\mathcal{N}'$ as the set of indeterminate test results. For this remaining set $\mathcal{N}'$ we use the following definitions:

N'	$= N - (a + b)$	(the number of nodes in set $\mathcal{N}'$)
T'	$= T - b$	(the maximum number of faulty nodes in $\mathcal{N}'$)
S'	$= S - b$	(the actual number of faulty nodes in $\mathcal{N}'$)
G'	$= N' - S'$	(the actual number of correct nodes in $\mathcal{N}'$)

Set $\mathcal{N}'$ contains G' correct nodes, all of which are put in the fault-set. In general, we do not know G'. We can only derive an upper bound to the number of correctly functioning nodes put in the fault-set. The following lemma is used for this purpose.

For every node $n \in \mathcal{N}'$, one or more presupposed correct-sets $\mathcal{P} \in PS(n,\mathcal{N}')$ with $|\mathcal{N}' - \mathcal{P}| \leq T - |\mathcal{F}|$ exist. Notice that such a presupposed correct-set with $|\mathcal{N}' - \mathcal{P}| \leq T - |\mathcal{F}|$ does not necessarily contain correct nodes only. (In order to see this, recall example 1 from section 2.2. In this example, two such presupposed correct-sets can be found, viz. $\mathcal{P}_1 = \{1\}$ and $\mathcal{P}_2 = \{2\}$. Since $T = 1$, one of the nodes 1 and 2 may be faulty. In that case there is a presupposed correct-set containing a faulty node).

In the following lemma, we will show that if for the nodes in $\mathcal{N}'$, presupposed correct-sets with $|\mathcal{N}' - \mathcal{P}| \leq T - |\mathcal{F}|$ exist such that every presupposed correct-set contains at most one faulty node, then the number of correct nodes present in the remaining sets of nodes is maximal.

Lemma 1:
If for every node $n \in \mathcal{N}'$, a presupposed correct-set $\mathcal{P} \in \mathcal{PS}(n,\mathcal{N}')$ with $|\mathcal{N}' - \mathcal{P}| \leq T - |\mathcal{F}|$ exists such that it does not contain more than one faulty node, the number of correctly functioning nodes present in the sets $\mathcal{N}' - \mathcal{P}$ of nodes, is maximal.

Proof:
Assume we have a set $\mathcal{N}'$ of nodes with indeterminate test results. From the definition of indeterminate test results we know that, for every node $n \in \mathcal{N}'$, there exists a presupposed correct-set $\mathcal{P} \in \mathcal{PS}(n,\mathcal{N}')$ with $|\mathcal{N}' - \mathcal{P}| \leq T - |\mathcal{F}|$. Thus:

$$\forall n \in \mathcal{N}': \exists \mathcal{P} \in \{\mathcal{P} | S(\mathcal{P}, \mathcal{N}') \cap \mathcal{P} = \emptyset \wedge S(\mathcal{P}, \mathcal{N}') \cup \mathcal{P} \subset \mathcal{N}' \wedge |\mathcal{N}' - \mathcal{P}| \leq T - |\mathcal{F}|\} \wedge n \in \mathcal{P}$$

We will now show that for every node $n \in \mathcal{N}'$, there exists a presupposed correct-set $\mathcal{P} \in \mathcal{PS}(n,\mathcal{N}')$ with $|\mathcal{N}' - \mathcal{P}| \leq T - |\mathcal{F}|$, and $S(\mathcal{P}, \mathcal{N}') \cup \mathcal{P} = \mathcal{N}'$. Every node $x \in \mathcal{N}'$ with $x \notin S(\mathcal{P}, \mathcal{N}') \cup \mathcal{P}$ can be added to $\mathcal{P}$, resulting in a new set $\mathcal{P}'$ with $S(\mathcal{P}', \mathcal{N}') \cup \mathcal{P}' = \mathcal{N}'$. This can be seen as follows:

1. $\qquad S(\mathcal{P}, \mathcal{N}') \cup \mathcal{P} \neq \mathcal{N}' \Rightarrow (\exists x \in \mathcal{N}' : x \notin S(\mathcal{P}, \mathcal{N}') \wedge x \notin \mathcal{P})$
i.e. if $S(\mathcal{P}, \mathcal{N}') \cup \mathcal{P}$ is a subset of $\mathcal{N}'$, there must be a node x which is not in $S(\mathcal{P}, \mathcal{N}') \cup \mathcal{P}$.

From the definition of $S(\mathcal{P}, \mathcal{N}')$ we know:
2. $\qquad \forall x \in \mathcal{N}': (x \notin S(\mathcal{P}, \mathcal{N}') \Rightarrow (\forall m \in \mathcal{P}: M_{m,x} = C \wedge M_{x,m} = C))$

For every $x \in \mathcal{N}'$ with $x \notin S(\mathcal{P}, \mathcal{N}') \wedge x \notin \mathcal{P}$, it holds that:
3. $\qquad (\mathcal{P}' = \mathcal{P} \cup \{x\}) \wedge (\forall m \in \mathcal{P}: M_{m,x} = C \wedge M_{x,m} = C) \wedge (S(x, \mathcal{N}') \cap \{x\} = \emptyset)$
$\Rightarrow$

$\qquad (S(x, \mathcal{N}') \cap \{x\} = \emptyset) \wedge (S(x, \mathcal{N}') \cap \mathcal{P} = \emptyset) \wedge$
$\qquad \qquad (S(\mathcal{P}, \mathcal{N}') \cap \{x\} = \emptyset) \wedge S(\mathcal{P}, \mathcal{N}') \cap \mathcal{P} = \emptyset$
$\Rightarrow$

$\qquad (\mathcal{P} \cup \{x\}) \cap (S(\mathcal{P}, \mathcal{N}') \cup S(x, \mathcal{N}')) = \emptyset$
$\Rightarrow$

$\qquad S(\mathcal{P}', \mathcal{N}') \cap \mathcal{P}' = \emptyset$

So, for every node $n \in \mathcal{N}'$, there exists a presupposed correct-set $\mathcal{P} \in \mathcal{PS}(n,\mathcal{N}')$ with $|\mathcal{N}' - \mathcal{P}| \leq T - |\mathcal{F}|$, $S(\mathcal{P}, \mathcal{N}') \cap \mathcal{P} = \emptyset$ and $S(\mathcal{P}, \mathcal{N}') \cup \mathcal{P} = \mathcal{N}'$. For this set, it holds that $|S(\mathcal{P}, \mathcal{N}')| \leq T - |\mathcal{F}|$ (since $S(\mathcal{P}, \mathcal{N}') = \mathcal{N}' - \mathcal{P}$ and $|\mathcal{N}' - \mathcal{P}| \leq T - |\mathcal{F}|$). Thus:

$$\forall n \in \mathcal{N}': \exists \mathcal{P} \in \{\mathcal{P} | S(\mathcal{P}, \mathcal{N}') \cap \mathcal{P} = \emptyset \wedge S(\mathcal{P}, \mathcal{N}') \cup \mathcal{P} = \mathcal{N}' \wedge |S(\mathcal{P}, \mathcal{N}')| \leq T - |\mathcal{F}|\} \wedge n \in \mathcal{P}$$

We define the set of all presupposed correct-sets $\mathcal{P}$ within $\mathcal{N}'$ for which $S(\mathcal{P}, \mathcal{N}') \cup \mathcal{P} = \mathcal{N}'$ and $S(\mathcal{P}, \mathcal{N}') \cap \mathcal{P} = \emptyset$ and $|S(\mathcal{P}, \mathcal{N}')| \leq T - |\mathcal{F}|$ as $CPS(\mathcal{N}')$. Thus:

$$CPS(\mathcal{N}') = \{\mathcal{P} | S(\mathcal{P}, \mathcal{N}') \cap \mathcal{P} = \emptyset \wedge S(\mathcal{P}, \mathcal{N}') \cup \mathcal{P} = \mathcal{N}' \wedge |S(\mathcal{P}, \mathcal{N}')| \leq T - |\mathcal{F}|\}$$

From the definition of $\mathcal{N}'$ and the definition of $S(\mathcal{P}, \mathcal{N}')$ we know that:

$$\forall\, n \in \mathcal{N}' : \exists\, m \in \mathcal{N}' : n \in S(m, \mathcal{N}')$$

i.e. every node in $\mathcal{N}'$ is element in a set of suspicious nodes for another node in $\mathcal{N}'$ within $\mathcal{N}'$.

Thus, for every correct node y in $\mathcal{N}'$, there is presupposed correct-set $P \in CPS(\mathcal{N}')$ with $y \in S(P, \mathcal{N}')$. An upper bound to the maximal number of correct nodes put in the fault-set, can therefore be given by:

$$upperbound = \left| \left\{ y \middle| \left(y \in \left(\bigcup_{P \in CPS(\mathcal{N}')} S(P, \mathcal{N}') \right) \right) \right\} \right|$$

Notice that for a node $x \in \mathcal{N}'$, in every presupposed correct-set $P \in CPS(\mathcal{N}')$, for which $x \in P$, the set of suspicious nodes $S(x, \mathcal{N}')$ is the same. If node x is correct, then, by assumption A1, its set of suspicious nodes $S(x, \mathcal{N}')$ contains no other correct nodes. Now, since all nodes in $\mathcal{N}'$ are element in a set of suspicious nodes $S(x, \mathcal{N}')$ for some $x \in \mathcal{N}'$, and only the sets of suspicious nodes $S(x, \mathcal{N}')$ for faulty nodes x contain correct nodes, an upper bound to the maximal number of correct nodes put in the fault-set, is given by:

$$upperbound = \left| \left\{ y \middle| \left(\left(y \in \left(\bigcup_{x \in \mathcal{N}'} S(x, \mathcal{N}') \right) \right) \wedge faulty\,(x) \right) \right\} \right|$$

We will calculate the maximal number of correct nodes that may be put in the fault-set in the case that X $(X > 1)$ presupposed correct-sets contain only one faulty node, and also in the case that one presupposed correct-set contains X faulty nodes.

The case: X presupposed correct-sets containing one faulty node
Assume a presupposed correct-set $P \in CPS(\mathcal{N}')$ contains several nodes, of which at most one may be faulty. Then, the other $(S' - 1)$ faulty nodes must be in $S(P, \mathcal{N}')$. Furthermore, $|\, S(P, \mathcal{N}')\,| \leq T'$. Thus, the set of suspicious nodes $S(P, \mathcal{N}')$ can not contain more than $T' - (S' - 1)$ correct nodes. So by selecting a presupposed correct-set with one faulty node, a maximum of $T' - (S' - 1)$ correct nodes can be put in the fault-set. So by X of these presupposed correct-sets, $X*(T' - (S' - 1))$ correct nodes can be put in the fault-set.

The case: one presupposed correct-set containing X faulty nodes
If a presupposed correct-set containing X faulty nodes $(X \geq 1)$, the remaining set of nodes $\mathcal{N}' - P$ contains at most $T' - (S' - X)$ correct nodes.

Provided that $T' \geq S'$ and $X \geq 1$, it can be derived that $X * (T' - (S' - 1))$ is always greater than or equal to $T' - (S' - X)$. It follows then, that the number of correctly functioning nodes being put in the fault-set is maximal, if each presupposed correct-set contains only one faulty node. ❑

We will now use the result of this lemma in the following theorem.

Theorem 1:
In the diagnosis algorithm, the number of correct nodes accused of being faulty, is always less than or equal to $\mathrm{Min}[\, G', S' * (T' - (S' - 1))]$.

Proof:

From assumption A1, we know that a correct node does not accuse other correct nodes of being faulty. So a presupposed correct-set containing only correct nodes only accuses faulty nodes of being faulty. Thus, in order to calculate the maximum number of correct nodes accused of being faulty, we need only consider presupposed correct-sets containing one or more faulty nodes.

From lemma 1, we know that the number of correctly functioning nodes accused of being faulty is maximal, if each presupposed correct-set contains at most one faulty node. The number of faulty nodes in $\mathcal{N}'$ is S'. Thus at most S' of these presupposed correct-sets can be found. From the foregoing, we know that these S' presupposed correct-sets can accuse a maximum of $S' *(T' - (S' - 1))$ correct nodes of being faulty.

Of course, the number of correct nodes accused of being faulty can never become greater than the total number G' of correct nodes in $\mathcal{N}'$. So, in the diagnosis algorithm, the number of correct nodes accused of being faulty, is always less than or equal to Min[G', $S' *(T' - (S' - 1))$]. ❑

4. Determining the maximum number of nodes in the service that are accused of being faulty

If we assume that $G' \geq S' *(T' - (S' - 1))$, we find the maximal number of *correct* nodes marked faulty, which is equal to $S' *(T' - (S' - 1))$. In the table below, for some practical values of S' and T', we have calculated the maximal number of correct nodes accused of being faulty.

	$S' = 1$	$S' = 2$	$S' = 3$	$S' = 4$
$T' = 5$	5	8	9	8
$T' = 4$	4	6	6	4
$T' = 3$	3	4	3	-
$T' = 2$	2	2	-	-
$T' = 1$	1	-	-	-

The maximum number of *faulty* nodes marked faulty in the algorithm is equal to S. By definition, $S = S' + T - T'$ (because $S' = S - b$, and $T' = T - b$). The maximum number of (either faulty or correct) nodes marked faulty in the algorithm is the sum of the maximum number of correct nodes marked faulty and the maximum number of faulty nodes marked faulty, and is equal to $S' *(T' - (S' - 1)) + S' + T - T'$.

By differentiating this function on S', we can find the value for S' for which the number of correct nodes accused of being faulty, is maximal.

$$f(S') = S'*(T' - (S' - 1)) + S' + T - T' = -S'^2 + (T' + 2)*S' + T - T'$$
$$f(S') \text{ is maximal for } S' = 1/2*(T' + 2).$$

For *even* T', the maximum value for $f(S')$ is indeed reached at $S' = 1/2*(T' + 2)$. Since S' is always an integer value, for *odd* T', the maximum value for $f(S')$ is reached at $S' = 1/2*(T' + 1)$ and $S' = 1/2*(T' + 3)$ respectively.

If we calculate the value of $f(S')$ for these values of S', in all cases, we find that the maximum number of nodes marked faulty is $\lfloor 1/4*T'^2 + T + 1 \rfloor$.(For any positive real value r, $\lfloor r \rfloor$ is defined as the smallest integer value less than or equal to r.). For fixed value of T, the number of nodes marked faulty increases with increasing T'. The value of T' is limited by the requirement $T \geq T'$. So, for any value of T, the maximum number of nodes marked faulty is found by selecting $T' = T$ in $\lfloor 1/4*T'^2 + T + 1 \rfloor$. In the table below, for some practical values of T, the maximum number of nodes marked faulty is given

T	1	2	3	4	5
#nodes marked faulty = $\lfloor 1/4*T^2 + T + 1 \rfloor$	2	4	6	9	12

5. Determining the minimally required number of nodes in the service

After having performed the above-described diagnosis algorithm, the correct nodes have a consistent view of the set of nodes that must be removed from the service. The only way in which the correct nodes can exclude this set of possibly faulty nodes is by creating some secret information which is kept within the set of correct nodes. This secret information is the new identification of the service to the clients. The remaining nodes must form a majority in order to be able to convince clients who use the service that the identification of the service has changed. So the number of nodes required in the service must be more than twice the number of nodes marked faulty by the diagnosis algorithm. In the table below, for some values of T, we have calculated N, being the minimally required number of nodes in the service.

T	1	2	3	4	5
N	5	9	13	19	25

6. Conclusion

In this paper, we have described a new diagnosis algorithm, by means of which we can guarantee that all nodes behaving in a faulty way are removed from a fault-tolerant service. Timely removing all faulty nodes is very important in order to be able to guarantee the correctness of a fault-tolerant service despite the presence of up to T maliciously functioning nodes. Our algorithm is based on the realistic assumption of imperfect tests, therefore, indeterminate test results may occur. In this case, in order to be able to exclude all faulty nodes from the service, it may be inevitable, that some correctly functioning nodes from the fault-tolerant service are also removed. We have derived an upper bound on the number of correctly functioning nodes that may be removed from the fault-tolerant service by execution of the algorithm. In order to be able to tolerate up to T maliciously functioning nodes, the minimally required number of nodes in the service is $2 * \lfloor 1/4*T^2 + T + 1 \rfloor + 1$.

Appendix 1: Proof of correctness of the reduction rules

In this appendix, we will prove that the reduction rules are correct, i.e. by application of the reduction rules only faulty nodes are put in the fault-set $\mathcal{F}$ and only correct nodes are put in the correct-set C. In other words, we prove, that application of the reduction rules preserves the correctness of:

$$\forall n \in \mathcal{F}: faulty(n)$$
$$\forall n \in C: correct(n)$$

Here, for a node n, $faulty(n)$ means that n is faulty, whereas $correct(n)$ means that the node n is correct.

Formally, we can denote the assumptions as follows:

A1. $\forall a,b \in \mathcal{N}:(correct(a) \wedge correct(b)) \Rightarrow \mathcal{M}_{a,b} = C$

A2. $\forall a \in \mathcal{N}: faulty(a) \Rightarrow (\exists b \in \mathcal{N}: correct(b) \wedge (\mathcal{M}_{a,b} = F \vee \mathcal{M}_{b,a} = F))$

A3. $\forall a \in \mathcal{N}: (faulty(a) \Rightarrow \neg correct(a)) \wedge (correct(a) \Rightarrow \neg faulty(a))$

A4. $\forall a,b \in \mathcal{N}: (\mathcal{M}_{a,b} = F \Rightarrow \neg (\mathcal{M}_{a,b} = C)) \wedge (\mathcal{M}_{a,b} = C \Rightarrow \neg (\mathcal{M}_{a,b} = F))$

A5. $|\{ a \in \mathcal{N}: faulty(a)\}| \leq T$

By applying reduction rules to the elements of set $\mathcal{N}$, the number of elements in $\mathcal{F}$ resp. C increase. In our proofs, we will use the notations $\mathcal{F}_i$ resp. C_j, to indicate the fault-set $\mathcal{F}$ containing i nodes, respectively the correct-set C containing j nodes. Analoguously, we use the notation $\mathcal{P}_{i,j}$ to indicate a presupposed correct-set which is element of $\mathcal{PS}(n, \mathcal{N} - \mathcal{F}_i - C_j)$.

By induction on the number of elements i resp. j in $\mathcal{F}_i$ and C_j, we prove that the predicates: $(\forall n \in \mathcal{F}_i: faulty(n))$ and $(\forall n \in C_j: correct(n))$ are invariant under application of the reduction rules.

Proof (By induction):

For arbitrary fault-set $\mathcal{F}_i$ and correct-set C_j, the reduction rules are as follows:

R1. $\forall n \in \mathcal{N} - \mathcal{F}_i - C_j : (\mathcal{M}_{n,n} = F \Rightarrow \mathcal{F}_{i+1} = \mathcal{F}_i \cup \{n\})$

R2. $\forall n \in \mathcal{N} - \mathcal{F}_i - C_j : |\{ m \in \mathcal{N} - \mathcal{F}_i | \mathcal{M}_{m,n} = F \vee \mathcal{M}_{n,m} = F \}| > (T - | \mathcal{F}_i |) \Rightarrow \mathcal{F}_{i+1} = \mathcal{F}_i \cup \{n\}$

R3. $\forall n \in \mathcal{N} - \mathcal{F}_i - C_j : (\forall m \in \mathcal{N} - \mathcal{F}_i : \mathcal{M}_{m,n} = C \wedge \mathcal{M}_{n,m} = C) \Rightarrow C_{j+1} = C_j \cup \{n\}$

R4. $\forall n \in \mathcal{N} - \mathcal{F}_i - C_j : (\neg (\exists P_{i,j} \in PS(n, \mathcal{N} - \mathcal{F}_i - C_j) : |\mathcal{N} - \mathcal{F}_i - C_j - P_{i,j}| \leq T - |\mathcal{F}_i|)) \Rightarrow$
$$\mathcal{F}_{i+1} = \mathcal{F}_i \cup \{n\}$$

Basis:
The basis of the proof by induction is the case $i = 0$ and $j = 0$. Since $\mathcal{F}_0 = \emptyset$ and $C_0 = \emptyset$, we may conclude that:

$$\forall n \in \mathcal{F}_0 : faulty(n)$$
$$\forall n \in C_0 : correct(n)$$

Induction step:
The induction hypothesis is:

$$\forall n \in \mathcal{F}_i : faulty(n) \qquad \text{(C1)}$$
and
$$\forall n \in C_j : correct(n) \qquad \text{(C2)}$$

Assuming the induction hypothesis holds, we must prove the correctness of:
$$\forall n \in \mathcal{F}_{i+1} : faulty(n)$$
and
$$\forall n \in C_{j+1} : correct(n)$$

From the definition of the reduction rules, we know that:
$\forall n \in \mathcal{N} - \mathcal{F}_i - C_j : (n \in \mathcal{F}_{i+1} - \mathcal{F}_i \Rightarrow$
$$(\mathcal{M}_{n,n} = F \vee$$
$$|\{m \in \mathcal{N} - \mathcal{F}_i | \mathcal{M}_{m,n} = F \vee \mathcal{M}_{n,m} = F\}| > (T - |\mathcal{F}_i|) \vee$$
$$(\neg (\exists P_{i,j} \in PS(n, \mathcal{N} - \mathcal{F}_i - C_j) : |\mathcal{N} - \mathcal{F}_i - C_j - P_{i,j}| \leq T - |\mathcal{F}_i|))) \qquad \text{(C3)}$$
i.e. a node n is only added to fault-set $\mathcal{F}_i$, if at least one of the premises of the reduction rules R1, R2, or R4 holds for node n with respect to $\mathcal{F}_i$.

We will now prove that if one of the premises of the reduction rules R1, R2, or R4 holds for node n with respect to $\mathcal{F}_i$, then n is faulty, i.e.
$\forall n \in \mathcal{N} - \mathcal{F}_i - C_j : (\mathcal{M}_{n,n} = F \vee$
$$|\{m \in \mathcal{N} - \mathcal{F}_i | \mathcal{M}_{m,n} = F \vee \mathcal{M}_{n,m} = F\}| > (T - |\mathcal{F}_i|) \vee$$
$$(\neg (\exists P_{i,j} \in PS(n, \mathcal{N} - \mathcal{F}_i - C_j) : |\mathcal{N} - \mathcal{F}_i - C_j - P_{i,j}| \leq T - |\mathcal{F}_i|))) \Rightarrow faulty(n) \quad \text{(C4)}$$
From C3 and C4, we may conclude that:
$$\forall n \in \mathcal{N} - \mathcal{F}_i - C_j : (n \in \mathcal{F}_{i+1} - \mathcal{F}_i \Rightarrow faulty(n)) \qquad \text{(C5)}$$
From C1 and C5, we may conclude that:
$$\forall n \in \mathcal{F}_{i+1} : faulty(n) \qquad \text{(C6)}$$

Analoguously, from the definition of the reduction rules, we know that:
$$\forall n \in \mathcal{N} - \mathcal{F}_i - C_j : (n \in C_{j+1} - C_j \Rightarrow (\forall m \in \mathcal{N} - \mathcal{F}_i : \mathcal{M}_{m,n} = C \wedge \mathcal{M}_{n,m} = C)) \qquad \text{(C7)}$$
i.e. a node n is only added to correct-set C_j, if the premise of reduction rule R3 holds for node n with respect to C_j.

We will now prove that if the premise of reduction rule R3 holds for node n with respect to C_j, then n is correct, i.e.
$$\forall n \in \mathcal{N} - \mathcal{F}_i - C_j : (\forall m \in \mathcal{N} - \mathcal{F}_i : \mathcal{M}_{m,n} = C \wedge \mathcal{M}_{n,m} = C) \Rightarrow correct(n) \qquad \text{(C8)}$$
From C7 and C8, we may conclude that:
$$\forall n \in \mathcal{N} - \mathcal{F}_i - C_j : (n \in C_{j+1} - C_j \Rightarrow correct(n)) \qquad \text{(C9)}$$

From C2 and C9, we may conclude that:

$$\forall\, n \in C_{j+1} : correct(n) \tag{C10}$$

Proof of C4 and C8:

R1. We must prove that:

$$\forall\, n \in \mathcal{N}\text{-}\,\mathcal{F}_i\text{-}\,C_j : (\mathcal{M}_{n,n} = F \Rightarrow faulty(n))$$

From A1 and $\mathcal{N}\text{-}\,\mathcal{F}_i\text{-}\,C_j \subset \mathcal{N}$, we know: $(\forall\, a,b \in \mathcal{N}\text{-}\,\mathcal{F}_i\text{-}\,C_j : (\,correct(a) \wedge correct(b)) \Rightarrow \mathcal{M}_{a,b} = C)$

$$(\forall\, a,b \in \mathcal{N}\text{-}\,\mathcal{F}_i\text{-}\,C_j : (\,correct(a) \wedge correct(b)) \Rightarrow \mathcal{M}_{a,b} = C)$$
$\Rightarrow$ {Select $a = b$}
$$(\forall\, a \in \mathcal{N}\text{-}\,\mathcal{F}_i\text{-}\,C_j : correct(a) \Rightarrow \mathcal{M}_{a,a} = C)$$
$\Rightarrow$ {assumption A3 and A4: $(\neg faulty(a) \Rightarrow correct(a))$ and $(\mathcal{M}_{a,a} = C \Rightarrow \neg (\mathcal{M}_{a,a} = F))$}
$$(\forall\, a \in \mathcal{N}\text{-}\,\mathcal{F}_i\text{-}\,C_j : \neg faulty(a) \Rightarrow \neg \mathcal{M}_{a,a} = F)$$
$\Rightarrow$
$$(\forall\, a \in \mathcal{N}\text{-}\,\mathcal{F}_i\text{-}\,C_j : \mathcal{M}_{a,a} = F \Rightarrow faulty(a))$$

R2. We must prove that:

$$\forall\, n \in \mathcal{N}\text{-}\,\mathcal{F}_i - C_j : |\,\{\, m \in \mathcal{N}\text{-}\,\mathcal{F}_i \,|\, \mathcal{M}_{m,n} = F \vee \mathcal{M}_{n,m} = F \,\}\,| > (T - |\,\mathcal{F}_i\,|) \Rightarrow faulty(n)$$

$|\,\{\, m \in \mathcal{N}\text{-}\,\mathcal{F}_i \,|\, \mathcal{M}_{m,n} = F \vee \mathcal{M}_{n,m} = F \,\}\,| > (T - |\,\mathcal{F}_i\,|)$
$\Rightarrow$ {assumption A3 $\Rightarrow \forall\, n \in \mathcal{N} : (\,faulty(n) \vee correct(n))$ }
$(\,faulty(n) \vee correct(n)) \wedge (|\,\{\, m \in \mathcal{N}\text{-}\,\mathcal{F}_i \,|\, \mathcal{M}_{m,n} = F \vee \mathcal{M}_{n,m} = F \,\}\,| > (T - |\,\mathcal{F}_i\,|))$
$\Rightarrow$ { distributivity }
$(\,faulty(n) \wedge |\,\{\, m \in \mathcal{N}\text{-}\,\mathcal{F}_i \,|\, \mathcal{M}_{m,n} = F \vee \mathcal{M}_{n,m} = F \,\}\,| > (T - |\,\mathcal{F}_i\,|)) \vee$
$\qquad\qquad (correct(n) \wedge |\,\{\, m \in \mathcal{N}\text{-}\,\mathcal{F}_i \,|\, \mathcal{M}_{m,n} = F \vee \mathcal{M}_{n,m} = F \,\}\,| > (T - |\,\mathcal{F}_i\,|))$
$\Rightarrow$ { $A \wedge B \Rightarrow A$ }
$(\,faulty(n)) \vee (correct(n) \wedge |\,\{\, m \in \mathcal{N}\text{-}\,\mathcal{F}_i \,|\, \mathcal{M}_{m,n} = F \vee \mathcal{M}_{n,m} = F \,\}\,| + |\,\mathcal{F}_i\,| > T)$
$\Rightarrow$ {assumption A1 $\Rightarrow \forall\, m \in \mathcal{N} : (correct(n) \wedge (\mathcal{M}_{m,n} = F \vee \mathcal{M}_{n,m} = F) \Rightarrow faulty(m))$ }
$(\,faulty(n)) \vee (|\,\{\, m \in \mathcal{N}\text{-}\,\mathcal{F}_i \,|\, faulty(m) \,\}\,| + |\,\mathcal{F}_i\,| > T)$
$\Rightarrow$ { induction hypothesis $\Rightarrow \forall\, n \in \mathcal{F}_i : faulty(n)$ }
$(\,faulty(n)) \vee (|\,\{\, m \in \mathcal{N}\text{-}\,\mathcal{F}_i \,|\, faulty(m) \,\}\,| + |\,\{\, m \in \mathcal{F}_i \,|\, faulty(m)\}\,| > T)$
$\Rightarrow$ {assumption A5 $\Rightarrow (|\,\{\, m \in \mathcal{N}\,|\, faulty(m) \,\}\,| \leq T)$ }
$faulty(n)$

R3: We must prove that:

$$\forall\, n \in \mathcal{N}\text{-}\,\mathcal{F}_i - C_j : (\forall\, m \in \mathcal{N}\text{-}\,\mathcal{F}_i : \mathcal{M}_{m,n} = C \wedge \mathcal{M}_{n,m} = C) \Rightarrow correct(n)$$

$(\forall\, m \in \mathcal{N}\text{-}\,\mathcal{F}_i : \mathcal{M}_{m,n} = C \wedge \mathcal{M}_{n,m} = C)$
$\Rightarrow$
$\neg\, (\exists\, m \in \mathcal{N}\text{-}\,\mathcal{F}_i : \mathcal{M}_{m,n} = F \vee \mathcal{M}_{n,m} = F)$
$\Rightarrow$
$\neg\, (\exists\, m \in \mathcal{N}\text{-}\,\mathcal{F}_i : correct(m) \wedge (\mathcal{M}_{m,n} = F \vee \mathcal{M}_{n,m} = F))$
$\Rightarrow$ {induction hypothesis $\Rightarrow \forall\, n \in \mathcal{F}_i : faulty(n)$ }
$\neg\, (\exists\, m \in \mathcal{N} : correct(m) \wedge (\mathcal{M}_{m,n} = F \vee \mathcal{M}_{n,m} = F))$
$\Rightarrow$ {assumption A2 }

$\neg faulty(n)$
$\Rightarrow$ {assumption A3 }
$correct(n)$

R4. We must prove that:

$\forall n \in \mathcal{N} - \mathcal{F}_i - C_j : (\neg (\exists \mathcal{P}_{i,j} \in \mathcal{PS}(n,\mathcal{N} - \mathcal{F}_i - C_j) : |\mathcal{N} - \mathcal{F}_i - C_j - \mathcal{P}_{i,j}| \le T - |\mathcal{F}_i|)) \Rightarrow faulty(n)$

We prove the following equivalent predicate:

$\forall n \in \mathcal{N} - \mathcal{F}_i - C_j : (correct(n) \Rightarrow (\exists \mathcal{P}_{i,j} \in \mathcal{PS}(n,\mathcal{N} - \mathcal{F}_i - C_j) : |\mathcal{N} - \mathcal{F}_i - C_j - \mathcal{P}_{i,j}| \le T - |\mathcal{F}_i|)$

Let $\mathcal{P}_{i,j} = \{n \in \mathcal{N} - \mathcal{F}_i - C_j \mid correct(n)\}$. Clearly, $correct(n) \Rightarrow n \in \mathcal{P}_{i,j}$. For this set $\mathcal{P}_{i,j}$, we prove that $\mathcal{P}_{i,j} \in \mathcal{PS}(n,\mathcal{N} - \mathcal{F}_i - C_j)$ and $|\mathcal{N} - \mathcal{F}_i - C_j - \mathcal{P}_{i,j}| \le T - |\mathcal{F}_i|$.

$\mathcal{P}_{i,j} \in \mathcal{PS}(n,\mathcal{N} - \mathcal{F}_i - C_j)$
$\Leftarrow$ {definition of $\mathcal{PS}(n,\mathcal{N} - \mathcal{F}_i - C_j)$ }
$\quad n \in \mathcal{P}_{i,j} \wedge \mathcal{S}(\mathcal{P}_{i,j}, \mathcal{N} - \mathcal{F}_i - C_j) \cap \mathcal{P}_{i,j} = \emptyset$
$\Leftarrow$ {definition of $\mathcal{S}(\mathcal{P}_{i,j}, \mathcal{N} - \mathcal{F}_i - C_j)$ }
$\quad n \in \mathcal{P}_{i,j} \wedge \{m \in \mathcal{N} - \mathcal{F}_i - C_j \mid i \in \mathcal{P}_{i,j} \wedge (\mathcal{M}_{m,i} = F \vee \mathcal{M}_{i,m} = F)\} \cap \mathcal{P}_{i,j} = \emptyset$
$\Leftarrow$ { $correct(i) \Leftarrow i \in \mathcal{P}_{i,j}$ }
$\quad n \in \mathcal{P}_{i,j} \wedge \{m \in \mathcal{N} - \mathcal{F}_i - C_j \mid correct(i) \wedge (\mathcal{M}_{m,i} = F \vee \mathcal{M}_{i,m} = F)\} \cap$
$\qquad\qquad\qquad\qquad\qquad \{n \in \mathcal{N} - \mathcal{F}_i - C_j \mid correct(n)\} = \emptyset$
$\Leftarrow$ {assumption A1 $\Rightarrow \forall m \in \mathcal{N} - \mathcal{F}_i - C_j : (correct(i) \wedge (\mathcal{M}_{m,i} = F \vee \mathcal{M}_{i,m} = F) \Rightarrow faulty(m))$ }
$\quad n \in \mathcal{P}_{i,j} \wedge \{m \in \mathcal{N} - \mathcal{F}_i - C_j \mid faulty(m) \} \cap \{n \in \mathcal{N} - \mathcal{F}_i - C_j \mid correct(n)\} = \emptyset$
$\Leftarrow$ {assumption A3, and $\mathcal{N} - \mathcal{F}_i - C_j \subset \mathcal{N}$}
$\quad n \in \mathcal{P}_{i,j}$
$\Leftarrow$ {definition of $\mathcal{P}_{i,j}$ }
$\quad correct(n)$

$\quad |\mathcal{N} - \mathcal{F}_i - C_j - \mathcal{P}_{i,j}| \le T - |\mathcal{F}_i|$
$\Leftarrow$ {assumption A3, and def. of $\mathcal{P}_{i,j} \Rightarrow \forall m \in \mathcal{N} - \mathcal{F}_i - C_j - \mathcal{P}_{i,j} : faulty(m)$ }
$\quad |\{m \in \mathcal{N} - \mathcal{F}_i - C_j - \mathcal{P}_{i,j} \mid faulty(m) \}| \le T - |\mathcal{F}_i|$
$\Leftarrow$ {induction hypothesis $\Rightarrow \forall n \in \mathcal{F}_i : faulty(n)$ }
$\quad |\{m \in \mathcal{N} - \mathcal{F}_i - C_j - \mathcal{P}_{i,j} \mid faulty(m) \}| \le T - |\{m \in \mathcal{F}_i \mid faulty(m) \}|$
$\Leftarrow$
$\quad |\{m \in \mathcal{N} - C_j - \mathcal{P}_{i,j} \mid faulty(m) \}| \le T$
$\Leftarrow$ { $correct(i) \Leftarrow i \in \mathcal{P}_{i,j}$ and assumption A3 }
$\quad |\{m \in \mathcal{N} - C_j \mid faulty(m) \}| \le T$
$\Leftarrow$ {induction hypothesis $\Rightarrow \forall n \in C_j : correct(n)$ and assumption A3}
$\quad |\{m \in \mathcal{N} \mid faulty(m) \}| \le T$
$\Leftarrow$ {assumption A5 }
$\quad$ TRUE $\qquad\qquad\qquad\qquad\qquad\qquad\qquad\qquad\qquad\qquad \Box$

Appendix 2: Proof of consistency of the reduction rules

In this appendix, we will prove the consistency of the reduction rules as formulated below:
1. $\forall n \in \mathcal{N} - \mathcal{F}_i - C_j : (\mathcal{M}_{n,n} = F \Rightarrow \mathcal{F}_{i+1} = \mathcal{F}_i \cup \{n\})$

2. $\forall\, n \in \mathcal{N} - \mathcal{F}_i - C_j: |\{\, m \in \mathcal{N} - \mathcal{F}_i \,|\, \mathcal{M}_{m,n} = F \vee \mathcal{M}_{n,m} = F \,\}| > (T - |\mathcal{F}_i|) \Rightarrow \mathcal{F}_{i+1} = \mathcal{F}_i \cup \{n\}$

3. $\forall\, n \in \mathcal{N} - \mathcal{F}_i - C_j: (\forall\, m \in \mathcal{N} - \mathcal{F}_i: \mathcal{M}_{m,n} = C \wedge \mathcal{M}_{n,m} = C) \Rightarrow C_{j+1} = C_j \cup \{n\}$

4. $\forall\, n \in \mathcal{N} - \mathcal{F}_i - C_j: (\neg(\exists\, \mathcal{P}_{i,j} \in \mathcal{PS}(n, \mathcal{N} - \mathcal{F}_i - C_j): |\mathcal{N} - \mathcal{F}_i - C_j - \mathcal{P}_{i,j}| \le T - |\mathcal{F}_i|) \Rightarrow$
   $\qquad \mathcal{F}_{i+1} = \mathcal{F}_i \cup \{n\}$

First, reduction rule 1 is applied to all nodes for which $\mathcal{M}_{n,n} = F$. Then, reduction rules 2 through 4 may be applied in any order. In this appendix, we will prove that:

C1. $\forall\, a \in \{1,2,3,4\}: (\exists\, x \in \mathcal{N} - \mathcal{F}_i - C_j: $ reduction rule a can be applied to node x for fault-set $\mathcal{F}_i$)

$\qquad \wedge\, \mathcal{F}_{i+1} = \mathcal{F}_i \cup \{y\} \wedge (y \ne x) \Rightarrow$ (reduction rule a can be applied to node x for fault-set $\mathcal{F}_{i+1}$)

i.e. putting a node y in the fault-set does not change the applicability of the reduction rules 1 through 4 for node x.

C2. $\forall\, a \in \{1,2,3,4\}: (\exists\, x \in \mathcal{N} - \mathcal{F}_i - C_j: $ reduction rule a can be applied to node x for correct-set C_j)

$\qquad \wedge\, C_{j+1} = C_j \cup \{y\} \wedge (y \ne x) \Rightarrow$ (reduction rule a can be applied to node x for correct-set C_{j+1})

i.e. putting a node y in the correct-set does not change the applicability of the reduction rules 1 through 4 for node x.

Furthermore, we must prove that the reduction rules 2 through 4 are consistent, i.e. it must be impossible to classify a node both in the fault-set and in the correct-set. A node x is put in the correct-set only if the premise of reduction rule 3 is satisfied. We prove that if a node y satisfies the premise of reduction rule 2 or 4, node x and y must be two different nodes. Thus:

C3. $\forall\, a \in \{2,4\}: \quad (\exists\, x \in \mathcal{N} - \mathcal{F}_i - C_j: $ reduction rule a can be applied to node x) $\wedge$

$\qquad\qquad (\exists\, y \in \mathcal{N} - \mathcal{F}_i - C_j: $ reduction rule 3 can be applied to node y) $\Rightarrow (y \ne x)$

Proof of C1:

$a = 1$

$\exists\, x \in \mathcal{N} - \mathcal{F}_i - C_j: (\mathcal{M}_{x,x} = F) \wedge \mathcal{F}_{i+1} = \mathcal{F}_i \cup \{y\} \wedge (y \ne x) \Rightarrow (\mathcal{M}_{x,x} = F)$

$a = 2$

$\exists\, x \in \mathcal{N} - \mathcal{F}_i - C_j: |\{\, k \in \mathcal{N} - \mathcal{F}_i \,|\, \mathcal{M}_{k,x} = F \vee \mathcal{M}_{x,k} = F \,\}| > (T - |\mathcal{F}_i|) \wedge \mathcal{F}_{i+1} = \mathcal{F}_i \cup \{y\} \wedge (y \ne x) \Rightarrow$

$|\{\, k \in \mathcal{N} - \mathcal{F}_{i+1} \,|\, \mathcal{M}_{k,x} = F \vee \mathcal{M}_{x,k} = F \,\}| + 1 \ge |\{\, k \in \mathcal{N} - \mathcal{F}_i \,|\, \mathcal{M}_{k,x} = F \vee \mathcal{M}_{x,k} = F \,\}| >$

$(T - |\mathcal{F}_i|) \ge (T - |\mathcal{F}_{i+1}| + 1) \Rightarrow |\{\, k \in \mathcal{N} - \mathcal{F}_{i+1} \,|\, \mathcal{M}_{k,x} = F \vee \mathcal{M}_{x,k} = F \,\}| \ge (T - |\mathcal{F}_{i+1}|)$

$a = 3$

$\exists\, x \in \mathcal{N} - \mathcal{F}_i - C_j: (\forall\, m \in \mathcal{N} - \mathcal{F}_i: \mathcal{M}_{m,x} = C \wedge \mathcal{M}_{x,m} = C) \wedge \mathcal{F}_{i+1} = \mathcal{F}_i \cup \{y\} \wedge (y \ne x) \Rightarrow$

$(\forall\, m \in \mathcal{N} - \mathcal{F}_{i+1}: \mathcal{M}_{m,x} = C \wedge \mathcal{M}_{x,m} = C)$ since $\mathcal{N} - \mathcal{F}_{i+1} \subset \mathcal{N} - \mathcal{F}_i$

$a = 4$

$\exists\, x \in \mathcal{N} - \mathcal{F}_i - C_j: (\neg(\exists\, \mathcal{P}_{i,j} \in \mathcal{PS}(x, \mathcal{N} - \mathcal{F}_i - C_j): |\mathcal{N} - \mathcal{F}_i - C_j - \mathcal{P}_{i,j}| \le T - |\mathcal{F}_i|) \wedge$

$\mathcal{F}_{i+1} = \mathcal{F}_i \cup \{y\} \wedge (y \ne x) \Rightarrow (\neg(\exists\, \mathcal{P}_{i,j} \in \mathcal{PS}(x, \mathcal{N} - \mathcal{F}_{i+1} - C_j): |\mathcal{N} - \mathcal{F}_{i+1} - C_j - \mathcal{P}_{i,j}| \le T - |\mathcal{F}_{i+1}|)$

since $\mathcal{PS}(x, \mathcal{N} - \mathcal{F}_{i+1} - C_j) \subset \mathcal{PS}(x, \mathcal{N} - \mathcal{F}_i - C_j) \wedge |\mathcal{N} - \mathcal{F}_{i+1} - C_j - \mathcal{P}_{i,j}| \le T - |\mathcal{F}_{i+1}|$

The predicate $|\mathcal{N} - \mathcal{F}_{i+1} - C_j - \mathcal{P}_{i,j}| \le T - |\mathcal{F}_{i+1}|$ is implied by:

$|\mathcal{N} - \mathcal{F}_{i+1} - C_j - \mathcal{P}_{i,j}| + 1 = |\mathcal{N} - \mathcal{F}_i - C_j - \mathcal{P}_{i,j}|$ and $|\mathcal{N} - \mathcal{F}_i - C_j - \mathcal{P}_{i,j}| \le T - |\mathcal{F}_i|$ and

$T - |\mathcal{F}_i| = T - |\mathcal{F}_{i+1}| + 1$

Proof of C2:

$a = 1$

$\exists\, x \in \mathcal{N} - \mathcal{F}_i - C_j: (\mathcal{M}_{x,x} = F) \wedge C_{j+1} = C_j \cup \{y\} \wedge (y \ne x) \Rightarrow (\mathcal{M}_{x,x} = F)$

$a = 2$

$\exists\, x \in \mathcal{N} - \mathcal{F}_i - C_j : |\{k \in \mathcal{N} - \mathcal{F}_i | \mathcal{M}_{k,x} = F \vee \mathcal{M}_{x,k} = F\}| > (T - |\mathcal{F}_i|) \wedge C_{j+1} = C_j \cup \{y\} \wedge (y \neq x) \Rightarrow$
$|\{k \in \mathcal{N} - \mathcal{F}_i | \mathcal{M}_{k,x} = F \vee \mathcal{M}_{x,k} = F\}| \geq (T - |\mathcal{F}_i|)$

$a = 3$

$\exists\, x \in \mathcal{N} - \mathcal{F}_i - C_j : ((\forall\, m \in \mathcal{N} - \mathcal{F}_i : \mathcal{M}_{m,x} = C \wedge \mathcal{M}_{x,m} = C) \wedge C_{j+1} = C_j \cup \{y\} \wedge (y \neq x) \Rightarrow$
$(\forall\, m \in \mathcal{N} - \mathcal{F}_i : \mathcal{M}_{m,x} = C \wedge \mathcal{M}_{x,m} = C)$

$a = 4$

We must prove that:

$\exists\, x \in \mathcal{N} - \mathcal{F}_i - C_j : (\neg (\exists\, \mathcal{P}_{i,j} \in \mathcal{PS}(x, \mathcal{N} - \mathcal{F}_i - C_j) : |\mathcal{N} - \mathcal{F}_i - C_j - \mathcal{P}_{i,j}| \leq T - |\mathcal{F}_i|) \wedge$
$C_{j+1} = C_j \cup \{y\} \wedge (y \neq x) \Rightarrow (\neg(\exists\, \mathcal{P}_{i,j} \in \mathcal{PS}(x, \mathcal{N} - \mathcal{F}_i - C_{j+1}) : |\mathcal{N} - \mathcal{F}_i - C_{j+1} - \mathcal{P}_{i,j}| \leq T - |\mathcal{F}_i|)$
Proof:

We distinguish two cases: $y \in \mathcal{P}_{i,j}$ and $y \notin \mathcal{P}_{i,j}$

Case $y \in \mathcal{P}_{i,j}$

$\quad \exists\, x \in \mathcal{N} - \mathcal{F}_i - C_j : (\forall\, \mathcal{P}_{i,j} \in \mathcal{PS}(x, \mathcal{N} - \mathcal{F}_i - C_j) : |\mathcal{N} - \mathcal{F}_i - C_j - \mathcal{P}_{i,j}| > T - |\mathcal{F}_i|) \wedge$
$\quad C_{j+1} = C_j \cup \{y\} \wedge (y \neq x) \wedge (y \in \mathcal{P}_{i,j})$
$\Rightarrow \{ C_{j+1} = C_j \cup \{y\} \wedge (y \in \mathcal{P}_{i,j}) \Rightarrow |\mathcal{N} - \mathcal{F}_i - C_j - \mathcal{P}_{i,j}| = |\mathcal{N} - \mathcal{F}_i - C_{j+1} - \mathcal{P}_{i,j}|\}$
$\quad (\forall\, \mathcal{P}_{i,j} \in \mathcal{PS}(x, \mathcal{N} - \mathcal{F}_i - C_j) : |\mathcal{N} - \mathcal{F}_i - C_{j+1} - \mathcal{P}_{i,j}| > T - |\mathcal{F}_i|)$
$\Rightarrow \{ \mathcal{PS}(x, \mathcal{N} - \mathcal{F}_i - C_{j+1}) \subset \mathcal{PS}(x, \mathcal{N} - \mathcal{F}_i - C_j) \}$
$\quad (\forall\, \mathcal{P}_{i,j} \in \mathcal{PS}(x, \mathcal{N} - \mathcal{F}_i - C_{j+1}) : |\mathcal{N} - \mathcal{F}_i - C_{j+1} - \mathcal{P}_{i,j}| > T - |\mathcal{F}_i|)$

Case $y \notin \mathcal{P}_{i,j}$

$\quad \exists\, x \in \mathcal{N} - \mathcal{F}_i - C_j : (\forall\, \mathcal{P}_{i,j} \in \mathcal{PS}(x, \mathcal{N} - \mathcal{F}_i - C_j) : |\mathcal{N} - \mathcal{F}_i - C_j - \mathcal{P}_{i,j}| > T - |\mathcal{F}_i|) \wedge$
$\quad C_{j+1} = C_j \cup \{y\} \wedge (y \neq x) \wedge (y \notin \mathcal{P}_{i,j})$
$\Rightarrow \{ R3 \Rightarrow (y \in C_j \Rightarrow (\forall\, m \in \mathcal{N} - \mathcal{F}_i : \mathcal{M}_{m,y} = C \wedge \mathcal{M}_{y,m} = C), \text{definition } \mathcal{PS}(x, \mathcal{N} - \mathcal{F}_i - C_j)\}$
$\quad (\forall\, \mathcal{P}_{i,j} \in \mathcal{PS}(x, \mathcal{N} - \mathcal{F}_i - C_j) : \mathcal{P}_{i,j+1} = \mathcal{P}_{i,j} \cup \{y\} \Rightarrow \mathcal{P}_{i,j+1} \in \mathcal{PS}(x, \mathcal{N} - \mathcal{F}_i - C_j) \wedge$
$\quad (\forall\, \mathcal{P}_{i,j+1} \in \mathcal{PS}(x, \mathcal{N} - \mathcal{F}_i - C_j) : |\mathcal{N} - \mathcal{F}_i - C_j - \mathcal{P}_{i,j+1}| > T - |\mathcal{F}_i|)$
$\Rightarrow \{((\mathcal{P}_{i,j+1} = \mathcal{P}_{i,j} \cup \{y\}) \wedge (C_{j+1} = C_j \cup \{y\})) \Rightarrow |\mathcal{N} - \mathcal{F}_i - C_j - \mathcal{P}_{i,j+1}| = |\mathcal{N} - \mathcal{F}_i - C_{j+1} - \mathcal{P}_{i,j}|\}$
$\quad (\forall\, \mathcal{P}_{i,j} \in \mathcal{PS}(x, \mathcal{N} - \mathcal{F}_i - C_j) : |\mathcal{N} - \mathcal{F}_i - C_{j+1} - \mathcal{P}_{i,j}| > T - |\mathcal{F}_i|)$

Proof of C3:

$a = 2$

$\quad \exists\, x \in \mathcal{N} - \mathcal{F}_i - C_j : |\{k \in \mathcal{N} - \mathcal{F}_i | \mathcal{M}_{k,x} = F \vee \mathcal{M}_{x,k} = F\}| > (T - |\mathcal{F}_i|) \wedge$
$\quad \exists\, y \in \mathcal{N} - \mathcal{F}_i - C_j : (\forall\, m \in \mathcal{N} - \mathcal{F}_i : \mathcal{M}_{m,y} = C \wedge \mathcal{M}_{y,m} = C)$
$\Rightarrow \quad \{ \text{Assumption 4} \Rightarrow ((\forall\, a, b \in N : \mathcal{M}_{a,b} = C) \Rightarrow \neg \mathcal{M}_{a,b} = F)\}$
$\quad |\{k \in \mathcal{N} - \mathcal{F}_i | \mathcal{M}_{k,x} = F \vee \mathcal{M}_{x,k} = F\}| > (T - |\mathcal{F}_i|) \wedge |\{k \in \mathcal{N} - \mathcal{F}_i | \mathcal{M}_{k,y} = F \vee \mathcal{M}_{y,k} = F\}| = 0$
$\Rightarrow \quad \{ \text{Appendix 1} \Rightarrow (\forall\, f \in \mathcal{F}_i : faulty(f) \Rightarrow \mathcal{F}_i = \{f \in \mathcal{F}_i | faulty(f)\}) \}$
$\quad |\{k \in \mathcal{N} - \mathcal{F}_i | \mathcal{M}_{k,x} = F \vee \mathcal{M}_{x,k} = F\}| > (T - |\{f \in \mathcal{F}_i | faulty(f)\}|) \wedge$
$\quad |\{k \in \mathcal{N} - \mathcal{F}_i | \mathcal{M}_{k,y} = F \vee \mathcal{M}_{y,k} = F\}| = 0$
$\Rightarrow \quad \{ \text{Assumption 5} \Rightarrow (|\{f \in \mathcal{F}_i | faulty(f)\}| \leq T) \Rightarrow (T - |\{f \in \mathcal{F}_i | faulty(f)\}| \geq 0)) \}$
$\quad |\{k \in \mathcal{N} - \mathcal{F}_i | \mathcal{M}_{k,x} = F \vee \mathcal{M}_{x,k} = F\}| > 0 \wedge |\{k \in \mathcal{N} - \mathcal{F}_i | \mathcal{M}_{k,y} = F \vee \mathcal{M}_{y,k} = F\}| = 0$
$\Rightarrow$
$\quad (y \neq x)$

$a = 4$

$\quad \exists\, x \in \mathcal{N} - \mathcal{F}_i - C_j : (\neg (\exists\, \mathcal{P}_{i,j} \in \mathcal{PS}(x, \mathcal{N} - \mathcal{F}_i - C_j) : |\mathcal{N} - \mathcal{F}_i - C_j - \mathcal{P}_{i,j}| \leq T - |\mathcal{F}_i|)) \wedge$

402

$$\exists\, y \in \mathcal{N} - \mathcal{F}_i - C_j : (\forall\, m \in \mathcal{N} - \mathcal{F}_i : \mathcal{M}_{m,y} = C \wedge \mathcal{M}_{y,m} = C)$$

$$\Rightarrow \{\text{App.1, proof R3} \Rightarrow (\forall\, n \in \mathcal{N} - \mathcal{F}_i \cdot C_j : (\forall\, m \in \mathcal{N} - \mathcal{F}_i : \mathcal{M}_{m,n} = C \wedge \mathcal{M}_{n,m} = C) \Rightarrow correct(n))\}$$

$$\exists\, x \in \mathcal{N} - \mathcal{F}_i - C_j : (\neg\, (\exists\, \mathcal{P}_{i,j} \in \mathcal{PS}(x, \mathcal{N} - \mathcal{F}_i - C_j) : |\, \mathcal{N} - \mathcal{F}_i - C_j - \mathcal{P}_{i,j}\, | \leq T - |\, \mathcal{F}_i\, |)) \wedge$$

$$(y \in \mathcal{N} - \mathcal{F}_i - C_j) \wedge correct(y)$$

$$\Rightarrow \{\text{Appendix 1, proof R4}: \forall\, n \in \mathcal{N}: correct(n) \Rightarrow (\exists\, \mathcal{P}_{i,j} \in \mathcal{PS}(n, \mathcal{N} - \mathcal{F}_i - C_j) :$$

$$|\, \mathcal{N} - \mathcal{F}_i - C_j - \mathcal{P}_{i,j}\, | \leq T - |\, \mathcal{F}_i\, |)\}$$

$$\exists\, x \in \mathcal{N} - \mathcal{F}_i - C_j : (\neg\, (\exists\, \mathcal{P}_{i,j} \in \mathcal{PS}(x\,, \mathcal{N} - \mathcal{F}_i - C_j) : |\, \mathcal{N} - \mathcal{F}_i - C_j - \mathcal{P}_{i,j}\, | \leq T - |\, \mathcal{F}_i\, |) \wedge$$

$$\exists\, y \in \mathcal{N} - \mathcal{F}_i - C_j : ((\exists\, \mathcal{P}_{i,j} \in \mathcal{PS}(y\,, \mathcal{N} - \mathcal{F}_i - C_j) : |\, \mathcal{N} - \mathcal{F}_i - C_j - \mathcal{P}_{i,j}\, | \leq T - |\, \mathcal{F}_i\, |)$$

$$\Rightarrow$$

$$(y \neq x)$$

References.

[1]   Preparata, F., Metze, G., Chien, R., On the connection assignment of diagnosable systems, in: **IEEE Transactions on Electronic Computing**, EC-16, 6(Dec. 1967), pp.848-854.

[2]   Barborak, M., Malek, M., Dahbura, A., The consensus problem in fault tolerant computing, in: **ACM Computing Surveys**, Vol 25, 2(Jun. 1993), pp.171-220.

[3]   Blough, D.M., Sullivan, G.F., Mason G.M. Intermittent fault diagnosis in multi processor systems, in: **IEEE Transactions on computers**, vol 41, 11(Nov. 1992), pp.1430-1441.

[4]   Bauch, A., Maehle, E., Self diagnosis, Reconfiguration and Recovery in the Dynamical Reconfigurable Multiprocessor System DAMP, in: **Fault-tolerant computing systems: tests, diagnosis, fault-treatment: 5th international GI/ITG/ GMA Conference Nürnberg, September 25-27, 1991: Proceedings**, Dal Cin, M., and Hohl, W. (Eds.), Springer-Verlag, Berlin, 1991, ISBN 3 540 54545 x, pp. 18-29.

[5]   Bianchini, R., Goodwin, R., Nydick, D.S., Practical application and implementation of distributed system level diagnosis theory, in: **Fault-tolerant computing: the twentieth international symposium**, IEEE Comp. Soc. Press, Los Alamitos, California, 1990, pp. 332-339, ISBN 08186 2051 x.

[6]   Chen, Y., Bucken, W., Echtle, K., Efficient algorithms for system diagnosis with both processor and comparator faults, in: **IEEE Transactions on parallel and distributed systems**, vol 4, 4(Apr. 1993), pp.371-381.

[7]   Lee, S., Shin, K.G., Optimal multiple syndrome probabilistic diagnosis, in: **Fault-tolerant computing: the twentieth international symposium**, IEEE Comp. Soc. Press, Los Alamitos, California, 1990, pp. 324-331, ISBN 0 8186 2051 x.

[8]   Maheshwari, S.N., Hakimi, S.L., On models for diagnosable systems and probabilistic fault diagnosis, in: **IEEE Transaction on computers**, vol 25, 3(March 1976).

[9]   Kime, C.R., An analysis model for digital system diagnosis, in: **IEEE Transactions on computers**, vol c-19, 11(Nov. 1970).

[10]   Jalote, P., **Fault tolerance in distributed systems**, Prentice Hall, 1994, pp.115-125.

[11]   Lee, S., Shin, K.G., On probabilistic diagnosis of multiprocessor systems using multiple syndromes, in: **IEEE Transactions on parallel and distributed systems**, vol 5, 6(Jun. 1994), pp.630-638.

[12]   Lee, S., Shin, K.G., Optimal and efficient probabilistic distributed diagnosis schemes, in: **IEEE Transactions on computers**, vol 42, 7(Jul.1993), pp.882-886.

Constraint Based System-Level Diagnosis of Multiprocessors

J. Altmann[1], T. Bartha[2], A. Pataricza[2], A. Petri[2] and P. Urbán[2]

[1] University of Erlangen, Dept. of Computer Science III, Martensstr. 3,
91058 Erlangen, Germany
[2] Technical University of Budapest, Dept. of Measurement and Instrument Eng.,
Műegyetem rkp. 9, H-1521 Budapest, Hungary

Abstract. The paper presents a novel modelling technique for system-level fault diagnosis in massive parallel multiprocessors, based on a re-formulation of the problem of syndrome decoding to a constraint satisfaction problem (CSP). The CSP based approach is able to handle detailed and inhomogeneous functional fault models on a similar level as the Russel-Kime model [18]. Multiple-valued logic is used to describe system components having multiple fault modes. The granularity of the models can be adjusted to the diagnostic resolution of the target without altering the methodology. Two algorithms for the Parsytec GCel massively parallel system are used as illustrations in the paper: the centralized method uses a detailed system model, and provides a fine-granular diagnostic image for off-line evaluation. The distributed method makes fast decisions for reconfiguration control, using a simplified model.

1 Introduction

The large number of components built into *massively parallel multiprocessor systems* increases the probability of component faults. Since reliable operation over a long time period is also necessary for complex computations, the system must be able to mask the effect of occurring errors by *fault tolerance*. The underlying diagnostic principle is generally *system-level diagnosis*, followed by reconfiguration and recovery in case of a detected fault.

Different models and algorithms were developed for system-level diagnosis, typically originating from the first graph theory based "system-level models" (PMC for symmetric and BGM for asymmetric test invalidation) published in the late-sixties. Their mathematical apparatus is simple and well-elaborated; practical implementations also proved their usefulness. However, the implicit limitations – for instance the over-simplification of the test invalidation mechanism in order to assure a proper mathematical treatment – decrease the level of reality in these models. Moreover, the rapid development of electronic technology and computer architectures radically modified the basic assumptions used in diagnostic models [16]:

- fault rates are in general low and the dominating part of faults is *transient*;
- the complexity of additional components of the system (interface and communication circuits) is comparable with that of the processing elements;

- the number of the components in the systems drastically increased.

The majority of insufficiencies result from the hardest simplification of the PMC-type models: the assumption of a homogenous system and test structure (identical components with the same test invalidation over the entire system). This reduces their applicability due to the increasing practical importance of inhomogeneous systems.

1.1 Required Features of a New Diagnosis Method

The new requirements involved by the latest results in multiprocessor system design characterize the expected features of a general purpose self-diagnosis method:
- it should be applicable to inhomogeneous systems as well as to homogenous ones (components with different test invalidation models are to be considered);
- neither the actual system topology nor the test invalidation model should limit the diagnostic resolution (current methods use rigid, inadaptive algorithms seriously restricting the target system features);
- the algorithm should extract all of the useful information from the elementary diagnostic results (e.g. for estimating the level of diagnosis at run-time);
- it should be able to work in massively parallel computers with several hundreds or even thousands of system components, thus the algorithm should have an excellent efficiency even for a very high number of units under test;
- many applications demand "on-the-fly" diagnosis for a maximal performance, able to identify the fault states of certain units even from partial syndrome information (i.e. before receiving all of the test results).

These requirements necessitate a new approach. A generalized test invalidation model and syndrome decoding algorithm for inhomogeneous systems is published in [1]. However, the efficiency of the algorithm becomes to a crucial factor in case of large-scale systems due to the employed mathematical apparatus—operations on matrices of the dimension of the number of processor in the system.

Syndrome decoding is the most important step in diagnosis, determining the actual fault states of system components from the syndrome. This systematic search is in general NP-complete. The main intention of "artificial intelligence" (AI) methods is to find efficient solutions for difficult to solve problems. A group of them, the CSP (Constraint Satisfaction Problem) solving methods seem especially useful for system-level diagnosis [2].

2 System-level Diagnosis and CSP

2.1 Definition of the CSP

Constraint satisfaction problems (CSP) deal with the estimation of a single or all consistent solutions in large-scale relation systems. More formally, a CSP is a (X, D, C) tuple, where $X = \{X_1, X_2, ..., X_n\}$ is a *set of variables*, defined over the set $D = \{D_1, D_2, ..., D_n\}$ *domains*; and $C = \{C_1, C_2, ..., C_k\}$ is a *set of constraints*. Constraints are *relations* between the variables, that is they are subsets of the Cartesian product of the corresponding variables' domains ($C_i \subseteq D^* = D_p \times D_q \times ... \times D_z$). A *solution* of a CSP is a vector $x = [x_1, x_2, ..., x_n]$ of values that satisfies all the constraints.

The structure of CSPs can be represented by a $G = (X, C)$ hypergraph where the variables are represented by *nodes* and the relations defined between them by *edges* of the network. *Binary* CSPs constitute a special subclass of CSPs, where each constraint affects at most two variables and the network becomes to a simple graph. *Loop edges* represent unary constraints (affecting only a single variable), *multiple parallel edges* are different constraints affecting the same variables.

The CSP is *static* if both the constraint network topology and the constraints themselves are fixed, and *dynamic* if they can change during the search for solutions.

2.2 CSPs solution methods

Solving discrete CSPs is proved to be NP-complete [10], so exhaustive algorithms are impractical for large-scale systems. Intelligent search algorithms (using backjumping, conflict based backtracking, forward checking, etc.) [14] offer a better average time complexity, yet their worst-case complexity is still exponential.

Let us assume for simplicity, that each of the n variables in the CSP has a discrete domain of the same cardinality d, so the search space is $D^* = D^n$. The worst-case complexity of a simple exhaustive search is $O(d^n)$. This complexity can be reduced only by decreasing d. (A decrease in n would imply that the CSP contains redundant variables, i.e. the CSP was improperly formulated). Decreasing of d can be achieved by preprocessing the CSP problem prior to the solution procedure. The so-called *consistency algorithms* [10, 11, 12] exclude locally inconsistent value combinations from the domains of variables, since these values surely cannot appear in a globally consistent solution. These methods work generally only on binary CSPs, because every variable can be evaluated independently in this subclass of CSPs. Moreover, such an evaluation of the variables guarantees the global consistency as well.

Consistency algorithms can be grouped according to the number of the nodes they consider during an elementary step, while searching for local inconsistencies:

- **Node-consistency or 1-consistency** considers only a single node at a time. It simply checks unary constraints, and deletes all values not complying to them. As unary constraints can be previously eliminated by restricting the domains, this algorithm is used only as a supplementary step in more complex algorithms.
- **Arc-consistency or 2-consistency** considers at a time two variables X_i and X_j and a binary relation R_{ij} between them. Every value is excluded from the domain of X_i without a value of X_j satisfying R_{ij}. Full consistency can be achieved by checking appropriate vertex pairs and relations. There are three basic versions of general purpose arc consistency algorithms (enlisted in the order of decreasing worst case time complexity):
  - **AC-1** updates all the variables whenever any of the variable domains has changed. Its time complexity is $O(d^3nc)$, where c is the number of constraints;

- **AC-3** updates only the domains of the variables adjacent to the changed variable. Its complexity is $O(d^2n)$;
- **AC-4** updates only those adjacent variables which are affected by the change of a variable domain. It reaches the proven optimal complexity of $O(d^2c)$, at the price of some bookkeeping of the relations and the variable domains [10].

- **Path consistency or 3-consistency** algorithms check the transitivity of the consistency of a candidate value assignment, thus path consistency between two variables X_i and X_j connected by a binary relation R_{ij} means that all value pairs in a solution allowed by R_{ij} must be also allowed by *all* paths between X_i and X_j. The entire constraint network is path consistent if every vertex pair is path consistent. Full path consistency in a complete constraint graph is equal to the consistency for length 2 paths. Checking path consistency requires only the checking of all length 2 paths, since any constraint network can be virtually extended to a complete constraint graph by inserting dummy ("always true") constraints.

  There are also three basic versions of path consistency algorithms similarly to arc consistency algorithms:
  - **PC-1** updates domains of every vertex, vertices along every arc and every length 2 path if any vertex has changed. Its time complexity is $O(d^5n^5)$;
  - **PC-2** updates domains of those length 2 paths that contain the changed vertex. Its complexity is $O(d^5n^3)$;
  - **PC-3** updates only the length 2 path affected by the changes of a vertex domain. It uses similar bookkeeping about the influence of variables and edges like AC-4 [10]. It is also proven to be optimal, its complexity is $O(d^3n^3)$.

- **k-consistency** examines a set S_k of k variables is considered at a time. If a completely consistent subset of value $k - 1$ tuples exist on $S_{k-1} \subset S_k$ (with $k - 1$ variables), then any value from the domain of the kth variable can be eliminated which cannot form a consistent value set with any one of the consistent $k - 1$ tuples. Global consistency can be achieved by successive elimination for increasing values of k until all variables are involved or a domain becomes empty indicating the insatisfiability of the CSP. The most widely used k-consistency algorithm, the *invasion procedure* [9] has a time complexity of $O(cd^{f+1})$, where f is the maximal number of new nodes found traversing the graph.

2.3 Formulating the Diagnosis Problem as a CSP

The ultimate goal of syndrome decoding and CSP is very similar: the algorithm must classify the fault state of system components in a consistent way that conforms to the given diagnostic model, test invalidation rules and the actual outcomes of the elementary tests (syndrome elements). These restrictions can be represented as binary relations between the fault state of the tester and the tested units. Note that the use of *relations* instead of *logical functions* supports the handling of diagnostic uncertainty appearing in some test invalidation models (e.g. in symmetric invalidation the outcome of a test executed by a faulty tester is non-deterministic).

A diagnosis problem can be very easily reformulated to a constraint satisfaction problem. The *variables* of the CSP represent the *fault states* of the system components.

The *constraints* correspond to the restrictions derived from the *test invalidation model* and the current *syndrome elements*, thus the test invalidation rules determine a set of candidate relations, from which the actually used one has to be selected, when knowing the actual test outcome. For instance, the relation over the tester-tested unit fault state value pair in the case of asymmetric test invalidation consists of $\{(0, 0), (1, 0)\}$ if the test outcome is 0, and of $\{(0, 1), (1, 0), (1, 1)\}$ if the test outcome is 1, respectively.

If *one-pass diagnosis* is required, simply a static binary CSP is produced after performing all tests. However, in the case of *on-the-fly* diagnosis, newly generated test results must be processed immediately. Only a few syndrome elements are present at the beginning, so the complete set of relations cannot be created at once. Every incoming test result adds new relations to this set, while the previously constructed ones remain still valid. Thus the solution space is gradually reduced, in other words a *monotone* dynamic CSP is produced.

The resulting constraint network is a "clear" mathematical structure, details such as the applied fault model or the system topology appear only implicitly in the relations and the variable domains. This representation is extremely flexible and applicable to a wide range of systems. Moreover, a well-elaborated toolset of CSP solution methods is available, so the diagnosis problem can be solved computationally efficiently.

If not all the components have a sure classification after the transitive closure, the remaining ones are classified using further restrictions on the fault model (limitation on maximal number of faults, exclusion of certain faults, etc.).

3 The Modelled System

The diagnosis model of the algorithms presented in this paper were derived from the Parsytec GCel massively parallel reliable multiprocessor (Fig. 1).

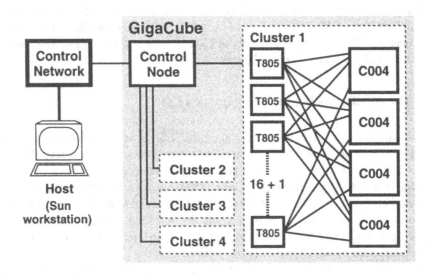

Fig. 1. The structural layout of the Parsytec GCel

The processing elements are Inmos T805 transputers. Sixteen transputers are grouped together in one *cluster*, forming the basic building block of the machine. Each transputer has 4 physical data links, and they are connected to C004 link switch chips. Each cluster incorporates 4 link switch chips, each of them having 32 connection ports, so inside a cluster arbitrary interconnection topology can be realized.

Four clusters constitute a so-called *GigaCube*. The topology of the clusters is a static 2×2 two-dimensional grid. A GigaCube forms a physical unit: it has its own temperature and voltage monitoring facilities, and a separate transputer working as a *control node*. GigaCubes can be arranged in a $4 \times 4 \times 8$ spatial array, so in its full configuration the system is scalable up to 16,384 transputers.

As a default, transputers are connected in a two-dimensional grid topology. Yet, despite the only 4 physical data connections every transputer can communicate with an arbitrary number of other transputers via *virtual links*.

The machine has built-in fault-tolerant mechanisms. In every cluster, there is an additional spare processor, replacing the faulty one in case of a detected error. The local memory of the transputers is ECC-protected, and soft memory errors are eliminated by memory scrubbing. These actions, as well as booting, job control and dynamic configuration management are supervised by control nodes. They communicate over a separate interconnection network called the *Control Network* (C-Net).

Peripheral I/O management is done by a stand-alone host computer (usually a Sun workstation) connected to the Parsytec GCel machine.

4 Fault Model

Different diagnostic goals require this complex multiprocessor to be modelled at separate abstraction levels. A centralized diagnostic algorithm is intended for off-line monitoring of the system. Diagnosis is made at the replacement unit level, hence the fault model should provide a detailed view about the multiprocessor. The model can be rather complex, as no tight time limits are imposed on the algorithm.

On the other hand, the system should take reconfiguration measures quickly in the case of faults, in order to minimize the effects of *fault propagation* and the error-related loss of performance. The efficiency of the diagnosis algorithm is crucial, necessitating a simple fault model, which supports a diagnostic resolution only down to the reconfiguration unit level. Also, the diagnosis algorithm should avoid using any central resources to maintain scalability and hence be executed locally at every processing element (i.e. distributed diagnosis is needed).

These fault models can be constructed by a *stepwise model refinement*; gradually refining a basic initial model to provide a more sophisticated view of the system.

4.1 Centralized Diagnosis

The modelled system is a simplified version of the Parsytec GCel massively parallel multiprocessor (see Fig. 2) consisting of processing elements and communication links in the form of a two-dimensional grid. Each processor mutually tests all of its neighbors. Test results are sent to the host computer performing syndrome decoding.

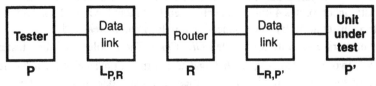

Fig. 2. Components involved in a test

For simplicity, host—transputer communication facilities are assumed to be reliable in the model. The used fault model (shown in Table 1) includes the faults in inter-processor links and routing chips as well, additionally to the processor faults [4].

Table 1. Component fault states

Unit	Fault state and its notation		Behavior	Possibly faulty component(s)
Processor	fault-free	0_P	correct operation	-
	faulty	1_P	incorrect test result evaluation	memory
	dead	c_P	no communication	CPU configuration, virtual link, Control Network, hardware exceptions
Data link	live	$\overline{L}_{P,R}$	correct message transfer	-
	broken	$L_{P,R}$	no message transfer	wires/connectors, CPU data link circuit
Router	fault-free	0_R	correct operation	-
	single port fault	$1_{R,P}$	no transfer via the faulty port	router data port circuit
	dead	c_R	all ports are faulty	internal routing scheme, clock

Testing of system components is done by time-out protected mutual <I'm alive> messages, sent periodically between neighboring processors. Asynchronous transfer mode is used for message exchange, because it does not block the sender processor. The possible test results are included in Table 2.

Table 2. Possible test results and their notation

Test result	Notation	Description
good	0	correct <I'm alive> message within time-limit
faulty	1	corrupted <I'm alive> message within the time-limit
dead	c	no message within the predefined time-limit

An extended PMC-like test invalidation [17] is used (see Table 3) to describe the fault state–test result relationships.

Table 3. Test invalidation model used in diagnosis (X indicates a *don't care* value)

Diagnosis	Tester	Data links	Router	UUT	Test result
centralized	0_P	$\overline{L}_{P,R} \wedge \overline{L}_{R,P'}$	0_R	$0_{P'}$	0
				$1_{P'}$	1
				$c_{P'}$	c
		$L_{P,R} \vee L_{R,P'}$	X	X	c
		X	$c_R \vee 1_{P,R} \vee 1_{R,P'}$	X	c
	1_P	X	X	X	1
	c_P	X	X	X	c
distributed	0_P	$\overline{L}_{P,R} \wedge \overline{L}_{R,P'}$		$0_{P'}$	0
				$1_{P'}$	1
		$L_{P,R} \vee L_{R,P'}$		X	1
	1_P	X		X	1

4.2 Distributed Diagnosis

Diagnosis is made in the distributed case concurrently on each individual transputer of the multiprocessor. Processors broadcast their results across the network after performing the tests. At the end, every processor receives every *syndrome message*. The dynamic specification of the broadcasting mechanism (e.g. an upper limit on the communication delays) assures that after a specific time limit there are no pending messages [7].

Only syndrome messages containing a "faulty" test result will be sent by the testers to their neighbors and no message transfer is invoked in the "fault-free" case. This is a significant reduction in the number of messages, as typically only a few faults occur.

Broadcast messages require the interaction of intermediate processors, due to the limited neighborhood of the message source processor. Syndrome messages from other processors will be potentially altered or lost by a faulty processor during this broadcast. Corrupted messages can be detected by a simple error detecting protocol; altered messages are ignored[1]. Thus the diagnosing program assumes that no undetected changes will occur.

---

[1] Theoretically, an altered message indicates a fault in the message forwarding chain of elements, but in order to avoid cross-interference between test and syndrome decoding time faults, we neglect corrupted messages.

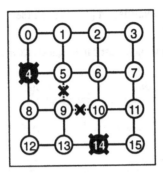

Fig. 3. The system is cut into two isolated parts (Processor 0 never receives messages from Processor 12)

The other type of syndrome losses cannot be detected in such a simple way, so the diagnosing processor will never or only occasionally receive fault reports from unfortunately placed – good or faulty – processors [6]. (Fig. 3 is an example for such a situation).

No routers are considered in the fault model, as router faults are assumed to make reconfiguration within a processor cluster impossible; so faulty routers must be handled by reconfiguration at cluster level. Also, no distinction between "faulty" and "dead" fault states and test outcomes is made for simplicity. The lower part of Table 3 describes the simplifications to the fault model in the centralized approach.

5 Implementation

5.1 Centralized Diagnosis

5.1.1 Transformation of the Implication Rules into Constraints

Syndrome decoding is driven by implication rules, represented by constraints. They originate from the system structure, the test invalidation model and the actual test outcomes. All the constraints are binary over the fault state of the tester and the tested component, to achieve a greater simplicity: the test results (syndrome bits) are eliminated from them as variables after receiving the test outcome [3].

The constraints originated from the implication rules are the following ($S_{P,R,P'}$ denotes the result of the test made by P on P' via router R):

- *Forward implication* (from the state of the tester to the state of the tested)
    - $S_{P,R,P'} = 0 \wedge 0_P \Rightarrow 0_{P'}$ (if the tester processor is fault-free and the test result is "good" then the tested processor is also fault-free);
    - $S_{P,R,P'} = 1 \wedge 0_P \Rightarrow 1_{P'}$ (if the tester is fault-free and the test is "faulty" then the tested unit is faulty);
    - $S_{P,R,P'} = c \wedge 0_P \Rightarrow L_{P,R} \vee c_R \vee L_{P',R} \vee c_{P'}$ (if the tester is fault-free and the test is "dead" then the links between them are broken, the router involved is dead or the tested unit is dead).

- *Backward implication* (from the state of the tested to the state of the tester)
  - $S_{P,R,P'} = 0 \wedge 1_{P'} \Rightarrow 1_P$ (if a faulty unit is tested as good then the tester is faulty);
  - $S_{P,R,P'} = 1 \wedge 0_{P'} \Rightarrow 1_P$ (if a good unit is tested as faulty then the tester is faulty);
  - $S_{P,R,P'} = c \wedge \overline{c_{P'}} \Rightarrow L_{P,R} \vee c_R \vee L_{P',R} \vee \overline{0}_P$ (if a unit is tested as dead and it is not dead then the links are broken, the router is dead or the tester is not fault-free).

5.1.2 One Pass and "On-the-Fly" Diagnosis

The diagnostic algorithm has the ability to create diagnosis "on-the-fly", using only partial syndrome information. In this case the diagnostic part is invoked several times at the arrival of partial test results. Implications from new syndrome elements are added to this dynamic constraint network during each call and a path-consistency based preprocessing of the network is performed, successively restricting the solution domain. If few syndromes are available, the solution process is expected to be fast (see Section [7]). Table 4 summarizes this process:

Table 4. "On-the-fly" diagnosis

initialization
process the list of already known faults
while there are syndrome messages **do**
read some syndrome messages
process the list of syndrome messages
preprocess the constraint network
solve the constraint network
generate output from the solution set

5.2 Distributed Diagnosis

5.2.1 Modelling the Constraints

First of all, implication rules should be created on the basis of the system structure, the applied test invalidation model and the actual syndrome elements [5]. These implication rules can then be represented by constraints. Moreover, some syndrome-independent constraints can be generated before receiving any fault reports:

- Known faulty components C of the system – for instance those on the list of a priori known faults obtained by the power-on self-test – are predefined in this model as faulty (1_C).
- The diagnosing processor P is fault-free (0_P) in his own local diagnostic image; this assumption is justified by the fact that a diagnosis produced by a faulty processor is worthless anyway.

- The processors on the cluster boundary have unconnected links; these are considered by the algorithm as virtually existing, always fault-free links ($\overline{L}_{P,0}$) in order to keep a total symmetry of the structure.

- If a processor is faulty, the fault states of its links cannot be determined in the applied fault model, i.e. processor faults dominate the faults of the associated links. Links are assumed to be fault-free to reduce the number of solutions and speed up the algorithm:

$$\text{Links } L_i \text{ are connected to } P: 1_P \Rightarrow \overline{L}_{P,1} \wedge \overline{L}_{P,2} \wedge \overline{L}_{P,3} \wedge \overline{L}_{P,4}.$$

The implication rules depend on the actual test results, so they can be produced only at "run-time". In the following paragraphs P stands for the processor performing the test, P' for the processor under test and L for the link connecting them.

Table 5. Implication rules generated from test results

Test result	Implication rules	Constraint(s)
0	$0_P \Rightarrow \overline{L}_{P,P'} \wedge 0_{P'};\quad L_{P,P'} \vee 1_{P'} \Rightarrow 1_P$	$\neg(0_P \wedge L_{P,P'});\quad \neg(0_P \wedge 1_{P'})$
1	$0_P \Rightarrow \overline{L}_{P,P'} \vee 1_{P'};\quad L_{P,P'} \wedge 0_{P'} \Rightarrow 1_P$	$\neg(0_P \wedge \overline{L}_{P,P'} \wedge 0_{P'})$

A compact representation has a low number of variables, with a domain kept small, and a simple structure of the constraint network. These are contradictory aspects, so a compromise had to be made: a variable is assigned to a processor and the links to its eastern and northern neighbors. The variable does not include the fault states of the western and southern links in order to avoid modelling links twice, together with each of the two processors connected by the link.

This representation ensures that the constraint $\neg(0_P \wedge \overline{L}_{P,P'} \wedge 0_{P'})$ becomes binary. Now, as P and P' are neighboring processors, the link L between them is assigned to either the variable representing P or to the one representing P'.

Even the implication expressing the dominance of a processor fault over the link faults in the form of $1_P \Rightarrow \overline{L}_{P,1} \wedge \overline{L}_{P,2} \wedge \overline{L}_{P,3} \wedge \overline{L}_{P,4}$ is now binary. Additionally, a part of it becomes unary, i.e. the values **101**, **110** and **111** are not allowed, reducing the domain size from $2^3 = 8$ to 5.

It did not seem worthwhile to integrate more components into a single variable, as the domain size would have become intolerably large (growing exponentially with the number of components).

5.2.2 A Priori Known Faults

A list of already known faults could be generated by the power-on self-test, or by a previous diagnosis. This list is processed on the first invocation of the diagnostic part: the initialization of the constraint network includes restricting the domains of variables by node consistency, conforming to a faulty component of the list. This simplifies the constraint network, thus speeding up the diagnosis algorithm.

5.2.3   Detection of Message Losses

The constraint network built on the basis of the received syndrome messages has - in most practical cases – a huge number of solutions. This prevents the algorithm from generating any useful diagnosis. The reason for this: despite of the relatively low fault rate, no limitation on the number of faulty elements is used in an intrinsic way by the algorithm. If only a few of the components fail, most processors test all of their neighbors as fault-free and broadcast no syndrome messages. Thus, there are too few syndrome messages, the constraints and the solution space remains large. To overcome this problem, an inference engine reconstructs the results of tests performed by "silent" processors.

Silent processors can be classified the following way:

- *Reachable* processors have a live connection to the diagnosing processor. They are silent because there is nothing to broadcast (their neighbors are fault-free).
- *Non-reachable* processors cannot communicate with the diagnosing processor; they are isolated from it by faulty components.

The algorithm has to find the processors, which are reachable but were silent in the previous round. Numerous new constraints can be formulated by using this additional information and consequently the solution space shrinks.

Table 6.   Detection of message losses

determine the "union" of possible faults
find some reachable silent processors
produce new constraint from new information
do while there is new information

The identification of these processors and addition of new constraints can be solved by means of reachability constraints. The transitivity of the relation "reachable" can be described by simple implication rules such as "if x is reachable and y, a neighbor of x is fault-free, then y is reachable". However, this would make the constraint network much more complex, by introducing ternary constraints.

Therefore the problem of processor reachability is handled by a non-CSP based iterative process, shown on Table 6. In the first step, the existing constraints are satisfied. Components, which were faulty in all the solutions of the network are marked as faulty. Then the silent and reachable processors are identified by a simple backtracking algorithm starting from the diagnosing processor. If such processors were found, new constraints are formulated and the first step is repeated; the subsequent processing of the extended constraint network will generate fewer solutions. The iteration terminates when there are no more silent and reachable processor candidates. In this case no further reduction of the solution space is possible. Note, that this process is strictly *monotone*, i.e. no constraint is removed from the network, only new ones are added, and the solution space is cut by the new constraints. Test runs show that the algorithm terminates after at most 5 steps, even in the case of the most complicated fault patterns.

This strategy contains the implicit assumption that links have only permanent faults. Without this assumption no diagnostic correctness is ensured. An example is

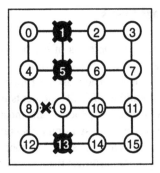

Fig. 4. Fault pattern in a system; failure of link 8-9 is transient

shown in Fig. 4; if the faulty link behaves fault-free when processor 9 tests processor 8 but blocks communication during the distribution of messages, the diagnosis program comes to the wrong conclusion that every processor is reachable. Therefore the observation seen by the program (on processor 0) that processors 1, 5, and 13 are tested faulty from the left and fault-free from the right leads to a global contradiction.

5.2.4 Implementation Characteristics

In its present form the distributed algorithm runs on a single processor. A tool simulating a cluster of the Parsytec machine and a random fault injector were developed. The diagnostic part itself could be used on a multiprocessor without any modification.

5.3 The Applied CSP Solver

A diagnostic purpose CSP solver should be written in a low-level, effectively compilable language, as it is expected to be run fast and require relatively few resources. Due to the "benign" nature of the employed special class of CSPs, there is no need to apply a full-featured, general purpose CSP solver system. The majority of known constraint-oriented languages and systems (CLPR, CONSTRAINTS, etc.) are strongly related to resource-hungry, interpreter-based languages like Prolog or LISP; a solver for special CSP classes, written in the more effective C programming language was much more promising. The applied CSP solver is based on a public domain CSP library [14], intended for solving static binary CSPs. Fortunately, its built-in preprocessing methods made it applicable for the class of dynamic CSP appearing in the developed model as well [15].

The solver was added the ability to prune obviously useless branches of the decision tree. This involves checking of an explicit upper bound on the number of faults (diagnostic t-limit), based on a priori knowledge about the system. Typically, uncorrelated faults affect only a few processors. The assumed testing frequency is by several orders of magnitude higher than the fault rate, thus the accumulation of many faulty components is highly improbable. If, in spite of this, the number of faults exceeds the predefined upper bound, the constraint network becomes unsatisfiable: a global contradiction occurs. This way the incorrect assumption about the behavior of the system can be detected.

6 Reconfiguration Control

The goal of *reconfiguration* is to exclude the faulty components from the system. Usually the architecture of a multiprocessor does not allow the exclusion of an arbitrary set of components; if multiple neighboring components fail, the exclusion of a larger group of components might be necessary. Therefore, the list of components to be excluded may differ from the list of the faulty components identified by the diagnosis algorithm.

The implemented distributed diagnosis algorithm is able to generate the list of components to be excluded, based on the following modification of the system model:

- groups of 2×2 neighboring processors form so-called *reconfiguration entities*;
- a reconfiguration entity must be excluded if it has less than 3 processors that are
  - fault-free
  - connected by fault-free links
  - reachable via fault-free links and processors (see Section 5.2.3).

Moreover, all faulty components – links or processors – not contained in the excluded reconfiguration entities must be excluded one by one. Generating the list of components to be excluded is a simple task and is performed by means of conventional methods. It may be worthwhile to implement it using constraint-based methods in the case of a more complicated reconfiguration policy.

The program extends the list of the faulty components with the reconfiguration measures that remove the corresponding fault. These may be the exclusion of the component or the exclusion of the whole enclosing reconfiguration entity.

7 Measurement Results

The CSP-based diagnosis algorithm was tested by means of a logic fault injector: the host machine generated a random fault pattern for the Parsytec processors and downloaded it as part of the test initialization messages. The low-level testing mechanism on the Parsytec processors interpreted the fault pattern and acted according to the fault state: "fault-free" processors tested their neighbors and sent the results back to the host, "faulty" processors performed the test but reported a random result and "dead" processors remained totally inactive. This construction was necessary because no physical fault injection was available for the Parsytec machines equipped with T805 transputers and the fault injector developed for the final model based on T9000 was unusable due to the difference in the hardware structure.

The results of a typical test run for the centralized algorithm are shown at first on Fig. 5. In this case the fault pattern contained a single faulty processor. Fig. 6 displays the number of the candidate solutions found by the CSP solver and the number of pro-

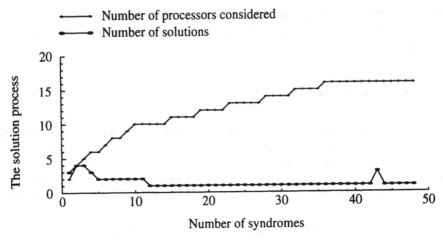

Fig. 5. Centralized diagnosis: the solution process

cessors considered at various stages of the solution process. Fig. 7 displays the number of consistency checks made, as a measure for the computational efficiency.

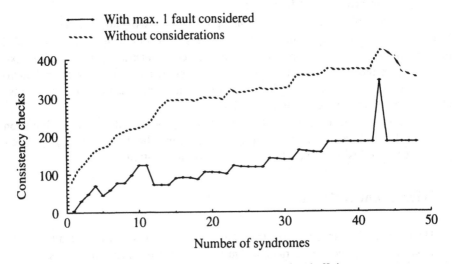

Fig. 6. Centralized diagnosis: computational efficiency

It was examined how a t-limit-like upper bound on the number of faults affects the efficiency of the distributed algorithm by diagnosing the same fault pattern with a variable fault limit (Fig. 8).

The efficiency of the algorithm is strongly influenced by the t-limit. The proper selection depends on the failure characteristics of the system: a high t-limit unnecessarily increases the execution time, while an excessively low one can lead to a contradiction in the constraint network and thus to no diagnosis, if there are more faults than the preset t-limit.

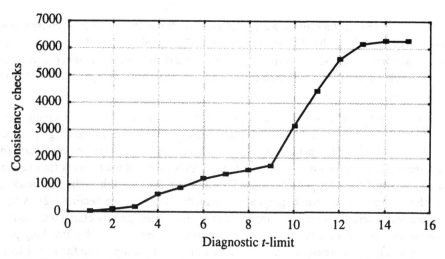

Fig. 7. Distributed diagnosis: effect of a diagnostic *t*-limit on computational efficiency

Moreover, detection of a global inconsistency – in the case when the number of faults exceeds the *t*-limit – is by some orders of magnitudes faster than finding the correct diagnosis. At values slightly greater than the actual number of faults the gradient of the curve is high. This property suggests an adaptive fault number minimization oriented diagnosis algorithm: the testing is started with the assumption of a single fault; the limit can be increased if global contradiction was detected. This strategy will result in low computational cost for the most frequent cases, while the diagnostic capabilities of the algorithm are preserved.

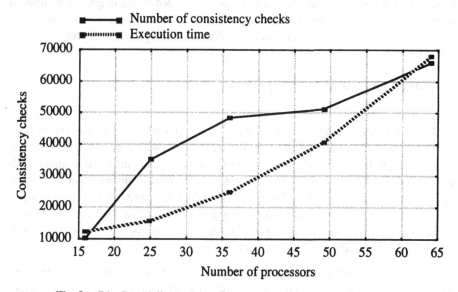

Fig. 8. Distributed diagnosis: performance versus the scale of the system

It was examined how the scale of the system affects the number of consistency checks performed by the diagnosis algorithm. The number of faults and its upper bound was fixed; the fault pattern was generated randomly. As the number of consistency checks strongly varies with the actual fault pattern, the averages of 40 test runs were taken.

The statistically fitted curves suggest that the algorithm is of a complexity $O(n^{2.52})$ (execution time) and the complexity of the backtracking part is $O(n^{1.61})$ (number of consistency checks), where n is the number of processors. In fact, the majority of the time is spent with the preprocessing of the network (this task is of complexity $O(n^3)$ for general binary CSPs). The reason for this is the CSP library, which contains only inoptimal preprocessing methods (**PC-2**, see Section 2.2). A significant improvement is expected from implementing faster preprocessing techniques. The number of consistency checks, measuring the efficiency of the backtracking part has exponential worst-case complexity. In fact, it varied strongly with the actual fault pattern, hence the 5 highest and the 5 lowest values were omitted from the analysis. The most important task in the future is to find a good heuristic function to decrease this fluctuation. Also, the CSP library is written for general binary networks and cannot make use of the special properties of the constraint network used for diagnosis. Theoretical investigations could help to find a more efficient constraint solver for this special class of CSPs.

Another possibility is to employ an approximate diagnosis method as a heuristic for the reduction of the search space. The algorithm described in [8] introduces the number of implications supporting a fault state hypothesis as a decision factor. Additional assumptions about the fault model can be included in the diagnosis by using a weighted sum instead of simply counting the implications. This heuristic could contribute to decrease the number of fruitless backtracks during the search process.

8   Conclusions and Further Work

The CSP-based diagnosis approach proved the correctness of the basic concepts, in both a centralized and a distributed environment. It is capable of handling situations which cause problems in traditional diagnosis algorithms; in particular, complex fault models and situations when a part of the system is isolated from other parts by faulty components. It was demonstrated that a t-limit affects the speed of the algorithm significantly. Adjusting this upper bound adaptively during the diagnosis enables to exploit this fact. In the distributed model the inter-processor communication was reduced radically, at the expense of a moderate performance degradation.

Further work involves selecting an optimal constraint solver focusing on memory use, fast preprocessing and exploiting the special properties (e.g. sparseness) of diagnostic constraint networks. Another task is studying the applicability to large-scale systems. Hierarchical diagnosis and stepwise fault model refinement could help reducing the time complexity.

References

1. E. Selényi, "Generalization of System-Level Diagnosis Theory," D.Sc. Thesis, Budapest, Hungarian Academy of Sciences, 1985.

2. A. Pataricza, K. Tilly, E. Selényi, M. Dal Cin, "A Constraint Based Approach to System-Level Diagnosis," Internal report 4/1994, University of Erlangen-Nürnberg, 1994.

3. A. Petri, "A Constraint Based Algorithm for System Level Diagnosis," Diploma Thesis, Technical University of Budapest, 1994.

4. A. Pataricza, K. Tilly, E. Selényi, M. Dal Cin, A. Petri, "Constraint-based System Level Diagnosis of Multiprocessor Architectures," Proc. of *8th Symp. on Microprocessor and Microcomputer Applications*, vol. 1, pp. 75-84, 1994.

5. P. Urbán, "A Distributed Constraint Based Diagnosis Algorithm for Multiprocessors," *Scientific Conference of the Students*, Technical University of Budapest, Faculty of Electrical Engineering and Computer Science, 1995.

6. J. Altmann, T. Bartha, A. Pataricza, "An Event-Driven Approach to Multiprocessor Diagnosis," Proc. of *8th Symp. on Microprocessor and Microcomputer Applications*, vol. 1, pp. 109-118, 1994.

7. J. Altmann, T. Bartha, A. Pataricza, "On Integrating Error Detection into a Fault Diagnosis Algorithm For Massively Parallel Computers," Proc. of *IEEE IPDS '95 Symposium*, pp. 154-164, 1995.

8. T. Bartha, "Effective Approximate Fault Diagnosis of System with Inhomogeneous Test Invalidation," submitted to the *Euromicro '96 Conference*, 1996.

9. K. Tilly, "Constraint Based Logic Test Generation," Ph.D. Thesis, Hungarian Academy of Sciences, 1994.

10. U. Montanari, "Networks of Constraints: Fundamental Properties and Applications to Picture Processing," *Information Sciences*, vol. 7, pp. 95-132, 1974.

11. R. Mohr, T. C. Henderson, "Arc and Path Consistency Revisited," *Artificial Intelligence*, vol. 28, pp. 225-233, 1986.

12. A. Mackworth, E. C. Freuder, "The Complexity of Some Polynomial Network Consistency Algorithms for Constraint Satisfaction Problems," *Artificial Intelligence*, vol 25, pp. 65-74, 1985.

13. R. Seidel, "A New Method for Solving Constraint Satisfaction Problems", *IJCAI '81*, pp. 338-342, 1981.

14. P. van Beek, "A Binary CSP Solution Library," available by FTP from ftp.cs.alberta.ca.

15. G. Kondrak, "A Theoretical Evaluation of Selected Backtracking Algorithms," M.Sc. Thesis, University of Alberta, Edmonton, 1994.

16. M. Barborak, M. Malek, A. Dahbura, "The Consensus Problem in Fault-Tolerant Computing," *ACM Computing Surveys*, vol. 25, no. 2, pp. 171-220, June 1993.

17. F. Preparata; G. Metze; R. Chien, "On the Connection Assignment Problem of Diagnosable Systems," *IEEE Trans. Comput.*, vol. EC-16, no. 6, pp. 848-854, Dec. 1967.

18. C. Kime, "System Diagnosis," in *Fault-Tolerant Computing: Theory and Techniques*, D. Pradhan ed., Prentice-Hall, New York, pp. 577-623, 1985.

A Unified Theory for f_1/f_2-Diagnosable Communication Networks

Guy G. Berthet, Henri J. Nussbaumer

Industrial Computing Laboratory, Department of Computer Science
Swiss Federal Institute of Technology
EPFL-DI-LIT, CH-1015 Lausanne, Switzerland

Abstract

We propose a new diagnosis model that allows a continuum between the two classical invalidation models in system-level diagnosis, namely, the PMC and BGM models. This new invalidation model assumes that there is no maximal set of connected faulty units of cardinality greater than f_2 ($1 \leq f_2$) in which all the faulty units can declare other faulty unit in this set to be fault-free out of a total of up to f_1 faulty units in a network with n units ($f_1 \leq n$). This f_1/f_2-invalidation model provides a realistic representation of behavior of faulty units in the diagnosis of heterogeneous communication networks. A complete characterization theorem provides the necessary and sufficient conditions for a network to be one-step f_1/f_2-diagnosable. We propose an adaptive algorithm for the diagnosis of communication networks of arbitrary topologies using the f_1/f_2-invalidation model.

1 Introduction

The probability of occurrence of faults in large communication networks grows as they become widespread, complex and heterogeneous. One of the ways to ensure high dependability of communication networks is by minimizing the time taken to detect and isolate the faulty unit. Reliability and availability constraints of the communication network require that faulty units be rapidly diagnosed and suitable steps be taken to recover from the failure. If the faulty units are quickly diagnosed, the network can be reconfigured to exclude these faulty units and the services provided by these faulty units can be shifted to other fault-free units. This can be achieved by incorporating an automatic diagnosis procedure and by reconfiguring or repairing the faulty units based on the results of the diagnosis.

The theory of system-level diagnosis (SLD) [1] was initially developed to diagnose nodes in multiprocessor [2], [3] and distributed systems [4]. In SLD, diagnosis is based on testing the units of the system. The result of the test is used to infer about the status of a unit. The application of the SLD theory to the diagnosis of communication networks has been proposed in [5]. In SLD, the assumption about the inability of a faulty unit to correctly test other units is known as the principle of *fault invalidation model*. The diagnosability of a system starts with the definition of a fault invalidation model which models the behavior of faulty and fault-free units in the diagnosis of the system. Despite the firm theoretical framework and the abundance of invalidation models provided by the SLD theory, there has been little discussion on the implication of the choice of a fault model for diagnosis in heterogeneous communication networks. In this paper, we first discuss the unification of different fault invalidation models proposed in SLD theory to represent the behavior of a faulty node in the diagnosis of heterogeneous communication networks. The rest of the paper is organized as follows. Section 2 discusses the classical fault models in SLD theory and their application to network faults and we propose a truly continuum f_1/f_2-invalidation model such that there are at most f_1 faulty units in a network with n units ($f_1 \leq n$) among which at most f_2 ($1 \leq f_2$) faulty units can declare other faulty unit to be fault-free in the same maximal connected subgraph of the network. Following this discussion, the one-step f_1/f_2-diagnosability concept is developed in Section 3. A generalized characterization theorem is proved in Section 4. This theorem provides the conditions under which a network is one-step f_1/f_2-diagnosable in terms of all possible combinations of pair of distinct consistent fault subsets. Two other theorems are shown which characterize a f_1/f_2-diagnosable communication network in terms of vertex connectivity. Based on these characterizations, an adaptive fault diagnosis algorithm is described and proved in Section 5 and compared to other adaptative algorithms. The last section concludes the paper and discusses some open research issues.

2 Communication Network and Fault Model

The communication network is modeled as an undirected graph as proposed in [6]. This is called the *system graph* $S = (U(S), E(S))$. A system graph S is composed of the finite set of vertices $U(S)$ corresponding to the units or nodes of the network and the finite set of edges $E(S) = \{(u_i, u_j) : u_i, u_j \in U(S)\}$ such that there is a direct communication path between u_i and u_j in the network. In this paper, the term unit and node refers to the smallest subsystem to which the faults can be isolated. The nodes in the network are heterogeneous but are assumed to be able to test other nodes for correct functioning. While the model makes no assumption about the nature of the tests and how they are performed, the fault coverage of the tests is supposed to be 100%. It implies that the tests certainly discover a faulty node.

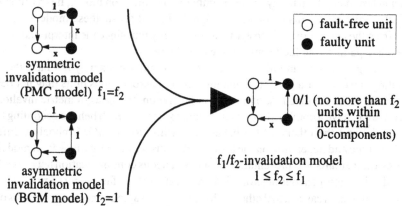

Fig. 1. f_1/f_2-**Invalidation Model for Permanent Faults**

To perform automatic fault diagnosis of S, each unit $u_i \in U(S)$ is capable of testing units of a particular subset of the remaining units in S. The *test connection assignment* of S is the complete collection of ordered pairs of units (u_i, u_j) where u_i (the *tester* unit) tests u_j (the *tested* unit) in S. We assume that no unit tests itself. The test connection assignment is represented by a simple directed graph[1] referred to as *test digraph*. Let

$D = (U,E)$ denote the test digraph, where each considered unit $u_i \in U(S)$ is represented by a vertex and each ordered pair $(u_i,u_j) \in E(S)$ is represented by a *directed edge* or *arc* $(u_i,u_j) \in E$ if the unit u_j is tested by the unit u_i. The test digraph $D(U,E)$ is a directed subgraph of the undirected system graph $S(U(S),E(S))$. The result of the test of u_j by u_i is called *test outcome* and may be 0 or 1 corresponding to tester u_i evaluating u_j as fault-free or faulty, respectively. The test outcome may be arbitrary (either 0 or 1) regardless of the fault status of u_i and u_j when the outcome is unpredictable. In this case the value of the test outcome is denoted by x as shown in Fig. 1.

The well known invalidation models in the theory of system-level diagnosis are the symmetric and asymmetric invalidation models. The *symmetric invalidation model* considers that a faulty unit evaluates another tested unit regardless of its actual fault status. In this category, the PMC model [1] assumes that a faulty unit evaluates another units arbitrarily as fault-free or faulty as shown in Fig. 1. These models do not assign an interpretation to the obtained test results in which the tester is faulty irrespective of the state of the tested unit. In that sense, from the perspective of a tester which is a faulty unit, the interpretation of the test result is symmetric. The *asymmetric invalidation model* is based on the premise that a diagnostic evaluation (or test) involves a large number of tests (stimuli) and the observation of the corresponding responses. In this category, the BGM model [2] shown in Fig. 1 is based on the assumption that if a tested unit is faulty even if the tester is faulty there is likely to be a mismatch between the actual and expected responses. On the other hand, by assuming a diagnostic evaluation involving a large number of tests, the responses a faulty tester expects will not agree with the responses provided by a fault-free unit. Therefore the asymmetric invalidation model involves a complex diagnostic tests in terms of computing capacity of the units compared to the symmetric invalidation model. This model differs from the symmetric invalidation models only in the case when both the tester and tested units are faulty. In the asymmetric invalidation model, it is assumed that two faulty units cannot match on all test signals. In that sense, these models are asymmetric from the perspective of a tester which is a faulty unit since the interpretation of the test result depend on the fault status of the tested unit.

In heterogeneous communication networks, all faulty units may not have the same computing capacity for a given test and thus these heterogeneous units may not behave according to only one invalidation model; either symmetric or asymmetric invalidation model. We can have a combination of faulty units some of which behave according to the PMC model and the others which behave according to the BGM model at different instants of time and depending on the tested unit. Thus we propose a new fault model that provides a more realistic representation of heterogeneous communication networks. With this model, in heterogeneous network S there are at most f_1 faulty units among which at most f_2 faulty units can test to 0 other faulty units in the same connected subgraphs of test digraph $D(U,E)$. This model is the so called f_1/f_2-*invalidation model*.

2.1 Preliminaries

For the terminology of graph theory used in this paper and proofs of theorems the reader has to refer to [7] and [8]. A digraph D is said to be *weakly connected* if its corresponding

---

1. A simple directed graph is an oriented graph with neither self-loops nor parallel arcs according [7].

undirected graph is connected. A digraph D is said to be *strongly connected* if there is at least one dipath[1] from every vertex to every other vertex. Each maximal connected (weakly or strongly) subgraph of a digraph D is called a *component* of D. Within each component of D, the maximal strongly connected subgraphs will be called the *fragments* of D. We note that a fragment is obviously a component of D.

For a given test digraph $D(U,E)$ and each unit $u_i \in U$, we have the following definitions:

Definition 1: The set $\Gamma(u_i)$ of adjacent units from u_i (set $\Gamma^{-1}(u_i)$ of adjacent units to u_i) is defined formally as $\Gamma(u_i) = \{u_j \in U : (u_i,u_j) \in E\}$ ($\Gamma^{-1}(u_i) = \{u_j \in U : (u_j,u_i) \in E\}$).

Since we assume that no unit tests itself, we have: $\forall u_i \in U, u_i \notin \Gamma(u_i) \cup \Gamma^{-1}(u_i)$. In the terminology of system-level diagnosis, $\Gamma(u_i)$ is the set of (tested) units tested by the unit u_i whereas $\Gamma^{-1}(u_i)$ is the set of (tester) units testing the unit u_i. In the same manner for each subset of units $U_i \subseteq U$:

Definition 2: The set $\Gamma(U_i)$ of adjacent units from a subset U_i (set $\Gamma^{-1}(U_i)$ of adjacent units to U_i) is defined formally as $\Gamma(U_i) = \bigcup_{u_i \in U_i} \Gamma(u_i) - U_i$ ($\Gamma^{-1}(U_i) = \bigcup_{u_i \in U_i} \Gamma^{-1}(u_i) - U_i$).

A function $\sigma : E \to \{0, 1\}$ represents the collection of all outcomes associated with the set of arcs $(u_i,u_j) \in E$ resulting from all tests in the test digraph $D(U,E)$ so called a *syndrome* for D. For a given syndrome σ, we have the following definitions:

Definition 3: A 1-arc (0-arc) is an arc (u_i,u_j) such that $\sigma(u_i, u_j) = 1(0)$.

Definition 4: A 0-spanning closed walk is a spanning closed walk[2] composed only by 0-arcs.

Definition 5: A 0-dipath is a dipath composed only by 0-arcs.

Definition 6: With each unit $u_i \in U$, we associate the sets: $\Gamma_\alpha(u_i) = \{u_j, (u_i,u_j) \in E : \sigma(u_i, u_j) = \alpha\}$ and $\Gamma_\alpha^{-1}(u_i) = \{u_j, (u_j,u_i) \in E : \sigma(u_j, u_i) = \alpha\}$ for $\alpha = 0, 1$.

Definition 7: The 0-derived digraph $D^0 = (U^0,E^0)$ is the graph derived from $D(U,E)$ by deleting all the 1-arcs.

The digraph $D^0(U^0,E^0)$ may be disconnected and split into several disjoint weakly connected components and split in their turn to several disjoint strongly connected fragments $D_1^0(U_1^0,E_1^0), ..., D_k^0(U_k^0,E_k^0)$ with $\bigcup_{i=1,k} U_i^0 \subseteq U^0$.

Definition 8: A 0-component (0-fragment) of D is a component (fragment) of $D^0(U^0,E^0)$

2.2 f_1/f_2-Invalidation Model for Permanent Faults

In this paper we restrict ourselves to the study of permanent faults. Intermittent faults in heterogeneous communication networks is currently under study [9].

Large communication networks are usually heterogeneous. The computing capacity and functionality of the units in a network are different. The units may be computers, switches, routers, bridges, communication lines, satellite links, modems, etc. For a given test, some units may be more sophisticated in terms of their computing capacity to satisfy the asymmetric BGM invalidation model of faults, whereas others may be simple and fol-

---

1. A directed path or dipath is a directed walk in which all vertices are distinct.
2. A spanning closed walk of a digraph D is a walk which has the same first and last vertices and contains all the vertices of D.

low the symmetric PMC invalidation model of faults. Therefore depending on the tester and on the tested unit, it is more realistic to represent the behavior of the faulty units in a network using a model that includes both the PMC and BGM invalidation models.

Now we describe our new f_1/f_2-invalidation model providing a truly continuum of invalidation models that stands between classical PMC symmetric and BGM asymmetric invalidation models. This fault model considers only the *permanent faulty units* for which the source of a fault condition is permanent and testing is complete to the extent that any fault-free unit which tests a faulty unit will always detect its failed state. If units u_i and u_j are permanent faulty units, repeated applications of test of u_j by u_i will always yield the same outcome.

Our modified invalidation model is shown in Fig. 1. It is nearly identical to the symmetric PMC invalidation model, and in particular it allows two faulty units to test to 0. However there is no 0-component of faulty units greater than f_2 faulty units ($1 \leq f_2$) out of a total of up to f_1 faulty units in a network with n units ($f_1 \leq n$). Suppose that the 0-derived subgraph is disconnected and that there are k 0-components of faulty units in the 0-derived subgraph. We have: $\forall k, 1 \leq k \leq f_1: kf_2 \leq f_1$. The maximum value of f_2 is obtained when the 0-derived subgraph is connected ($k = 1$). In that worst case, we have: $f_2 \leq f_1$. Thus we have the following inequality between f_1 and f_2 parameters: $1 \leq f_2 \leq f_1 \leq n$. We note that since a 0-fragment is a 0-component the same upper bound f_2 applies for all 0-components which are 0-fragments of faulty units in test digraph with the f_1/f_2-invalidation model. It follows the definition of the f_1/f_2-invalidation model:

Definition 9: In a syndrome under the f_1/f_2-invalidation model, there is no 0-component of faulty units with cardinality greater than f_2 faulty units out of a total of up to f_1 faulty units in a network with n units ($1 \leq f_2 \leq f_1 \leq n$).

If $f_2 = f_1$ then the 0-derived subgraph is connected ($k = 1$). This model reduces to the conventional symmetric PMC invalidation model because there exists no 0-component of cardinality greater than f_1 faulty units in which all faulty units can test indistinctly to 0 or 1 other faulty units. If $f_2 = 1$ then there is no nontrivial[1] 0-component of faulty units in test digraph D which implies that no distinct faulty units are allowed to test to 0. This corresponds to the asymmetric BGM invalidation model, where all faulty units test other faulty units to 1. When $1 < f_2 < f_1$, each tester faulty unit may behave according to one of the two invalidation models (PMC or BGM) depending on tested faulty unit. Hence the f_1/f_2-invalidation model provides a continuum of models between the symmetric and the asymmetric invalidation models. The characterization can be expected to yield results that stand between those corresponding to the symmetric PMC model and those corresponding to the asymmetric BGM model.

Once the f_1/f_2-invalidation model defined, we define now the diagnosability of the network.

3 One-Step f_1/f_2-Diagnosability

On the basis of a given syndrome σ, a *diagnosis* can be defined as the identification of faulty units in the system on the basis of the information contained in this syndrome σ produced by test set applications. A *fault set* is a subset of the units of system S which are faulty. A fault set is usually denoted by F, $F \subseteq U$. If all faulty units of any fault set when

---

1. A nontrivial component consists of more than one vertex.

present in a system can be diagnosed completely as faulty and no fault-free units are incorrectly diagnosed as faulty based on a single syndrome σ produced by the system, then this system is known as *one-step diagnosable*.

From Definition 9, we can deduce the following theorem:

Theorem 1: In a network S with test digraph $D(U,E)$ given any syndrome σ under the f_1/f_2-invalidation model, for every 0-dipath P_j^0 of length[1] L greater than or equal to f_2 ($|P_j^0| \geq f_2 + 1$) the last $L - f_2$ units are fault-free.

Proof: Let P_j^0 be a 0-dipath of length $L \geq f_2$. Since a 0-dipath is a 0-component according to Definition 9 there exist no more than f_2 successive distinct faulty units in 0-path P_j^0. Suppose that there exists a faulty unit $u_j \in P_j^0$ in the $L - f_2$ last units in P_j^0. According to the f_1/f_2-invalidation model, the unit u_i adjacent to unit u_j in P_j^0: $(u_i, u_j) \in P_j^0$ such that $\sigma(u_i, u_j) = 0$ if and only if u_i is a faulty unit. By induction, we can deduce that there exists a 0-dipath of length greater than f_2 consisting of only faulty units. Then there exists a 0-component of distinct faulty units with a cardinality greater than f_2. This results in a contradiction. ∎

A well known result in graph theory (Theorem 16.1, [8]) is that a component is a fragment if and only if it has a spanning closed directed walk. Thus in any 0-spanning closed walk of length less or equal to f_2, either all the units are fault-free or all the units are faulty for a given syndrome σ for the f_1/f_2-invalidation model. This is stated in the following theorem.

Theorem 2: In a network S with test digraph $D(U,E)$, given any syndrome σ under the f_1/f_2-invalidation model, every 0-fragment F_j^0 consists of either only fault-free units or only faulty units.

The reader can refer [9] for a detailed proof of this theorem. ∎

We can deduce from Theorem 2 that for a given syndrome σ if the diagnosis can surely determine the fault status of at least one unit as fault-free or faulty in a 0-fragment of cardinality less or equal to f_2 then all units in this fragment are fault-free or faulty respectively. Moreover for the f_1/f_2-invalidation model, if there exists a 0-fragment of cardinality greater than f_2 then all the units in this 0-fragment are fault-free. This can be easily demonstrated in the following corollary.

Corollary 1: In a network S with test digraph $D(U,E)$, given any syndrome σ under the f_1/f_2-invalidation model, every 0-fragment F_j^0 of cardinality greater than f_2 ($|F_j^0| > f_2$) consists of only fault-free units.

The proof of Corollary 1 is a straightforward consequence of Theorem 2 and the definition of the f_1/f_2-invalidation model. ∎

A fault set $F \subseteq U$ is called an *consistent fault set* for a syndrome σ if and only if the assumption that the units in F are faulty and the units in $U - F$ are fault-free is consistent with this syndrome and the invalidation model. From Theorem 1, Theorem 2 and Corollary 1 we can deduce the following definition of a fault set F which are consistent with the f_1/f_2-invalidation model for a given syndrome σ. Let $H = (F,L)$ be a subgraph of $D(U,E)$ with $F \subseteq U$, $L \subseteq E$ and $H^0 = (F^0, L^0)$ be the 0-derived graph of H with 0-components $F_1^0, ..., F_k^0$ for the syndrome σ.

Definition 10 (CFS): In a network S with test digraph $D(U,E)$, a non-empty fault set F is a consistent fault set (CFS) for a syndrome σ under the f_1/f_2-invalidation

---

1. The length of a walk (dipath) is the number of occurrences of arcs in this walk (dipath).

model if all the following four conditions holds:

(1) $|F| \leq f_1$

(2) $\sigma(u_i, u_j) = 1$ for all $u_i \in U - F$, $u_j \in F$

(3) $\sigma(u_i, u_j) = 0$ for all $u_i, u_j \in U - F$

(4) $|F_j^0| \leq f_2$ for all 0-components F_j^0 of $F \subseteq U$.

The first three conditions of the definition of CFS are straightforward consequences of Definition 10. Condition (4) makes sure that there does not exist any 0-dipath of length greater than f_2 units in a consistent fault set F for a syndrome σ. Otherwise by Theorem 1 some of these units are fault-free and the set F cannot be a consistent fault set.

The definition of CFS applies immediately to the symmetric PMC invalidation model [10] by setting $f_2 = f_1$ since condition (4) becomes $|F_j^0| \leq f_1$ and is always satisfied if condition (1) is satisfied and conversely. With the asymmetric BGM invalidation model, two faulty units cannot test mutually to 0 in a fault set F. Since $F_j^0 \subseteq F$, we have: $|F_j^0| = 1$, F_j^0 is a trivial 0-component. Thus condition (4) is always satisfied by setting $f_2 = 1$. This implies that $\forall u_i, u_j \in F: \sigma(u_i, u_j) = 1$ and together with condition (2) this is equivalent to $\forall u_j \in F: \sigma(u_i, u_j) = 1$. Thus the CFS Definition 10 applies to the BGM model [5] by setting $f_2 = 1$.

From Definition 10, it follows a necessary and sufficient condition for the *one-step* f_1/f_2-*diagnosability* of a network S for a given syndrome σ is that this syndrome σ must be producible by only one consistent fault set:

Definition 11: A network S is one-step f_1/f_2-diagnosable for the f_1/f_2-invalidation model if and only if, given any syndrome σ, there exists no two distinct consistent fault sets in S.

4 Characterization of f_1/f_2-Diagnosable Communication Networks

We now present a theorem of complete characterization with the necessary and sufficient conditions for one-step f_1/f_2-diagnosability of communication networks.

Theorem 3: A n-unit network S and the test digraph $D(U,E)$ is one-step f_1/f_2-diagnosable for the f_1/f_2-invalidation model if and only if for every pair of distinct sets $U_1, U_2 \subset U$ with $|U_1|, |U_2| \leq f_1$, one of the following conditions is valid:

(3.1) $\exists (u_i, u_j) \in E: u_i \in U - (U_1 \cup U_2)$ and $u_j \in U_1 \oplus U_2$ [1]

(3.2) *Let* $Z_1 = U_1 - U_2$ *and* $Z_2 = U_2 - U_1$ *be a partition of* $U_1 \oplus U_2$, *one of both following conditions holds:*

$$\exists Z_{1i}: Z_{1i} \subseteq Z_1 \text{ is a component of subgraphs } H_1(Z_1, E_1) \text{ and } |Z_{1i}| > f_2$$

$$\exists Z_{2j}: Z_{2j} \subseteq Z_2 \text{ is a component of subgraphs } H_2(Z_2, E_2) \text{ and } |Z_{2j}| > f_2$$

Proof of necessity (by contradiction): Assume that there exists a pair of distinct sets $U_1, U_2 \subset U$ with $|U_1|, |U_2| \leq f_1$, for which neither condition (3.1) nor condition (3.2) is satisfied and let $Z_1 = U_1 - U_2$ and $Z_2 = U_2 - U_1$ be a partition of $U_1 \oplus U_2$:

$$\forall (u_i, u_j) \in E: u_i \in U - (U_1 \cup U_2) \text{ and } u_j \notin U_1 \oplus U_2 \tag{3.3}$$

$$\forall Z_{1i}, Z_{2j}: |Z_{1i}|, |Z_{2j}| \leq f_2, Z_{1i} \text{ and } Z_{2j} \text{ are components of } Z_1 \text{ and } Z_2 \text{ resp.} \tag{3.4}$$

There exists no arc $(u_i, u_j) \in E: u_i \in U - (U_1 \cup U_2)$, $u_j \in (U_1 \cup U_2) - (U_1 \cap U_2)$ and no component in Z_1 and Z_2 with cardinality greater than f_2. We show that for some syndrome $\sigma: E \to \{0, 1\}$, U_1, U_2 are two distinct consistent fault sets. Suppose first that:

---

1. $U_1 \oplus U_2$ is defined as: $U_1 \oplus U_2 = (U_1 \cup U_2) - (U_1 \cap U_2)$.

$$U_1 \cap U_2 \neq \varnothing \tag{3.5}$$

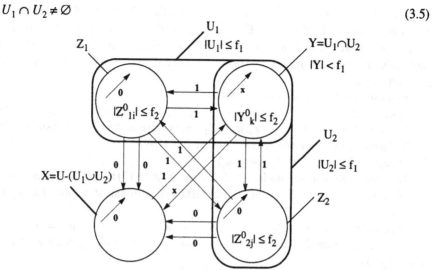

Fig. 2. **Proof of Necessity of Theorem 3.**

Let Y, Z_1, Z_2, and X be a partition of U defined as follows:
$$Y = U_1 \cap U_2, \; Z_1 = U_1 - Y, \; Z_2 = U_2 - Y, \; X = U - (U_1 \cup U_2) \tag{3.6}$$
From (3.3) and (3.6), we obtain:
$$\Gamma(X) \subseteq Y \tag{3.7}$$
Since $|U_1|, |U_2| \leq f_1$, from (3.6) note that:
$$|Y| \leq f_1 \tag{3.8}$$
Then we can assume that Y contains only faulty units since it pertains to the two sets U_1 and U_2 that are candidates for being CFSs. Let X contain only fault-free units. Thus given (3.4) and (3.7), there exists a syndrome σ such that sketched in Fig. 2 for which it can be seen easily that the two sets U_1 and U_2 satisfy all the conditions of CFS Definition 10. The case where U_1 and U_2 are two disjoint sets ($U_1 \cap U_2 = \varnothing$) is straightforward. Hence U_1 and U_2 are two distinct CFS by building and S is not one-step f_1/f_2-diagnosable.

Proof of sufficiency (by contradiction): Assume that S is not one-step f_1/f_2-diagnosable and at least one of the conditions (3.1) or (3.2) is satisfied for any partition of U in two distinct non-empty sets U_1, U_2 with $|U_1|, |U_2| \leq f_1$:
$$S \text{ is not one-step } f_1/f_2\text{-diagnosable} \tag{3.9}$$
Since we have (3.9) and by Definition 10 then there exists a syndrome $\sigma : E \rightarrow \{0, 1\}$ such that at least one pair of sets U_1, $U_2 \subset U$ with $|U_1|, |U_2| \leq f_1$ are both consistent fault sets. Suppose first that:
$$U_1 \cap U_2 \neq \varnothing \tag{3.10}$$
Let Y, Z_1, Z_2, and X be a the partition of U already defined in (3.6)-(3.6). It follows from (3.6) that:
$$U_1 \oplus U_2 = Z_1 \cup Z_2 \tag{3.11}$$
Suppose first that the condition (3.1) is satisfied for two sets U_1, U_2:
$$\exists (u_i, u_j) \in E : u_i \in X, \; u_j \in Z_1 \cup Z_2 \tag{3.12}$$
From (3.12), we can have: $\exists (u_i, u_j) \in E$, $u_i \in X$, $u_j \in Z_1 \subset U_1 \oplus U_2$. If $\sigma(u_i, u_j) = 0$, U_1 is not a CFS by condition (2) of CFS Definition 10 and if

$\sigma(u_i, u_j) = 1$, U_2 is not a CFS by condition (3) of CFS Definition 10. In the same manner, it is shown that if: $\exists (u_i, u_j) \in E$, $u_i \in X$, $u_j \in Z_2 \subset U_1 \oplus U_2$ then the existence of the arc (u_i, u_j) breaks the simultaneous fault consistency of sets U_1 and U_2. Thus (3.12) and furthermore condition (3.1) of Theorem 3 is in contradiction with (3.9) the non-diagnosability of S.

Suppose now that condition (3.2) holds:

$$\exists Z_{1i} : |Z_{1i}| > f_2 \text{ or } \exists Z_{2j} : |Z_{2j}| > f_2, Z_{1i}, Z_{2j} \text{ are components of } Z_1, Z_2 \quad (3.13)$$

Note first that: $\forall (u_i, u_j) \in E : u_i, u_j \in Z_1$, the syndrome σ must be consistent with set Z_1 being either faulty or non-faulty. Thus we must have:

$$\forall (u_i, u_j) \in E : u_i, u_j \in Z_1, \sigma(u_i, u_j) = 0 \quad (3.14)$$

The same argument applies for Z_2. It follows from (3.13) and from the assumption of f_1 / f_2-invalidation model in which there exists no 0-component of more than f_2 faulty units that:

$$\exists (u_i, u_j) \in E : u_i, u_j \in Z_1, \sigma(u_i, u_j) = 1 \text{ or } u_i, u_j \in Z_2, \sigma(u_i, u_j) = 1 \quad (3.15)$$

which contradicts the simultaneous consistency of U_1 and U_2 since $Z_1 \subset U_1$ and $Z_2 \subset U_2$ (3.6).

Hence condition (3.2) of the theorem which implies the existence of a component of cardinality greater than f_2 in Z_1 or Z_2. This is in contradiction with the assumption that S is not one-step f_1 / f_2-diagnosable (3.9). The case where U_1 and U_2 are two disjoint sets ($U_1 \cap U_2 = \emptyset$) is straightforward. This completes the proof of sufficiency. ∎

We can observe that the existence of the arc $(u_i, u_j) \in E$ with $u_i \in U - (U_1 \cup U_2)$ and $u_j \in (U_1 - U_2) \cup (U_2 - U_1)$ in every pair of distinct sets $U_1, U_2 \subset U$ with $|U_1|, |U_2| \leq f_1$ breaks the simultaneous fault consistency of U_1 and U_2. In the same manner, the existence of 1-arc in $U_1 - U_2$ or $U_2 - U_1$ implied by condition (3.2) breaks the fault consistency of U_2 or U_1 respectively.

Note that when $f_1 = f_2 = t$, condition (3.2) of Theorem 3 disappears since $|Z_{1j}| > f_1$, $|Z_{2j}| > f_1$ with $Z_{1j} \subseteq Z_1 \subseteq U_1$, $Z_{2j} \subseteq Z_2 \subseteq U_2$ implies $|U_1| > f_1$ and $|U_2| > f_1$ which contradicts the preconditions on U_1 and U_2. Then Theorem 3 reduces to Theorem 3.1 reported in [11] for one-step t-diagnosability with a directed test graph for the symmetric invalidation model. When $f_1 = t$, $f_2 = 1$, condition (3.2) of Theorem 3 means there exists at least one arc within either Z_1 or Z_2. In this case Theorem 3 reduces to Theorem 3.2 reported in [11] for one-step t-diagnosability with a directed test graph for the asymmetric invalidation model. The existence of this test within Z_1 or Z_2 makes certain to obtain a 1-arc since two faulty units test to 1 for the asymmetric invalidation model which breaks the simultaneous consistency of two CFS U_1 and U_2.

We now give the sufficient and necessary conditions for f_1 / f_2-diagnosability based on the connectivity of a digraph, which may be verified using known methods [12].

According to the f_1 / f_2-invalidation model depicted in Fig. 1, a test outcome of zero implies that either both units are fault-free or the tester unit is faulty, while a test outcome of one implies that one or both units are faulty. Thus the orientation of the edges is important for the f_1 / f_2-invalidation model. Following Hakimi in [10], we define a vertex connectivity for digraph which takes into account the orientation of edges. The *strong vertex connectivity* $k'(D)$ of a digraph $D(U, E)$ is the minimum number of vertices whose removal from D results in a digraph that is not strongly connected or trivial. Note that if $D(U, E)$ is a weakly connected digraph then $k'(D) = 0$ and if $D(U, E)$ is a complete digraph of n vertices then $k'(D) = n - 1$. We now present a characterization theorem for f_1/f_2-diagnosability where $0 < f_2 \leq f_1$ with the following Theorem 4. Due to lack of space a sketch of proof is presented in this paper. A detailed proof can be found in [9].

Theorem 4: Let $D(U,E)$ be the strongly connected test digraph of a network S of n units ($|U| = n$) for the f_1/f_2-invalidation model where $1 \leq f_2 \leq f_1$. S is one-step f_1/f_2-diagnosable if and only if both the following conditions hold:

(4.1) $n \geq 2f_1 + 1$

(4.2) $k'(D) \geq f_1$

The necessity of conditions (4.1) and (4.2) with $f_2 = f_1$ (PMC symmetric invalidation model) is known (Theorems 1 and 2 [1] and Corollary 1 [10]). The proof of the necessary condition (4.1) with $0 < f_2 < f_1$ consists in supposing the contrary $n < 2f_1 + 1$ and proving the existence of a syndrome $\sigma : E \to \{0, 1\}$ for which there exists two distinct CFS. For this purpose we present a partition F_1 and F_2, $|F_1|$, $|F_2| \leq f_1$ such that the condensation[1] digraph D_c of digraph $D(U,E)$ is bipartite and every fragment of F_1 and F_2 has at most f_2 vertices. Thus there exists a syndrome σ such that all arcs between F_1 and F_2 are 1-arcs and all arcs within F_1 and F_2 are 0-arcs thus F_1 and F_2 are two distinct CFS. By Definition 11, S is not one-step f_1/f_2-diagnosable.

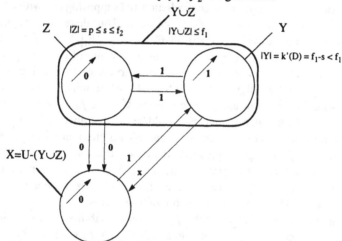

Fig. 3. **Proof of Necessity of condition (4.2) of Theorem 4.**

The proof of necessary condition (4.2) with $0 < f_2 < f_1$ consists in supposing the contrary $0 < k'(D) = f_1 - s < f_1$, $0 < s \leq f_2$ and proving the existence of a syndrome σ for which there exists two distinct CFS. For this purpose we present a partition X, Y and Z of fragments of the strongly connected digraph $D(U,E)$ such that $|Y| = k'(D) = f_1 - s$, $0 < |Z| = p \leq s$ and $X = U - (Y \cup Z)$. It follows that Z is a fragment with $|Z| \leq f_2$. Since $k'(D) > 0$, $U - Y$ is not a strongly connected component. To satisfy this statement we suppose $\Gamma(X) \cap Z = \varnothing$. Given this structure, we present a syndrome σ such that sketched in Fig. 3 for which it can be seen easily that Y and $Y \cup Z$ are two distinct CFS.

---

1. The *condensation* D_c of a digraph D is a digraph in which each fragment is replaced by a vertex in D_c, and all arcs from one fragment to another in D are replaced by a single arc in D_c.

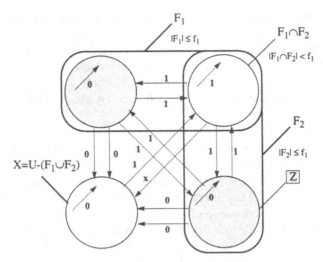

Fig. 4. Proof of Sufficiency of Theorem 4.

The proof of sufficiency is done by contradiction and supposing that with $n \geq 2f_1 + 1$ and $k'(D) \geq f_1$, S is not one-step f_1/f_2-diagnosable. Thus there exists a syndrome σ: $E \rightarrow \{0, 1\}$ such that there exist two distinct CFS F_1, F_2, $|F_1|, |F_2| \leq f_1$. First we suppose $F_1 \cap F_2 \neq \varnothing$. We show that the simultaneous consistency of F_1 and F_2 implies that $\Gamma^{-1}(Z) \subseteq F_1 \cap F_2$ where $Z = F_1 \oplus F_2$. We get the structure shown in Fig. 4. It follows that $|F_1 \cap F_2| < f_1$ and the digraph formed from the set of units $U - (F_1 \cap F_2)$ is not strongly connected which contradicts the condition $k'(D) \geq f_1$. The remaining case is when $F_1 \cap F_2 = \varnothing$ for which F_1 and F_2 would be two disjoint consistent fault sets. In that case the simultaneous consistency of F_1 and F_2 implies that $\Gamma^{-1}(F_1 \cup F_2) = \varnothing$. But condition $n \geq 2f_1 + 1$ guaranties that there is a third set $X = U - (F_1 \cup F_2)$, $X \neq \varnothing$ and condition $k'(D) \geq f_1$ implies that this set X is strongly connected to at least one of the sets F_1 or F_2 since $|F_1|, |F_2| \leq f_1$. This is in contradiction with $\Gamma^{-1}(F_1 \cup F_2) = \varnothing$. This completes the proof of Theorem 4. ∎

We give now a theorem that states the f_1/f_2-diagnosability conditions in terms of connectivity for a network S of n units when $f_1 + f_2 + 1 \leq n < 2f_1 + 1$. Thus $0 < f_2 < f_1$ and Theorem 5 does not apply for symmetric invalidation models ($f_1 = f_2$). Due to lack of space a sketch of proof is presented in this paper. A detailed proof can be found in [9].

Theorem 5: Let $D(U,E)$ be the strongly connected test digraph of a network S of n units ($|U| = n$) for the f_1/f_2-invalidation model where $0 < f_2 < f_1$. S is one-step f_1/f_2-diagnosable if and only if both the following conditions hold:

   (5.1) $f_1 + f_2 + 1 \leq n < 2f_1 + 1$

   (5.2) $k'(D) \geq f_1 + 1$

The proof of necessary condition (5.1) consists in reducing the contrary condition $n < f_1 + f_2 + 1$ *ad absurdum*. We do not consider the case where $n \geq 2f_1 + 1$ which has already been proved in Theorem 4. We suppose the existence of a syndrome σ in which F is the actual fault set such that F and $U - F$ is a partition of the strongly connected test digraph $D(U,E)$ such that $|F| \le f_1$, $|U - F| \le f_2$ and $F^\sim \subseteq F$ a 0-fragment of exactly f_2 faulty units: $|F^0| = f_2$.

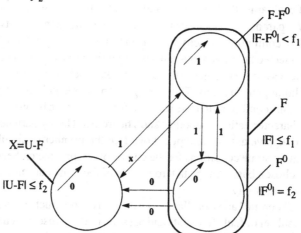

Fig. 5. Proof of Necessity of Condition (5.1) of Theorem 5

Since $0 < f_2 < f_1$, we have: $|F - F^0| \le f_1 - f_2 < f_1$. Moreover if $\Gamma(U - F) \subseteq F - F^0$ then there exists a syndrome σ as shown in Fig. 5 such that F and $F - F^0$ are two distinct CFS. Thus by Definition 11, S is not one-step f_1 / f_2-diagnosable if $n < f_1 + f_2 + 1$.

The proof of necessity of condition (5.2) consists in supposing the contrary $k'(D) = f_1 - s \le f_1, 0 \le s < f_1$ and proving the existence of a syndrome σ for which there exists two distinct CFS. We suppose that $2k'(D) \le n$ and that F_1 and F_2 is a partition of $D(U,E)$ such that $|F_1| = k'(D) \le f_1$ and $k'(D) \le |F_2| = k'(D) + p \le f_1, 0 \le p \le s$. It follows that F_1 and F_2 are not strongly connected components. Suppose here that F_1 and F_2 are two subsets of bipartite graph $D(U,E)$. Thus F_1 and F_2 are totally disconnected. Then there exists a syndrome σ such that all arcs between F_1 and F_2 are 1-arcs and thus F_1 and F_2 are two CFS.

The proof of sufficiency of conditions (5.1) and (5.2) is done by supposing the contrary $f_1 + f_2 + 1 \le n < 2f_1 + 1$ and $k'(D) > f_1$, S is not one-step f_1 / f_2-diagnosable. This proof can be obtained from the proof of sufficiency of Theorem 4 by replacing $k'(D) \ge f_1$ with $k'(D) > f_1$. Only the case where $F_1 \cap F_2 = \emptyset$ is different since the condition $f_1 + f_2 + 1 \le n < 2f_1 + 1$ does not allow to suppose the existence of a third non-empty set. Since $|F_1|, |F_2| \le f_1$, F_1 and F_2 are strongly connected. Thus there exists a syndrome σ for which F_1 or F_2 has a 0-fragment of cardinality greater than f_2 units which contradicts the hypothesis S is not one-step f_1 / f_2-diagnosable. This completes the proof of Theorem 5. ∎

By comparing conditions of Theorem 5 with Theorem 4, we can see that when the cardinality constraint of network S relatively to the number of faulty units is relaxed ($f_1 + f_2 + 1 \le n < 2f_1 + 1$) and when the invalidation model is in-between the asymmetric invalidation model and the symmetric invalidation model excluded ($0 < f_2 < f_1$) then the conditions on the network S in terms of vertex connectivity $k'(D)$ must be stricter in order to have one-step f_1 / f_2-diagnosability.

5 An Adaptive Network Diagnosis Algorithm

The problem of evaluating the bounds f_1 and f_2 must be addressed for the diagnosis of network. The f_2 parameter can be seen as a measure of the connectivity of the heterogeneity in terms of computing capacity for a given test. For example, the f_2 parameter for a large set of connected heterogeneous units is larger than the f_2 parameter for the same set of heterogeneous units but sparse in the test digraph which is larger than the f_2 parameter for a set of homogeneous units. Thus for a given network and a test digraph, we have shown the additional conditions that are required for a network to be one-step diagnosable network in the characterization Theorem 4 and Theorem 5. The f_2 parameter is evaluated in two steps. Firstly, we assume an upper bound on the number of simultaneous faulty units f_1. This gives some conditions for the choice of f_2 parameter. Secondly, an exact value for f_2 is chosen based on the heterogeneity of the units participating in the diagnosis and their connectivity.

Theorem 1, Theorem 2 and Corollary 1 can be used to construct an adaptive algorithm that discovers a subset of fault-free units and uses the units so discovered to diagnose the rest of the network. The classical adaptive approach [5], [13] is based on the assumption that each unit is capable of testing every other unit, with the tests being conducted one at a time in such a way that the choice of the next test to be performed depends on the results of the previous tests, rather than on a preselected pattern of tests. The principal idea of the existing adaptive diagnosis algorithms proposed by Hakimi [5], [13] and by Chutani [6] is based of efficiently identifying one fault-free unit. Due to the complete connectivity assumption the identified fault-free unit can be used in a second step to diagnose the remaining units of the system. It is obvious that this approach does not apply to networks of arbitrary topologies. Our algorithm is pseudo-adaptive since the choice of the next test to be performed depends on the result on the previous test but in a preselected pattern of tests. It is less restricted in terms of connectivity since it does not suppose a complete test digraph. This is a generalization of the previous adaptive algorithms [5], [13], [6] to networks of arbitrary topologies with a strongly connected test digraph. We show that our algorithm can find all the fault-free and faulty units if the *conditions of the characterization* of Theorem 4 are satisfied and those of Theorem 5 are satisfied with a stricter condition on connectivity of the test digraph $D(U,E)$.

We use the f_1/f_2-invalidation model described in Section 2. The network is assumed to have a strongly connected test digraph $D(U,E)$ with a vertex-connectivity $k'(D) \geq f_1 + 1$ and with a cardinality $n \geq f_1 + f_2 + 1$. Even for a cardinality $n \geq 2f_1 + 1$, we note that the condition on connectivity is $k'(D) \geq f_1 + 1$. This is different from the conditions of Theorem 5. The structure of the test digraph and all the outcomes resulting from the tests are collected at a central unit. This central unit is assumed to be reliable and determines the status of all the units in the communication network using our algorithm.

Since the test digraph $D(U,E)$ is supposed to be strongly connected, this digraph has at least one tree which contains all the vertices of D. Furthermore, by knowing the topology of test assignment digraph $D(U,E)$, we can initially identify such a spanning tree in D by using a Depth-First Search (DFS) algorithm [14]. This algorithm has a complexity $O(|E|)$. It can be computed before starting the diagnosis procedure. The results of this algorithm are given in the form of two disjoint subsets $Palm(D)$ and $Fron(D)$ into which the arcs of D are partitioned. The set of arcs $Palm(D)$ defines a subdigraph of D which is a spanning tree referred to as *palm tree* of D because every vertex in this subdigraph, except the root, has an indegree equal to one, and the indegree of the root is zero. Arcs not in any palm tree $\exists (u_i, u_j) \in E$, $(u_i, u_j) \notin Palm(D)$ belongs to the arc set $Fron(D)$ and fall into three classes. Some arcs going from descendants to ancestors in the tree are called *fronds*. Other arcs going from one subtree to another in the tree are called *cross-links*. Other arcs goes from ancestors to descendants in the tree. We assume that the result $Palm(D)$ is stored in an preorder traversal of the spanning tree.

The strategy of the algorithm sketched below consists in identifying as many fault-free units as soon as possible with a minimum number of tests $\sigma(u_i, u_j)$ in the following way.

As soon as a unit u_j is diagnosed as fault-free ($u_j \in FF(U)$) the algorithm uses this reliable fault-free unit u_j to identify the fault status of all the units in the already identified 0-fragments which contain u_j. To do so, the algorithm tries to construct all maximal 0-dipaths $maxPath(Oarc(D))$ by traversing first the spanning tree $Palm(D)$ stored in a preorder manner. In the second step, by traversing the set of all the frond and cross arcs $Fron(D)$, the algorithm search for all maximal 0-dipaths $maxPath(Oarc(D))$ and 0-closed walk $maxClosedWalk(Oarc(D))$.

Secondly, this algorithm exploits the reliable diagnosed fault-free unit u_j as tester for the set of all the units $\Gamma(u_j)$ incident from u_j. The fault status of the units in $\Gamma_0(u_j)$ and $\Gamma_1(u_j)$ are identified as fault-free and faulty respectively.

In the following algorithm all additional operators on set have the type of the left part and are idempotent for already existing element in the corresponding set. The parameters qualified with the prefix "Var" are passed by reference as in the description of a procedure in a high-level language. This means that recursive calls of this procedure can modify these parameters. In this algorithm $\sigma(u_i, u_j)$ is the outcome of the conducted test of u_j by u_i. The first call of the Af_1f_2D recursive procedure initializes the parameters in the following way:

1 $Oarc(D) \leftarrow \varnothing$, $Iarc(D) \leftarrow \varnothing$, $FF(U) \leftarrow \varnothing$, $F(U) \leftarrow \varnothing$

2 $Af_1f_2D(Elmt(Palm(D))$, $Palm(D) - Elmt(Palm(D))$, $Fron(D)$, f_1, f_2, $Oarc(D)$, $Iarc(D)$, $F'(U)$, $FF'(U))$

Diagnosis Algorithm.

Input: set of vertices $U(D)$, set of arcs $Palm(D)$, set of arcs $Fron(D)$, the maximum number of faulty units f_1 in the network, the maximum cardinality f_2 of 0-components of faulty units.

Output: set of all fault-free units $FF(U)$, set of all faulty units $F(U)$.

3 Procedure Af_1f_2D ((u_i, u_j), Var $Palm(D)$, Var $Fron(D)$, f_1, f_2, Var $Oarc(D)$, Var $Iarc(D)$, Var $F(U)$, Var $FF(U)$)

4   If $|F(U)| = f_1$ then $FF(U) \leftarrow U(D) - F(U)$

5   Else (* $|F(U)| < f1$ *)

6   If $(u_i, u_j) = \varphi$ then (* $Palm(D) = \varnothing$ or $Fron(D) \neq \varnothing$ *)

7   If $Fron(D) \neq \varnothing$ then (* $Palm(D) = \varnothing$ *)

8          $Af_1f_2D(Elmt(Fron(D))$, $Fron(D) - Elmt(Fron(D))$, $\varnothing$, f_1, f_2, $Oarc(D)$, $Iarc(D)$, $F(U)$, $FF(U))$ Fi

9   Else

10   If $\sigma(u_i, u_j) = 0$ then

```
11    If u_i ∈ FF(U) then (* u_j ∈ FF(U) *)
12        FF'(U) ← FF(U) + u_j
13        For each maxClosedWalk(Oarc(D)) Do
14            If u_j ∈ maxClosedWalk(Oarc(D)) then (* Theorem 2 or Corollary 1*)
15                FF'(U) ← FF(U) + maxClosedWalk(Oarc(D)) Fi
16        Od
17    Else (* u_j ∈ FF(U) *)
18        FF'(U) ← FF(U)
19        For each maxClosedWalk(Oarc(D)) Do
20            If Length(maxClosedWalk(Oarc(D) + (u_i,u_j))) ≥ f_2 then(*Corollary 1*)
21                FF'(U) ← FF(U) + maxClosedWalk(Oarc(D) + (u_i,u_j)) Fi
22        Od
23        For each maxPath(Oarc(D)) until u_j ∈ FF'(U) Do
24            If Length(maxPath(Oarc(D) + (u_i,u_j))) > f_2 then (* Theorem 1 *)
25                FF'(U) ← FF(U) + u_j Fi
26        Od
27    Fi
28    F'(U) ← F(U) , Oarc'(D) ← Oarc(D) + (u_i,u_j) , Iarc'(D) ← Iarc(D)
29    If FF'(U) ≠ FF(U) then
30        For each u_j ∈ FF'(U) − FF(U) Do (* for each new diagnosed fault-free unit *)
31            If (u_j,u_k) ∈ Oarc(D) then FF'(U) ← FF'(U) + u_k Fi
32            If (u_j,u_k) ∈ Iarc(D) or (u_k,u_j) ∈ Iarc(D) then F'(U) ← F'(U) + u_k Fi
33        Od
34    Fi
35    Else (* σ(u_i, u_j) = 1 *)
36        If u_i ∈ FF(U) then
37            F'(U) ← F(U) + u_j
38            For each maxClosedWalk(Oarc(D)) Do
39                If u_j ∈ maxClosedWalk(Oarc(D)) then (* Length < f_2 *)
40                    F'(U) ← F(U) + maxClosedWalk(Oarc(D)) (* Theorem 2 *) Fi
41            Od
42            FF'(U) ← FF(U) , Oarc'(D) ← Oarc(D) , Iarc'(D) ← Iarc(D) + (u_i,u_j)
43        Fi
44    Fi
45    If u_i ∈ FF'(U) and (u_i, u_k) ∈ Palm(D) then
46        Af_1f_2D((u_i, u_k),  Palm(D) − (u_i, u_k),  Fron(D),  f_1,  f_2,  Oarc'(D),
                Iarc'(D), F'(U), FF'(U))
47    Fi
48    If u_i ∈ FF'(U) and (u_i, u_k) ∈ Fron(D) then
49        Af_1f_2D((u_i, u_k),  Palm(D),  Fron(D) − (u_i, u_k),  f_1,  f_2,  Oarc'(D),
                Iarc'(D), F'(U), FF'(U))
50    Fi
51    Af_1f_2D(Elmt(Palm(D)),  Palm(D) − Elmt(Palm(D)),  Fron(D),  f_1,  f_2,
            Oarc'(D), Iarc'(D), F'(U), FF'(U))
52    Fi
53 Fi
```

Before we present the proof of the validity of the algorithm we make some preliminary observations. Before diagnosing any fault-free unit and thus any unit, the algorithm:

1) either has to find at least one 0-dipath of length greater than f_2. It is easy to

verify that by storing all the 0-arcs in Oarc(D) then it will be possible to find out all maximal 0-dipaths.

2) ot has to go through at least one 0-closed walk of length greater than f_2. At worst case all the frond arcs are examined thus all 0-cycles are examined since adding any frond arc to any directed tree creates a cycle. Since a closed walk is composed by several distinct cycles intersecting in one or two vertices, all maximal 0-closed walk are examined.

Moreover, the algorithm:

3) terminates and at worst case will examine all arcs of $D(U, E)$. This is a straightforward consequence of the termination conditions on $Palm(D)$ and $Fron(D)$.

Theorem 6: Let S be a network of n units with a strongly connected test digraph $D(U,E)$ which satisfies the conditions $n \geq f_1 + f_2 + 1$ and $n - 2 \geq k'(D) \geq f_1 + 1$. Then the Af_1f_2D algorithm correctly identifies the fault status of every unit using at most n^2 tests.

Proof: First we have to show that this algorithm correctly identifies the fault status of all considered units. Secondly we show that all units are considered. The proof by induction that the computation of the set of fault-free units $FF(U)$ and the set of faulty units $F(U)$ is correct can be found in [9]. It remains to be shown that every unit of $D(U,E)$ is diagnosed by our algorithm in at most n^2 tests.

We first prove that at the end of algorithm: $\forall u_i \in U$, $u_i \in FF(U) \cup F(U)$ with $FF(U) \cap F(U) = \emptyset$. Since S with test digraph $D(U,E)$ is supposed to be f_1/f_2-diagnosable according to Definition 11 there exists only one consistent fault set F, $|F| \leq f_1$ in S. Let $k'(D) \geq f_1 + 1$ be the vertex-connectivity of test digraph $D(U,E)$ with $n \geq f_1 + f_2 + 1$. The set of fault-free units $U - F$ is strongly connected since removing all units of CFS F, $|F| \leq f_1$ leads a digraph that is strongly connected. Moreover we have: $|U - F| \geq n - f_1 \geq f_2 + 1 > f_2$. Thus there exists a 0-spanning closed walk of length greater than f_2 in $U - F$. Since F is a CFS this 0-spanning closed walk of $U - F$ is maximal otherwise there exists a unit $u_j \in F$ such that $u_i \in U - F$ and $\sigma(u_i, u_j) = 1$ which is a contradiction. Since the diagnosis of any unit begins with the diagnosis of fault-free unit and from observation 3), whatever the root selected to apply the prediagnosis DFS algorithm our algorithm will examine the 0-arcs of this maximal 0-closed spanning walk of $U - F$. Thus all the units of $U - F$ will be diagnosed as fault-free by Af_1f_2D procedure.

Once fault-free units of $U - F$ has been diagnosed as fault-free, we need to show that the algorithm can diagnose all the remaining units in F as faulty. We know that if $k'(D) \geq f_1 + 1$ then for all u_i belonging to U: $|\Gamma^{-1}(u_i)| \geq f_1 + 1$. In particular: $\forall u_i \in F$: $|\Gamma^{-1}(u_i)| \geq f_1 + 1$. Thus we have: $\forall u_i \in F$: $\Gamma^{-1}(u_i) \cap (U - F) \neq \emptyset$. Then each units of F is diagnosed as faulty by an already fault-free diagnosed unit of $U - F$ and at the end of algorithm we have: $\forall u_i \in U$: $u_i \in FF(U) \cup F(U)$ with $FF(U) \cap F(U) = \emptyset$. From observation 3) our algorithm terminates and at worst case will examine all arcs of $D(U, E)$. The maximum of arcs is obtained for a test digraph which has one arc less than a complete test digraph. For such a test digraph $k'(D) = n - 2$. The number of test is bounded by $n^2/2 + n/2 - 1$. This completes the proof of the theorem. ∎

Using the adaptive approach and a complete test digraph $k'(D) = n - 1$, Hakimi and Nakajima [5] were able to identify all faulty units in at most $n + 2t - 2$ tests ($t = f_1$) for the symmetric PMC invalidation model and in at most $(2n-2-mq-m)(q/2) + (n-1)$ tests for the asymmetric BGM invalidation model where m is the number of complete asymmetric digraphs constructed by the algorithm and $q = \lfloor (n-1)/m \rfloor$. Blecher [15] improved the bound for the symmetric PMC invalidation model by using a different adaptive procedure which identified the status of all units in at most $n + t - 1$. Blecher also proved that this number of tests is optimal for identifying the correct status of all units. By allowing the selection of the next test to be performed before the results of all the previous tests Hakimi and Schmeichel [13] relaxed this bound to $\log_2(n - t + 1) + t + \log_2 t$. The most important limitation of these algorithms is the assumption that the test digraph is complete. This limitation is partly overcome in [5] by proving that the proposed adaptive algorithm is applicable to $D_{\delta t}$ test digraphs for which $k'(D_{\delta t}) = t \leq n$ and $\forall u_i \in U$: $|\Gamma^{-1}(u_i)| = t$.

Our adaptive algorithm relaxes the requirement on connectivity because it can be applied to a test digraph of any topology with the condition $k'(D) \geq f_1 + 1$. Moreover our algorithm diagnoses all the units of the network for the f_1/f_2-invalidation model. The f_1/f_2-invalidation model is a continuum of invalidation models and it does not restrict the outcome of a test to only one invalidation model (PMC or BGM) when the tester is faulty irrespective of the fault status of the tested units. By using the number of tests to be performed as the measure of complexity, our algorithm diagnoses an entire n-nodes network in $O(n^2)$ tests. This complexity is greater than those of the above adaptive algorithms for the symmetric PMC invalidation model and equal to the algorithm of Hakimi and Nakajima [5] for the asymmetric BGM invalidation model. This expresses the trade-off between the topology of the test digraph, the combination of invalidation models and the efficiency in terms of the maximum number of tests to be performed.

6 Conclusions

In this paper, we have shown the use of automatic fault diagnosis in communication networks as the means to achieve dependability in terms of availability of the network resources. For this purpose we have introduced a new concept of f_1/f_2-diagnosability for heterogeneous communication networks by defining a truly continuum of PMC symmetric invalidation model and BGM asymmetric invalidation model. We have discussed the suitability of this f_1/f_2-invalidation model to represent the fault behavior for the diagnosis of heterogeneous communication networks. A generalized characterization theorem is proved in Section 4. This theorem provides the conditions under which a network is one-step f_1/f_2-diagnosable in terms of all possible combinations of pair of distinct consistent fault subsets. Two other characterization theorems in terms of vertex connectivity have been proved. These theorems give the necessary and sufficient conditions for f_1/f_2-diagnosability of networks with arbitrary topologies but with a strongly connected test digraph. This requirement is more realistic than a complete test digraph for communication networks. The conventional $D_{\delta t}$ optimal design for test digraphs proposed in [5] is a particular case of our characterization. Using the results of the characterization theorems, an adaptive algorithm for identifying the fault status of all the units in the network is proposed. By using the number of tests to be performed as a measure of complexity, this algorithm diagnoses a network with n nodes in $O(n^2)$ tests. The comparison of this complexity with other existing adaptive algorithms expresses the trade-off between the topology of the test digraph, the combination of invalidation models and the efficiency in terms of the maximum number of tests to be performed.

The diagnosis of communication path is as important as the diagnosis of the nodes in a network. The extension of this unified theory to develop characterization theorems and diagnosis algorithms to take into account faulty links is currently under study [9]. The diagnosis algorithm presented here works for arbitrary network topologies and we are currently working [9] on a distributed diagnosis algorithm to avoid the strong assumptions about reliability of the central unit which collects the result of the tests and performs the diagnosis.

References

[1]   Preparata, F. P., Metze, G., Chien, R. T., On the Connection Assignment Problem of Diagnosable Systems, IEEE Trans. Electr. Comp., Dec. 1967, Vol.EC-16, No.6, pp.848-853.

[2]   Barsi, F., Grandoni, F., Maestrini, P., A Theory of Diagnosability of Digital Systems, IEEE Trans. Computers, June 1976, Vol. C-25, No. 6, pp. 585-593.

[3]   Somani, A. K., Agarwal, V. K., Avis, D., A Generalized Theory for System Level Diagnosis, IEEE Trans. Computer, Vol. C-36, No.5, May 1987, pp. 538-546.

[4]   Kuhl, J.G., Reddy, S.M., Fault-diagnosis in fully distributed systems, in Proc. 11th Symp. on Fault-Tolerant Comp. IEEE Comp. Society Pub., pp. 100-105, June 1981.

[5]   Hakimi, S.L., Nakajima, K., On Adaptive System Diagnosis, IEEE Trans. Computers, Vol. C-33, No. 3, pp. 234-240, 1984.

[6]   Chutani, S., A Framework for Fault Diagnosis of Networks, Ph. D. Thesis, Swiss Federal Institute of Technology, Switzerland, 1995.

[7]   Deo, N., Graph Theory with Applications to Engineering and Computer Science, Prentice-Hall Ser. in Auto. Comp., 1974.

[8]   Harary, F., Graph Theory, Addison-Wesley Series in Mathematics, 1972.

[9]   Berthet, G.G., Extension and Application of System-Level Diagnosis for Distributed Fault Management in Communication Networks, Ph. D. Thesis (under preparation), Swiss Federal Institute of Technology, Switzerland, 1996.

[10]   Hakimi, S.L., Amin, A.T., Characterization of Connection Assignment of Diagnosable Systems, IEEE Trans. Computers (Corresp.), January 1974, pp. 86-88.

[11]   Das, A., Lakshmanan, K.B., Thulasiraman, K., Agarwal, V.K., Generalized Characterization of Diagnosable Systems based on Kohda's Theorem, in Proceedings of the 21th Conference Inform. Sci. Syst., Baltimore, MD, March 1987.

[12]   Kleitman, D.J., Methods for investigating connectivity for large graphs, IEEE Trans. Circuit Theory (Corresp.), Vol.CT-16, pp. 232-233, May 1969.

[13]   Hakimi, S.L., Schmeichel, E.F., An Adaptive Algorithm for System Level Diagnosis, Journ.Of Algo.5, pp. 526-530, 1984.

[14]   Tarjan, R., Depth-First Search and Linear Graph Algorithms, Society for Industrial and Applied Math. (SIAM) Journal on Comp., June 1972, Vol.1, No.2, pp.146-160.

[15]   Blecher, P.M., On A Logical Problem, Discrete Mathematics, Vol. 43, pp. 107-110, 1983.

Author Index

Springer-Verlag
and the Environment

Lecture Notes in Computer Science

For information about Vols. 1–1081

please contact your bookseller or Springer-Verlag